EASTERN WISEDOME AND LEARNING

EASTERN WISEDOME AND LEARNING

The Study of Arabic in Seventeenth-Century England

G. J. TOOMER

CLARENDON PRESS · OXFORD
1996

Oxford University Press, Walton Street, Oxford OX2 6DP

Oxford New York
Athens Auckland Bangkok Bombay
Calcutta Cape Town Dar es Salaam Delhi
Florence Hong Kong Istanbul Karachi
Kuala Lumpur Madras Madrid Melbourne
Mexico City Nairobi Paris Singapore
Taipei Tokyo Toronto
and associated companies in
Berlin Ibadan

Oxford is a trade mark of Oxford University Press

Published in the United States
by Oxford University Press Inc., New York

British Library Cataloguing in Publication Data
Data available

Library of Congress Cataloging in Publication Data
Toomer, G. J.
Eastern wisedome and learning: the study of Arabic in seventeenth-
century England / G. J. Toomer
p. cm.
Includes bibliographical references (p.) and index.
1. Arabic language—Study and teaching (Higher)—Great Britain—
History—17th century. 2. Arabists—Great Britain—History—
17th century. I. Title
PJ6068.G7T66 1995
492'.78'0071141—dc20 95-32746
ISBN 0-19-820291-1

1 3 5 7 9 10 8 6 4 2

Typeset by Regent Typesetting, London
Printed on acid-free paper by
Biddles Ltd., Guildford and King's Lynn

'The Country is miserably decay'd, and hath lost the Reputation of its Name, and mighty stock of Credit it once had for Eastern Wisedome and learning: It hath followed the Motion of the Sun and is Universally gone Westward.'

(Robert Huntington, from Aleppo, to John Locke, 1 April 1671)

Acknowledgements

THIS book could not have come to be without the help of numerous people and institutions, which I wish to acknowledge here. Corpus Christi College, Oxford (where I am proud to have been, like Edward Pococke, undergraduate and fellow) appointed me to a Visiting Fellowship in 1990, enabling me to spend time in Oxford to consult a significant part of the vast unpublished material there relevant to my topic. I am very appreciative of the assistance I received from the staff of the Bodleian Library. I was also privileged to have access to the libraries of Cambridge University and the School of Oriental and African Studies, the British Library, and the Public Record Office. I am grateful to Mr John Field, Librarian of Westminster School, for showing me the Busby Library, and to Mr Stephen Gregory, Librarian of Sion College, for providing me with access to the oriental manuscripts and copies of a unique document in the library. I thank the Librarian of the University Library, Sheffield for the use of the Hartlib Papers. Access to the resources of the libraries of Brown University and Harvard University has helped me greatly. I am grateful to the staff of Oxford University Press, especially Richard Jeffery and Michael Belson, for the care which they expended on this book.

I thank Dr Monika Asztalos, Mr Ian Christie-Miller, Professor Hans Daiber, Dr David Howarth, Professor Michael Hunter, Dr J. Robert Jones, Dr George Molland, and Dr Lawrence Principe for answering my queries and sending me copies of documents and printed materials. Mr Rijk Smitskamp offered me, besides several useful publications, the benefit of his unique knowledge of early Arabic printing. I am particularly grateful to Professor Alastair Hamilton for providing me not only with his published papers, but with a copy of his article on Abudacnus in advance of publication. I thank my colleagues Professor Owen Gingerich (for copies of seventeenth-century publications), Professor William Newman (for information on some obscure personages of the period), and Professor A. I. Sabra (for help with documents written in colloquial Arabic). Jonathan Sachs spent much time and effort on improving the illustration used for the dust-jacket. It would be impossible for me to enumerate the places in this book which owe something to my discussions with Professor Mordechai Feingold, who has been extraordinarily generous in allowing me to exploit his unrivalled knowledge of the byways of the intellectual history of England in the seventeenth century, and in giving, lending, and pointing out to me relevant books and documents. He also read and commented on a draft of the whole book. Let me here express, once and for all, my particular gratitude for the multiple ways in which he has improved it.

Above all, I wish to express my grateful appreciation for everything that my dear wife, Janet Sachs-Toomer, has done to make this book possible. Not only did she read it all as it was written, using her expert proofreader's eye to remove many slips and infelicitous expressions, but she was always with me to provide support, companionship, and encouragement on both sides of the Atlantic during its long gestation. It belongs to her as much as to me: κοινὰ τὰ τῶν φίλων.

Contents

Contents   xi

Editorial Procedures

Bibliographical references in the footnotes are invariably abbreviated in such a way that the full descriptions may easily be found in the Bibliography (less obvious designations are given in the abbreviations listed below).

References to manuscripts, except where otherwise indicated, are to items in the Bodleian Library.

Dates in the seventeenth century can be ambiguous. After the Gregorian calendar reform of 1582 the date assigned to a given day in the British Isles fell ten days earlier than in most of the rest of Europe,[1] so that 14 December 1615 in England corresponded to 24 December 1615 in Holland or France. The dates in this book are to be understood as applying to areas in which the events to which they are attached occurred, so that '14 December' is Old Style for an event in England and New Style (hence ten days earlier) for an event in Holland. In most cases the difference is immaterial. Occasionally 'double dates' of the form 14/24 December are given (usually when the date is in that form in the document referred to). The matter is complicated by the fact that in England during the seventeenth century the new year began on 25 March, so that for instance the execution of Charles I on 30 January (1649 by modern reckoning) took place in 1648 according to contemporary reckoning. Somewhat inconsequentially, I have used the modern reckoning of the year from 1 January throughout, while keeping the Old Style dating for month and day number for English events. Thus I would give the above date as '30 January 1649', and not '30 January 1648' (as a contemporary Englishman would have), nor '9 February 1649' (like a contemporary Dutchman). Occasionally for dates between 1 January and 24 March a 'double year date' of the form '1648/9' is given (again taken from the document).

Quotations from contemporary books and documents are given in the spelling and punctuation of the originals, but abbreviations are usually resolved, so that e.g. 'y^e' and 'y^t' are transcribed as 'the' and 'that'.

---

[1] All of Catholic Europe immediately, and many Protestant countries soon afterwards, with important exceptions in Protestant German and Scandinavian areas.

Abbreviations

BL	British Library
CSP	*Calendar of State Papers*
CUL	Cambridge University Library
DNB	*Dictionary of National Biography* (see Bibliography)
DSB	*Dictionary of Scientific Biography* (see Bibliography)
NS	New Style (i.e. using the Gregorian calendar)
OS	Old Style (i.e. using the Julian calendar)
PO	*Philologia Orientalis* (see Bibliography s.v. Smitskamp)
PRO	Public Record Office
SC	*Summary Catalogue of Western Manuscripts in the Bodleian Library* (see Bibliography)
TCD	Trinity College, Dublin

Introduction

THE topic of this book, the study of Arabic in England during the seventeenth century, has to be put in the context of similar efforts elsewhere in Europe in the same period and immediately before. Accordingly Chapter 2 presents a survey of Arabic studies in other European countries during the sixteenth and seventeenth centuries, which necessarily omits many details. To compensate for the brevity of this summary I have supplied abundant references to the work of others (on which this part of my book relies almost exclusively). For the history of Arabic studies in Europe as a whole the only adequate general treatment is that of Fück, *Die arabischen Studien in Europa*. Although this was published in 1955, the first part, covering the medieval period and the seventeenth and eighteenth centuries, is essentially a reprint of an earlier essay written in 1944. The picture it presents has been supplemented by many detailed studies over the last fifty years, but the work has not been replaced. Although it suffers from the disadvantages of an almost exclusively biographical approach, it is a well-informed and judicious book. For the sixteenth and early seventeenth centuries the recent work of Jones, 'Learning Arabic in Renaissance Europe', provides much useful and interesting material, but attempts to be comprehensive only in the area of grammatical studies. For the late fifteenth and sixteenth centuries Dannenfeldt's 'The Renaissance Humanists and the Knowledge of Arabic' is a much more general survey which, although superficial, has many useful references. Levi della Vida's masterly *Ricerche sulla formazione del più antico fondo dei manoscritti orientali della Biblioteca Vaticana* contains a great deal of valuable information on Arabic studies in the sixteenth and seventeenth centuries, not only in Italy, but also in the rest of Europe.

Examination of the modern literature on the history of oriental, and in particular Arabic studies in the various parts of Europe reveals a wealth of detailed essays but a dearth of general treatments. The only country for which there is anything approaching a satisfactory discussion is the Netherlands, where for the seventeenth century Juynboll's *Zeventiende-eeuwsche Beoefenaars van het Arabisch in Nederland* provides a useful if superficial account.[1] No good book has

---

[1] Brugman's survey of the 17th century in Brugman and Schröder, *Arabic Studies in the Netherlands*, 3–21 adds little of significance.

been written on Arabic studies in Italy. The posthumous work of
Colomesius, *Italia et Hispania Orientalis*, is so slight as to be useless;
much more information can be found in de Gubernatis's *Matériaux
pour servir à l'histoire des études orientales en Italie*, but this is
sporadic and poorly documented. Particularly distressing is the lack of
a general history of the pursuit of Arabic and related topics from the
sixteenth century onwards in France, which would be of extraordinary
interest. Recent detailed studies, for instance those of Duverdier, have
given us some glimpses of the wealth of unpublished material, but the
only general treatment, Colomesius' *Gallia Orientalis*, was unsatisfactory even for its own time (1665), being derived almost exclusively
from printed sources; even so it is occasionally useful.

The core of the book (Chapters 3 to 9), which is devoted to
seventeenth-century England, is based, as far as was feasible, on the
original sources, that is the books written by those involved in Arabic
studies, and their correspondence and other documents relevant to
those studies. While the wealth of unpublished material available for
the period makes it inevitable that I have missed much that would
supplement or correct the details of my account,[2] I am confident that
the general outline will not be changed by future discoveries. I have
not in general attempted to narrate the lives of the men whose work I
discuss, except as they were related to their Arabic interests, for I
judge that the *DNB* and (for Oxford scholars) Wood's *Athenae
Oxonienses* provide an adequate background. Only for John Viccars
(for whose life these secondary sources are seriously defective) and
for Edward Pococke and John Greaves (who are central to the narrative) have I supplied more biographical detail. Although my account
emphasizes the primary sources, I hope that it will be clear from the
references in the footnotes how much I owe to the work of others
whose publications have guided me to those sources. In particular, the
Oxford B.Phil. thesis of Holt, 'Arabic Studies in Seventeenth-Century
England', is truly remarkable for its time, and I am indebted to it in
many ways. Although perfunctory in its treatment of important figures
other than Pococke, it is particularly valuable in drawing attention to
the remains of Pococke's unpublished notes and lectures in the
Bodleian Library, and in exploiting his Arabic correspondence that
survives there. The thesis was never published, but the author extracted
some particularly interesting parts in three articles now collected as the

---

[2] For instance I have examined only part of the vast correspondence of Edward
Bernard preserved in the Bodleian Library.

first three chapters in his *Studies in the History of the Near East*. Several of the essays in the recent book edited by Russell, *The 'Arabick' Interest of the Natural Philosophers in Seventeenth-Century England*, are useful contributions to my topic, but the book as a whole cannot serve as an overview of it.

For details on the printing and publishing of Arabic books in the early modern period the work of Schnurrer, *Bibliotheca Arabica*, superb for its time (1811), remains unsurpassed, although it needs correcting and supplementing in many details. Most useful for this purpose is the publication *Philologia Orientalis* by Smitskamp, whose knowledge of such matters is unrivalled in our times. For Arabic printing in England in particular the article by Roper, 'Arabic Printing and Publishing in England before 1820', although marred by some strange errors, is a vast improvement over what can be found in older works of reference such as Reed's *History of the Old English Letter Foundries*. For Oxford publications in particular Falconer Madan's great *Oxford Books* has been a constant source of information and amusement.

The growth of the Arabic and other oriental collections in English libraries is an important element in my narrative. At this period only the libraries of the two universities are significant (although items of interest occur in other libraries, such as those of the Earl of Arundel, Sion College, and Westminster School). For Cambridge University Library in the seventeenth century Oates's *History* is a model of erudition, wit, and curiosity. There is nothing comparable for the (admittedly far more complex) history of the Bodleian Library during this period; but Macray's *Annals of the Bodleian Library* provides much useful material, and the brief account of Philip, *The Bodleian Library in the Seventeenth and Eighteenth Centuries*, frequently corrects and supplements that. For the history of the collections of Arabic manuscripts the recent article by Wakefield, 'Arabic Manuscripts in the Bodleian Library', is valuable but far from exhaustive.

Edward Pococke is necessarily the central figure in this account, and we are fortunate to possess a detailed biography based closely on primary material, namely that by Leonard Twells. Unhappily, Twells's principal source, Pococke's extensive scholarly correspondence, vanished soon after the publication of the biography in 1740, and no trace of it has ever been found,[3] although diligent search has been

---

[3] Although a number of letters *from* Pococke survive in various collections, almost no letters *to* him (and absolutely none that were in Twells's hands) have been found. The nearest thing we have (in MS BL Add. 6193, fos. 73–7) is the careful copies of three

made several times in the last 150 years. Since the letters provided so much of value, I give a brief sketch of their history.[4] Evidently Pococke carefully kept all of his scholarly correspondence, at least from his later life (the correspondence from the 1620s and early 1630s, including the seminal period as chaplain at Aleppo, seems to have survived only sparsely). He also kept drafts of some of his own letters. On his death almost all of this correspondence, numbering, at a conservative estimate, over 200 documents, passed into the hands of Arthur Charlett, later Master of University College, who was already interested in having a biography of Pococke written.[5] (Only the letters written in Arabic and Hebrew, with a few associated documents, remained in the possession of Pococke's eldest son Edward.) However, when some years later Humfry Smith started to collect materials for his projected life of Pococke, Charlett was unable to produce the letters, and Smith, supposing them lost, never completed the biography, although his rough draft and other materials were preserved by the younger Pococke after Smith died in 1708. More than twenty years later[6] the letters were rediscovered among Charlett's papers by his nephew, the antiquarian Thomas Rawlins of Pophills. By this time Edward Pococke junior was dead, and his son John had succeeded him as Rector of Minall or Mildenhall in Wiltshire. Rawlins communicated the letters to him via the Oxford antiquary Thomas Hearne, and encouraged him in his hitherto desultory attempts to find someone to write his grandfather's life. The task, and the letters, were entrusted in 1734 to Twells, who as vicar of a church in Marlborough was John Pococke's neighbour. The project was stretched out for several years through delays engendered principally by the decision to issue the

letters from John Greaves to Pococke, made by John Ward in the 1730s for the biography of Greaves in his *Lives of the Gresham Professors*, from the originals then being used in London by Twells; and Sir Simonds D'Ewes's own copy of the letter he sent to Pococke (mentioned by Twells, p. 266) thanking him for some Arabic transcripts with Latin translation, preserved in MS BL Harley 377, fo. 144ʳ.

[4] The following account is based mainly on Twells's preface to the original (1740) edition of the biography, which is omitted in the 1816 reprint. It also relies on letters from John Pococke and Twells to Thomas Rawlins preserved in MS Ballard 28 and on inferences from Twells's *Life*.

[5] Hearne's *Diary* for 8 Nov. 1710 (iii. 77): 'Dr. Charelett (or Varlett) prevail'd with Mr. Pocock for the Papers that Dr. Pocock had by him, such as Letters &c. promising to write his Life. Dr. Charlett told me several times he had a great Number of Dr. Pocock's Letters.' Cf. x. 464.

[6] The approximate date is given by Hearne's *Diary* for July 1731 (x. 462), at which time Rawlins himself was contemplating writing a life of Pococke based on the letters. He did not send them to John Pococke until 1733.

biography as the introduction to a reprint of Pococke's *Theological Works*, in the hope that subscriptions would be more forthcoming (both Twells and John Pococke expected to make money from the enterprise). In 1737 Twells moved to London, where he had been made rector of St Matthews, Friday Street, taking the letters with him in order to complete the biography. While the letters were in London they were consulted by John Ward for his *Lives of the Professors of Gresham College* (1740), and by Thomas Birch for the biography of John Greaves prefixed to his edition of Greaves's *Miscellaneous Works* (1737). After the publication of Twells's biography no trace of the letters has been found. It seems certain that they were not returned by Twells to the man who had the best claim to be their owner, John Pococke.[7] None of them are to be found with the other remains of his grandfather (including the Arabic and Hebrew correspondence) which he kept faithfully at Minall Rectory and which remained there after his death (he being the last of that branch of the family) until they were donated by a later incumbent, Charles Francis, in 1821 to the Bodleian,[8] where they now repose among the Pococke manuscripts. Twells died in poverty in 1742, and it is possible that the letters were simply destroyed then or later. It is also possible that they still exist in an uninvestigated private collection:[9] they are certainly not in any public one.

Although the letters would constitute a precious source for the intellectual history of the seventeenth century, their loss is not as

---

[7] This is not surprising, since the two men were on very bad terms by the time the *Theological Works* was finally published, Pococke blaming Twells for his dilatoriness, and Twells accusing Pococke of rapacity. This is evident from the letters of both to Rawlins in MS Ballard 28. Cf. Twells's letter to Zachary Grey of 22 Mar. 1740, quoted by Nichols, *Literary Anecdotes*, i. 469–70: '. . . Pocock, at last, is finished, and will be delivered on Tuesday next, . . . if 300 sets are taken off by Subscribers, the reward of the Editor, for writing the Life, compiling Indexes, collating and correcting the errors of the old Edition (which with soliciting for subscriptions, travelling to London, Oxford, &c. have more or less employed his time and patience for five years last past) will be but 50*l*. . . . In order to explain my assertion above, that 50*l*. at the most will be all my gains on the foot of the subscription, you may please to know that Mr. Pocock, the proprietor of his grandfather's copies, may, and I fear will insist on half the clear profits of the Edition.'

[8] Macray, *Annals*, 161, 311.

[9] One might conjecture that they were acquired by Thomas Hunt, Laudian Professor of Arabic at the time, and a great admirer of Pococke, who collaborated with Twells in the edition of the *Theological Works* by correcting the proofs for the *Porta Mosis* (since Twells knew no Arabic). But the letters are not among the manuscripts bequeathed by Hunt to the Bodleian in 1775, and the only quotation that I have seen of a Pococke letter by Hunt (in *De usu dialectorum orientalium*, 21) appears to have been taken from Twells's *Life* (p. 22 of the 1816 edition).

damaging as it might have been, for Twells, who was an unimaginative man, frequently quotes or paraphrases important passages in them, and indeed whole stretches of his narrative consist of rather bald summaries of their contents. Nevertheless, there is no doubt that, could they be recovered, they would illuminate many passages in the lives of others,[10] if not of Pococke himself, and would clear up a number of chronological and other uncertainties in Twells's narrative. The fact remains that his is the essential basis for all subsequent accounts of Pococke, including the excellent article in the *DNB* by Stanley Lane-Poole.[11] However, I believe that the need to use Twells's reconstruction of the facts of Pococke's life, which is unavoidable,[12] has often led to uncritical acceptance of Twells's complacent view of his character. There is good reason to think that Pococke was a far more complex man than the pious and orthodox Anglican parson (not unlike himself) presented for our edification by Twells.[13] Certainty in such matters is impossible, since one trait of Pococke's that is unquestionable is his hatred of controversy (in marked contrast to his great friend John Greaves). One cannot expect from him statements overtly challenging common opinion on matters of morality or doctrine. But there are enough hints to suggest to the alert reader that Pococke held some views that were neither conventional nor uninfluenced by his experiences of the East in life and his vast knowledge of its literature.

[10] For instance Ward (*Lives of the Gresham Professors*, 151) tells us that there were no less than 42 letters from John Greaves. That number is far more than could be directly inferred from Twells's narrative.

[11] However, this adds some interesting items, including Pococke's planting cedars from cones he brought back from Syria (for further information on his botanical activities see Harvey, 'Coronary Flowers and their "Arabick" Background', 300).

[12] In general, wherever in this book a statement is made about Pococke's life for which the evidence is not obvious from the context, it may safely be assumed that it is derived from Twells.

[13] The character sketch of Pococke supplied to Humfry Smith by John Locke (*Correspondence*, viii, no. 3321, pp. 37–42), who knew him in his later years at Christ Church, is disappointingly vague, and suggests an acquaintance based on affable high table conversation rather than the 'close relationship' which Russell ('The Impact of *The Philosophus Autodidactus*', 240) finds in it.

I

The Medieval Background

THE study of Arabic in Europe during the Middle Ages was pursued for two motives: the acquisition of scientific knowledge, and Christian missionary and apologetic activities. For both of these the most important focus of activity was Spain, which had long been a centre of Islamic culture,[1] and thereby provided to other parts of Europe ready access to Arabic speakers and literature. Also essential to the Latin-speaking scholars and missionaries who undertook the study of Arabic were the safety and resources afforded by the Christian kingdoms of Castile and Aragon,[2] which grew out of the remnants which had survived the Arab conquest in the north of the peninsula, and accomplished the slow process of the 'Reconquista' over the centuries from 718 to 1492. Thus it was only after the conquest of Toledo by Alfonso VI of Castile in 1085 that significant activity, either of translators or missionaries, began in Spain. Another area where transmission of the Arabic language and culture took place was Sicily and southern Italy, which had also been under Islamic influence (and partly under Arabic rule) from the tenth century onwards. After the Norman conquest, beginning in the late eleventh century, Sicily experienced a fusion of Greek, Latin, and Arabic culture, particularly under two rulers who were patrons of Arabic literature, Roger II (1130–54) and his grandson the Emperor Frederick II (King of Sicily 1197–1250).[3] The reign of Frederick's son Manfred is also notable for the activity of translators from the Arabic in Sicily and southern Italy. But the contribution of this part of the world to both Islamic and Latin culture was never comparable to that of Spain. As for the crusades, and the Crusader Kingdom of Jerusalem which existed from the late eleventh century onwards, one need only note that they were of small importance in this respect.[4]

[1] The Arabic conquest of Spain began in 710. The Emirate (later Caliphate) of Cordoba was founded in 756, and from the time of the Caliph al-Ḥakam II (961) was the seat of a brilliant civilization.

[2] This point is well made by Metlitzki, *The Matter of Araby in Medieval England*, 6.

[3] See Haskins, *Studies in the History of Medieval Science*, chs. 9, 12. Hartwig's 'Die Uebersetzungsliteratur Unteritaliens', although antiquated in many respects, is still worth reading.

[4] One of the earliest translators, Adelard of Bath, visited Syria, as well as Sicily and southern Italy, not long after 1100. There is no direct evidence that he visited Spain, but

(I) THE SCIENTIFIC TRANSLATIONS

The translation of scientific works from Arabic into Latin[5] was carried out mainly in the twelfth and early thirteenth centuries, although occasional isolated examples can be found as early as *c.*1000 and as late as the fourteenth century. The main purpose of these translations was to recover the heritage of antiquity, much of which had been lost in the Latin West during late antiquity and the 'dark age' of the sixth and seventh centuries. Since communication of Western Europe with the Byzantine Empire was poor, and knowledge of Greek almost non-existent, the 'Carolingian Renaissance' of the ninth century was confined to the recovery of works in Latin. Meanwhile there had sprung up at Baghdad and elsewhere in the Arabic-speaking world an intense interest in the translation of Greek works into Arabic. This began in the later eighth century and lasted for about 150 years, during which period many hundreds of treatises were translated.[6] For religious and cultural reasons these were confined to scientific texts, but 'scientific' in the ancient and medieval sense was a term of wide embrace, including not only mathematics, astronomy, medicine, and geography, but also philosophy and pseudo-sciences such as astrology, alchemy, and geomancy. Furthermore, on this foundation a huge number of new scientific works, some of considerable originality and very high quality, were produced in the Islamic world; most of these were written in Arabic. This body of work in its turn, as well as treatises originally written in Greek, formed the material on which the medieval translators from Arabic into Latin drew. Although not comparable either in extent or in philological competence with the earlier translations from Greek into Arabic, the work of these translators was impressive in quantity and of fundamental importance for the development of science and philosophy in Latin-speaking Europe.

it is significant that the work which made his fame as a translator, the astronomical tables of al-Khwārizmī, was derived from Spain. For recent work on Adelard see Burnett, *Adelard of Bath*, and for the meagre evidence on 'Translators in Syria during the Crusades' see Haskins, *Studies in the History of Medieval Science*, ch. 7.

[5] There is no adequate general treatment of the translation movement. The best available is the series of separate articles by Haskins collected in his *Studies in the History of Medieval Science*, which needs to be corrected and supplemented in many details by the work of the last 70 years.

[6] For a good introduction see Rosenthal, *The Classical Heritage in Islam*; for mathematics Toomer, 'Lost Greek Mathematical Works in Arabic Translation'; in general Steinschneider, *Die arabischen Übersetzungen aus dem Griechischen*.

(II) MISSIONARIES AND APOLOGISTS

The serious study of Islam in Western Europe[7] begins with the activity of Peter the Venerable, Abbot of Cluny, who in 1141 visited Spain to inspect the Cluniac monasteries there. Anxious to combat the 'heresy' of Islam and convert the heretics to Christianity, he recruited to his cause, amongst others, Robert of Ketton and Herman of Dalmatia, both experienced translators from the Arabic, who happened to be in Spain at the same time, engaged in the study of scientific texts. With their aid he had translated a body of texts to be used in his missionary and apologetic programme.[8] The chief of these was Robert's translation of the Koran, which, for all its faults, was the form in which that work was mainly known in Europe not only in the Middle Ages but down to the seventeenth century.[9]

The mendicant orders, Franciscans and Dominicans, were also interested in missionary activity amongst Muslims, and established centres for teaching Arabic,[10] especially in Spain. But by far the most ambitious programme was conceived by Ramon Lull (Ramón Llull, Raimundus Lullus), much of whose life and many of whose voluminous writings were devoted to the task of converting the Muslims.[11] He not only learned Arabic himself, but spent much time advocating that it be taught systematically as part of the missionary efforts. He even travelled to Islamic lands in an effort to personally convert the populace. In 1292 he went to Tunis and in 1306 to Bougie in Algeria,

---

[7] The best survey of the interest in Islam during the medieval period is Monneret de Villard, *Lo Studio dell'Islam in Europa nel XII e nel XIII secolo*, to be corrected and supplemented by articles by d'Alverny, notably 'Deux traductions latines du Coran' and 'La Connaissance de l'Islam en Occident'. Much additional material, notably on the later medieval period, can be found in Daniel, *Islam and the West*, but this is not organized in an accessible way.

[8] Some of these, together with Peter's own 'Refutation of Islam' based on them, were published with English translation by Kritzeck, *Peter the Venerable and Islam*, a useful albeit flawed collection.

[9] It is the version which was printed by Bibliander (1543; 2nd edn. 1550: see *PO* no. 12), from which was derived the Italian version of Arrivabene (1547), which in turn was the basis for the German version of Schweigger (1616), itself translated into Dutch in 1641: see Schnurrer, pp. 425–7. The more accurate version by Mark of Toledo (1209–10: see d'Alverny, 'Deux traductions latines du Coran', 113ff.) was little known.

[10] Monneret de Villard, *Lo Studio dell'Islam*, 35–42 is far more useful than the sententious article on the Dominican schools by Coll, 'Escuelas de lenguas orientales en los siglos XIII y XIV'.

[11] The enormous literature on Lull cannot be surveyed here. On his Arabic studies in particular see Fück, 16–22. On his missionary activities see Monneret de Villard, *Lo Studio dell'Islam*, 42–4.

from both of which he was quickly expelled. Undaunted, he returned in 1316, at an advanced age, to Tunis, where he finally met the martyr's death that he had courted. His knowledge of Arabic was alleged to have been good enough for him actually to write works in that language, but since none of these have survived it is impossible to assess his linguistic competence. Despite untiring advocacy directed towards popes and monarchs over many years, Lull had very little success in promoting the study of Arabic for missionary activity. He did indeed establish a seminary for that purpose in 1276 at Miramar on his native Majorca, but it did not last long. Undoubtedly the most famous result of his efforts[12] was the canon of the Council of Vienne in 1311–12, decreeing that professorships for teaching Greek, Hebrew, Chaldee,[13] and Arabic be established at the papal court and the Universities of Paris, Oxford, Bologna, and Salamanca.[14] The decree is frequently cited later by those interested in promoting Arabic,[15] but in fact had remarkably little effect. As far as Arabic is concerned, nothing was done at Oxford, and the decree seems to have been used in England only as an occasional excuse to collect ecclesiastical taxes.[16] Elsewhere there is more evidence,[17] but nothing that points to real implementation of the decree anywhere during the Middle Ages.

(III) KNOWLEDGE OF ARABIC

Concerning the level of competence, linguistic and otherwise, of those who undertook the study of Arabic it is hard to generalize. Nothing of

[12] There is no doubt that Lull was the prime mover in this affair: see e.g. Altaner, 'Raymundus Lullus und der Sprachenkanon des Konzils von Vienne', which gives a useful survey of Lull's advocacy of similar schemes in the preceding years.

[13] An ambiguous term, which was used during the period with which we are concerned both for Biblical Aramaic (written in Hebrew characters) and Christian Aramaic (written in Syriac characters, but also spoken by Eastern Christians). In this context it is certainly the latter which is intended. See Altaner, 'Raymundus Lullus und der Sprachenkanon des Konzils von Vienne', 217–18, who rightly stresses that the aim of the decree was missionary, not scholastic.

[14] The full text of the decree is in Hefele–Leclercq, 688–9.

[15] Examples in 17th-century England are Pasor (see below, p. 99), Thomas Greaves, *De Linguae Arabicae Vtilitate*, 18, and Walton, *Introductio ad lectionem linguarum Orientalium*, 9. For Pococke's comment see below, p. 214. Jones, 'Learning Arabic in Renaissance Europe', 220 n. 10 gives references to the decree by Postel, Raimondi, and Erpenius.

[16] See Weiss, 'England and the Decree of the Council of Vienne'.

[17] Altaner, 'Die Durchführung des Vienner Konzilsbeschlusses', has collected some instances, many of them dubious.

significance emerged in the way of grammatical or lexicographical study. Two meagre lexicographical compilations survive from medieval Spain. The first, a Latin–Arabic glossary of uncertain date (perhaps from the twelfth century), was intended to help Arabic-speaking Christians understand Latin, according to the most recent study of it.[18] The second, the *Vocabulista in Arabico* from the thirteenth century,[19] was designed to aid Latin-speakers to make themselves understood in the vulgar Arabic of Spain. Both of these would be of very little use in interpreting Arabic texts (although Scaliger, who owned the former manuscript, used it for that purpose[20]). All the medieval students of Arabic had to rely, at least initially, on native speakers, who were familiar with both Arabic and the vernacular (usually a Spanish dialect). If these interpreters were Muslims or Jews, they did not know Latin, and if they were Christian Arabophones ('Mozarabs') they were rarely educated men, and were equally ignorant of Latin. Thus the process of translation was often a laborious procedure from Arabic through the common vernacular to Latin. Nevertheless, some of the translators attained a respectable level of competence in Arabic, for instance Gerard of Cremona (d. 1187), who spent most of his long life in Spain and completed an astonishing number of translations, including such basic works as Ptolemy's *Almagest*.[21] Most of the medieval Latin translations from the Arabic are uncouth by virtue of their excessive literalism, with frequent Arabisms not only of vocabulary but also of syntax; but some are faithful enough to the original to be of help to the modern scholar in elucidating and occasionally correcting surviving Arabic texts.[22] The knowledge of the culture of Arabic-speaking lands which filtered through to the West was sparse, and the picture was distorted by the lens of religious prejudice and polemic. But there were a few individuals who had a surprisingly detailed knowledge of the practice of Islam, derived not only from the Koran, but from some of the Arabic commentators thereon and from the collections of traditions about the

[18] By van Koningsveld, *The Latin-Arabic Glossary of the Leiden University Library*. The glossary, now MS Leiden Or. 231, was published by C. F. Seybold (Berlin, 1900).

[19] Edited by Schiaparelli; see Fück, 22–5.

[20] The manuscript was owned by other 16th-century Arabists before it came into Scaliger's possession: Postel, Andreas Masius, and Franciscus Raphelengius; for the latter's use of it in his Arabic lexicon see Hamilton, 'Nam Tirones Sumus', 559–60. Van Koningsveld's account of the history of the manuscript in the 16th century (*The Latin-Arabic Glossary of the Leiden University Library*, 6) is very summary.

[21] Kunitzsch, *Der Almagest*, 104–12 gives a good analysis of Gerard as a translator.

[22] This is notably so in parts of ibn al-Haytham's *Optics*.

Prophet (the *ḥadīth*). Besides Lull and Ricoldo da Montecroce[23] in the early fourteenth century, there was the Spanish Dominican Raimundo Martini, whose *Pugio Fidei adversus Mauros et Judeos* of 1278, a polemical work mainly directed against the Jews, reveals a remarkable knowledge of Islamic religious and philosophical treatises,[24] which Martini certainly knew at first hand. His command of Arabic is impressively demonstrated by a dialogue between a Christian and a Muslim which he composed in the style of the Koran.[25] But these men too, for all their superior knowledge, were concerned to present the 'heresy' of Islam in the worst light. In general, the picture of Islam, and especially of its Prophet, derivable from medieval Latin texts is an unedifying farrago of myth and invective leavened with a few facts and historical events.[26] Western knowledge of the history of the Arabs, even during the time of Muḥammad, was extremely defective,[27] and indeed there was no interest in it except for the purposes of polemic.

That several of the most prominent translators from the Arabic in the medieval period came from England, or the British Isles, is a matter of curiosity rather than significance,[28] given the international nature of Latin European culture. In the twelfth century Adelard of Bath travelled widely in Arabic-speaking areas, and Robert of Ketton was active in Spain. In the thirteenth century Michael Scot, after working at Toledo and Salerno, was patronized by Frederick II in Sicily;[29] Alfred of Sareshel (also known as Alfred the Englishman) visited Spain. There is reason to believe that some medieval Latin manuscripts (for instance of the translations of al-Khwārizmī's astronomical tables) in which the scribe betrays knowledge of the Arabic language or even script, were written in England. Certainly there were occasional individuals in England from the early twelfth century onwards with some

[23] On the Florentine Dominican Ricoldo, who studied Arabic and Islam on his journey to the East, especially Baghdad, about 1291, and later wrote an attack on the Koran, see Monneret de Villard, *Il Libro della Peregrinazione di Frate Ricoldo da Montecroce*, and the works mentioned ibid. 12.

[24] For details see Fück, 15–16; Monneret de Villard, *Lo Studio dell'Islam*, 55–6.

[25] Printed and translated by Schiaparelli in his edition of the *Vocabulista in Arabico*, pp. xvi–xviii.

[26] The standard work on this is Daniel, *Islam and the West*.

[27] The situation was different among the Greeks and among the Eastern Christians, but their accounts were as yet virtually unknown to Latin-speaking Europe.

[28] Metlitzki, *The Matter of Araby in Medieval England*, which is mainly concerned with 'Arabic' influences in Middle English literature, gives (ch. 2) a well-informed and sympathetic account of individuals with knowledge of Arabic who came from or visited England at this time.

[29] Haskins, *Studies in the History of Medieval Science*, ch. 13.

knowledge of Arabic,[30] but they had no influence whatever on the developments in the period that concerns us.

[30] For instance the converted Spanish Jew Petrus Alfonsi, author of the famous *Disciplina Clericalis*, was doctor to King Henry I: see Metlitzki, 21 ff. for other evidence, in an astronomical manuscript, of his activity in England. Roger Bacon, for all his strictures on the errors of contemporary translators from the Arabic, was not among the English Arabists: see the references given by Metlitzki, 257 n. 75.

2

The Study of Arabic in Europe during the Sixteenth and Seventeenth Centuries

TWO new factors favouring the study of Arabic in Europe were operative during the sixteenth and seventeenth centuries. The first was the
involvement of the European nations with the Ottoman Empire, which
continued vigorous and partially successful efforts to expand westward
during this period. Relations between Europeans and Turks were in
part hostile (for instance the Ottomans made war on both the Emperor
and the Venetians in the seventeenth century), but trade also became
increasingly important. During the later Byzantine Empire trade with
Constantinople and the Ottomans had been largely in the hands of the
Venetians and Genoese, but now the countries of northern Europe also
became heavily involved. This, combined with the need for formal
diplomatic relations with the Ottoman power, led to the 'capitulations'
of the sixteenth century. These were treaties by which the Sultan
granted certain privileges to a country, which allowed merchants to
reside permanently and conduct their business in specific areas, as self-
governing communities under the supervision of an ambassador at the
Porte and consuls in the more important trading locations elsewhere,
such as Aleppo and Smyrna. The first nation[1] to negotiate these privileges was France, when Suleiman the Magnificent concluded with
King François I a treaty of commerce and friendship in 1536.[2] This
formed the model for the treaty concluded between Murad III and
Queen Elizabeth of England in 1580[3] (which was followed in 1581 by
the chartering of the Levant Company), and for that between Ahmet I
and the Dutch Republic in 1612. The merchant communities in
Constantinople, Asia Minor, Syria, Egypt, and elsewhere in the Ottoman dominions constituted safe havens for Europeans (who otherwise

---

[1] The capitulations which Venice and Genoa had long possessed with the Byzantine
Empire were renewed by the Ottomans after they captured Constantinople in 1453.

[2] Charrière, *Négociations de la France dans le Levant*, 283–94.

[3] For details of the negotiations and terms see Wood, *History of the Levant Company*,
7–13.

would have been at considerable risk as alien Christians in Muslim dominions) wishing to visit the East in search of manuscripts as well as knowledge of the languages. The resources that these communities provided were thus an essential element in the phenomenal growth of Arabic studies in seventeenth-century Europe.

The second new factor was the growth of interest among Western Europeans in establishing contacts with the Eastern Churches (Orthodox, Nestorian, Melkite, Maronite, Jacobite, and Coptic Monophysite Christians).[4] These Eastern Christians used a number of different languages (Greek, Syriac, Arabic, Turkish, and Coptic) either as liturgical or vernacular tongues. Both Catholics and Protestants were anxious to enlist the Eastern Churches as allies against each other (thus in England in the seventeenth century hopes of establishing communion between the Church of England and the Greek Orthodox Church were long entertained). However, the Catholic Church, particularly after the revival of purpose and discipline following the Council of Trent, was far more vigorous and systematic in these activities. Small communities of Jesuit and other missionaries were maintained in a number of places in the Ottoman Empire. More importantly, several colleges were established in Rome under the papal aegis in order that Eastern Christians might study and be indoctrinated in the Catholic faith. Of these the most influential for Arabic was the Maronite College founded by Pope Gregory XIII in 1584. Among those who came to study there were priests whose native language was Arabic or Syriac,[5] but who in any case knew Arabic well, and were men of considerable education. As will be seen below in the survey of Italy and France, they were of fundamental importance as instructors and editors in the early period of the revival of Arabic studies.

Also fundamentally different from the medieval period were the new approaches to texts and history which had been introduced in the Renaissance. It is true that certain aspects of the Renaissance in Europe were prima facie unfavourable to the study of Arabic. The recovery of the original Greek texts of many works which had hitherto been known only from barbarous translations from the Arabic resulted in new translations made directly from the Greek, which were rapidly

[4] Hamilton, 'The English Interest in the Arabic-Speaking Christians', gives a useful overview of this phenomenon.

[5] On the question whether the native language of the Lebanese Christians around 1600 was still Syriac, or had already changed to Arabic, the evidence of a contemporary witness, Savary de Brèves, is ambiguous: Duverdier, 'Les Impressions orientales en Europe et le Liban', 197.

diffused by the recent invention of the printing-press. Many humanists expressed contempt for the learning of the 'Arabs'.[6] On the other hand, the more sophisticated methods of scholarship which were developed in the Renaissance, especially in the realm of textual criticism, led eventually to the demand for the oriental versions of the Bible, which became a primary motive in the seventeenth century for searching out and publishing oriental manuscripts. Likewise in medicine, where Arabic authors such as Avicenna were still held in high repute, there was considerable interest in consulting the original Arabic texts rather than the corrupt medieval Latin translations. Furthermore, the 'new astronomy' of Copernicus and Kepler brought about renewed interest in recovering ancient and medieval observations which had been transmitted by the Arabs. It is no accident that some of the most prominent Arabists of the seventeenth century were physicians or (especially in England) astronomers.[7] But above all, that expanded curiosity, that sense of history, which men had learned in the Renaissance to bring to the treatment of classical antiquity, was applied by the best of the seventeenth-century Arabists to the literature, history, and civilization of the lands of Islam as well.

In the following survey of the study of Arabic in Europe (outside England) individual countries or areas are treated separately, but this is merely for convenience of organization. As will appear from my narrative, there were multiple links and influences between the different areas. Indeed some of those involved were active in more than one area; for instance Postel, who began his career in France, also worked in Italy and Austria. Conversely the Maronites Gabriel Sionita and Abraham Ecchellensis moved from Italy to France. Joseph Scaliger was a Frenchman and learned Arabic in France, but since his greatest influence was in the Netherlands he is treated here under that heading, as is the Frenchman Salmasius, whose principal publications connected with Arabic were done in the Netherlands.

---

[6] From the extensive literature on the disputes between 'humanists' and 'Arabists' in 15th- and 16th-century Europe, especially among medical writers, I cite only Klein-Franke, *Die klassische Antike in der Tradition des Islam*, ch. 1, and Siraisi, *Avicenna in Renaissance Italy*, 65 ff. The term 'Arabist' in this context implies no knowledge of the language, but was applied to those who continued to favour the old Latin translations from the Arabic.

[7] The Germans Kirsten and Elichmann were Arabist physicians, as was the Frenchman Vattier and the Flemish Vopiscus Fortunatus Plempius. English Arabist astronomers include John Bainbridge, John Greaves, Edward Bernard, and Edmund Halley. Elsewhere we may mention Schickard in Germany and Golius in Holland.

(I) SPAIN

The country where Arabic studies were most energetically and successfully pursued during the Middle Ages contributed very little during the early modern period. The reason for this lies in the political and social policies of the ruling powers. The last independent Islamic enclave, Granada, fell to the Reconquista in 1492. There were many 'Moriscos' (as the Muslim Spaniards were called)[8] left, not only in Granada, but in other parts of the Iberian peninsula, for some time after. But the centuries of war between Christian and Islamic states had left a legacy of hatred and suspicion, which soon led to a policy of eradication, not only of the religion of Islam, but of all aspects of its culture, including the Arabic language.[9] As early as 1499 we hear of about 5,000 Arabic manuscripts being burned in the public square at Granada on the orders of Ximénez de Cisneros, Archbishop of Toledo.[10] In 1567 a decree of Philip II, repeating and enforcing an earlier edict which had remained a dead letter, forbade the Muslims of Granada the use of their traditional dress and customs, including the use of the Arabic language,[11] which led to the last great rebellion of the Arabic-speaking population of Granada. This, and its suppression by the royal forces, were accompanied by horrifying atrocities in which ethnic hatreds were intensified by religious zeal. The final unhappy act was the expulsion of all Moriscos in 1609, in imitation of the example of Ferdinand and Isabella, who expelled the Jews in 1492.

In the preceding period missionary activity did leave its mark on Spanish Arabic scholarship. This appears in two works written, at the behest of the Archbishop of Granada, by Pedro de Alcalá, and printed at Granada in 1505: the *Vocabulista aravigo en letra castellana* and the *Arte para ligeramente saber la lengua araviga*, respectively a vocabulary and grammar intended for the use of missionaries in the newly conquered territories. For lack of any but Gothic letter-types

---

[8] In Spain the term 'Morisco' was narrowed to apply only to former Muslims who had been converted to Christianity and their descendants, while those who retained their allegiance to Islam were termed 'Mudéjares' (Arabic مدجّن).

[9] This was a secular policy, but was vigorously advocated and enforced by the religious authority, the Inquisition, whose excesses in Spain need not be rehearsed here.

[10] Gómez de Castro, *De Rebus Gestis a Francisco Ximenio*, fo. 30b (according to Dannenfeldt, 'The Renaissance Humanists and the Knowledge of Arabic', 105 n. 61); p. 99 of Oroz Reta's translation.

[11] For a vivid account see Prescott, *History of the Reign of Philip the Second*, iii. 20–35.

Arabic words are printed in transcription, with only crude woodcut representations of the letters of the alphabet.[12] The Arabic in these books is the vulgar dialect of Granada, and is of more interest to modern students of dialectology[13] than it can have been of use to sixteenth-century students of classical Arabic, although some of them used the books *faute de mieux*.[14] It is significant that in the table of imprints containing Arabic listed in order of date by Schnurrer[15] there is no book printed in Spain between these two (which comprise the first item in the list) and Cañes's *Grammatica arabigo-española*, published in Madrid in 1775. Once the missionary problem of dealing with the Muslims had been solved by forcible conversion and expulsion, since reading not only the Koran but any other Arabic book was forbidden, and use of the Arabic language was banned not only from legal contexts but absolutely, the practical uses which had driven the study of Arabic in medieval Spain were no longer operative. A partial exception is the use of Arabic texts by medical practitioners, which required some knowledge of the language. The only books which Archbishop Ximénez spared from the pyre were some Arabic medical texts, which he donated to the library at Alcalá. The edition of the first part of Avicenna's *Canon* by Ledesma (Valencia, 1547–8) is allegedly based in part on the original Arabic.[16] But even this kind of knowledge was scarce by the end of the sixteenth century.[17] The drastic decline in Spain of competence in Arabic can be illustrated by two anecdotes. When Nicolaus Clenardus, anxious to learn Arabic, came in 1531 to Salamanca (relying on its status in the decree of the Council of Vienne), he was told that no one there was able to give instruction in the language.[18] In 1609 a commission appointed by King Philip III to

---

[12] Reproduced in *Le Livre et le Liban*, 117.

[13] See Jones, 'Learning Arabic', 134–43 for a detailed analysis of the grammar, with references to modern literature. Fück, 29–35 is still useful.

[14] Jones, 'Learning Arabic', 143. For Raphelengius' use of the *Vocabulista* in his Arabic lexicon see Hamilton, 'Nam Tirones Sumus', 565.

[15] *Bibliotheca Arabica*, 515–29. This omits the last gasp of Spanish missionary activity towards the Moriscos, the *Doctrina Christiana*, in Arabic and Castilian, printed at Valencia in 1566 for Archbishop Martín Pérez de Ayala. In this the Arabic is again printed in transliteration.

[16] Siraisi, *Avicenna in Renaissance Italy*, 139, 364.

[17] See the informative article by Garcia Ballester, 'The Circulation and Use of Medical Manuscripts in Arabic in 16th Century Spain', with further literature.

[18] See Bataillon, 'L'Arabe à Salamanque', 10. (The whole of this article is a valuable commentary on the state of Arabic instruction in Spain in the 16th century, summed up on p. 17: 'L'Espagne de la Renaissance était à la fois le pays le mieux désigné pour devenir une pépinière d'arabisants et le pays le moins disposé à jouer ce rôle.') On Clenardus' partial success thereafter see below, p. 40.

deal with some mysterious lead tablets inscribed in Arabic, purporting to be early Christian writings, which had been dug up at Granada in 1595, could only recommend that experts be summoned from Italy or elsewhere abroad to examine them.[19] However, there were humanists in sixteenth-century Spain who advocated the study of Arabic, like Vives,[20] or even undertook it, like Benito Arias Montano,[21] who while librarian of the Escorial in the early 1580s advocated collecting Arabic manuscripts for that library.[22]

One might have supposed from the existence of great libraries at Cordoba and elsewhere under Muslim rule that Spain would be a major source of Arabic books in the sixteenth and seventeenth centuries, but this was not so: Archbishop Ximénez's bonfire helps to explain why.[23] It is true that the library of the Escorial, founded by Philip II in 1563, began to accumulate Arabic manuscripts almost from the beginning,[24] but these were neither numerous nor, for the most part, of any great value until the accession of the library of the Sultan of Morocco, Mawlāy Zaydān, by an act of piracy in 1611.[25] This acquisition did indeed give the Escorial the largest and most varied collection of Arabic manuscripts in Europe at a stroke,[26] and even after the disastrous fire of 1671 and the accumulation of large numbers of Arabic manuscripts at Oxford, Leiden, Paris, and elsewhere, the Escorial Arabic collection remained one of the most impressive.[27] But

[19] Jones, 'Learning Arabic', 22–3 summarizes the evidence for this strange story. It is discussed at length by Cabanelas Rodríguez, *El Morisco Granadino Alonso del Castillo*, 197–232. The tablets were forgeries by contemporary Moriscos, perhaps Miguel de Luna and Alonso del Castillo.

[20] *De tradendis disciplinis*, quoted by Dannenfeldt, 'The Renaissance Humanists and the Knowledge of Arabic', 106–7. Other examples of Spanish humanists who knew or advocated Arabic, ibid. 104–8.

[21] Much more important for Hebrew than for Arabic studies; his chief contribution was the assistance he gave in the editing of the Antwerp Polyglot Bible: see Lloyd Jones, *The Discovery of Hebrew in Tudor England*, 43–4, with references to further literature.

[22] The passage is quoted by Justel Calabozo, *La Real Biblioteca de El Escorial*, 154.

[23] Clenardus, in Spain in the 1530s, found it virtually impossible to get Arabic books out of the hands of the Inquisition, and reported that Christians who possessed Arabic manuscripts were selling them to North Africa: Chauvin and Roersch, *Étude sur la vie et les travaux de Nicolas Clénard*, 135.

[24] See Justel Calabozo, 133–69 for a summary account of the collections that came to the library.

[25] See Justel Calabozo, 172–7; Jones, 'Learning Arabic', 55–7.

[26] This incidentally explains why the script of so many of the most interesting manuscripts in the present collection of the Escorial is Maghrebine (North African).

[27] Mawlāy Zaydān's manuscripts numbered about 4,000, making a total of about 4,500 Arabic manuscripts in the Escorial. After the fire about 2,000 remained (Justel Calabozo, 183, 190).

there is little sign of its being used in the period we are examining. Access to it was extremely difficult,[28] and there was no published catalogue until Casiri's of 1760–70.[29] It is no exaggeration to say that the Escorial Library was of no importance whatever for Arabic studies in the seventeenth century.

(II) ITALY

During the sixteenth century Italy was in the forefront of Arabic studies. This is particularly evident in the printing of Arabic. The first book printed with Arabic movable type is the Fano book of hours of 1514.[30] This was followed by the magnificent polyglot Psalter (in Hebrew, Greek, Arabic, Chaldee, and Latin), published at Genoa in 1516, and edited over many years by Agostino Giustiniani, Bishop of Nebbio in Corsica, who was a remarkable linguist for his time.[31] The most astonishing achievement of early Arabic printing, however, is the publication of the complete Koran by the Venetian printer Paganino de Paganinis in about 1538. This was evidently intended as a commercial venture, the publisher hoping to make great profit by selling the book to Muslims in the Ottoman dominions: hence it was printed entirely in Arabic, with no indication of its European origin. But attempts to sell it must have failed in face of the contemporary Muslim suspicion of printing (fostered by the powerful guilds of professional scribes), for only one copy has survived,[32] and Paganino soon went bankrupt, no

[28] This naturally led to overestimation of its extent and importance: *omne ignotum pro magnifico*. In 1692 Thomas Hyde, in his inaugural Arabic lecture, related how the Moroccan ambassador assured him that the Moroccan library which had been taken to Spain contained 20,000 Arabic books. See below on John Bainbridge's futile attempts to get access to or information about the treasures of ancient astronomy which he imagined might be at the Escorial, p. 72. One Englishman who did manage to get access in the early 17th century, Robert Ashley, described it as a 'glorious golden librarie of Arabian books' (Wood, *Athenae Oxonienses*, iii. 20).

[29] The list published by Hottinger, *Promtuarium*, Appendix A, merely reproduces that in Ravius, *Alcoran*, which came from a copy owned by Golius of a catalogue compiled, allegedly in 1583, by the Morisco doctor Alonso del Castillo, and contained only 261 items (Justel Calabozo, 217–20). On the difficulties of the date, and the compiler, see Cabanelas Rodríguez, *El Morisco Granadino Alonso del Castillo*, especially 121–37.

[30] Schnurrer no. 235; the beginning is reproduced *Philologia Arabica*, 68. Although the imprint is the small papal city of Fano, the work was published by a Venetian printer, and in all probability was printed in Venice: see Duverdier's note in *Le Livre et le Liban*, item 54, p. 188.

[31] On him, and the book, see Aboussouan in *Le Livre et le Liban*, 110–16, with good illustrations; for an example of the book, *PO* no. 236.

[32] See Nuovo, 'Il Corano arabo ritrovato', for the remarkable story of the recent

doubt overwhelmed by the costs of having a special fount designed and cast for a press run which produced no return at all. A much more successful production was the revised Latin translation of Avicenna's medical encyclopedia (*Canon*) made by Andrea Alpago of Belluno, who had spent many years in the East at Damascus (where he was attached to the Venetian consulate as its doctor) and elsewhere, learning Arabic and looking for manuscripts. This was published posthumously (Venice, 1527). Alpago also produced translations from the Arabic of some of Avicenna's philosophical works, which were published by his nephew Paolo in 1546.[33]

A figure of some importance for the information he provided on the geography and history of the Arabic-speaking world was Leo Africanus. A Spanish Muslim who had migrated to Fez at an early age, and was moderately well educated there, he was captured by Christian corsairs in 1518, and brought to Rome, where he was handed over to Pope Leo X. After a two-year imprisonment, during which he was allowed to use the Arabic manuscripts in the Vatican Library,[34] he was baptized, changing his name from al-Ḥasan b. Muḥammad b. Aḥmad al-Wazzān to Johannes Leo, in honour of his patron the Pope. After his release he lived in Italy for a while, where he taught Arabic to Cardinal Aegidius of Viterbo,[35] before eventually returning to Morocco and Islam. He wrote a number of works in and on Arabic, including a grammar. Most of these have not survived, but a version of his 'Description of Africa', which he composed in Italian, was published in Ramusio's *Navigationi et viaggi*.[36] This work of Leo's was republished many times, in Latin and other languages, in the sixteenth and seventeenth centuries, and long remained a principal source for European knowledge of the Islamic world.[37] Leo wrote

recovery of this, after the book had disappeared so completely that as early as the 17th century there were those who doubted whether it had ever really existed.

[33] On Alpago and his translations of Avicenna see d'Alverny, 'Avicenne et les médecins de Venise', 184–97; Lucchetta, *Andrea Alpago*, is exhaustive on his life. The Arabic text of the *Canon* was not printed until 1593 (see below).

[34] Levi della Vida, *Ricerche*, 99–108. On Leo Africanus in general see Codazzi, 'Leone Africano', and Jones, 'Learning Arabic', 65–6.

[35] For other evidence on Aegidius of Viterbo's Arabic studies see Hamilton, 'Nam Tirones Sumus', 561–2. For the slender evidence that he taught Arabic to Widmanstetter in 1532 see Müller, *Johann Albrecht v. Widmanstetter*, 21–2.

[36] First edition Venice, 1550. Reprinted in Ramusio, vol. 1. The best modern translation is Épaulard's (see vol. 1, pp. vi–vii for some account of the recently discovered manuscript, which is independent of Ramusio's version).

[37] For details of the kind of geographical, biographical, and bibliographical information it contains see Jones, 'Learning Arabic', 67–72, who stresses its importance for Erpenius.

another work on the Arabic philosophers, which was apparently the source for the short treatise 'De viris quibusdam illustribus apud Arabes' published by Hottinger in 1664.[38]

It is no accident that the earliest Arabic imprints in Italy are associated with Venice and Genoa, both of which had a long tradition of commerce with the East. Those which appear later in the century all come from Rome, reflecting the shift of emphasis to missionary activity, mainly, although not exclusively, connected with the papacy. Although there are forerunners, the great event for our story was the founding of the Medicean oriental press[39] by Cardinal Ferdinando de' Medici, with the encouragement of Pope Gregory XIII, in 1584. The Arabic type for this press, far superior to any previously used, was designed by the great French typographer, Robert Granjon.[40] The expressed intention of this foundation was to promote the Catholic faith amongst Eastern Christians,[41] and this is indeed consistent with some of its productions, such as the first book issued by the press, the four Gospels in Arabic of 1590.[42] But the director of the press, Giovanni Battista Raimondi, was a man of wide interests, with considerable knowledge of Arabic and Persian.[43] In its early years the press also produced a number of secular works in Arabic. Apart from some native Arabic grammars, these comprised the *Canon* of

[38] Hottinger, *Bibliothecarius Quadripartitus*, 245–91, from a copy made in 1527.

[39] Jones, 'The Medici Oriental Press', provides a good short account of the press and its aims, with an extensive bibliography of modern publications about it, 102–3. Of these the most useful are Saltini, 'Della Stamperia Orientale Medicea e di Giovan Battista Raimondi', and Tinto, *La Tipografia Medicea Orientale* (which provides reproductions of title-pages of many of the publications of the press).

[40] See Vervliet, 'Robert Granjon à Rome'. Some of the type had already been used by Domenico Basa, for instance in the edition of the *Kitāb al-Bustān* (Rome, 1584; Schnurrer no. 189), which has the distinction of being the first secular Arabic book ever printed. On Basa as a printer of orientalia see Tinto, *La Tipografia Medicea*, 19–22, with some corrections to Vervliet's discussion of Granjon's types, 22–43.

[41] This is expressed in the memorandum drawn up by Raimondi published by Tinto, *La Tipografia Medicea*, 94. In the same passage the printing of Arabic books in 'the humane sciences' is naïvely justified on the grounds that it would introduce printing to Muslims, and by this means gradually 'vi possi penetrare la notizia dell'errori di mahumettani, et la verità della fede christiana'.

[42] Schnurrer no. 318; for the date 1590, rather than Schnurrer's '1591', see Fück, 54 n. 118.

[43] See Saltini, 'Della Stamperia Orientale'. Some more material on Raimondi's tenure at the press can be found in Tinto, *La Tipografia Medicea*, and in the unpublished dissertation of Jones, 'The Arabic and Persian Studies of Giovan Battista Raimondi' (most of which is devoted to Raimondi's works on Arabic grammar).

Avicenna[44] and an Arabic translation of Euclid,[45] and also a geographical work, printed without the author's name, which was part of the treatise of al-Idrīsī, but was known to seventeenth-century Europe as 'the Nubian Geography', after the title ignorantly applied to it by Gabriel Sionita and Johannes Hesronita, who published a Latin version.[46] The ostensible rationale for these publications was to make money for the press by selling them in Muslim countries: accordingly a licence to import books printed in Arabic was obtained from Sultan Murad III in 1587, and printed at the end of the Euclid.[47] This venture seems to have been as unsuccessful as Paganino's earlier attempt,[48] but even these three works furnished a valuable resource to Europeans who wished to study Arabic outside the narrow orbit of Christian liturgy and scripture to which the printed texts had hitherto been confined.[49] In fact Raimondi had conceived an ambitious programme of printing no less than eighty works, mainly in the sciences, in Arabic and other oriental languages. For this to succeed he needed access to the relevant manuscripts,[50] and in fact we know that a valuable collection of oriental manuscripts was available to him in the library which Ignatius Ni'matallah, Jacobite Patriarch of Antioch, brought with him to Rome in 1577, and eventually donated to Cardinal Ferdinando to be used by the Medicean Press.[51] Amongst these was an Arabic

[44] 1593: Schnurrer no. 393; the title-page is reproduced *Philologia Arabica,* 75, and Gabrieli and Scerrato, *Gli Arabi in Italia,* 686. Tinto, *La Tipografia Medicea,* 16, reproduces an Arabo-Latin title-page unknown to Schnurrer.

[45] 1594: *PO* no. 31, Schnurrer no. 401 (title-page reproduced Tinto, *La Tipografia Medicea,* 57; another page in Gabrieli and Scerrato, *Gli Arabi in Italia,* 672). The version is stated in the title to be that of aṭ-Ṭūsī, but this is denied by Sabra, 'Simplicius's Proof of Euclid's Parallels Postulate', 18. Cf. John Murdoch in *DSB* iv. 440.

[46] *Geographia Nubiensis* (Paris, 1619; see below, p. 31). For the original Arabic imprint see *PO* no. 29; a modern facsimile of the whole is al-Sharīf al-Idrīsī, *Kitāb Nuzhat al-Mushtāq.* John Selden seems to have been the first to point out that the work is from al-Idrīsī (in *Uxor Ebraica,* 1646), soon followed by John Greaves, preface to his *Tabulae Geographicae* (1648): see below, pp. 68, 173.

[47] Reproduced in Russell, *The 'Arabick' Interest of the Natural Philosophers,* 99, and (better) *Le Livre et le Liban,* item 133, p. 248. Duverdier's note ad loc. on the failure of Raimondi's plans for scholarly publications is relevant to what follows here.

[48] In the 1670s or 1680s Galland saw an exemplar of the Medicean Press Avicenna in a bookshop in Constantinople, which the proprietor had offered for sale for a long time, in vain, although it was much cheaper than manuscripts of that work: Galland's preface to d'Herbelot, *Bibliothèque orientale,* p. xix.

[49] Some examples of such use of the Medicean Press books are collected by Jones, 'The Medici Oriental Press', 92.

[50] For efforts by Raimondi to obtain manuscripts from the East see Jones, 'Learning Arabic', 36 ff.; cf. Tinto, *La Tipografia Medicea,* 8, 93–4.

[51] On Ni'matallah and his manuscripts see Jones, 'Learning Arabic', 42 ff., and for full details Levi della Vida, *Documenti,* 1–113.

translation of Apollonius' *Conics*, including three books which were lost in the original Greek, which Raimondi expressed his intention of publishing.[52] However, after the Euclid of 1594 only one other secular Arabic book was printed at the Medicean Press, namely the native grammar *Taṣrīf* with a Latin translation by Raimondi, in 1610.[53] In the introduction to this, addressed to Pope Paul V, Raimondi alleges the death of Gregory XIII and the removal of Cardinal Ferdinando to Florence when he succeeded to the Grand Duchy of Tuscany as the reasons for the intermission of publication.[54] But since these events occurred in 1585 and 1587 respectively, well before any publication at all emerged from the press, we may suspect that the commercial failure of the scholarly publications was the real determining factor.[55] In any case, when Raimondi died in 1614 the Medicean Press effectively ceased operation. However, its Arabic types were preserved and later used elsewhere, for instance in the Vatican Press[56] and by the press of the Sacra Congregatio de Propaganda Fide,[57] founded in 1622 to exercise general oversight over missionary activity, which was the most prolific source of oriental publishing in Italy from 1626 onwards.

Through the efforts of this and other religious institutions, Arabic works continued to be printed in Italy during the seventeenth century, and in fact in terms of the actual number of works published Italy probably outstripped all other areas of Europe in the production of Arabic books. But the types of literature published were very circumscribed, being principally liturgical and homiletic. This was in accordance with the missionary and apologetic goals of those who controlled the presses; rigid supervision and censorship by the ecclesiastic authorities stifled any tendencies to further enquiry.[58] There was some

---

[52] Giovannozzi, 'La versione Borelliana di Apollonio', 3; cf. Toomer, *Apollonius*, p. xxii.

[53] *PO* no. 32. This work is discussed at length by Jones, 'The Arabic and Persian Studies of Raimondi', 78–97, and more briefly in 'Learning Arabic', 176 ff.

[54] To these Jones ('Learning Arabic', 43) adds the death, *c*.1595, of Patriarch Niʿmatallah, who was supposed to aid in the publications of the press. More relevant is the contract which Ferdinando's agents forced on Raimondi in 1596, by which he took over financial responsibility for the press (Saltini, 278–9).

[55] In 1772, among the stock of the press, were 810 copies of the Avicenna, 1,129 of the Geography, and 1,967 of the Euclid: Saltini, 293 n. 2.

[56] See Vervliet, *The Type Specimen of the Vatican Press 1628*, Introduction, 21–2 and 12.

[57] On this press in general see Henkel, *Die Druckerei der Propaganda Fide*.

[58] In a letter of 1588 Raimondi describes at length the difficulties he experienced in getting oriental books passed by the 'Congregation of the Index': Tinto, *La Tipografia Medicea*, 68 (the full text 107).

talk of publishing the Koran, but so great was the fear of its corrupting influence that it was not printed until the very end of the century, by Ludovico Marracci (Padova, 1698), and even then only after he had previously published, at the press of the Propaganda Fide, a huge 'refutation' of the detested book.[59] Meanwhile the publication had been anticipated by the edition of Hinckelmann (Hamburg, 1694). Italy also produced Arabic grammars and lexicons, e.g. the *Breves arabicae linguae institutiones* of Guadagnoli (Rome, 1642)[60] and the enormous but unsatisfactory *Thesaurus linguae Arabicae* of Giggei (Milan, 1632),[61] but none of much merit, nor any able to compete with the products of Dutch Arabic scholarship, the grammar of Erpenius and the lexicon of Golius. It is significant that the one secular Arabic work published in Italy in the seventeenth century, the translation of Books V–VII of Apollonius' *Conics*, when it finally appeared in 1661 (made from the very same manuscript which Raimondi had promised to print seventy years earlier), contained only a Latin translation and not the Arabic text.[62]

Italy, and in particular Rome, was hospitable to a number of Eastern Christians with considerable skill in Arabic. I will mention only those who recur in my account: the Maronites Victor Scialac, Johannes Hesronita, and Gabriel Sionita early in the century, and later Abraham Ecchellensis. The Copt Josephus Abudacnus was in Rome even earlier. All of them except Scialac later migrated northwards and were important in promoting the study of Arabic there, Hesronita, Sionita, and Ecchellensis in France, and Abudacnus in France, England, the Spanish Netherlands, and Austria. Also important for the ultimate progress of the study of Arabic was the considerable growth during the seventeenth century in the oriental collections of the Vatican Library,[63] but these collections were as yet little exploited.[64]

---

[59] Schnurrer no. 377. This *Prodromus* revealed Marracci's wide learning in Arabic literature: for his debt to Pococke in particular see Nallino, 'Le fonti arabe manoscritte dell'opera di Ludovico Marracci sul Corano'.

[60] Schnurrer no. 72.

[61] *PO* no. 226.

[62] See Toomer, *Apollonius*, p. xxii, to which the note by Duverdier, *Le Livre et le Liban*, item 142, pp. 252–3, although inaccurate in details, adds some interesting information. The fullest discussion is by Giovannozzi, 'La versione Borelliana di Apollonio'.

[63] On this the standard work is Levi della Vida, *Ricerche*.

[64] For use of the oriental manuscripts in the Vatican Library by the Englishmen John Greaves and John Viccars in the 1630s see below, pp. 141, 76.

(III) FRANCE

France has the distinction of being both the first European country to establish formal relations with the Ottoman Empire, and also the first to institute formal instruction in Arabic. Both occurred under the same king, François I.[65] The lecturer in Arabic at what was later to be the Collège de France was Guillaume Postel, who deserves, if anyone, to be called the father of Arabic studies in Europe. Here is not the place to describe, even in outline, the extraordinary career of this strange man;[66] I will confine myself to those aspects which are directly relevant to my topic. The rationale that he gave for his interest in Arabic, as in other exotic languages, was his (genuine) desire to promote universal world peace through the spread of the Gospel to all nations, by preaching it in their own languages. But he was clearly fascinated by the philological study of languages. He obtained his knowledge of Arabic (and other languages) on journeys to the East: the first was from 1534 to 1537, when he accompanied the French ambassador de la Forest to Constantinople, where the treaty between France and the Porte was concluded.[67] Returning to France via Italy, where he met amongst others the famous Venetian printer of Hebrew texts Daniel Bomberg and the orientalist Teseo Ambrogio,[68] he was appointed royal lecturer in Arabic at the recently founded Collège Royal in 1538. However, he was dismissed from this post in 1542, and in 1544 returned to Italy, where he joined the Jesuit order, but was soon expelled for heterodoxy. In 1549 to 1550 he undertook a second journey to the orient, during which he received the protection of the

[65] François had made an abortive attempt to establish Hebrew and Arabic studies in Paris as early as 1517, by summoning Agostino Giustiniani to teach the languages. However, the bishop did not remain there long.

[66] The literature on Postel has increased enormously in this century, but little of it has to do with his career as an Arabist. For an outline of his life see e.g. Bouwsma, *Concordia Mundi*, 1–29. On his Arabic studies see Fück, 36–44. Secret, 'Guillaume Postel et les études arabes à la Renaissance', adds some interesting information, but is not comprehensive.

[67] See above, p. 14. Postel also visited Egypt on this journey: Levi della Vida, *Ricerche*, 309 n. 1. On the chronology of Postel's eastern journeys the fundamental discussion is Vogel, 'Ueber Wilh. Postel's Reisen in den Orient'.

[68] Or Theseus Ambrosius: he contributed more to the study of Syriac than of Arabic, but his *Introductio in Chaldaicam linguam . . . et decem alias linguas* (Pavia, 1539; see *PO* no. 240 for a full description; illustrated in Hamilton, 'Eastern Churches and Western Scholarship', 237) contains Karshūnī (Arabic text in Syriac script) and a short analysis of Arabic grammar (on which see Jones, 'Learning Arabic', 153–5). Ambrogio owned the unique surviving copy of the Venice edition of the Koran (see above, p. 20).

French ambassador in Constantinople, but visited other places, including Jerusalem and Syria. By the time he returned he had assembled what was undoubtedly the best contemporary collection of Arabic manuscripts in Europe. Financial straits later in life compelled him to sell or pawn most of these. A large number were pledged to Ottheinrich, the Elector Palatine, in 1555, and Postel was frustrated in his later attempts to recover them. Most passed to the Vatican, with the rest of the Palatine Library, after the sack of Heidelberg in 1622.[69]

Postel was teaching in France only from 1538 to 1542 and again from 1551 to 1553, and seems to have had little influence there; but in 1562, before he was confined to the monastery of St Martin in Paris for the rest of his life, his teaching bore fruit: Joseph Scaliger, later to become the greatest scholar of his time, lived with him for a short time in order to study Arabic. Others who studied Arabic with Postel included Bibliander and Franciscus Raphelengius. However, Postel's publications were more important than his teaching. In 1538 he published *Linguarum duodecim characteribus differentium alphabetum introductio ac legendi modus longe facilimus*,[70] which among other exotic languages (such as Samaritan and Ethiopic) includes a section on Arabic, with the Lord's Prayer and other short texts in that language, rendered in crude woodcut blocks. This was soon followed by his *Grammatica Arabica*,[71] specifically intended as a replacement for that section: in this the Arabic was printed with movable types, but the result was still clumsy. The grammar, based on the native Arabic tradition, was unsatisfactory in many ways.[72] Nevertheless it long remained one of the chief tools available for the study of Arabic in Europe: thus the 'Compendium of Arabic Grammar' appended by Ruthger Spey to his 1583 edition of an Arabic version of the Epistle to the Galatians was little more than an (unacknowledged) excerpt from Postel's grammar. Neither the brief rules in the *Alphabetum Arabicum* produced by the Medicean Press in 1592 (anonymous, but probably by

[69] See Levi della Vida, *Ricerche*, 290 ff., especially 307–27 on Postel's manuscripts. For the fate of some see below, p. 45.

[70] *PO* no. 241, with illustrations; Jones, 'Learning Arabic', 149–53.

[71] Schnurrer no. 38. The book is undated: Schnurrer assigns it to 1538 or 1539; Claude Postel, *Les Écrits de Guillaume Postel publiés en France*, 13–17, more plausibly to 1540.

[72] Fück (40–1) gives a brief analysis; possible Arabic grammatical sources are discussed by Jones, 'The Arabic and Persian Studies of Raimondi', 88, 93. See also his 'Learning Arabic', 155–7. Postel acquired a copy of Leo Africanus' Arabic grammar (Levi della Vida, *Ricerche*, 311, 313), but probably only after he had published his own.

Raimondi)[73] nor the latter's edition of the *Kitāb al-Taṣrīf* (1610) could fully replace it, and it was only the grammar of Erpenius (1613) which made Postel's work obsolete. Postel also intended to publish an Arabic lexicon,[74] but it seems that this was never completed.

One of the Arabic manuscripts which Postel had acquired in the East contained the *Geography* of Abū 'l-Fidā', a work of the early fourteenth century that gives an extensive description of the known world, with latitudes and longitudes of many places. Recognizing its importance for geographical knowledge, Postel prepared a summary of the work for Ottheinrich, which came into the hands of Ramusio, who gave an account of it in the second volume of his *Navigationi et viaggi* (1559) and strongly recommended publication of the whole work.[75] Information about it passed to other European geographers, including Ortelius,[76] and inspired the interest of many seventeenth-century Arabists, including Erpenius, Wilhelm Schickard,[77] and John Greaves, all of whom planned to produce a complete edition and translation of this Arabic *Geography*.

After the dismissal of Postel there was no successor in the post of royal lecturer in Arabic for many decades.[78] However, in the late sixteenth and early seventeenth century the lectureship was held by men of distinction. Arnoult de Lisle[79] was appointed in 1587, but in the following year went as physician to the Sultan of Morocco, where he remained until 1599. Even after his return he could have done little teaching, since he spent much time on diplomatic missions until his death in 1613. His successor as the Sultan's physician was Étienne Hubert,[80] who during his year's stay in Morocco learned Arabic well, and on his return to Paris in 1600 was appointed royal lecturer in

---

[73] Schnurrer no. 41; Jones, 'The Arabic and Persian Studies of Raimondi', 28 ff., and 'Learning Arabic', 169–72.

[74] He was discussing this as late as 1565: Lossen, *Briefe von Andreas Masius*, 202.

[75] Ramusio, vol. 2, Preface fo. 4ʳ, written in Venice, 7 July 1553. On p. 18 he gives a list of longitudes and latitudes taken from Abū 'l-Fidā'.

[76] See Levi della Vida, *Ricerche*, 314, 326–7. Postel's manuscript of Abū 'l-Fidā' is now MS Vat. Arab. 266: ibid. 294–5.

[77] Schickard's transcript and partial translation of the *Geography* is now MS Paris Arab. 2242: see Ullmann, 'Arabische, türkische und persische Studien', 121–6, and Oehme, 'Der Geograph und Kartograph', 364–73 for a good analysis.

[78] See the list of professors in the Collège Royal printed in Lefranc, *Histoire du Collège de France*, 381 ff., which is, however, notoriously incomplete and inaccurate for the early period.

[79] On his career see de Castries, *Sources inédites de l'histoire du Maroc. Archives et Bibliothèques de France*, vol. 3, Introduction, pp. xiii–xxi.

[80] Ibid., pp. xxii–xxvii.

Arabic, a post he held until about 1613.[81] Unlike Arnoult de Lisle, he seems to have taught regularly. Although Savary de Brèves had a low opinion of his attainments as an Arabist,[82] he was admired by Casaubon, Scaliger, and especially Erpenius, whom he helped in his formative years in France. Despite Casaubon's encouragement,[83] Hubert never published anything in Arabic. Gabriel Sionita, who succeeded him as royal lecturer from 1614 to 1648, was undoubtedly competent in Arabic, and was responsible for some important publications, but his influence on Arabic studies in France was less than it might have been. He seems to have avoided lecturing as much as possible,[84] and his laziness is well attested. The completion of the great Paris Polyglot Bible, which began in the early 1620s, was dragged out until 1645 by his dilatoriness in producing the Arabic text. Peiresc complains about him several times in this regard.[85]

Printing that Bible required oriental types, which brings us to the history of printing Arabic in France. After Postel's *Grammatica Arabica*, with its clumsy types, nothing printed in Arabic appeared in France until the very end of the sixteenth century. Cayet de la Palme's *Paradigmata de Quatuor Lingvis Orientalibus Praecipvis* (Paris, 1594) employs woodcuts for its Arabic excerpts.[86] Then the printer Guillaume Le Bé had Arabic types made for a specimen.[87] Le Bé (who

[81] A most interesting account by Aḥmad b. Qāsim al-Ḥajarī (on whom see below, p. 44) of his meeting with Hubert in Paris in 1611 is translated from the Arabic by Jones, 'Learning Arabic', 108. Aḥmad had met Hubert earlier in Marrakesh (Wiegers, *Aḥmad b. Kâsim al-Andalusî*, 40). Presumably Aḥmad's statement that Hubert had been in Marrakesh 'many years' rests on a misunderstanding.

[82] As quoted by Duverdier, 'Les Impressions orientales en Europe et le Liban', 165. See further Jones, 'Learning Arabic', 33–4.

[83] e.g. in his letter from London of 22 Sept. 1612 (Casaubon, *Letters*, no. 831, p. 485), in which he urged Hubert and Le Bé to co-operate in publishing 'aliquid . . . quod studia illa promoveat'.

[84] Matthias Pasor studied with him for a short while (see below, p. 98), but I have found little else concerning his teaching activities. In a letter to Ravius of 1647 (Ravius, *Sesqui-Decuria*, 18) Sionita complains of 'la lecture que i'ay esté obligé de faire dans le College Royal, de laquelle i'avois esté cy deuant dispensé' (the excuse for the dispensation being his work on the Polyglot).

[85] e.g. Peiresc, *Dupuy Correspondence*, i. 599: [the recently deceased Johannes Hesronita] 'estoit beaucoup plus laborieux que le sieur Gabriel, son compagnon, et de beaucoup plus de resolution quand il falloit entreprendre et mettre à execution quelque bon dessein en matiere de libvres', and the passage quoted by Duverdier, 'Les Impressions orientales en Europe', 170–1 (where the absurd 'Père Gaultier' is Tamizey de Larroque's misreading of 'Psaultier').

[86] Illustrated and described in *L'Europe et le monde arabe*, 64–5.

[87] Le Bé's Arabic type specimen of 1599 is reproduced *Le Livre et le Liban*, item 93, pp. 222–3, q.v. for further literature.

himself composed an unpublished Arabic grammar) was interested in publishing Arabic texts, and in 1610 urged Erpenius to give him the Arabic grammar that he was then working on at Saumur to print.[88] The only use made of the types during Le Bé's lifetime was to print some Arabic words in the posthumous edition of Scaliger's *Opuscula varia*, edited by Casaubon in 1610. However, they were occasionally used, both in France and elsewhere, as late as 1805.[89]

The Le Bé types, although not inelegant, were too large to print extended texts in Arabic conveniently. Of vastly greater use and significance were the Arabic types of Savary de Brèves. But these were only part of their owner's plan to introduce oriental studies into France.[90] François Savary de Brèves was French ambassador to the Ottoman Porte, where in 1604 he negotiated the treaty of alliance between Ahmet I and Henri IV. While in Constantinople he had learned Turkish and Arabic, and acquired a good collection of oriental manuscripts. From 1608 he was ambassador to the Papal See, where he used the resources available in Rome to set up an Arabic printing-press (the 'Typographia Savariana'). The types which he had made for this, in several sizes, are in the estimation of many the finest Arabic types ever produced, in Europe or elsewhere.[91] Two books were printed with these at Rome: an Arabic translation of Cardinal Bellarmino's catechism in 1613, and an edition of the Psalms in Arabic, with Latin translation, in 1614.[92] For both of these the work of editing and translating was performed by two Lebanese priests, former students in the Maronite College, Jibrā'īl aṣ-Ṣahyūnī and Naṣrallāh Shalaq al-ʿĀqūrī, or Gabriel Sionita and Victor Scialac, to use the Latinized names by which they were usually known. Returning to Paris in 1614, Savary de Brèves took with him not only his press and manuscripts, but also his Italian printer, Stefano Paolino,[93] as well as Gabriel Sionita and

---

[88] Erpenius to Casaubon, in Casaubon, *Letters*, no. 662, p. 345.

[89] For the history of the Le Bé Arabic types see Schnurrer, pp. 506–12. To the books printed with them mentioned there add *PO* nos. 287 and 345.

[90] On Savary de Brèves and his Arabic types see the informative articles by Duverdier, 'Les Impressions orientales en Europe et le Liban', 159–78, and 'Savary de Brèves et Ibrahim Müteferrika'.

[91] It is certain that they were cut in Italy, but it is not known who the craftsman was. However, Vaccari, 'I Caratteri Arabi della «Typographia Savariana»', identified the model for the types as a manuscript psalter that had been sent by the Maronite patriarch from the Lebanon to be printed at Rome, which was also the exemplar used for the 1614 edition of the Psalms.

[92] *Le Livre et le Liban*, item 61, p. 195, and item 66, pp. 199–200, respectively.

[93] Paolino (Stephanus Paulinus) had worked under Raimondi at the Medicean Press. After instructing the Frenchman Jérome Blageart in oriental printing, he returned

another Maronite priest, Johannes Hesronita (Yūḥannā al-Ḥaṣrūnī). With his press he hoped to publish not only a polyglot bible (containing *inter alia* the Arabic and Syriac versions), but also other works, including secular ones, in Arabic, Persian, and Turkish, and an Arabic dictionary. For this his manuscripts would provide a resource; but there would also be need for learned men to edit them, and for this purpose he had previously planned the institution of an oriental college in Paris.[94] But these plans required funding, and de Brèves, who had already spent a great deal of his own money on setting up the press, did not possess sufficient resources, despite his lucrative post as governor of the King's brother, the Duc d'Anjou. He did manage to procure pensions from King Louis XIII for Hesronita and Sionita, as royal interpreter and professor of Arabic and Syriac at the Collège Royal, respectively. But no more funds were made available from royal or other sources, and the Typographia Savariana was able to print very little. Apart from the Turkish text of the 1604 treaty which de Brèves had negotiated,[95] the only work printed by the press in Paris was the *Grammatica Arabica Maronitarum* of 1616, the first part of a projected five-part Arabic grammar by Sionita and Hesronita, the rest of which never appeared.[96] In 1618 Savary de Brèves fell out of favour and was dismissed from his post. Sionita and Hesronita retained their positions, but did not have the resources to undertake the publication of Arabic texts. They did, however, produce a Latin translation of the Medicean Arabic geography of 1592, under the title *Geographia Nubiensis*. This was published at their own expense in 1619, and sold well, especially because they added an appendix on modern oriental geography drawn from Arabic authors.

Although the Typographia Savariana effectively ceased operation in 1618, the oriental types survived, and were used elsewhere.[97] The Arabic types were employed in the great Paris Polyglot Bible, published by Michel Le Jay and printed (beginning in 1628) by André Vitray, who in 1630 was designated as the King's printer for oriental languages. After de Brèves died in 1627, there were fears in Paris that

to Rome, where he was later employed by the Propaganda Press: *Le Livre et le Liban*, 192.

[94] See his letter to de Thou of 27 Nov. 1611, quoted by Duverdier, 'Les Impressions orientales', 164.

[95] In 1615: *Le Livre et le Liban*, item 101, p. 226.

[96] Ibid., item 72, pp. 202–3.

[97] The Syriac types were used in the edition of the Syriac Psalter by Sionita (Paris, 1625): see Strothmann, *Die Anfänge der syrischen Studien in Europa*, Tafeln VI–VII.

his manuscripts, and especially his press, would be sold to 'foreign Huguenots', namely the Dutch or the English.[98] Accordingly, in 1632 Vitray was compelled by royal order to buy both the types and the manuscripts from de Brèves's heirs.[99] The Arabic and Syriac texts for the Paris Polyglot, with their Latin translations, were prepared by Hesronita[100] and Sionita. At a late stage another graduate of the Maronite College at Rome took part. This was Ibrahīm al-Ḥāqilānī, or Abraham Ecchellensis, who spent most of his life in Italy, but lived and published in Paris from 1640 to 1641 and again from 1645 to 1653. However, the greatest part of the work fell to Sionita, whose dilatoriness led to quarrels and eventually lawsuits with Vitray and Le Jay. Sionita was even imprisoned for a time in 1640, emerging only after promising to finish the Bible by Easter.[101] Even so, the Polyglot was not finally finished until 1645. The ten stately volumes were a major achievement both of printing and of scholarship, but they also represented a cul-de-sac in Arabic studies in seventeenth-century France. No more books in Arabic were published in that country for the rest of that century and most of the next, and in 1656 the splendid types of Savary de Brèves were transferred to the Imprimerie Royale, where they vanished from public view so completely that many supposed them to have been destroyed, until they were reintroduced by de Guignes in 1787.[102]

This sorry state of affairs was not due to the lack of able Arabists in France, both among the professors at the Collège Royal, such as Pierre Vattier (1658–67), and elsewhere. Some of these had acquired their linguistic expertise outside France, for instance André du Ryer, who was French consul in Alexandria for many years. J.-B. Duval, after learning the elements of Arabic from Hubert in Paris, travelled to Italy to study with Raimondi, Sionita, and Scialac, and also to the Levant, before returning to Paris, where he became the King's interpreter in oriental languages.[103] Others, such as Claude Hardy and Gilbert

---

[98] Although this is likely enough, given the current lack of Arabic type in England, and the interest in acquiring it (see below, p. 83), I have not been able to confirm it from English sources.

[99] On this and the subsequent events see Bernard, *Antoine Vitré*, and *Le Livre et le Liban*, items 102, 108, and 109, and pp. 265–71.

[100] Hesronita had returned to the Lebanon in 1621, and died there in 1626; but work on the Polyglot had evidently been going on for many years before the printing began.

[101] See the documents summarized in *Le Livre et le Liban*, items 126–9, pp. 242–3.

[102] See his *Essai historique sur l'origine des caractères orientaux de l'Imprimerie Royale*.

[103] His curious *Dictionarium latino-arabicum* (see *Le Livre et le Liban*, item 76) was

Gaulmyn, were amateurs who pursued Arabic as an intellectual diversion from their professions[104] and never published anything concerning that language. It is notable that what was published in France after 1645 was only translations, never originals. Du Ryer's French translation of the Koran from the original Arabic (1647)[105] was popular enough to be translated into English[106] and Dutch. Vattier translated into French Erpenius' edition of the *History* of al-Makīn,[107] Golius' edition of ibn ʿArabshāh's life of Timur, the *Logic* of Avicenna, and Ṭughrāʾī's poem.[108] Efforts were indeed made by Frenchmen to print in Arabic; the most curious of these was the affair of the seizure of the 'clandestine press' at Caen in 1644.[109] The Protestant operators of this had contrived (with the assistance of Sionita and his nephew) to obtain types made from the Savary de Brèves matrices, which they proposed to use in printing the *Hierozoicon*[110] of Samuel Bochart, a Calvinist minister of Caen, who was a pupil of Erpenius and no mean Arabist.[111] In March 1669 Melchisédech Thévenot wrote to Colbert, for whom he was buying oriental manuscripts in Amsterdam, about his plan to do a complete edition and translation of the geographical work of Abū 'l-Fidāʾ.[112] But Edward Bernard, who was in Holland at the time, informed Pococke that Thévenot was unable to find anyone in the Netherlands willing to undertake the publication.[113] Evidently Thévenot knew that it was hopeless to expect his work to be printed in France;[114] in the event it remained unpublished. Toward the end of the century d'Herbelot

---

printed by Vitray in 1632, but his 'Dictionarium arabo-latinum' (ibid., item 75) was never published.

[104] The letter from Chasteigner to Christianus Ravius (printed in the latter's *Sesqui-Decuria*, 18–23) gives an interesting portrait of the small circle of mostly amateur Arabists in Paris in 1648.

[105] See *L'Europe et le monde arabe*, 96–8.

[106] See below, p. 200.

[107] Paris, 1657: Fück, 73 n. 193. On Erpenius' edition see below, p. 46.

[108] Paris, 1658, 1658, and 1660 respectively. For other translations published or proposed by him see [Michaud], *Biographie universelle*, xlii. 705–6.

[109] The story is narrated by Duverdier, 'Les Impressions orientales', 267–8.

[110] This eventually saw the light in London in 1663; 3rd edn. Leiden, 1692.

[111] Fück, 84–5. See Hamilton, *William Bedwell*, 52 with n. 123, for Bochart's visit to England in 1623.

[112] MacLaughlin, 'Une lettre de Melchisédech Thévenot', with further literature in n. 3 on p. 126.

[113] Twells, *Life of Pococke*, 255–6.

[114] In his *Gazophylacium linguae Persarum* (Amsterdam, 1684), Angelus a S. Joseph describes his vain attempts to get the work printed at Paris in 1680 'ob dissuetum jam, penèque abolitum Persicorum, seu Arabicorum typorum usum': see *PO* no. 345.

compiled his *Bibliothèque orientale* in Arabic, and Colbert intended to have oriental types cut to print it, but this came to nothing with Colbert's death in 1683,[115] so that the published version is printed entirely in French.

The mention of Colbert is a reminder that a prominent phenomenon in seventeenth-century France was the accumulation of Arabic and other oriental manuscripts in the collections of the King's ministers and other wealthy and influential men. Savary de Brèves's manuscripts were eventually absorbed into Cardinal Richelieu's library.[116] Particularly interesting is the organization of expeditions to the East in search of manuscripts, coins, and other archaeological items. This was done by Cardinal Mazarin and especially by Colbert,[117] for whom the German convert Wansleben collected an immense booty from Egypt, Asia Minor, and Constantinople from 1671 to 1675. Earlier in the century the great scholar and collector Fabri de Peiresc was remarkably successful in procuring oriental manuscripts. Possibly he was inspired by the report he received of the treasure of Arabic manuscripts brought back from the East by Jacobus Golius.[118] In any event, by means of his connections with the Levant through the merchants of Marseilles he soon acquired some interesting Arabic manuscripts; although not himself able to read these, he freely communicated them to others. For instance he sent a musical manuscript to Mersenne in Paris, where Mersenne (equally ignorant of Arabic) hoped to get the help of Sionita in interpreting it.[119] He also supplied Salmasius with manuscripts, as is abundantly attested in the published letters of Salmasius.[120] It is a testimony to the effectiveness of Peiresc's relations with the orient that Jacobus Golius, in Leiden, used Peiresc as an intermediary to communicate with his brother Petrus in Aleppo, even though there was a Dutch consulate in that city.[121]

---

[115] Cousin's life of d'Herbelot, *Bibliothèque orientale*, Introduction, 22–3. This is further proof that the de Brèves Arabic types had effectively disappeared by that time.

[116] On this, and their later history, see *Le Livre et le Liban*, item 79, pp. 209–11.

[117] A very detailed account of these expeditions is provided by Omont, *Missions archéologiques françaises en Orient*, vol. 1. For Wansleben in particular see pp. 54–174.

[118] Peiresc, *Dupuy Correspondence*, ii. 168, Aug. 1629.

[119] Ibid. iii. 285, Mar. 1635. Gaulmyn had volunteered his services as a translator, but Peiresc was unwilling to let the book into the hands of a rival collector who might never return it.

[120] e.g. Salmasius, *Epistolae*, 73 (Nov. 1631): Salmasius is impatiently awaiting the Coptic New Testament, with an Arabic unprinted version, from Peiresc.

[121] See for instance Peiresc, *Dupuy Correspondence*, iii. 614 (2 Dec. 1636), or Salmasius, *Epistolae*, 185: in a letter of Feb. 1636 Salmasius tells Golius that, according to Peiresc, his brother has made great progress in the oriental tongues. On Petrus Golius see further below, p. 123.

Almost all such manuscripts eventually ended up in major libraries in France, the majority in the Royal Library,[122] thus forming the basis of the splendid collection of Arabic manuscripts in the Bibliothèque Nationale. Without them Silvestre de Sacy could not have achieved the revival of Arabic studies in France and ultimately in Europe in the late eighteenth and nineteenth centuries. But even earlier the royal collection was an important resource for the *Bibliothèque orientale* of Barthélemy d'Herbelot,[123] which provided eighteenth-century Europe with its standard reference work on the Near East. Published posthumously in 1697, it drew on Arabic texts published by Erpenius and Golius in the Netherlands, and by Pococke in England, but also on a number of unpublished Arabic and Persian books available in manuscript in Paris, especially the huge bibliographical work *Kashf al-Ẓunūn* of Ḥajjī Khalīfa.[124] It is a testimony to the learning of d'Herbelot that no less a scholar than J. J. Reiske thought it worth his efforts to produce a revised edition of his book.[125]

(IV) GERMANY

Considering the central role played by Germans (for instance Reuchlin and Sebastian Münster) in the flowering of Hebrew studies in sixteenth-century Europe,[126] it may appear surprising that those Germans involved in Arabic studies during the sixteenth century and the first half of the seventeenth were few and not very influential. In the sixteenth century this may be explained by factors which affected all of Europe outside Italy, namely the dearth of texts and teachers of Arabic.[127] In the seventeenth century, however, the reason for the comparative backwardness of the German-speaking areas in this respect may be not so much their political and religious fragmentation as the devastating effects on Germany of the Thirty Years War,[128] which was

---

[122] Delisle, *Le Cabinet des Manuscrits*, remains the standard work on the growth of that library in this period, but it is inadequate for the oriental collections.

[123] On d'Herbelot and his encyclopaedic work see Fück, 98–100.

[124] There were manuscripts of this in both the Royal and Colbert's libraries. Galland lists d'Herbelot's sources on p. xi of his preface to the *Bibliothèque orientale*.

[125] This was never achieved, but his notes were incorporated in the French edition published at The Hague and the German version published at Halle: see d'Herbelot (Reiske).

[126] See Lloyd Jones, *The Discovery of Hebrew*, especially chs. 2 and 3.

[127] The situation was very different for Hebrew in Germany, where the presence of Jews provided resources which were totally lacking for Arabic.

[128] Schickard's pitiable letter to John Bainbridge telling him how he had to hide away

raging at just the period when these studies were flourishing elsewhere in Protestant Europe, notably in the Netherlands and England. Before that war broke out in 1618, a promising start had been made by the establishment of an Arabic printing-press at Breslau by Peter Kirsten, who was drawn to Arabic by his interest in medicine.[129] With this he published a number of Arabic works on grammar, medicine, and Christian theology, from 1608 to 1611.[130] But after the outbreak of the war he was forced to move to Prussia, taking his press with him. In 1632 he wrote to Bedwell from Danzig[131] saying that he had hoped to move to England with his family and press, but having received no answer to his letters was now thinking of returning to Germany. In 1636 he went to Sweden, still transporting his Arabic press, as physician to Queen Christina, and died at Uppsala in 1640, having produced nothing further.

Another casualty of the Thirty Years War was the Palatine Library at Heidelberg, which, thanks largely to the items acquired from Postel, was one of the principal sources of Arabic manuscripts for scholars in northern Europe in the sixteenth and early seventeenth centuries.[132] Among those who borrowed manuscripts from it for the purpose of making their own copies were Erpenius in the Netherlands and Tengnagel in Austria. However, in 1622 Heidelberg was besieged and sacked by the army of Tilly. The great library was captured and eventually removed to the Vatican, where the Arabic manuscripts became virtually inaccessible. Among the defenders at the siege of Heidelberg was Matthias Pasor, who was later to make a name for himself as an Arabist at Oxford,[133] but who was at that time barely acquainted with the language. He, like a number of Germans after him, was to find instruction in Arabic not in Germany but elsewhere, usually Leiden. For example Johann Elichmann came from Silesia, but

his work on Abū 'l-Fidā' from the Imperial soldiers ravaging Württemberg in 1634 is quoted by Oehme, 'Der Geograph und Kartograph', 374 n. 213.

[129] Fück, 57–9; *PO* nos. 110–13. For his Arabic grammar (a wretched production) see Jones, 'Learning Arabic', 182–3.

[130] The last work that he published using his Arabic types appears to have been the first part of Megiser's Turkish grammar (Breslau, 1613): see *PO* no. 346, where a specimen of the type is reproduced.

[131] Hamilton, *William Bedwell*, 51 and 104–5 gives a reproduction and transcript of the letter.

[132] Levi della Vida, *Ricerche*, 327–33 gives some examples of those who used the Palatine oriental manuscripts; see ibid. 290 ff. for the essential discussion of the Arabic manuscripts in that collection and their later history.

[133] See below, pp. 98–101.

settled in Leiden.[134] German pupils of Golius at Leiden included Levinus Warner[135] and J. H. Hottinger, who after studying with Pasor at Groningen in 1639 and with Golius in 1640–1[136] became Professor of Oriental Languages at his native Zurich. There, and while professor at Heidelberg from 1655 to 1661, he produced several works on Arabic biography and bibliography which, although mediocre, were of some importance in oriental studies for the lack of anything better.[137] Finally among the Germans who studied with Golius at Leiden we may mention Theodorus Petraeus of Flensburg, who worked with Edmund Castell in England, and Christianus Ravius of Berlin, who had a remarkable career in the Netherlands, the orient, England, and Sweden. Both will be dealt with later.

Earlier, in the sixteenth century, Arabic studies in northern Germany were mainly centred on the Palatine Library at Heidelberg. It was there that the converted Jew Immanuel Tremellius and his associate Franciscus Junius (François du Jon, from Bourges) produced a new translation of the Old Testament from the Hebrew, and that Junius made a Latin translation from the Arabic of the Acts of the Apostles and the Epistles to the Corinthians.[138] At least two pupils of Junius at Heidelberg worked in Arabic. One was Ruthger Spey, who published in 1583 the Epistle to the Galatians in Arabic from the same Palatine manuscript (originally Postel's) that Junius had used, with a summary of Arabic grammar; in this book the Arabic text was done in wood-cut.[139] The other pupil was Jakob Christmann,[140] who published a brief introduction to reading and writing Arabic, *Alphabetum Arabicum* (also with woodcut Arabic letters) in 1582.[141] In 1590 he produced a Latin translation of the astronomical work of al-Farghānī, made from a Palatine manuscript not of the Arabic original but of the medieval Hebrew version.[142] However, the commentary does contain Arabic

---

[134] See below, p. 51.

[135] See below, p. 51.

[136] Juynboll, 209–10.

[137] See Fück, 91–2 for details. Hottinger's *Historia orientalis* is criticized at length for the author's ignorance of the Arabic language and its literature by Abraham Ecchellensis, *Eutychius Vindicatus*, i. 76 and ii, chs. 28 ff.; even when discounted for *odium theologicum*, the criticisms have merit.

[138] Published Lyons, 1578: see Schnurrer, p. 20. In 1592 Junius became Professor of Theology at Leiden, where he lent Arabic books and manuscripts to Raphelengius.

[139] Schnurrer no. 317; *Philologia Arabica*, 104. On the grammar see Jones, 'Learning Arabic', 163–6.

[140] Fück, 45–6.

[141] Schnurrer no. 39; *Philologia Arabica*, 101; Jones, 'Learning Arabic', 161–3.

[142] *PO* no. 100.

text, also in woodcut, and in the preface, addressed to the Elector Palatine Johann Kasimir, Christmann urges the establishment of a Professorship of Arabic and the publication of Arabic texts from the Palatine Library. In 1607 we learn from a letter from the librarian of that library, Jan Gruter, to Tengnagel[143] that because of the lack of Arabic types and the general neglect of Arabic studies Christmann was ceasing to work on the manuscripts at Heidelberg. In fact, although he was appointed Professor of Arabic at Heidelberg in 1608 (the first such post in Germany), he published nothing more after the 'Alfraganus'. Curiously, Arabic types did exist in Germany at least as early as 1587,[144] but these were used only to print one line of type in Elias Hutter's edition of the Hebrew Bible at Hamburg in that year.[145] It was apparently only from 1639 onwards that they were used for substantial printing, by which time they had migrated to Altdorf, where they appear in the *Locutiones Sacrae* of Theodoricus Hackspan[146] and several other works of the seventeenth and eighteenth centuries.[147]

Other sixteenth-century manifestations of Arabic in northern Germany are sparse and little more than curiosities, for example the *Introductio in Linguam Arabicam* of Bartholomaeus Radtmann, an exceedingly rare work published at Frankfurt an der Oder in 1592.[148] In Austria, however, where relations with the Ottoman Empire, although often hostile, were close, there was considerable interest in the languages and customs of this formidable neighbour. Although Turkish was more studied there, Arabic also received attention, for instance from Johann Albrecht von Widmanstetter, a pupil of Teseo Ambrogio, but most famous as the publisher of the Gospels in Syriac (Vienna, 1555).[149] Widmanstetter was responsible for the appointment

143 Excerpted by Jones, 'Learning Arabic', 225 n. 50.

144 The first representation of Arabic letters in a printed book was done in Germany; this was the woodcut of the Arabic alphabet in Bernhard von Breydenbach's *Peregrinatio in terram Sanctam* (Mainz, 1486, often reprinted: see Davies, *Bernhard von Breydenbach Bibliography*). This alphabet table has been reproduced e.g. in Davies, pl. 39, *PO*, p. 257, and *Philologia Arabica*, 17.

145 See *PO* no. 101.

146 *PO* no. 358, with illustration of the types on p. 322. Cf. Schnurrer no. 74.

147 The crude Arabic types which Schickard himself cut in 1623 and which were used in his *Tarich*, printed Tübingen 1628 (Ullmann, 'Arabische, türkische und persische Studien', 114, reproduction 119) remained a mere curiosity.

148 On Radtmann and his tutor in Arabic, a captured Turk baptized as Paul Willich, see Jones, 'Learning Arabic', 72–4. Radtmann's grammar is analysed ibid. 167–9.

149 Müller, *Johann Albrecht v. Widmanstetter*, is exhaustive on his career. On his oriental studies see also *Le Livre et le Liban*, item 55, p. 189 and for the history of the publication of the Syriac Gospels ibid. 122–34; also Strothmann, *Die Anfänge der syrischen Studien in Europa*, 9–16. Widmanstetter's Syriac grammar is reproduced ibid. 63–114.

of Postel to teach Arabic in Vienna in 1554, although Postel remained only a few months. Widmanstetter's Latin translation of the Koran seems not to have survived, and the Arabic grammar which he promised was probably never written.[150] Ultimately more influential for oriental studies at Vienna was Sebastian Tengnagel, who was librarian of the Imperial Library there from 1608 to 1636.[151] His linguistic skills were great enough for Lucas Holsten to rate him the best master of oriental languages in Europe.[152] Although he published nothing himself, he assiduously collected oriental manuscripts for the library from the Emperor's dragomans and other agents in Constantinople.[153] He also acquired Arabic texts by borrowing manuscripts from Heidelberg and other European collections and having them copied. For this purpose he employed for a time the services of Darwīsh Ibrāhīm, a Turkish captive.[154] He also tried unsuccessfully to get Wilhelm Schickard, who had a reputation as an orientalist, to move from Tübingen to the Emperor's court at Vienna.[155] Publication of his voluminous correspondence with scholars in all parts of Europe, Protestant as well as Catholic, would be of great interest for the history of oriental studies and scholarship in general, but this has been done only in small part.[156] Tengnagel greatly increased the oriental resources of the Imperial Library, but these were not much utilized until the time of Meninski, who published his great *Lexicon Turcico-Arabico-Persicum* in 1680,[157] and even then more for Turkish than for Arabic.

Not until the later seventeenth century do we see the first signs of that position in Arabic studies which Germany was later to achieve, ranking second only to the Netherlands in the eighteenth century, and rivalling France for pre-eminence in the nineteenth. Hottinger's

[150] Müller, *Johann Albrecht v. Widmanstetter*, 48, 76–8.

[151] Unterkircher, 'Sebastian Tengnagel', gives some account of his life, but is of little use for his oriental scholarship, being mainly concerned with his work as librarian.

[152] Letter to Peiresc of 21 June 1630, Holsten, *Epistolae*, 187.

[153] Jones, 'Learning Arabic', 38–9.

[154] Ibid. 74–85. Jones's suggestion (e.g. 78) that Tengnagel may have had more than one Turkish scribe is unsupported by the texts he quotes.

[155] Holsten, *Epistolae*, 187. On Schickard's correspondence with Golius concerning Arabic astronomy see below, p. 48, and on his oriental studies in general see Ullmann, 'Arabische, türkische und persische Studien'.

[156] The few surviving letters from Kepler to Tengnagel are published in Kepler, *Gesammelte Werke*, vols. 17 and 18 (see especially the letter of 1620, vol. 17 no. 873, in which Kepler consults him about the content of an Arabic book). A number of Tengnagel's letters at Vienna relating to oriental manuscripts have been excerpted by Jones, 'Learning Arabic'.

[157] On Meninski, originally François Mesgnien, a Frenchman from Lorraine, see Baranowski, 'F. Mesgnien-Meninski'; Fück, 93–4.

publications of the 1650s and 1660s, although careless, were far from negligible. The Augsburg physician Georgius Hieronymus Velschius was an eccentric[158] but learned Arabic scholar. That is apparent from his published *Exercitatio de vena Medinensi* (the preface of which contains a text and translations of a short section of Avicenna's *Canon*) and from his commentary on the Ruzname.[159] Especially notable was the first (effective) publication of the Arabic text of the Koran, by Abraham Hinckelmann, at Hamburg in 1694.[160]

(V) THE NETHERLANDS

In the earlier sixteenth century interest in Arabic in the Netherlands was confined to the southern areas (the later Spanish Netherlands, modern Belgium). Here, even before Postel in France, Nicolaus Clenardus[161] (or Cleynaerts, from Diest in Brabant) conceived a passionate interest in Arabic.[162] After imbibing the first elements of the language at Louvain by heroic and unaided study of Giustiniani's Polyglot Psalter, he travelled abroad in search of a teacher of the language. He found no one to instruct him in Paris in 1530–1, but did learn that there was supposed to be a chair of Arabic at Salamanca. Arriving there at the end of 1531, he was disappointed to find that the chair was not filled. Eventually he did get some Arabic lessons and even access to some Arabic manuscripts[163] from Hernán Núñez (who taught Greek at the university but had learned Arabic many years before). However, the difficulties of finding a teacher of Arabic in

---

[158] As is apparent from his *Dodecas Epistolarum*, a collection of his letters to other scholars which are at least partly fictitious. The first of these, an open letter addressed to the publishers of the Holy Roman Empire, offers no less than 70 of his own works for publication.

[159] Augsburg, 1674 and 1676 respectively: see Schnurrer no. 395 (with details on his career, including his studies with a 'learned Aleppan' in Italy) and p. 465; Siraisi, *Avicenna in Renaissance Italy*, 127, 155.

[160] On this see *Le Livre et le Liban*, 135–43, with a good discussion of Hinckelmann's preface by Jean Aucagne; title-page illustrated, *L'Europe et le monde arabe*, 103.

[161] For his life see Chauvin and Roersch, *Étude sur la vie et les travaux de Nicolas Clénard*, particularly 118–28 on his Arabic studies. There is a brief summary in Juynboll, 18–19.

[162] His declared motivation, like Postel's, was conversion of Muslims, for which he hoped to set up a teaching establishment at Louvain: Chauvin and Roersch, *Nicolas Clénard*, 133.

[163] On these Jones, 'The Arabic and Persian Studies of Giovan Battista Raimondi', 66–7 is of interest.

Spain are illustrated by the refusal of a Morisco who had formerly taught Núñez to instruct Clenardus, since he had renounced the Arabic language at the same time as he had abjured Islam: to speak it again would be to invite the suspicion of the Inquisition.[164] Nevertheless, Clenardus did manage to get instruction from a Moroccan captive at Granada, whom he acquired as his slave. What he learned from this man concerning Islam determined him to devote the rest of his life to studying Arabic in order to combat that religion.[165] In 1540–1 he spent a year learning the language and collecting manuscripts at Fez. But while still in North Africa he was robbed of all that he had collected. Undaunted, he planned a second journey to Morocco, but on his way there he died at Granada in 1542. None of his works on Arabic, including a grammar and a lexicon, survive,[166] but his letters, which are full of interest for contemporary scholarship,[167] were printed not long afterwards, and were a source of inspiration to other early Arabists.

A major achievement of oriental scholarship which took place in the southern Netherlands was the great Polyglot Bible printed at the Plantin Press at Antwerp from 1568 to 1572. Although this was the first of the polyglots to include the Chaldee paraphrases of the whole Old Testament, as well as the Syriac New Testament, it did not contain the Arabic versions. However, some of the contributors had knowledge of Arabic, for instance the Fleming Andreas Masius[168] (who had studied the language with Postel in Rome) and especially the chief editor, the Spaniard Benito Arias Montano. Furthermore, one of those who helped to print this Bible, Franciscus Raphelengius (the son-in-law of Christopher Plantinus), became an important figure in the growth of Arabic studies in the Dutch Republic.[169]

After the revolt of the Dutch from Spanish rule, and particularly after the foundation of the University of Leiden in 1575, the centre of

---

[164] Bataillon, 'L'Arabe à Salamanque', 12–13; Clénard, *Correspondance*, no. 47, p. 152.

[165] Letter to Latomus from Fez, 9 Apr. 1541 (Clénard, *Correspondance*, no. 54, p. 172).

[166] His reputation as a linguist rests on his influential Greek, Latin, and Hebrew grammars.

[167] Modern edition by Roersch (Clénard, *Correspondance*).

[168] A short account of Masius' life is given by Lossen on pp. xvi–xx of his edition of *Briefe von Andreas Masius*. Although there are references to Arabic studies in those letters, Masius was primarily interested in Syriac (see Strothmann, *Die Anfänge der syrischen Studien in Europa*, 12–13, 50–3) and in 1554 confessed to Postel 'ego in arabicis . . . sum adhuc infirmus' (Lossen, 161).

[169] Juynboll, 36–45.

Arabic studies in the Netherlands became Holland,[170] in particular Leiden and Amsterdam. In 1585 Raphelengius moved to Leiden to found his own branch of the Plantin Press. He soon became not only the official printer for the University, but also Professor of Hebrew. His interest in Arabic was further stimulated by the arrival in Leiden of the greatest scholar and one of the foremost Arabists of his time, Joseph Justus Scaliger, who was appointed to a professorship there in 1593. Partly for the purpose of reprinting books by Scaliger containing Arabic, Raphelengius had Arabic types cast for his press, of which he issued a specimen in 1595.[171] Being very large (30-point), these types were ill suited to print extensive Arabic texts, or even short Arabic quotations in the middle of other text,[172] and during Raphelengius' lifetime they were used only to print short passages in learned works such as the re-edition of Scaliger's *De emendatione temporum*.[173] Raphelengius spent many years compiling an Arabic lexicon, but this remained unpublished when he died in 1597.[174]

Scaliger, although intensely interested in Arabic from an early age (we saw that he studied with Postel while a young man), was well aware of the inadequacy of his knowledge of the language. However, his attitude towards its study was well in advance of his time.[175] His predecessors and contemporaries among European Arabists had all emphasized Christian and especially biblical texts. Also, recognizing the close affinity of Arabic to Hebrew, they assumed that Hebrew was the 'mother' and Arabic the 'daughter',[176] and that each could be used

[170] The very few Arabists from the Spanish Netherlands in the 17th century, such as Petrus Golius (the younger brother of Jacobus Golius), and Vopiscus Fortunatus Plempius (who published a translation of part of Avicenna's *Canon* at Louvain in 1658, see Juynboll, 188; Siraisi, *Avicenna*, 154, 366), learned the language elsewhere (in Italy and Holland respectively).

[171] Schnurrer no. 44; the specimen is reproduced in *Philologia Arabica*, 128. Best described and illustrated by Vervliet, *Sixteenth Century Printing Types of the Low Countries*, 315–17.

[172] The incongruity of the Raphelengian Arabic type in the middle of a normal-sized Latin text can be seen for instance in the distortion of the line-spacing on p. 39 of the notes in the 1600 edition of Scaliger's *Manilius*, or on p. 237 of Spencer's *De Legibus Hebraeorum* (1683), probably the last book in which it was used. The clumsiness of the type is apparent even in Raphelengius' own *Lexicon* (see the reproduction of a page, *Philologia Arabica*, 132).

[173] For other books in which they were used see Hamilton, 'The Victims of Progress', 97. On the later history of the types see below, pp. 60, 271.

[174] On the sources and history of the lexicon see Hamilton, 'Nam Tirones Sumus'.

[175] Grafton, *Scaliger*, provides little on his Arabic studies. Scaliger's notions on the proper way to study Arabic are well characterized by Hamilton, *William Bedwell*, 83–5.

[176] This was connected with the belief that Hebrew was the original language of

to help interpret the other. Scaliger rejected both approaches, stressing instead the necessity of reading the Koran, not for the purpose of confuting Muslims (a common contemporary justification for learning Arabic), but as the only possible introduction to the language and history, which should be studied for their own sake. Scaliger's own contributions in this field were modest,[177] although the Arabic thesaurus which he compiled was utilized by Raphelengius and later by Erpenius, who also completed and published Scaliger's edition of a collection of Arabic proverbs from a manuscript which Casaubon had sent him. More important was the example which Scaliger set to those whom he advised at Leiden, above all Erpenius, and the collection of oriental manuscripts which he had assembled over many years, from sources in Europe, Constantinople, Cairo, and elsewhere, which on his death in 1609 was bequeathed to the University Library of Leiden, thus forming the foundation of what was to become one of the foremost Arabic collections in Europe.

In Thomas Erpenius (van Erpe)[178] we meet the first native European to achieve true excellence in Arabic. Born of a prosperous family of Brabantine origin, he entered the University of Leiden in 1602, where he distinguished himself academically, and was encouraged by Scaliger in his interest in oriental languages, although as yet he knew only Hebrew, not Arabic. After receiving the degree of MA in 1608, he embarked on a foreign tour. He went first to England,[179] and after visiting Oxford and Cambridge he began to learn Arabic in London

mankind (and of God) from which all contemporary languages were descended after the 'confusion of tongues' at the destruction of the Tower of Babel. This theory, which was almost universally accepted in the early modern period (see Benfey, *Geschichte der Sprachwissenschaft*, 224 ff.), despite occasional doubts by Leibniz and others, hindered comparative philology down to the 19th century.

[177] In works published in his lifetime, little more than the calendars in *De emendatione temporum* and the Arabic star-names in the *Manilius*. For his correspondence with Patriarch Ignatius Ni'matallah about calendrical matters see Grafton, *Scaliger*, ii. 107–8 and 211–13, and especially Levi della Vida, *Documenti*, 22–4, with the Arabic quotation from Ni'matallah's letter in the *De emendatione temporum* (p. 246 of the Paris, 1583 edition).

[178] A full-scale modern biography of Erpenius remains a desideratum. Vossius' *Funeral Oration* of 1625 provides valuable information, but is only a sketch. Juynboll devotes a section (pp. 59–118) of *Zeventiende-eeuwsche Beoefenaars van het Arabisch in Nederland* to his career, but this relies entirely on printed materials and was incomplete even in that respect. Recent publications have enlarged and corrected many aspects of her account.

[179] Erpenius had family connections with England: his sister Maria had married Daniel van Hasevelt, a deacon of the Dutch church in London. But he also formed close connections with scholars there. He visited England at least five times.

with William Bedwell.[180] He could have learned little more than the elements from the English Arabist, for in January 1609 he moved on to France, first to Paris, where Isaac Casaubon encouraged him in his Arabic studies and loaned him books.[181] Erpenius also became acquainted with Étienne Hubert, Professor of Arabic at the Collège Royal, and improved his Arabic by taking lessons from the Copt Josephus Abudacnus, whom we will meet later in England. He recognized that Abudacnus could teach him only the vulgar, not the learned language, as he wrote to Bedwell in a letter of 14 September 1609, couched in hesitant Arabic.[182] From November 1609 to October 1610 he stayed at the Protestant Academy in Saumur, nominally studying theology but in fact spending much time working on an Arabic grammar which Le Bé had promised him to publish.[183] Returning to Paris, he spent the next year there or in nearby Conflans. There, in September 1611, he was visited by another native Arabic speaker, Aḥmad b. Qāsim al-Ḥajarī,[184] who was learned in the classical tongue and the Koran, and was able to give him better instruction than any he had hitherto received. Erpenius acknowledged this in a letter to Aḥmad written in that same month, which incidentally reveals how much his Arabic had improved in the two years since he wrote to Bedwell.[185] He continued his travels in October 1611. At one time he had intended to go as far as Constantinople, but in the event he did not get beyond Venice. On his return journey he visited the Palatine Library at Heidelberg, where he examined the Arabic manuscripts. He later borrowed from that library two important manuscripts which had formerly belonged to Postel, the *Geography* of Abū 'l-Fidā', of which

---

[180] Erpenius remembered the date (17 Dec. 1608) of his introduction to what was to be his life's work, and twelve years later recorded it in the preface to his *Orationes* (Juynboll, 63 n. 1).

[181] The encouragement is handsomely acknowledged in the dedication to the second edition of the Arabic proverbs (Leiden, 1623): Juynboll, 64 n. 3. Casaubon had long been interested in Arabic, and had collected printed books and manuscripts in the language, but his own knowledge of it never progressed very far, as he admits in his letter to Erpenius of Feb. 1610 (Casaubon, *Letters*, 341–2). We later find Erpenius encouraging him to take it up again and offering his help (ibid. 344, Apr. 1610).

[182] Houtsma, *Uit de Oostersche Correspondentie*, 6–12.

[183] Casaubon, *Letters*, no. 662, 1 Apr. 1610. The grammar was not published until 1613, at Leiden.

[184] On this most interesting man, a Morisco who had emigrated from Spain to Morocco, and was currently in France on behalf of some compatriots who had suffered in the expulsion of 1609, see Wiegers, *Aḥmad b. Kâsim al-Andalusî*, and Jones, 'Learning Arabic', 98–120, which makes good use of Aḥmad's autobiography.

[185] Jones, ibid. 116–19 and 300. Hamilton (*William Bedwell*, 32–3, 135 n. 7) mistakenly supposes the letter to be addressed to Bedwell.

he made a copy, and the *History* of al-Makīn, which was never restored.[186]

When Erpenius returned to Leiden in July 1612, he found that the question of teaching Arabic at the university was under discussion. The Curators, mindful of the importance of the language for commercial as well as academic purposes, had, at Scaliger's instigation, appointed Philippus Ferdinandus, a converted Jew, as Professor of Arabic in 1600,[187] but on his death in 1601 he had not been replaced. Now, however, Jan Theunisz. (Johannes Antonides), who in this very year published the Epistle to Titus in Arabic at the Raphelengius press,[188] was anxious to become Arabic professor, and had been granted permission by the Curators to lecture for one year. But he had the disadvantage of being a Baptist from a plebeian family, with no university education and poor knowledge of Latin.[189] In February 1613, aided by recommendations from Casaubon, Hugo Grotius, Daniel Heinsius, and other influential supporters, Erpenius was appointed extraordinary professor of oriental languages. In the eleven years that he held the post, until his death in 1624, he laid the foundations for the serious study of Arabic in Europe.

The first step was the publication of his Arabic grammar, printed at the Raphelengius press in 1613.[190] Although it incorporates material derived from the native grammatical tradition, Erpenius based his descriptions primarily on his already wide reading, and gave the book a structure which would be familiar to students schooled in Latin and

---

[186] See Levi della Vida, *Ricerche*, 334. Erpenius' copy of the Abū 'l-Fidā' is now at Cambridge with his other manuscripts. The manuscript of al-Makīn has a curious history. It was still in Erpenius' possession when the Palatine Library was removed to Rome, and no doubt he felt disinclined to put it in the hands of the papists, particularly since he had pledged a large sum of money as security for it (ibid. 296). Golius borrowed the manuscript in order to complete Erpenius' posthumous edition of the *History*, and 'forgot' to return it to Erpenius' widow. It was eventually bought with most of Golius' Arabic manuscripts by Narcissus Marsh in 1696, and thus, in 1714, came to the Bodleian Library (MS Marsh 309).

[187] Juynboll, 52. I am at a loss to reconcile this with the information in Adler, *Jews of Medieval England*, 334–6 that Philippus was in the Domus Conversorum in London in 1599 and died there in 1600.

[188] Schnurrer no. 321. On this publication, which embroiled Antonides with Abudacnus and Bedwell, see below, p. 60.

[189] See Wijnman, 'De Hebraicus Jan Theunisz.', who argues that Antonides' replacement by Erpenius was due to class prejudice and Erpenius' powerful connections. While this may be true, there can be no doubt that Erpenius was greatly superior as an Arabist. Jones, 'Learning Arabic', 196–7 describes a unique copy of a brief publication by Antonides on Arabic grammar.

[190] *PO* no. 68; illustrated in *Philologia Arabica*, 144. There is a good analysis of the book in Jones, 'Learning Arabic', 197–205.

Greek grammar. The result was infinitely superior to all earlier European Arabic grammars, and deservedly achieved the status of a standard work, which it retained for two centuries (in numerous revisions by Erpenius himself and later scholars). Later versions, beginning with Erpenius' own *Rudimenta linguae Arabicae* of 1620,[191] included short Arabic texts as reading exercises. The most influential was that published by Golius in 1656,[192] which contained *inter alia* a collection of Arabic proverbs, the first *Maqāma* of al-Ḥarīrī, and a poem of Abū 'l-ʿAlā al-Maʿarrī. But Erpenius also tried to supply the lack of printed texts for students of Arabic by editing a number of elementary texts with Latin translation, for instance the book of Arabic proverbs (a posthumous publication of Scaliger),[193] the *Fables* of Luqmān,[194] and Sura 12 of the Koran.[195] He also produced texts for scholarly purposes: the New Testament and Pentateuch in Arabic,[196] and the first printed Arabic historical work, the *Ta'rīkh al-Muslimīn* ('Historia Saracenica') of al-Makīn.[197]

The earliest of these books, the grammar and Scaliger's edition of proverbs, were printed at the Raphelengius press by the sons of Franciscus Raphelengius, who in 1613 finally brought out their father's Arabic *Lexicon*. Erpenius co-operated in this to the extent of adding an appendix, and his own Arabic grammar was printed in the same quarto format as a complement to the *Lexicon*. However, in 1614 the only compositor at the press who was competent to print Arabic died,[198] and the Raphelengius brothers were no longer interested in publishing Arabic works. Erpenius took the bold step of setting up his own oriental press. This, though costly, had the advantage that he could be his own publisher, and also that he could have types designed to suit his own needs instead of relying on the large and clumsy Raphelengian characters. Accordingly, beginning with the *Fables* of Luqmān of 1615, his later publications were printed with the elegant smaller 'Erpenian' Arabic types, which became the model for many other typefaces in northern Europe, including England.

---

[191] Schnurrer no. 55; *PO* no. 88. This edition includes Sura 64 of the Koran, with an interlinear Latin version and notes.   [192] Schnurrer no. 81.

[193] *PO* no. 267; illustrated in *Philologia Arabica*, 146.

[194] Schnurrer no. 219; illustrated in *Philologia Arabica*, 152.

[195] *PO* no. 89; illustrated in *Philologia Arabica*, 158. This is an interesting example of Erpenius' didactic methods, since it includes not only his own interlinear Latin translation, but also the version published by Bibliander (to exhibit its inadequacies).

[196] *PO* nos. 79 and 86.

[197] *PO* nos. 83, 84, and 85.

[198] Hamilton, 'The Victims of Progress', 102.

Erpenius also assembled a collection of Arabic manuscripts, buying some from the estate of Hubert after his death in 1614, and acquiring others from Constantinople with the help of Cornelis Haga, the Dutch ambassador. The high cost of these reinforced his conviction that the most pressing need was to provide students of Arabic with reliable and comparatively cheap printed texts of a wide variety of Arabic literature.[199] He did much towards this end, and undoubtedly would have done much more had he not died from plague at the early age of 40.[200] Even so, in his short lifetime he transformed the study of Arabic in Europe. The superiority of his grammar was recognized almost universally. For instance, when Cardinal Richelieu decided to distribute an Arabic grammar for the use of French missionaries, the work chosen was simply a reprint of Erpenius' *Rudimenta* of 1628.[201] Erpenius' pre-eminence was recognized even in Italy, where the 'Congregatio de Propaganda Fide' tried in vain to acquire his services in producing their own Arabic Bible,[202] and reprinted his grammar as late as 1829. In the Netherlands the tradition founded by Erpenius thrived. Although his manuscripts were carried off to England, despite the efforts of the Leiden Curators,[203] his oriental types were sold to the Elzevir printing-house, which continued to put them to good use. Above all, the teaching of Arabic at Leiden University was assured by the appointment as Arabic professor of the man who was to hold the post for more than forty years, Jacobus Golius.

This man (Jacob Gool),[204] born in 1596 into an influential family

[199] He expresses his opinions about the proper way to study Arabic in his *Oratio II de lingua arabica*, summarized by Juynboll, 98–100, and about the importance of providing printed books in the language in his letter to the Leiden Curators of 1620 (ibid. 79–80).

[200] For some account of his unfulfilled plans, including editions of the whole Old Testament in Arabic, the *Geography* of Abū 'l-Fidā', and the *Dīwān* of al-Mutanabbī, see Juynboll, 92–3 and 107–11, derived mainly from Vossius, *Funeral Oration*, 88.

[201] Paris (Vitray), 1638: see *Le Livre et le Liban*, no. 68, pp. 200–1. The supervisor was Gabriel Sionita, who thus abandoned his own *Grammatica Arabica Maronitarum* in favour of Erpenius' manual.

[202] The strange story is recounted by Cornelissen, 'Thomas Erpenius en de "Propaganda"'.

[203] On the Duke of Buckingham's purchase of the manuscripts and their eventual transfer to Cambridge see below, p. 91.

[204] Golius' scholarly career (which extends beyond Arabic to other oriental languages, including Chinese, and to the mathematical sciences and geography) has never received the extended treatment it deserves. Any such treatment will have to make full use of his Arabic correspondence preserved in MS Leiden Or. 1228, only partially published by Dozy, *Catalogus*, pp. iv–x and Houtsma, *Oostersche Correspondentie*. Gronovius' funeral oration gives a good sketch of Golius' life, on which Juynboll has drawn in her chapter on him (119–83). A brief but useful treatment of his Arabic manuscripts is in Witkam, *Jacobus Golius en zijn Handschriften*.

with noble connections, devoted himself more to mathematics than to languages in the earlier years of his studies at Leiden, when he was instructed by the notable mathematicians Willebrord Snellius and Frans Schooten the elder. But from 1618 onwards he learned Arabic from Erpenius, whose favourite pupil he became. From 1622 to 1624 he was attached as an engineer to a Dutch mission to Morocco, where he improved his skills in the language and collected manuscripts, aided by Aḥmad b. Qāsim (the same learned Morisco who had instructed Erpenius in France and Holland, now attached to the Sultan Mawlāy Zaydān).[205] Golius returned to Leiden in time to attend Erpenius on his deathbed, and, supported by the latter's recommendation, was appointed his successor as Professor of Arabic in 1625. But he very soon embarked on another journey to the East. On the grounds that he needed to improve his knowledge of oriental languages, he persuaded the Curators not only to give him leave of absence while continuing to pay his salary, but also to spend up to 2,000 guilders[206] buying manuscripts on behalf of the university. Accompanying the newly appointed Dutch consul to Aleppo in 1625 as his assistant, he spent some time in Syria and Mesopotamia. In 1627 he moved to Constantinople, where he lived with Ambassador Haga. By consorting with learned men in both Aleppo and Constantinople, he became expert in Arabic, Turkish, and other languages. When he returned to Leiden in 1629, the oriental manuscripts which he brought with him, acquired by purchase, gift, or copy, constituted a treasure richer than any collection available in northern Europe. News of this hoard soon spread to other parts of Europe, especially after a partial catalogue of it was printed at Paris in 1630 by the enterprise of Pierre Gassendi.[207] Numerous applications were made to him for information about items in this. We shall see John Bainbridge asking him for astronomical data, apparently without success. Wilhelm Schickard was luckier, for Golius sent him information about observations of three eclipses found in the astronomical treatise of ibn Yūnus; these were published much later.[208] Particular

---

[205] See Wiegers, 64–8. There is a good deal of information on Golius' stay in Moroccco in de Castries, *Sources inédites de l'histoire du Maroc. Archives et Bibliothèques des Pays-Bas*, vol. 3, e.g. 268.

[206] This sum was eventually increased to 3,195 guilders 8 stuivers: Witkam, *Jacobus Golius*, 55–6.

[207] Golius, *Catalogus*.

[208] By 'Lucius Barrettus' (i.e. Albert Curtz) in his 1666 edition of Brahe's *Historia Coelestis*, preface, p. xxxiv, from Schickard's manuscript notes. For other information on Arabic subjects which Golius afforded to Schickard see Ullmann, 'Arabische, türkische und persische Studien', 123.

interest was aroused by the presence in the collection of Arabic translations of several Greek mathematical works that were wholly or partly
lost in the original, such as Apollonius' *Conics*, Heron's *Barulcus*, and
Ptolemy's *Planetary Hypotheses*. There were high hopes that Golius
would enrich the 'Republic of Letters' by publishing some of these
with a Latin translation, as he promised, and as he was well equipped
to do, being a superb Arabist and a competent mathematician. Snellius,
the Professor of Mathematics at Leiden, died in 1626. Golius, who had
lobbied for the position while still in Turkey, was appointed as his
successor soon after his return, and held both professorships until his
death.

Golius proved himself a worthy successor to Erpenius in providing
teaching materials in Arabic. Not only did he reissue Erpenius'
grammar with a greatly expanded reading-list,[209] but he had several
other Arabic texts printed which he read with his pupils, and which
were used for teaching Arabic in England and elsewhere. As early
as 1629 he published a collection of proverbs attributed to 'Alī (the
Prophet's son-in-law), with the poem of Ṭughrā'ī[210] and a philosophical text of Avicenna. Another instructional publication was his
edition of ibn 'Arabshāh's life of Timur (1636), but this was of much
greater length, and of considerable historical and scholarly interest.[211]
But undoubtedly the greatest contribution of Golius to the teaching of
Arabic was his *Lexicon*, which appeared, after many years' labour, in
1653.[212] Given the immense wealth of the Arabic language, and the
paucity of Arabic texts available in Europe, the only hope of producing
a comprehensive dictionary was to utilize the native Arabic lexicographical tradition, which is both rich and ancient.[213] Golius was not
the first European to do so: Giggei had excerpted the *Qāmūs* of
al-Fīrūzābādī for his huge *Thesaurus*. Golius also referred to the
Qāmūs, but relied principally on the *Ṣaḥāḥ* of al-Jawharī. Moreover,

---

[209] See above, p. 46. Golius was undoubtedly also responsible for the reprint of 1636
(*PO* no. 70) edited by his pupil Anton Deusing (on whom see Juynboll, 189–91).

[210] On this see below, p. 212. The poem was commonly used for educational purposes
by contemporary Muslims.

[211] Schnurrer no. 166. On Golius' (unfulfilled) plan to produce a translation and commentary on this see Juynboll, 150–1.

[212] See Bibliography (Golius, *Lexicon*) for full details, and Juynboll, 152–7 for an
account of the work. Erpenius had intended something similar, and had actually printed
a specimen of three leaves, which showed that he too intended to use al-Jawharī and the
Qāmūs: Vossius, *Funeral Oration*, 88, cf. Golius, *Lexicon*, preface.

[213] Haywood, *Arabic Lexicography*, gives a good short survey of the native tradition,
but is of little use for Golius and other early European publications.

he supplemented and corrected his Arabic lexicographical sources from his own wide reading. The result, although far from perfect, as Golius himself acknowledged, was so superior to any previously published Arabic dictionary that it immediately became the standard work, a position which it retained until the nineteenth century.

The Republic of Letters was disappointed, however, in its expectation that Golius would publish the Arabic versions of lost Greek texts. The disappointment was greatest in the case of Books V to VII of Apollonius' *Conics*, which he frequently vowed to produce, but never did. In 1646 Constantijn Huygens complained to Mersenne that it was now seventeen years that Golius had been promising to publish it.[214] Golius was not idle: he did in fact work on the Apollonius, to the extent of having figures engraved for all three books,[215] and actually completed a Latin translation of Heron's *Barulcus*.[216] But he published none of these. He was distracted by the wide range of his interests and occupations, and especially by the demands of compiling his *Lexicon*, which took more than twenty years. He can, however, be blamed for his selfishness in denying others, who were willing and able to edit these works, access not only to his own manuscripts but to those which were the property of Leiden University, but which he treated as his own preserve.[217]

Golius was responsible for the accumulation of a large number of Arabic and other oriental manuscripts, not only in his travels in the East, but subsequently by purchase through agents, including his brother Petrus Golius, who spent many years in Syria. He also employed native speakers of Arabic at Leiden as amanuenses to copy manuscripts for him (including Nicolaus Petri and Shahin Qandi, both of whom we shall meet later). The result of all this enriched his own collection more than that of the university: in at least one case (Apollonius' *Conics*) we know that he kept the original for himself and

---

[214] Mersenne, *Correspondance*, xiv, no. 1577, p. 718. Mersenne had been interested in it for many years, and had tried in vain to obtain a copy for Gilbert Gaulmyn or Claude Hardy (ibid. xi, no. 1127, pp. 266–7, 13 Sept. 1642; cf. vii, no. 684, 8 July 1638).

[215] See below, p. 239. On the specimen page of his translation of Book V which he had printed in 1659 see Toomer, 'Apollonius', pp. lxxxvi–lxxxvii. I have not yet located a copy of this document, although it is now clear that Edward Bernard too owned one.

[216] Printed only in 1785: see Juynboll, 139–40. For other editions and translations which Golius started but left incomplete, some of which have now vanished, ibid. 138–43, 150–2, 172.

[217] For his successful efforts to dissuade John Pell from publishing his translation of the Arabic Apollonius see below, p. 184. Job Ludolf's complaint about Golius' reluctance to permit access to his manuscripts is printed by Dozy, *Catalogus*, p. xiii n. 3.

put the copy in the university library.[218] By the time he died in 1667, he had one of the finest collections of oriental manuscripts in Europe, rivalled among those in private hands only by Pococke's in England.[219] These manuscripts did not go to Leiden University, but (largely through the greed of Golius' heirs) remained unsold until 1696, when they were auctioned and the lion's share went to Britain and ultimately to the Bodleian Library. Nevertheless, Leiden had one of the finest collections of Arabic manuscripts in the later seventeenth century. This was due less to Golius than to a former pupil of his, Levinus Warner.[220] Warner was a German from Lippe, who after studying at Bremen enrolled at Leiden in 1638, where he devoted himself to oriental languages, and published three small tracts on orientalia before going to Constantinople in 1645. There he eventually became Dutch resident, but continued his studies and diligently collected manuscripts. Very little of his scholarly work ever saw print,[221] but on his death in 1665 he bequeathed his magnificent library to Leiden University.

Among other foreign pupils of Golius who made their mark in Arabic studies Hottinger has been mentioned above, and Ravius and Petraeus, both of whom had connections with England, will be discussed later. Yet another was Johann Elichmann,[222] who, after studying at Zwickau with Johann Zechendorf,[223] enrolled at Leiden in 1631. Later he practised medicine there, and was host to several students of Arabic, but he died young in 1639. His edition of the Greek, Latin, and Arabic text of the 'Tabula Cebetis', together with an Arabic version of a poem attributed to Pythagoras,[224] was published posthumously through the efforts of his patient and friend Claudius Salmasius (other projected Arabic publications by Elichmann, such as editions of a

[218] That he was capable of sharp practice in acquiring manuscripts is also suggested by his possession of several manuscripts which had belonged to Erpenius (see above, p. 45, for one case). It was probably by an oversight of his executors that several manuscripts which (according to the 1640 printed catalogue) belonged to the university and which were in his house at his death were sold with the rest of his collection. For an example see Dozy, *Catalogus*, pp. xiii–xiv.

[219] The two men had at times competed to acquire the same manuscript in Aleppo: see below, p. 123.

[220] On his career see Juynboll, 222–33; on his legacy G. W. J. Drews, 'The Legatum Warnerianum of Leiden University Library', in *Levinus Warner and his Legacy*, 1–31.

[221] For those that did see *Levinus Warner and his Legacy*, nos. 6–9.

[222] Juynboll, 191–5.

[223] On Zechendorf as an Arabist see Schnurrer, pp. 405–6, and Worthington, *Correspondence*, ii/1. 33, quoting Crinesius, *De Confusione Linguarum*.

[224] Leiden, 1640: Schnurrer no. 409; *PO* no. 322; *Philologia Arabica* no. 97. The manuscript used was one of those that Golius had brought back.

commentary on the Hippocratic oath and of al-Mubashshir's flori-
legium of philosophical sayings,[225] remained uncompleted). Salmasius
(Claude Saumaise), one of the most learned men of his time, began to
learn Arabic fairly late in life in his native France, but undertook it
seriously only after coming to Leiden, where he was appointed in 1632
to the same kind of position which Scaliger had held. His preface to
Elichmann's book is noteworthy for the scepticism it expresses about
the value of Arabic translations of Greek works for establishing the
original text.[226] His own reading in Arabic is exhibited incidentally
in such works as *De Annis Climactericis* (1648)[227] and *Plinianae
Exercitationes*, published posthumously in 1689.[228] After Golius' death
the study of Arabic at Leiden declined drastically. Thomas Marshall,
writing from Dordrecht to Samuel Clarke in Oxford less than a month
after Golius' death, expresses scepticism that any press in Holland
would print the Turkish Bible 'here, where those studies are half dead,
if not half buryed also'.[229] Similar sentiments are expressed by
Hieronymus Harder in a letter to Pococke from Leiden, 28 November
1671,[230] in which he assigns the blame partly to Golius, who 'did not
exercise the students, not even those that were maintained at the public
expence . . . nor use his authority to make them take pains therein'.
There are even earlier indications of Golius' disinclination to teach: in
1643 he tried to get a dispensation from giving lectures in order to
perfect his Persian.[231] But the true reason for the decline is more
probably the other cause assigned by Harder: 'the avarice of the age,
which gave no attention to any sciences, that were not greatly lucrative'. In fact after Golius no professor of Arabic was appointed at
Leiden until 1710, despite occasional efforts by the Curators, including
a short stint by Harder from 1671 to 1673 as extraordinary professor,
and overtures to Edward Bernard in 1683.[232] It was only with the
advent of Albert Schultens in 1729 that Arabic underwent even a
partial revival there.

---

[225] See Rosenthal, 'An Ancient Commentary on the Hippocratic Oath', 52, and
'Al-Mubashshir ibn Fâtik', respectively.

[226] Salmasius' work on the book is discussed, and parts of his preface translated, by
Klein-Franke, *Die klassische Antike in der Tradition des Islam*, 57–62.

[227] There are many astrological terms in Arabic script in the preface.

[228] *PO* no. 320; Fück, 91.

[229] MS BL Add. 22905, fo. 67.

[230] Twells, *Life of Pococke*, 283.

[231] Juynboll, 165: the Curators refused him the dispensation.

[232] Smith, *Life of Bernard*, 44.

3
The Earliest Period of Arabic Studies in England

(I) THE SIXTEENTH CENTURY

The new intellectual interests typical of the Renaissance, which originated in Italy, came later to England than to France and other countries
of northern Europe. Nevertheless, by the end of the sixteenth century the
study of Greek was well established at the two English universities, and
proficiency in Hebrew too was quite widely diffused.[1] Thus there was no
difficulty in assembling a competent body of scholars to translate the
Bible for the Authorized Version which was published in 1611.

The state of Arabic studies in the late sixteenth and early seventeenth
centuries, however, was quite different. Not only was there no provision
for teaching it at the universities, but even those who wished to study it
privately faced formidable difficulties. Printed grammars were few and
miserable, and there was no dictionary worth the name. Indeed there
were very few printed books in Arabic at all, and those that existed were
hard to obtain in England. Access to Arabic manuscripts, apart from
stray copies of the Koran, was virtually impossible.[2] There were no native
speakers at hand to give instruction in the language; this again contrasts
with the situation in Hebrew, where despite the ban on Jews in England
since the Middle Ages, occasional converts and others did give lessons.[3]

The few instances that I can cite of knowledge of Arabic among
sixteenth-century Englishmen before William Bedwell are items of
curiosity rather than significance. The earliest, and the one whose
merits as an Arabist can best be judged, is Robert Wakefield, who
became the first Regius Professor of Hebrew at Oxford in 1540. In

---

[1] An important step was Henry VIII's establishment of the Regius Professorships in
both languages at Oxford and Cambridge. On these and their antecedents see Lloyd
Jones, *The Discovery of Hebrew*, 190–3.

[2] Even that great book collector, John Dee, possessed just one Arabic manuscript
(which he could not read): Roberts and Watson, *John Dee's Library Catalogue*, 183
[DM166]. In contrast, Dee owned a respectable Hebrew library: Lloyd Jones, *The
Discovery of Hebrew*, 169–70.

[3] See Roth, 'Jews in Oxford after 1290'. On Philippus Ferdinandus, a converted Jew
who taught at both Oxford and Cambridge in the late 16th century, see Lloyd Jones, *The
Discovery of Hebrew*, 206–7.

1524 he delivered a lecture at Cambridge entitled 'De laudibus et utilitate trium linguarum', the three languages being Hebrew, Chaldee, and Arabic. Most of the treatise, as printed,[4] is devoted to Hebrew, but there is a section on the value of Arabic, primarily for biblical studies (the author asserts, like others before and after him, that the book of Job was virtually written in Arabic). Despite Wakefield's claim to have introduced the teaching of Chaldee and Arabic to the University of Tübingen (where he succeeded no less a Hebraist than Reuchlin), to have composed a trilingual dictionary and grammar, and to be ready to teach Arabic at Cambridge, one does not form a high opinion of his competence in Arabic from the book.[5] Arabic quotations in the text consist of crude woodcuts of the 'bismillah' and a few other words. His discussion of the language is mainly a series of implausible etymologies, and one gets the impression that his knowledge of the Arabs was derived almost entirely from classical sources, and of Arabic from rabbinical writings.

In 1555 Richard Argentine delivered a speech advocating the teaching of Arabic at both Oxford and Cambridge. As was appropriate for a Cambridge MD, he stressed the benefits of learning Arabic for those practising medicine. Not having seen the original, which exists only in manuscript,[6] I cannot say what it tells us about Argentine's own knowledge of Arabic. Seventy-five years were to pass before his plea for instruction in the language at the universities was answered.

In at least two places Bedwell lists the names of English contemporaries who were interested in Arabic.[7] From these we can form a composite list: John Montfort, John Aylmer, Richard Hooker, George Drywood, Edward Lively, William Thorne, Francis Burley, Lancelot Browne, and Lancelot Andrewes. Except for the last two, it can safely be said that we know nothing whatever about their Arabic accomplishments, although several of them were distinguished Hebraists.[8] It is

[4] Wakefield, *De laudibus trium linguarum* (see Bibliography for details). The approximate date of 1528 is given by Rex, 'The Earliest Use of Hebrew'; modern edition and translation by Lloyd Jones, *Robert Wakefield on the Three Languages*.

[5] He was undoubtedly far more familiar with Hebrew: Lloyd Jones calls him the 'first Hebraist worthy of the name in sixteenth-century England' (*The Discovery of Hebrew*, 181). But one of the auditors of his Hebrew lectures at Tübingen expressed a low opinion of them (ibid. 182–3).

[6] MS e Museo 200, 'Ad Oxonienses et Cantabrigienses pro lingua arabica beneficio principum restituenda'; cf. Hamilton, *William Bedwell*, 8.

[7] In the prefaces to his editions of the Arabic texts of the Epistles of John (Hamilton, *William Bedwell*, 110) and of the Epistle to Titus (ibid. 116).

[8] On the first seven see ibid. 6, 8, 19.

noteworthy that most were Cambridge men, and this is probably to be attributed, not to Bedwell's partiality for his fellow alumni, but to the greater interest in Arabic at Cambridge in the late sixteenth century. Notably absent from the list is the name of Thomas Comber, who came up to Trinity College, Cambridge (of which he was later Master) in about 1592, and according to his biographer[9] was taught Hebrew, Syriac, and Arabic there by his tutor, Titchburn, and later was 'dexterous in Hebrew, Arabick, Coptick, Samaritane, Syriack, Chaldee, Persian', and many modern languages (none of which I have been able to verify). Lancelot Browne, like Andrewes a Fellow of Pembroke Hall, Cambridge, became a distinguished physician, whose fascination with Arabic medical writings led him to compile a dictionary of the works of Avicenna.[10] This was never printed, but the manuscript was used some seventy years later by Edmund Castell as one of the sources for his Heptaglot Lexicon, in the preface of which he refers to Browne as 'Avicennistae incomparabilis, atque viri ob praecellentiam in hisce literis summe admirandi'. Since Browne's dictionary is apparently no longer extant, it is impossible to say whether Castell's estimation of him is coloured by piety towards another Cambridge Arabist. Bedwell also says that, when an embassy from the Sultan of Morocco came to England (in 1600), Browne was the only one who understood their language.[11] One would like to know how he had acquired this understanding of the spoken language, and whether Bedwell himself was one of those who could not understand the ambassadors.

Lancelot Andrewes's skill in oriental languages is attested to by others besides Bedwell.[12] He received an early introduction to them under Richard Mulcaster at Merchant Taylors' School, for that was one of the few English grammar schools to teach Hebrew at that period. His expertise in Hebrew at least is well attested by his extant Hebrew prayers,[13] and by his supervision, in 1604, of the first Westminster group responsible for the translations of the Old Testament in the Authorized Version. His Arabic studies probably belong to his Cambridge period, where he became Fellow of Pembroke Hall in 1576

---

[9] Lloyd, *Memoires*, 447–51.

[10] Perhaps compiled from the Medicean Press edition of the *Canon* (1593).

[11] Preface to the Epistles of John (Hamilton, *William Bedwell*, 112). On the Moroccan embassy see ibid. 15–18.

[12] e.g. Thomas Fuller, quoted by Lloyd Jones, *The Discovery of Hebrew*, 147; and Isaacson, *Lancelot Andrewes*, fo. [**3]ʳ.

[13] See Lloyd Jones, *The Discovery of Hebrew*, 147–8.

and Master in 1589. It was during this time, in about 1585, that he regularly consulted an expert in 'Hebrew, Chaldee, Syriac, Arabic' called Hopkinson, who lived in Grub Street in London.[14] According to Bedwell, Andrewes had begun to compile an Arabic dictionary, but had desisted, overcome by the difficulties, including 'more important duties'.[15] Since this was written in about 1604, these 'graviores occupationes' must comprise the duties connected with his advancement in the Church under James I, by whom he was appointed to the bishoprics of Chichester, Ely, and Winchester in succession. No trace survives of Andrewes's work in Arabic, but in any case there can be no doubt that his own linguistic studies were of far less significance than his activity as a patron and promoter of scholars. Isaacson lists the European scholars whom he entertained, including [Isaac] Casaubon, Cluverius, [G. J.] Vossius, Grotius, [Pierre] du Moulin, and especially Erpenius, to whom he offered a position in England.[16] In a letter he wrote to Selden in 1621, mention of the Dutch scholars Franciscus Junius and Doublet, who were then staying with him, leads him to wish that Erpenius were there.[17] Andrewes's attachment to Erpenius (as well as his ability to read Arabic) is also attested by a letter in Arabic, written by Golius in the name of Erpenius' widow and children, and addressed to the bishop.[18] Another Arabic scholar whom Andrewes welcomed to England was Josephus Abudacnus.[19] But above all it was through his encouragement, patronage, and financial support of Bedwell that Andrewes advanced the cause of Arabic in England.

(II) BEDWELL

William Bedwell was the first Englishman after the Middle Ages to undertake the serious study of Arabic. We are fortunate to have a full-

[14] According to the autobiography of James Whitelocke, who was reading Hebrew with the otherwise unknown Hopkinson at the same time: see ibid. 231. In this context it is interesting that in 1612 Sir George Buc (*The Third Vniversitie of England*, 1082) claimed: 'There bee also in this Cittie [London] Teachers and Professors of the holy or Hebrew Language, of the Caldean, Syriake, and Arabike or Larbey Languages.'

[15] 'Solus D.D. Andrewsius strenuam in hoc navabat operam foelicibus auspiciis: sed graviores occupationes, operis magnitudo, librorum penuria, incoeptum opus retardabant': preface to the Epistles of James (Hamilton, *William Bedwell*, 111).

[16] Isaacson, *Lancelot Andrewes*, fo. [**3]ʳ. This was as early as 1612, as appears from Vossius, *Funeral Oration*, 88.

[17] MS Selden supra 108, fo. 122ʳ. Doublet is presumably Georgius Rataller Doublet (see below, p. 74).

[18] *PO* no. 84, giving the correct date (end of May 1625).

[19] See below, p. 96.

length recent monograph on his life and his work, especially his work on Arabic (Hamilton, *William Bedwell the Arabist*). My account owes much to that, and adds very little: I refer the reader to it for a detailed biography, and for Bedwell's work outside of Arabic, especially in mathematical education.

After Bedwell graduated from Cambridge (MA 1588), where he learned Hebrew and Chaldee at Trinity College, and had begun to study Arabic under the influence of Andrewes, little is known of his external life until he obtained the living of St Ethelburgha, Bishopsgate, in 1601. However, he was certainly deeply engaged in the study of Arabic in the last decade of the sixteenth century, for the first extant specimen of the work which occupied a large part of his scholarly life, his Arabic dictionary, is dated 1596.[20] Although he had as yet published nothing, he already had a reputation as an Arabist outside England, as is attested by the signatures which appear from 1597 on in his 'album amicorum'. Many of these were entered by European scholars visiting England, who made a detour to Bedwell's house to admire his recondite knowledge.[21] In 1607 Andrewes (then Bishop of Chichester) gave Bedwell the vicarage of All Hallows' Church in Tottenham High Cross, at that time a village some six miles north of London, which became his usual place of residence for the rest of his life.

After he left Cambridge, Bedwell's study was solitary (apart from his brief journey to Holland in 1612). He did indeed have occasional pupils for short periods, and came into contact with scholars visiting him at his house or elsewhere (for instance at the Westminster sessions of the Bible translators). At least towards the end of his life these included such luminaries as John Selden and Archbishops Ussher and Laud. Moreover, he acted as interpreter for the Government's correspondence with Arabic-speaking potentates.[22] He was also in epistolary communication with European scholars, some of them eminent (Casaubon initiated a correspondence with him in 1603[23]). Nevertheless, Bedwell's work in Arabic was hampered by lack of texts

---

[20] This is MS Bodl. Or. 372: Hamilton, *William Bedwell*, 12, 127. For evidence that Bedwell began work on it in 1592, see n. 41 below.

[21] See ibid. 13 ff. and *passim*.

[22] De Castries, *Sources inédites de l'histoire du Maroc, Archives et Bibliothèques d'Angleterre*, vol. 2, pp. 418–21, prints Bedwell's English translation of a letter from Sultan Mawlāy Zaydān to James I of 1609; ibid. 610–13, Bedwell's faulty copy of an Arabic letter of 1611 from the same ruler.

[23] Casaubon, *Letters*, no. 344, p. 183. The letter is reprinted by Hamilton, *William Bedwell*, 97.

and difficulties in getting access to those which did exist. He did indeed consult Arabic manuscripts at the Bodleian Library after 1611,[24] but, as we shall see, during his lifetime these were few and insignificant. We know that he also occasionally exchanged books and manuscripts with other English scholars, for in 1622 Selden told Ussher that he was unable to return the bishop's copy of 'Nubiensis Geographia' because Bedwell had borrowed it from him,[25] and in May 1632 Ussher informed Louis de Dieu that he had little hope of recovering an Arabic Psalter of his own which was still in Bedwell's possession at his death.[26] On the whole, however, Bedwell had to rely on those printed books which he bought for himself,[27] and whatever manuscripts he could somehow obtain. He did in fact manage to assemble a number of Arabic manuscripts over the course of his lifetime. Since these were dispersed after his death, no complete list has been compiled, but many, perhaps most, were bought by Laud,[28] others by Selden, and all of these are now in the Bodleian. Other manuscripts owned by Bedwell reached the Bodleian by some other route, for instance Or. 298 (Nicoll–Pusey no. 24, pp. 484–7), Arabic letters sent to or copied by Bedwell; Or. 575 (Nicoll–Pusey no. 407, pp. 397–402), Arabic letters, including Bedwell's copy and translation of a safe conduct given by Mawlāy Zaydān in 1615; and Or. 372 (Nicoll–Pusey no. 240, p. 195), the 1596 version of Bedwell's Arabic dictionary. The source of Bedwell's manuscripts is not known, but we may suspect that many of them came to him through the agency of merchants in the Levant Company.

Bedwell, like his pupil Erpenius, learned from his own experience that students of Arabic were in desperate need of two things: a good grammar and dictionary, and a supply of printed texts in Arabic, with Latin translations. To supply the former need he worked on his dictionary; towards the latter he prepared a number of editions and translations of Arabic texts. With one exception (*Mohammedis Imposturae*), these are all Arabic translations of the Scriptures, mostly

[24] For details of these see ibid. 90.
[25] Ussher, *Letters*, no. 46, p. 78. The work in question is probably the Latin translation published by Sionita and Hesronita.
[26] Ibid. no. 174, p. 462.
[27] For these, primarily the Medicean Press publications, see Hamilton, *William Bedwell*, 12, 87.
[28] See Hunt, *Laudian Manuscripts*, pp. xii–xiii for a list of the Laudian manuscripts known to have belonged to Bedwell. This is certainly not complete, since it omits the MSS Laud Or. 278 (ibn al-Bannā''s *Minhāj*, see below, p. 73), and Laud Or. 319, 372, 819, and 829, listed by Hamilton, *William Bedwell*, 126–8.

of Epistles from the New Testament.[29] If one asks what dictated this choice of texts, the obvious answer, that he wished to promote biblical studies, may not be the right one. It is true that in justifying the study of Arabic in his preface to the Epistles to Titus and Philemon[30] he gives prominence to this aspect of it.[31] But a more compelling reason may have been that these were the texts (amongst those available to him) that he felt the most confidence in handling and offering to his readers, since, having the Greek original, both he and they would know what the Arabic ought to mean. Although he was proud of the most unusual manuscript he possessed, the *Minhāj* (a set of astronomical tables and canons) of ibn al-Bannā', he seems to have made no attempt to edit or translate it. The editions that he did complete are a respectable achievement.

Having produced these editions, he was faced with the problem of having them published. Since there were no facilities for printing Arabic in England, it was necessary either to send them abroad, or to set up an Arabic printing-press at home. Either course would require expense, which meant the support of patrons. It is not surprising, then, to find Bedwell dedicating his editions to influential men: the Epistle to the Colossians is dedicated to Richard Bancroft, Bishop of London and soon to be Archbishop of Canterbury; the Epistles to Titus and Philemon to Bishop Andrewes; and the Epistles of John to no less a personage than King James I.[32] The latter contains an outright appeal for the monarch's support in publishing Bedwell's Arabic dictionary. Andrewes was the only one to help Bedwell, and it was with his financial aid that Bedwell was able to achieve publication of the only Arabic text of his which ever saw print, the Epistles of John, printed with Bedwell's Latin translation at the Raphelengius Press in Leiden, 1612.[33]

Bedwell had considered the Medicean Press as a possibility,[34] but that

---

[29] For details see Hamilton, *William Bedwell*, 126–7. It is unlikely that the translations and transcriptions of small parts of the Koran listed there were intended for publication; even less does the obscure sentence in Erpenius' letter to Bedwell of 1609, written in stumbling Arabic (Houtsma, *Oostersche Correspondentie*, 8), support the notion that Bedwell had any intent that Le Bé should publish the 'three suras of the Koran with commentary' which he had sent to Erpenius.

[30] Unpublished, but the preface is printed in Hamilton, *William Bedwell*, 112–18: see especially 115.

[31] Hamilton has a good discussion of Bedwell's professed and actual motivations for studying Arabic, ibid. 69 ff.

[32] Ibid. 106, 112, and 108 respectively.

[33] Schnurrer no. 322, cf. Hamilton, *William Bedwell*, 124.

[34] Ibid. 24. There is no evidence that he ever contemplated offering his work to Kirsten at Breslau to publish, although Kirsten had visited him in England in 1602, and

could only have been through ignorance of its circumstances. The Raphelengius Press offered the advantages of the good communications between England and Holland, and the presence in Leiden of Bedwell's friend and former pupil Erpenius, who had recently returned to Leiden in the summer of 1612. Armed with recommendations from Casaubon (who had moved to England in 1610), and funded by Andrewes, Bedwell made the journey to Leiden in August 1612. His purpose was not only to entrust his book to the brothers Raphelengius, but also to consult the Arabic manuscripts which Scaliger had bequeathed to the university. He was given free access to these by the librarian, Daniel Heinsius, and made a very careful collation of one which contained the same text that he was about to publish.[35] No doubt his interest in lexicography also led him to examine Scaliger's Arabic thesaurus. But while in Leiden he discovered that the Raphelengii were already engaged in printing their father's Arabic dictionary, thus frustrating his hopes to be the first to produce one. Even more disturbing was his discovery that they were publishing an edition of the Arabic text of the Epistle to Titus prepared by the current lecturer in Arabic at Leiden, Jan Theunisz. For Bedwell had long before prepared such an edition, for which he would hardly now find a publisher, and to add insult to injury, the Arabic text had been supplied to Theunisz. by Abudacnus, whom Bedwell had recently entertained in his own house.[36]

Bedwell's visit to Leiden did achieve one result which must have given him great satisfaction: he persuaded the Raphelengius brothers to sell him their Arabic type (which Andrewes had agreed to pay for). With this he hoped to print his Arabic dictionary in England, where he returned in October 1612. Although Erpenius obtained his permission for the Raphelengii to keep the type a while longer in order to finish printing some books that they had already undertaken, including Franciscus Raphelengius' dictionary and Erpenius' grammar, the types were finally sent to Bedwell in 1614. When he received them, however, he found them a disappointment. This is reported by John Greaves (who knew Bedwell for a short period before his death), in a letter to Peter Turner of 10 February 1637:

was in correspondence with him as late as 1632 (ibid. 19, 104). The only other Arabic press in Europe at the time was that of Le Bé; the odd remark by Casaubon in his letter to Hubert of 22 Sept. 1612 (*Letters*, 485), that Andrewes would be willing to buy Le Bé's types for Bedwell, probably means only that he was aware of their current negotiations for buying those of the Raphelengii.

[35] Leiden Or. 217: Hamilton, *William Bedwell*, 138 n. 56.
[36] On this curious and obscure incident see below, p. 96.

The onely danger is that some of the puncheons [of the recently purchased Oxford Arabic types] being wanting, and it may be also some of the matrices, which answer those puncheons, it will be a difficult matter, either in the Low countries, or here, to supply them. Mr. Bedwell, when he bought Raphelengius his Arabicke presse, found some characters defective, which he desired to haue perfited, and made suitable to the rest, but was neuer able to effect it.[37]

Greaves was right to be concerned about the possible deficiency of matrices, for it seems that what the Raphelengii sent Bedwell was not the matrices from which new types could be cast, but only a set of actual types, and those were used and worn.[38] Bedwell never used the types to print his dictionary or anything else; he did, however, bequeath them to Cambridge for the express purpose of printing his dictionary.

The only other work of Bedwell's relating to Arabic which was published in his lifetime was his *Mohammedis Imposturae: That is, a Discovery of the Manifold Forgeries, Falshoods, and horrible impieties of the blasphemous seducer Mohammed* [etc.].[39] This was an English translation of an Arabic text printed in Italy some time after 1566,[40] purporting to be a centuries-old record of a dialogue between two Muslims, one of whom casts doubt on the Koran and the character of Muḥammad. In fact it is an impudent forgery by a sixteenth-century Christian, perhaps not even a native Arabic speaker, but Bedwell took it at face value. The title is a good indication of the polemical purpose of the work, and it was received well enough by the pious in England to be reissued in 1624. Bedwell attached to it two small treatises of his own: *The Arabian Trudgman*, a list of the names for offices and dignities used among Muslims, and other terms which the reader of 'Orientall histories' might find unfamiliar; and an *Index Assuratarum*, a catalogue of the chapters of the Koran as numbered and used among the Muslims. This would assist those who wanted to compare the

---

[37] PRO, SP 16,381 no. 75. The date of 1638 given by Hamilton, *William Bedwell*, 47, derives from an error in the printed *Calendar of State Papers*.

[38] The evidence on this from the Dutch side is ambiguous: see Hamilton, 'The Victims of Progress' and *William Bedwell*, 45–7. But the judgements about the types expressed at Cambridge in the 1640s by Thomas Smith and Wheelock support the interpretation that no matrices were available: see below, p. 180.

[39] London, 1615: *PO* no. 59. See Hamilton, *William Bedwell*, 124–5 for the full title of this and the 1624 reissue.

[40] There is no date on the original, which is entirely in Arabic: see Schnurrer no. 236, and Levi della Vida, *Ricerche*, 257–9, who diffidently suggests a date after 1584. I do not know on what grounds Smitskamp assigns the date 1579 (*PO* no. 59c, p. 56). Bedwell's annotated copy of this book is in the Bodleian Library (Nicoll–Pusey, p. 487 n. c).

original Koran with the standard translation of Bedwell's time, Bibliander's printing of Robert of Ketton's medieval Latin version, in which a confusingly different system of numbering and naming the suras had been introduced.

Bedwell undoubtedly considered his most important contribution to Arabic studies to be his dictionary, on which he began working in about 1592,[41] and continued until his death forty years later. Various versions of it exist in manuscript dating from various epochs, the earliest from 1596,[42] but even the latest of these, the version which was eventually bequeathed to Cambridge, is a kind of palimpsest written over many years, with innumerable additions and corrections in the margins and on inserted slips of paper.[43] When he began the work Bedwell had very few Arabic texts to work from, and his knowledge of the language was limited. Over his lifetime he became acquainted with many more Arabic works, and he corrected and enlarged the dictionary as his reading progressed. However, as late as 1612 Bedwell is still referring to Averroes (ibn Rushd) as 'Abin-Rhoi',[44] a desperate guess at the true form of the name which reveals his unfamiliarity with Arabic philosophical or biographical sources. Erpenius recognized quite early in his career as an Arabist that Bedwell's dictionary was vitiated by his inadequate grasp of grammatical forms.[45] Four years later he criticized it on the grounds that Bedwell could not determine the correct meaning or vocalization of many words because he did not have access to the dictionaries of the Arabs themselves.[46] In fact references in the latest version of the dictionary to the *Qāmūs* (of al-Fīrūzābādī) and to al-Jawharī (presumably the *Ṣaḥāḥ*) show that Bedwell did have access to these works in the latter part of his life,[47] but unlike Golius (who used them as a foundation), Bedwell seems to have consulted them only sporadically. The imperfections of the dictionary's content are aggravated by those of its form. Led astray,

[41] In his dedicatory epistle to James I of about 1604 (Hamilton, *William Bedwell*, 108) he describes the dictionary as 'duodecim annorum partum'.

[42] For details of these see ibid. 127.

[43] Some idea of this confusing presentation is given by plates 12 and 13, ibid.

[44] Preface to his edition of the Epistles of John (reprinted ibid. 119).

[45] Erpenius to Casaubon, 10 Apr. 1610 (Casaubon, *Letters*, no. 662, p. 344): 'Mirum fortassis tibi videri potest, verissimum tamen est, solas istas chartas, quas habes [Erpenius' first outline of his grammar], utut sunt imperfectae, ex doctissimi Bedwelli Dictionario millia aliquot erratorum delere posse.'

[46] Erpenius to Casaubon, quoted by Hamilton, *William Bedwell*, 152 n. 111.

[47] Ibid. 88. Selden owned a copy of the *Qāmūs*, which he later lent to Golius for his lexicon; conceivably Bedwell had borrowed it earlier. I have not attempted to investigate Bedwell's sources for his dictionary, and can refer only to Hamilton, pp. 87–91.

like many of his contemporaries and successors, by the supposed daughter–mother relationship of Arabic to Hebrew, Bedwell chose to arrange his dictionary in the order of the Hebrew alphabet instead of the Arabic. He also inserted numerous etymological remarks connecting the Arabic words not only to Hebrew and Syriac, but also to Greek, English, and other languages. This demonstrates the author's learning more than it helps the user. In fact, in the form in which Bedwell left it, the dictionary is unusable, and would have required years of work by a skilled Arabist to reduce it to a publishable book. In the mean time the printed works in Arabic emanating from Leiden and elsewhere, to say nothing of the increasing availability of Arabic manuscripts, including lexicographical works, in England, made Bedwell's dictionary ever more obsolete as the years passed. It is not surprising that Cambridge University, which had inherited the dictionary, together with Bedwell's types, on the condition that it be printed, did nothing whatever with it. It was indeed lent to Edmund Castell to help compile his Heptaglot Lexicon, but to judge from Castell's private remarks about it, he found it more a hindrance than a help:

it wold have required at least a quarter of a year to make him [Bedwell] fit and ready to bee used by us, no les than 21. or 2300. loose papers without any order at al in him, many obscure expressions which seem to allude to som other piece written by him, in Avicen numberles misquotations according to any the Copies wee have etc. . . . . Infinite are the words of which the great Bedwel almost in every leafe professes himself ignorant.[48]

Bedwell's own attainments in Arabic were modest, but his contributions to the promotion of the study of the language and its literature, especially in England, were substantial. He enjoyed a reputation both in England and abroad as one of the few competent European Arabists of his time. Before the study of Arabic had any status at either university, Bedwell's house at Tottenham provided a place where those who were interested in it could resort for instruction and to consult manuscripts. Among those who did so whose names occur later in this book were Josephus Abudacnus, Selden, John Bainbridge, and John Greaves. He has the distinction of having taught two of the most renowned and influential Arabists of the seventeenth century, Thomas

---

[48] Castell to Samuel Clarke, 7 Mar. 1659 (MS BL 22905, fo. 27). Later the same month (ibid. fo. 29) he complains about 'Mr Bedwels MS. which being very intricate to understand especially in regard of his so many 100s some thousands of litle loos papers without any order at al scatteringly inserted & som in wors order stitched together'.

Erpenius and Edward Pococke; and although both soon outstripped their teacher in knowledge of the language, they owed much to the example he gave them of devotion to it.

(III) SELDEN

John Selden's name will recur often in these pages, in many contexts: as patron, as statesman, as scholar. It is impossible within the limitations of my chosen topic to do justice to one who ranks among the greatest of seventeenth-century Englishmen.[49] It would be far too extensive a digression even to summarize the scholarship of one of the most learned men of his time in many fields, including Hebrew, the ancient world, and legal and constitutional history. His Arabic studies, although a minor aspect of his intellectual activity, deserve our attention. They extend over almost the whole period of his literary career, up to *De Synedriis Liber Tertius* (published posthumously in 1655), but since they begin as early as *Titles of Honor* (1614), it is appropriate to treat them here.

Selden's earlier publications reveal little more than an interest in the Arabic language. In the first edition of *Titles of Honor* (1614), when discussing Eastern titles, he gives appellations such as 'al-Shaykh' and 'Sulṭān' in Arabic script. For lack of Arabic types these are rendered in woodcut.[50] The first work of Selden's in which Arabic is a prominent feature is the second edition of *De Dis Syris* (1629).[51] He had been requested by the Elzevirs in Leiden to prepare a revised edition of this treatise (originally published in London in 1617). Since the publishers, who had acquired Erpenius' types, were able to print Arabic, Selden took the opportunity to insert long Arabic quotations. It is of some interest to see what Arabic works Selden had read by this time. He quotes the Koran in the original, using it not only to give the proper references to suras instead of those in Bibliander, but even on occasion

---

[49] The literature on Selden is very large, but for the printed biographies, including that by Wilkins prefaced to Selden's *Opera Omnia*, Crossley's verdict (Worthington, *Correspondence*, ii/1, 27) remains true 150 years later: 'Certainly a better is deserved by him who has been styled "the glory of the English nation" than that or any other which has been yet published.' For general purposes the account by Edward Fry in *DNB* is as good as any. I am preparing a book on Selden as a scholar.

[50] Roper, 'Arabic Printing', 12–13.

[51] The difference in this respect from the first edition is striking. There is nothing on Arabic in that except for the names of two Arabic deities rendered (incorrectly) in woodcut on pp. 161 and 164.

to correct the medieval Latin translation as printed.[52] His general opinion of Robert of Ketton's version can be seen on p. 134, where he says of it: 'Periocha est nullius sensus uti & quamplurimae apud eundem [Robert] aliae.' In elucidating the Koran he used an Arabic commentary on it which he consulted in a manuscript belonging to Sir Robert Cotton.[53] Selden knows the Arabic Pentateuch, not only in the printed text of Erpenius, but in a different version which he read in a manuscript in the library of the Earl of Arundel. In the 1620s the great library of Thomas Howard, second Earl of Arundel,[54] Earl Marshal from 1621, was one of the very few in England containing significant numbers of Arabic manuscripts and printed books. Some idea of its contents can be gathered from the present Arundel collection in the British Library, which would indicate that its Arabic holdings were mainly Christian works and grammars. However, the Arabic Pentateuch used by Selden is not among these, and was presumably a casualty of the severe losses from the collection, by theft and neglect, after the earl's death in 1646. Selden also elucidates a word in the Koran from the 'Geographia Nubiensis' (the Medicean Press edition of al-Idrīsī), and quotes from an anonymous Arabic manuscript in his own possession on the subject of talismans.[55] But he was especially interested in an Arabic treatise which he knew from a manuscript in Cotton's library, the ecclesiastical history of Eutychius, Patriarch of Alexandria from 933 to 938. This work was to occupy him on and off for the rest of his life. There are numerous quotations from it in his *De jure naturali & gentium* (1640).[56] In 1642 he published a long extract from Eutychius' annals, concerning the origin of the Patriarchate of Alexandria, with his own translation and commentary, as a contribution to the controversial subject of the positions of presbyter and bishop in early Christianity; Selden's commentary displeased those

[52] There are several examples on pp. 133–5, where the translations given by Selden are indeed far more accurate than those in Bibliander.

[53] On p. 134. I have not identified this 'Scholiastes' in any of the Cottonian manuscripts presently in the British Library. Perhaps he is the same as 'praestantissimus Alcorani paraphrastes Mahumedes ben Achmed' (i.e. Jalāl al-Dīn al-Maḥallī, see below), quoted by Selden on p. 95 of *Mare Clausum*.

[54] For a brief account of the history of his library see de Ricci, *English Collectors of Books and Manuscripts*, 25–6. For Ussher's use of Arabic manuscripts in it in 1625 see below, p. 78. Selden had rendered services to the earl (who gave him a pension of £50 in 1634; Hervey, *Earl of Arundel*, 358 n. 3), and had recently published the Greek inscriptions owned by him (*Marmora Arundelliana*, 1628).

[55] pp. 129, 116. I have not succeeded in identifying the latter work among the present Selden MSS in the Bodleian.

[56] *PO* no. 369.

asserting the primacy of the bishops.[57] This book is notable as the first Arabic text (as distinct from isolated quotations) printed in England. Towards the end of his life Selden brought about the publication and translation (by Pococke) of the whole work, having apparently abandoned a plan to do this himself.[58]

Selden explicitly tells us that his attention was drawn to the Eutychius by Henry Jacob, to whom he owed many other hints.[59] According to Wood,[60] Jacob taught Selden Hebrew. That formulation of their relationship is definitely incorrect, since Selden's interest in Hebrew long predates his acquaintance with Jacob; but it is certainly possible that Jacob assisted him with Hebrew, and it seems very probable that Selden's increasing familiarity with Arabic from the time of this book onwards (the preface is dated 1628) was due in large part to this man.[61] Jacob had only recently come to England from Holland,[62] where his father, a prominent Protestant sectary, had spent many years of exile, and where he himself was educated, studying Arabic with Erpenius. His reputation for oriental studies was great, according to Wood, but from his published work one would infer only that he had some knowledge of Arabic.[63] But at least one of Selden's

---

[57] Selden, *Eutychius* (*PO* no. 369). I cannot go into the arguments on both sides of this topic, which was arousing great passions in England at the very time that Selden published that book; I note only that the great scholars Salmasius (*Dissertatio de foenere trapezitico*, Leiden, 1640) and Petavius (*Dissertationes Ecclesiasticae de Episcoporum dignitate*, Paris, 1641) had published on opposite sides of the question, and that many years later Abraham Ecchellensis, in defence of the papacy, was to publish a lengthy polemic directed mainly against this work of Selden's (*Eutychius Vindicatus*).

[58] See below, pp. 164–5.

[59] 'Observavit mihi primo, libentissime fateor, juramentum illud, uti solet & alia compluria, doctissimus juvenis & de me optime meritus, Henricus Jacobus', *De Dis Syris*, 46.

[60] *Athenae Oxonienses*, iii. 330. Wood associates this with the publication of Selden's *Mare Clausum* (1635), because Selden later acknowledged that Jacob had acted as his amanuensis for that book.

[61] It certainly did not begin with him, however. Selden had met Erpenius on one of his visits to England (probably in 1621: letter of Selden to Erpenius of 17 Feb. 1622, MS Selden supra 108, fo. 208ʳ), and, at his request, Erpenius had sent him a copy of the printed Arabic text of al-Makīn before the latter was published (letter of Bainbridge to Erpenius of 1 Sept. 1624, MS Savile 47, fo. 35). For the story that Ussher instructed Selden in the 'elements of the Eastern tongues' see below, p. 78.

[62] Probably in 1628: he became BA Oxon. (Queen's) on 20 Jan. 1629, through the intercession of Bedwell with the Chancellor. See below for proof that Jacob was still in Leiden in 1627.

[63] This is *Philologiae* ἀνακαλυπτήριον, his inaugural lecture at Merton. See Madan, *Oxford Books*, iii, nos. 2184–5. The copy 4° S 4(2) Art. Seld. in the Bodleian was presented by Jacob to Selden. It consists largely of futile 'learned etymologies' characteristic of the period, but on p. 88 is a badly printed Arabic quotation from Avicenna, and on p. 89 a reference to al-Makīn.

manuscripts contains Arabic texts with translations by Jacob, his annotations in his copy of Bainbridge's *Canicularia* (1648)[64] display
Hebrew and Arabic learning, and he was employed to catalogue the
rabbinical Hebrew manuscripts in the Bodleian in 1629.[65] His learned
notes on *De Dis Syris* were in the possession of David Wilkins, the
editor of Selden's *Opera Omnia*, in 1726,[66] but seem to have disappeared. With the help of Selden and Peter Turner, Jacob was
appointed as Praelector in Philology at Merton College,[67] but because
he had been intruded into his post by Laud he earned the enmity of the
Warden, Sir Nathaniel Brent, and was ejected from his fellowship by
the Visitors, of whom Brent was chairman, in 1648.[68] Wood maintains
that Edmund Dickenson's *Delphi Phoenicizantes* was plagiarized from
a manuscript which Jacob left behind at Merton,[69] and perusal of the
book reveals a remarkable similarity to *Philologiae* ἀνακαλυπτήριον
in style and perverse misapplication of learning. Moreover, the Arabic
authorities quoted are the very same that Jacob refers to elsewhere,
versions of the scripture and Eutychius' annals. However, Dickenson
at least brought the book up to date by giving the references to
Eutychius in Pococke's recent edition, and also refers to the notes to
his *Specimen* and apparently consulted him in person. He published it
only after Jacob had died in obscurity at Canterbury in 1652.

Selden's command of Arabic was never really good. In his earliest
reference to the work of Eutychius[70] he gives it the meaningless title
تطم الجوهر, instead of نظم الجوهر ('string of pearls'). The second word is
merely a misprint, but Selden's translation '*involuens gemmam*, seu
Theca gemmaria' suggests that he may have read the first word as it is
printed, deriving it from طمّ or even (impossibly) طوي. By the time he

[64] Tanner 934 in the Bodleian Library.

[65] MS Arch. Seld. B super. 80 (Nicoll, p. 85) is prayers and proverbs in Arabic, with
Jacob's Latin version, dated 1627. Jacob signs himself هنريكو يعقوب الانقليسى من لوندرا
'Henry Jacob the Englishman from London'. MS Rawl. D. 1171 is the catalogue com-
piled by Jacob: see Wheeler, 'Bibliotheca Rabbinica'.

[66] Selden, *Opera*, i/1, p. xv.

[67] According to Brodrick, *Memorials of Merton College*, 78, Laud, as Visitor of the
College, ordered the readmission of Jacob to Merton as 'Grammar Master'.

[68] On the factions at Merton see below, pp. 107, 155.

[69] *Athenae Oxonienses*, iii. 331. One should be cautious in accepting everything that
Wood says about Dickenson, since he detested him, blaming his mother's death on
Dickenson's inept medical treatment.

[70] *De Dis Syris*, 46. Selden refers to him as 'Said Aben-Batrich'. As late as 1640, in
De jure naturali & gentium (*Opera*, i/1, 504) he misreads the Greek form of his name as
'Apthisius'. By the time of his *Eutychius* (1642) he has it right (no doubt informed by
Pococke).

came to publish an excerpt from the work in his *Eutychius* he had the title right, but his translation of the text contains several blunders.[71] Arabic quotations in his other works also exhibit solecisms. Nevertheless, he had a working knowledge of the language, and by the end of his life his reading in it was remarkably wide. This can be illustrated by his last book, *De Synedriis Liber Tertius*.[72] He refers to a number of Arabic and Persian printed works. Besides biblical publications, such as Erpenius' edition of the Pentateuch and the versions of the Psalms published by Giustiniani and Savary de Brèves, he quotes all the principal secular texts: the Medicean editions of Avicenna and al-Idrīsī's *Geography*, Erpenius' edition of al-Makīn, Abū 'l-Faraj in Pococke's *Specimen*, John Greaves's editions of Ulugh Beg and Naṣīr al-Dīn, and de Dieu's *Historia Christi Persice ab Hieronymo Xaverio conscripta*.[73] He also quotes from numerous manuscripts belonging to himself and others: the Koran, with at least two Arabic commentaries, one 'Mahumed Ben Achmed perpetuus Alcorani sed compendiosior paraphrastes' (i.e. the well-known 'Tafsīr' by Jalāl al-Dīn Muḥ. b. Aḥmad al-Maḥallī), the other described merely as 'a more ample commentary on the Koran which I own';[74] Maimonides' *Guide of the Perplexed* in the original Arabic, which he took from a manuscript belonging to Pococke;[75] the *Geography* of Abū 'l-Fidā', from the Cambridge manuscript (this had previously enabled him to identify the 'Nubian Geographer' as al-Idrīsī[76]); the Arabic Councils from the Roe manuscript in the Bodleian; a long extract on Christian feasts from a manuscript of al-Qalqashandī which he owned;[77] and the astronomical work of ibn al-Shāṭir, in the manuscript formerly owned by John Greaves, from which he extracts a table on pp. 414–17. For

[71] Scornfully analysed by Abraham Ecchellensis in his *Eutychius Vindicatus*, i. 22 ff. By the time this was printed (1661) Selden was dead and Pococke had already (silently) corrected the errors in his edition of the whole Eutychius. Prideaux, *Mahomet*, pt. II, pp. 165–6 comments harshly on Selden's *Eutychius*, but also remarks about Ecchellensis (p. 176): 'The greatest skill which he shews in this Book, is in railing.'

[72] The following list is far from exhausting Selden's Arabic reading. For instance in *De jure naturali* (*Opera*, i/1, 405) he quotes at length from 'Abu Walid Mahumed Ben Elshecina, historico veteri MS.', i.e. ibn al-Shuḥna's روضة المناظر (now MS Arch. Selden A 19, Uri no. 666, p. 151); and in *Uxor Hebraica*, ii. 26 (*Opera*, ii/1, 815) from Muḥ. b. ʿAbd al-Bāqī's account of the Abyssinians in a Bodleian manuscript (Uri no. 859, p. 185, SC no. 1600).

[73] Leiden, 1639: *PO* no. 310.

[74] *De Synedriis Liber Tertius*, 158, 159.

[75] Ibid. 433.

[76] *Uxor Hebraica*, ii. 26 (*Opera*, ii/1, 814); cf. *Judicium de Decem Scriptoribus Anglicanis* (ibid. ii/2, 1160).

[77] *De Synedriis Liber Tertius*, 347–74. The manuscript is now MS Arch. Seld. A 17.

Eutychius he is now able to refer not only to his manuscripts, but to the page numbers of the printed edition then in progress. His lexicographical aids include not only the very recent printed Arabic lexicon of Golius and the older one of Raphelengius, but a manuscript of al-Jawharī which he had consulted in the Arundel Library.

In a letter to Francis Tayler of 25 June 1646, Selden gives an interesting appraisal of the value of oriental studies for the early history of Christianity, comparing it to the use of the telescope in astronomy.[78] It is characteristic of Selden that when he became interested in a subject he began to acquire books about it for his splendid scholarly library. In the case of Arabic, this meant primarily manuscripts.[79] When he composed the second edition of *De Dis Syris* he already owned at least two Arabic manuscripts[80] (the Koran and the work on talismans), but he probably began to collect Arabic manuscripts seriously at about that period. When *De Dis Syris* was published the only manuscript of Eutychius that Selden knew about was the one in the Cottonian Library. Thirteen years later he himself owned two manuscripts of the work; as Pococke later informs us, both of these were contemporary copies made by Michael Thaljah, a professional scribe whom Pococke had known at Aleppo.[81] Selden acquired one from his friend George Gage, and the other from a prominent Aleppo merchant, William Corderoy.[82] Selden's use of the facilities provided by the Levant Company to procure Arabic manuscripts is also illustrated by a letter to him dated 26 November 1632

[78] The letter is printed from a Lambeth Palace MS by Todd, *Life of Walton*, i. 40–2. Selden's expression 'sidereis nuntiis' (p. 41) is an oblique reference to Galileo's astronomical discoveries.

[79] However, Selden also bought such printed books as were available. The handwritten list of his library made after his death, not long before it came to the Bodleian (MS Selden supra 111), reveals that he owned almost all books printed in Arabic to that date, including the publications of the Medicean Press and other 16th-century imprints, some of them already rare.

[80] I noted above the possibility that the manuscript of the *Qāmūs* which Selden lent to Golius might have already been available to Bedwell. Golius had been using this for some time before 26 Jan. 1648, according to the letter from William Boswell to Selden, MS Selden supra 108, fo. 35ʳ.

[81] Pococke, *Eutychius*, preface, fo. ¶¶2ᵛ. There are Arabic letters from Thaljah to Pococke in MS Poc. 432, fos. 14–16 (cf. Twells, 59).

[82] Corderoy appears during the years from 1628 to 1640 in the Court Minute-Book of the Aleppo merchants (PRO, SP 110,54, Levant Company's Records: Minutes, 1616–48). He was treasurer for several years, but was rebuked and dismissed from his post by the Company's Court in London for failing to send in his accounts (PRO, SP 105,148, p. 55). He was also of service to Pococke in obtaining manuscripts: Twells, 57–8.

from John Wandesford, consul at Aleppo from 1630 to 1638.[83] One particularly interesting passage not only illustrates the search after manuscripts but throws a sidelight on the young Edward Pococke:

you commended a diligent and able gent: Mr Pococke to me who hath inabled himselfe verye much in Arabb though these parts have forgott there learninge. I have not other comforte but in ?his for Converse and indeed his nature is sweete and amirable. I owe much too you for the Commande you laide upon me to receive him I should have been desirous too make use of his paynes to inquire you out some books to present you withall but indeed he himselfe made Arabb his mistresse & is soe amorous that he is not willinge to part with any booke yet I gained one which I shall intreate you to accept from me[84] I suppose Mr Goole hath it I doe but in this lett you see I carrye a deutifull obsarvation of you & begin the way wheerein I would be sarviceable to you but least I should not make a good choice for you I pray you direct me for wee often have opportunityes heere for books which are not sould in shopps but from the liberaries of ?particular upon death or necessity[85]

The Arabic manuscripts assembled by Selden (now in the Bodleian Library) are very heterogeneous, including both Muslim and Christian religious texts, and secular works on historical and scientific subjects. The latter include some extremely rare and interesting items, for instance the Arabic translation of Apollonius' *Cutting off of a Ratio*,[86] and the unique copy of al-Hāshimī's *'Ilal al-Zījāt* ('Reasons behind the· Astronomical Tables').[87] However, the credit for recognizing the value of these and bringing them to England must go to John Greaves, from whose brother, Thomas, Selden acquired them after John's death in 1652.[88] We have seen that Selden likewise bought some of Bedwell's Arabic manuscripts after he died.

[83] Wandesford was the brother of the better-known Christopher Wandesford, who was associated with Selden in the attack on Buckingham in the Parliament of 1626. Selden must have long known John Wandesford, at least since the Parliament of 1624 in which they both sat, and probably earlier in the Inns of Court.

[84] This is probably MS Arch. Seld. A 38 (Uri no. 667, p. 152), a biographical work by Tāj al-Dīn al-Subkī, which is annotated by Selden: 'Ex Oriente dono accepi ab humanissimo mihique amicissimo V. Johanne Wandesford, Mercatorum in Alepia Anglicorum Consule, 1 Maij 1633.'

[85] MS Selden supra 108, fo. 25ʳ.

[86] MS Arch. Seld. A 7 (Uri no. 877, p. 190). The Greek original is lost, and the Arabic survives only in this and a manuscript in Istanbul. On translations of the treatise see Toomer, *Apollonius*, p. xii n. 4.

[87] MS Arch. Seld. A 11 (Uri no. 879, pp. 190–1). See the edition by Kennedy and Pingree, which, however, has no discussion whatever about the history of the manuscript.

[88] On the manuscripts collected by John Greaves see below, pp. 176ff.

Selden's services to the promotion of Arabic studies went beyond his own scholarship, his collection of books, and his patronage of others (especially Pococke). He was also responsible for the introduction of Arabic type into England. The circumstances surrounding this are far from clear; but on present evidence the first book published in England containing Arabic words printed with movable types is Selden's *Mare Clausum* (London, printed by William Stansby, 1635). The type used is an imitation of Erpenius' Arabic fount, but no examples of it are known in Holland or elsewhere outside England, so it seems certain that (unlike Bedwell's types previously and the Oxford Arabic in 1636–7) it was not imported from Holland. Therefore it must have been cut and cast in England; although there is no evidence as to the typefounder, the most probable candidate is Arthur Nicholls, since it was his son and successor, Nicholas Nicholls, who performed similar services later for Oxford. Although there is, again, no evidence, it seems probable that the considerable expense of cutting punches, producing matrices, and casting types for a complete Arabic fount was undertaken, not by the printer or publisher, but by Selden, who by 1635 was a wealthy man. It is conceivable that for the publication of this work, undertaken in part to support the claim of the Crown of England to sovereignty over the English Channel and other parts of the high seas, Selden received a subvention via Laud or one of the King's ministers, which he then employed for his own scholarly ends. But like much else in this affair, that is pure conjecture. The type, however, was put to good use: it was also employed in Selden's later books, *De successionibus in bona defuncti* (1636), *De jure naturali & gentium* (1640), and *Eutychius* (1642).[89] After that, apart from a few words in John Greaves's *Pyramidographia* (1646), it vanishes from view[90] until 1683, when it appears in John Spencer's *De Legibus Hebraeorum*, and thereafter sporadically in Cambridge publications of the late seventeenth and early eighteenth centuries.[91]

[89] For details see Roper ('Arabic Printing', 13–14). The appearance of Arabic type in Selden's books as early as 1635 had already been pointed out by Carter and Ricks in their edition of Rowe Mores's *Dissertation upon English Typographical Founders*, 9 n. 6.

[90] So that for instance the frequent Arabic quotations in *De Synedriis Liber Tertius* (see above) are printed with the types which the printer, Jacob Flesher, had pirated from the Oxford matrices with the connivance of John Greaves.

[91] See below, p. 271.

(IV) BAINBRIDGE

John Bainbridge[92] illustrates another aspect of the interest in Arabic in the seventeenth century. A physician by training, but with astronomy as his primary interest, he was appointed as the first Savilian Professor of Astronomy at Oxford in 1619. Like his patron Sir Henry Savile, he was firmly convinced of the value of ancient astronomy, as embodied in Ptolemy's *Almagest*, of which he promised an edition and translation. However, he knew from the results of Brahe and Kepler that Ptolemy's work needed correction and revision in many respects. For that purpose he proposed a programme of observations (for instance simultaneous observations of lunar eclipses at places far removed from each other, to establish longitudes). He also wanted to redetermine, by new and accurate methods, the latitudes of such places as Rhodes and Alexandria, where important astronomical observations had been made in antiquity by Hipparchus and Ptolemy. He was anxious too to obtain further observational material transmitted from earlier times; thus he was hopeful of getting the work of Hipparchus 'On the Length of the Year', which he believed to be in the Vatican and Escorial libraries.[93] Most of these efforts came to nothing, although John Greaves's activities in the East from 1637 to 1639 are certainly connected with them. However, in the 1620s Bainbridge came to realize that valuable material might be recovered from medieval Arabic astronomical works, and he undertook to learn Arabic in order to extract what he could from such works. His letter to Ussher of 3 October 1626 is particularly revealing:

Being at London, I procured an Arabick Book of Astronomy, the Tables whereof I do perfectly understand, but the Canons annexed are more difficult, and yet do so much the more incite me to find out that particular meaning, which is not possible without knowledg in the Arabick; wherefore I have made

---

[92] Bainbridge's life was written by Thomas Smith. Like most of Smith's biographical writings, this is a slovenly piece, and tells us no more about Bainbridge's work on Arabic than that he came to it when he was more than 40 years old (i.e. after 1622), and that it was inspired by his interest in Greek astronomy (Smith, *Vitae*, Bainbridge, 10–11).

[93] See his letter to Ussher of 7 Apr. 1628 (Ussher, *Letters*, no. 125, p. 390). Bainbridge was mistaken: that work of Hipparchus is lost except for quotations in the *Almagest*. An earlier fruitless effort by Bainbridge to get information from the Escorial Library is attested by a letter to him from William Goddard, then in Madrid with Prince Charles in his equally fruitless pursuit of the hand of the Spanish Infanta (MS TCD 382, fo. 84, 5 Sept. 1623).

entrance into the Rudiments thereof, and hope (labore & Constantia) at length to be able to translate any Arabic Book of Mathematicks. It is a difficult thing which I undertake, but the great hopes I have in that happy Arabia to find most precious Stones, for the adorning and enriching of my Σύνταξις μαθηματικὴ, do overcome all difficulties besides the great satisfaction to see with mine own eyes (videre est octava scientia) and not be led hoodwinked by others, who though they may be expert in that tongue, yet without special skill in these particular sciences, cannot truly translate the Arabic; besides that every one hath a special purpose in his study of that language, taking no delight to follow another's course; stultum est ducere invitos canes ad venandum. I relate this to your Grace in assurance of your Favour herein, if you please in your enquiry at Aleppo, and other Eastern Places for Syriack Books, to take in all Arabick Books of the Mathematicks and Chronology, and amongst the rest a good Arabick Copy of the Alkoran, the only Book whereby that Language is attained. If your Grace have one already, I humbly request the use thereof for some time, for ours are bound Prisoners in the Library, wherin are many Arabic Books, but authore nescio quo, de re nescio qua. I hope to bring them in lucem meliorem, and with them many others, if I may have the gracious rays of your favorable assistance[94]

We shall return to the matter of the Arabic books in the Bodleian Library at that time. Here I note that the 'Arabick Book of Astronomy' was Bedwell's manuscript of ibn al-Bannā's *Minhāj*, as is clear from Bainbridge's letter to Selden of 27 August 1627:

The Arabicke tables (which you desire to see) I returned a Monthe since to my good frende Mr Bedwell, they are for the most part collected out of the Toletan tables of Arzachel, and reduced to the meridian of Marocco by Albinna, about the year 1234: although hee profess to followe one Isaack of Morocco. The Geographicall Table is very erroneous in the Longitudes, the Chronographicall is all according to Arzachell, and refuteth the conceits of Scaliger. They are a precious Treasure bothe for matter, and Language. I have ernestly entreated Mr Bedwell to translate the Canons affixed; desiring you to enforce my request.[95]

These remarks about the content of the tables demonstrate Bainbridge's acuteness: they are indeed derived from al-Zarqāllu via ibn Ishāq.[96] His close study of Bedwell's manuscript is also evident from the excerpts he made from it, now in MS TCD 383, especially fo. 45ᵛ, where his careful transcription of the title and introduction imitates the North African hand of the original.[97]

[94] Ussher, *Letters*, no. 110, p. 370.
[95] MS Selden supra 108, fo. 236ʳ.
[96] See Toomer, 'The Solar Theory of az-Zarqāl', 330–1.
[97] The manuscript is one of those that was bought by Laud after Bedwell's death, and is now MS Laud Or. 278 (Uri no. 873, p. 188; see also Nicoll–Pusey, p. 283 n. d).

Before he himself embarked on the study of Arabic Bainbridge had endeavoured to obtain the kind of information he needed from an expert, namely Erpenius. In 1622, at the instigation of Georgius Rataller Doublet, a young Dutchman who had been studying at Oxford, Bainbridge gave him letters to take back to Leiden, addressed to Erpenius and Snellius.[98] In the letter to Snellius he explains that he hopes that Erpenius will be able to provide him with ancient observations of lunar eclipses and solar or stellar meridian altitudes made at Alexandria, from Arabic sources ('nam de Graecis despero'). Erpenius did not reply, and two years later Bainbridge wrote again, encouraging him to complete the editions of Abū 'l-Fidā''s *Geography* and al-Makīn's *History* which he had promised. He also asked Erpenius to send him the geographical coordinates of Alexandria, Babylon, and London from Abū 'l-Fidā'. [99] Bainbridge probably never received a reply to this letter either, since Erpenius died not long afterwards. But that did not discourage him from applying to Erpenius' successor Golius. In a letter of 17/27 December 1632, Bainbridge informed him that his enthusiasm had been aroused by two lists of oriental manuscripts that had come into his hands. The first was a catalogue of those manuscripts formerly owned by Ignatius Ni'matallah, Patriarch of Antioch.[100] The second was the printed list of the manuscripts brought back to Leiden by Golius (Paris, 1630). From this Bainbridge singled out the references to works by 'Nasir Eddyn', 'Ali Escherif', and 'Aben Ionis Aegyptii',[101] requesting specific information about astronomical parameters in them. Ironically, Bainbridge does not appear to have noticed the item 'Coeli descriptio, Claudio Ptolomaeo autore, nunquam nobis visa, ex Graeco Arabica facta':[102] this was the Arabic translation

[98] MS TCD 382, fos. 87, 82. John Greaves's transcription of the latter is in MS Savile 47, fos. 34 and 36.

[99] MS TCD 382, fo. 87 (transcript in MS Savile 47 fo. 35). Bainbridge's information that these were available in the *Geography* came from Bedwell, who may have seen Erpenius' copy of Abū 'l-Fidā' on his visit to Leiden in 1612.

[100] By then in the Laurentian Library at Florence. Copies of such a list, compiled by Marco Dobelo about 1610, were in the Vatican and in the hands of the brothers Dupuy in Paris: see Levi della Vida, *Documenti*, 43 n. (2), and *Ricerche*, 287 (cf. 217). It is likely that Bainbridge's list came from the same source, since a letter from Dobelo in Arabic, sent to Casaubon in London, was copied by Bedwell and is now in the Bodleian (ibid. 282; cf. Nicoll–Pusey no. 24, pp. 486–7, MS Bodl. Or. 298).

[101] These are: the famous astronomer Naṣīr al-Dīn al-Ṭūsī (cf. Golius, *Catalogus*, p. 4, [q 7] 'Tabulae Astronomicae Nassir Eddyn Persae'); 'Alī b. Muḥ. al-Jurjānī (ibid., p. 5, [q 42] 'Tabulae expeditae Motuum caelestium, autore Ali Esscherif'); and ibn Yūnus (ibid., p. 8, [o 1] 'Methodice Chronologica, & Astronomica Aben Ionis Ægyptii, in qua etiam variae Orientalium Observationes coelestes').

[102] Ibid., p. 11, [o 44].

of Ptolemy's *Planetary Hypotheses*. Bainbridge himself had published in 1620 the *editio princeps* of the Greek text, but in that version the whole of Book 2 and the extremely important end of Book 1 is lost. Golius had brought back with him one of the two surviving manuscripts of the Arabic version, but neither he nor anyone else investigated it until the late nineteenth century, and it was not fully published until 1967.[103] Had Bainbridge been able to gain access to it, the startling information about ancient astronomical theory that it contains might have been revealed three centuries earlier. However, Golius would not in any case have permitted him to look at it. We know that he never responded to Bainbridge's modest request for information.[104]

Bainbridge himself achieved very little by his pursuit of Arabic, but the aspects of its study which he emphasized were taken up, with much greater success, by his pupil, friend, and colleague at Merton, John Greaves (who also succeeded him as Savilian Professor of Astronomy). We cannot doubt that Bainbridge's influence was formative on Greaves, and we may guess that it also had an effect on his colleague, as Fellow of Merton and (later) Savilian Professor of Geometry, Peter Turner.

(V) JOHN VICCARS

Among those who made a mark on Arabic studies in the earlier part of the century was John Viccars. We know little about his life, except for one episode.[105] Educated at both Cambridge (matriculated Christ's College in 1618, BA 1621/2) and Oxford (commoner at Lincoln College 1624, MA 1625),[106] he became Vicar of St Mary's, Stamford in Lincolnshire. He was denounced by some of his parishioners in 1628 for what appear to have been Puritan tendencies, and in 1631 was condemned by the Court of High Commission 'for holdinge and publishing sundry hereticall schismaticall and pernitious and erroneous opinions and tenetts'[107] to be excommunicated, defrocked, and fined

---

[103] Goldstein, *Planetary Hypotheses*.

[104] This is explicitly attested by Christianus Ravius (whose information must have come ultimately from John Greaves) in a letter to Isaac Vossius of 1641 (MS d'Orville 470, p. 278: 'Sed quod Cl. Golius ad tot ejus literas non responderet, indignè tulit sperni suam diligentiam persuasus').

[105] I give the evidence for this in detail below, since the whole episode, which ruined seven years of his life, is omitted in the worthless article on Viccars in *DNB*.

[106] Wood, *Athenae Oxonienses*, ii. 657.

[107] PRO, SP 16,261, fo. 1r. The details of the charges and sentence are in SP 16,203 no. 30 (fos. 39–42).

£100. His judges included Sir Nathaniel Brent and William Laud (then Bishop of London). These punishments were eventually all revoked or remitted,[108] but Viccars was forbidden to exercise his priestly function in Stamford, and he himself says that he had spent seven years in prison.[109] Instead of seeking another living, he went abroad (probably early in 1636) on an extended scholarly tour of France and Italy.

The results of his researches were published after his return to England in 1638. This was his *Decapla in Psalmos* (London, 1639), a folio of more than 400 pages, commenting on all 150 Psalms, for which Viccars compared ten different versions: Hebrew, Arabic, Syriac, Chaldee, rabbinical Hebrew, Greek, Latin, Italian, Spanish, and French. For the oriental versions especially he had examined manuscripts in many different libraries. As he explains at length in his preface, besides the manuscripts available at Oxford and Cambridge, he saw some in Paris, but above all in Italy. In Rome he gained entry to the Vatican Library and the College of Maronites, and in Florence to the Laurentian Library and the libraries attached to San Marco and Santa Maria Novella. He also saw manuscripts in Bologna, Livorno, and Venice (in the latter two places perhaps only in the private possession of Jews). Of the Arabic versions he says specifically: 'Arabicos MS. consului multos in Collegio Maronitarum Romæ & Parisiis, 300. aut 400. An. vetustate gaudentes. Sunt duae editiones, una apud Nebiensem, Romana altera,[110] cum versione Latina dicti Sionitae. Haec Arabica versio citatur proprio & novo Caractere.' This brings us to the most remarkable feature of the book. As Viccars proudly boasts, even on the title-page, he had had new Syriac and Arabic types made for this publication, at great expense to himself and his recently deceased brother Samuel. Specimens of the types are conveniently included.[111] The Arabic fount is yet another imitation of the Erpenius types,[112] and

---

[108] Absolved from excommunication 3 Mar. 1634 (SP 16,261, fo. 5ᵛ); fine remitted because of his 'povertie & long imprisonment', 1 July 1634 (ibid. fo. 71ʳ); restored to his ministerial function, 19 Nov. 1635 (ibid. fo. 295ᵛ).

[109] Viccars, *Decapla*, preface. The seven years are presumably between 1628 and 1634 inclusive: summaries of his tribulations from 1628 to 1635 may be found in the printed Calendars of State Papers for those years.

[110] He is referring to Giustiniani's and Savary de Brèves's editions.

[111] Partially reproduced, *PO* no. 368.

[112] Roper ('Arabic Printing', 15) supposes that Viccars's book used the Oxford Arabic types (whereas a cursory comparison of Viccars's type specimen with those in Morison's *John Fell* shows notable differences), and claims that Viccars mentions the 'Arabic types which had been provided by Laud's endeavour'. In fact Viccars, in praising Laud, speaks only of his founding the Arabic lectureship and donating oriental manuscripts: 'linguas Orientales promoventi, gravibúsque impensis Bibliothecam

was used thereafter, as far as I can determine, only for a few words in Greaves's *Roman Foot* and John Gregory's *Posthuma*;[113] for the 'second edition' of Viccars's work in 1655 is merely a reissue of the sheets of the first edition, with none of its faults corrected, but with the title-page altered to contain the name of the new publisher. Since the only Arabic texts contained in the book are brief excerpts from the different versions of the Psalms, they tell us little about Viccars's knowledge of the language. Certainly the use of the Arabic types does not reflect well on the printer or on the author (if he had any supervision at all over the printing). There are frequent misprints and use of the wrong letter forms (final letter instead of medial, et cetera).

The preface to the 1639 edition contains a grovelling dedication to Laud, calling the book 'τεκμήριον gratitudinis & devotissimae observantiae erga Clementiam Tuam, quae post septennii vincula captivo, primam liberationis scintillulam accendit, accensamque gradatim perfecit'. This evidently had the desired effect, for in May 1640 Viccars again obtained a living, becoming Vicar of South Fambridge in Essex. Unluckily for him the fall of Laud and the collapse of Laudianism quickly ensued. He was charged before the Essex County Committee in 1644 with, among other things, being a Roman priest (since he had been at Rome), and was sequestered.[114] In 1652 he was among those named in the original proposals for the Polyglot Bible as editors and overseers,[115] but it is unclear what part he played, and it seems unlikely that he had anything to do with the Arabic in that work. When the *Decapla in Psalmos* was reissued in 1655 the dedication to Laud was omitted. It would in any case have been prudent to avoid praise of the late archbishop in a work published during the Protectorate, but probably Viccars was glad enough to discard the flattery of his former tormentor which the times had demanded. After that we hear no more of him, and it is probable that he died before the Restoration.[116]

Oxoniensem MSS. Arab. Syr. aliisque libris celeberrimam, locupletanti', and specifically says that he and Samuel had paid for the new types.

[113] London, 1647 and 1649–50: see below, pp. 171, 102.

[114] Matthews, *Walker Revised*, 166.

[115] Todd, *Life of Walton*, i. 49.

[116] The statement by Venn and Venn, *Alumni Cantabrigienses*, iv. 301 (an article which is in other respects faulty and incomplete), that he died in 1660, is a misrepresentation of the statement of Peile, *Register of Christ's College*, i. 324, that he must have been dead by 1660, when South Fambridge was assigned to another incumbent.

(VI) USSHER

James Ussher,[117] a product of the Protestant Ascendancy in Ireland, was one of the most learned men of his time. He was educated at Trinity College, Dublin, of which he later became Fellow and Professor of Divinity, and was appointed Bishop of Meath in 1621 and Archbishop of Armagh in 1625. He held this office, with (from 1634) the title of 'Primate of all Ireland', until his death in 1656, but after the Irish rebellion of 1641 he lived in various places of refuge in England,[118] and even after Cromwell restored order in Ireland Ussher never returned, since the abolition of episcopacy by the Parliament had deprived him of his ecclesiastical functions and estates. Even before 1640 he spent much time in England pursuing his scholarly interests. He is an important figure in Arabic studies, but not as an Arabist. There is no doubt that he knew the language quite well, for his scholarly correspondents[119] freely intersperse their letters to him with Arabic words, and he was prepared to read Arabic grammatical texts in the Earl of Arundel's library in manuscript form.[120] A somewhat dubious source[121] alleges that Ussher claimed that Selden learned 'the elements of the Eastern tongues from him', although he soon surpassed his instructor. However, Arabic was of minor importance to Ussher in his own work, which was primarily concerned with British and Irish antiquities, ancient (especially biblical) chronology, and the text of the Bible. And even here he relied at times on the help of others. For instance John Greaves supplied him with data about the length of the year in various Arabic and Persian astronomical works,[122] information

---

[117] Several biographies of Ussher have been published: I mention only Thomas Smith's in his *Vitae*, Nicholas Bernard's (1656), Richard Parr's (published with Ussher, *Letters*), and Elrington's in vol. 1 of his edition of Ussher's *Works*. None of these deal adequately with Ussher's oriental studies. The last three biographies are well characterized in Trevor-Roper's essay, 'James Ussher, Archbishop of Armagh', in his *Catholics, Anglicans and Puritans*.

[118] During the Civil War he was with the King at Oxford until 1645.

[119] These include many Arabists who occur elsewhere in this book, including Selden, Bainbridge, John Greaves, Wheelock, and Ravius. The earliest Arabic quotation in a letter to him is by William Eyres of 1608 (Ussher, *Letters*, no. 3, p. 3, cf. below, p. 85).

[120] Letter from Bourgchier of 12 May 1625 (Ussher, *Works*, xvi. 428–9; the original is MS Rawl. letters 89, fo. 50ʳ).

[121] An anonymous contemporary account of Selden's death published by Macray, *Annals of the Bodleian Library*, 110 n. 2. If this is to be believed, Ussher's instruction of Selden took place about 45 years earlier, i.e. about 1610 to 1614.

[122] Letter of 19 Sept. 1644 (Ussher, *Letters*, no. 211, p. 509). See also 'An Account of the Latitude of Constantinople and Rhodes' which he sent to Ussher (Greaves, *Works*,

which Ussher used in his *De Macedonum et Asianorum anno solari Dissertatio*, 1648.[123] But more pertinent to the topic of this book are Ussher's activities as a collector of manuscripts, and as a patron and promoter of scholarship.

From 1624 to 1628 Thomas Davis, an English merchant[124] at Aleppo, acted as agent for Ussher in obtaining manuscripts from Syria and Mesopotamia. The search for these is recounted in the letters of Davis to Ussher, which are full of interest for the conditions under which such quests were conducted at the time. I quote two extracts, the first from a letter of 16 January 1626:[125]

I perceive that my Letter of the 29th of September, 1624. together with the five Books of Moses in the Samaritan character came in safety to your hands, being very glad it proves so acceptable to your Lordship; however find my self to have been abused by a Jew, who pretends to have knowledg in that Tongue, affirming to me that it contained all the Old Testament. How they read those books I have enquired (having no better means) of him, who I perceive knows no more (if so much) than their Alphabet, and to hear him read the first two Verses of Genesis I could not, because another of those books is not here to be had. The name of God, *Jehovah*, is pronounced by them, as saith he, Yehueh. And the fift, eight and sixteen of these Letters of their Alphabet are pronounced hei, chei, ei; the ch of the eight Letter must be pronounced deep in the throat, chei.

I sent to Damascus to see if I could procure the Grammer, Chronicles and Calendar which your Lordship desires, but could not obtain any of them, there being but one poor Man of the Samaritan race left in Damascus, who is not able to satisfy me in any thing you desire; only he said there were certain Books in their Language pawned to a great Spahee of that city, but what they contained the poor Fellow knew not. The Spahee would not part with them under 200 Dollers, which is 60l. Sterling: so I durst not venture upon them, being ignorant of their worth; yet I will not cease labouring as occasion shall

ii. 364–71). Excerpts from the original in MS Add. A 380 were published by Mercier, 'English Orientalists and Mathematical Astronomy', 170–2, in apparent ignorance of the three previous printings.

[123] Ussher, *Works*, vii. 408.

[124] This should be emphasized, since although Ussher's first biographer, Nicholas Bernard, correctly describes him as a 'Factor' (*Life of Usher*, 86), more than one modern work (e.g. Trevor-Roper, *Catholics, Anglicans and Puritans*, 138) refers to him as a chaplain. In fact the Levant Company chaplain at Aleppo for most of the time covered by these letters was Charles Robson (on whom see below, p. 117). Thomas Davis appears in the Minute Book of the Aleppo merchants (PRO, SP 110,54) between 27 Nov. 1623 and 18 Oct. 1630. Todd, *Life of Walton*, i. 186, says that he was afterwards 'Sir Thomas', but I suspect that this is by confusion with the later Lord Mayor of London, a different man.

[125] Ussher, *Works*, xv. 323–6 = *Letters*, no. 81, pp. 323–4.

sèrve to give satisfaction to your Grace in what you require touching the Samaritans, and I hope to prevail in some things, unless the troubles in and about Jerusalem do hinder the free passage of caravans this ensuing Spring.

A former Letter, which it seems your Lordship writ and sent away by Marcelles, I never received: but as for the Old Testament in the Chaldean tongue, my diligence hath not wanted to procure, and to this end sent divers times to Tripoly and Mount Libanus; but could not prevail. I have seen here the first two Books of Moses; but, examining them according to your Direction, I found them to be out of the Greek; whereupon I resolved to sent to Emmit and Carommit a city in Mesopotamia, where divers of the Sect of the Jacobites do remain; and after a long time there was sent me (which I received eight days past) the five Books of Moses only, in an old Manuscript, and according to the Hebrews, with a promise ere long to send the rest of the Old Testament: the Party that sent me this is the Patriarch of the Jacobites in those Parts who writ also that I should have Eusebius his Chronicle, with some of the Works of Ephræm; which if he do, shall be sent by the first good conveyance. Those parcels of the New Testament, viz. the History of the Adulterous Woman, the second Epistle of St. Peter, the second and third of John, the Epistle of Jude, with the Book of the Revelation, I have procured, and sent them together with the five Books of *Moses*, and a small tract of Ephræm, by the ship *Patience* of *London*. . . . I have sought the Old Testament in that Tongue, which is out of the Greek, and distinguished by certain Marks and Stars;[126] but I cannot hear of any such. From *Emmit* I hope to have some good News to write your Lordship, and to send you a catalogue of such books as be here to be had. When this Book which I now send shall be received, I beseech your Grace to give your Secretary order to advise me thereof: in the mean time, if any of the Books you desire shall be brought or sent unto me, I will not let them go for a small matter more or less; such Books are very rare, and esteemed as Jewels by the owners, tho they know not how to use them, neither will they part with them but at dear rates, especially to Strangers who they presume would not seek after them, except they were of good worth: and indeed they give a kind of superstitious Reverence to all Antiquity.

The second was sent on 13 March 1627:[127]

Most Reverend Sir≈ Maie it please your Grace to take notice that my last unto you was of the 20th 8ber, per the shipp Rainbowe, when isent you such Bookes in the Siriacke tounge as then could procure, the which I hope are in saftie come to your hands and to content. I doe not cease to procure those

[126] Fourteen years later, in his letter to Ravius, Ussher was still asking for this ('obelis et asteriscis distinctum', i.e. containing the diacritical marks introduced by Origen into his *Hexapla*).

[127] Ussher, *Works*, xvi. 444–6, but my version is transcribed from the original in MS Rawlinson letters 89, fo. 111. For other letters of Davis see Ussher, *Letters*, no. 69, p. 311; no. 83, p. 326; no. 111, p. 371; no. 120, p. 225; and *Works*, xv. 225 and xvi. 472.

other Bookes your Lordship writt for; The old Testament in the Siryacke is not as yett finished, in 40 daies I hope to haue it in my possession, with the Bookes in the Samaritan Language that were granted to the Spahee in Damascus, A Venetian that liues there promiseth to procure them for me, and att easie rates, The Psalter in the Syriacke accordinge to the Greeke I cannot finde as yett, this cittie and hereabouts beinge very bare of ancient Bookes, the reason I conceive to bee, is that the Christians bee much keept under, But in the parts of Mesopotamia where Christians have more liberty there bee found diuers ancient Bookes, But the truth is I canot deuise anie meanes to obtaine them, the place beinge very remote, and not a Franke passeth that way, diuers letteres I have caused to bee written to the Patriarks and Bishopps that liue there, but haue noe Answer of them, soe doubt that manie of them miscarry, yett I will not giue ouer to solicite them in this maner; Neyther am I unmind-full of the new Testament in the Ethiopian tongue, I hope in tyme to procure it; I am hartily glad when can light upon anie of the Bookes maie doe seruice to the Church of Christ and your Lordship. The reward I expect and desire is the Benifit of your faithfull prayers, and in truth I haue much neede thereof ≈ I perceiue by your Lordships letter of the 31st July from Oxford, that you had the Bookes sent per the shipp Patience; By the shipp Barbary Constance of London that may departe Scanderoon in 4. or 5. daies ihaue sent you some fewe loose sheetes of paper and Copies of some of Ephraems workes, and another Booke that I ventured to buy, and as am informed is noe other then a Grammar in the Syriacke, it cost not much, and it maie proue usefull, I will not bee too bould in this kinde for the time to come, for this if haue done amisse I craue pardon, the Cost of theise Bookes and them sent per the Rainbowe will aduise your Lordship off when shall send the bookes I expect from Damascus and Mount Libanus≈ . . . pardon the rudenes of my stile and in what offend impute to my ignorance, and take me for no other then aplain merchant.

These and other letters reveal that among the manuscripts which Davis obtained for the Archbishop were the Samaritan Pentateuch (i.e. in the Samaritan script, although the language used was Hebrew), the Syriac New Testament, the Syriac Old Testament (translated from the Hebrew), and works of Ephraim in Syriac. Ussher himself kept other scholars informed about his acquisitions. Thus in his letter to Selden of 30 November 1627,[128] accompanying Ussher's transcription of a passage from the Samaritan Pentateuch for Selden's *Marmora Arundelliana*, he says that besides the Pentateuch in Syriac and Arabic (the latter translated from the Greek of the Septuagint), 'I have had also an other booke latelye sent unto me from the East, intituled Otzar Raza (or rather *Razaja*) a threasure of secrets: contayning a briefe

---

[128] Ussher, *Works*, xv. 380–7=*Letters*, no. 122, pp. 383–6. The original letter is preserved in MS Selden supra 108, fos. 174–5.

Commentarye in the Syriack language upon the whole Old Testament.'
An even longer list can be found in a letter to Louis de Dieu at Leiden,
dated 9 June 1632.[129] In addition to the works mentioned above,
Ussher says that he has, in Syriac, the complete Old Testament (which
Golius had seen when it was being purchased in Syria), besides
treatises of Ephraim. In Arabic he had part of the Pentateuch translated
from the Samaritan, the Psalter, Genesis translated from the Greek,
commentaries on biblical history, sermons of John Chrysostom, and
canons from the ancient Church Councils.[130]

Ussher was extremely generous, even by the standards of his time,
in making the manuscripts he owned available to other scholars. From
the letter just mentioned we learn that he had sent one of his copies of
the Samaritan Pentateuch, and the Syriac Pentateuch, to Leiden to
be used, and perhaps published, by de Dieu and L'Empereur (the
successor to Erpenius as Professor of Hebrew). He sent all of his
Samaritan material to Selden for aid in writing his notes to *Marmora
Arundelliana*,[131] and in the preface to the Polyglot Bible Walton makes
particular mention of the many manuscripts and books which Ussher
had lent the editors.[132] He would even give texts of which he had more
than one copy to others. Besides the Arabic Psalter which he donated
to Laud for the Bodleian, he gave the oldest and best of his five or six
copies of the Samaritan Pentateuch to Sir Robert Cotton, in gratitude
for Cotton's allowing him the use of his library.[133] He was concerned
in other ways to enrich the libraries of England and Ireland. His
correspondence bears witness to his efforts to obtain Erpenius' printed

[129] Ussher, *Works*, xv. 550–4 = *Letters*, no. 174, pp. 462–3.

[130] 'Arabici Psalterii tria habui exemplaria, satis antiqua: quorum unum D. Londinensi
Episcopo, Academiae Oxoniensis dignissimo Cancellario, cum aliquam multis aliis
MSS. nuper a me donatum est. alterum quod D. Gulielmo Bedwell commodaveram,
eo jam vita functo, vix est ut recuperari a me posse sperem: Bibliotheca mea
tertium adhuc conservat. Habeo & Genesim Arabice ex Graeco versam, et amplo
commentario explicatam: Arabicas quoque Homilias in Sacrae Historiae partem, a
Josepho incipientes. Eadem lingua Chrysostomi Conciones Quadragesimales habeo,
quae in nostris desiderantur libris, et Graecis et Latinis. Arabicum quoque Nomo-
canonem possideo; in quo veterum synodarum canones ad certos titulos reducti conti-
nentur.'

[131] Cf. also Selden, *De Synedriis Liber Primus* (*Opera*, i/2, 805), on a Christian
Arabic manuscript 'quem mecum, ut assolet alia, . . . communicavit praestantissimus vir,
Jacobus Usserius'.

[132] Quoted by Todd, *Life of Walton*, i. 182 n. i.

[133] The manuscript is now in the Cotton collection in the British Library, Claudius
B.VIII. Cf. Ellis, *Original Letters of Literary Men*, 138–9 for the dedication to Cotton
written in the manuscript by Ussher, according to which he had bought it for the equivalent of £75, an enormous sum at that date.

Hebrew books and oriental types for Cambridge.[134] Alerted by the bookseller Henry Fetherston that he had bought and was bringing to England the magnificent collection of Greek manuscripts assembled at Venice by Giacomo Barocci,[135] he urged an unnamed nobleman to persuade the King to get them, and also the manuscripts of Erpenius currently in the hands of the widow of the Duke of Buckingham, for the Royal Library.[136] This attempt too failed, for a few months later the Earl of Pembroke, at the instigation of Laud,[137] bought the Barocci manuscripts for Oxford, and Erpenius' manuscripts were eventually donated to Cambridge.

Ussher appears in the dual role of collector of manuscripts and patron of oriental studies in his dealings with Christianus Ravius. He had no agent in the East for several years after Davis ceased this function. Bainbridge did indeed suggest to Ussher that he recommend Samson Johnson, who was skilled in oriental languages, as chaplain at Aleppo, promising 'his best Endeavours to do your Grace all respective Service',[138] but for some reason that came to nothing, and the man who did go out as chaplain, Edward Pococke, was buying manuscripts only for himself and (later) Laud. In 1639 Ussher received a letter from Ravius, a young German who wished to travel to the East. Since Ravius will reappear in these pages more than once, I give a brief outline of his career up to that time.[139] Born in Berlin in 1613, he studied theology and oriental languages at various German universities, but principally at Wittenberg, where he became MA in 1636. After a period in Scandinavia he went (probably late in 1637) to Holland, where he ingratiated himself with G. J. Vossius at Amsterdam, and studied Arabic under Golius at Leiden while staying in the house of Elichmann. In the summer of 1638 he embarked on a journey

---

[134] Letter to Cotton of 12 July 1625 (Ellis, *Letters of Literary Men*, 133–4 = Ussher, *Works*, xv. 283–4); letter to Samuel Ward of 16 June 1626 (Ussher, *Letters*, no. 98, p. 342). Ussher did not succeed, since Erpenius' books were auctioned in Holland and his types bought by the Elzevirs: see Oates, 167 n. 33.

[135] Ussher, *Works*, xvi. 466–7 (30 Apr. 1628).

[136] Ussher, *Letters*, no. 133, p. 400 (22 Jan. 1629). Could the nobleman have been the Earl of Arundel?

[137] Who did not fail to remind Ussher of this in his letter of 5 July 1630 in response to Ussher's congratulations on Laud's election as Chancellor of Oxford (Ussher, *Works*, xvi. 525–8).

[138] Ussher, *Letters*, no. 144, p. 411 (20 July 1629).

[139] By far the best account of Ravius' life is still that in Moller, *Cimbria Literata*, ii. 680–8, although much could be added, for instance from Annerstedt's *Upsala Universitets Historia* for the years he spent in Sweden. I hope to deal elsewhere at greater length with the career of this repulsive but fascinating man.

to the East, but went first to England. He wrote to Ussher (then in Ireland) from London, enclosing recommendations from de Dieu, Elichmann, and Vossius, outlining his travel plans, and asking for Ussher's support not only for his journey, but also for his candidature for the Professorship of Hebrew at Trinity College, Dublin. Ussher replied on 15 January 1639,[140] explaining that there was no such post, but promising financial support for Ravius' eastern journey. He later guaranteed him £24 annually for as long as he was in the East, remitting the money via Samuel Hartlib in London.[141] On 12 November 1639 (by which time Ravius was in Constantinople), Ussher sent him a list of the books he wanted him to obtain:

Vetus Testamentum Syriacum, non ex Hebraeo factum (illud quod jam habeo) sed ex Graeco versum, atque obelis et asteriscis distinctum. Polycarpi & Ignatii Epistolae Syriace conversae. Eusebii (non Historia Ecclesiastica quae passim prostat) Chronicum Graecum, vel etiam Syriace versum. Si quid etiam versionum Symmachi, Aquilae & Theodotionis reperiri possit. Julii Africani Chronicon, Hegesippi Historia Ecclesiastica, Clementis Alexandrini Hypotyposeôn libri, & de Paschate libellus Anatolii. Aniani & Panodori computi Paschales. Georgii Syncelli Graecum Chronicon. Apollodori Graecum Chronicon. Phlegon de Olympiadibus. Diodori Siculi, Polybii, Dionysii Halicarnassei, Dionis Cocceiani libri illi, qui apud nos desiderantur. Hipparchi Astronomica, Graece.[142]

Most of these works had long since vanished completely, but Ussher's list is an interesting testimony to the hopes of finding lost treasures of antiquity which were still entertained in the seventeenth century. Ravius had little chance of finding any of these desiderata, and we do not know whether he procured anything for Ussher in return for his support during the two years that he stayed in the East.[143] He continued, however, to refer to him gratefully as his patron for many years afterwards.[144]

John Evelyn visited Ussher at Lady Peterborough's house in Reigate on 21 August 1655, and reports the conversation that he had with the aged man in the last year of his life.[145] Ussher expressed disillusion

---

[140] I know this letter only from Ravius' publication on p. 2 of his *Specimen Lexici Arabico-Persici-Latini*.

[141] See the letter from Ussher to Hartlib, 12 Nov. 1639: *Letters*, no. 304, p. 623.

[142] Ibid. no. 305, pp. 623–4.

[143] On the numerous manuscripts that Ravius acquired for himself see below, pp. 145, 152.

[144] e.g. his letter to Ussher written on his way to Sweden, 3/13 May 1650 (Ussher, *Letters*, no. 252, p. 550): 'Patrono suo aetatem Colendo'.

[145] Evelyn, *Diary*, iii. 156–7.

with the study of Arabic: 'he told me how greate the losse of time was to study much the Eastern languages, that excepting *Hebrew*, there was little fruite to be gatherd of exceeding labour; that besides some *Mathematical* bookes, the *Arabic* itselfe had little considerable.' As can be deduced from the oriental manuscripts that he acquired, Ussher had always viewed Arabic, Syriac, and the other oriental languages from the narrow perspective of their utility for biblical and patristic studies and especially the text of the Bible. Despite the efforts of many, including Ussher himself, towards editing the oriental versions for the London Polyglot (which was emerging from the press at the very time of this interview), Ussher was right in his opinion that these were of little importance for establishing the original text. But in thinking that there was no point in studying Arabic except for this and perhaps for mathematics, he shows that he had neither understanding nor sympathy for the new approach to Arabic literature, history, and philosophy of a Golius or a Pococke. This was not entirely a reflection of his belonging to an older generation.

(VII) THE ESTABLISHMENT OF ARABIC STUDIES AT CAMBRIDGE

In the sixteenth century the most productive place in England of Arabic scholarship had been Cambridge: thence came Andrewes, Lancelot Browne, and Bedwell. The situation there early in the seventeenth century is illuminated by a letter to Ussher from William Eyres of Emmanuel College, who was trying to learn Arabic as a help to his biblical studies.[146] He is grateful to Ussher for sending him Postel's grammar, and to Ussher's younger brother Ambrose (like Ussher, then at Trinity College, Dublin) for copying out some passages of the Koran for him.[147] The only Arabic text he appears to have is the Psalms in Giustiniani's Polyglot Psalter. Previously he had a teacher of Arabic, an unnamed Jew[148] whose presence had led him to hope

[146] Ussher, *Letters*, no. 3, pp. 3–11 (24 Mar. 1608).

[147] Ambrose Ussher never published anything on Arabic, but an Arabic dictionary and grammar are among various collectanea compiled by him which are preserved in manuscript at Trinity College, Dublin. The very work to which Eyres refers here may be that described among the Trinity manuscripts in *Catalogi Manuscriptorum Angliæ et Hiberniæ*, ii/2, as '541. 401 Liber quidam Arabicus exscriptus & translatus per Ambrosium Usserium: Surata Cavernae Alcorani'.

[148] This can hardly have been Philippus Ferdinandus, who left Cambridge for Leiden in 1598.

that the study of the language might have some place at Cambridge ('specula aliqua affulserat, qualemcumque hujus linguae scientiam in Academia nostra hac ratione, locum aliquem habere potuisse'). Having lost him, Eyres despairs of making progress in the language, for lack of a teacher such as Christmann, Bedwell, or Ambrose Ussher. Clearly would-be Arabists at Cambridge were destitute both of books and of teachers. Nevertheless, we do know that in the 1620s some managed to learn Arabic there. Brian Walton and Edmund Castell, who will be discussed in connection with the Polyglot Bible, are examples. Another is John Lightfoot (BA, Christ's College, 1620/1), who in his *Miscellanies Christian and Judaical* of 1629 handsomely acknowledges his debt to Bedwell: 'Of the largenesse of the Arabic alphabet . . . or indeed any thing of the tongue I cannot say, which I have not received of . . . Master William Bedwell.'[149] Furthermore there was Robert Sheringham (BA, Caius College, 1622/3), who was ejected from his fellowship at the college in 1643, and a little later, according to Wood,[150] went 'into Holland, where he taught the Hebrew and Arabic tongues to young men at Rotterdam, and in other places', returning to Cambridge only after the Restoration. I know nothing more of his prowess in Arabic, but his skill in Hebrew is evidenced by his translation, with commentary, of the Mishnaic tractate 'Yoma', published in London (1648). However, the man most responsible for Cambridge becoming the first place in England to have a Professor of Arabic, and a significant collection of Arabic manuscripts, was the first Arabic Professor himself, Abraham Wheelock.[151]

Coming from humble origins in Shropshire, Wheelock took his BA and MA degrees from Trinity College, but from 1619 onwards was a Fellow of Clare Hall. He became vicar of St Sepulchre's church in Cambridge in 1622, and was appointed University Librarian in 1629. How he became interested in or learned Arabic is not known, but by 1624 he was already well versed in the language, for in that year John

---

[149] p. 127, quoted by Todd, *Life of Walton*, i. 107.

[150] Fasti, i. 145 (in Bliss's edition of the *Athenae*, vol. ii).

[151] There is some useful information on Wheelock in the funeral sermon by Sclater, *Crown of Righteousnes*; but the other contemporary 'life', by Wheelock's pupil Thomas Hyde, in Barksdale, *Memorials of Worthy Persons*, iv. 133–5, is worthless. Oates, in his history of Cambridge University Library, especially chs. 7 and 8, gives a detailed and sympathetic account of Wheelock, to which the reader is referred for his Anglo-Saxon studies and activities as University Librarian. His name is spelled in various ways, including 'Wheloc', 'Whelock' (so invariably by Oates), and even 'Whillock' (by Thomas Adams). But in all English letters of his that I have seen he signs himself 'Wheelock'.

Foorthe (or Ford), a minister at Wheelock's native Whitchurch, wrote congratulating him on his progress in oriental languages, mentioning particularly the use of Arabic in elucidating the Book of Job.[152] It is probable that Wheelock spent some time studying with Bedwell, for in March 1632 Mrs Bedwell assured Thomas Adams that Wheelock (whom Adams was contemplating as the Professor of Arabic) was 'as able as any in the kingdom'.[153]

From the surviving correspondence of Thomas Adams[154] it is clear that the initiative for setting up the Arabic Professorship at Cambridge came from Wheelock himself. He approached Adams, probably in late 1631, not only because Adams was a wealthy and influential merchant in the City of London, but also because they were both Shropshire men.[155] Wheelock's initial proposal is not preserved, but it seems probable that he stressed to Adams, a man of great piety, the value of Arabic for the propagation and defence of Christianity.[156] Wheelock had suggested that the City of London or one of the merchant companies might provide the necessary funds; Adams told him that this was impractical, but that individuals might be found who would do so. Soon he himself promised to provide a stipend of £40 for three years, but only after being assured that the proposal was supported not only by the university (as represented by the Vice-Chancellor and the heads of colleges), but also by Richard Holdsworth. This man, currently Professor of Divinity at Gresham College and Rector of St Peter-le-Poer in London, had been a Fellow of St John's College, Cambridge, and was later to become Master of Emmanuel College and Vice-Chancellor, and a great benefactor to the University Library.[157] By

---

[152] Cf. Oates, 177. The letter is preserved with other correspondence of Wheelock in MS CUL Dd.3.13.

[153] Holt, 'The Study of Arabic Historians', *Studies in the History of the Near East*, 40. Presumably it was Mrs Bedwell who gave the assurance because Bedwell, who died not long after, was already too feeble to write.

[154] MS CUL Dd.3.12, from which excerpts were published by Holt, *Studies,* 37–42; also partially published by Ellis, *Letters of Literary Men*, from Baker's copies in MS BL Harley 7041.

[155] The importance of this county connection was pointed out by Arberry, *The Cambridge School of Arabic*, 9.

[156] Compare the letter of the Vice-Chancellor and Heads to Adams four years later: 'The worke itselfe wee conceive to tend not onely to the advancement of good Literature, by bringing to light much knowledge which is as yet lockt upp in that learned tongue; but alsoe to the good service of the King and State in our commerce with those Easterne nations, and in Gods good tyme to the enlarging of the borders of the Church, and propagation of Christian Religion to them who now sit in darkenesse' (Arberry, ibid. 7–8; previously published by Todd, *Life of Walton*, i. 236–7, from a copy at Lambeth Palace).   [157] See Oates, 304 ff.

23 March 1632 Wheelock was duly installed as 'Professor Linguae Arabicae', with the duty of lecturing twice a week in term time. The appointment was *ad hominem*, although Adams expressed the hope 'to perpetuate the same publicke lecture by a setled maintenance for ever'.[158] He did not in fact do this until 1666, thirteen years after Wheelock's death, but he did continue to maintain the Arabic lecture by paying the annual stipend for the rest of Wheelock's life.

Wheelock conscientiously read his lecture, usually to a sparse audience,[159] but his scholarly contribution to the advancement of Arabic was small indeed. This is partly to be attributed to the pressures of supporting his numerous family (in 1632, against Adams's advice,[160] he married a widow with one child, and fathered five more offspring). His other occupations included not only his office of Librarian (which he took very seriously), but from 1638 onwards duties connected with a lectureship in Anglo-Saxon which Sir Henry Spelman wished to set up. The lectureship was never formally established, but was, like the Arabic one, an *ad hominem* arrangement.[161] Spelman gave Wheelock a stipend, and later the vicarage of Middleton in Norfolk, in return for studying Anglo-Saxon, and assisting him in his own researches. This patronage was continued by Henry Spelman's son John and grandson Roger; and Wheelock's own contributions to the study of Anglo-Saxon are considerable, especially his edition of the Old English version of Bede's *Historia Ecclesiastica*.[162] Wheelock also spent much time and effort consulting and transcribing manuscripts at Cambridge and arranging the loan of books for other scholars.[163] Even before he became University Librarian, he was busy at Emmanuel College library trying to locate a Talmud for Ussher.[164] He performed similar services for Selden, but it was above all Sir Henry Spelman and Sir Simonds D'Ewes who called on his assistance in their Anglo-Saxon researches. Wheelock was always obliging (not to say obsequious), but not entirely altruistic in answering these demands. Spelman was his patron, and his sufferance of the importuni-

---

[158] Letter of 3 Mar. 1632 (Holt, *Studies*, 38).

[159] In a letter to Thomas Greaves in 1639, Wheelock says: 'I am ashamed to tell you few do Arabicari in this university' (printed by Birch in Greaves, *Works*, i, p. lxix); and writing to Sir Simonds D'Ewes on 4 Nov. 1641 he says that he was flustered by an unusual number of auditors at his 8 a.m. lecture (MS BL Harley 374, fo. 164).

[160] See Oates, 182–3.

[161] For details see Oates, 185–8.

[162] On this see Oates, 204–9.

[163] These activities are abundantly illustrated by Oates, 194 ff.

[164] Ussher, *Letters*, no. 85, p. 329 (12 July 1625).

ties of the insufferable D'Ewes may have been made easier by the hope of reward from him too. When he sent D'Ewes a copy of his edition of Bede he mentioned a benefice which D'Ewes had in gift whose occupant was about to expire, and begged for it in grovelling terms ('mei, viri pauperrimi, et famuli vestri obsequentissimi'), while assuring him that alleviation of his wants would benefit the publication of D'Ewes's Anglo-Saxon lexicon.[165]

Wheelock's one serious attempt to publish something connected with Arabic was a translation and 'refutation' of the Koran. This is mentioned in published letters of Wheelock to Ussher and Ravius,[166] but is described at greatest length in unpublished extracts of communications from Wheelock to Samuel Hartlib preserved in the Hartlib Papers. From all this we can gather that it consisted of parts of the Koran translated into both Latin and Greek, together with a commentary consisting of virulent attacks on Islam and its prophet. The following quotations may give some idea of Wheelock's approach:

I would not set out the Alcoran onlie to tell the Latin Church, who know it to well alreadie, nor yet put it into Greeke to boast of that skil be it what litle soever, in that Language; but by the helpe of our Merchants I would have the Methode of confutinge it, and the discoverie of the plaine falacies thereof, be without noise, if it may bee, be communicated to some well minded Christians at Aleppo &ce and in Persia and other places as the hand and providence of Christ shal direct, who said, ite et prædicate Evangelium cuique nationi. Set aside some grosse idolatries of the church of Roome, & their Tyrannicall government, the onlie pressure on the bodie of the Church of Christ is Mahomets Alcoran, I desire to breath out my Last breth in this cause, and to my poore skil, I would endeavour to write Notes against the Alcoran in the Language of the Alcoran, which is the Arabick.[167]

as you see neither have I given my selfe sattisfaction either for the Language or Method, or for the writers part. But all these by the assistance of the Almighty, may bee easily perfected, if it be once agreed upon by the most approved judgments that the wicked and pernicious Alcoran's hypocrises, soe full of good wordes under divelish endes ought to bee confuted. I have translated a great and considerable portion thereof into the Latin and greeke, & would give a specimen of my poore tallent to Christian universities: that they would assist and helpe the Lord against the mightie. But instead of helping wee should hinder gods cause, if it be not discovered to be full of hipocrisie,

---

[165] MS BL Harley 374, fo. 209 (23 Sept. 1642).

[166] Ussher, *Letters*, no. 248, p. 546, undated, but on internal evidence from about December 1649; Ravius, *Sesqui-Decuria*, 28–32 (12 Nov. 1647 and 11 Feb. 1648).

[167] Hartlib Papers, 33/4/2 (12 Nov. 1647).

falshoode, savage crueltie against the world of mankinde, which it would subdue; & against the sonne of God whom it pretends to advance, to be fulle of blasphemie; yet soe subtillie convaied are all his assertions that where the sword of the Turke is drawen, they seeme to be truely christian. I have given a Taste of his craft, in shewing that he begins his hellish fained scriptures, with these wordes. IN THE NAME OF GOD THE GRATIOUS AND MERCI-FULL Good wordes in themselves; if they had not beene intended to blot out the Trinitie, AND THE NAME OF THE FATHER, OF THE SONNE AND OF THE HOLY GHOST;[168] I have briefly layd downe my apprehension of Mahomets meaning in these.[169]

Wheelock sent his specimen to Hartlib because he hoped that he would use his influence with the Parliament to get the funds for publishing this pious work. He also asked him to show the specimen to competent judges, naming Ravius, Pococke, Greaves, and Boncle.[170] Hartlib seems to have done nothing about it for some time, for in September and October 1648 Wheelock was anxiously enquiring, through Thomas Smith of Christ's College, what had happened to his specimen.[171] This appeal at last stirred Hartlib to action, for by the next month he had returned Wheelock's papers with the message that 'they were not approved'. Wheelock preferred not to know who had rendered this judgement, but he probably suspected, as we may, that it was his professed 'friend' Ravius, then in London as Professor of Oriental Languages,[172] and a crony of his fellow-countryman Hartlib. Ravius would probably have been more sympathetic to the tenor of Wheelock's 'refutation' than either Pococke or Greaves, but he himself had recently published a small part of the Koran,[173] and promised to publish more. It is in keeping with the man's character that he would secretly suppress a rival work while professing devotion towards its author. In any case, this reception of his specimen utterly discouraged Wheelock from continuing the work, despite the fact that, according to Thomas Smith,[174] 'a vote is passed already [by 11 October 1647] for printing the Alcoran at the university charge', which can only refer to

---

[168] Wheelock's odd notion that Muḥammad deliberately substituted the 'Bismillah' for the invocation of the Trinity is repeated in his letter to Ussher mentioned above.

[169] Hartlib Papers, 33/4/3 (undated, but not long after the preceding).

[170] On John Boncle, Fellow of Eton College and a correspondent of Pococke, see Katz, *Philo-Semitism*, 209 with n. 62. Wheelock was probably thinking of John Greaves rather than Thomas.

[171] Hartlib Papers, 15/6/18 and 15/6/20.

[172] On this post see below, p. 190.

[173] Ravius, *Alcoran* (Amsterdam, 1646; Schnurrer no. 371). I have not seen this rare publication.　　　　　　　　　　　　　　　　　　　　　　[174] Hartlib Papers, 15/6/27.

endorsement of Wheelock's proposed book at Cambridge. The work seems to have vanished; it would have been interesting to see Wheelock's efforts to annotate it 'in the Language of the Alcoran'.

Wheelock's disenchantment with teaching Arabic at Cambridge in the late 1640s is reflected in an anecdote retailed by Edmund Calamy.[175] When the young Isaac Barrow and another Trinity student approached Wheelock 'to discourse with him about the Arabick Language, which they were desirous to learn', he discouraged them from proceeding further by telling them 'how great Difficulties they were to encounter, and how few Books there were in that Language, and the little Advantage that could be got by it'. However, Wheelock was among those who signed the first printed proposals for the London Polyglot, and according to Todd was supposed to join Castell in correcting the Syriac and Arabic versions for that publication.[176] But before the work was under way he died on 25 September 1653 in London, where he was engaged in preparing for the press his own edition and translation of the Gospels in Persian. This appeared posthumously in 1657, at the expense of Thomas Adams.[177]

During Wheelock's term as Librarian, Cambridge acquired significant numbers of Arabic books and manuscripts, and although this was not due to his efforts alone, he did much to help.[178] By far the most important acquisition of this kind was that of Erpenius' manuscripts, numbering about eighty-four items, of which some fifty-six are Arabic or Persian.[179] After Erpenius' death in 1624, these were bought by the Duke of Buckingham, who happened to be in the Netherlands on a special embassy, and outmanœuvred both the Curators of Leiden and, allegedly, 'the Jesuits of Antwerp', by paying without hesitation the sum of £500.[180] In 1626 Cambridge elected Buckingham as its Chancellor, and one of the inducements mentioned by his supporters was the likelihood that he would donate Erpenius' manuscripts to the

[175] *An Account of the Ministers who were Ejected*, 340; cf. Feingold, 'Isaac Barrow', 17.

[176] Todd, *Life of Walton*, i. 54, 231. On Wheelock's enthusiastic promotion of the project see ibid. 55–7.

[177] Oates, 209–11, with details of the manuscripts used by Wheelock for his edition.

[178] Oates, ch. 9, deals at length with the acquisition of oriental items during Wheelock's tenure.

[179] For details see Oates, 222–31, and Oates, *The Manuscripts of Thomas Erpenius*.

[180] Oates, 164–6. The manuscripts were, by the standards of the time, grossly overvalued: later in the century Golius' manuscripts, far superior both in number and quality, were offered by his heirs for the equivalent of £400 (and found no takers at that price); Oxford paid only £600 for the 420 choice manuscripts in Pococke's collection.

University.[181] The duke's assassination in August 1628 put an end to the hopes that he would become a benefactor to the University Library in this and other ways. But in 1632, just at the time when the Arabic Professorship was being established, negotiations were opened with Buckingham's widow to persuade her to carry out the duke's intention (or so it was claimed) to donate the manuscripts to Cambridge. The proceedings can be followed in Wheelock's surviving correspondence,[182] from which it is clear that the principal negotiator was Richard Holdsworth, who reported to the anxious Wheelock through Adams. The university, writing to the dowager duchess on its own account, used the argument that now that Cambridge had an Arabic lectureship, it lacked only 'matter & store of Bookes to encourage & cherish this new Studdy amongst us'. Fears were expressed that the books might be diverted to Oxford, and given the interest of Laud (who had great influence with the King) in acquiring Arabic manuscripts for his own university, these were probably justified. However, on 8 June 1632 Holdsworth was able to congratulate Wheelock and the university on the dispatch of the 'Arabick books' to Cambridge, where Erpenius' manuscripts were housed in a specially built bookcase in the library.

Before this, Wheelock had been instrumental in persuading Bedwell to donate a manuscript of the Koran to the university.[183] After Bedwell's death he was in communication with John Clerke (Bedwell's son-in-law), and seems to have had some hopes of obtaining more Arabic books from Bedwell's estate: for Clerke tells him 'I praye you saye nothing to the universitye touching the Avicene, for in lookeing over the Alminakes, where my Father noted all his remarkable things, there was found some mencion of Pococke for that Booke, & therefore my mother will give itt to him, if hee comes home, if not the universitye may have itt.'[184] This book was the Medicean Press imprint of Avicenna's *Canon*, and it seems likely that Bedwell's copy did go to Pococke (then in Aleppo), for the copy in Cambridge Library was purchased in 1635–6; Oates remarks that it is heavily annotated by

---

[181] Oates, 163, notes that Wheelock's name heads the list of those who voted for the duke, although this may merely reflect his usual submissive attitude to authority, since the Master of his college, Dr Paske, was one of Buckingham's strongest backers.

[182] There is a full account in Oates, 217–22.

[183] Oates, 213. Bedwell's letter of 12 Oct. 1630, promising the gift, is printed by Hamilton, *William Bedwell*, 103.

[184] Letter of 31 Aug. 1632, MS BL Harley 7041, fo. 59ᵛ (Baker's transcription of the original in MS CUL Oo.6.113).

Wheelock.[185] In fact the rest of Bedwell's books and manuscripts were dispersed after his death, with the exception of his dictionary, which in accordance with the terms of his will went to Cambridge, together with the types with which to print it. We have already seen that this was an impractical request. Certainly Wheelock is not to blame for the university's failure to fulfil it; we shall see below how he and others attempted to improve the resources for printing Arabic at Cambridge.[186]

Wheelock's indexes and annotations in two Cambridge manuscripts of the Koran which had belonged to Erpenius[187] attest to his diligence in utilizing the new resources in Arabic that he had helped to obtain for Cambridge. But his view of the utility of Arabic (essentially religious and polemical) became outdated; he seems to have taken no notice of the new directions being taken at Leiden and Oxford. Two other Arabic manuscripts of Erpenius at Cambridge were studied during Wheelock's tenure: a copy of Eutychius' ecclesiastical history, and Erpenius' transcript of Postel's manuscript of the *Geography* of Abū 'l-Fidā'. It is significant that these secular treatises were examined not by Wheelock (nor, as far as I know, by any of his pupils), but by three Oxford men, John Gregory, Pococke, and John Greaves, and by Selden. However, Wheelock's limitations as an Arabist do not detract from his initiative and devotion in promoting the study of the language and improving the facilities for it at Cambridge.

(VIII) ARABIC AT OXFORD BEFORE POCOCKE

In 1600 Oxford was even more poorly equipped than Cambridge for the study of Arabic. Not only was no instruction in that language available, but the university library consisted of a room in which there were no books in any language. However, in that year Sir Thomas Bodley was already busy refurbishing the building and collecting books and donations for the library which was to bear his name, and which was formally opened two years later. Much of the intellectual history of seventeenth-century Oxford is connected with the growth and use of the Bodleian Library, and by the end of the century it was to contain one of the foremost collections of oriental manuscripts in Europe. In

---

[185] p. 254 n. 14.
[186] Ch. 7, where I also deal with later accessions of Arabic manuscripts and with Wheelock's pupils.   [187] See Oates, 224–5.

its early years, however, obtaining Arabic books was certainly not among the principal objectives either of the founder or of the first librarian, Thomas James (although the interest of both men in Hebrew is reflected in the early holdings of the library). However, Arabic was not entirely neglected. When the library opened in 1602 the single Arabic manuscript it possessed was a copy of the Koran.[188] But the first printed catalogue of the library, published in 1605, reveals that its shelves already contained Giustiniani's polyglot Psalter and the Medicean Press editions of Avicenna and Euclid. For help with Arabic vocabulary and grammar it offered, besides Pedro de Alcalá's *Vocabulista*, Postel's *Linguarum duodecim alphabetum* and Raimondi's *Alphabetum Arabicum*.[189] Moreover, several more Arabic manuscripts were donated to the library in its early years, including three more copies of the Koran.[190] Bodley himself was alert to the possibilities of obtaining such material from the East. As early as 7 June 1603 he wrote to James: 'Because I haue bin disappointed of my hopes of bookes from out of Turkie, I doe intend er be long, to send a scholler of sette purpose, who is very well studied both in the Hebr. and Arabick tongues, whose errand shall be onely, to seek out bookes for the Libr.'[191] We hear nothing further of this scheme, but in 1608 Bodley, perhaps encouraged by the recent donation of two Greek manuscripts by Sir Henry Lello, who had just returned from Constantinople where he had been ambassador,[192] wrote to Paul Pindar, consul of the Levant Company at Aleppo. This request for oriental material was rewarded by the donation of no less than twenty oriental manuscripts (eight of them Arabic) in 1611, when Pindar was about to become ambassador at Constantinople. Bodley announced the gift in a letter to the Vice-Chancellor.[193]

We have little other information about interest in Arabic at Oxford before 1610, but since a pamphlet published there in 1597, Richard Brett's *Theses*, was actually intended to contain Arabic (although lack

---

[188] MS Bodl. Or. 322, given by John Wrothe in 1601: see Macray, *Annals,* 421, and Wakefield, 'Arabic Manuscripts in the Bodleian Library', 128. This, and the miniature Koran donated by Sir Henry Wotton in 1604, are listed in James, *Catalogus,* 11.

[189] James, *Catalogus,* 112, 181, 316, 588, 365, and 282.

[190] For details see Wakefield, 'Arabic Manuscripts in the Bodleian Library', 129.

[191] Bodley, *Letters to James,* no. 83, p. 88.

[192] Macray, *Annals,* 36.

[193] Bodley, *Letters to Oxford,* 21, quoted by Wakefield, 'Arabic Manuscripts', 129; Macray, *Annals,* 42. For details of the Arabic manuscripts donated by Pindar see Wakefield, ibid.

of the proper types meant that this had to be filled in by hand),[194] we may be sure that some Oxonians could read the language. This is confirmed by the reception given to the first teacher of Arabic in seventeenth-century Oxford, Josephus Abudacnus. This man,[195] Yūsuf Abū Dhaqn ('father, i.e. possessor, of a beard'), known in Europe as Josephus Abudacnus or Barbatus, was a Copt, i.e. a Monophysite Christian from Egypt. He was born in Memphis, probably in the 1570s, and was sent by his patriarch to Pope Clement VIII in Rome in 1595. There he converted to Catholicism (an event which he seems to have prudently suppressed during his stay in England), and learned Italian, some Latin, and possibly Hebrew and Syriac. Arabic was his native language, but, as Erpenius found and as his extant Arabic letters from the years 1608 to 1611 testify, he knew only the vulgar dialect of Egypt, at least at that time.[196] By 1608 he was in Paris, where he worked as an interpreter for Arnoult de Lisle, the Professor of Arabic at the Collège Royal, and was befriended by Étienne Hubert and Isaac Casaubon, amongst others. We have already seen how Erpenius took Arabic lessons from him in 1609.

In 1610, armed with recommendations from Erpenius and perhaps others,[197] he came to England, where he was welcomed by Bedwell

---

[194] Madan, *Oxford Books*, i. 230. On Brett (1560–1637), who was a Fellow of Lincoln College and 'appointed one of the translators of the Bible into English by King James I in 1604', see Wood, *Athenae Oxonienses*, ii. 611–12, where he is described as 'skill'd and versed . . . in the Latin, Greek, Hebrew, Chaldaic, Arabic and Ethiopic tongues'. This is probably based entirely on his *Theses*, a single sheet containing three theses in Latin, each followed by paraphrases in one or two other languages, Greek, Chaldee, Syriac, Arabic, and Ethiopic (the last three written in, no doubt by Brett himself). The Latin and Greek are metrical, the rest not. The four lines in Arabic, in an unpracticed hand, show only that Brett had mastered the elements of the language. I have not seen the Arabic poem which Brett wrote on the Gunpowder Plot in MS Selden supra 84 (*SC* no. 3472).

[195] The whole history of Abudacnus is discussed at length by Hamilton, 'An Egyptian Traveller', to which the reader is referred for information and source material on his career in Italy, France, the Spanish Netherlands, Bavaria, Austria, and Constantinople, and his published and unpublished writings.

[196] Erpenius to Bedwell in Houtsma, *Oostersche Correspondentie*, 6–7. Abudacnus' letter to Erpenius of 8 July 1611 is published ibid. 13–14. His letter to Bedwell of 28 Aug. 1610 is printed by Hamilton, *William Bedwell*, 99–100 (to be corrected from ibid. pl. 5, e.g. for والله العوض read ولله العون). His letter to Scaliger of 25 Sept. 1608 is partially printed in Hamilton, 'An Egyptian Traveller', 127 n. 14 (omitting the Arabic summary). Later, at Louvain, Barbatus composed an Arabic grammar (unprinted, but surviving in two copies at Vienna). In this both the Latin and the classical Arabic show a great advance on his letters, but he may have had help with the Latin, and the grammar is mainly plagiarized from Erpenius.

[197] Abudacnus mentions the recommendations from Erpenius to his sister Maria and to Bedwell in his letter to Erpenius from London (Houtsma, *Oostersche*

and introduced by him to Lancelot Andrewes. Soon Abudacnus was moving in exalted circles. Not only was he entertained by Andrewes and introduced to Miles Smith, the future Bishop of Gloucester,[198] but the Archbishop of Canterbury, Richard Bancroft, in his capacity as Chancellor of Oxford, gave him a letter to the Vice-Chancellor, John King, recommending him as Arabic lecturer at Oxford. We know this from a letter which Bodley gave him to take to James, reinforcing Bancroft's recommendation with his own: 'I would be glad to vnderstand, that he might be provided of a competent intertainment, to keep him in Oxon, lest Cambridge should endeuour, as I make account they would, to drawe him vnto them.'[199] The letters had their effect, and Abudacnus was soon ensconced in St Mary's Hall, and lecturing on Arabic with financial support from the university. He stayed at Oxford for three years, with occasional visits to London and to Bedwell, but nothing is known about whom or what he taught.[200] The only record of his activity there is his contribution to the volume of verses published at Oxford in 1612 to commemorate the death of Henry Prince of Wales, *Eidyllia in Obitum Fulgentissimi Henrici Walliae Principis*.[201] This consists of four couplets (all saying much the same thing), in Aramaic, Syriac, Arabic, and Turkish. The Aramaic is printed in Hebrew characters, but the other three, for lack of proper types, are given in transcription, which makes them rather enigmatic.

Abudacnus did, however, make an indirect contribution to Arabic studies while he was in England. It appears that Bedwell showed him a manuscript of some New Testament Epistles in Arabic which he was engaged in editing, and that Abudacnus copied out the Epistle to Titus from this. Later (probably in 1611), back in Oxford, he gave his transcript to Matthew Slade, Rector of the Latin School at Amsterdam,

---

Correspondentie, 13–14). It is probable that he received the recommendation from Casaubon mentioned there after he arrived in England, for Casaubon himself left Paris in 1610, and Abudacnus reports in his letter to Bedwell of 28 Aug. 1610 that he had seen Casaubon in London (Hamilton, *William Bedwell*, 100).

[198] Who evidently knew some Arabic, since in the above-mentioned letter to Bedwell Abudacnus promises to send Smith a letter in that language.

[199] Bodley, *Letters to James*, no. 188, pp. 193–4, 14 Aug. 1610. It should be remarked that this letter is the sole source of Wood's account of Abudacnus in his 'Fasti', i. 301–2 (in *Athenae Oxonienses*, ed. Bliss, vol. ii). Since Bodley's letter is dated only by month and day, Wood made the bad guess of 1603 for the year, which has led to confusion about Abudacnus' English visit ever since.

[200] Feingold, 'Oxford Oriental School', conjectures that his students may have included Richard Kilbye and Arthur Lake, both of whom owned Arabic printed books, the latter a good collection for his time (1617) (ibid., n. 87).

[201] Madan, *Oxford Books*, i. 80.

and himself something of an Arabist,[202] who was on a visit to England. Slade in turn communicated it to Jan Theunisz., who published it at Leiden in 1612, much to the chagrin of Bedwell, who had intended to publish it himself.[203]

Abudacnus styled himself, now and later, 'Professor Arabicae linguae Oxoniae', but he never held any formal post, and no doubt realized that his prospects were tenuous there, particularly after the death of the patrons to whom he owed the position, Bancroft in November 1610, and Bodley early in 1613. Seizing the opportunity afforded by a meeting in London with Ferdinand de Boisschot, ambassador of Archduke Albert of the Spanish Netherlands, he left England for ever in the autumn of 1613. Resuming the Roman Catholic confession, he was welcomed at Antwerp. His later eventful career does not concern us here. I note only that he taught oriental languages at Louvain (where he published a Hebrew primer plagiarized from that of Elias Hutter), and was patronized by such luminaries as Herwarth von Hohenburg, Kepler, and Tengnagel in his passage through Altdorf, Munich, Augsburg, Linz, and Vienna until he finally came to Constantinople, where he served as an impoverished dragoman in the service of the Imperial resident from 1623 to 1643. It is piquant to observe that Abudacnus, who proclaimed himself 'Professor of Arabic at Oxford', must certainly have met Edward Pococke, then actually Professor of Arabic at Oxford, during Pococke's stay in Constantinople from 1637 to 1640. Although I have found no mention of Abudacnus at Constantinople in English records, we shall see[204] that his book on the Coptic Christians, which was published in Oxford long after his death, was probably obtained from Abudacnus himself in Turkey.

After Abudacnus left, there was no instruction in Arabic at Oxford for thirteen years, but some there managed to learn the language, for

---

[202] On the Arabic grammars which Slade donated to the Amsterdam city library in 1612, and which are annotated by Theunisz., see Jones, 'Learning Arabic', 180. There are many letters from Slade to Sibrand Lubbert in the MSS BL Add. 22961 and 22962, but neither these nor the letters published in Nijenhuis, *Matthew Slade*, shed any light on his attainments in Arabic. His elder brother Samuel Slade was taught Hebrew by Leone da Modena, according to a letter he wrote to Tengnagel from Venice, 1 Aug. 1608: A. Z. Schwarz, 'Aus der Briefsammlung Sebastian Tengnagels', *Zeitschrift für hebräische Bibliographie*, 20 (1917), 73.

[203] For a full discussion of this incident, many details of which are unclear (for instance, whether Abudacnus had Bedwell's permission to copy the text, and precisely what version was copied), see Hamilton, 'An Egyptian Traveller', 130 with n. 26.

[204] Below, p. 280.

instance William Pinke of Magdalen College, who is said to have been chosen by Lord George Digby as one of his 'Readers' at Magdalen, especially because of his 'skill in languages, Hebrew, Greek, Arabick'.[205] University lectures in Arabic were resumed in 1626, by Matthias Pasor. He has left a brief but remarkable account of his own life up to his fifty-fifth year, which was printed together with a funeral oration on him at Groningen in 1659.[206] The son of Georg Pasor (also a scholar of some note) he was born at Herborn in 1599. He became Professor of Mathematics at Heidelberg, where he took part in the defence of the city in the Thirty Years War, and describes its sack by Tilly's forces in 1622. Exiled from Germany by the war, he came to Leiden in 1624, where he studied Arabic for a month with an amanuensis of Erpenius, but then went on to England. He arrived at Oxford in May 1624, and was incorporated MA, but finding employment with Peter von Spreckelfen, who was tutor to two noble youths from Hamburg, he accompanied them to Paris in October of that year. However, von Spreckelfen died, so Pasor took the opportunity while in Paris to study Arabic and Syriac for a time with Gabriel Sionita; he also met Grotius and Claude Hardy. Returning to England in 1625, he eventually made his way again to Oxford, where he gave instruction in Arabic to John Prideaux (Rector of Exeter College) and Thomas Clayton (the Regius Professor of Medicine).[207] In the summer of 1626 Ussher met Pasor in the Bodleian Library and urged him to accompany him back to Ireland, telling Juxon (President of St John's and Vice-Chancellor) that if Oxford could not employ Pasor, Ussher would. Pasor had already supplicated the Vice-Chancellor and Heads for permission to give public lectures in Arabic,[208] and when this was granted, he delivered his inaugural lecture on 25 October 1626. This was later published,[209] and provides some useful information about his attainments in Arabic and the facilities for studying it at Oxford.

According to his autobiography, Pasor in fact taught Arabic only in

[205] William Lyford's dedicatory epistle to Pinke's *Triall of a Christian's Sincere Love unto Christ*. Wood's remarks about Pinke's linguistic skills (*Athenae Oxonienses*, ii. 475) are derived from this.

[206] Pasor, *Vita*, 19–59.

[207] Laud acquired an Arabic medical manuscript from Clayton in 1636: see below, p. 110.

[208] The emolument for these was not provided by the university, but, as Twells says (p. 5) by 'a pension collected from his auditors'. However, Wood (*History and Antiquities*, ii/2, 903) notes that Merton College contributed and supposes that other colleges did so too.

[209] Pasor, *Inaugural Lecture* (Madan, *Oxford Books*, ii. 109).

the year 1626/7. In 1627/8, responding to the demand for 'a more useful study of the authentic text' (i.e. the Bible), he turned to Chaldee,
and in 1628/9, having in the mean time been appointed Hebrew
praelector at New College, taught Syriac. In the year when he did
teach Arabic, the content of his lectures was 'Arabic grammar' (or 'an
Arabic Grammar', in either interpretation probably an explication of
Erpenius' handbook), together with the Arabic proverbs edited by
Erpenius (after Scaliger).[210] Pasor's Arabic lectures at Oxford must
have been a case of the one-eyed leading the blind, since his own education in the language consisted of some unspecified 'levia principia'
at Heidelberg, a month with a pupil of Erpenius at Leiden, and a few
months (at most) with the notoriously lazy Sionita in Paris. Pasor's
autobiography shows that he was ready to turn his hand to teaching in
any field where the opportunity was offered: mathematics, geography,
theology, philosophy, Hebrew, Syriac, and Arabic. From his published
inaugural lecture one derives no high estimate of his Arabic learning.
The single Arabic text of which he actually demonstrates knowledge is
the collection of proverbs that he was about to use as a reading-book.
Most of the lecture is a series of commonplaces about the utility of
Arabic studies that can be found in many such hortatory addresses
before and after this.[211] After invoking the decree of the Council of
Vienne concerning the teaching of Arabic at Oxford, Pasor notes that
Arabic is the 'daughter' of Hebrew. To sustain his theses that Arabic
is useful, and that it deserves especially to be taught at Oxford, he
stresses the elegance of its orthography, the copiousness of its vocabulary, the wide geographical distribution of those who speak it, and its
usefulness for theology and sacred literature.[212] Knowledge of Arabic
is particularly important, he says, for conversing with the peoples of
Asia and for confuting their errors (for which he cites the authority of
Peter the Venerable). The works of the Arabs in medicine, philosophy,
physics, mathematics, history, poetry, geography, and astronomy are
praised. Pasor then refers to Leo Africanus for the importance of the

[210] Probably the second edition published by Erpenius' press in 1623 (*PO* no. 67),
rather than the original edition printed by the Raphelengius press in 1614.

[211] Pasor's principal source was undoubtedly Erpenius' inaugural and second lectures,
printed in his *Orationes* (Leiden, 1621; see the English translation of the second by
Jones, 'Thomas Erpenius on the Value of the Arabic Language'). Many of the same
themes can be found (to confine ourselves to English sources) in the prefaces of Bedwell
(Hamilton, *William Bedwell*, Appendix II), and in the inaugural lectures of Thomas
Greaves (Oxford, 1637) and Edmund Castell (Cambridge, 1666).

[212] In this respect he notes that both Casaubon and Ussher had cited the Arabic text of
the Bible in their arguments against Baronius.

Arabs' libraries and academies, before summarizing the history of Arabic studies in Europe, with mentions of Frederick II, the Council of Vienne (again), Ramon Lull, Pope Gregory XIII and the Medicean Press, Pope Paul V and the foundation of colleges at Rome, Postel, Clenardus, Christmann, Scaliger, Raphelengius, Erpenius, and his own teacher Gabriel Sionita. He ends this list with a tribute to Bedwell, for whose dictionary he wishes a successful conclusion. Boldly proclaiming that his lectures will fulfil the decree of the Council of Vienne, he says that, unlike Clenardus, his auditors will have no need to go to Asia to find a teacher; we shall see that at least one of those present came to the opposite conclusion.

Perhaps the most revealing part of Pasor's lecture is his enumeration of the 'riches' of the Bodleian Library in Arabic. Besides grammars and lexicons, he says, you have the Pentateuch, Psalms, and New Testament from Leiden and Rome; Avicenna's *Canon*, the 'Geographia Nubiensis', and Euclid's *Elements* from the Medicean Press; and in manuscript the Pentateuch in Syriac letters,[213] four Korans, the works of Saint Ephraim, and 'Nazri de insomniis'.[214] Comparison of the list of printed books with that culled above from the earliest Bodleian catalogue reveals that very few such books had come to the Bodleian in the twenty years since, and that the library did not even possess all of Erpenius' publications; unless indeed Pasor missed noting these, as he missed some other interesting Arabic manuscripts which were there in his time.[215] But even when we make allowance for the lecturer's superficial acquaintance with the library holdings, his list is a telling indictment of the poverty of the materials available at Oxford in 1626 for the study of Arabic, and the idleness of his claim that with their aid he was able to fulfil the requirements set out in the decree of Vienne.

After invoking the memory of Robert Wakefield, Pasor ended his oration with an appeal for the establishment of a permanent chair in Arabic. This evidently met with no response, for in 1629 he accepted an offer to become Professor of Philosophy at the University of Groningen, where he remained until his death in 1658. Ravius, writing

---

[213] I have not identified this Karshūnī manuscript, which was used by John Gregory also.

[214] This book on dreams by Abū Saʿīd Naṣr al-Dīnawārī (MS Bodl. Or. 323) and the homilies of Ephraim (MS Bodl. Or. 571) were among the manuscripts donated by Paul Pindar in 1611.

[215] For these see Wakefield, 'Arabic Manuscripts', 129, who estimates that the total of Arabic manuscripts in the library in Pasor's time was nineteen.

to Ussher from Amsterdam in 1647, says that since moving to Groningen Pasor had done nothing at all in oriental studies.[216] His chief claim to fame in that field was that while at Oxford he had been the first to instruct Edward Pococke in Arabic, as he himself proudly records in his autobiography. Pococke himself acknowledged his debt to Pasor handsomely in after life, but we may suspect that he owed more to Pasor's enthusiasm than to his learning; for he soon applied for further instruction to a better master, Bedwell.

Pasor's lectures were well attended, according to Henry Briggs, who in 1627 wrote to Samuel Ward that 'his Arabicke lecture . . . findethe diverse constante hearers'.[217] However, the only man whom we can certainly name among the auditors of Pasor's Arabic lectures, besides Pococke, is Thomas Crosfield of Queen's College, who mentions in his diary that Pasor gave elementary instruction in Arabic grammar.[218] There were two contemporaries of Pococke at Oxford who contributed to Arabic studies, John Greaves and John Gregory. But Greaves seems to have become interested in oriental studies only later, and Gregory was probably too junior to have attended Pasor's lectures (and also too poor to pay the fees). Furthermore he was said to be essentially self-taught,[219] and indeed his published works display the contorted erudition characteristic of the autodidact. Anthony Wood[220] extols him as 'the miracle of his age for critical and curious learning' and mentions his 'exact skill in Hebrew, Syriac, Chaldee, Arabic, Ethiopic etc.', and certainly his wide reading in biblical and rabbinical Hebrew is attested in the two books described below.[221] Gurgany says that Gregory engaged in learned correspondence 'with divers famous Men abroad, aswel Jesuites and Jews, as others', and he himself mentions a letter he received from Menasseh ben Israel.[222] Gregory was also

[216] Ussher, *Letters*, no. 213 p. 511: 'nihil omnino praestat in Orientalibus, & eorum amorem penitus rejecit.'

[217] MS Tanner 72, fo. 211, quoted by Feingold, 'Patrons and Professors', 121.

[218] Feingold, 'Oxford Oriental School', cf. Crosfield, *Diary*, 12. For the suggestion that Richard Busby, who introduced Arabic into Westminster School while Headmaster, may have attended Pasor's lectures see below, p. 266.

[219] According to pp. 3–4 of Gurgany's 'Short Account of the Autor's Life and Death' in Gregory, *Posthuma*, he learned 'the Saxon, French, Italian, Spanish, and all Eastern Languages, through which hee miraculously travelled, without anie Guid, except Mr *Dod* the Decalogist, whose Societie, and Directions for the Hebrew Tongue, hee enjoied one vacation near *Banburie*'. David Lloyd's account of Gregory (*Memoires*, 86–90) is derived almost entirely from Gurgany's, and adds very little.

[220] *Athenae Oxonienses*, iii. 205–7.

[221] On this aspect of his learning see Feingold, 'Oxford Oriental School'.

[222] Gregory, *Notes and Observations*, 23.

known to Laud. When Laud as Chancellor was trying to get a 'learned press' established at Oxford, Gregory was one of the witnesses of an agreement between the university and the printer William Turner for the publication of the *Chronicle* of John of Antioch (Malalas), which Gregory was evidently going to edit, since the printer undertook to supply 'as much Arabicke letter as shall be needefull for the notes of that booke'.[223] However, nothing came of this.

Born in 1607 of humble parents, Gregory came to Christ Church as a servitor in 1624. After graduating MA in 1631, he took orders, and was patronized by Brian Duppa, Dean of Christ Church and later Bishop of Chichester and Salisbury. In March 1642 we find Brian Twyne recruiting Gregory to interpret some passages in the Bodleian manuscript of the Church Councils in Arabic for Selden.[224] But during the Civil War he lost his patron and his stipend as chaplain at Christ Church, and retired to the obscurity of an alehouse at Kidlington, where he died in 1647. Two books of his containing numerous quotations in Arabic with translations show that he had read in that language as widely as was possible with the resources available at Oxford during his lifetime. His *Notes and Observations upon Some Passages of Scripture* was published at Oxford (1646; reprinted London, 1650 and several times later). In this the Arabic quotations are printed with Hebrew types. After his death, by the efforts of his friends, a number of other short tracts which he wrote, mostly on scriptural topics but also dealing with geography, chronology, and astronomy, were published as *Gregorii Posthuma* (London, 1649, also reprinted several times). In this most of the Arabic quotations are printed with Viccars's Arabic types,[225] but the printer has mangled them almost beyond recognition.[226] Given the subjects that Gregory was treating, it is not surprising that the principal Arabic sources he refers to are the Christian scriptures and commentaries thereon. But he was also well

[223] The agreement is printed in Johnson and Gibson, *Print and Privilege at Oxford*, 13.

[224] MS Selden supra 109, fo. 278c. On this famous manuscript of the Councils see p. 106. Selden presumably wanted to consult it in connection with his *Eutychius* (published later that year), in which he printed a long extract from the manuscript on the participants in the Nicene Council (pp. 90–114).

[225] Viccars's Syriac types also appear, in the margins of pp. 195 and 201.

[226] The printer, William Dugard, was an educated man, who was currently Headmaster of Merchant Taylors' School (Rostenberg, 'William Dugard', 133–9), where he presumably taught Hebrew to the young Edward Bernard. However, it is obvious that he understood not a word of Arabic, but merely matched Gregory's handwritten copy with letters that he imagined were similar. He bought the types with other equipment from James Young, the son and heir of Robert Young, who had printed Viccars's book.

acquainted with the Koran and some of its Arabic commentators,[227] and made good use of the Laudian and other Arabic manuscripts in the Bodleian. For instance he refers to the manuscript of ibn al-Bannā''s *Minhāj*, although he calls it, obscurely, the 'Tables of Alkas', because he misread العباس (part of the author's name, Abū 'l-'Abbās, on the title-page) as القاس.[228] He also sought out manuscripts in other collections: from Cambridge the annals of Eutychius and Abū 'l-Fidā''s *Geography*;[229] from Balliol College the *Kitāb al-Burhān* (which he ascribes to 'James the Jew', and says was written 'to prove out of all the Prophets, &c. that our Saviour was the Christ'[230]); and other Christian Arabic texts at Queen's College[231] and in the possession of Henry King, Bishop of Chichester.[232] There are many indications in his work of his contacts with Selden, and each seems to have influenced the other. On p. 78 of *Notes and Observations* Gregory says: 'I have an Arabick Translation of the Psalmes[233] (the possession whereof I am bound here to acknowledge amongst many other favours to Learned Master *Selden*).' Gregory not only refers to Selden's printed extract from Eutychius, but himself gives several extracts from the Cambridge manuscript.[234] We saw that he consulted the Roe manuscript of the Arabic Councils in the Bodleian on Selden's behalf; but he also frequently cites it himself.[235] His surviving correspondence with Selden illustrates their common concern with matters of chronology.[236] Gregory also cites secular Arabic texts from printed books, not only the Medicean Press editions of Euclid and the 'Nubian Geographer'

[227] His comments on the Koran in the preface to *Notes and Observations* are remarkably unprejudiced for the time, e.g. 'the Book it self . . . would not heare altogether so ill, if it were looked upon in its own text or through a good Translation.'

[228] Bainbridge made exactly the same mistake in his Arabic transcription of that part of the manuscript in MS TCD 383, fo. 45ᵛ. Gregory mentions the 'Tables of Alkas' in *Notes and Observations*, 14, 31, 156, and *Posthuma*, 110.

[229] e.g. *Notes and Observations*, 75; *Posthuma*, 273.

[230] *Notes and Observations*, 85. The manuscript is still at Balliol (Mynors, *Catalogue of the Manuscripts of Balliol College*, no. 327) with a letter from Gregory pasted in saying that he is returning it after a long loan.

[231] Crosfield, *Diary*, 81 records that 'Mr Gregory came to borrow Theseus Ambrosius' (i.e. his *Introductio in Chaldaicam linguam et decem alias linguas*) from Queen's College library in 1635, in order to learn Armenian 'which he could doe by the helpe of an Armenian that was now in towne'.

[232] e.g. *Notes and Observations*, 46, 88.

[233] Presumably the 1614 (or 1619) printed version 'ex typographia Savariana' (Schnurrer no. 324) rather than a manuscript.

[234] MS Dd.5.35, formerly owned by Erpenius (Oates, 225). See e.g. *Notes and Observations*, 156–7; *Posthuma*, 8–9.

[235] e.g. *Notes and Observations*, 89, 155; *Posthuma*, 85, 108.

[236] MS Selden supra 108, fos. 52, 74, 243, 278a, 278e.

and Erpenius' edition of al-Makīn, but also extracts that he found in other works such as Kircher's *Prodromus Coptus* (Rome, 1636), Kirsten's *Vitae quatuor Evangelistarum* (Breslau, 1608),[237] and Schickard's *Tarich* (Tübingen, 1628).[238] Gregory's numerous translated Arabic quotations show that he understood the language quite well, but they are not without errors. Like Bedwell, he had no notion of the correct Arabic form of the name of Averroes.[239] In general his work is impressive for the width, but not the depth, of his Arabic learning. His influence on the field was negligible.

[237] *PO* no. 112.
[238] See Ullmann, 'Arabische, türkische und persische Studien', 115–21.
[239] Whom he calls 'Aben Rois' (impossible in Arabic), *Notes and Observations*, preface [15] and 74. This is an indication that he did not attend Pasor's inaugural lecture, which gives the correct Arabic form of the name.

4

Laud and Arabic at Oxford

THE situation of Arabic studies at Oxford after Pasor left appeared as unpromising as it was before he arrived. There was no provision for teaching the language in the university, and very inadequate resources for studying it in the form of printed books and manuscripts in the University Library. In 1629 no one would have guessed that within the next ten years Oxford would be well on the way to becoming one of the principal centres for these studies in Europe. This transformation was due above all to the efforts of William Laud, but also to those Oxford men who advised, worked for, and influenced him, namely Peter Turner, John Greaves, and Edward Pococke, as well as to the man whom Laud called 'olim academiæ nostrae alumnus, nunc decus',[1] John Selden.

When Laud[2] became Chancellor of the University of Oxford in April 1630, he was as yet only Bishop of London, but was already one of the most powerful men in the kingdom through his influence with the King. This position was enhanced by his elevation to Archbishop of Canterbury in 1633. One of his ambitions was to make the university, with which he had long been associated as alumnus, Fellow, and eventually President of St John's College, equal to any in Europe in prestige and scholarly reputation. Although his impeachment and fall from power in 1641, and the outbreak of the Civil War, prevented the completion of all of Laud's plans for Oxford, his achievement in the twelve years of his chancellorship probably had a greater effect on the university than that of any other chancellor in its whole history. Here is not the place to evaluate his entire chancellorship, for instance the effect of his radical revision of the Oxford statutes on the teaching, discipline, and governance of the university. I will concentrate rather on his promotion of scholarship in general and of Arabic in particular.

---

[1] Laud, *Works*, v/1, 135.

[2] Trevor-Roper, *Archbishop Laud*, remains the best account of his life, although its treatment of his promotion of scholarship at Oxford and elsewhere could be greatly amplified. The same author's essay 'Laudianism and Political Power' in his *Catholics, Anglicans and Puritans* should be read for its analysis of Laud's religious aims in his treatment of the Church and universities.

Although he was not a stranger to written controversy, Laud (unlike his fellow archbishop Ussher) was no scholar, but he had great respect for scholarship in others, and regarded it as essential for a university. Before becoming Chancellor he had grasped the importance to a university of having a well-equipped library and a learned press, and intended to establish both at Oxford. We have seen how, as early as January 1629, he had persuaded the then chancellor, the Earl of Pembroke, to buy the Barocci manuscripts for the Bodleian. In a letter that he sent to the Vice-Chancellor announcing this gift,[3] he informed him that at the same time he was sending twenty-eight manuscripts donated by Sir Thomas Roe, who had recently returned from being ambassador in Constantinople. Laud was undoubtedly instrumental in encouraging this donation too, which included the Arabic version of the early Church Councils, a manuscript of the highest importance.[4] Perhaps the most interesting collection of manuscripts which he elicited was that of Sir Kenelm Digby in 1634, many of them containing unique items.[5] However, it was Laud himself who was to donate the collection of manuscripts which was in quantity and quality the most splendid acquisition of the Bodleian to date. He began to buy manuscripts on a large scale soon after (if not before) he became Chancellor, and he passed these on to the library in a series of donations from 1635 to 1640.[6] It is noteworthy that these manuscripts were not confined to the usual categories of Latin, Greek, and Hebrew, but also included significant numbers of oriental and especially Arabic items.

It seems unlikely that Laud himself knew any Arabic at all. What then was the reason for his interest in advancing study of the subject? The answer must be conjectural, since I know of no pronouncements of his own which are relevant. He was on terms of friendship and respect with scholars who were enthusiastic in their study of Arabic, notably Bedwell and Selden. He also had a high regard for G. J. Vossius, who, although himself no Arabist, was, as we shall see, an

---

[3] Printed by Macray, *Annals*, 69–70.

[4] MS Roe 26. This had been given to Roe by the Patriarch Cyril Lucaris.

[5] See Macray, *Annals*, 78–9 for an evaluation of these. Digby's smaller collection of Arabic and other oriental manuscripts came to the library later, in 1640; these were mistakenly incorporated in the collection of Laud, who was only the conduit for them: see Wakefield, 'Arabic Manuscripts', 131.

[6] See Hunt, *Laudian Manuscripts*, Introduction for a very detailed discussion of the dates and origins of Laud's acquisitions, and when they came to the Bodleian. Of the total number of over 1,000 items about a quarter were oriental, of which no less than 147 were Arabic (Wakefield, 'Arabic Manuscripts', 130).

ardent promoter of the language. But I suspect that the principal influence on Laud's benefactions in this as in other respects was Peter Turner, Savilian Professor of Geometry and Fellow of Merton College. Anthony Wood informs us that Turner was 'much beloved of archb. Laud',[7] and this is borne out by Laud's extant correspondence. Turner, who had been known to Laud at least since 1629, was of great assistance to him in drafting the new University Statutes in 1633–4, and the confidence which the Chancellor reposed in him is amply illustrated by such passages as his letter to the Vice-Chancellor of 26 May 1637, where he not only accepts a suggestion of Turner's about the proposed University Press, but virtually instructs the Vice-Chancellor to deal with Turner on the matter as Laud's delegate.[8] Laud also, in the visitation which he inflicted on Merton College from 1638 onwards, favoured the faction of Turner and Greaves against that of the Warden, Sir Nathaniel Brent.[9] Wood describes Turner as 'well skill'd in the Hebrew and Arabic',[10] but unfortunately it is impossible to test this. For Turner published nothing,[11] and, probably as a result of his expulsion from Oxford by the Visitors in 1648,[12] very little written by him remains in manuscript.[13] What is beyond doubt is that he energetically advanced the careers of two men who were very interested in Arabic, Henry Jacob and John Greaves.[14]

[7] *Athenae Oxonienses*, iii. 306. Cf. Wood, *History and Antiquities*, ii/1, 369, where he says that the two men at Oxford with whom Laud as Chancellor regularly corresponded were Turner and William Chillingworth. It was no doubt through Laud's influence that Turner was, by the King's Letters, given leave to hold his Fellowship at Merton after being elected Savilian Professor (ibid. ii/2, 866).

[8] Laud, *Works*, v/1, 172.

[9] Trevor-Roper, *Archbishop Laud*, 354–7, especially 355 on Turner's activity.

[10] *Athenae Oxonienses*, iii. 306. On Turner see also Ward, *Lives of the Professors of Gresham College*, 131–5.

[11] Apart from some Latin poems in various congratulatory or commiserating publications of the university: Madan, *Oxford Books*, ii. 687.

[12] The plundering of his goods at Oxford by Parliamentary forces after he was taken prisoner in 1642 (Wood, *History and Antiquities*, ii/1, 449) may also have led to losses of this kind.

[13] Examination of some collations he made for Selden in MS Selden supra 121 reveals him as an exceedingly neat and accurate Greek scholar. According to Macray, *Annals*, 71–2, a catalogue of the Barocci and Roe MSS compiled by Turner is with Selden's printed books (MS AA. 1. Med. Seld.).

[14] For Jacob see above, p. 67. In a letter to Selden of 30 Dec. 1641, Turner expresses concern about keeping the Fellowship at Merton for Jacob, and incidentally reveals his hostility to Brent. Turner was one of those (for the others see below, p. 128) who recommended Greaves to be his own successor as Professor of Geometry at Gresham College. For Turner's recommendation of Greaves to Laud see below, p. 133. If Wood correctly identified his handwriting (*Life and Times,* i. 189 n. 2), Turner addressed Greaves not only as friend but also as 'my kinsman'.

(I) LAUD COLLECTS ORIENTAL MANUSCRIPTS

Whatever the source of his inspiration, Laud devoted much money and energy to collecting oriental manuscripts. We have already seen that he bought many of Bedwell's Arabic manuscripts after his death, and later both Pococke and Greaves, while in the East, were active on his behalf. Laud also launched a scheme (perhaps suggested to him by Turner) to assess a sort of manuscript toll on the ships of the Levant Company. A letter to the company issued under the King's name on 15 February 1634[15] commands that

euery Shippe of yours at euery Voyage that yt makes should bring home one Arab: or Persian MS. Booke to be delyuered presently to the Master of your Company, and by him carryed or sent to the Lord ArchBishop of Cant. for the time being, who shall dispose of them as Wee in our Wisdome shall think fitt.

The justification for this in the preamble is worth quoting:

There is a great deale of Learning and that very fitt and necessary to be knowne, that is written in Arabicke, and there is a great defect in both our Vniversityes, very few spending any of theyr time to attaine to skill eyther in that or other Easterne Languages. Which Wee impute not soe much to the fault of the Students there, as partly to the great scarcity and want of Arabicke and Persian Bookes, in which they might spend theyr paines; and partly to theyr lack both of opportunity and means to prouide and furnish them selves with such Bookes.

The Governor and Court of the company duly noted receipt of the letter and resolved to write to the ambassador and consuls about it.[16] But it is not surprising that this scheme, which contained no provision for supervision or choice of manuscripts,[17] was not very productive. On 10 February 1637, John Greaves, writing to Turner with an outline of the plans for Pococke and himself to travel to the East, for which he wanted Turner to enlist Laud's support, says: 'if I were at Constantinople I would take order that no ship should returne without strictly observing the kings iniunctions about Arabicke bookes: and for

[15] PRO, SP 16,260, no. 116.

[16] PRO, SP 105,149, fo. 63ᵛ. What was said to the ambassador and consuls is not known, since the 'out letters' for these years are not among the surviving records of the company.

[17] The only guidance in the original letter was the exclusion of copies of the Koran: 'because Wee haue choyce of them allready.' However, see below, p. 124, for proof that from 1634 to 1636 Pococke supervised the choice and dispatch of manuscripts, at least for ships departing from Aleppo.

such as are the best, and dearest, and may be worth his Grace's acceptance, I should do the Merchants so much service as to recommend
such to them.'[18] As we shall see, the arrival of Greaves and Pococke in
Constantinople was succeeded by an unusually large influx of Arabic
manuscripts in Laud's donations to Oxford, but this was not because
the merchants were obeying the King's order. For in the Levant
Company's Court of 18 April 1640 was read 'a Letter from my Lords
Grace of Canterburie & another from Secretary Windebanke
Signifieing his Majesties pleasure in requiring the Companie to be
more Carefull for the future, in giving order for prouition of Arabicke
bookes in Turkey'. Laud's letter does not survive, but Windebanke's
draft[19] reveals that 'very few Bookes haue beene brought to him
[Laud] upon this Order. And that he hath scarce receaued two Bookes
in these last two yeares.' In this letter the justification for the King's
order was couched in terms which were designed to appeal more to
merchants: 'His Majestie hauing a great desire to increase the knowledge of the Eastern languages within his kingdome; And that as well
for the knowledge of those parts, as for some Accomodacion to Trade.'
This time the Court selected the company's chaplains to see to the
matter, ordering that it 'should be strictly recommended vnto the
Ministers residing in the Companies' priviledges, & particularly unto
the Minister that is to goe for Alleppo vpon the next General Shipp'.[20]
Laud's fall from power within the year put an end to what the
merchants must have regarded as a nuisance.

The researches of Hunt have thrown some light on the sources from
which Laud acquired his manuscripts.[21] Although more undoubtedly
remains to be discovered,[22] I summarize what can be learned from this
about the Arabic manuscripts in particular. We have already seen that
some were obtained from the Levant Company as a kind of tribute,
and we shall see that Pococke while at Aleppo (and later both Pococke
and Greaves at Constantinople) exercised some kind of supervision
over the choice of these; but, given the slackness of the merchants in
carrying out this royal command, such items cannot have been
numerous. Laud did, however, acquire some manuscripts from indivi-

[18] PRO, SP 16,381, no. 75, fo. 159ᵛ.

[19] PRO, SP 16,383, no. 43, fo. 83ʳ; undated, but obviously written March or April
1640. It is wrongly dated Feb. 1638 in the printed *Calendar of State Papers Domestic*
(Charles I, 1637–8, 285).

[20] PRO, SP 105,149, fo. 201.

[21] Hunt, *Laudian Manuscripts*, pp. x–xxxi.

[22] See above, p. 58, on manuscripts of Bedwell owned by Laud which are absent from
Hunt's list.

dual merchants, e.g. MS Or. 22, in which he recorded that he received
it on 5 May 1634, 'sent me Edward Tynes from Aleppo in Siria'.[23]
Other individuals who gave him Arabic manuscripts included Ussher,
Thomas Clayton (Regius Professor of Medicine at Oxford, who appropriately donated 'Rhazes in Arabic'), and Patriarch Cyril Lucaris.[24]
Laud appears to have used Samson Johnson, chaplain of Sir Robert
Anstruther, ambassador to the Diet of Frankfurt am Main, as his agent
for collecting manuscripts in Europe.[25] Johnson was interested in
oriental languages (at one point he had contemplated applying for the
chaplaincy at Aleppo which Pococke eventually obtained). Among the
items which Laud acquired from him were two Arabic manuscripts,
and he also corresponded with Laud about the sale of Elichmann's
Arabic books after that scholar's death in 1639. I have already
mentioned that after Bedwell's death Laud bought many of his manuscripts, and that others came later through Selden. Hunt failed to draw
the obvious conclusion from the list he gives on p. xxxiii of the
numbers of western and oriental manuscripts which accrued to Laud's
collection in each of the years from 1634 to 1640 (before 1634 he had
assembled a total of 56 oriental manuscripts). The totals for oriental
manuscripts in 1635 and 1638 (93 and 55 respectively) are far greater
than in any other year, and together comprise well over half of
all Laud's oriental acquisitions.[26] It is surely no coincidence that in
1635 Pococke at Aleppo, and in 1638 Pococke and Greaves at
Constantinople were active on the archbishop's behalf. The same
picture is displayed in Laud's household accounts: £12. 7s. 6d. 'for
Arabian Books' on 6 May 1636 and £50 to 'Daniel Harvey for
Manuscriptes' on 26 October 1638.[27] Although there is explicit
evidence to connect only one manuscript of Laud's with Greaves,[28]
and none with Pococke, we cannot doubt that between them the two

---

[23] Hunt, p. xix, q.v. for information on Tynes (from whose widow Sir Simonds
D'Ewes later bought most of his oriental manuscripts).

[24] Hunt, pp. xii, xxii, xxvii. Cyril's gift was an Arabic Pentateuch, sent to Laud in
1638, shortly before the Patriarch's murder, while Greaves and Pococke were both in
Constantinople (Hunt, who misdates Greaves's activities in the East, is wrong when he
says, p. xv, that it was probably sent before Greaves reached Constantinople).

[25] Hunt, pp. xx, xxx.

[26] If we add the 25 oriental manuscripts of 1636, probably also due to Pococke, the
proportion increases to two-thirds of the total.

[27] Hunt, pp. xxii, xxvii. On Harvey, who acted as Laud's intermediary with the
Levant Company, see below, p. 138. Laud's extant accounts begin on 18 Dec. 1635,
hence there is no record of the large expenditures which must have accompanied the
enormous acquisitions of that year.

[28] See below, p. 138.

were responsible for sending Laud the majority of the Arabic manuscripts which he was to donate to Oxford.

(II) LAUD ESTABLISHES THE ARABIC PROFESSORSHIP

Laud's other service to Arabic studies at Oxford was his establishment of a professorship in the subject. Since this followed Thomas Adams's action at Cambridge by four years, it is often assumed that Laud was simply emulating him. While it would be foolish to deny that rivalry between the two universities played a part, the known facts reveal a more complex situation. Laud wrote to Pococke in Aleppo on 30 October 1631, on the strength of their common friendship with Bedwell, asking him to buy coins and manuscripts on his behalf.[29] Thus, well before Wheelock was made Arabic lecturer at Cambridge, Laud was in contact with the man for whom he later designated the professorship, and was already concerned with collecting Arabic manuscripts destined for the university. It is impossible to say precisely when Laud determined to create an Arabic lectureship at Oxford, but it must have been before 21 May 1634, when he wrote to Pococke: 'I hope you will, before your return [from Aleppo], make yourself able to teach the Arabic language.' Among the 'things which I have projected to do, if God bless me in them' listed by Laud on a page at the end of his diary is the intention to 'erect an Arabic lecture in Oxford, at least for my life-time, my estate not being able for more: that this may lead the way'.[30] Although the list was probably started at the time of his election as Chancellor, in April 1630, Laud added to and annotated it later, and this item appears to be one of the additions. Hence one can say only that the intention was formed some time between 1630 and 1634. However, I do not believe that it was to Cambridge that Laud looked for inspiration in this matter. Rather, as he sought to make Oxford the peer of any European university, it was Leiden that would have drawn his attention, with its universally admired school of Arabic and impressive collection of oriental manuscripts. Laud greatly respected the opinion of G. J. Vossius (as is apparent from their printed correspondence), and Vossius, although he knew little Arabic himself, was convinced of its importance to scholarship. Writing to Meursius in October 1625 concerning Golius' plans to travel to the East in order to improve his knowledge of Arabic, he

---

[29] Twells, 27.   [30] Laud, *Works*, iii. 255.

wishes him success 'cum Bataviae, tum praecipue studiorum causa. Multa enim ex Arabum monumentis erui possunt, quae à nostris sciantur, juxta ac ab ignarissimis.'[31] Later he sent his son Dionysius, a youth of extraordinary promise, to live and study Arabic with Golius. Laud had met Vossius in London on the occasion of the latter's visit to England to be installed as a prebendary of Canterbury, through Laud's influence, in 1629,[32] when their conversation surely touched on the treasure of Arabic manuscripts brought back to Leiden by Golius barely a month before Vossius travelled to England.

Laud formally established the Arabic Professorship on 8 August 1636, soon after Pococke returned to Oxford from Aleppo. Like the lectureship established at Cambridge for Wheelock, this was an *ad hominem* creation, for which Laud pledged an annual stipend of £40 for the term of his own life. However, from the beginning Laud expressed his intention of making it a permanent endowment, if possible. The following extract from a letter written to Laud in November 1639 by Thomas Greaves (then deputy for Pococke, who was away in Constantinople) illustrates Laud's careful attention to detail and the circumstances and success of the lecture:

At the first institution of the Arabick Lecture, your Grace thought fitt to prae-scribe these orders (which have beene duly observed) that it should be read in times of vacation, & in Lent, ones every weeke upon Wednesday, betweene the houres of nine, & ten. Moreover that upon every Monday & Friday in the afternoone the Reader should be in readines for one houres space, privately to direct in the language all students that would repare unto him. When your Graces pleasure was certified to the Convocation, certaine Delegates were nominated to consider what further orders might be requisite, who have yet added nothing more. Neither are any bound to be Auditors, which freedome makes the company the lesse, yet I can truly affirme, that there is now a greater frequency then heretofore. The most of them are Masters of Arts. Diverse have come unto me for private directions, of whose proficiency I can give good testimony. One (a servitour) long since praesented unto me an epistle in Arabick of his own composing. If it please your Grace it may be moved unto the Heades of Houses, at there meeting to speake unto such as they conceiue most capable to apply themselves unto these studies, unto whom I shall with all willingnes & alacrity give my best assistance and directions.[33]

[31] Vossius, *Epistolae*, i, no. 51. The whole passage, important for Vossius' attitude towards the study of Arabic, is quoted and translated by Rademaker, *Life of Vossius*, 158.

[32] On Vossius' visit to England see Rademaker, ibid. 231–4. See further below, p. 117.

[33] PRO, SP 16,432, no. 11, fo. 19ʳ. The letter is in reply to a request from Laud for information (Laud, *Works*, v/1, 237).

On 25 June 1640, with the clouds already gathering of the political storm which was to bring Laud's impeachment, foreseeing that he would have little time to make further changes at Oxford, he endowed the Arabic Professorship with lands that he owned at Bray.[34] Thus Oxford obtained a permanent chair of Arabic some twenty-five years before Cambridge.

Shortly afterwards, on 2 July, Laud promulgated the permanent statutes governing the duties of the Arabic Professor and his audience.[35] The provisions outlined above by Thomas Greaves were somewhat altered. Although the lecture was still to be held once a week in vacations and Lent, the professor was otherwise obliged to be available for private consultation only after the lecture and for three hours in the afternoon of that day. More significantly, attendance was no longer voluntary. It was made incumbent on 'all bachelors of arts, until they stand advanced . . . to the master's degree' and 'all students in medicine, until they are presented for the bachelor's degree in that faculty'. Anyone else was at liberty to attend. Thus the statute embodied Laud's conviction that Arabic was suitable in general only for graduates, with the exception of those undergraduates who intended to pursue a career in medicine, for whom (he believed) it had a practical application in aiding their study of Avicenna's medical works. But did it operate as he intended? I know of no explicit evidence one way or another. But the very lack of evidence about large audiences of BAs attending Pococke's lectures leads me to suspect that (even if there was some attempt to force attendance on the few students in medicine), as far as the bachelors were concerned the statute was a dead letter already in the seventeenth century (as it certainly was in the eighteenth). Laud provided penalties in the form of a fine of sixpence per person for each lecture missed, the proceeds to be spent on buying Arabic books for the Bodleian. As far as I can determine, there is no trace of any such income for the library during this period. We should not, however, conclude that all bachelors dutifully attended all lectures,[36] for imposition of the fines required the attendance of the Vice-Chancellor or one of the proctors at the lecture

[34] Laud, *Works*, v/1, 272.

[35] Griffiths, *Statutes of Archbishop Laud*, 317–18; translated by Ward, *Oxford University Statutes*, i. 295–7.

[36] The naïve assumption that because a statute prescribed a course of conduct it must have been followed is the sole basis of Bourne's assertion (*Life of John Locke*, i. 56) that Locke regularly attended Pococke's Arabic lectures and thus learned the language. This is taken seriously by Russell, '*The Philosophus Autodidactus*', 239 (cf. below, p. 267).

in question, and we may doubt whether these officials were so mindful of their responsibilities. Everything that we know suggests that the vast majority of senior students at Oxford had no knowledge whatever of the Arabic language, and that Pococke's lectures were attended only by those few who were really interested in learning it.

(III) LAUD AND THE 'LEARNED PRESS'

There was another important respect in which Arabic studies at Oxford lagged behind Leiden, namely facilities for printing in Arabic. Indeed here even Cambridge was supposedly better off, having inherited Bedwell's Arabic types in 1632. Although these were hardly used (and were probably unusable for extensive printing) it was well known that they were in the university's possession. The steps which Laud took to remedy this were part of his plans to establish a 'learned press' at Oxford.[37] As early as 1634 the university printer, William Turner, agreed to provide 'Arabicke letter' for printing Gregory's edition of Malalas,[38] but he never obtained any. Equally abortive was the proposal for 'the procuring of a sufficient composer and corrector for the eastern languages' from Leiden, mentioned in Laud's letter to the Vice-Chancellor of 5 May 1637.[39] However, in 1636 Samuel Brown, a bookseller and publisher in London, and the brother of one of the Oxford proctors for that year, went to Leiden and bought, on behalf of the university, a number of punches and matrices from the stock of Arent Cornelisz. van Hoogenacker, a typefounder who had recently died.[40] These included both Hebrew and Arabic founts. Although the purchase was made by the university, there can be no doubt that the impulse, and probably the funds, came from Laud. This is clear from John Greaves's letter to Turner of 10 February 1637, which incidentally reveals that Greaves, while in Leiden in 1636, had conducted preliminary negotiations on behalf of Laud:

I cannot but approue of that bargaine, which hath beene made by your Proctors brother Mr Browne. As I remember the summe doth not much exceede that,

---

[37] On these see Carter, *History of the Oxford University Press*, ch. 3. Although these plans did not reach fruition in Laud's lifetime, some important parts were incorporated in the statutes and carried out later, for instance the institution of an 'Architypographus' to oversee all publications licensed by the university.

[38] See above, p. 102.   [39] Laud, *Works*, v/1, 168.

[40] Full details are given by Morison, *John Fell*, Appendix IV, pp. 233–43. The contract specifying the types is dated 7 Jan. 1637.

which was proposed to me at my being in Leyden, with which, after my returne, I gaue my Lords Grace information. . . . I hope now, since that my Lords Grace hath taken such honourable care, for the furnishing of the Vniversity with all sorts of types, and procuring so many choice MSS. of the Orientall languages, as are no where els to be found, (unlesse it be in the Escurial in Spaine) that some will endeavour to make true use of his Graces noble intentions, and publish to my Lords honour and to the improuement of learning, some of those incomparable peeces of the East.[41]

The opinion of modern experts is less favourable than Greaves's cautious approval of the Arabic type bought by Brown.[42] The fount was an inferior imitation of Erpenius' types, and in far from perfect condition.[43] Nevertheless, unlike the Cambridge Arabic types, it was serviceable enough for printing whole books in Arabic, and was used for all the pioneering works of Pococke and John Greaves, and for everything else printed in Arabic at Oxford until 1768. For reasons which I cannot explain, it was not used for some years after its acquisition, even when it would have been appropriate. For instance, in Thomas Greaves's inaugural lecture, printed at Oxford in 1639, the occasional Arabic quotations are represented by blanks (filled in by hand in some copies),[44] and John Gregory's *Notes and Observations upon Some Passages of Scripture*, printed at Oxford in 1646, has the frequent Arabic quotations set in Hebrew type.[45]

[41] PRO, SP 16,381, no. 75, fo. 159[r].

[42] Morison, *John Fell*, 22 describes the punches and matrices as 'rather indifferent'. Carter, *History of Oxford University Press*, 34, says: 'A less complacent critic would have said that Brown was a bad judge of typefounder's material.'

[43] For specimens of it in modern books see e.g. Morison, *John Fell*, 240–2, and Carter, *History of Oxford University Press*, 33, although these incorporate some additions that were made later in the century, especially under Fell.

[44] Greaves, *De Linguae Arabicae Vtilitate & Praestantia*. According to Madan, *Oxford Books*, ii. 142, some copies have the Arabic printed with Hebrew type.

[45] See above, p. 102.

5

The Early Career of Pococke

EDWARD POCOCKE[1] was born on 8 November 1604 in Oxford, the city where he was to spend the greater part of his life. As the eldest son he was named after his father, who had been a Fellow of Magdalen College, but had recently become Vicar of Chieveley in Berkshire. The name Pococke[2] is common in Berkshire, but the branch of the family with which we are concerned also appears to have Hampshire connections.[3] Pococke's early education was at the grammar school at Thame,[4] where he learned Latin, and perhaps Greek, under the headmaster Richard Boucher or Butcher. He matriculated at Magdalen Hall, Oxford, in 1619, but soon after his sixteenth birthday was admitted as a scholar of Corpus Christi College, with which he was to be associated for more than twenty years. As an undergraduate at Corpus, where the teaching of the 'three languages' was traditional,[5] he would certainly have studied Hebrew as well as Latin and Greek. Graduating BA in 1622, and MA in 1626, he was elected probationer-fellow of the college on 24 July 1628. But before that, as we have seen, he embarked on the study of the language to which he was to devote his life, learning the elements of Arabic while attending Pasor's lectures in 1626–7, and soon afterwards applying to Bedwell in Tottenham for private instruction. It was probably in Bedwell's house that he first met Selden,[6] who was later to be of importance to him as protector and patron. Pococke may also have attended Pasor's lectures on Syriac; certainly by 1628 he had mastered

[1] For a good outline of Pococke's life see Holt, 'An Oxford Arabist'.

[2] Frequently spelled 'Pocock'. Since no less a scholar than Nallino ('Filosofia d'Avicenna', 224 n. 1) discussed the correct form of the Arabist's name, and came to the conclusion that it should be 'Pocock', I note that although his contemporaries more often than not use the latter form to refer to him, he himself invariably signs his name as 'Pococke', which I have adopted.

[3] The Arabist Pococke's wife came from Hampshire, and he owned property there. The many links between the families of Pococke and Greaves (from Hampshire) are probably to be explained not by the close friendship between Edward Pococke and John Greaves, but by the county connection.

[4] Among later pupils of note were John Fell and Anthony Wood.

[5] Lloyd Jones, *The Discovery of Hebrew*, 94–5, cf. 204–5.

[6] Selden certainly knew Pococke before he went to Aleppo, since he recommended him to the consul, John Wandesford (see the letter quoted above, p. 70).

the language sufficiently to prepare an edition of some apostolic Epistles which had been omitted from the Syriac New Testament published by Widmanstetter. These were 2 Peter, 2 and 3 John, and Jude, which Pococke found in a Bodleian manuscript. The prospects of getting this published at Oxford, or even in England at that time, were poor. A happy accident led not only to publication, but to another turning-point in Pococke's life.

In October 1629 G. J. Vossius came to England to be installed as a canon at Canterbury.[7] He took the opportunity to visit Oxford, where on 12 November he was given an honorary degree. As a matter of course, being a distinguished guest, he was shown around the Bodleian Library by the librarian, John Rous. When he happened to admire the manuscript containing the Syriac epistles, Rous informed him of Pococke's edition. Thereupon Vossius insisted on meeting Pococke, and after talking with him and examining his edition, urged him to publish it, promising to arrange for it to be printed at Leiden. Pococke assented to what must have been a most flattering invitation for a 25-year-old scholar, and the work was duly published in the following year, supervised at Leiden by Louis de Dieu.[8] In the mean time Pococke had been ordained, on 20 December 1629. In the normal course of events he would have continued as a fellow of his college until he obtained a living.

Instead, he almost immediately applied for the post of chaplain to the merchants of the Levant Company at Aleppo, which had become vacant some time before when Charles Robson had left to return to Oxford, where he was Fellow of Queen's College.[9] The decision to undertake this employment was a momentous one, for the six years which Pococke was to spend there were crucial to his intellectual development. Aleppo, a centre of learning as well as trade, provided the best opportunity (among those places where a European might live in safety) to learn Arabic from native speakers and scholars. Nevertheless, to take such a step was by no means obvious or enticing

---

[7] For a detailed account of his visit see Rademaker, *Life of Vossius*, 231–5.

[8] See Pococke, *Syriac Epistles*. It was accompanied by a transcription in Hebrew characters, with below it the Greek text and Pococke's Latin translation of the Syriac, followed by 43 pages of notes, in which the Arabic version is occasionally quoted (presumably from Erpenius' 1616 edition of the New Testament).

[9] Robson, who arrived at Aleppo some time before July 1624, returned to his college on 12 Dec. 1628 (Crosfield, *Diary*, 31). In the same year he published a small pamphlet entitled 'Newes from Aleppo' (see Hamilton, 'English Interest in Arabic-Speaking Christians', 36). He donated two oriental manuscripts to the Bodleian in 1631 (Macray, *Annals*, 74, 128).

for one in his position. The chaplain's salary (£50 a year)[10] could have been no attraction for the eldest son of a substantial family. He would have to exile himself from friends and libraries at Oxford. Some of the chaplains welcomed the opportunity to travel and see strange places: such were Robert Huntington, Pococke's pupil and also chaplain at Aleppo from 1671, who travelled widely in Syria, the Holy Land, and elsewhere; or John Luke, chaplain at Smyrna for two periods between 1664 and 1683, and later Professor of Arabic at Cambridge, who obviously enjoyed his rambles in Asia Minor and Syria.[11] Pococke was not one of these. Twells says 'he did not (as many travellers do) carry with him a violent desire of viewing strange countries', and supports this by a quotation from a letter that Pococke wrote to Thomas Greaves soon after arriving in Aleppo: 'My chief solace is the remembrance of my friends, and my former happiness, when I was among them. Happy you that enjoy those places where I often wish myself as I see the barbarous people of this country. I think that he that hath once been out of England, if he get home, will not easily be persuaded to leave it again.'[12] One may discount these sentiments as the homesickness of one who has recently left his native land for the first time; but there is other evidence for Pococke's dislike of travel. He seems never to have left Aleppo and the immediate environs in the years he spent there; and in his second trip to the East he likewise spent the whole time in one place, Constantinople, in contrast to his companions there, John Greaves and Ravius, who both travelled extensively. Yet Pococke stayed in Aleppo for nearly six years, despite all inconveniences. He himself later claimed that 'his continuance at Aleppo . . . had been a thing of charge and difficulty to him'.[13] John Greaves elaborates in his letter to Turner: 'It was not possible for him, during his stay in Aleppo, to bring these his intentions to perfection, his College calling vpon him continually to returne home, and thereby disquieting him, and the Merchants tying him to too strict termes of preaching, besides the performing of other Ministeriall offices.'[14] The

[10] For such details as the chaplains' emoluments Pearson, *Chaplains to the Levant Company* is of use, since he consulted the records of the company preserved in the Public Record Office, but in general it is a slovenly work.

[11] Various unpublished travel diaries of his survive in the British Library, MS Harley 7021.   [12] Twells, 14–15.

[13] Twells, 99–100, paraphrasing a letter of Pococke to those in the Parliament who had sequestered Laud's estates after he was executed in 1645.

[14] PRO, SP 16,381, fo. 159ʳ. The normal period for a fellow's leave of absence, which Corpus had presumably granted Pococke, was three years. Pococke was originally appointed chaplain for four years.

sole reason for his continuing stay was, as the consul Wandesford told Selden, that Pococke 'made Arabb his mistresse', not too strong a term for the passion with which he pursued the object of his scholarly affection.

It was this same desire which led him to apply for the post. Pococke was not the first to consider the possibilities of the chaplaincy at Aleppo for an Arabist. Bainbridge, writing to Ussher on 20 July 1629, says:

Whereas our Turky Merchants, trading at Aleppo, being now destitute of a Minister, have referr'd the choice of one unto yourself, may it please you to understand, that there is one Mr. Johnson, a Fellow of Magdalen-Colledg, who hath spent some Years in the Oriental Languages, and being desirous to improve his Knowledg therein, is content to adventure himself in the Voyage; he would take pains to preach once a week, but not oftner; being desirous to spend his time in perfecting his Languages, and making such other Observations as may tend to the advancement of Learning.[15]

Samson Johnson, for reasons unknown, did not in the end present himself as a candidate for Aleppo. Instead in 1631 he went to Germany as chaplain of Sir Robert Anstruther, ambassador to the Diet of Frankfurt, and later was chaplain to the exiled Queen Elizabeth of Bohemia at The Hague, where, as we saw, he acted as agent for Laud in purchasing manuscripts. Pococke may have heard about Johnson's proposal from their common friend, John Greaves.[16] But I suspect that the impulse to go himself came from the 'much discourse' which he held with Vossius during the latter's fateful visit to Oxford. We have already noted the high regard of Vossius for Arabic studies and also for the achievement of Golius, whose triumphal return from the East with his treasure of manuscripts had occurred shortly before Vossius' visit to England. It is inconceivable that Vossius, hearing of Pococke's interest in Arabic, would not have discoursed to him about Golius' expertise in Arabic and his manuscripts, for which Aleppo, where he had used the resources of the Dutch merchant community, had been a principal source. It is surely not a coincidence that Pococke applied for the post at Aleppo shortly thereafter. On his return he reported to Vossius on his achievements there, telling him that he had 'a right to expect' such a report.[17]

[15] Ussher, *Letters*, no. 144, p. 411.
[16] Johnson mentions Greaves as his friend in a letter to Bainbridge from Vienna, 28 Feb./9 Mar. 1632 (MS TCD 382, fo. 104ᵛ).
[17] Letter of 5 Dec. 1636, MS Rawlinson letters 82, fo. 155 (printed in Vossius, *Epistolae*, ii, no. 239): 'Si rationem exacti in Syria temporis ut reddam (quod iure poteris) expectes'.

Pococke was present at the General Court of the Levant Company held in London on 25 March 1630, at which his candidature was announced, and, as was customary for those aspiring to be chaplains for the company, preached a sermon before them at St Andrew's Undershaft on the following Wednesday. His appointment was confirmed in the court held on the same day.[18] There were no other candidates, but Pococke needed, and got, recommendations. Unfortunately the minutes of the court state only that they had 'receiued very good testymony & recommendacions both for his abilitie in Learning, Soundness in the Studdy of devynitie, conformitie to the constitucions of the Church & integritie of Lyfe & conversacion', without naming those who recommended him. It has been suggested that Pococke was put forward by Laud. However, not only is it improbable that the name of such a powerful patron would remain unmentioned in the minutes, but Twells (who was at a loss on this question) specifically notes that Laud's first letter to Pococke at Aleppo in 1631 'plainly discovers that they had then no acquaintance with each other'. I conjecture that, besides the usual testimonials from his own college, Pococke had the support of members of the Fettiplace family, of Rampayns Manor in Childrey, Berkshire. They came to Pococke's aid in 1655 when, as Rector of Childrey, he was accused of 'insufficiency'. However, his connection with them long predates his tenure at Childrey, for when he was at Constantinople from 1637 onwards his salary as Arabic Professor was transmitted to him by Charles Fettiplace, then one of the 'Assistants' at the Court of the Levant Company in London. This man had also been responsible for the choice of Pococke's predecessor as chaplain at Aleppo, having sent Robson out on his own initiative, much to the displeasure of the Governor and Court in London (which delayed paying Robson's salary for more than a year before confirming the appointment).[19] Charles Fettiplace himself went as a factor to Aleppo in 1626, and was the treasurer there for most of the time that Pococke was chaplain. I suspect, however, that the county connection between the Fettiplace and Pococke families was of long standing.

Pococke arrived at Scanderoon (Iskenderun, Alexandretta, the port of Aleppo) on 14 October 1630, and at Aleppo itself three days later.[20]

[18] PRO, SP 105,148, fos. 218ᵛ, 219ᵛ, excerpted by Holt, 'An Oxford Arabist', 4–5.

[19] PRO, SP 105,148, fos. 119ʳ, 125ʳ, 138ʳ: 'the Court takeing into consideracion and understanding that hee was a man well deserueing that Place did not so much dislike of him as the manner of Mr ffetiplace his sending him without acquainting the Company.'

[20] Twells could not ascertain when he left England. Wood, *History of the Levant Company*, 211, says that 'general ships' usually sailed before 1 June. But a con-

It was customary for the chaplain to live in the consul's house, and Wandesford's account of his familiarity with Pococke may be taken as confirmation that the two did indeed live together. Twells's narrative of Pococke's years in Aleppo is rather thin, which suggests that comparatively few letters from that period were preserved.[21] We may believe, as Twells asserts, that he carried out his ministerial duties conscientiously, but all the time that he could claim as his own must have been devoted to improving his knowledge of oriental languages. These included Syriac, Ethiopic, and Hebrew. For the latter he employed a Rabbi Samuel as a teacher, but seems to have derived little satisfaction from him or other Jewish instructors. Most of his efforts, however, were directed towards Arabic. To improve his knowledge of the spoken language he hired a native speaker called Ḥamīd to be his personal attendant, and for the literary language made an arrangement with a Muslim 'shaykh' called Fatḥallāh,[22] with whom he became very friendly. He also got to know some educated Arabic-speaking Christians, including Michael Thaljah, a professional scribe who was brother of the Greek Orthodox bishop at Aleppo. Either in Aleppo or during his later stay in Constantinople, he made the acquaintance of another professional scribe, Nicolaus Petri, whom we will meet again later in England.

Besides his intensive study of Arabic language and literature, Pococke began to assemble the magnificent collection of manuscripts which was to become one of the chief ornaments of the Bodleian Library after his death. Since he continued to collect manuscripts through agents for the whole of his life, it is not in general possible to

temporary source (Ravius in Vossius, *Epistolae*, ii, no. 295) says that in 1640 the general ship would sail from Dover at the end of July or the beginning of August. Even with the earlier date, a voyage of 20 weeks, although long, was not unthinkable. The ship *Sampson* took 17 weeks to sail from Smyrna to London in 1641 (Ravius, *Discourse*, 69). In 1668 Thomas Smith, on the ship taking the ambassador to Constantinople, records that it took three and a half months to travel from the Downs to Smyrna (Smith, '*Journal of a Voyage from* England *to* Constantinople').

[21] Smith, *An Account of the Greek Church*, 287, says that Pococke's copy of the letter he sent to Laud about the death of Cyril Lucaris 'was unhappily lost in the time of the Civil Wars'. Probably Pococke's correspondence suffered other losses at that time.

[22] Holt, 'An Oxford Arabist', 23 n. 9, says that this man has been identified by Sāmī al-Kaylānī (*Ṣafḥa min ta'rīkh Ḥalab al-adabī*, 8) as the poet Fatḥallāh al-Ḥalabī, called ibn al-Naḥḥās. Not having seen that work, I do not know what the grounds for this identification are, but it seems utterly implausible, since the poet died at Medina in 1642, whereas Huntington wrote to Pococke from Aleppo in 1671 that his 'old scheich', who died 'several years since', remembered Pococke with his last breath. It is inconceivable that this could refer to an event that took place nearly thirty years before in another country.

determine when he acquired any particular item. However, those manuscripts which were copied by or acquired through 'al-Darwīsh Aḥmad' certainly belong to the earlier stages of his career.[23] This engaging and enterprising character lived in Aleppo, where documents from 1626 to at least 1638 attest to his activities in copying and also trading in manuscripts. This has long been known from his published correspondence with Golius,[24] which shows that he acted as the latter's agent for buying manuscripts after he returned to Leiden. He also transcribed manuscripts for Golius between 1627 and 1629, when Golius was in Aleppo, notably the copy of the famous manuscript of Apollonius' *Conics*.[25] It may have been Golius who first brought this dervish to Aleppo, since in another letter[26] to him Aḥmad complains that Golius had persuaded him to leave his home, received instruction from him, and then dismissed him 'with the shoes of Ḥunayn' (i.e. empty-handed). More recently Holt has summarized and partially translated five letters from the dervish to Pococke that survive in MS Pococke 432.[27] These date from the period after Pococke had returned to Oxford and while he was on his later visit to Constantinople (i.e. between 1636 and 1638–40). Since Aḥmad occasionally addresses Pococke as his 'dear pupil', we may presume that he instructed him too in Arabic. The letters are full of interest for the traffic in books at Aleppo, but one extract must serve as an example for all.

Truly the most decorative are the necklaces of words which decorate the necks of papers, and the most beautiful are what the pickaxes of pens extract from the mines of souls. Salutation spreads its fragrance like amber [etc.] . . . Besides this, there arrived the desired letter, written in the fairest style, so we were refreshed because of its arrival and satisfied with the scent of its lush-

[23] Wakefield, 'Arabic Manuscripts in the Bodleian Library', 142 n. 86, lists three manuscripts of Arabic poetry belonging to Pococke that were copied by the dervish.

[24] Houtsma, *Oostersche Correspondentie*, 48–50.

[25] The copy was finished, according to the subscription, on Friday 15 Dhū 'l-Hijja AH 1036 (corresponding to 17 Aug. 1627). This was made for Golius before Leleu de Wilhem bought the original for him, on 19 Sept. of that year. Golius deposited the copy in the Leiden Library, where it is now MS Or. 14(1), and kept the original for himself (now MS Marsh 667 in the Bodleian).

[26] MS Leiden Or. 1228, no. 90. I know this only from the summary of Houtsma, *Oostersche Correspondentie*, 49–50.

[27] Holt, 'Arabic Historians in Seventeenth-Century England', 42–5. A very inaccurate translation of the introduction to the first of these, done by the younger Edward Pococke after his father's death, was printed long ago by Twells, 31–3. Twells's notion that 'the poor Dervise Ahmed' might be the same person as Pococke's house-servant 'Hamed' may be dismissed out of hand, since Aḥmad was a man of education who was far above menial labour.

ness: it took the place of spring and the smell . . . And we understood its contents, and what answers you sought in it. And if you ask about us, to God the
praise and favour, we are well and safe, and we ask God that you may be likewise. However, since we were separated, it is as if we were separated from a
brother or a child, or the spirit which is in the liver. But perfect joy came to us
when we heard the news of your health and of your arrival in your country. So
we praised God, who brought you to your people in health and safety, and his
abundant favour. And we inform you also that we have taken to wife a camel-
woman to be a help in our affairs; and that we[28] have obtained Ikhwān al-Ṣafā',
[the copy] which you saw previously, an illustrated one, for sixty piastres. We
have obtained it at this price only because Guglielmo[29] asked us for it as that
one which you saw on the day you travelled from Aleppo was unobtainable, so
that you may know. As for the history of al-Jannābī the judge, some quires of
which you saw and said to me that I must take it to the consul when I had
finished writing it out, when it is finished, we will take it to him, if God on
high wills. The commentary on the *Gulistan* has been completed and I have
sent it to you. If God on high wills I shall strive on your behalf in sending the
history of ibn Khallikān and *Ma'āhid al-Tanṣīṣ*, and I will send you every
book which in my opinion is suitable for you. You must send us a reply to
this letter and with it something of the rarities of your home and send us the
printed geography.[30] And whatever requirements you have in this respect, send
and let me know about them, so that I may successfully accomplish them.

The poor Dervish Aḥmad

In a later letter Aḥmad explains with relish how he outbid the
brother of Golius the Fleming for a book that both Golius and Pococke
wanted. This man was Petrus Golius, Jacobus' younger brother, who
was brought up by his maternal uncle, Johannes Hemelarius, at
Antwerp, and converted by him to Catholicism at an early age. He
joined the order of the barefoot Carmelites, adopting the name
'Celestinus de Sancta Liduina'. Like his brother, he studied Arabic, but
in his case for missionary purposes, in the pursuit of which he came
out to Aleppo before 1636, while Pococke was still there, and the two
became friends despite their rivalry over books and their confessional
differences. Forty years later another chaplain at Aleppo, Robert
Huntington, wrote to Pococke that Father Celestinus, on his way to

[28] From here to the end I follow Holt's translation (with slight variations). For the
books mentioned see Holt's notes ad loc.

[29] Holt interprets this as 'Girolamo', but the Arabic (جرليمو, جرليمو, or جليلمو) must
surely be interpreted as Guglermo or Guglielmo. In either case the man must have been,
as Holt says, a dragoman attached to the English factory.

[30] This must be the Medicean Press edition (*Nuzhat al-Mushtāq*, 1592) of the geographical work of al-Idrīsī, rather than, as Holt says, the 1619 Latin translation, which
would have been of no interest to the dervish.

missionary work in India, 'made Mr. Huntington a visit, on purpose to understand the Doctor's welfare' and 'enquired most affectionately after him'.[31]

We saw above that in 1631 Laud asked Pococke to buy manuscripts for him that would be appropriate for the university library. Twells was unable to say whether any of the oriental manuscripts which the archbishop later gave to the Bodleian were acquired in this way, and doubtfully conjectures that none were. The more recent investigations of Hunt and Wakefield have also failed to disclose any proven examples. However, it seems likely that the fairly large numbers of manuscripts in Laud's collection with the acquisition dates of 1633 and 1635 reflect Pococke's activity on his behalf (just as the big influx in 1638 is certainly the result of Pococke and Greaves being in Constantinople).[32] Moreover, it is apparent that after 1634 Pococke personally supervised the dispatch (and no doubt the choice) of the manuscripts which by the King's letter of that year each of the Levant Company's ships were to bring back for Laud. This is shown by a letter of Turner to the archbishop of 25 July 1636:[33] while Turner and Pococke were unpacking the recent consignment of manuscripts which Laud had sent to the Bodleian, Pococke had noticed that two books were missing, and encloses for Laud's information a note of their titles and value. Turner remarks: 'It seemes but a slouenly part to present the furnishing of your Grace with rarities in this kind, & then to suppresse the best of them.' That this is a reference to the Levant Company's 'tribute' is made certain by Pococke's addition: 'The latter brought to the Gouernour of the Turkey Merchants this summer, the former more than twelve months since.' For the King's letter had specified that the books brought back on the company's ships were 'to be delyuered presently to the Master of your Company' in London.

While in Aleppo Pococke was also engaged in actually preparing editions of Arabic texts. On 12 September 1635 he completed an edition and Latin translation of some 6,000 proverbs collected by al-Maydānī.[34] He had presumably chosen this as his first effort because it was a type of Arabic text made familiar in Europe by the publications of Scaliger, Erpenius, and Golius. In the report on his progress in

---

[31] Twells, 300. Father Celestinus' passage through Basra is recorded by Huntington's correspondent there, Agathangelus a S. Theresia (Gollancz, *Chronicle of Events relating to the Order of Carmelites in Mesopotamia*, 17–18).

[32] See above, p. 110.

[33] PRO, SP 16,329, no. 39, fo. 64^r.

[34] Now MS Pococke 392. See Holt, 'An Oxford Arabist', 5.

Aleppo that he sent to Vossius after his return to Oxford he expressed hopes of publishing it,[35] and soon after, when about to leave for his second journey to the East, he entered in the manuscript of his edition an indication that it might be published in the future:

> If it please God that I returne not otherwise to dispose of this translation of Proverbes I desire that it may be put in the Archives of Corpus Christi College Library. there though very rude and imperfect to be kept for some helpe of those that study the Arabicke language. hopeing that Mr. Thomas Greaves or some other may at some time perfect the worke for an edition. per me Edwardus Pococke April 10th. 1637.[36]

Yet it was never published, despite efforts by his friends and pupils later in the century.[37] The reason was that in the mean time, while still at Aleppo, he had found something which interested him far more. In the same letter to Vossius he describes this as 'historia quaedam compendiosa à creatione ad annum Hegirae ultra 600um, Saracenicae isti Erpenianae et stili elegantiâ et iudicio (si quid ego censeam) longè praeferenda'. This was the 'History of the Dynasties' of Gregorius Abū 'l-Faraj (also known as Bar Hebraeus), a Christian author of a late date (thirteenth century), but valuable because he used older Islamic sources, such as the Fihrist, which were then completely unknown in Europe. As an account of Islamic history, both political and literary, it is far superior to what was available in Europe at the time, the jejune chronicle of al-Makīn published in 1625 by Erpenius (as Pococke indicated in his letter to Vossius), or the partial and unreliable Eutychius (later to appear by the efforts of Selden). Pococke was to spend much of the next twelve years working on his elucidations of Abū 'l-Faraj, work which was to culminate in his masterpiece, *Specimen Historiae Arabum*, and eventually he would publish the whole text.[38]

He had already stayed at Aleppo well beyond the time originally envisaged, but was still unsatisfied with what he had achieved. It may only have been the direct command of Laud that finally moved him to return. The archbishop, anxious to settle the Arabic Professorship at Oxford, wrote to Pococke, probably late in 1635, informing him that he had chosen him for that post, and ordering him to return soon. Accordingly, Pococke embarked on a ship going to England via Italy,

---

[35] 5 Dec. 1636 (MS Rawlinson letters 83, fo. 155, printed in Vossius, *Epistolae*, no. 239).

[36] Holt, 'An Oxford Arabist', 23 n. 10, cf. Twells, 44.

[37] See below, p. 271. A small specimen of Pococke's work was published by H. A. Schultens in 1773: Schnurrer no. 223.

[38] Pococke, *Abū 'l-Faraj*.

and arrived in Oxford in time to take his BD on 8 July 1636.[39] There he also resumed his Fellowship at Corpus and was formally installed in the Arabic Lectureship, for which, on 10 August, he delivered his inaugural lecture. Unfortunately this is lost, except for a small portion which was printed at the end of his edition of *Carmen Tograi* in 1661, 'so as not to leave an empty page'. Interestingly, in contrast to the themes of the inaugural lecture of his predecessor Pasor and his successors Thomas Greaves and even Thomas Hunt in the eighteenth century,[40] this excerpt dwells on the love of the ancient Arabs for poetry. Pococke seemed to be well launched in his scholarly career at Oxford, and would in all probability have pursued it there tranquilly, but for the intervention of John Greaves.

---

[39] The date when he left Aleppo is not recorded by Twells. From the surviving records of the Levant Company all that can be gleaned is that it must be earlier than 25 Apr. 1636, on which date a will was witnessed at Aleppo by Pococke's successor, the minister 'Thomas Prichett' (PRO, SP 110,54, fo. 216ʳ).

[40] *De Antiquitate, Elegantia, Utilitate, Linguæ Arabicæ, Oratio Habita Oxonii, in Schola Linguarum, VII Kalend. Augusti, MDCCXXXVIII* (Oxford, 1739).

6

Greaves and Pococke in the East

ONE of the most interesting characters in the intellectual history of that most interesting of English centuries, the seventeenth, was John Greaves. His enormous energy, curiosity, and breadth of vision combined to make him extremely effective in extending the bounds of scholarship. Generous to his friends, he could be ruthless in promoting their and his own interests, and in so doing he aroused enmities which eventually cost him all of his academic positions. However, it was not his loss of these, but rather his early death (at the age of 50) which prevented him from fulfilling his ambitious plans. His published work, although far from contemptible, is but a promise of what he might have achieved had he lived another ten or twenty years.

(i) EARLY TRAVELS OF GREAVES

Greaves[1] was born in 1602, the eldest of the four sons of John Greaves, Rector of Colmore near Alresford in Hampshire, and his wife Sara. He matriculated at Balliol College on 12 December 1617, but was at St Mary Hall when he graduated BA on 6 July 1621.[2] In 1624 he was placed first in the fellowship examinations for Merton College, where he remained for the rest of his academic career. Evidently he was awarded one of the 'secular' fellowships, for, unlike most of his academic contemporaries, he was never ordained. It was at Merton that he developed his interests in mathematics and astronomy (taught and encouraged by his colleagues Briggs and Bainbridge), and in oriental

[1] A full biography of John Greaves, which, besides his travels, should include his intellectual activities in astronomy, geography, mathematics, metrology, Egyptology, and the history of science, all of which were connected with his oriental studies, is an urgent desideratum. The short biography by Thomas Smith in his *Vitae* is superficial and erroneous, but incorporates some useful material which Edward Bernard assembled on his great predecessor in the Savilian Chair of Astronomy. The unassuming account by John Ward in his *Lives of the Professors of Gresham College*, 135–53, is more accurate, and the life prefixed by Birch to his edition of Greaves's *Works* (i, pp. i–lxxii) adds some more details. On Greaves as an Egyptologist see below, p. 167. On the astronomical aspect of his oriental interests much useful material is presented in a muddled way by Mercier, 'English Orientalists and Mathematical Astronomy', 161–77.

[2] Foster, *Alumni Oxonienses*, ii. 596.

languages (under the influence of Turner and again of Bainbridge). In January 1631 Henry Briggs died, and Turner (then Professor of Geometry at Gresham College) was chosen to succeed him as Savilian Professor of Geometry at Oxford. Greaves applied for the post that Turner had vacated, and it is not surprising that he obtained it,[3] for he was supported by recommendations not only from Bainbridge, Turner, William Boswell, and the Warden of Merton, Sir Nathaniel Brent,[4] but also from the Archbishop of Canterbury, George Abbot, as well as from Laud, then Bishop of London but already one of the most influential men in the land.[5] After obtaining the Gresham Professorship Greaves, like Turner before him, retained his fellowship at Merton and continued to reside for the most part at Oxford, travelling to London in order to give his lectures at Gresham College. He seems to have treated the Gresham position, if not exactly as a sinecure, as a minor distraction from his scholarly pursuits. In his letter to Turner of 10 February 1637, he even claims that 'none of the Readers by the Founders will are obliged either by oath, or by any explicit promise, to the performance of anything'.[6] In the ten years following his appointment he was to be out of England on three separate journeys, for a total of about six years.

His interest in astronomy at this time is attested by eclipse observations that he made in Oxford from 1630 onwards and recorded in his notebook on 'Elementa omnium scientiarum, praesertim mathematicarum'.[7] It cannot be determined exactly when he began to learn Arabic and other oriental languages. We may guess that this too belongs to the early 1630s, since John Clerke, Bedwell's son-in-law, in dedicating the posthumous publication of the latter's *Via Regia ad Geometriam* to Greaves, says 'Your acquaintance with the Author before his death was not long'. This suggests that Greaves, in pursuit of his Arabic interest (and perhaps as a result of his journeys to London to lecture at Gresham College), sought out Bedwell in 1631. Interest in Arabic was probably also a primary motive for Greaves's first journey abroad in 1633. After being incorporated at Cambridge,

---

[3] Appointed 22 Feb. 1631.

[4] These are printed by Ward, *Gresham Professors*, 136.

[5] These testimonials are unpublished, but according to a personal communication from Prof. Feingold they are in the Gresham archives at Mercers' Hall in London.

[6] PRO, SP 16,381, fo. 159ᵛ.

[7] This is the title assigned by Ward, *Gresham Professors*, 149–50, who gives a good description of its multifarious contents. The notebook is now MS Smith 15. Some eclipse observations are excerpted from it by Mercier, 'English Orientalists and Mathematical Astronomy', 169–70.

he went to Holland and was enrolled as a student in 'Letters' at Leiden on 8 October.[8] It was almost certainly then that he attended Golius' Arabic lectures.[9] In any case, either on this occasion or when he returned to Leiden in 1636, he got to know Golius well enough to appeal to the 'old friendship between us at Leiden' in a letter he sent to him on 1 June 1642 introducing his younger brother Edward.[10]

I have not succeeded in determining at what date Greaves came back to Oxford from this journey, but there could only have been a short interval before he embarked on a longer, more ambitious, and far better documented voyage. On 31 July 1635, he obtained a passport certifying that

Whereas the bearer hereof John Greaues Master of Artes of the Universitie of Oxforde, is desirous to spend some tyme in the parts beyonde the Seas, the Better to enable him selfe to doe his Majesty and Country Service thereafter, and to that purpose hath humbly desired our Liecence and Passeporte to remayne there for the space of twoe yeares next ensuing the date hereof, wee hereby thinke fit to grant unto him, provided that he repaires not to the Citie of Rome without Liecence from his Majesty.[11]

Greaves took ship from Rye to Dieppe on 20 August,[12] and made his way to Paris, where he got to know Claude Hardy, with whom he maintained a friendly correspondence for the rest of his life. He also either attended Arabic lectures by Gabriel Sionita, or at least talked with him long enough to form an opinion about his competence in Arabic. We next find Greaves in Italy: on 10 November 1635 he enrolled as a student at the University of Padua, together with George Ent.[13] This man, who was to be his lifelong friend, became well known as a physician,[14] and was knighted in 1665. Greaves could not

[8] Innes Smith, *English-Speaking Students of Medicine at the University of Leyden*, 101. This first journey of Greaves is unknown to his 17th- and 18th-century biographers, but is proven beyond any doubt by the Leiden records.

[9] Golius later called Greaves 'auditor quondam meus' (Smith, *Vitae*, Life of Greaves, 38).

[10] MS Savile 47, fo. 53; 'pro veteri amicitiâ, quae inter nos Lugduni Batavorum intercessit'. From the same letter it appears that Greaves had also made the acquaintance at Leiden of the Persian scholar Louis de Dieu, the Hebraist Constantijn L'Empereur, and the two Boxhorns.

[11] PRO, SP 16,294, no. 64, the original passport carried by Greaves, with the signatures of Windebank and others.

[12] PRO, SP 318,21, fo. 43ʳ.

[13] Innes Smith, *English-Speaking Students*, 101. Greaves contributed verses to the volume celebrating Ent's graduation as MD at Padua in 1636 (*DNB* s.v. 'Sir George Ent', 795).

[14] He submitted Greaves's account of the method of incubating chicken eggs in ovens at Cairo to the *Transactions of the Philosophical Society* (Jan.–Feb. 1678).

have stayed in Padua long, for a letter from George Middleton to Thomas Greaves of 18 January 1636 informed him that his brother had been in Venice for some time. Characteristically, in spite of the prohibition in his passport, Greaves did go to Rome and talked to the Maronites there.[15] It was probably at Rome, before July 1636, that he encountered William Petty, the agent of the Earl of Arundel, who had already spent many years in Italy, Greece, and other Turkish dominions collecting books, paintings, statuary, and other antiquities for his master.[16] Greaves himself tells what followed:

When I was in Italy Mr Petty seeing me not altogether vncurious in observing buildings, pictures, statues, and antiquities, would faine haue enterteined me in his Lords service, to which purpose he offred me a liberal pension of 200 lb yearely, in his Lords name, and the expectation of more. It was his desire that for the present I should haue accompanied him in Italy, and this winter, or the next, to haue gone with him to Athens. I thank[ed] him for his profer; and required some time to consider of it. Afterwards I told him my resolutions were, as soone as ye heates would permit (for it was then July) to returne for England, and that I rather thought of making a iourny from thence to Constantinople, and so to Alexandria in Ægypt, where besides the meeting with Antiquities, and MSS (which in Italy are rare, and excessiue deare, by reason so many Cardinals and great men buy them at any price) I might improue those studies, which I had begun in the Orientall languages, and make some Astronomicall observations, a thing that hath beene much desired by the Astronomers of this age, but neuer vndertaken by any. He very much approued of my intentions, and would gladly haue persuaded me to haue vndertaken the voyage in his Lords name, with what conditions I would myselfe; which when he saw that I would not assent to he then proposed another course for the facilitating of the buisines.[17]

(II) GREAVES'S PLANS FOR A JOURNEY TO THE EAST

The interest of the above narrative lies not only in Petty's generous offer, but also in the indications that Greaves had already conceived the plans of travelling to the East for the triple purpose of collecting manuscripts, improving his knowledge of Arabic and other languages, and making astronomical observations. Reluctant to cut himself

[15] Letter to Pococke of 23 Dec. 1636.

[16] On Petty see e.g. Howarth, *Lord Arundel and his Circle*, ch. 6.

[17] Greaves to Turner, 10 Feb. 1637 (PRO, SP 16,381, fo. 159). Greaves had given much the same account in an earlier letter to Pococke, summarized by Twells, 39–40.

off from academic advancement by entering Arundel's service, he returned home, stopping at Leiden *en route*, where, as we saw, he inspected the oriental types which were later to be bought by Oxford. He was back in England late in 1636. There he found that Pococke had in the mean time returned from Aleppo. He immediately acquainted him with his own plans to travel in the East. This is the first we hear of the friendship between John Greaves and Pococke, but it was probably already of very long standing. Greaves's younger brother Thomas had entered Corpus as a scholar in 1627, and Pococke, although seven years his senior, and a fellow from 1628, was his friend, corresponded with him from Aleppo, taught him Arabic, and (in 1637, if not earlier) shared rooms with him in College. I suspect that Thomas Greaves had been put under Pococke's wing because the families were acquainted long previously.[18]

Petty had suggested to Greaves that 'he should, by the Archbishop's means, go consul to Aleppo, and procure leave of the Grand Seignior to have a consular power at Alexandria, as often as he should go thither',[19] but he wanted to ask his friend's advice about it before approaching Laud. No doubt Pococke informed him that the consulship was no sinecure, for that plan was soon abandoned; but Pococke also seems to have indicated his own interest in returning to the East, for in his next letter, of 23 December 1636,[20] Greaves is already busy with plans for the two of them to travel there together. The motives of both men for undertaking this journey, Greaves's schemes for financing it and dealing with the awkward fact that both would be absent for a long time from their academic duties, and the inducements he offered, especially to Laud, to facilitate this, appear best in an extraordinarily interesting long letter that he sent to Turner on 10 February 1637, from which I have already cited several passages.[21] After praising the archbishop's bounty in providing Oxford with oriental types and manuscripts, Greaves expresses the hope that 'some of those

[18] In his will John Greaves bequeathed to Pococke 'in memorie of his and of his ffathers ffreindshipp one of my best gold rings' (PRO, PROB 11,223, fo. 147ᵛ). Richard Pococke, grandfather of the famous traveller of the same name, and a distant relative of Edward, was Rector of Colmore in Hampshire in 1660, as John Greaves's father had been earlier in the century.

[19] Twells, 40.

[20] Quoted verbatim by Twells, 42–3, and (more fully) by Ward, *Gresham Professors*, 137–8.

[21] PRO, SP 16,381, no. 75, fo. 159. The reason that the letter survives in the Public Record Office is that Turner passed it on to Laud (as Greaves intended), and that it was confiscated with the rest of Laud's papers in 1643, after the archbishop's impeachment.

incomparable peeces of the East' may be published. For this he knows 'no man so able, or more willing to serue my Lord, then Mr Pococke, who hauing liued some yeares in those Countries, and being furnished with good abilities before he undertooke his iourny, doth as far exceede Golius, and Sionita, and the best maisters of Europe, as they exceede other men'. This is high praise indeed (even if partial) from one who had personally encountered both Golius and Sionita. However, he proceeds, Pococke is dissatisfied with himself, and

confesses that, in the translation of Gregorius Abulpharagius his history out of Arabicke into Latine, which he intends to dedicate to my Lords Grace, he is often to seeke, often, I say, in matters of Geography of the remoter parts of Asia, often in the lineal descents of many of the gret monarches there, of which the Greekes, and Latines hitherto, as you are best able to iudge, haue beene vtterly ignorant. His desires therefore are, with submission to his Graces pleasure, once more to goe into those Parts, and to get farther light for the perfit edition of that same excellent authour, with which he is in hand.

After explaining why his distractions at Aleppo prevented Pococke from doing this, Greaves considers the financial side:

Yet doth he not desire by this iourny to draw any greater expense vpon his Grace, then what his Grace hath already beene pleased to bestowe vpon him, or els in lieu of this the addition, if it might be, of some Prebendary, or some good living sine curâ: so that his purpose is the labour shall be his owne, and the honour my Lords. To whome I conceiue it will be a greater honour, to employ a man of such eminent parts in forrein Countries, vnder the title of procuring Bookes, as the States did Golius . . . then it can be in staying at home, and making Profession of a bare language.

That is, Laud should allow Pococke at least his salary while he is on leave, in return for Pococke's buying manuscripts for him. The problem of delivering the Arabic lecture while Pococke is away is easily solved: Greaves's brother Thomas[22] will take his place, for a suitable reward:

And yet I would not that the Profession of so learned a tongue, and for which after times will blesse my Lords memory, should cease, and therefore I dare undertake that my brother of C. C. C. shall most willingly supply Mr Pocockes absence, if my Lord so please, without any farther reward, then that my Lord will graciously protect him in his right to the next Living in the Charter House

---

[22] John Greaves was always eager to promote his family's interest: in 1643, after Bainbridge's death, while he himself succeeded to the Savilian Professorship of Astronomy, his youngest brother Edward, who had the necessary medical qualifications, took Bainbridge's place as Senior Linacre Lecturer in Physic at Merton.

gift, which God and the Founder hath giuen him, by being the seniour scholar of that Foundation.

Greaves next turns to his own plans. After recounting his meeting with Petty in Italy and the offer to enter the Earl of Arundel's service, he says that instead

I intend to lay out 250 lb of my owne, in making the fairest and largest instruments of brasse that I can procure, and if I had more, more I would expend. For my maintenance abroad for 3 or 4 yeares for my selfe, and a man to assist me, I thinke my stipend here,[23] my allowance from Merton College a litle enlarged, and 20 lb a yeare that I shall receiue from my mother, with that frugality which I have vsed, may in a reasonable manner be sufficient. The greatest difficulty will be the being assured of Sir Thomas Greshams stipend, since the court of Aldermen gaue order it should not be payd in my absence in Italy, though I deputed my brother[24] in my place. . . . But I suppose by his Maiesties gracious dispensation, there anger, or at least the sting of it, may be avoided: and I do verily beleeue that if the honourable Founder were now aliue, he would haue giuen mee a speciall liberty, for such ends as I proposed, to goe, as I did, into Italy, and as I now intend the next August into Constantinople, without defalcation of halfe my stipend by a deputation.

After requesting Turner's good offices with Laud on behalf of himself and Pococke '(for I know my Lord deservedly loues and respects you)', he adds as a final inducement the promise quoted above,[25] that while at Constantinople he would make sure that the ordinance for the Levant Company's ships to bring back Arabic manuscripts was enforced, and would recommend choice manuscripts to the merchants' notice.

These applications, no doubt backed by Turner, had the desired effect. On 28 July 1637 Laud curtly informed the Vice-Chancellor: 'Sir, Mr. Greaves of C.C.C. began to read the Arabic lecture upon Wednesday July 19, as deputy to Mr. Pocock, to whom I gave leave to travel to Constantinople and the eastern parts for the better perfecting himself in the Arabic and Eastern languages, and I allowed him the stipend of the lecture towards his travels.'[26] How Thomas Greaves was compensated for his three years' stint of Deputy Professor of Arabic is not known.[27] He may have had to be contented with the 'preferments

---

[23] In London, at Gresham College. [24] Probably Nicholas Greaves.
[25] p. 108. [26] Laud, *Works* v/1, 176–7.
[27] A year before, Turner had suggested to Laud that Thomas Greaves might replace Pococke on a permanent basis. On 25 July 1636 (while John Greaves was still abroad, but certainly at his instigation) he wrote: 'If your Grace shall hereafter provide some preferment for [Pococke], which will call him from the Lecture, he hath a chamber-

bestowed on him' mentioned in a letter from Charles Fettiplace to Pococke in 1640.[28] Pococke, besides his professor's salary and his allowance for his Corpus fellowship, paid part of his expenses by some private trading in bales of cloth exported to Constantinople on the Levant Company's ships. This was possible only because a special privilege was granted him by the company's London court (no doubt also at Laud's insistence).[29] Even so, he was obliged to spend much money of his own, as he wrote to the Parliament in 1645 after it had sequestered Laud's estates: 'to qualify himself better for this employment, he had been at the hazard of a voyage to Constantinople, the necessary expences of which amounted to a sum sufficient, even for the purchase of a revenue for life, of much greater value.'[30] Greaves too undertook the voyage at considerable personal expense, for the help which he hoped to obtain from London merchants was not forthcoming, as he wrote to Turner from Constantinople on 2 August 1638:

Since the city of London failing me in my expectation of their contributions towards mathematical instruments, I have been necessitated to sell most of the bookes I brought with me. But the love and care of my brothers straining their owne occasions to supply mine, have enabled me, in despight of the city, to go on with my designs.[31]

(III) GREAVES AND POCOCKE AT CONSTANTINOPLE

The two friends embarked together on a ship going to Constantinople early in July 1637. At Livorno, however, Greaves got off to go to Rome, leaving Pococke to travel by himself 'in the prison of his ship' to Constantinople. Here he spent the next three years, living in Galata

fellowe, Mr Greaues, allready by his owne industry & his Brothers helps communicated from beyond seas, so well initiated in that Language that by Mr Pococks assistance, which he imparts to him very freely, I make no doubt but that you may be provided of a fitt successor in his roome, whensoever it shall become voide' (PRO, SP 16,329, no. 39, fo. 64ʳ).

[28] Twells, 74. These preferments, which certainly included the rectorship of Dunsby in Lincolnshire, were presumably the work of Laud.

[29] PRO, SP 105,149, fo. 157ᵛ (Court of 19 May 1638): 'Mr. Fettiplace moued the Court on the behalfe of Dominico the Secretary at Constantinople, that they would permit 20 clothes to be laden for his account free of Imposicions, which is consented unto. And the like is also graunted for 7 clothes for the use of Mr Pocock the late preacher at Aleppo, he being now in Turky upon some employment for his Majesty.'

[30] Twells, 99–100. Twells, 74, states that Pococke's stay in Constantinople 'had cost him between five and six hundred pounds'.

[31] MS Savile 47, fo. 45, printed in Greaves, *Works*, ii. 434–8.

in the house of the ambassador,[32] to whom he and Greaves had been recommended by Laud. He occupied himself principally with his studies and with collecting books and manuscripts both for himself and for Laud. In seeking out native teachers he found the situation different from Aleppo: there he had enjoyed the conversation of learned Arabs, but got little satisfaction from the Jews, whereas in Constantinople he had difficulty in finding some learned Turk to converse with, but encountered several educated Jews, whom he employed to buy and transcribe books. In particular he enjoyed the company of the Jewish scholar Jacob Roman, with whom he discussed the Christian sects, and whom he later praised as 'second to none, among the Jews whom I have known, in learning or integrity (ingenuitate)'.[33] It was probably he who first inspired Pococke's lifelong interest in Judaeo-Arabic, for Roman was an expert in Arabic as well as Hebrew, and planned to print Maimonides' *Guide of the Perplexed* in Arabic, Hebrew, and Latin at Constantinople.[34] Moreover, he was familiar with ibn Ṭufayl's *Ḥayy ibn Yaqẓān* not only in the Hebrew translation but in the Arabic original, and possessed the *Maqāmāt* of al-Ḥarīrī in Arabic and in a partial Hebrew translation, all of which suggest connections with Pococke.[35] In the pursuit of manuscripts Pococke was also aided at Constantinople by Domenico Timone, the experienced secretary of the Levant Company;[36] by Nathaniel Conopius (Protosyncellus of Patriarch Cyril Lucaris);[37] and by Giorgio Cerigo, a physician in

[32] Namely first Sir Peter Wyche (for whom Pococke served as chaplain) and after October 1638 his successor Sir Sackville Crowe.

[33] Pococke, *Porta Mosis*, 90. On Roman's acquisition of manuscripts for Pococke and his later correspondence with him see Roth, 'Edward Pococke and the First Hebrew Printing in Oxford'.

[34] Letter of Roman to the younger Buxtorf printed by Kayserling, 'Richelieu, Buxtorf père et fils, Jacob Roman', 93–4. The plan was never carried out. For Pococke's own abortive plan to do the same thing see below, p. 277.

[35] Kayserling, 91. On Pococke and ibn Ṭufayl's work see below, p. 218. Pococke's manuscript of al-Ḥarīzī's Hebrew translation of the *Maqāmāt* (the only one known to Steinschneider, *Die hebräischen Übersetzungen*, 851), MS Poc. 50 (Neubauer no. 1976), from which the work was published by Chenery in 1872, is almost certainly the very one mentioned by Roman in his letter to Buxtorf of 1633, since it too breaks off half-way through. Other Pococke manuscripts owned by Jacob Roman include nos. 131, 134, and 343 (Neubauer nos. 1345, 1453, and 1322).

[36] His name appears frequently in the Levant Company records. In the report of his death to the London court on 15 Apr. 1649, mention is made 'of his long service even from a Child and totall dependance on the Company, and of his great and generall experience: as well in the way of an Interpreter, as otherwise' (PRO, SP 105,112, fo. 48ʳ).

[37] This man came to England after Cyril's death, and was settled by Laud in Balliol: Twells, 55–6. Like Pococke, he was one of the earliest coffee-drinkers in Oxford: Wood, *Life and Times*, ii. 334.

Galata who also helped Greaves with his astronomical observations. However, Pococke was also greatly assisted by his old friends in Aleppo. Besides the dervish Aḥmad, Pococke's 'sheikh' Fatḥallāh, and Michael Thaljah and his brother the bishop, the English merchants William Corderoy and Richard Hill were active on his behalf.

In the mean time Greaves, having spent some time in Rome (where he again saw Petty and explored monuments with him),[38] had by December 1637 arrived in Constantinople and joined Pococke in the ambassador's house. He stayed there less than a year, and, like Pococke, was disappointed in his hopes of finding a suitable teacher of Arabic, but the letters he wrote from Constantinople (and other incidental information) reveal that he was very active. In a letter sent probably to Turner after he had been in Constantinople five months he says:[39] 'tho' I have sent to many places, and gone my selfe to some, yet have I not seen, besides Liturgies and some few imperfect pieces of the fathers, any thing worthy the taking up. And yet the Greeks would have me believe, that at Mount Athos, where there are some 3000 Monks, that they have store of MSS.' Greaves is sceptical whether there is anything worth his trouble there, but at this time had hopes of the library in the Seraglio, where, he had been assured by the Patriarch, was still kept 'the Library of the Greek Emperors, in which were also many Latin MSS'. He continues:

In my inquiry after Turkish and Arabick books I have been a little more fortunate, than in those of Greek, tho' with some danger. For finding my selfe often cheated by the brokers, who are Jews, whom I secretly imployed, I ventured once or twice to the shops, where the Turks sell them, where I have bought some few, tho' at excessive prices, and might have had many more choice copies, if I had had sufficient mony to have disbursd. . . . These books, when it pleases God that I return home, I shall lay them down at his Grace's feet. Onely two of them besides some other small traces, I hope, I shall be able to publish, if I could find better Masters, than I have hitherto don. Those are Abulfeda his Geography in Arabick, and Ulug Beg his canons and Astronomical tables in Persian.

Despite his doubts about the manuscripts on Mount Athos, Greaves intended to go there, but his plans were spoiled by the sudden

---

[38] See Howarth, *Lord Arundel and his Circle*, 138. Ward, *Gresham Professors*, 138 is right in saying that Smith (*Vitae*, Life of Greaves, 8) has assigned events from Greaves's travels in Italy on his way back from the East to his journey out; but he is wrong in denying that Greaves stopped in Italy at all in 1637.

[39] Greaves's draft of this letter is in MS BL Add. 34727, fo. 63. There is a copy in MS Smith 93, pp. 137–8.

execution of Patriarch Cyril Lucaris. In his letter announcing this catastrophe,[40] he says:

having procured out of a blinde and ignorant Monastery, which depends upon the Patriarchate, 14 good MSS. of the Fathers, I was compelled privatly to restore the bookes, and loose my mony, for feare of a worse inconvenience. Yet if P.S.P.K. Cyrill had lived a litle longer, I might have sent to my Lord's Grace, not only these, but many other choice copies without any extraordinary expense. For my purpose was to have gone to mount Athos, . . . whither I should have been recommended by the Patriarke, and have had liberty of entring into all the libraries in that place, to have collected a catalogue of such bookes, as either were not printed, or els, by the help of some there, might have been more correctly sett out. These (by dispensing with the anathemas which former Patriarkes have layd upon all Greeke library's, thereby to preserve the books from the Latines) the Patriarke purposed to have presented to his Grace, for the better prosecution of his Grace's honourable designes in the edition of Greeke Authors.

Greaves goes on to narrate how he had supervised the dispatch by the Levant Company of some Arabic manuscripts to Laud, but that they had been unwilling to pay the price for 'very choice ones' (some of which he had himself bought). He promises to have

most of the Greeke Mathematicians, translated into Arabicke, brought home and, it may be, some of those, that are lost in the Greeke, stil extant in the Arabick.[41] Amongst others, I have procured Ptolemies almagest, the fairest book that I have ever seene, stolne by a Spahy (as I am informed) out of the King's Library in the Serraglio.[42]

We shall see that Greaves did manage to bring back a remarkable collection of manuscripts from the East. Despite the difficulties he experienced in getting the Levant Company to send the Arabic manuscripts which they owed the archbishop, the joint efforts of himself and Pococke resulted in a large accession of oriental manuscripts to Laud's

[40] MS Savile 47, fo. 45, printed in Greaves, *Works*, ii. 434–8. Birch's conjecture there that the addressee was Peter Turner is certainly correct. Kemke, *Patricius Junius*, 85–6 printed the letter from Thomas Smith's copy in the mistaken belief that it was sent to Patrick Young.

[41] See below, p. 177.

[42] According to Ravius, in a letter written to Isaac Vossius from Constantinople (MS d'Orville 470, p. 279), this was a Greek manuscript (which Greaves had obtained from Cerigo). However, Greaves's words above surely imply that it was Arabic. In that case it must be the Arabic manuscript which Hottinger saw in Greaves's library in 1641 and described as 'opusculum *Arabicum* Astronomicum, adeò eleganter exaratum, ut vix credam, simile inter Christianos Europaeos reperiri. Bibliotheca Imperatoria dignum!' (*Bibliothecarius Quadripartitus*, 31). I fear that it was one of the manuscripts irretrievably lost in the ransacking of Greaves's rooms during the Civil War.

collection. This is best seen by the number of Arabic and other oriental manuscripts which Laud acquired in 1638.[43] Furthermore, the exceptionally large sum of £50 which Laud paid to Daniel Harvey in that same year[44] is certainly connected with the dispatch of manuscripts from Constantinople. For Harvey was a prominent member of the Levant Company in London,[45] as well as being a friend of Laud,[46] and was thus well placed to act as intermediary in transferring the funds being spent by Laud in the East. A manuscript in Laud's collection of the Persian translation of al-Ṭabarī's history has an inscription stating that it was bought at Constantinople by John Greaves, and given to Laud 'together with many other Arabic, Persian and Greek manuscripts'.[47] We may believe that Greaves did obtain many other manuscripts for Laud, but his straitened finances, by his own account, would not have allowed him to 'give' them to the archbishop, who must have reimbursed him.

(IV) GREAVES'S JOURNEY TO EGYPT AND ITALY

Greaves's other main purpose in his eastern journey was to make astronomical observations. In this he was carrying out the programme of his mentor Bainbridge (which both, perhaps, had derived from Sir Henry Savile himself). The observations were of two kinds. Firstly, he wanted to determine precisely the latitudes of places which were significant in ancient astronomy, notably Constantinople (Byzantium), Rhodes (where Hipparchus had observed), and Alexandria (where Ptolemy's observations were made). He and Bainbridge hoped that this would enable them to evaluate the ancient observations that had been transmitted. For this purpose Greaves carried observational instruments with him, and at least one more was sent out to him later.[48] With these

---

[43] See above, p. 110.

[44] Hunt, *Laudian Manuscripts*, p. xxxiii.

[45] He was chosen assistant to the court in London on 5 Feb. 1638 (together with Charles Fettiplace): PRO, SP 105,149, fo. 145ᵛ. He was a brother of the famous physician William Harvey, and his son, Sir Daniel Harvey, took Pococke's pupil Thomas Smith with him as his chaplain when he went to Constantinople as ambassador in 1668.

[46] See Wood, *History of the Levant Company*, 128 n. 3.

[47] MS Laud Or. 323. See Hunt, *Laudian Manuscripts*, p. xiv, and Wakefield, 'Arabic Manuscripts in the Bodleian Library', 140 n. 24. As Wakefield notes, this is the manuscript mentioned by Twells (p. 86) among those given by Laud in 1640 as 'Persick . . . written in very large folio, contain[ing] the History of the World'. Cf. Hunt, p. xxx.

[48] This was the 'brass quadrant of 7 feet radius' with which he observed the altitude

he did in fact find new values for the latitudes of those three places, which were considerably more accurate than those of the ancient astronomers, except for that of Rhodes.[49] The second type of observation which Greaves planned was simultaneous sightings of eclipses (preferably lunar eclipses) performed in places far distant from each other. The purpose of this was the determination of longitudes and ultimately the improvement of contemporary maps. This type of observation required considerable advance planning and organization, and it is interesting to read the evidence for this kind of activity in his letters. Writing to Turner in August 1638 he says:

the eclipse of the moone in December next will be observed (if it please God) at Bagdad, Constantinople, Smyrna, and Alexandria: All which places I have furnised with convenient instruments, and given them instructions according to Tycho Brahe's, how they should observe. I presume at Bagdad it will be punctually and carefully done, since the Physician to the King's Favorite, a Christian, hath undertaken the busines, who hopes to get reputation by doing of it in the sight of the Grand Segnore and of his army. I doubt not it will be as carefully observed in England, and could wish (as by my letters I earnestly desired) that at the same time observations might be made at the Azôres.[50]

Greaves was not as successful as he hoped in this, since for the eclipse in question (10/20 December 1638) he records in his notebook, besides his own observation at Alexandria, only those made by Panagiotes in Constantinople and by Samuel Foster in Coventry.[51] This may also be the eclipse mentioned by Greaves in an (undated) letter to Pococke from Egypt: 'He desired him [Pococke] to be careful in procuring for him several observations, especially of eclipses, which were to be made by Dr. Cerigo, at Galata, by a Ragusa doctor, who went with the

of Spica at Alexandria in April 1639 (Mercier, 'English Orientalists and Mathematical Astronomy', 168). This instrument is still extant in the Museum of the History of Science at Oxford, signed 'Elias Allen fecit Londini 1637' (Gunther, 'The First Observatory Instruments of the Savilian Professors', 192–3). For in a letter to Turner from Constantinople in 1638 (MS BL Add. 34727, fo. 63) Greaves expresses his anxiety about not yet having received his 'brass Quadrant' from Mr Allen.

[49] For details see Mercier, 'English Orientalists and Mathematical Astronomy', 164–5, according to whom the poor result for Rhodes is due to a calculating error on Greaves's part, rather than a bad observation.

[50] MS Savile 47, fo. 45, printed in Greaves, *Works*, ii. 434–8.

[51] MS Smith 15, p. 50, as reported by Mercier, 'English Orientalists and Mathematical Astronomy', 170. Panagiotes was a Greek, known to both Greaves and Pococke, who sought out manuscripts for them in Constantinople (MS BL Add. 6193, fo. 72ʳ). Samuel Foster, Gresham Professor of Astronomy, later revised Greaves's translation from the Arabic of the *Lemmata* attributed to Archimedes; this was published in Foster's posthumous *Miscellanea*.

army to Bagdat, and by a certain consul of his acquaintance at Smyrna.'[52] Greaves's interest in oriental astronomy led him to seek out Turkish astronomers in Constantinople, as he recounts in the preface to his *Tabulae Geographicae*.[53] The encounter was mutually instructive: Greaves showed these men the *Progymnasmata* of Tycho Brahe, whose fame had reached them,[54] and was in turn shown by them that many of Tycho's observations were in agreement with those of Ulugh Beg. They further informed him about the enormous observational instruments which Ulugh Beg had constructed.

Greaves took ship for Alexandria, with the annual Turkish fleet, in late August or early September 1638. The ship stopped for a few days at Rhodes on the way, which gave him the opportunity to make clandestine astronomical observations in a garden under the city walls.[55] He stayed at Alexandria some six months, mainly employed in making astronomical observations, having bribed the Jewish customs officials to allow his instruments into Egypt. But he also took two short trips to Cairo, whence he visited the pyramids at Saqqara, and took measurements of them. He paid special attention to the Great Pyramid, penetrating into the interior. He also looked for manuscripts, and although he complained to Pococke that he was very disappointed in the results,[56] he obtained at least some very old fragments of the Koran in Kufic script,[57] and 'a fair manuscript of Euclid, in Arabic, with vowels', which he lost to bedouin robbers while travelling from Rosetta to Alexandria.[58] Egypt also gave him the opportunity to

[52] Twells, 71–2. The difficulties with this identification of the eclipse are that it was Panagiotes, not Cerigo, who observed it at Constantinople, and that the 'consul of his acquaintance at Smyrna' is almost certainly Edward Stringer (who while treasurer at Constantinople had assisted Greaves with astronomical observations there), and Stringer did not arrive at Smyrna until the summer of 1639. So possibly this is a later event, e.g. the solar eclipse of 1 June 1639.

[53] Greaves took care to contradict the prejudices of his countrymen about the Turks by describing these scholars as 'hominibus, meo judicio, neque moribus agrestibus, neque ingenio efferato'.

[54] Ravius at Constantinople also noticed the Turkish admiration of Brahe, whom, he says, they call 'Tinchuna' (Ravius, *Panegyrica Prima*, 36). For interesting parallels between the instruments of Tycho Brahe and those in the contemporary observatory of Tāqī al-Dīn at Constantinople see Sayili, *The Observatory in Islam*, 375 ff.

[55] Letter to Hardy of May 1641 (MS Smith 93, p. 111, printed in Greaves, *Works*, ii. 442–6). This letter gives Greaves's own overview of his purposes in undertaking the journey and what he accomplished. For the Rhodes observation see also ibid. ii. 371.

[56] Twells, 64; Ward, *Gresham Professors*, 141.

[57] He gave these to Pococke, who records his gratitude, *Specimen*, 158 (original edition); 163 (1806 edition); now MS Pococke 287, item 13.

[58] Twells, 71. Whether his manuscript of al-Idrīsī (now MS Greaves 42), which he

collect, *inter alia*, hieroglyphic inscriptions from mummy wrappings, to examine mummies,[59] and to observe the customs of the natives. He also found native informants on scholarly matters at Cairo: in the notes he wrote in his manuscript of Abū 'l-Fidā''s *Geography*[60] he refers to a Copt whom he calls 'mio Maestro Giorgio a Gran Cairo' for information about the Coptic Martyrs' Era, and gives a list of 'What bookes are to be read by a student of astronomy' according to a man he calls 'my Sheic . . . at Cairo', presumably one of the ulema he met there.

In late March or April 1639 Greaves took ship for Livorno, a journey which lasted no less than two months. From there he wrote to Pococke on 14 June, telling him of his ill success in finding books in Egypt. In this and subsequent correspondence he urged Pococke to buy manuscripts on his behalf in Constantinople,

not only by soliciting the assistance of their common friends at Galata, but even by going over the water himself to the Bezars, and shops at Stambol; which he supposed might be done without hazard, provided a due caution were used about such books as relate to religion. He intreated him also to make a further enquiry after the libraries of private men, and to attend to the return of the then victorious army from Persia, which, perhaps, among other spoils, might bring with them many books in the language of that country.[61]

Greaves spent the next nine months in Italy, visiting the monuments and libraries, and cultivating the acquaintance of learned men, in Siena, Florence, Rome, Naples, and elsewhere. It was presumably at this time that he became friendly with Lucas Holsten, Librarian of the Vatican, and gained access to that library. There he collated the manuscript of Abū 'l-Fidā''s *Geography* which had belonged to Postel and had migrated to the Palatine Library, and thence to Rome.[62] He also carefully examined an unusual manuscript of the Gospels in Persian,

claimed to have been written in Egypt, was bought by him in Egypt is not clear from his mention of it in *Tabulae Geographicae*, preface.

[59] Dr Howarth informs me that he was mistaken in saying (*Lord Arundel and his Circle*, 138) that Greaves was responsible for sending the Egyptian mummy in its sarcophagus which the Earl of Arundel, accompanied by Selden, saw unpacked at the docks in London in February 1638.

[60] MS Greaves 2, transcribed by Mercier, 'English Orientalists and Mathematical Astronomy', 173–4. His opinion of these informants cannot have been high, for he later told Pococke that in Egypt 'for books, I saw few; and for learned men, none' (Ward, *Gresham Professors*, 142).

[61] Twells, 64–5; the whole passage is a valuable illustration both of the difficulties and the opportunities for a European trying to buy books in Constantinople at that epoch.

[62] Greaves, *Chorasmiae Descriptio*, preface. It is possible that he had succeeded in doing this on his first visit to Rome in 1635. Cf. Levi della Vida, *Ricerche*, 335.

made at the Mogul court and donated by Hieronymus Xavier.[63] To
ease his path into the Medicean Library in Florence Greaves had composed a Latin ode in praise of the Grand Duke Ferdinando II of
Tuscany, celebrating his victory over the Barbary pirates.[64] In March
1640 he embarked on the *Golden Fleece*, which carried him back to
England.

Pococke remained in Constantinople for a while longer. His reports
to Laud, of which he kept copies, provided Twells with an outline of
the principal events there during his stay. Of these the most dramatic
was the execution of Cyril Lucaris, Patriarch of Constantinople, on
27 June 1638.[65] This event, which was engineered by the faction within the Greek Orthodox Church opposed to Cyril's rapprochement with
the Protestant churches, was a hard blow to Laud, who was among
those who had hoped for a union between the Anglican and Orthodox
churches through Cyril's influence. It was also a setback to Greaves
and Pococke in their quest for manuscripts on behalf of the archbishop,
for which Cyril had promised his help;[66] shortly before his murder he
had sent Laud (no doubt through Pococke) a manuscript of the
Pentateuch in Arabic.[67]

(V) RAVIUS IN THE EAST

Another event of which Pococke informed the archbishop was the
arrival at Constantinople of Christianus Ravius. We saw in Chapter 3
how his journey was financed by Ussher in return for a promise to look
for manuscripts. Ravius travelled via France, where he stopped for a
while in Paris and was introduced by Hugo Grotius to Cardinal

[63] Greaves's account of the manuscript is reported by Selden, *Uxor Hebraica*, iii. 11
(*Opera*, ii/1, 732). It is apparently no longer in the Vatican, since it is mentioned neither
by Rossi, *Elenco dei manoscritti persiani*, nor by Levi della Vida, *Ricerche*.

[64] Twells, 73. The ode is preserved in MS Savile 47, fo. 91ʳ, where Greaves records
that he had composed it at Alexandria in 1638; printed in Greaves, *Works*, ii. 533–4.

[65] Pococke's letter to Laud about this had been lost, but Twells was able to use a
letter describing the event that Pococke wrote to Thomas Greaves in 1659, as well as the
oral version which Thomas Smith obtained from Pococke for his *Account of the Greek
Church*, 287 ff. (also in Latin in his *Miscellanea*, 126–9, and in his *Collectanea de
Cyrillo Lucario* etc., London, 1707). The event is described in detail by Greaves too in
his letter to Turner, MS Savile 47, fo. 45 (printed in Greaves, *Works*, ii. 434–8).

[66] See the quotation from Greaves's letter above, p. 137.

[67] See above, p. 110. The Patriarch had long before donated the famous 'Codex
Alexandrinus' of the Greek Bible to King Charles, and the Arabic manuscript of the
Church Councils to ambassador Roe (whence it had passed to the Bodleian).

Richelieu, who, according to Ravius himself,[68] tried to seduce him into his own service in the East. He also spent time with Mersenne and was introduced by him to Desargues.[69] He then took ship from Marseilles for Constantinople, where he arrived after a fortnight's voyage about the beginning of July 1639. Pococke takes up the story:

He came thither, without either clothes befitting him (of which he said he had been robbed in France) or money, or letters of credit, to any merchant. He had letters of recommendation from some of the states to the Dutch ambassador, who was departed before his arrival. Sir Sackvil Crow, the English ambassador, finding that he brought the Archbishop's recommendation, generously took him into his house and protection, and gave him all due furtherance; requiring of him that, if occasion so present itself, England may enjoy the benefit of what time he shall here employ, in the study of the eastern tongues.[70]

Ravius very soon began to assemble[71] manuscripts on his own account. When Edward Stringer moved from Constantinople, where he was treasurer of the Levant Company, to Smyrna, where he had been appointed consul, Ravius took the opportunity to accompany him.[72] On 8 September 1639 Ravius bought at Smyrna an Arabic manuscript giving a description of Jerusalem which he later donated to Sion College library, where it still remains.[73] While at Smyrna he also witnessed the funeral service of a young English merchant, of which he gave a long and interesting account in a public lecture at Utrecht in 1643.[74] He soon returned to the company of Pococke in Constantinople. While there he composed a 'treatise on the Turkish

---

[68] Ravius, *Generall Grammer*, preface. One has to treat with caution any unsupported statement by Ravius tending to his own credit, since, as his Arabic-speaking amanuensis averred, he was 'a treasury of lies'.

[69] Ravius, *Apollonius*, preface [*7ᵛ].

[70] Twells, 60–1. The 'Archbishop' whose recommendation Ravius brought must be Ussher, although Twells's narrative makes it look like Laud. Ravius also brought a recommendation from Vossius to Pococke (Vossius, *Epistolae*, ii, no. 295, p. 195).

[71] I use the word advisedly, for he certainly did not 'buy' all those that he acquired. A letter from Ravius' amanuensis Nicolaus Petri to the Turkish scholar Shaikh-zādeh Muḥammad Efendī reveals that Ravius, in Constantinople, had borrowed or taken on approval books which Shaikh-zādeh Muḥammad was vainly trying to retrieve or be paid for several years later (Houtsma, *Oostersche Correspondentie*, 100–2).

[72] Stringer, whom we have already noticed as an assistant to Greaves in his astronomical observations, was clearly a cultivated man. According to Ravius, 'de Linguâ Turcicâ' (see below), fo. 100ʳ, he had composed a Turkish lexicon. He was related to Henry Stringer, who was later Warden of New College and interested in Arabic, to judge from his donation of Arabic printed books to the college in 1654 (see Feingold, 'The Oxford Oriental School').

[73] MS Cod. Or. 4 (see below, p. 191). [74] Ravius, *Panegyrica Secunda*, 24–7.

Language', which was never printed, but which survives, in his autograph copy, in the British Library.[75] Although philologically negligible, it is interesting for Ravius' warm feelings towards the Turks, whose dignity and helpfulness to strangers he contrasts with the fraudulence of the Armenians and Jews.

It was probably also in Constantinople that Ravius met Nicolaus Petri,[76] a silk-weaver from Aleppo, Greek Orthodox in religion, but educated in writing Arabic (which was probably his native language) and Turkish. Promising Nicolaus a profitable career as his amanuensis,[77] Ravius persuaded him to accompany him back to Europe, where Nicolaus's disgust at his treatment by his employer led him to write to Pococke and Golius letters in Arabic which are of unusual interest and poignancy. Ravius was still in Constantinople, and buying manuscripts, when he wrote separate letters to G. J. Vossius and his son Isaac on 13 April 1640.[78] In the former he looked forward to leaving for Persia in a month or so, but he also complained about lack of funds, which may explain why he was still there when Ussher wrote to Hartlib on 30 September 1640 about Ravius' desire to travel further east.[79] Apparently he did not leave until early 1641, for in that year he bought, in Constantinople, the manuscript which was to be the pride of his collection and the envy of mathematicians. This was a copy of the Arabic translation of Apollonius' *Conics* in the recension of 'Abd al-Malik al-Shīrāzī, with more than thirty other mathematical treatises.[80] Before returning to Europe he spent some months visiting Ephesus and other sites in Asia Minor (probably the 'Seven Churches of Asia' which later became a popular tour for the Christian merchant

[75] MS Harley 3496, fos. 90–118.

[76] Although Nicolaus came from Aleppo, his letter to Shaikh-zādeh Muḥammad (Houtsma, *Oostersche Correspondentie*, 101) shows that he was with Ravius in Constantinople. Cf. also Nicolaus's letter to Pococke: 'in Istanbul I had land and dirt, until I went and became his servant, and took the books from Istanbul to Galata, and from Galata until we put them in the ship' (MS Pococke 432, fo. 12, my translation).

[77] Ravius probably got this idea from Golius, who as early as August 1627 had expressed to Vossius his hope 'virum aliquem orientalis literaturae peritum, in patriam mecum perducere, meisque impensis ibidem alere'. Golius did not in fact bring anyone back from the East, although he did later employ the services of several native scribes (including Nicolaus) at Leiden. It is interesting that another pupil of Golius, John Greaves, expressed exactly the same intention in a letter from Constantinople (MS Smith 93, p. 138): 'I intend if I can light upon any Greek, that writes a faire hand, & can speak Arabick, to bring him home with me, who shall copy out such things as you require.'

[78] Vossius, *Epistolae*, ii, no. 295, pp. 195–6; MS d'Orville 470, pp. 278–84.

[79] Ussher, *Letters*, no. 60, p. 624.

[80] Now MS Thurston 3 in the Bodleian. On the later vicissitudes of this manuscript see below, pp. 183, 238.

communities at Smyrna), in the company of Charles Cavendish[81] and other English noblemen.[82] In the summer of 1641 he embarked on the ship *Sampson*, together with Nicolaus Petri and what he called 'my Orientall library of above 300 manuscripts',[83] including not only Arabic, Persian, and Turkish, but also Greek, Russian, and even Chinese items. Stopping in Cyprus on the way, where Ravius was given an Arabic anti-Christian tract by an obliging Muslim physician,[84] the ship reached London probably in November 1641.

(VI) POCOCKE'S RETURN AND INTERVIEW WITH GROTIUS

Pococke had already returned to England, although he came back long after John Greaves. As the year 1640 drew on, the system of government erected by King Charles, with the support and encouragement of Laud, looked ever more precarious, and prudent men in the City of London saw which way the wind was blowing. Charles Fettiplace wrote to Pococke urging him to return while Laud could still do him favours, and Laud himself, informing Pococke on 4 March that he was about to settle the Arabic lectureship on a permanent basis, also expected him to come back. Pococke used the excuse that he was waiting for a visit by his 'sheikh' from Aleppo to delay until August. Even then he took ship not directly for England, but only as far as Livorno, whence he proceeded overland through Italy and France. As Twells aptly remarks, Pococke 'was never fond of travelling', and this detour is explained only by what happened when he got to Paris. There, early in 1641, he sought an interview with Hugo Grotius,[85] who (as Pococke could have learned from Ravius if he did not already know) was resident there as ambassador of Queen Christina of Sweden. The purpose of Pococke's visit was to discuss his Arabic translation of Grotius' *De*

---

[81] This man (not to be confused with the Charles Cavendish who was Pell's correspondent in the 1640s) was second son of the Earl of Devonshire, and was killed by Cromwell's troops in 1643 while a royalist commander at Gainsborough.

[82] Moller, *Cimbria Literata*, ii. 681.

[83] Ravius, *Discourse*, 69. I cannot discuss here the problem of the number of manuscripts in Ravius' collection, about which he and others gave different accounts at different times. He probably added to it later, for Pococke, writing to Selden in August 1652, in response to an invitation to view Ravius' manuscripts, says 'which I take to be not only a collection of his in Turky, but more at London of bookes by the directions of others gotten by merchants, who by reason of the disturbance of the times knew not how to dispose of them' (MS Selden supra 109, fo. 341ʳ).

[84] Ravius, *Panegyrica Secunda*, 13.

[85] The only other person he is known to have seen in Paris was Gabriel Sionita; this was a courtesy visit to a fellow Arabist.

Veritate Religionis Christianae. To explain Pococke's reasons for doing this translation I prefer to give Grotius' own version of the interview rather than rely on Twells's tendentious account.[86] Grotius writes to his brother Willem on 16 February 1641:

Recently I was visited by a very learned Englishman, who has lived long in the Turkish empire and has translated my book *On the Truth of the Christian Religion* into Arabic, and will see that it is printed in England, if he can. He thinks that no book is more useful either for instructing the Christians in those parts, or even for converting the followers of Muḥammad who live in the Turkish, Persian, Tartar, North African, or Indian dominions. Moreover, this truly pious man urgently requested me to be true to the vow which I made at the end of that book, and not to allow myself to be deterred by any factions or calumnies from offering to all Christians the cup of concord. For, [he said], nothing turns those outside Christianity away from it more than the great number of divisions within it.[87]

Pococke's motives for making this Arabic translation, and the changes he made in Book VI (for which he asked and received Grotius' permission on this occasion), will be treated more fully in my discussion of the published version of the translation, which appeared nearly twenty years later. Here it is sufficient to note that Pococke's admiration for Grotius' book, the purpose of which 'was to unite all Churches, and reconcile non-Christians to Christianity by placing Christianity clearly on the basis of non-sectarian, universal human reason',[88] put him in a minority. In Europe *De Veritate* and its author were denounced by Catholics and Calvinists alike. In the England of Archbishop Laud to hold such views was still respectable, but in the years that followed it became increasingly dangerous to voice them, and Pococke was to suffer at the hands of those who denounced such tolerance.

The Long Parliament which presided over the English Revolution was already in session when Pococke came to Paris. Grotius gave him a message for Laud, who had been impeached and was in the custody of Black Rod. By the time Pococke reached London to deliver it, the archbishop had been moved to the Tower (1 March 1641).

[86] It seems probable to me that Twells had exactly the same evidence about this incident as we do, namely Grotius' letter to his brother, Pococke's own preface to the printed translation, a passage in the *Specimen* (186 of the original edition, 191–2 of the 1806 edition), and (possibly) letters of Pococke to Boyle about the publication. In the light of this it is instructive to read Twells's elaborations on 'so great a part of the world . . . being enslaved to the foolish opinions of that grand impostor Mahomet'.

[87] Grotius, *Correspondence*, xii, no. 5061, p. 103 (my translation from the Latin).

[88] Trevor-Roper, *Catholics, Anglicans and Puritans*, 197–8.

7

Arabic Studies during the English Revolution

THE 'English Revolution' is a convenient term to denote not only the Civil War itself, but also the turbulent period preceding it (beginning with the summoning of the Long Parliament) and the struggle for power following it, culminating in the Protectorate of Oliver Cromwell. It was a difficult time in England for the pursuit of scholarship. Both universities were shaken not only by the disruptions of the war but by rough intrusions into their affairs by the Parliament, which resulted in many losing their academic positions or livings. The patrons of Arabic studies were also affected. Laud was impeached for treason on 18 December 1640, imprisoned in the Tower, and resigned the Chancellorship of Oxford on 28 June 1641; he was executed early in 1645. Ussher was deprived of most of his revenues by the Irish rebellion of 1641, and spent much of the time until his death in 1656 at various places of refuge in England. This did not prevent him, however, from publishing many learned works, for some of which he enlisted the aid of John Greaves. Selden, on the other hand, was very important as a patron and protector of scholarship, including Arabic studies, in this period. He was elected as burgess representing Oxford University[1] in the Long Parliament, where he was one of the true moderates. While approving many of the measures taken to curb the arbitrariness of royal power, he was equally opposed to the abuse of power by the Parliament. He was one of the very few in the Commons to vote against the attainder of Strafford, not because he approved of the actions of that hated minister of Charles I, but on the grounds that the bill of attainder flouted the rule of law which he reverenced. When open hostilities broke out, he remained in London with the Parliament instead of decamping with the royalist members to the King at Oxford. The respect in which he was held by the Parliament and his good relations with some of the influential Parliamentarians enabled him to help both universities and to mitigate the sufferings of some of their members at the hands of their persecutors.

[1] From 1644 onwards he was the sole representative of Oxford, since his colleague Sir Thomas Roe, who died in that year, was not replaced.

(I) THE CIVIL WAR AND ARABIC AT OXFORD

Before he fell from power, Laud had taken care to make the Arabic Professorship at Oxford permanent, and had completed the transfer of his manuscripts to the Bodleian Library.[2] Both Greaves and Pococke communicated with their fallen patron. A letter from Laud to Greaves written from the Tower on 13 January 1642 shows that the two had been in consultation about the disposition of the coins and manuscripts which Laud had given to the library.[3] Laud's accusers later tried to use a letter which Greaves had written to him from Italy to incriminate the archbishop.[4] However, of the two it was Pococke who was the real subversive, for he carried a verbal message from Grotius to Laud when he visited him in the Tower in March 1641. Grotius urged the archbishop to use any opportunity to escape from his captivity and go overseas.[5] Laud refused to give his accusers this satisfaction, preferring to stay and meet his fate.[6]

Pococke returned to normal life at Oxford. To support him he had his fellowship at Corpus and his Arabic Professorship. To these was added, in 1643, the Rectorship of Childrey, a charming village on the edge of the Berkshire Downs some twelve miles from Oxford, the living of which was in the gift of Pococke's college. This offered, besides the proximity of his friends the Fettiplaces, the advantage of easy travel to Oxford to deliver his Arabic lectures in vacation. It also enabled him to marry, which he did not long after. Early in 1646 he took to wife Mary Burdet of West Worldham in Hampshire, who between 1648 and 1661 bore him six sons and three daughters. Exceptionally for that time, all but one of these survived to adulthood, and five sons and two daughters were still living at their father's death

---

[2] The final donation was made on 6 Nov. 1640, three days after the Long Parliament met. The accompanying letter begins: 'Dum sic fluctuant omnia' (Hunt, *Laudian Manuscripts*, p. xxx).

[3] For other evidence of Greaves's arranging and identifying the oriental manuscripts of Laud's gift, see ibid., pp. xiv–xv. This activity certainly belongs to the period after his return from the East.

[4] Laud, *Works*, iv. 325. The letter was printed by Laud's chief tormentor, William Prynne (*Canterburies Doom*, 421).

[5] Grotius himself had escaped from life imprisonment in the Netherlands, with the help of Golius' uncle Johannes Hemelarius among others.

[6] Twells (81–5) gives the story in substantial detail, including a long speech by Laud in direct quotation. If this is authentic, the only possible source for it must have been an oral account by Pococke himself, as relayed by one of his Oxford colleagues after his death to his first biographer, Humfrey Smith. One wonders how much the story was embellished in the telling.

in 1691.[7] The only one with whom we will be concerned is the eldest son, Edward Pococke junior.

The 'normal life' at Oxford did not last long. In 1642 both King and Parliament raised armies, and hundreds from the University enlisted for the King. Most were undergraduates, but they were joined by some ardent Royalists among the senior members. One of these was Peter Turner, who at the age of 55 enlisted in the cavalry under Sir John Byron. He was taken prisoner near Stow-on-the-Wold (10 September 1642), and spent time in prison at Banbury and Northampton, until he was freed in July 1643. Oxford was occupied briefly by Parliamentary forces in September 1642, but after the battle of Edgehill the King reoccupied it (29 October 1642) and established his court there. The years from this occupation until the surrender of the city on 24 June 1646 were even more disruptive to university life than the purges which followed. The disturbances caused by the soldiers quartered in Oxford, and the dissolute behaviour of the followers of the courtiers, made it difficult to maintain the discipline of the university. The studies of many undergraduates were cut short either by their joining the royal forces or by their being withdrawn by parents reluctant to expose them to the rampant corruption of morals, and enrolment at the university dropped precipitously.[8] Teaching was also interrupted: writing to Ussher on 19 September 1644, John Greaves remarks of his lecture as Savilian Professor that 'as yet it cannot be read'.[9] The colleges were subjected to demands for money from the King, and most of them lost their best plate, which they were forced to 'donate' for melting down. This process at one college, Merton, is illuminated by a deposition made by Thomas Greaves when his brother John was accused by the Visitors in 1648 of using college funds to aid the King: 'I Thomas Greaves do testify . . . that Mr. John Greaves, fellow of Merton college, when the plate of the said college was demaunded by the king, kept himselfe private in his chamber for many dayes, that he might not be present, nor give his consent, neither did hee go abroad, till hee had heard, that the plate was already delivered.'[10] Anthony Wood gives a vivid summation of the general decay of the university which he witnessed during the royal occupation:

[7] This appears from Pococke's will, PRO, PROB 11,406, 1691 146, fo. 52[v].
[8] Mallet, *History of the University of Oxford*, ii. 353–60, gives a good picture of this state of affairs.
[9] Ussher, *Letters*, no. 211, p. 509.
[10] Ward, *Gresham Professors*, 145; cf. Greaves, *Works*, vol. i, p. xxix. Both Ward and Birch transcribed this deposition from Pococke's correspondence.

Lectures and Exercises for the most part ceased, the Schools being employed as Granaries for the Garrison, which was the reason why so many Scholars were superannuated at the Surrender. . . . Those few also that were remaining, were for the most part, especially such that were young, much debauched, and become idle by bearing Arms and keeping company with rude Soldiers . . . The Colleges were much out of repair by the negligence of Soldiers, Courtiers and others that lay in them, a few Chambers that were the meanest (in some Colleges none at all) being reserved for Scholars use. Their treasure and plate was all gone . . ., the books of some Libraries imbeziled, and the number of Scholars few, and mostly indigent . . . The Halls (wherein as in some Colleges, ale and beer were sold by the penny in their respective Butteries) were very ruinous, occasioned through the same ways as the Colleges were, and so they remained, except Magdalen Hall and New Inn, (which upon the Surrender replenished with the Presbyterian faction) for several years after. Further also, having few or none in them, except their respective Principals and Families, the Chambers in them were . . . rented out to Laycks. In a word, there was scarce the face of an University left, all things being out of order and disturbed.[11]

The tense situation in London before hostilities broke out is illustrated incidentally in two letters sent from that city to Pococke in Oxford late in 1641[12] by Nicolaus Petri. We saw above how Ravius had persuaded him in Constantinople to come to Europe as his amanuensis. Ravius liked to parade him around as a kind of trophy of his travels, calling him 'my Arab'.[13] But Nicolaus was already disillusioned with Ravius' promises, seeing his master penniless and at a loss to find employment for himself. In his letters to Pococke, written in a colloquial Arabic which is difficult to understand in places, he tells him of his own unhappiness as a stranger in London, unable to speak either English or Latin, and of Ravius' financial straits and mistreatment of him. Ravius hoped to make some money from his cherished manuscript of Apollonius, either by selling it or getting Nicolaus to make a copy of it for people in France.[14] His amanuensis, however, was reluctant:

---

[11] Wood, *History and Antiquities*, ii/1, 487–8.

[12] The letters bear no date, but can be approximately dated by the statement in the later one that Ravius has now got his books out of the ship. Ravius himself informed Greaves on 6 Dec. 1641 that he had got possession of his manuscripts two days earlier (MS Smith 93, p. 109).

[13] Ravius, *Panegyrica Prima*, 22: 'Doctissimus, & mille Arabibus Muhammedanis contra Eruditus ille meus Arabs, Nicolaus Petri'. Cf. L. de Dieu to G. J. Vossius, 25 Mar. 1642: 'Ravius . . . quem promptissime hic cum suo, quem adduxit Arabe Christiano loquentem, non sine admiratione audivi' (Vossius, *Epistolae*, ii, no. 338).

[14] These were Mersenne and Claude Hardy, as we learn from Ravius' letter to Greaves, MS Smith 93, p. 109.

But I ?curse the book and its owner, for the book is not like some books: its script is corrupt, . . . it is very old, its letters small, its ink faded, and it is written in the margins and can only be read with great effort.[15] And he wants me to sit down and labour and revise [it] so that he will give me six Ottomans[16] daily. And he is better off than I if he owns two Ottomans . . . and he is at a loss what to do: he hopes to get someone to buy it from him for however much he can get. But in the present situation in London these days there is no one to buy all his books[17] for a quarter of a kurush, and from despair he is at a loss what to say: one moment he says 'I want to travel to Holland', next moment he says 'I want to travel to France', but it is not in his power for us to travel anywhere, because he hasn't a penny.[18]

The 'situation in London' is further described in the next letter: 'we have had the intention of going to the land of the Franks, the land of France, because London is very disordered at this time, and the people of the place, night and day, are patrolling with weapons, so we are afraid lest war arise in the place.'[19]

Although Nicolaus's letters are rambling and disjointed, one can glean a fairly coherent picture from them. Ravius and his amanuensis had visited Pococke at Oxford soon after reaching England, but were now back in London, staying at Gresham College. With his first letter to Pococke Nicolaus sent a gift of a manuscript written in Kufic script, and in the second letter promised an Arabic geographical work.[20] He also sent Pococke, for whose understanding of Arabic he expresses an admiration as great as his contempt for Ravius', a list of the latter's manuscripts (which he kept secret from his master). The bearer of the packets between London and Oxford was John Greaves,[21] who had brought a letter and a 'gift' (i.e. money) from Pococke to Nicolaus. Ravius had also taken Nicolaus to see a man of rank in London whose

---

[15] This is an accurate description of Ravius' MS of Apollonius.

[16] A Turkish coin.

[17] About this time Ravius must have sent a handwritten catalogue of his manuscripts, with the price of each in pounds sterling, to scholars in Europe. For on 31 Mar. 1642 Vopiscus Fortunatus Plempius wrote from Louvain offering to buy from him, *inter alia*, Avicenna's *Canon* for £12 (Ravius, *Specimen Lexici*, 3).

[18] MS Pococke 432, fo. 11 (my translation).

[19] Ibid., fo. 12.

[20] The title of this was سبط الأرض في طوله والعرض. I do not know whether there is any such work among the Pococke MSS in the Bodleian.

[21] Nicolaus refers to him as 'al-Jalabi'. One might have expected 'Jarāwī' (from Greaves's Latin name 'Gravius'). But Nicolaus liked to assimilate the European names he heard to a *kunya* which had meaning in Arabic. Thus he refers to Ravius as 'al-Rāwī', which can be interpreted as 'the story-teller'. Likewise 'al-Jalabī' is the Arabic form of the Turkish *çelebi*, 'educated man'. The identification with John Greaves is assured by numerous details in the first letter.

name is hopelessly garbled in the letter,[22] but who can only be Selden; for Nicolaus says that Ravius went again to him later to ask for money, and we know that Selden did indeed give Ravius £15 on 15 February 1642.[23] Before getting his manuscripts off the ship Ravius had spent nine days in Cambridge, and had now sent 'three small books' to Cambridge, one a gift to the university,[24] the other two to a person whose name (or more probably title) I am unable to decipher,[25] in the hope that he would get Ravius a post at Cambridge.

Like Ravius' other hopes of employment in England, this proved vain. On 9 February 1642 Patrick Young, the King's Librarian, gave Ravius a letter of recommendation to Peter Turner, asking him as Savilian Professor to allow Ravius to consult a Greek manuscript of Apollonius' *Conics* in the Savilian Library at Oxford, for comparison with his own Arabic exemplar. Probably very little came of this, for not long afterwards Ravius, still accompanied by Nicolaus Petri, went to Leiden, where Louis de Dieu admired the two in Arabic or Turkish conversation before 25 March (15 March OS). Ravius was forced to leave some 200 of his manuscripts behind in England as pledges for his debts.[26] Five years were to pass before he returned in triumph to England to begin redeeming them, and also to teach Arabic.

We have almost no information about the scholarly activity of Pococke, and little about that of John Greaves, at this time and during the Civil War. The main reasons for this are that the political situation made scholarly publication difficult, and that both men were resident in or near Oxford, and communicated in person rather than by letter. In 1642 John Greaves was indeed still travelling between Oxford and London to give his lectures at Gresham College, but his absences must

---

[22] I dubiously read فسجنسلوس.

[23] His letter to Ravius, regretting that he could do no more, and refusing to take any pledge, is printed in Ravius, *Specimen Lexici*, 3, and thence in Selden, *Opera*, ii/2, 1709.

[24] This must be the manuscript recorded in the Cambridge Donors' Book (CUL MS Oo.7.52, p. 46): 'Ex dono Clarissimi Christiani Ravii Berlinatis #B.β.3 Razis Institutiones logicae. Arabicè. M. S.'

[25] I can only conjecture that it was Richard Holdsworth, currently Vice-Chancellor of Cambridge, who in 1647 was holding some of Ravius' manuscripts, according to Ravius himself.

[26] Ravius, *Specimen Lexici*, 1. One gets a glimpse of the tangled state of his affairs in his letter to Isaac Vossius of 6 July (NS) 1647, whence it appears that he had left manuscripts as pledges in Oxford, Cambridge, and Constantinople. There is an amusing exchange of letters between Ravius and Sir Simonds D'Ewes in 1645 in which Ravius asks D'Ewes to retain the Greek manuscripts he had pledged to the baronet until he is able to redeem them, and D'Ewes indignantly replies that the manuscripts belong to him, since he had received one in exchange for a Chinese book, and had bought the other four (MSS BL Harley 364, fo. 272, and 378, fo. 86).

have been brief. Even this changed in November 1643, when Bainbridge died and Greaves was chosen Savilian Professor of Astronomy
in his place. On the day following his election he was removed from
his professorship at Gresham College, allegedly 'for absence', but
according to Ravius (who presumably got this version from Greaves
himself) 'for being too obedient to the King at Oxford, and for pled-
ging the silver plate of his college for money for the King'.[27] It was
presumably on this occasion that, on the order of the Parliament, his
room at Gresham College was ransacked by soldiers looking for subversive materials.[28] All of his books and papers there were confiscated,
and although they were later returned to him through Selden's intercession, some valuable items were lost, including an illustrated manuscript of Abū Maʿshar's *Great Introduction* in Arabic, which Pococke
had brought back for him, and which must have been torn apart, since
Pococke later saw a few leaves of it in a collection of 'Orientall
rarities' in London.[29]

We have already seen that Greaves was engaged in ordering Laud's
collections at the Bodleian Library in 1642. Glimpses of his studies
and publication plans during the years 1642 to 1644 can be obtained
from two letters he wrote in those years. In a letter to Golius, written
June 1642, recommending his youngest brother Edward, who was
going to Leiden to study medicine, he enclosed a list of his oriental
manuscripts which he had made at the request of Claude Hardy.[30] In
return he asked Golius to send him some astronomical observations
contained in the Leiden codex of ibn Yūnus, and gives an Arabic
quotation from a work of Jalāl al-Dīn al-Suyūṭī about that author.[31]

[27] MS d'Orville 468, p. 215: 'quod putaretur Oxonii Regi fuisse obsequentior, et
argentea Collegii sui vasa pro rege deposuisse, pecuniae causa'.

[28] However, in a letter to Claude Hardy of late 1649 (MS Savile 47, fo. 38, printed in
Works, ii. 462–4), Greaves says that five years earlier, while actually on his way to Paris,
he had been robbed by soldiers (obviously from a Parliamentary force) of his money and
literary apparatus ('in ipso itinere à militibus nostris pecuniâ et supellectile meâ literariâ
exutus'). From what he says later in the letter it would appear that this 'supellex
literaria' included the choicest of the manuscripts he had brought from Constantinople,
but that he had hopes of recovering them. So perhaps he was plundered twice, once at
Gresham College (in 1643?) and once on the road (in 1644).

[29] Letter of Pococke to Selden of 11 Feb. 1653, in the Inner Temple MS 538, fo. 305,
published by Wakefield, 'Arabic Manuscripts in the Bodleian Library', 133 (from the
copy in MS Smith 21, p. 29).

[30] Letter of Hardy to Greaves, 1 Sept. 1641, MS Savile 47, fos. 43–4, printed (inaccu-
rately) in Greaves, *Works*, ii. 446–50. On Greaves's oriental manuscripts see below, pp.
176–9.

[31] MS Savile 47, fo. 53 (= Greaves, *Works*, ii. 456–8). He gives the title of the work
he quotes from as احیاء مصر والقاهره.

There is no indication that Golius was any more responsive to this request than he had been to Bainbridge's earlier. Greaves's letter to Ussher of 19 September 1644 is even more informative.[32] After repeating Bainbridge's earlier request for any information Ussher had about a mythical copy of Hipparchus' work 'On the Length of the Year' in the Vatican or Escorial, Greaves says:

in perusing of some of my Arabian and Persian MSS. I have found some Observations, which may much conduce to the clearing of that Argument. I have not now leisure to send your Grace those which were made by the Indians at Kôbah, and Kandahar, or those others, which were made by the Persians before Yezdegerd's time, and by Yezdegerd, and long after him in Almamon's time, as I find them mentioned by Alhashamy[33] an Arabian Author. Those of the Chatéans, and of Nassir Eddin, and of Aly Kôsgy, as later than the former, so exacter, I could not but send them to your Grace.

He then gives a list of the lengths of the year according to various oriental astronomers, some of which, as we saw, were later used by Ussher in his *De Macedonum et Asianorum anno solari Dissertatio.* Turning to his plans for publication, he says that he has completed, with considerable difficulty because of the corruptions in his manuscript, an edition and translation of the Arabic *Lemmata* of Archimedes.[34] He has also completed a Persian lexicon of some 6,000 words.[35] To complete this, and for other purposes, he intends to travel to Leiden to consult the manuscripts there, and asks for Ussher's help in obtaining the necessary permissions. Among the works he intends to publish is Bainbridge's work on the Sothic period. We shall see that he did bring this out in 1648, with considerable additions of his own. But he never accomplished his projected journey to Leiden, although he was still promising it two years later.[36] First lawsuits involving the

[32] Ussher, *Letters*, no. 102, pp. 509–10. Since Ussher (and also William Harvey, to whom Greaves offers his services) were in Oxford at that date, it is clear that Greaves was writing from London. This is an interesting indication that in the midst of the Civil War travel between London and Oxford, the headquarters of Parliament and King respectively, was still possible for non-combatants.

[33] On Greaves's use of al-Hāshimī see below, p. 177. The passage is important as proving that the unique manuscript of this work, MS Arch. Seld. A 11, belonged to Greaves. Since it came to the Bodleian from Selden's collection, it must have been one of those oriental manuscripts which Selden bought from Thomas Greaves after John's death. Further confirmation is provided by the many annotations in the manuscript in Greaves's hand (Mercier, 'English Orientalists and Mathematical Astronomy', 164).

[34] Published some years after Greaves's death in Foster's *Miscellanea.*

[35] I do not know what became of this. Greaves had compiled a Persian grammar some years earlier, but it was not to be published until 1649.

[36] Letter to Pococke, quoted by Ward, *Gresham Professors*, 145.

estate of Mrs Bainbridge, of which he was executor, and then troubles of his own, kept him in England for the rest of his life.

Greaves was also deeply involved in the political struggles within Merton College. These go back before 1638, when Laud invoked the right he claimed as Archbishop of Canterbury to hold a visitation of Merton, and took the side of the faction (in which Peter Turner was prominent) hostile to the Warden, Sir Nathaniel Brent.[37] After the Civil War broke out Brent, and some of the fellows who supported him, took the side of Parliament. Brent left Oxford before the King occupied it in October 1642. Later Greaves drew up a petition to the King, signed by the 'loyal' Fellows of Merton, requesting Brent's removal from the Wardenship.[38] This was ordered by Charles on 27 January 1645. In April Greaves's candidate for Warden, the famous physician William Harvey, was elected. Greaves thus earned Brent's implacable enmity, which he was later in an excellent position to exercise, as Chairman of the Visitors appointed to reform the University of Oxford. Not content with getting rid of the Warden, Greaves also was instrumental in having two of Brent's supporters among the fellows, Edward Corbet and Ralph Button,[39] removed from their fellowships. These too were to return in 1647 to have their revenge, Corbet as one of the Visitors, and Button as an assistant to the Visitors and (in 1648) University Proctor.[40]

(II) POCOCKE DURING THE REVOLUTION

Pococke, whatever his convictions, was of a far different temperament from Greaves and Turner, and refrained from any provocative demonstrations of loyalty to the Royalist cause. During the years from 1641 to 1646 we have very little direct evidence for his scholarly activity. Selden, in his *Eutychius* of 1642, acknowledges Pococke's help in

---

[37] See Brodrick, *Memorials of Merton College*, 78–84; Trevor-Roper, *Archbishop Laud*, 354–7.

[38] Brodrick, *Memorials of Merton College*, 88.

[39] On Button see Wood, 'Fasti', ii. 158–9, in *Athenae Oxonienses*, ed. Bliss, vol. iv, and Ward, *Gresham Professors*, 153–5, 338. He was appointed Gresham Professor of Geometry when Greaves was ejected from that post. Greaves expressed a low opinion of Button's competence in a letter to Dr Scarborough (MS Savile 47, fo. 50, printed in Greaves, *Works*, ii. 395): 'Hee that is in the place doth no way deserve it.'

[40] Burrows, *Register of Visitors*, p. lxi notes the prominence of Merton fellows (several of whom had suffered in Laud's 1638 visitation) among the Visitors. No doubt Brent used his influence to pack that body with those whose support he could count on in the purge which he proceeded to conduct at Merton.

transcribing a passage from a Bodleian manuscript of ibn Khallikān's biographical work.[41] It was unfortunate that he did not also consult him on the translation, which was far from faultless. In the same year Selden asked Brian Twyne to get some passages of the Arabic Councils transcribed for him from the Roe manuscript at Oxford, and Twyne (who knew little or no Arabic) consulted first Pococke and then John Gregory on the matter.[42] To do the actual transcription Twyne recruited two Bachelors of Arts, Hamilton of Brasenose and Davis of Balliol, who must have been current pupils of Pococke (although nothing more is heard of either in connection with Arabic). Other pupils from this time who did later make their mark in Arabic studies were Thomas Marshall (Lincoln College, BA 1645) and Samuel Clarke (matriculated Merton 1640, MA 1648). The two remained close friends despite Marshall's many years of exile in the Netherlands. Another man who must have attended Pococke's lectures during these years was Thomas Jones (BA Oriel, 1638, and in the same year Fellow of Merton, where he was an adherent of Brent). In his *Prolusiones Academicae*[43] of 1660 he incidentally displays some knowledge of Arabic, and his scholarship was praised by Edmund Castell.[44] As far as Pococke's own studies at this time are concerned, we may be sure that he was mainly occupied with the investigation of pre-Islamic and early Islamic history which was to bear fruit in his *Specimen*, and which had been the justification for his spending three years in Constantinople. But this was not his sole concern. The chance survival of some stray pages from a translation which he made at this time reveals that he was already deeply interested in an Arabic philosophical work. This was the treatise *Ḥayy ibn Yaqẓān* by ibn Ṭufayl. We shall discuss this at length below in connection with its publication in 1671, merely noting here that in July 1645 Pococke produced an English translation of at least part of the work from the manuscript which he owned.[45]

From 1644 onwards Pococke was subjected to a series of personal difficulties and persecutions.[46] First he was deprived of his stipend as

[41] Selden, *Eutychius*, p. xvii.

[42] Twyne to Selden, 7 Feb. and 16 Mar. 1642 (MS Selden supra 109, fos. 278a, 278c).

[43] Madan, *Oxford Books*, iii, no. 2502. On Jones see Wood, *Athenae Oxonienses*, iii. 708; Wood knew and disliked Jones: see his *Life and Times*, i. 391–5.

[44] e.g. in his letters to Samuel Clarke, MS BL 22905, fos. 29, 50 (March 1659 and April 1661).

[45] The few fragments that survive are in MS Pococke 429, fos. 1, 2, 16, 17. They were discovered by Holt, 'Arabic Studies in Seventeenth-Century England', 91.

[46] Since these are narrated at length by Twells, I merely summarize them here.

Arabic Professor for about three years, by the actions of those who, by order of the Parliament, had seized Laud's estates; they had also sequestered those properties which Laud had donated to the university to fund the Arabic lecture. These were eventually restored by the efforts of Selden, urged on by John Greaves, and of Gerard Langbaine, Provost of Queen's College, who drew up the university's protest. From now on Langbaine appears as one of Pococke's closest friends. In 1647, after the occupation of Oxford and environs by the Parliamentary forces, Pococke was harassed by depredations and quartering of soldiers in his rectory at Childrey. Again Greaves came to his rescue, using the influence of his friend George Ent with the Parliamentary commander, Sir Thomas Fairfax, to procure from him an order of protection for Pococke. Worse was to follow with the establishment by Parliament of the Visitation of Oxford. Although this was done on 1 May 1647, it took some time for the Visitors to make any headway, and at first they were preoccupied with more prominent 'malignants' than Pococke. However, attention was drawn to him by his appointment to the Hebrew Professorship. The incumbent, John Morris, died on 27 March 1648, and the King (then in captivity on the Isle of Wight) named Pococke to the position on the advice of his chaplains Gilbert Sheldon and Henry Hammond. In ordinary times this would have been sufficient, but Selden, who was a member of the Parliamentary Committee for regulating the universities, took the precaution of getting the committee to order Pococke's appointment. By an ordinance made under the Chancellorship of Laud the Regius Professorship of Hebrew had annexed to it a prebend at the cathedral, which brought with it the considerable advantage of a canon's lodgings at Christ Church for the incumbent and his family. However, instead of assigning the prebend which Morris had enjoyed to Pococke, to his great dissatisfaction the committee ordered that he succeed to that of Dr Payne (whom they had ejected). Pococke did not at this time occupy any lodgings, since he did not move back to Oxford, but rather took care to avoid the Visitors as much as possible. Nevertheless, he was among the very few professors who 'submitted' to the Visitors:[47] that is, he answered in the affirmative to the question 'Do you submit to the authority of Parliament in this present Visitation?' Langbaine

---

[47] This submission is glossed over by Twells, who prefers to concentrate on Pococke's avoidance of taking the oaths, i.e. swearing to the 'Solemn League and Covenant' and the 'Negative Oath', by which all connection with the King was abjured. But that Pococke submitted is plain from the records of the visitation: see Burrows, *Register of Visitors*, p. lxxxii.

also submitted, but Greaves and Turner did not, no doubt because they well knew that submission would not save them from expulsion.

Pococke's policy of avoiding confrontation with the Visitors as long as he could do so without injury to his conscience kept him unscathed for a while. However, after the execution of the King (30 January 1649), and the abolition of the House of Lords, Parliament was determined to demonstrate its authority, and passed an act requiring everyone to subscribe to the 'Engagement', whereby he promised to be loyal to the government as established.[48] This was particularly sternly enforced at the universities, and order was given to the Visitors to return the names of all those who had refused or failed to take the Engagement. Pococke, following the advice of Selden and Greaves, who continued to exert themselves in London on his behalf, simply kept away from the Visitors. But in the end events overtook him. On 24 October 1650 the committee removed him from his prebend at Christ Church, and soon appointed Peter French (Cromwell's brother-in-law) in his place. Pococke expected to be turned out of both professorships as well,[49] and indeed in December of that year a vote was passed by the committee to that effect. However, a petition was immediately addressed to them, signed by the Vice-Chancellor, several heads of colleges, both proctors, and many others, urging the committee, in view of Pococke's learning and harmlessness, to suspend the execution of the vote at least until someone should be found competent to succeed him. It is interesting to see, as Twells remarks, that all but Langbaine and one other signatory were men who had been 'intruded' into their places by the Visitors; one was Greaves's enemy Ralph Button. This petition, no doubt supported, if not inspired, by Selden, had its effect, and Pococke was quietly permitted to continue as Hebrew and Arabic Professor until he was rehabilitated at the Restoration. No attempt was made to find a 'fit successor'. Twells, indeed, suggests that Ravius would have been eager to do so, and was only dissuaded from the attempt by the rebukes of Selden and Ussher. But although Ravius very probably did have such hopes earlier, by the time of the committee's vote he was long gone to take up a professorship in Sweden. It was probably fortunate for Pococke that he was no longer in England.

---

[48] 'I doe declare and promise that I will be true and faithfull to the Commonwealth of England as the same is now established without a King or House of Lords' (ibid. 274).

[49] As he wrote to Hornius on 30 Nov. (Twells, 134). Langbaine was of the same opinion on 29 Oct., when he wrote to Selden recommending the unnamed bearer of the letter as a possible successor in the Arabic Professorship 'if there be no hopes of Mr Pococks continuance, as I feare there is not' (MS Selden supra 109, fo. 323ʳ).

Pococke spent the next ten years at Childrey, travelling to Oxford (where he stayed in Balliol College) to give his lectures. But even in the rural retirement of Berkshire he was not left in peace. Some of his parishioners, who held grudges concerning payment of tithes, denounced him before the County Commissioners 'for ejecting ignorant, scandalous, insufficient and negligent ministers' appointed by an act of Cromwell in 1654. Pococke was occupied with defending himself against these frivolous and malicious charges[50] for several months. Pococke's former protector Selden died on 30 November 1654, but he did not lack supporters, for at a meeting of the Commissioners at Wantage on 27 March 1655 Charles Fettiplace and three other members of his family were among the numerous witnesses testifying for Pococke. However, it took the personal intervention of some eminent members of the university, headed by John Owen, the puritanical Vice-Chancellor, and himself one of the Commissioners appointed by Cromwell, to convince the County Commissioners 'of the infinite contempt and reproach which would certainly fall upon them, when it should be said, that they had turned out a man for insufficiency, whom all the learned, not of England only, but of all Europe, justly admired for his vast knowledge, and extraordinary accomplishments'.[51]

Pococke had indeed by that time acquired a reputation for scholarship throughout Europe. These years, although full of tribulation, were nevertheless the most productive period of his scholarship. Pococke belonged to the scholarly type recognizable to all members of the Republic of Letters: immensely learned, but reluctant to publish, ever certain that there is more to be discovered, and at last publishing only because pressed into print by someone else. So it was with Pococke's greatest book, the *Specimen Historiae Arabum*. When this appeared in 1650 Pococke was already 45 years old, and had published nothing since his juvenile edition of the Syriac Epistles twenty years earlier. Even then it is unlikely that he would have gone to print with this work, had it not been for his friend Gerard Langbaine. Writing to Ussher on 20 March 1648, Langbaine says: 'I have prevailed with Mr. Pocock to publish that remarkable piece of Alkadi Saed, of the sects of the Arabians, which I am now perusing before they go to press.'[52] This

---

[50] In the preface to his *Eutychius*, published about this time, he refers to the 'malitia planè insuperabili' which had distracted him from his work on that book.

[51] Twells, 174–5.

[52] Ussher, *Works*, xvi. 547; not in Ussher, *Letters*.

is a reference to the *Specimen*, the Arabic part of which consists of an extract from Abū 'l-Faraj's *History of the Dynasties* (the section on pre-Islamic history of the Arabs and the early history of Islam). 'Alkadi Saed' is Saʿīd al-Andalūsī, whose book *Ṭabaqāt al-Umam* is quoted by Abū 'l-Faraj at the very beginning of the extract.[53] The title of Pococke's book, 'A specimen of Arabic history', is intended, I think, to describe not the extract itself, but Pococke's notes on it (which indeed make up the great bulk of the work).[54]

(III) POCOCKE'S *SPECIMEN HISTORIAE ARABUM*

Pococke had been studying Abū 'l-Faraj's book for at least twelve years, so it is not surprising that this is the kind of work, embodying sound judgement and wide reading, that one would expect from a mature scholar. But it is much more: it is no exaggeration to say that it represents a revolution in Arabic studies. The notes illuminate the bare narrative of Abū 'l-Faraj with a wealth of information on points of history, geography, mythology, religion, and cultic practice, drawn from a large number of original sources, almost all available only in manuscript and the great majority unexploited by any European before Pococke.[55] The title 'Specimen' is well chosen to emphasize the pro-grammatic nature of the work. It is a remarkable attempt to claim the field of Arabic and Islamic history, literature, and culture as one that can and should be treated as equal in interest and validity, and be assessed by the same historical and philological criteria, as the Greek and Roman culture which had hitherto been the standard for European scholarship. Pococke does indeed consider Arabic rhetoric inferior to Greek and Latin, applying to it Caligula's characterization of Seneca's prose, 'sand without limestone'.[56] However, he emphatically denies that the Arabs lacked the facility for philosophy, and devotes a long note to the Caliph al-Ma'mūn's role in its development,[57] quoting

[53] The original was not available to Pococke, nor indeed was it known in Europe before the 20th century.

[54] The notes were printed first, in 1648 (Madan, *Oxford Books*, ii, no. 2007), but the book as a whole was not officially published until 1650 (ibid. no. 2034).

[55] These cannot be enumerated here. Most are listed and identified in Holt, 'Arabic Studies in Seventeenth-Century England', appendix 9. Some idea may be gained from the list of authors on pp. 345–73 (all references to the *Specimen* are to the 1806 edition, unless otherwise indicated).

[56] 'arena sine calce', p. 167.

[57] pp. 170–3.

with approval Henry Savile's judgement that the Arabs made such progress that they may be considered not inferior to the Greeks in 'bonae literae'. He is at pains throughout to illustrate his claim in the Preface that the Arabs possess 'treasures as yet unrevealed in every kind of literature',[58] drawing his illustrations from historians, poets, biographers, philosophers, geographers, zoological writers, belletrists, lexicographers, and grammarians as well as the many kinds of religious and ethical texts. But it is at the very end of the book that the comparison with classical culture is made most explicit:

If anyone should be amazed that not only those [Arabs] who were in former times considered wise, but also other races of antiquity outstanding for their wisdom, who indeed gave wisdom its very name, should have embraced such ridiculous superstition, let him be grateful to God that he had the good fortune to be brought up in a better tradition, and learn to cling closely to that and to be wise in sobriety, lest he fall, like them, by the just judgement of God, into the same or equally ridiculous beliefs. Even he who has the highest opinion of his own wisdom ought to fear such a fate, when he shall find that those whose foolishness in matters pertaining to religion surprises him, in matters pertaining to human wisdom are no whit inferior to himself or anybody else in genius and acuity.[59]

One contemporary reference in the book was noted by Twells, who drew attention to Pococke's remark about those stunted creatures of his own time ('apud nos homunciones') who despised learning and asserted that knowledge of other languages besides English was useless for the study of Christianity and should be banished.[60] But in a sense the whole long section of the notes on the Islamic sects,[61] with their quarrels over dogma and behaviour, could be taken by the alert reader as a commentary on contemporary divisions within Christianity, especially in England. This section is based mainly on al-Shahrastānī's *Kitāb al-Milal wa 'l-Niḥal*, but has additions from many other sources (Pococke is notable as the first European with significant knowledge of the Kalām, much of which he derived from al-Ījī's *Mawāqif*). Although Pococke's account is generally objective in tone, many of the disputes among Islamic sects which he chooses to describe are on topics which would have contemporary resonance, such as quarrels between the proponents of free will and predestination; the source of authority in religious matters, and in particular the status of the holy

[58] p. xv.
[59] pp. 326–7 (my translation).
[60] Twells, 176, citing *Specimen*, 166 (original edition; 172 of 1806 edition).
[61] pp. 199–269.

book; whether one has the right to kill those whom one considers heretics; and on what basis (if any) one might suppose people to be condemned to eternal damnation. In this connection Pococke repeats with obvious pleasure the response that silenced one theologian who was always ready to condemn to damnation those who disagreed with him: 'So Paradise, which is as great as the whole heavens and earth, will be reserved for the sole use of you and the three who agree with you?'[62] It is interesting to read the long quotation from al-Ghazālī on the excesses of certain Sufi enthusiasts in the light of such contemporary English sects as the Ranters:[63]

Some of them boast about their union with God, and having familiar speech with him . . . This kind of talk is the cause of great evils among the vulgar, so that some peasants stop cultivating the soil and make such claims for themselves . . . There is nothing to stop even the most stupid of men from saying such things, and readily applying this kind of talk to themselves; and when someone denies the truth of what they say, their response is: such incredulity comes from science and logic, but science is a veil, and logic the work of the mind, whereas what they say is revealed only from within by the light of truth.[64]

The *Specimen* was immediately recognized as a monumental achievement, and established Pococke's scholarly reputation throughout learned Europe. Pococke undoubtedly intended to edit and translate the whole of Abū 'l-Faraj's history. Whether he contemplated a commentary on the whole work on the same scale as the *Specimen* may be doubted. In the event he was side-tracked by Selden and Walton. When he did publish the complete work, in 1663, he added very little commentary apart from a factual account of Islamic history, drawn from other Arabic historians, to serve as a chronological continuation of his author's narrative down to his own time.[65]

(IV) OTHER ARABIC EDITIONS BY POCOCKE

The *Specimen* was (with the possible exception of Bainbridge's *Canicularia*)[66] the first book printed at Oxford with the Arabic types

[62] pp. 222–3.
[63] See e.g. Hill, *The World Turned Upside Down*, ch. 9.   [64] p. 264.
[65] See Pococke, *Abū 'l-Faraj*. In the preface to that work he credits Langbaine (by then dead for some years) with persuading him to publish it.
[66] On John Greaves's publication of this see below, p. 169. It was technically the earlier of the two, since the date on the title-page is 1648, whereas the *Specimen* is dated 1650. But, as we saw, Pococke's notes were printed earlier, in 1648.

which the university had acquired in 1636. As yet the university had no press of its own, but licensed printers (in this case Henry Hall) to produce works under its aegis, and, as here, lent them its exotic types where necessary. Immediately after this publication, in 1650, Pococke set to work on preparing for the press another edition which he had undoubtedly been contemplating before. This was the first book to be printed with the Hebrew types that the university had acquired at the same time as the Arabic. However, the work was written not in Hebrew but in Arabic. Entitled *Porta Mosis*, it consisted of the six prefatory sections of Maimonides' commentary on the Mishna, with Latin translation and extensive learned notes.[67] Arabic was the native language of Maimonides and most other Jews living in Islamic lands from the tenth century onwards, and there is a vast learned Jewish literature from the earlier medieval period written in Arabic with Hebrew characters. Pococke,[68] who lamented the neglect of this literature by contemporary Jews, was always interested in that branch of Arabic,[69] and this publication is a brilliant pioneering work.[70] It was well under way by 16 March 1652, when Langbaine told Selden about it,[71] and on 31 March, through Langbaine's efforts, an agreement was signed with the London typefounder Nicholas Nicholls to cast Hebrew type from the university's matrices.[72] However, the book did not appear until 1655.[73] Undoubtedly the main reason for the delay was that in the mean time Pococke had been persuaded, much against his inclination, to undertake another publication.

[67] See Roth, 'Edward Pococke and the First Hebrew Printing in Oxford'. Roth failed to note that Pococke's own manuscript, from which he made the translation, was an autograph of Maimonides: see Stern, 'Autographs of Maimonides in the Bodleian Library', 182.

[68] Twells's edition, p. vi: 'cum lingua *Arabica* apud *Judæos* in desuetudinem abierit, metus sit, ne prorsus perirent thesauri isti. Nescio enim quo pacto factum sit, ut paucorum jam manibus terantur quae Arabicè scripta sint, blattisque solùm & tineis comedentur, iis etiam in regionibus ubi ante aliquot saecula, non aliam, ut vidimus, dialectum facilè intelligerent vel eorum doctissimi.'

[69] See his requests to Boyle in 1661 and Huntington in 1671 and 1673 to find for him the *Kitāb al-Bayān* of Tanḥūm Yerūshalmī (Boyle, *Works*, vi. 324; Twells, 289, 295).

[70] Hitherto the only published work in Judaeo-Arabic was the special case of Saʿadya Gaon's Arabic translation of the Pentateuch (printed Constantinople, 1546).

[71] MS Selden supra 109, fo. 465ʳ.

[72] Carter, *History of Oxford University Press*, 40. According to Pococke the only reason that the Vice-Chancellor agreed to this was because Pococke's book, which would use the type, was in preparation (letter to Selden of 14 May 1652, MS Selden supra 109, fo. 349ʳ).

[73] Madan, *Oxford Books*, iii, no. 2277; the notes were also published separately in 1654 (ibid. no. 2259).

The mover in this was Selden, who wished to produce a complete edition and translation of the *Annals* of Eutychius, for which he had long borne an affection.[74] At one time he contemplated doing this himself, for his own Latin translation of a large part of the work survives among his manuscripts in the Bodleian Library.[75] However, in April 1652 he approached Langbaine with the proposal that the edition be printed at Oxford, at his own expense but under the supervision of Langbaine and Pococke, with a Latin translation which Pococke should make for the purpose.[76] On 11 May he put the same request to Pococke himself, who was reluctant, but felt that he could not refuse, since Selden had been so active in his promotion and defence.[77] Twells has a long discussion of the reasons for Pococke's reluctance, which he attributes primarily to Selden's attempt (in his *Eutychius*, 1642) to use Eutychius to 'bear down Episcopacy', an attempt which Twells himself refutes at length.[78] It is true that Pococke heartily disliked controversy, especially of the theological variety, but there was nothing of the kind in the book now projected by Selden, and it is absurd to suppose that he would feel himself compromised by the association with Selden's earlier work. Rather, he must have disliked the delays in the publication of the *Porta Mosis* that this new task would entail. Furthermore, Selden had idiosyncratic ideas about the right way to edit a text, and, although he had three manuscripts of the work available, insisted that the printed text should follow one of them to the letter, with any variants in the other two being consigned to the notes;[79] Pococke was clearly unhappy with this practice, but perforce adopted it in the printed work. Above all, he knew how inferior as a historical source Eutychius' *Annals* were[80] in comparison with

[74] See above, p. 65.

[75] MS Arch. Selden A 74* (*SC* no. 3212c).

[76] Langbaine's reply to this letter, on 21 April, is in MS Selden supra 109, fo. 339ʳ. Virtually the whole correspondence from the side of Langbaine and Pococke concerning the printing of the Eutychius is preserved in that manuscript, and Twells summarizes several letters about it from Selden to Pococke. It should be noted that Twells also had access to MS Selden supra 108/9, which at the time he wrote belonged to the physician and antiquary Richard Mead.

[77] He had publicly acknowledged these obligations in the preface of the *Specimen*, which was dedicated to Selden.

[78] Twells, 225–9. This version is repeated unquestioningly by some authoritative modern writers, e.g. Madan, *Oxford Books*, iii, no. 2297, followed by Carter, *History of Oxford University Press*, 41.

[79] This is explained by Pococke in his preface to the publication. This rule, and others which he insisted on, are listed by Selden in MS Selden supra 109, fo. 348.

[80] Twells draws attention to the remarks that Pococke makes about Eutychius' unreliability as a historian, but only as part of his own denigration of Eutychius' account

Abū 'l-Faraj, and must have resented having to spend his time on this author when the other was still unpublished as a whole.

Pococke worked intermittently on the translation and correction of the text of the Eutychius from 1652 to 1654, by which time the book was substantially finished, and the title-page to the second volume already printed.[81] Selden not only provided the paper for the edition, but also paid for Arabic type to be cast from the university's matrices. Twells mentions that a new puncheon and matrix were made for one letter at Pococke's instance, and this story seems to have been generally accepted.[82] The matter is indeed discussed by both Langbaine and Pococke in their correspondence with Selden (which reveals that the letter in question was *dāl*[83]). But the form of that letter in the printed Eutychius appears to be identical with that in earlier texts printed with the Oxford fount (e.g. those of John Greaves), so the plan must have been abandoned. The publication of the work was delayed by the death of Selden, which occurred on 30 November 1654. In a codicil to his will he had bequeathed the whole edition of the Eutychius (500 copies) to Langbaine and Pococke, but it was published only in 1656, after Pococke had completed the notes (mainly listing variant readings), written the preface, and compiled extensive indices and a list of errata. In the interval between 1654 and 1656, besides the distractions caused by the accusations of 'insufficiency' and by completing *Porta Mosis*, he had also been occupied with supervising the transfer of Selden's oriental and other manuscripts to the Bodleian, where they had been donated. Pococke's preface to the Eutychius betrays his personal dissatisfaction with the work. He is distressed by the solecisms of the printed text which Selden's editorial methods had imposed on him, and takes pains to document Eutychius' untrustworthiness as a historian. Nevertheless, the translation is reliable, and given the paucity of any printed editions of Arabic historians at the time, it was a valuable contribution.

of early episcopacy. The distortion is carried further by Madan, who says (p. 52) that Pococke 'had also found out meanwhile' that Eutychius was not a dependable historian, as if Pococke (who assisted Selden in his 1642 publication) had not known that for many years.

[81] Copies of the printed sheets were sent to Selden in London as they emerged from the press. The separate copy of pp. 1–244 of vol. 2, dated 1654, which is in the Bodleian was no doubt, as Madan surmises, Selden's own.

[82] Even by historians of printing, e.g. Carter, *History of Oxford University Press*, 41.

[83] Pococke's objection to the form of the Oxford *dāl*, according to Langbaine, was that 'he bears his head (or, to give it you in his expression, Kicks up his heels) too high' (MS Selden supra 109, fo. 343a).

Although, as we shall see, Pococke provided help in the great English Polyglot Bible, the only other Arabic text that he himself published before the Restoration was in a kind of *jeu d'esprit*. This was a tiny anonymous pamphlet entitled *The Nature of the drink Kauhi, or Coffe . . . Described by an Arabian Phisitian*. It is a short extract from a sixteenth-century Arabic work, the author of which has been identified by Margoliouth[84] as Dā'ūd ibn 'Umar al-Anṭākī. The extract, which was printed by Henry Hall in Oxford in 1659, using the Oxford Arabic types, was accompanied by an English translation. Pococke himself had learned to drink coffee in the East, and continued to do so ever afterwards, to the extent that a 'palsy in his hand' which afflicted him late in life was ascribed to this addiction.[85] The little work aroused some interest among the scientifically curious.[86] On 5 April 1659 Hartlib thanked Boyle for sending him a copy (which presumably Pococke, who became friendly with Boyle at Oxford in the 1650s, had given to him).[87] Hartlib promptly made handwritten copies of the English translation[88] and sent them to others, including Worthington at Cambridge, to whom he explained that 'Mr. Pococke has lately translated out of Arabick something of an Arabian physitian concerning coffee, of which papers, because he will suffer very few to be printed, I enclose you one'.[89] The work was already scarce in 1668, when Edmund Castell asked Samuel Clarke to search for a copy at Oxford, offering to pay a groat (fourpence) or as much as sixpence for it.[90] As late as 1671 the Hamburg physician Martin Vogel was trying to get the pamphlet through Oldenburg, and John Wallis, to whom Oldenburg applied, had to turn to Pococke himself for a copy.[91] The extract, after describing the coffee plant, lauds the effects of drinking its product,

[84] In Madan, *Oxford Books*, iii, no. 2438. Madan's note there needs slight corrections: there is at least one other copy extant besides the Bodleian's (Wood 679), namely the one in the British Library, from which Pococke's translation was published by Chew, *The Crescent and the Rose*, 185; the attribution to Pococke is put beyond all doubt by the contemporary references quoted here.

[85] Twells, 336–7.

[86] Coffee-drinking was a recent pastime at Oxford. Wood, *Life and Times*, i. 168–9, records that 'Jacob a Jew' opened a coffee-house there in 1650/1. Bliss's note ad loc. adds recondite information on the topic.

[87] Boyle, *Works*, vi. 117.

[88] Such a copy was published from the Hartlib Papers, 42/4/4, in *The Hartlib Papers Project Newsletter* (October 1990), 9.

[89] Hartlib to Worthington, 20 Apr. 1659 (Worthington, *Correspondence*, i. 127). Cf. ibid. 131–2, which makes it clear that Hartlib sent only the English without the Arabic.

[90] MS BL Add. 22905, fo. 75.

[91] Oldenburg, *Correspondence*, viii. 331, 372, 387.

but warns of its dangers, e.g. 'it allayes the ebullition of the blood, is good against the small poxe and measles, and bloudy pimples; yet causeth vertiginous headheach, and maketh lean much, occasioneth waking, and the Emirods, and asswages lust, and sometimes breeds melancholly.'

After the disturbances of the Civil War and the early years of the Visitation, Oxford in the 1650s returned to a semblance of normality. Whereas the best of Pococke's pupils in the 1640s had been forced out of or voluntarily left Oxford in the early years of the Visitation,[92] in the 1650s a new generation of pupils arrived to study Arabic. Of those who were prominent later we should mention Edward Bernard (St John's, BA 1659), Robert Huntington (Merton, BA 1658), and Narcissus Marsh (Magdalen Hall, BA 1658). Slightly junior to these, but a friend of all three, was Thomas Smith, who matriculated at Queen's College in 1657, and graduated BA after the Restoration, but appears to have studied oriental languages while still an undergraduate.

(V) GREAVES'S ORIENTAL PUBLICATIONS

All the other Arabic publications emanating from Oxford during the Revolution were prepared by John Greaves. Although all but one of these books were printed not in Oxford but in London, and although Greaves himself was expelled from the university in 1648,[93] it is appropriate to consider his work while discussing Arabic at Oxford, for not only was much of the preparation done there, but the Oxford Arabic types were used to print most of his books. None of these was published during the royal occupation of Oxford, but Greaves must have been preparing the first for the press at that time, for it appeared in 1646, soon after Oxford surrendered to the forces of Fairfax. This was *Pyramidographia or a Description of the Pyramids in Ægypt*.[94] Most of this extraordinary book is devoted to Greaves's own exploration and measurements of the pyramids in 1638–9. But in the first part he gives an overview of the history of the pyramids, as far as it can be

---

[92] I refer to Thomas Marshall and Samuel Clarke.

[93] Since Sir Nathaniel Brent resumed the Wardenship of Merton immediately upon the surrender of Oxford, the college could not have been congenial to Greaves, and it is not surprising that thereafter he seems to have spent most of his time in London or elsewhere.

[94] Greaves, *Pyramidographia*, reprinted in Greaves, *Works*, vol. i. For an evaluation of its importance in the history of Egyptology see Wortham, *British Egyptology*, 19–23.

derived from written records. Amongst these he includes Arabic
sources, although he attaches no great credence to the fabulous
accounts they give. The Arabic works that he quotes and translates are
'Morat Alzeman' and 'Ibn Abd Alhokm an Arabian, where he dis-
courses of the wonders of Ægypt'.[95] He also quotes from the Persian
author he calls 'Emir Cond': this is the well-known Persian history of
Mīr Khwānd.[96] Greaves produced another book in the following year,
*A Discourse of the Romane Foot and Denarius: From whence, as from
two principles, the Measures and Weights, used by the Ancients, may
be deduced.*[97] The contents of this are far more diverse than the title
would suggest, and range far and wide over ancient, medieval, and
modern metrology, which was one of Greaves's favourite studies, and
to which, as he boasts, he had devoted much effort in his travels. He
had also recruited the unfortunate Pococke to drudge for him in this
arena. Twells (p. 72) describes the instructions he sent him 'to measure
the west end of S. Sophia very exactly, with a very fine small wire of
brass or iron'. In another letter written to Pococke in Constantinople
Greaves gives him lengthy and minute directions for taking various
weights and measures, from which two short extracts must suffice as
examples: 'for more security upon a dry and straight sticke you may
exactly marke the length of the Persian dirah, especially that of
Bagdad, for Almamon's sake who lived Calif there, and by that
measured the earth'; 'I remember your litle Jew told me that he had the
waight of a shekel in lead, if he will not part with his, by a true and
fine balance, take the waight of it in another peice of lead and put it up
with such care as that it may not loose of its waight'.[98]

As the first of the above extracts indicates, Greaves was particularly
interested in Arabic measures of length in connection with the famous
measurement of one degree of the earth's surface by astronomers
under the patronage of the Caliph al-Ma'mūn.[99] In the seventeenth
century the precise size of the earth was still a matter of uncertainty,
and Greaves was not alone in considering that ninth-century measure-

[95] pp. 6, 44 (*Works*, i. 9, 60–1, with translation 110–15).

[96] 'The Garden of Purity', written in the 15th century: see A. Jourdain in *Notices et
extraits des manuscrits*, 9 (1812).

[97] Greaves, *Roman Foot*, reprinted, *Works*, i. 165–356.

[98] Pococke noted on this: 'He had the forme, not the waight, but said that silver one
of which he tooke the waight for me weighed 27 dragms of Turkish silver.' The letter is
one of those copied by Ward: MS BL Add. 6193, fos. 73–5, written from Livorno, 28
Feb. 1640.

[99] The best treatment of this is still Nallino's 'Il valore metrico del grado di meridiano
secondo i geografi arabi', although some details need correction.

ment relevant to modern geography. In his work on the Roman foot he cites two different accounts of it, one by 'Muhammed Ibn Mesoud . . . in his book intituled in the Persian, Gehandanish'.[100] He knew this astronomical work, Kitāb-i-Jahāndānish, by Muḥammad b. Mas'ūd al-Mas'ūdī, from a manuscript of his own.[101] He also gives a translation and partial text of the circumstantial account of the measurement in Abū 'l-Fidā''s *Geography*,[102] a work which he was engaged in editing. Although Greaves's book is mainly concerned with the precise length of the Roman foot, there are other incidental references to Arabic and Persian treatises, including 'Aly Kushgy, who assisted Vlug Beg in compiling his astronomical tables in Persian',[103] to whom Greaves would also return later. Perhaps the most notable feature of the work is the list at the end, of measurements, in current metrical units, that Greaves had taken on some 'remarkable and lasting monuments', including the pyramids. The purpose of these was to ease the way of some future enquirer who might encounter the same difficulties in determining the exact length of, for example, the English foot as Greaves had with the Roman. Only in the seventeenth century could such a 'modern' conception of the changes that the future might bring be combined with a belief that investigation of the discoveries of past ages could still be of use for the development of science.

In 1648 Greaves supervised the printing at Oxford of the *Canicularia* of John Bainbridge. Ussher had commissioned the work from Bainbridge, and he now requested Greaves to complete it. It is concerned with the Sothic period attributed to the ancient Egyptians, of 1,460 Julian years, which is connected with the heliacal rising of the star Sirius (the 'dog-star'). Bainbridge's discussion is drawn exclusively from Greek and Latin sources. However, Greaves took the opportunity to add material of his own, which illuminates his wide reading in Arabic and Persian astronomical authors. On pp. 43–8 he cites a number of values for the obliquity of the ecliptic from various medieval authors. These include 'Ibn Shater . . . sedulus cœli, siderumque inspector, è multis observationibus Damasci factis', i.e. ibn al-Shāṭir's *Zīj al-Jadīd*, of which Greaves possessed a manuscript

---

[100] *Works*, i. 192.

[101] Now MS Greaves 11, with many marginal notes and paraphrases by Greaves.

[102] *Works*, i. 220–1. An earlier account had been published by Christmann (from Postel's manuscript of Abū 'l-Fidā', at that time in the Palatine Library) in the notes to his edition of *Alfragani Chronologica et astronomica elementa*, Frankfurt, 1590.

[103] *Works*, i. 194.

which he annotated heavily;[104] al-Ṣūfī's star catalogue, which he consulted in a manuscript belonging to Pococke; 'Aly Kushgius in instit.
Astr. Persicâ', i.e. the Persian *Risālah dar 'ilm-i-hai'at* by 'Ali 'Alā
al-Dīn al-Qūshjī,[105] an assistant in the observatory of Ulugh Beg; and
'Nassir Eddinus Persa, in civitate Maragâ', for which the authority is
'Cod. Ms. Persicus Nassir Eddin cum Comm. Shah Cholgii in Tabb.
ejus Astronom.' Greaves is referring here to the Persian *Zīj-i-Īlkhānī*
of Naṣīr al-Dīn al-Ṭūsī, with the fifteenth-century commentary of
Maḥmūdshāh Khalajī.[106] Extracts of another Persian work by the latter,
his *Zīj-i-Jāmiʿ*, were published by Greaves in *Astronomica quaedam*[107]
(see below). Finally, he not only refers to the astronomical tables of
Ulugh Beg, but on pp. 82–116 gives a list of coordinates selected from
the star catalogue in that great work, for the epoch AH 841 = AD 1437.
This is preceded by a short account of Ulugh Beg and his observatory
at Samarkand, and a promise to produce an edition of the whole star
catalogue. Greaves did not live to publish this, but we shall see that his
work was incorporated into the edition of Thomas Hyde (Oxford,
1665).

On 30 October 1648, after refusing to answer the charges of the
Visitors,[108] Greaves was formally deprived of his fellowship at Merton
and the Savilian Professorship, and expelled from the university. He
did not go without a fight. The records of the Visitation show that he
sought to be restored, and in July 1649 the articles against him were
formally exhibited.[109] He was unsuccessful, but did manage to obtain
some of his arrears of salary. His successor as Savilian Professor of
Astronomy was Seth Ward, who was allegedly appointed by Greaves's
influence, in return for which Ward turned over his professorial salary
to Greaves as long as he lived. However, since the only authority

[104] Now MS Arch. Seld. A 8; this is one of Greaves's manuscripts which was purchased after his death by Selden.

[105] Greaves's manuscript of this, heavily annotated by him, is now MS Greaves 21.

[106] Greaves evidently possessed a manuscript of this, which is not now identifiable
(the suggestion of Mercier, 'English Orientalists and Mathematical Astronomy', 163,
that he used MS Huntington 143, which was somehow in the Bodleian in Greaves's
time, has nothing to recommend it). It may have been one of the manuscripts which
Greaves lost when his room at Gresham College was ransacked.

[107] The statement in Sachau–Ethé, col. 930, no. 1513 that this is his commentary on
the *Zīj-i-Īlkhānī* appears to be an error.

[108] These are given in detail by Wood, *Athenae Oxonienses*, iii. 325, and in Greaves,
Works, vol. i, p. xxvii. Not surprisingly his behaviour at Merton towards Sir Nathaniel
Brent and Ralph Button (both associated with the Visitors) is a prominent feature.

[109] Burrows, *Register of Visitors*, 252–3; this document was the source of Wood's and
Birch's information. The matter was dragging on as late as January 1650 (ibid. 284).

for this seems to be Ward himself, as recorded by his sycophantic biographer,[110] one may suspect that the account is not impartial. Greaves went to live in London, and there, in 1650, married Elizabeth Gibbon. He died two years later without issue. Yet between his remove from Oxford and his death he managed to get another four books published,[111] despite the distractions caused by his encounters with the Visitors, and by many years of lawsuits connected with his position as executor of Bainbridge's and then Mrs Bainbridge's estate, into which he had been manœuvred by his enemy Sir Nathaniel Brent, acting as probate judge.[112] He had also spent much time defending himself against the charges for which he was dismissed from his Gresham Professorship.

To print the Arabic and Persian quotations in his first two books Greaves (or his printers) had to scrounge for types. The two quotations in the book on the pyramids are set in the Selden types,[113] while those in the *Roman Foot* employ both the types of John Viccars and the Oxford Arabic fount.[114] It seems that by that time there were no matrices for Arabic type available in London, so the printers were forced to use such cast type as they found lying around or whatever Greaves could borrow from Oxford. This *ad hoc* method was obviously inadequate for Greaves's subsequent books, which were publications of Arabic and Persian texts, and required a complete fount. To this end Greaves borrowed the university's Arabic matrices (which were in the hands of Langbaine, the Keeper of the Archives), took them to London, and got the typefounder Nicholls to cast type for the printer Jacob Flesher (who undertook the books published by Greaves in London from 1648 to 1652). According to Gerard Langbaine, Greaves deceived the university by pretending that his motive in borrowing the matrices was merely to examine them in order

[110] Pope, *Life of Seth, Lord Bishop of Salisbury*, 20–3. A useful antidote to Pope's hagiography is Wood's malicious paragraph on Ward's 'cringing' before and after the Restoration (*Life and Times*, i. 363).

[111] Five if we count the publication of Robert Withers's *Description of the Grand Signor's Seraglio* (London, 1650) from a manuscript which Greaves had obtained in Constantinople. He did not know that this had been imperfectly published before in Purchas's *Pilgrims*, Lib. IX, c. 15, pp. 1580 ff. (London, 1625). It was reprinted in Greaves, *Works*, ii. 541–800.

[112] Ward, *Gresham Professors*, 145, quotes a letter from Greaves to Pococke of 28 Oct. 1646, in which he says: 'My journey [to Leiden] still holds, tho retarded by my losses, and by Sir N[athaniel Brent], who hath put me to play an after game with the three brothers, by giving them the administration.'

[113] *Pyramidographia*, 44, 57.

[114] e.g. pp. 57 and 10 respectively.

to have the defects in them remedied, and his allowing Flesher to have a fount cast from them was entirely unauthorized.[115] However dubious the means, the result was of considerable benefit to scholarship, since it made possible the publication not only of Greaves's own works but also of the later works of Selden, for instance his *De Synedriis Liber Tertius* (1655, also printed by Flesher).[116]

When Greaves published the extract from Ulugh Beg's star catalogue in 1648, he explained that the orthography was incorrect because some of the letters peculiar to Persian were not available to the printer. By the following year he had remedied this (presumably by arranging for Nicholls to cut the punches), for in 1649 he published a Persian grammar. As he explained to Selden,[117] this had been prepared long before, but he had postponed the publication because he lacked facilities for printing it and then took his journey to the East. The precise time of composition is fixed by Greaves's preface to another little work which was published with it (although the title-page and dedication are dated 1648). This is an anonymous Persian tract, explaining the abbreviations used in Arabic and Persian astronomical works, which Greaves had found in Constantinople. Addressing Claude Hardy, he mentions that he had composed his Persian grammar in Paris long before, at Hardy's exhortation. This must have been in 1635, at which time there was no grammar of Persian in print. In the mean time, however, Greaves had been anticipated by de Dieu's *Rudimenta linguae Persicae*.[118]

For several years Greaves had been working on an edition of Abū 'l-Fidā''s *Geography*. This had been desired by European geographers since some knowledge of the manuscript brought back by Postel had been disseminated in the sixteenth century.[119] Editions had been promised by Erpenius, and later by Wilhelm Schickard, who made some use of a copy of the Vienna codex which Tengnagel had provided for him.[120] Greaves expressed his intention of producing an

---

[115] Langbaine's note is printed by Johnson and Gibson, *Print and Privilege at Oxford*, 27 n. 2. According to the same authors Greaves's receipt for the matrices is dated Jan. 1648.

[116] For the original intention to use these types for printing the Polyglot Bible see below, p. 204.

[117] Greaves, *Elementa*, preface.

[118] Leiden, 1639: *PO* no. 312, cf. no. 310.

[119] Greaves, *Chorasmiae Descriptio*, preface Aa 3, mentions the use made of it by Ramusio, Castaldus, and Ortelius.

[120] See above, p. 28. Greaves had been in correspondence about this with Schickard before the latter's death in 1635.

edition as early as 1638.[121] We have seen already that one of the reasons for his visit to the Vatican Library in 1639 was to collate Postel's manuscript there. By 1645 he had made considerable progress, but had also encountered difficulties, as one sees from a letter he wrote to Pococke on 7 August:

Abulfeda goes on but slowly, having had so many impediments, & I feare, unless the copy at Leyden can give me better assistance then that at Cambridge, it will go on much slowlier. Besides somethings in the text, which certainly are corrupted, the numbers of all that I ever saw, even of yours, which is the best of them, are so different and false, (as I found by reducing the cities into maps) that it will be a most difficult peece of work to restore them. Wherefore I now see that to be true, which Schavenius long since writt to me, that it would be almost impossible to publish his mappes.[122]

A year later he was having doubts about the value of the work for modern geography. He wrote to Pococke on 28 October 1646:

to speake the truth, those maps, which shall be made out of Abulfeda, will not be so exact, as I did expect; as I have found by comparing some of them with our modern and best charts. In his description of the Red sea, which was not far from him, he is most grossely mistaken; what may we then think of places remoter? However there may be good use made of the book for Arabian writers.[123]

It must have been such doubts that influenced his choice of the excerpts of the *Geography* that he eventually published. These covered parts of the world that were virtually unknown to Europeans, for which Abū 'l-Fidā''s coordinates and descriptions, even if faulty, were better than nothing. In 1650 appeared Greaves's edition and translation of sections 25 and 26 of the *Geography*, dealing with two regions of Central Asia, Khwārezm and Mā warā'a al-Nahr ('the region beyond the River', i.e. the Oxus). The book also included Abū 'l-Fidā''s introduction to the whole work, and Greaves's preface to the reader. In this he explains that the present work is merely a specimen of the complete edition that will appear shortly, based on his collation of five manuscripts: the Palatine (now Vatican), Erpenius' copy of that (now at Cambridge), two manuscripts owned by Pococke, and one by Greaves himself.[124] He provides a well-informed discussion of the work and its

[121] In his letter to Turner from Constantinople in 1638 (MS Smith 93, p. 138), after Greaves had acquired his own manuscript of the *Geography*.

[122] MS BL Add. 6193, fo. 76ʳ; cf. Ward, *Gresham Professors*, 152 (wrongly dated to 1646).   [123] Ward, *Gresham Professors*, 151.

[124] Now MS Greaves 2. There are some useful collectanea on these manuscripts in Mercier, 'English Orientalists and Mathematical Astronomy', 173–4.

author, unfortunately marred by the wrong dates that he assigns to Abū 'l-Fidā''s accession as ruler of Hamah and death, namely AH 743 and 746. Pococke had already assigned the correct date of AH 710 to the accession.[125] Twells, indignant at the aspersion on Pococke's accuracy which this discrepancy elicited in Bayle's *Dictionary*, explains Greaves's error at length.[126] He had taken the dates from a work which he called 'AlSacerdan',[127] which refers to a completely different Abū 'l-Fidā', one of the Mameluke sultans of Egypt.

Greaves completed his translation of one other section of the *Geography*, that on Arabia, but did not live to see it published. However, his handwritten version later came to the Bodleian, whence it was printed in Hudson's *Geographiae Scriptores*.[128] His annotation to this suggests that by then he was thoroughly tired of the work: 'Non minus arida, et inculta est haec Abulfedae descriptio, quam ipsa Arabia Petraea.' He also used his knowledge of Abū 'l-Fidā''s work to annotate another geographical book which he published in 1648. This contained the short lists of geographical coordinates found in two sets of astronomical tables in Persian, al-Ṭūsī's *Zīj-i-Īlkhānī* and Ulugh Beg's *Zīj-i-jadīd-i-Sultānī*. In this work he also refers to the geographical treatise of al-Idrīsī, mentioning that both he and Pococke had manuscripts of it.[129]

In 1650 Greaves published the Persian text and Latin translation of a long extract from the astronomical work, *Zīj-i-Jāmiʿ*, of Maḥmūdshāh Khalajī.[130] This was reissued in 1652 with some small additions from the elementary astronomical work, in Arabic, of al-Farghānī, and other matter. Further editions which he planned, including the complete *Geography* of Abū 'l-Fidā' and at least the star catalogue from Ulugh Beg's *zīj*, were cut short by his early death on 8 October 1652. We have already mentioned the posthumous publication of his translations of the pseudo-Archimedean *Lemmata* and the Arabian section of

---

[125] *Specimen*, 363 (original edition); 349 (1806 edition).

[126] Twells, 257–63, following Gagnier and Sale.

[127] Greaves's manuscript of this is another of those that were later sold to Selden. It is now MS Selden superius 69, *Kitāb al-Sukkardān*, a work on the geography and history of Egypt by al-Talamsānī.

[128] Vol. iii, seventh item. The text for this edition was prepared by John Gagnier. The original is MS Greaves 13.

[129] Greaves, *Tabulae Geographicae*, preface. His manuscript is now MS Greaves 42, described by Wakefield, 'Arabic Manuscripts in the Bodleian Library', 133 as 'a fine North African copy of vol. I of al-Idrīsī'. See Gabrieli and Scerrato, *Gli Arabi in Italia*, 23, for a reproduction of one of the maps in this manuscript.

[130] Or Khiljī: Greaves, *Astronomica quaedam*. His manuscript of this is now MS Greaves 6: see Mercier, 'English Orientalists and Mathematical Astronomy', 162.

Abū 'l-Fidā"s *Geography*. Some other minor relicts were published by Birch in Greaves's *Works*.

In his approach to Arabic and Persian texts, Greaves was old-fashioned compared with Pococke. Although he was aware of their historical and cultural interest, his primary motive in studying and publishing them was that of his teacher Bainbridge, ultimately stemming from Sir Henry Savile. He wanted to use them to advance the contemporary study of astronomy and geography. This was not absurd at the time, but in fact the scientific data that could be derived from this kind of text were already partially obsolete or irrelevant in the Europe of the 1640s, and by the end of the century had been almost completely overtaken by the rapid advance of science and exploration. Today Greaves's publications are of interest primarily as contributions to the history of science in Islamic lands. In his knowledge of Islamic astronomy Greaves far surpassed all his European predecessors, and indeed had no successor until the nineteenth century.[131]

Greaves's oriental interests were not confined to scientific works. As we saw, he produced a Persian dictionary and grammar. He also worked on a Turkish dictionary, according to his letter to Pococke of 15 November 1649:[132] 'Mr. Seaman and myself are both in hand with a Turkish Dictionary.' I am uncertain whether to interpret this as a joint effort or rival efforts by Greaves and William Seaman,[133] but in either case have found no trace of the work. However, a literary translation by Greaves does survive: this is 'The Questions of Abdalla Ebn Salam the Jew and the answers of Mahomet, written in Arabicke by Abdalla Ebn Abbas, and translated into English by J[ohn] G[reaves]'.[134] According to Ward, Greaves also translated this Islamic apologetic work into Latin:

Quaestiones Abdallae Ebn Salan Judaei cum Mohammedis responsis, a Johanne Gravio ex Arabica lingua in Latinam traductae, et notis illustratae

---

[131] Until Caussin de Perceval's publication of major extracts from the astronomical work of ibn Yūnus in *Notices et extraits des manuscrits*, 7 (1804), the only contribution, and that a minor one, was Golius' edition and translation of al-Farghānī, published posthumously in 1669 (Schnurrer no. 402).

[132] Excerpted by Birch: Greaves, *Works*, vol. i, p. xxxiv.

[133] On this man see below, pp. 216–17.

[134] MS Locke c. 27, fos. 3–9 (Long, *Catalogue of the Lovelace Collection of the Papers of John Locke*, 27). 'Abdallāh b. Salām was allegedly the chief of a Jewish community to which Muḥammad wrote a letter. On this (probably fictitious) person see the note on Sura 16 in Sale, *Koran*. This is the 'Doctrina Mahumet' (or 'Questions of 'Abdallāh ibn Salām') translated by Herman of Dalmatia and available in printed editions of the Latin Koran (Bibliander): Nicoll–Pusey, pp. 508–9.

. . . a curious manuscript in Arabic and Latin, now in the possession of Sir Richard Ellys baronet. It contains certain questions taken out of the Jewish law by Ebn Salan, and proposed to Mahammed, which being answered by him, this rabbi is there said to have become one of his principal followers.[135]

Since Greaves transcribed the Arabic for this, I assume that he copied it from a manuscript already in the Bodleian.[136]

(VI) GREAVES'S COLLECTION OF ORIENTAL MANUSCRIPTS

This brings us to the topic of Greaves's oriental manuscripts. The manuscript collection in the Bodleian Library labelled 'Greaves' is so called because it was purchased, in 1678, from the estate of Thomas Greaves, who had died in 1676.[137] But it has always been assumed that all or most of the oriental items in it had belonged to his brother John, and we shall see that there is evidence for this assumption. Wakefield says that the collection contains twenty-one Arabic and seventeen Turkish and Persian manuscripts, and expresses surprise at its smallness.[138] In fact this was just the remnant of a much larger collection that John Greaves had owned. In his will (dated 5 June 1651 and proved 19 October 1652), after certain bequests, Greaves left the remainder of his estate, including his books, to be divided between his three brothers.[139] In the division his oriental manuscripts were taken by Thomas Greaves, as was natural, given his own interest in Arabic and Persian. However, he was soon approached by Selden, who had corresponded with him as early as 1636. On 25 October 1652 Langbaine wrote to Selden, in response to a letter informing him of Greaves's death: 'you know he was owner of some Arabick bookes which (I believe) are not to be found in Europe againe; unlesse you think fitt to buy them your self, I wold willingly putt in for this University.'[140] Selden did just this, as Samuel Clarke informed Ravius on 25 March 1656 in response to an enquiry about what had happened to Greaves's books, telling him that Thomas Greaves had obtained the entire library and sold or given very many Arabic books from it to Selden.[141] We

---

[135] Ward, *Gresham Professors*, 150. I do not know whether this version survives.
[136] MS Bodl. Or. 224, Nicoll no. 27, item 3, pp. 68–9.
[137] Macray, *Annals*, 147–8.
[138] Wakefield, 'Arabic Manuscripts in the Bodleian Library', 132–3.
[139] PRO, PROB 11,223, fo. 147ᵛ.   [140] MS Selden supra 109, fo. 372.
[141] MS BL Add. 29747, fo. 30: 'ea fratri ejus Thomae Gravio integra cessit, qui

have already noted several manuscripts in the Selden collection in the Bodleian which belonged to John Greaves. The list can be lengthened from other sources. In a letter to Claude Hardy of May 1641 reporting his doings in the East, Greaves mentions his success in obtaining manuscripts, and in particular 'quatuor [*sic*] libros Apollonii Pergaei, Geometrae subtilissimi فى قطع الخطوط علي النسب quorum Pappus aliique meminerunt'.[142] This is the Arabic version of Apollonius' *On the Division of a Ratio*, now MS Arch. Seld. A 7, from which Halley later made the first published translation. In his letter to Ussher of 19 September 1644, Greaves says that he has extracted observations of the Indians and Persians from a manuscript he owns of 'Alhashamy an Arabian Author'.[143] This shows that he was the owner of the present MS Arch. Seld. A 11, which contains the unique copy of al-Hāshimī's '*Ilal al-Zījāt*, a work of great interest for the early history of Islamic astronomy. That manuscript, which is annotated by Greaves, also contains al-Farghānī's 'Elements of Astronomy', from which Greaves published extracts in 1652. In his posthumously published letter to Ussher on the latitudes of Byzantium and Rhodes Greaves mentions 'the Geography of Said Ibn Aly Algiorgani'.[144] This must be the Persian treatise *Kitāb-Masālik-almamālik* by Abū 'l-Ḥasan Ṣā'id b. 'Alī al-Jurjānī (now MS Selden superius 95). The above are merely a few cases that I have incidentally documented of Selden manuscripts which had belonged to John Greaves; I have no doubt that the great majority of the scientific Arabic and Persian manuscripts in Selden's collection (of which there are many more than those mentioned) come from the same source.

Moreover, Selden was not the only one to whom Thomas Greaves sold manuscripts after his brother's death. On 23 May 1668 he sent a parcel of books to Samuel Clarke, with a letter[145] which makes it clear

plurimos exinde libros Arabicos Seldeno vel dedit vel vendidit.' Clarke was in an excellent position to know, for he had been in touch with Selden in London, and was familiar with Thomas Greaves not only from his participation in the Polyglot Bible (which Clarke was currently supervising the printing of), but as an old friend from Oxford: Thomas Greaves inscribed the copy of his brother's *Astronomica quaedam* which he gave to Clarke (now in Cambridge University Library, U.13.20) 'Amico suo charissimo D. Samueli Clerke Linguarum Orientalium peritissimo'.

[142] MS Smith 93, p. 111, printed in Greaves, *Works*, ii. 442–6. I have corrected the faulty Arabic in the transcript. The manuscript is also mentioned by Hottinger (*Bibliothecarius Quadripartitus*, 31) amongst those he saw in Greaves's library in 1641.

[143] Ussher, *Letters*, no. 211, p. 509.

[144] Greaves, *Works*, ii. 371, cf. Mercier, 'English Orientalists and Mathematical Astronomy', 172.

[145] MS BL 22905, fo. 77.

that he was selling manuscripts from his brother's legacy. The only item mentioned by name is 'Kamus', i.e. a copy of the well-known Arabic dictionary of al-Fīrūzābādī (presumably one of the lexicons which Greaves had told Hardy that he had bought in the East), valued by John Greaves at 40 crowns. Although there is no record of this transaction either in Macray, *Annals*, or in Philip, *Bodleian Library in the Seventeenth and Eighteenth Centuries*, there can be little doubt that Clarke was buying the books on behalf of the university in his capacity as Architypographus, at a time when it was acquiring exotic types and manuscripts as part of Dr John Fell's revival of the 'learned press'. A Greaves manuscript which came to the Bodleian by yet another route is MS Bodl. Or. 516, an important exemplar of al-Bīrūnī's major astronomical work, *al-Qānūn al-Masʿūdī*. Greaves refers to his manuscript of al-Bīrūnī in Bainbridge, *Canicularia*, p. 44, and to the table of ascensions for Ghazna from the *Qānūn* in *Tabulae Geographicae*, pp. 30 and 62. The manuscript came to the Bodleian by purchase from the estate of Edward Bernard in 1698, but how Bernard obtained it is less clear. He could have bought it from Thomas Greaves in 1672, at which time the two were in correspondence concerning an attempt by Bernard (then Deputy Professor of Astronomy) to get some of John Greaves's instruments for the Savilian Museum.[146] More probably he bought it from Thomas Greaves's estate after his death. On 26 October 1676 John Lamphere wrote from Oxford to Bernard (then in Paris): 'I have sent you over a Catalogue of diuers. Ms. of Dr Greeues once of Corpus Christi College';[147] so one may guess that Bernard bought some of the items in this catalogue for himself, and then persuaded the university to buy all or most of the rest. It is likely that some of the other Arabic astronomical manuscripts that came to the Bodleian from Bernard's library had formerly belonged to Greaves.

When we further consider that Greaves, while in Constantinople, had been active on behalf of Laud both in buying manuscripts and in selecting and supervising the transmission of the tributes of the Levant Company, we can see that the Bodleian Library owes a significant part of the great oriental collection which it assembled in the seventeenth century to his enthusiasm and judgement. In this respect he ranks only behind Pococke and Huntington. Since several items in his own collection were lost during his lifetime by the pillaging of soldiers, and the collection itself was dispersed in various ways after his death, it may

---

[146] Thomas Greaves's letter on the subject, of 26 Feb. 1672, is in MS Smith 45, p. 81.
[147] Ibid., pp. 55–6.

never be possible to reconstruct it as whole,[148] unless by some good
fortune a copy of the catalogue which he compiled at the request of
Claude Hardy and later sent to Golius[149] survives somewhere unnoticed.

(VII) ARABIC STUDIES IN CAMBRIDGE DURING THE REVOLUTION

Cambridge too was subjected to disturbances during the Civil War and
afterwards, although these were not as rude as at Oxford, since Parliament controlled that region almost from the beginning. Wheelock,
always submissive to authority, retained his positions (including the
Arabic lectureship) undisturbed, although others with whom he was
associated were neither so pliant nor so fortunate. Among these was
Richard Holdsworth, who had been instrumental in obtaining
Erpenius' manuscripts for Cambridge and was later to be a great benefactor of the University Library.[150] Master of Emmanuel College from
1637, and in the early 1640s Vice-Chancellor, he was imprisoned in
London and removed from office. Although there were a number of
scholars at Cambridge in this period besides Wheelock who had some
command of Arabic, and, as we shall see, Cambridge men played a
major part in the production of the Polyglot Bible, no publications
relevant to Arabic studies emerged from Cambridge.[151] One reason for
this was certainly the lack of appropriate printing facilities there. The
university had indeed inherited Bedwell's Arabic types with the
implicit promise of printing his dictionary with them. But these were
ill suited for printing an Arabic text of any length, as is clear from the
comments of contemporaries. Writing to Hartlib on 11 October 1647,
Thomas Smith of Christ's College says:

Mr Ravius desired me to speake to Mr Wheelock to print Mr Bedwels great
Lexicon, I spake to him & Mr Cudworth[152] & other his friends & they had all

---

[148] The list of oriental manuscripts which Hottinger reports having seen in the
libraries of John and Thomas Greaves in 1641 (*Bibliothecarius Quadripartitus*, 31–2) is
too incomplete and vague to afford much help.

[149] Letter of Hardy, 1 Sept. 1641, MS Savile 47, fos. 43ʳ–44ᵛ, printed in Greaves,
Works, ii. 446–50; letter of Greaves to Golius, 1 June 1642, MS Savile 47, fo. 53,
printed in *Works*, ii. 456–8.

[150] On Holdsworth's bequest of his great library, which eventually came to
Cambridge, see Oates, ch. 13.

[151] For the abortive efforts of Wheelock and Thomas Smith see pp. 89 and 199
respectively.

[152] Ralph Cudworth, Master of Clare Hall and Regius Professor of Hebrew.

a desire he should rather first consumate the Alcoran . . . What I said to Mr Ravius concerning our Arab. Raphelengius letters I said to our friends here, that they are not fit to print the Alcoran, much lesse Bedwel. Mr Cudworth said it would spoyle much paper, & Mr Whelock desired me to speak to the Senior Proctor (my very good friend) to have his consent that new small letters might be made at the University charge, he approved my motion very well, & I hope to get by my friends a vote paste the Regent-house to that purpose, as a vote is passed already for printing the Alcoran at the university charge.[153]

We have already seen that Wheelock later abandoned his plans to 'refute' the Koran, and we hear nothing more of this attempt to replace the Raphelengius types with a more suitable smaller Arabic fount. However, Wheelock too pressed Hartlib to use his influence to get Arabic types for Cambridge. In a letter he wrote at about the same time concerning his work on the Koran, he says: 'if once wee had a Typographie of faire Arabick Characters by noble benefactors here procured'.[154] Another communication from the same period openly begs for help to do this from 'the London Merchants': 'Our universitie wants a Typographie for Arabick & Syriack Samaritanes &c. that of Hebrew is very poore. . . . Worthy Sir be a benefactor to us in pro-curing us typographies . . . London is now soe wise that they would thank God if their monyes were all soe expended.'[155] No such help was forthcoming from London or elsewhere, and thirty-five years were to pass before any Arabic type was used at Cambridge.

Wheelock's Arabic lectures did attract some pupils. Thomas Smith[156] entered Christ's College from St Paul's School (one of the few in England where Hebrew was taught) in 1640, and graduated BA in 1643/4. He was appointed lecturer in rhetoric at the college, and University Librarian in 1659, but died of the plague in 1661, aged only 37. His ventures in Arabic, which will be discussed below in connection with Ravius, are known only from his correspondence with Hartlib partially preserved in the Hartlib Papers. Sclater, in his funeral oration on Wheelock, celebrates his teaching of Arabic as follows: 'Nor can his memory die, whilst so many hopefull plants of his setting,

---

[153] Hartlib Papers 15/6/27 and 28.

[154] Hartlib Papers 33/4/3, undated, but certainly from the time that Ravius was in London, i.e. 1647–8.

[155] Hartlib Papers 33/4/4. Similarly, writing to Ravius on 12 Nov. 1647 Wheelock says: 'Sed Arabici characteres nostri, novit claritas vestra, ut grandiores sint, quàm ora libri imprimendi ferre possit. Ut fiant aliquot minutiores, & aptiores margini, destinato operi nostro, ut & negotiis vestris multum proderit' (Ravius, *Sesqui-Decuria*, 28–9).

[156] See Peile, *Biographical Register of Christ's College*, i. 468, and Hammond, 'Thomas Smith', neither of whom mentions his oriental studies.

spring up after him, and daily grow famous in Cambridge.'[157] Isaac
Barrow too, in an oration delivered soon after Wheelock's death,[158]
praises those Cambridge students who have studied Arabic, although
he envisages no fruit of their labours beyond the recovery of ancient
science through Arabic translations. The only pupils of Wheelock
whose names Sclater mentions are Richard Hunt and Robert Austin,
Fellows of King's College. Hunt became Gresham Professor of
Rhetoric in November 1654, and accordingly Ward gives a brief
account of his career.[159] This was in part derived from a 'character'
sent to him by Hunt's nephew, according to whom Hunt never
published anything, but was 'esteemed one of the best orientalists of
his time' in both Arabic and Hebrew (having studied with learned Jews
in Holland),[160] and on a visit to Oxford with his nephew in 1676 was
'admired by all the great men of the university, as Dr. Pocock, Wallis,
Hide, Alestry, the great rabby Abendany . . . and Dr. Marshal'. Austin
too seems to have left no trace of his Arabic studies, but when he was
barely 20 Wheelock bestowed great praise on him in a letter to
Pococke of 1650: 'This young man, in the space of two months
time, not knowing a letter in Arabic, or Persick, at the beginning, sent
a letter to me in Norfolk of peculiar passages. So that, of his age, I
never met with the like; and his indefatigable pains, and honesty, or
ingenuity, exceed, if possible, his capacity.'[161] Twells further informs
us that Austin was at the time assisting Wheelock in his edition of the
Persian Gospels, and was designated to complete it when Wheelock
died, but himself succumbed in 1653 to 'distraction and death' brought
on by excessive application to his oriental studies.[162] Wheelock's most
famous pupil was Thomas Hyde, who entered Queens' College in
1652, and collaborated in the Polyglot Bible before he reached the age
of 20. However, the teaching of Arabic and Persian lapsed at
Cambridge after Wheelock's death, and in 1657 Hyde migrated to the
greener fields of Oxford, where he became Praelector of Hebrew at

---

[157] Sclater, *Crown of Righteousnes*, 32.

[158] 'Oratio ad Academicos in Comitiis' (Barrow, *Theological Works*, ix. 38). Barrow
himself never learned Arabic (even though he visited Constantinople in 1658), but
warmly advocated its study not only in this speech but in his 'Oratio Moderatoria in
Auspiciis Termini, April. 30, 1651' (ibid. 30).

[159] *Gresham Professors*, 317–18.

[160] The notes that Castell transcribed from 'Mr. Hunts Oriental Collections' in CUL
MS Dd.6.4, fo. 23 all have to do with Hebrew.

[161] Twells, 181.

[162] Austin was still alive and well on 1 Nov. 1653, when he wrote to Oughtred that he
had attended Wheelock's deathbed and funeral (*Correspondence of Scientific Men*, i. 76).

Queen's College, MA 1659, and eventually Bodley's Librarian. The man who was to revive Arabic at Cambridge, Edmund Castell, was not a pupil of Wheelock, since he was already MA in 1628, four years before Wheelock started lecturing on Arabic. Castell, who seems to have been essentially self-taught in oriental languages, had left the university for various country livings before 1638, and returned to Cambridge only after he was appointed Arabic Professor in 1666. As we shall see, he was extremely active in London during the 1650s, first with the Polyglot Bible, and then with his *Lexicon Heptaglotton*.

After the accession of Erpenius' manuscripts, very few Arabic items entered Cambridge University Library for twenty-five years.[163] During that period the library was enormously enlarged by the accession of the Lambeth Library formerly belonging to the Archbishops of Canterbury, mainly by the efforts of Selden, who managed to divert it from Sion College, to which Parliament had voted to give it.[164] The library did not arrive in Cambridge until 1649, although the transfer had been approved in 1647. Evidently archbishops Bancroft and Abbot (by whom most of the Lambeth collection had been bequeathed) had little interest in Arabic, for the library contained few Arabic books.[165] In any case Cambridge was forced to return it after the Restoration. Selden was also the prime mover in the vote of the Parliament, in March 1648, to appropriate £500 to buy for Cambridge a major collection of Hebrew books which the bookseller George Thomason had imported from Italy,[166] but it was only in 1655–7 that a significant number of Arabic and Persian manuscripts came to the library, from Nicholas Hobart, Fellow of King's College. He had collected these while serving as secretary to the ambassador at Constantinople, Sir Thomas Bendysh, from 1647 to 1650.[167] Even with this accession, which was considerably smaller than the Erpenius collection, Cambridge remained far behind Oxford (where Selden's bequest had recently enhanced Laud's gift), in the number and quality of Arabic manuscripts available for study, and this disparity continued to widen for the rest of the century. It was not until 1727 that George Lewis's gift brought another large increase in the oriental manuscripts at Cambridge.[168]

---

[163] Some individual accessions are recorded by Oates, ch. 9 ('Orientalia').

[164] For the whole episode see Oates, ch. 10, following Cox-Johnson, 'Lambeth Palace Library'.

[165] I have not attempted to determine which Arabic items currently in Lambeth Palace Library were there in 1647.   [166] Oates, 231–40.

[167] For some details see Oates, 290–2.

[168] See McKitterick, *Cambridge University Library*, ii: *The Eighteenth and Nineteenth Centuries*, 232–8.

(VIII) JOHN PELL AND ARABIC

During the period of the Revolution, in the years 1645 to 1647, a remarkable attempt to publish an important Arabic text was made, not indeed in England, but by an Englishman. This was John Pell, famous in the history of mathematics, and at the time Professor of Mathematics at Amsterdam and Breda. While at Amsterdam he met Christianus Ravius (then lecturing on oriental languages at Utrecht), and, learning from him about the Arabic version of Apollonius' *Conics* which he owned, borrowed the manuscript and, with his consent, made a Latin translation of Books V–VII. The main source of our knowledge of this is Pell's correspondence with Charles Cavendish.[169] Pell was faced with the difficulty that Golius had long promised his own translation of the Apollonius (albeit from a different Arabic version), and the rivalry was a delicate one. The following extracts illuminate the progress of events. On 7/17 August 1644 Pell wrote to Cavendish in Hamburg: 'Monsieur Hardy tells us, in a letter lately written, that Des Cartes met him in Paris, and blamed him for offering so much money to our Arabick professor at Utrecht, for his Arabicke manuscript of Apollonius.'[170] This letter of Hardy's may have inspired Pell's interest in the manuscript. At all events, by 19/29 October he was well launched on the translation. He told Cavendish:

in this instant there lyes under my hands Apollonius with 36 other autors which taken together make a bulke almost twice as great as Apollonius. All 37 in Arabicke. You smile and beleeve not that I have Arabicke enough to teach any of these to speake Geometricall Latine in any reasonable time. And if I had done it, the drawing of those Conicall diagrams is no childrens play nor can we every where finde a printer for such a crabbed & costly piece of worke. But some of these difficulties are over. Dr Blaeu[171] tells me he is ready to print Diophantus, Apollonius or what I will & how I will, in Arabicke & Latine if I will: He hath good Arabicke types, a compositor exercised in setting them & what not. But I have in a manner resolved to make lesse adoe, namely to

---

[169] This is among the Pell papers in the British Library, MSS Add. 4279 and 4280. Some parts of the correspondence were published by Vaughan, *Protectorate of Oliver Cromwell*, vol. ii, and Halliwell, *Collection of Letters* (both excerpted in Mersenne, *Correspondance*, vols. xiii, xiv). More recently van Maanen, *Facets of Seventeenth Century Mathematics in the Netherlands*, has published some important extracts. A complete annotated edition of this correspondence would be most useful.

[170] Vaughan, *Protectorate of Oliver Cromwell*, ii. 355; Mersenne, *Correspondance*, vol. xiii, no. 1292, p. 198.

[171] The well-known Amsterdam printer.

publish onely the 5t, 6t & 7th (not repeating Commandines 4) & those onely in Latine, adjoyning apt figures, some notes and Pappus his Lemmata upon the 5t, 6t & 7th & 8th book also: though the Arabicke booke wanteth the 8t. All which will require about 200 diagrams. To this purpose there lyes by me the whole fift booke translated into Latine but not faire written for the presse nor one figure yet drawen so well as I intend they shall be.[172]

Pell then gives a specimen translation from 'this Abdil Melik of Schiraz in Persia though he write Arabick', namely, the first proposition of Book VII, for Cavendish to compare with the version of the same proposition which Golius had sent to Mersenne, and which the latter had printed.[173]

By 9/19 May 1645 Pell had finished the translation, and this aroused the alarm of Golius.[174] Pell told Cavendish:

I have now the translation finished of those 3 latter bookes out of Arabicke and Dr Blaew hath a minde to print it and also to reprint Commandines edition of the first 4 bookes with my notes. Of which when mr Golius heard & that we began to talke with a graver about the diagrammes, he made a Journy from Leiden hither on purpose to dissuade or deterre both dr Blaew & me from that intention. He had been heere divers times in the city & inquired where I dwelt but never came to see me: till now he was in a manner constrained 6 dayes agoe. He brought his Arabicke 7 bookes of Apollonius with him, a goodly faire manuscript given him 18 years ago at Aleppo by a gentleman of this country,[175] to whom he sayes he hath given a faithfull promise to publish it or otherwise he would put it into my hands & give me all the assistance that he could in the publishing of it. Besides this promise, he hath been at some cost to pay for the delineating of all the figures and indeed they are exceeding neately drawn in paper by his Collegues sonne[176] & some of them are also graven.

Pell replied that he knew Golius was better able than he to do the translation, but he would rather do it himself than not see it done at all. Golius responded that he knew Ravius could not make an intelligible translation, and although Pell could produce one that made mathematical sense, he would be unable to reproduce the style of Apollonius from Ravius' manuscript, 'for saith he I have a copy of Ravius his Arabicke manuscript, which you use & know very well how bold that Persian makes with Apollonius'.[177] Pell concludes:

[172] MS BL 4280, fo. 109.

[173] Mersenne, *Synopsis*, 274.

[174] Cf. van Maanen, *Facets of Seventeenth Century Mathematics in the Netherlands*, 123, 136–7.   [175] David Leleu de Wilhem.

[176] Frans van Schooten the younger.

[177] Devious as his approach to Pell was, Golius spoke truly here: 'Abd al-Malik's version is indeed very far removed from that of the Banū Mūsā on which it was based.

Mr Golius was never in so much fear of losing much honour & I know not
what profit which he might have secured by publishing Apollonius as well 16
yeares agoe as now. The intention I perceive otherwise ran thus. First to finish
his Arabicke Lexicon, of which there are now perhaps 8 sheetes printed. Next
to get all his diagrams first graven & then to begin to translate into Latine not
onely those 3 bookes of Apollonius but also Barulcum Heronis & some other
things lost in the Greeke but preserved in the Arabicke & so come to his hands
and this he thought to doe at his best leisure, twenty years hence perhaps
because he thought no man could prevent him. What haste he will now make I
know not; but in the meane time Apollonius hath ill lucke, if betweene us both
he doe not now in short time obtaine his liberty to fly abroad.[178]

This was not to happen. On 11/21 May 1646 Pell told Cavendish
that Golius

lately wrote to me to let Apollonius alone for him, as having determined to goe
in hand with it, as soone as his Arabicke lexicon is done. Yesterday his
Arabian[179] comming to see me, I asked him how farre they were come, he
answered they were in Jîm, that is, words beginning with the fift letter. I asked
when he thought it would be finished; he said About 6 or 7 yeeres hence.[180] I
asked how old he thought Golius was; he replyed At least fifty years old. I
would I could persuade him to lend me a hundred pound upon condition to
receive two hundred for it, when he published Apollonius. For mine owne part
I have not promised to waite his leisure.[181]

This is the last we hear on the subject from Pell. Despite his justified
scepticism about Golius publishing the Apollonius, he never made his
own version public, and it seems to have vanished without further
trace. Pell did not indeed formally renounce his intention of publishing
it. On 23 December 1646 Constantijn Huygens wrote to Mersenne
lamenting Golius' seventeen years' delay in bringing out the work,
and saying that Pell would like to publish it,[182] but by 1648 Pell was
worrying about Claude Richard's version, allegedly of all eight
books.[183]

---

[178] MS BL 4280, fo. 112.

[179] At this date the 'Arabian' can only be Nicolaus Petri, who was living in
Amsterdam and copying manuscripts for Golius.

[180] This was a good estimate: Golius' Arabic lexicon was finally published in 1653.

[181] MS BL 4280, fo. 118b.

[182] Mersenne, *Correspondance*, vol. xiii, no. 1577, p. 718: 'Notre Pellius voudroit fort
l'auoir, et assurement en viendroit promptement a bout; mais le moyen de l'arracher au
premier sans picquer ou affronter?'

[183] Cavendish to Mersenne, 2 May 1648 (ibid. xvi, no. 1794, pp. 294–5). Pell need
not have been concerned, since Richard knew only the Greek version of Books I–IV,
and had 'reconstructed' the last four from the meagre indications in Pappus.

The attitude of Ravius to this matter is interesting. He had encouraged Pell in his undertaking, and continued to do so as late as 14/24 August 1651, when he wrote to Pell (now at Breda) from Stockholm. Still flush with the funds which Queen Christina had given him for the journey to his new post in Sweden, he offered to pay 100 florins for engraving the figures for Pell's edition.[184] Yet only a few months later, when sending the manuscript to Johannes Morianus in Amsterdam to transmit to Hardy, he told him that he would not have sold it if Pell had done his duty towards the public.[185] Other statements of Ravius concerning the translation of the Apollonius are, to say the least, ambiguous. On 3 March 1645 the Vroedschap (governors) of Utrecht granted Ravius leave to go to Amsterdam in order to get printed there some works which were allegedly ready for the press, including 'Apollonij Pergaei Conicarum Sectionum libros VII'.[186] On 21 October 1645 he told Mersenne that he himself had translated all seven books into Latin, at great expense, since he had had to pay Nicolaus Petri.[187] Since Pell was well embarked on his translation, and had already got a promise of publication in Amsterdam by the first of those two dates, and since he had completed at least Books V–VII by the second, one cannot escape the conclusion that Ravius was representing Pell's work as his own (a deception which was consonant with his character). Stranger still, when he did eventually publish his own translation of the Apollonius at Kiel in 1669, he claimed that he had done it in a few days in 1646.[188] This was when both Ravius and Pell were living in Amsterdam, and Pell was still talking about publishing his completed translation. It would be tempting to guess that Ravius simply appropriated Pell's translation for his 1669 edition, were the latter not so inept that it seems impossible to attribute it to a mathematician of Pell's calibre. I do not know what to make of the silence that both Ravius and Pell maintained about the Apollonius in an exchange of

[184] MS BL 4280, fo. 2: 'Quid de Apollonio tuo spei sit, scire aveo. jam ante scripsi centum florinos transmittere paratus sum, figuris aeri incidendis.'

[185] MS Lat. misc. c. 17, fo. 42: 'Non vendidissem illum Codicem si ea diligentia et erga publicum Amore Pellius fuisset quo esse posset' (12 Nov. 1651). On the later fate of the manuscript see below, p. 238.

[186] Wijnne, *Resolutiën, genomen bij de Vroedschap van Utrecht*, 56.

[187] Mersenne, *Correspondance*, vol. xiii, no. 1396, pp. 502–3: 'Ego interea non sine gravi inpensa in Arabem meum mecum Constantinopoli huc deductum totum Apollonium Pergaeum Conicorum scilicet libros septem verti in linguam latinam.'

[188] Ravius, *Apollonius*, preface, *5ʳ. This translation contains the whole of Books V–VII (less the last 10 propositions) and a few propositions from Books I and II, but lacks all figures.

letters between them in 1671.[189] Thus we have no means of assessing Pell's prowess as an Arabist.[190] There is no direct evidence as to how or where he learned Arabic, but if Wood[191] is right in saying that it was one of the many languages which Pell knew when he was incorporated at Oxford in 1631 at the age of 20, he must have learned it at Cambridge between 1624 and 1630, before Wheelock became Professor of Arabic there.

(IX) THE LONDON SCHOOL OF ORIENTAL LANGUAGES

Mention of Ravius brings us to a fascinating episode in the history of the study of Arabic during the Revolution, namely the attempt to set up a school for teaching oriental languages in London. This should be viewed in the context of calls to break the monopoly of the two universities on higher education which were characteristic of this period.[192] That topic is too extensive to treat within the framework of this book; I shall confine myself to two examples. Amongst the Thomason Tracts in the British Library is a short anonymous treatise,[193] dated in Thomason's hand 'Jan. 7th 1646':[194]

Motives grounded Upon the Word of God, and upon Honour, Profit, and Pleasure for the present Founding an University in the Metropolis LONDON: With Answers to such Objections as might be made by any (in their incogitances) against the same. Humbly Presented (in stead of Heathenish and Superstitious New-year Gifts) to the Right Honourable the Lord Major, and Right Worshipfull the Aldermen his Brethren, and to those faithfull and prudent Citizens which were lately chosen by the said City to be of the Common Counsell thereof for this year insueng, *viz.* 1647. By a true Lover of this Nation, and especially of the said City. Printed at London. 1647.

On p. 3 the author argues that

---

[189] MS BL Add. 4365, fos. 59, 62. The correspondence concerns Ravius' proposed biblical chronology, which obsessed him for the last eight years of his life.

[190] For evidence that he continued to be interested in the language see below, p. 268, on his association with Busby at Westminster School.

[191] 'Fasti Oxonienses', i. 462 (in vol. ii of Bliss's edition of the *Athenae*).

[192] Webster, *The Great Instauration*, for all its errors of detail, is a mine of information on such matters. See especially pp. 207–42 for attempts to expand higher education at this time (on London in particular, pp. 221–4).

[193] E.370 (17), *Thomason Tracts*, i. 486.

[194] i.e. the date '1647' on the pamphlet itself is, interestingly, New Style, and the pamphlet predates by little Ravius' call to London.

there is no City in any learned Nation, of *Londons* magnitude or magnificence, without an University in it; and by erecting an University in *London*; God offereth you now a golden opportunity to remedy this our lamentable defect, especially at this present, when so many great houses may be had and made Colledges of, with so little alteration, and *Pauls* Church, and *London*-House be the publike Schooles; and by reason of the Warres in other Countries, you may now have the choicest of their Professors of the *Arts*, and upon easie conditions.

Is it merely a coincidence that a few months later a German professor was lecturing at London-House, while the Thirty Years War was still being fought in Germany? On p. 5 the author proposes the foundation of three colleges, one where only Latin is spoken, another for Greek, and the third Hebrew. The reason for the third is that the Jews are about to be converted and come to England from the East (this reflects the millenary expectations which were rampant in England of the Revolution).[195]

Also addressed to the London City Council ('the honorable Court of common counsell') was a petition from 'our grave and judicious Ministry of *London*, . . . subscribed by the appointment and in the name of the society of Syon-Colledge, Ian. 12. 1647', part of which is printed by Ravius on p. 91 of his *Discourse* of 1648. There are some remarkable resemblances in the petition to the above-mentioned treatise, and although one would normally interpret the date as 22 January 1648 by modern reckoning, I am inclined to think that, like the other, the date is New Style.[196] The petition starts with the expectation that the conversion of the Jews, which is a necessary prelude to the second coming of Christ, is at hand, and goes on to emphasize the desirability of teaching oriental languages somewhere besides the two universities. The projected benefits are described as follows:

Thereby shall industrious men see more clearely with their owne eyes the very minde of GOD in that same Tongue, wherein himself uttered it, and bee not only better setled in the truth of our owne Translations, but able to understand those ancient versions of the holy Bible in those learned Languages, and other Authors of worth and use, as also with greater advantage to converse, and traffic with the Eastern Nations in their owne Languages, which marvelously winneth upon the Natives of any Kingdome, where ever Travailars or

[195] On contemporary millenarian expectations that the Jews would be converted in England see e.g. Katz, *Philo-Semitism*, 100 ff.

[196] Since Ravius gives only the preamble and not the petition itself, one cannot exclude the possibility that it belongs to 1648 and is a request for funds to support the lectureship which had already been established.

Merchants come. Besides it will greatly propagate this kinde of learning, whereby not onely the present age, but our posterity will be more capable of the spirituall advantages of the Jewes conversion, if not to contribute to it.

Since, as we shall see, the lectureship in oriental languages which was established later in 1647 was under the aegis of the London ministry centred on Sion College, it is tempting to interpret this petition as the first formal move in that direction.

There is a copy of the above-mentioned treatise advocating the establishment of a university in London among the Hartlib Papers.[197] Samuel Hartlib was prominent in the discussions of education in London, and at this time (1647) he exerted considerable influence in the Parliament, to which he had been serviceable. He was certainly one of the prime movers in the appointment of Ravius as lecturer in oriental languages in London. His association with Ravius began at least eight years earlier, when he acted as the liaison in London between Ussher (then in Ireland) and Ravius in the payment of Ussher's subsidy to the latter in his journey to the East in 1639 and 1640. In 1646 Dury discussed with Hartlib the possibility of employing Ravius, Adam Boreel, and Menasseh ben Israel to convert the Jews.[198] Both Dury and Hartlib were also in close contact with Johannes Matthiae,[199] tutor to Queen Christina of Sweden and later Bishop of Strängnäs, to whom Ravius undoubtedly owed his later appointment in Sweden, and whose niece he married in 1652.

Many aspects of the London school of oriental languages which existed from 1647 to 1649 remain obscure to me, but in what follows I present the facts as far as I have been able to determine them in some detail, since the whole episode has been largely ignored in standard histories of the period. In June 1647 Ravius returned to England, after five years in the Netherlands. During that time he had tried unsuccessfully to get a post teaching oriental languages, first at Utrecht, then at Amsterdam.[200] His ostensible reason for coming to England was to recover the manuscripts which he had left behind there as pledges for his debts, and he continued to urge his friends at Amsterdam to lobby

[197] Turnbull, *Hartlib, Dury and Comenius*, 49, with details of other related materials collected by Hartlib. A contemplated University of London was discussed in Sept. 1647, ibid. 263.
[198] Ibid. 257.
[199] See e.g. ibid. 178, 425.
[200] He was indeed permitted to lecture at both places, and given occasional honorariums for so doing. But efforts by himself and G. J. Vossius to make his position permanent had no result.

the Curators on his behalf.[201] As recently as 8 April he had expressed to Ussher his optimism that he would be appointed 'Professor Ordinarius' at Amsterdam.[202] But there is reason to think that he had received private assurances from Hartlib that a post would be created for him at London. Perhaps to demonstrate his fitness to teach oriental languages in England, in the previous year[203] he had contributed notes in English to a book published in Amsterdam. This was John Udall's *Key of the Holy Tongue*, first published in Leiden in 1593. It was the first Hebrew grammar in English, being a translation of Petrus Martinius' *Grammaticae hebraicae libri duo*.[204] Ravius, who as in all his English language publications Anglicizes his name to 'Christian Ravis', remarks at the end of his notes: 'This is the first thing that ever I did in English.'[205]

It is certain that the arrangements for Ravius to lecture in London had been made by August,[206] for on 14 August Thomason noted the receipt of a small rectangular handbill, obviously addressed to the members of the London clergy:

Sir, You are intreated to give notice in publick this next Lords day the 15 of *August*, that Master *Christianus Ravius*, heretofore publick Professor of the Orientall Tongues in some Universities beyond the Seas, will begin a Lecture of these Tongues in *London*-House, God willing, upon Thursday come seven-night the 26 of this instant *August*; and that he will preface to that Lecture on Thursday next at three of the clock in the afternoon in the place aforesaid.[207]

---

[201] Letter from Ravius in London to Isaac Vossius in Amsterdam, 6 July (NS) 1647 (MS d'Orville 468, pp. 214–19).

[202] Ussher, *Letters*, no. 213, p. 511.

[203] That the London position was already being discussed by Hartlib at least a year before it was established is suggested by John Dury's letter to Hartlib of 31 Aug. 1646, in which he mentions 'the many wayes which are now intended for the facilitating of the studie of the Orientall languages among Christians' and hopes that 'if God doth put it in the heart of this state or of the City of London to advance Godlines & Learning', Adam Boreel '& such as are qualified in this kind might bee sent for & employed' (Hartlib Papers 3/3/32–3, published by van der Wall, 'John Durie on Adam Boreel', 148–9).

[204] See Lloyd Jones, *The Discovery of Hebrew*, 257.

[205] Udall, *Key of the Holy Tongue*, 192. The copy I have seen of this, at Sion College, states that the work was printed at Amsterdam, but adds: 'Printed for C. P. and are to be sold by *David Frere*, at the Sign of the red Bull in little Britain London, 1648', which suggests that at least some copies were sent to London especially in connection with Ravius' lectures there. For evidence that Ravius did indeed use the work for teaching both at London and Oxford see below, p. 196.

[206] The earliest reference that I have found to Ravius' London appointment is in the letter of congratulation by Cornelius Tollius, dated 27 July (Ravius, *Sesqui-Decuria*, p. 27).

[207] BL E.401 (41), *Thomason Tracts*, i. 545, the only known copy.

The lectures were held at London-House in St Paul's churchyard, which was formerly the residence of the Bishop of London, but after the abolition of episcopacy had been appropriated to other uses. The sponsoring body was the London clergy, which had a centre for meeting and a library at Sion College, at that time located not far away on London-Wall.[208] This explains Ravius' connection with Sion College, to which, as we saw, he donated one of his manuscripts on 5 June 1648 'ad Gloriam Dei, Propagationem Evangelii, Studiorum Orientalium Fulgorem, Historiae claritatem, Angliae honorem, Reverendis Ministeriis Londinensis, Incitamentum ad haec studia'.[209] In the same year, and certainly in connection with Ravius' appointment, about twenty Arabic, Persian, and Turkish manuscripts and two Arabic printed books were given to the college by Sir Thomas Wroth.[210] In 1647 the college had been allocated the library of St Paul's Cathedral, evidently as a sort of consolation prize for its loss of the Lambeth Library to Cambridge. Although this too was taken back after the Restoration, in 1648 Sion College was beginning to look like a centre for serious scholarship.

The evidence for Hartlib's involvement in setting up the position for Ravius is in the correspondence of Thomas Smith of Christ's College. On 11 October 1647 he wrote to Hartlib (together with a letter in German to Ravius which he asked Hartlib to forward):

Sir Not my selfe only but the whole Common-wealth of learning are eternally obliged to you for your earnest & happy endeavours for the promotion of all kind of learning especially Oriental, which it hath pleased our good God to prosper, that we need no longer travaile with Clenard to Arabia, nor with others to other forreigne parts to learne the language, All the wealth & worth in Arabia begins now to be in London house.[211]

Precisely what Hartlib did remains unclear, but we may guess that he had some influence with the Provincial Presbyterian Synod of London, which met at Sion College from 1647 onwards.

As to Ravius' lectures, the best contemporary information about them is given by a Latin poem celebrating them composed by John

---

[208] Sion College had been founded in 1626 by the will of Thomas White (d. 1624) as 'a college for a corporation of all the ministers, parsons, vicars, lecturers and curates within London and the suburbs thereof'.

[209] Ravius' handwritten dedication in Sion College MS Or. 4.

[210] Sion College Benefactors Book, p. 52. Thirteen of these manuscripts which survived the Great Fire of London are still there (Reading, *Sion-College*, catalogue of MSS, nos. 5–17). Ravius praises Roth's gift in his *Discourse*, 92 [bis].

[211] Hartlib Papers 15/6/27.

Spencer, librarian of Sion College, published by Ravius in his *Sesqui-Decuria*, pp. 33–5. He addresses Ravius as 'Professor of the Hebrew and Arabic Tongues at London',[212] which was presumably his formal title. Concerning the lectures Spencer exults (p. 34)

> Mystarum auspiciis, Magni curaque Senatus,
> Ebræos, Arabesque videt resonare cathedra
> Hybleosque favos redolere in colle Sionis,
> Ad refluum Tamesim; Paulini & culmina templi

which I take to be a poetic way of saying that, sponsored by the [London] ministers, and supported by the Parliament,[213] Ravius is teaching Hebrew and Arabic at Sion College[214] in London and at London-House near St Paul's. Spencer goes on to say, if I interpret him rightly, that the lectures took place twice a week (presumably Tuesdays and Thursdays) at 3 p.m., and that on the intervening days the lecturer made himself available to all comers. This is confirmed by a letter of Ravius to Selden, undated but certainly written in 1648, in which he says that he lectures five times a week, twice in Latin and three times in English, the latter privately.[215] Spencer gives a clue to the justification offered for setting up the post:

> Omnipotens faveat conatibus hisce Jehovah,
> Vt convertantur pia per commercia gentes

that is, the hope of peaceably converting Jews and Muslims. This motive is confirmed and amplified in the petition to Parliament which will be mentioned later, asking for support for 'this kind of learning, on which the clearer knowledge of the sacred Scriptures, and our usefulnesse for the propagation of the Gospel, to such as understand those languages, and their usefulnesse to us so much dependeth'.[216]

Some idea of the content of Ravius' lectures may be found in the books that he published in London. It should be emphasized that

---

[212] 'Prosphoneticum In Sacras Orientalium Linguarum Praelectiones Clarissimi & Doctissimi Viri, Dn Berlinatis Marco-Branden Burgo-Germani; Londini Ebraeae & Arabicae Linguae Professoris, Amici & Fautoris Optimi'.

[213] We shall see that this merely expresses a hope. I do not believe that Spencer would call the Court of Common Counsel at London (which probably did approve Ravius' appointment) 'Magnus Senatus'.

[214] The biblical reference to 'Mount Sion' is presumably part of a laboured pun.

[215] MS Selden supra 108, fo. 48: 'quinque lectiones de septimanâ praestem, Latinas binas, ternas Anglicanas, (sed has privatim, ubi tamen aliquot ministri intersunt, coram quadraginta auditoribus).'

[216] BL 669.f.12(47), *Thomason Tracts*, i. 633.

whereas all his other publications before and after this were written in Latin, these are all in English (as were at least his informal lectures). The need to substitute the vernacular for Latin as the language of instruction in higher education is prominent among the themes of the educational reformers of the time, amongst whom Ravius' friend and promotor, Samuel Hartlib, was not the least. We have already noticed Ravius' English notes appended to Udall's Hebrew grammar in English. Another Hebrew publication of his is *A scheme of the orthography, etymology and syntax of the Hebrew language*, received by Thomason on 20 April 1648.[217] This is a single large sheet, purporting to give all the necessary data for Hebrew orthography in one column, for etymology in the second, and for syntax in the third. Although it is anonymous, the attribution to Ravius in the British Museum Catalogue is shown to be correct by a note at the bottom of the second column: 'See my notes on P. Martinius Grammar englished, printed at Amsterdam 1646.' According to Ravius himself he published an enlarged version of this entitled *The Rudiments of the Hebrew Grammar in English* in 1648.[218] However, the most informative book for Ravius' approach to teaching Arabic and other oriental languages is his *Generall Grammer For the ready attaining of the Ebrew, Samaritan, Calde, Syriac, Arabic, and the Ethiopic Languages*.[219] Ravius' main point of originality, which he had also maintained in his publications in Holland,[220] was that all six languages named in the title are not merely closely related, as was (and is) generally accepted, but are in fact the same language. Hence, if one knows Arabic (which, he had maintained as early as his student days at Leiden,[221] comes to one

---

[217] BL 669.f.12(9), ibid. 611.

[218] Ravius, *Discourse*, 20. I have not seen this, nor do I know where there is a copy.

[219] I have failed to completely disentangle the publication history of this book, which is very complicated. I have seen 1649 and 1650 imprints, both combined with Ravius' *Discourse of the Orientall Tongues*, but in a different order, and both containing his *Sesqui-Decuria*, but with a separate title-page dated 1648. There are references to a 1648 edition of the *Generall Grammer*, but the only copy of the 1648 edition of the *Discourse* that I have seen (Bodleian Library, 8° R 34(1) Art. Seld.) does not contain the *Grammer*, although it should according to the title-page. In the 1650 edition the engraved plates of various oriental scripts at the end are much more extensive and more beautifully executed than in the 1649 edition. Both books have, as frontispiece, a fine portrait of 'Christianus Ravius Berlinas, Aet. 32' (i.e. done in 1645, the only portrait of him that I know of).

[220] e.g. in his *Orthographia*; in *De scribendo Lexico*, 37 he asserts that 'Arabic' includes Hebrew, Chaldee, Syriac, Punic, Phoenician, Mauritanian, Lybian, Ethiopic, and even Turkish!

[221] Or so he claims, *De scribendo Lexico*, 11.

naturally), one knows Hebrew. The point is best made in the *Discourse,* which serves as a sort of protreptic to the *Grammer*:

Truly I say, if the English Nation would but once fall diligently upon true Divinity, and not trust so much unto their translations, and (which may be within a yeare for ought I know) perceive that Ebrew is Arabic, which being yet living and in use, is easie to be learnt, and being obtained, will give a more cleare and true interpretation of the Ebrew Bible (and that with greater ease too) than all the Rabbins, I doubt not but they would hereafter change their course of studying in dead bookes unto that of living persons in Asia and Africa, as *Nicolaus Clenardus* did begin, Mr *Pocoke* and Mr *Graves* those worthy men have folowed.[222]

Although some of Ravius' premisses are faulty, not to say absurd, his conclusions are not always contemptible, for instance his insistence that it is wrong to construct Arabic and Hebrew grammars on the pattern of Latin and Greek.[223]

I have seen nothing to indicate who paid Ravius' salary, although he does mention that Thomas Adams was his patron,[224] so perhaps the clergy had raised funds for the purpose from among sympathetic wealthy citizens of London. However, it soon became clear that if the school was to prosper, the students too would need financial support,[225] and the only possible source for this was by some grant from Parliament. This is made plain in a letter from Ravius to Selden, un-dated, but certainly not long before the petition to the House of Commons of June 1648 which will be discussed below. After explain-ing how his lectures are arranged, and claiming that in his private lectures in English he has forty auditors (although some of these are clergymen), he says that at the moment he is the sole professor, but more will be required. Furthermore, unlike the universities, where Bachelors and first-year Masters are required to attend such lectures, there are no graduates in London to supply an audience, so it will be necessary to support twelve or twenty students. Thirdly, a printing-press is essential for these studies. The letter is obviously designed as a plea for Selden's help in getting money voted by Parliament, but is

[222] Ravius, *Discourse,* 62.

[223] On this see the remarks in Salmon, 'Arabists and Linguists in Seventeenth-Century England', 63–4; ibid. 56 for the *Discourse.*

[224] *Discourse,* 92 [bis]: 'that renowned Citizen, And right Worshipfull, Alderman *Adams,* late *Lord Major* of *London* my especially respected and beloved patron and Friend'.

[225] Ravius had already expressed concern about this to Wheelock, who sympathizes in his letter of 11 Feb. 1648 (Ravius, *Sesqui-Decuria,* 31–2).

cast in the form of two questions: 1. What annual sum should we seek from the Parliament? 2. Should we seek this sum directly from the revenues of the deans and chapters?[226] Ravius notes that the 'Ministers and members of the Synod' had promised not to object to that procedure.

Unfortunately we do not have Selden's response to this, but in June 1648 a petition was addressed to the House of Commons '*Signed by about 40 Ministers, and 60 Citizens of quality in and about London*'.[227] The preamble states that

in *August* last, in *London-House* a Lecture was happily begun for the propagation of piety, and learning, in the discovery of the orientall Languages (to this nation remaining but yet obscure) which hitherto hath been elaborately performed twice a week, since that time neer fourscore Lectures in Latine, and highly approved by those of greatest parts and learning that frequent the same: And your Petitioners fearing lest a work of this nature, for the advancing such learning and Languages, should for want of maintenance and countenance from Authority fall to the ground. And forasmuch as an estimate hath been taken of the necessary charge which is requisite for the maintenance of Professors, and Students, as also for the erection of a Presse, for those Languages for the more effectuall prosecution of the desired ends, . . .

The petition does not state what that estimate amounts to, but expresses confidence that their Honours will support this kind of learning, and requests that they appoint a committee to consider the matter.

The published records of Parliamentary debates at this time are notoriously incomplete, so my failure to find any mention of this matter in them does not mean that it was not considered. But it is certain that no financial support was voted by Parliament, for nine months later Ravius, disappointed in his hopes that the 'Godly Parliament . . . would do great things for him',[228] left for a post in Oxford, and with the departure of its sole lecturer the first London school of oriental languages collapsed after lasting only a year and a half. It must have been obvious to Ravius that without some permanent endowment its continuance, and his career, were tenuous. He had friends on the Parliamentary Committee supervising the universities. At first he seemed to expect that he might succeed to one of those

---

[226] The former cathedral revenues which Parliament had sequestered for educational purposes when it had abolished episcopacy.

[227] The printed version of this was received by Thomason on 13 June 1648: BL 669.f.12(47), *Thomason Tracts*, i. 633.

[228] According to Twells, 138, Ravius had expressed such hopes in a letter to Pococke in 1648.

posts at Oxford which Pococke was in danger of losing, but was dissuaded by his patrons Ussher and Selden from seeking them. Instead, on 5 March 1649 he was chosen by the Visitors to be one of the Fellows of Magdalen College whom they intruded, replacing almost the whole of the existing governing body of the college.[229] He was also made Hebrew lecturer and librarian of the college. Not much is known about his activities during the short time that he was at Magdalen. In July 1649 the new fellows discovered a cache of gold coins in the college's muniment room which had been left there as a reserve fund, and promptly divided it up amongst all the members of the foundation, each fellow receiving about £30 worth. The scandal that this embezzlement caused was said to be the reason why Selden did not, as he had intended, leave all of his library to the university.[230] Apart from this exploit, in which Ravius was merely a participant, I know only what emerges from the exuberant attack on Ravius, as part of 'the dregs of all races that poured into Oxford', published by John Harmar, which deserves quotation in full:

Ex *Morauia Ravius* huc irrupit, qui primum *Londini*, Sellulariis aliquot nempe *Luke Harrony*,[231] & aliis ejusdem furfuris; deinde *Oxonii*, Neophytis quibusdam concionatorculis, & præcocibus Theologastis, pusilla quædam *primævæ Linguæ* rudimenta ab Udallo Anglo vernaculè conscripta, aut consimilia de suo, ad ravim[232] usque deblateravit. Et non ita multò post, apud *Cancellarium Academiæ* (renuentibus licèt, & refragantibus Magdalensis Collegii Sociis quibus illum consociârant Tempora) gratulatoriam Orationem habuit, ex sputuosa quadam Epithetorum farragine, *Nobilissime, Honoratissime, Clarissime, Celebratissime, Consultissime*, conflatam, nimirum ad insignem suam facultatem Oratoriam ostentandam.[233]

From this we see that Ravius taught Hebrew from Udall's and his own grammars, and delivered a speech, written in his usual bombastic style which Harmar aptly parodies, before the University Chancellor at Magdalen College.

There is one other initiative by Ravius which may belong to his time

[229] Burrows, *Register of Visitors*, 171 (where his name 'Ravis' is disfigured as 'Rains'); Macray, *Register of Magdalen College*, iv. 78–84.

[230] The story is told at length by Macray, *Annals*, 118–20. Most of Selden's printed books did eventually come to the Bodleian, by the act of his executors, to whom the decision was entrusted in Selden's will.

[231] I am baffled by this reference.

[232] 'hoarseness': a pun.

[233] Harmar, *Vindiciae Academiae Oxoniensis*, 39–40. This book, published in 1662, is from a speech delivered in the early 1650s. Harmar was himself a notorious trimmer: see Madan, *Oxford Books*, iii, no. 2581.

at Magdalen College, but is perhaps better attributed to his career in London. This is a handwritten copy of 'The humble motion of Christian Ravis the hebrew Lecturer', undated and with no addressee, among the Hartlib Papers.[234] The purport of this was 'That some who are well skilled in the hebrew & other orientall tongues, able also to expresse themselves in this English tongue to the full, may be encouraged & set a part, to joyne in the examination of all the various interpretations of the hebrew text, to show the true & proper meaning of every doubtfull word & phraze'. Amongst the aims of this enterprise were 'To prevent & correct many scruples, errors, & mistakes, whence many disputes, & some heresies are growne, which scandalize the Papists, Jewes, & Turks, & keep them from embracing Christianity' and 'To maintaine the Authority & Credit of the divinity, of the holy Scriptures against the objections of Atheists & Scoffers of religion'. This pious attempt by Ravius to find employment for himself was without effect, and less than a year after coming to Oxford he left England for ever. On 10 October 1649 Queen Christina wrote to him for the second time offering him a post in Sweden 'which your virtue and learning will deserve',[235] and on 6 February 1650 Ravius was granted leave of absence from Magdalen for six months. He may have already departed, since the pass granted by the Council of State 'to Dr Ravis, for himselfe servants and bookes, to bee transported into Sweden . . . being sent for thithere to bee professor of the Orientall Tongue' is dated 9 January 1650.[236] He resigned his fellowship at Magdalen later that year. His unhappy career at Uppsala and Stockholm does not concern us here.[237]

According to Anthony Wood, Ravius left Oxford because he found few persons in college or in Oxford who were 'inclined to the study of the tongues wherein was his excellency'.[238] Perhaps the reason (apart from the better salary and opportunities offered him in Sweden) was rather that he was thoroughly disliked by many of those who were inclined to the study of those tongues. Of these the most articulate was John Greaves, who had first met him in London in late 1641.[239] At that

---

[234] 10/8/1.

[235] The letter is printed by Knös, *Analecta Epistolarum*, iv. 68.

[236] PRO, SP 25,63, pp. 500, 502.

[237] It is treated best by Annerstedt, *Upsala Universitets Historia*, especially i. 330; ii/1, 20–39, 52–3, 85–90.

[238] Wood, *Athenae Oxonienses*, iii. 1131.

[239] See the letters of Nicolaus Petri excerpted above, p. 151. Ravius and Greaves could hardly have met in the East, since Greaves left Constantinople in August or September 1638, at least ten months before Ravius arrived there.

time Ravius wrote him an ingratiating letter offering to let him look at his manuscript of Apollonius.[240] Greaves, who was not a man to suffer fools gladly, expresses his contempt in a letter to Pococke of 7 August 1645:

I send you these papers (which I have lately received from Mr. Ravius) for your perusall. I have not been so merry since these sad distractions, as upon the reading of these, and how much mirth thinke you shall I have, when he shall blesse the world with the rest, as he promise? If I have laught (yet with some kind of pitty of the man) at his Persian, how much more will you smile at his Persian, and Arabicke? A little before, I received a letter from him by the hands of an honourable freind of yours, in which he writt that hee had dedicated a book[241] to me; the first noise of it almost put me into a cold swett, but after that I found it was dedicated to no lesse then sixescore, besides myselfe, and that you, and your frend, were in the number, I recovered myselfe, and grew warme again.[242]

When Ravius came to London in June 1647 the two were on friendly enough terms to spend the night together on a visit to Hampton Court Palace (where the King was soon to be removed).[243] By the middle of 1649, however, in response to an enquiry from Claude Hardy, who had heard that Ravius was in London and was still interested in his Apollonius manuscript, Greaves is coldly dismissive of the man and the manuscript:

You are right in thinking that I have often seen Ravius: hence I have some acquaintance with him, but no friendship. Whether he has lost or sold the Apollonius, I don't know for certain. Some years ago I saw the missing part of Apollonius' *Conics* in his collection; but it was written so badly, with words eaten away by age, that it could never be published, except very faultily. However, the diagrams are elegant enough.[244]

---

[240] MS Smith 93, p. 109 (6 Dec. 1641).

[241] This is Ravius' *Specimen Lexici Arabico-Persici-Latini* (Leiden, 1645). Greaves's 'six score' is an understatement. The list of addressees at the beginning, which must include all scholars whom Ravius knew in person or by correspondence, runs to 165 names. Selden's copy of this rare work is in the Bodleian, Arch. Seld. A 73.1.

[242] MS BL 6193, fos. 75ᵛ–76ʳ. This part of the letter is reproduced verbatim by Twells, 139–40.

[243] Letter of Ravius to Isaac Vossius, MS d'Orville 268 p. 214.

[244] MS Savile 47, fo. 38, printed in Greaves, *Works*, ii. 462–4: 'Ravium (ut recte iudicas) saepe vidi, inde cum eo notitia mihi aliqua est, amicitia nulla. Apollonium Pergaeum an vendiderit, an perdiderit, non certò scio. Ante annos aliquot in Musaeo ipsius vidi Apollonii Conica, quae desiderantur: sed adeò malè exarata, exesis prae vetustate vocabulis, ut nunquam possint, nisi mendosissimè, in lucem edi: Schemata tamen satis sunt elegantia.'

Pococke responded politely to a gift of some of Ravius' publications after he arrived in England,[245] but there is no trace of any commerce between them after Ravius cast greedy eyes on Pococke's professorships.

From Cambridge Ravius met with much more enthusiasm, at least to begin with. We have already seen how extravagantly Thomas Smith praised Ravius' appointment in London to Hartlib. Wheelock expressed similar sentiments to Ravius himself, congratulating him 'that you have now become ours and our fellow countryman; and that you will devote your efforts, for God and our most afflicted Church, that oriental literature may flourish in London through you'.[246] Ravius avowed great friendship for him, offering not only the use of his manuscripts but hospitality in London.[247] At the same time he was, in all probability, slandering Wheelock's version of the Koran to Hartlib.[248] Thomas Smith too was disappointed in his expectations of Ravius. He sent him through Hartlib some exercises of his own in Arabic and other languages, on the strength of which he hoped that he might receive a recommendation from Ravius which would help him get a fellowship at Emmanuel College.[249] Among those exercises was Smith's translation of the 'Proverbs of ʿAlī', part of an Arabic textbook which Golius had published in 1629[250] and which had become standard in the teaching of Arabic in Holland and England. By 22 September 1648 Smith, who hoped to publish the translation, was worried about what had happened to it. Ravius had said nothing about it except that he himself had also translated it.[251] The sad end to the story is told in Smith's letter to Hartlib of 29 January 1649:

I wonder I heare nothing of Mr Ravius who still detaines one of those bookes which you were pleased to deliver him a yeere agoe. viz. Alis his Arabick proverbs with my translation. I have sent severall letters to him about it but heare ne γρῦ in answer. . . . While I write, in comes a letter from an University man whom I desired to speake to Mr Ravius for my Alis, he sends me word 'tis lost. & it was the only coppy I had.[252]

---

[245] Letter to Ravius of 16 July 1647, printed by Ravius, *Sesqui-Decuria*, 11–12.

[246] Letter of 12 Nov. 1647, printed ibid. 28: 'te jam & nostrum, & nostratem factum esse: teque operam deo, & afflictissimae Ecclesiae nostrae tuam daturam, ut Orientales literae per te, vir egregie, Londini efflorescant.'

[247] Wheelock's letter of 11 Feb. 1648 (ibid. 30).

[248] See above, p. 90.

[249] Letter to Hartlib of 9 Dec. 1647, Hartlib Papers 15/6/7.

[250] Schnurrer no. 196.

[251] Letter of Smith to Hartlib, Hartlib Papers 15/6/18.

[252] Ibid. 15/6/24.

Whether Ravius deliberately 'lost' Smith's translation with the intention of appropriating it is not known.[253] It is not surprising that the only acquaintance in England, apart from Hartlib, with whom Ravius kept up any correspondence was Samuel Clarke, who was among the few Arabists whom he had not injured or offended during his stay of two and a half years in England.

(x) THE 'TURKISH ALCORAN'

One other minor sensation in London during this period deserves mention as throwing light on the attitude of government and populace towards a book which was a necessity for Arabic studies, namely the Koran. Early in 1649 an English version of this book (made from the mediocre French translation of du Ryer, Paris, 1647[254]) was published by the London bookseller John Stephenson. While it was still in the press the book was denounced to the House of Commons, which, ever on the alert for 'subversive' publications, on 19 March 1649 ordered the Sergeant at Arms to take soldiers and 'make search for the presse where the Turkish Alcaron is informed to be now printing and to seize the said presse & papers if there be any such & apprehend the printer and bring him in custody'. The bookseller was duly imprisoned, the books seized, and on 21 March the whole matter was 'referred to the Councell of State . . . to discharge the Prisoner or continue him in prison as they shall find cause; and to take what further order they thinke fitt for suppressing the bookes and further imprinting of them'.[255] The Council of State seems to have let the parties concerned

---

[253] I have speculated whether the British Library copy of the book from which the translation was made, *Proverbia quaedam Alis* (Leiden, 1629), 1075.m.5 (4), might be the actual book that Smith sent to Ravius with his translation. In the British Museum Catalogue of Arabic Printed Books this copy is said to be annotated by Pococke. The handwriting of the annotations shows that to be untrue, but the part of the book containing the proverbs has been interleaved, and is extensively annotated with Arabic quotations from other sources, including manuscripts, and the text of the proverbs has pencilled Latin glosses. When examining the book I was unable to check the handwriting of the annotations against Thomas Smith's. By 1656 the book had passed into the hands of someone else, who wrote notes of a much lower level, evidently taken from Pococke's lectures on the book, on the flyleaves in front.

[254] On this and later printings see *L'Europe et le monde arabe*, 96–101. The translation is commonly attributed to Alexander Ross, but the names of the English translator and printer are prudently omitted from the title-page, and Ross appears explicitly only as the writer of the postscript of 'Admonition, for them who desire to know what use may be made of, or if there be danger in reading the *Alcoran*'.

[255] PRO, SP 25,37, pp. 29 and 30.

off with a warning 'not to meddle more with things of that nature',[256] and in fact the book was formally published on 23 April 1649,[257] and went through two editions that year. Although the purpose of the book, according to the translator's preface 'to the Christian reader', is allegedly to confirm in him 'the health of Christianity', which is reinforced by a scurrilous 'Life of Mahomet' appended to the work, at least one reader regarded the publication as a covert assault on Christianity, and denounced it furiously. The pamphlet he published is entitled 'An Answer without a Question: *Or, The Late Schismaticall* Petition For a Diabolicall Toleration of Seuerall Religions Expounded', and is dated 'in the blessed yeer of the Admission of the *Turkish Alcaron* into this *Kingdom*, 1649', and foisted on Richard Holdsworth, who had conveniently died in August of that year. The writer presents the publication of the Koran as an example of what happens when the kind of religious toleration that Colonel Pride had advocated is practised. He claims that 'in the dayes of Queen *Elizabeth*, King *James*, and King *Charles* of blessed Memory' it was treasonable to import, much less translate the Koran; and (with equal mendacity) that the English translation deliberately omits 'all the most gross, absurd, ridiculous Blasphemies, and impossible Fictions which were wont to make that wicked volumn justly odious to the world', in order to favour 'the *Mahumetan* mis-religion'. This opinion was no doubt extreme, but the affair is of interest as a demonstration of the suspicion in which the holy book of Islam was held by many different kinds of Christians, which was one of the chief difficulties in getting it printed, despite the unanimous opinion of all practising Arabists that a printed version was highly desirable.[258]

---

[256] *CSP Domestic 1649–50*, 59, 63, 70, Proceedings of the Council of State between 29 March and 4 April 1649.

[257] *Stationers' Registers*, i. 317. It was received by Thomason on 7 May (*Thomason Tracts*, i. 742).

[258] On the obstacles put in the way of publishing it in Italy see above, p. 25. Even in Holland there was resistance: Daniel Heinsius, writing to Selden in 1633, tells him that Erpenius had intended to do an edition and translation of the whole Koran, and Golius too would like to, but 'Obstitere hactenus nonnulli, qui negotia religionis tractant. Arbitrantur enim librum ἑτεροδοξίας, & periculosæ, ut loquuntur ipsi, superstitionis plenum, neque edi, neque in Latinam linguam converti a Christianis debere' (MS Selden supra 108, fo. 114).

(XI) THE POLYGLOT BIBLE

The other important activity connected with Arabic and other oriental studies in this period was also centred in London, although it was directed by scholars from both universities. This was the publication of the Polyglot Bible in the 1650s. The project was conceived and overseen by Brian Walton, but his assistants and collaborators were a remarkable body of scholars, many of whom, like himself, had lost their ecclesiastical livings or university posts as a result of the purges brought about by the Revolution. They included most of those contemporaries who then or later made their mark in oriental studies, for the work was planned as the English response to the Paris Polyglot, and was to be even more comprehensive than the latter in its inclusion of the oriental versions of the Scriptures. I shall not attempt to give a complete survey of this work.[259] It deserves the accolades that it has received as a monument of seventeenth-century English scholarship, especially oriental scholarship. Here I shall mention only the work of those participants whose studies were relevant to the topic of this book, with some incidental remarks on the format and composition of the whole Polyglot.

Walton himself possessed considerable knowledge of the languages employed in the publication. This is apparent from the auction catalogue of his library, which contains a solid although not spectacular collection of Arabic printed books, and fifty-three manuscripts, most Arabic, but also Turkish, Persian, Russian, Armenian, and Greek.[260] His skill in oriental languages appears best, however, in the little book that he wrote as an aid to reading the Polyglot, an 'Introduction to reading oriental languages', which went through several editions.[261] It is printed in the eastern fashion, beginning at the 'back'. The section

---

[259] This has been done admirably by Todd, *Life of Walton*, especially i. 77–81. That book remains the best survey of the origin and progress of the work, and the contributions to it of the various participants.

[260] *Bibliotheca Waltoniana sive Catalogus Librorum (in omni Arte & Linguâ) Rarissimorum, Reverendissimi in Christo Patris Briani Waltoni Episcopi Cestriensis, qui Biblia Polyglotta edidit, cum variis MSS. ab eo diligenter collectis*, sold at London on 30 April 1683. Cf. Todd, *Life of Walton*, i. 161. There is a copy of this catalogue in the British Library.

[261] I cite the second revised edition; see Bibliography under Walton, *Introductio ad lectionem linguarum*. All the languages treated in that, with the exception of Armenian and Coptic, are represented in the Polyglot. Walton had hoped to include these too, but was disappointed in his hopes of obtaining the necessary manuscripts from Rome (Twells, 214–15).

on Arabic (pp. 56–84) contains the rudiments of the language, including Erpenius' oration of 22 March 1620, and an 'exercise' from Koran Sura 58 (the Arabic text and a word-for-word Latin version). Walton was a Cambridge man, but graduated before Wheelock became Arabic Professor (BA Peterhouse 1619, MA 1623). He left the university for ecclesiastical preferments, and in 1626 was installed as Rector of St Martin's Orgar in London. His high-handed Laudian attitude toward such matters as the payment of tithes and the position of the communion table alienated many of his parishioners, who took their revenge on him in 1641 by addressing a petition to the House of Commons, published as

The Articles and Charges proved in Parliament against Doctor Walton, minister of St. Martins Orgars in Cannonstreet. Wherein his subtile tricks, and popish Innovations are discovered; as also the consultations, and assistance he hath had therein by the Archbishop of Canterbury, the Bishop of Rochester, Mr. Brough and Mr. Baker to effect the same. Also his impudence in defaming the Honourable members of the house of Commons, by scandalous aspersions and abusive language.[262]

Walton was deprived of all of his ecclesiastical preferments in 1641, and removed to Oxford, where he was incorporated DD in 1645. We may presume that it was there that he met Ussher, Pococke, Clarke, and others who were later involved in the Polyglot Bible. After the fall of Oxford in 1646, he went to live in the house of his father-in-law, Dr William Fuller, in London. It was there, in 1652, that the project for the Polyglot Bible was announced.

Walton had taken the precaution of getting the Council of State to approve the work beforehand,[263] and enlisting the support of the two most eminent scholars of the day, Ussher and Selden. The printed prospectus for the Polyglot contains their 'Approbation'. It was accompanied by an invitation for subscriptions (at a cost of £10 per copy), dated '1652', and a letter signed by Ussher, Walton, and Wheelock, amongst others, dated 1 March 1653.[264] In the original proposals for

[262] BL E.173, no. 11 (*Thomason Tracts*, i. 36–7; London, 1641); excerpted by Todd, *Life of Walton*, i. 14–20.
[263] Their order, dated 11 July 1652, is cited in the prospectus (Todd, *Life of Walton*, i. 45–6). Cf. *CSP Domestic 1651–1652*, 328.
[264] A complete transcription of all three documents is given by Todd, *Life of Walton*, i. 31–54. The letter and invitation were previously printed by Twells, 197–205. The earliest notice of the prospectus that Todd was able to find is in Evelyn's *Diary* for 22 Nov. 1652 (op. cit. 31), but the project had been under discussion for some months before, as is shown by a letter from Selden to Pococke of February 1651/2 (Twells, 205).

subscriptions, among the 'persons to be employed in preparing of copies, correcting the press, overseeing the managing of the work, &c.' were, besides Walton, Wheelock, Pococke, [Thomas] Greaves, John Viccars, and Thomas Smith. Wheelock died too soon to play any part in the actual production of the Bible, and a number of others were recruited in the course of the work.

At the same time a specimen of the types to be used[265] was issued, printed in London by Jacob Flesher (who had recently printed most of John Greaves's books). I have not seen this (although I presume that the Arabic types used were those pirated from the Oxford matrices), but it was considered unsatisfactory. Wheelock, writing to the Vice-Chancellor of Cambridge on 5 January 1653 to recommend the Polyglot project, says that he had corrected eighty errata in the sheet. Walton noted at the bottom of the specimen seen by Todd: 'we shall acquire better Hebrew and Syriac types, with points.'[266] In the event Flesher's types were not used. The man who actually printed the Polyglot was Thomas Roycroft, and a whole new set of oriental types was cut especially for the work.[267] The Arabic fount was allegedly modelled on Savary de Brèves's types, and although less elegant than those, it is superior to any Arabic used for printing in England before or after until Caslon's in the eighteenth century. Walton was able to commission the founding of these types[268] because he had been very successful in attracting subscribers. Even before the prospectus was issued he had raised £4,000 in subscriptions, and by 4 May 1653, before the printing had begun, this had swelled to £9,000,[269] although this was money promised rather than cash in hand. Nevertheless, by the beginning of October 1653 the first volume was in the press, by which time Walton must have received the £1,500 which had been stated as the prerequisite for beginning the printing. Walton had

---

[265] Described by Todd, *Life of Walton*, i. 51–2, from a copy in Sidney Sussex College annotated by Walton himself. It contained Genesis 1: 1–12 in Hebrew, the Vulgate, Chaldee, Samaritan, Syriac, Arabic, and Persian, with Latin versions, all on a single sheet.

[266] 'Typos Hebr. et Syr. cum punctis meliores parabimus' (Todd, *Life of Walton*, i. 61).

[267] Walton treated these types as his own property, as Castell wrote to Clarke on 17 Nov. 1658 (MS BL 22905, fo. 20, see below, p. 261). He eventually sold them to Roycroft (ibid., fo. 22, 23 Dec. 1658), who thus established himself as the principal London printer with exotic types, and after the Restoration was granted the title of 'King's Printer for Oriental Languages'.

[268] Presumably from Nicholas Nicholls, and possibly from others as well. I know of no evidence on this point.

[269] Twells, 211, the latter sum according to a letter of Thomas Greaves to Pococke.

originally hoped to get a subsidy of £1,000 from the Council of State, as he wrote to Pococke on 28 July 1652,[270] but in the end had to be content with an exemption from duty on the paper imported for the work. This privilege was later confirmed by Cromwell as Lord Protector, for which he was duly thanked in the preface to the Polyglot. After the Restoration this caused Walton considerable embarrassment. The last two leaves of the preface had to be removed, and a dedication to Charles II substituted, in those copies not yet sold.[271]

The English Polyglot Bible is clearly modelled on the Paris Polyglot, and although inferior to it in stateliness and beauty of typography, it is superior in several other respects (and indeed hurt the sales of its great predecessor, the price of which was four or five times greater). Its six quarto volumes were much more convenient to handle than Le Jay's ten folios. Its arrangement was preferable from a scholarly viewpoint, since all the various versions were printed together on the same page,[272] instead of separately, and it also contained a critical apparatus to all the versions, lacking in the Paris Polyglot.[273] It also contained more of the old translations,[274] and the texts of the Arabic, Syriac, and Samaritan versions had been considerably improved over the Paris editions. Walton managed the difficult task of co-ordinating the work of numerous scholars, borrowing manuscripts,[275] and overseeing the whole production efficiently, if autocratically. The sixth and final volume emerged from the press in 1657,[276] less than four years after printing had begun, an astonishingly short time, especially compared with the twenty-odd years that the

---

[270] Twells, 208–9.

[271] On this episode see Todd, *Life of Walton*, i. 82–6.

[272] The reproduction of the first page in *Enciclopedia Italiana*, vi. 914, gives a good idea of the layout.

[273] According to Walton, *Introductio ad lectionem linguarum Orientalium*, 11, this omission was 'ex dissidia eorum qui operi præfuerunt' (i.e. Le Jay and Gabriel Sionita).

[274] Walton lists no less than nineteen areas in which the London Polyglot is superior to, or contains things missing in the Paris Bible (ibid. 92 ff.).

[275] Manuscripts were lent by individuals, such as Ussher and Pococke, and institutions, including the former King's Library and Cambridge University, which to Walton's displeasure required an enormous bond (see his letter to Lightfoot quoted by Oates, 229). Five Arabic, Syriac, and Samaritan manuscripts belonging to Ussher which were still on loan at the time of his death in 1656 are listed by Castell in MS BL 22905, fo. 103.

[276] The title-page to the whole work gives the publication date as 1657, but Walton's preface (the last thing to be printed, although it is bound first) must have been written in 1658, since it refers to the specimen for the Heptaglot Lexicon, which was printed in that year.

Paris Polyglot had taken. The first volume containing the Pentateuch, which emerged (without the preface) in 1654, already exhibits nearly the whole variety of exotic types used:[277] Hebrew (also used for Chaldee), Samaritan, Syriac, Arabic (used, with a few additional letters, also for Persian), and Greek. Like the Hebrew text, the Arabic is printed with full vocalization and diacritical points. Arabic is, after Greek and Latin, the language most prevalent throughout, since except for some books of the Apocrypha the whole of both Old and New Testaments were presented in an Arabic version. The variant readings for all the versions are collected in volume 6, together with a variety of other critical matter, including contributions by Pococke and Thomas Greaves.

The principal assistant in the supervision of the Polyglot was Edmund Castell, who had been a slightly junior contemporary of Walton's at Cambridge, and was currently Rector of Woodham Walter in Essex.[278] In the preface to the Polyglot Walton credits him with correcting the Samaritan, Syriac, Arabic, and Ethiopic texts, and translating the Ethiopic version of the Canticles into Latin. To these Todd adds the translation of several books of the New Testament, and of the Syriac version of Job.[279] Castell seems to have spent most of his time from 1653 onwards in London, preparing much of the work for the press, and correcting it after it was printed.[280] For this he received a salary. Castell, who was on bad terms with Walton by 1658 (and probably much earlier), was offended by Walton's mentioning this 'honorarium' in the preface to the Polyglot, but refrained from expressing his feelings, at least in public, while Walton was still alive. However, in his preface to the Heptaglot Lexicon he retorts that he had spent the whole sum he had received on the Polyglot, and had raised an additional £1,000 for it from solicitations and his own resources.[281] The Heptaglot Lexicon on which he spent so many years and so much

[277] The exception is Ethiopic, which was used very little outside the New Testament.

[278] For some details of Castell's life and career, with bibliography, see Norris, 'Professor Edmund Castell, Orientalist and Divine'.

[279] *Life of Walton*, i. 167–8.

[280] In his letter to Lightfoot of 9 June 1669 (MS BL Lansdowne 1055, fo. 96; Lightfoot, *Letters*, 393–5), Castell says 'A seventeen years' drudgery for the public I have now undergone.' Since he did not begin the Heptaglot Lexicon until 1657, he must be counting the four years of his work on the Polyglot. That these were spent in London is indicated by the phrase 'Annus jam agitur decimus septimus, ex quo relicto rure paterno . . .' in his preface to the Heptaglot Lexicon (1669).

[281] 'Honorarium illud quod in praefatione *Waltoniana* dicor accepisse, in illud ipsum opus non refundebam tantum omne, sed mille plus minus libras, ad promovendum illud, partim ab aliis solicitando procurabam, partim ipse donabam ultro.'

money grew out of his work on the Polyglot, but, since it was not published until long after the Restoration, will be treated in the next chapter.

The other principal assistant in London was Samuel Clarke. He had left Oxford, where he was considered the most promising of Pococke's pupils, but where his associations with Royalists made it impossible for him to get a fellowship at his college, Merton, after 1648.[282] By 1650 he was a schoolmaster in Islington, and was still there in June 1653, when Langbaine wrote to him and to Selden about getting him the headmastership of Northleach Grammar School.[283] Clarke seems to have refused this, and at some time before 25 March 1656 had moved to the City of London to work full-time on the Polyglot.[284] He had evidently given up hope of a fellowship at Oxford, since he had married. Walton, in his preface, credits Clarke with work on the Hebrew text, the Chaldee paraphrase, and the Persian Gospels. Clarke also made notable critical contributions in the appendices in vol. 6. Castell, in acknowledging Clarke's aid in his notes on the Ethiopic version of the New Testament, mentions his experience not only in philology but also in the mathematical sciences. This fits with Clarke's later interest in editing Abū 'l-Fidā''s *Geography*. We shall see how Clarke's connection with the Polyglot led to his association with Castell in the Heptaglot Lexicon, and also to the abortive 'seventh volume' of the Polyglot.

We have already noted the names of John Viccars and Thomas Smith in the original proposals as among those persons to be employed in preparing of copies, etcetera for the Polyglot. It is unclear what part, if any, they actually played, since Walton makes no mention of them in his preface. Viccars, after being ejected from his living at South Fambridge in 1644, migrated to Oxford, but (probably after its surrender) seems to have moved to London, since he donated an item

---

[282] In 1648 he submitted to the Visitors (Burrows, *Register of Visitors*, 152), and graduated MA. He was a friend of John and Thomas Greaves, both of whom were expelled from the university about that time. When in 1649 the university resolved that in accordance with the Laudian statutes the post of 'Architypographus' (controller of the University Press) should be attached to that of Superior Bedel of Law as soon as the latter fell vacant, it seems that Clarke was the person intended for that office, but that did not happen until 1658.

[283] MS BL Add. 4276, fo. 23, and MS Selden supra 109, fo. 418.

[284] Letter to Ravius, MS BL Add. 29747, fo. 39: 'in Bibliis polyglottis cudendis, inter alios viros eruditos, ipse licet omnium minimus atque indignissimus, totus sum'. Todd, *Life of Walton*, i. 243 is mistaken in saying that Clarke was still at the school in Islington when working on the Polyglot.

to Sion College library in 1650.[285] His *Decapla in Psalmos* was reissued in 1655, but he was not necessarily alive then, and we hear no more of him. Thomas Smith of Christ's College, on the other hand, was certainly alive and active during this period. In 1653 he published a translation of Jean Daillé's *Apology for Reformed Churches*. The only way in which he is known to have been of service to the Polyglot Bible is as intermediary between Walton and Cambridge University for the loan of manuscripts. For instance on 3 October 1655 Walton requests Lightfoot to deliver Bar Bahlul's Syriac lexicon to Smith, who will send it to London.[286] Smith later performed similar services for Castell's Heptaglot Lexicon in arranging the loan of Bedwell's Arabic dictionary.[287] In 1659 Smith was appointed University Librarian, but died after only two years' tenure.[288]

Thomas Greaves had been deprived of his fellowship at Corpus by the Visitors in 1648, but managed to retain the Rectory of Dunsby in Lincolnshire to which he had been preferred by Laud. We saw that Laud had appointed him Deputy Professor of Arabic while Pococke was absent in Constantinople, and that during that time he had published a hackneyed oration on the use of Arabic.[289] His only other published work appears in vol. 6 of the Polyglot. The first item consists of some observations on the Persian version of the Pentateuch, which he says are merely a specimen of a much larger collection which he has assembled and hopes to publish. The second is notes on the Persian translation of the Gospels, the meagreness of which he apologizes for in an accompanying letter, dated 22 December 1657, excusing it on the grounds of his remoteness at Dunsby from the aids available at London or the universities.[290] He had one other work in hand. In a letter to Richard Baxter of 5 August 1656 he tells him about his polemical anti-Islamic

treatise of their *Credenda* and *Agenda*, in part of which they are diametrically opposite to Christianity, I have composed out of their own writings; the translations now extant, and relations of the Greeks and Latins concerning Mahomet's original, and a great part of his doctrine, being very erroneous, which hath occasioned divers mistakes in Vives, Grotius, &c. Having therefore

---

285 Sion College Benefactors' Book, p. 52.
286 MS BL Lansdowne 1055, fo. 19.
287 Letter from Castell to Clarke, MS BL Add. 22905, fo. 13 (1 July 1658).
288 On his term as librarian see Oates, 300–3.
289 *De Linguae Arabicae Utilitate et Praestantia*: Madan, *Oxford Books*, i. 213.
290 The letter is reprinted by Todd, *Life of Walton*, i. 228.

shown some part of the work with other observations to the Reverend Bishop Usher, he often advised me to publish them.[291]

This was never published, and does not survive as such, but Greaves's translation of and commentary on the Koran is presumably related to it. This is extant as MS BL Add. 21901. Although neatly written, it is obviously intended for the writer's own use. The Latin text has numerous marginal annotations, with frequent Arabic quotations. The text is interleaved for extra notes, which are usually long Arabic quotations and mostly on purely factual matters. After Sura 13 some suras are omitted, and there is nothing at all between Sura 29 and Sura 81. The work is very far from complete. Greaves kept up a friendly correspondence until his death in 1676 with his old chamber-fellow Pococke, but his youthful enthusiasm for Arabic studies seems to have waned. We have seen how he alienated much of the splendid collection of oriental manuscripts which he had inherited from his brother. Such interest as he showed later in life remained within the traditional boundaries prescribed by religious dogma.

Pococke himself, although named in the proposals, played rather a small part in the Polyglot, despite Twells's attempt to magnify his contribution. He was otherwise occupied (with the Eutychius and *Porta Mosis*) during these years. It seems likely that he was not happy with the choice of the Arabic version which Walton decided on, and he was certainly dissatisfied with the Latin translation which accompanied it.[292] A suggestion that he made to add another version of the Syriac Gospels from a manuscript in his own possession was rejected. However, he did succeed in persuading Walton to use the version of the Persian Gospels (also in a manuscript belonging to him) made from the Syriac, rather than the version which Wheelock had published, made from the Greek. He also suggested improvements in the newly cut Hebrew types. The only printed contributions of Pococke to the Polyglot are his preface to the notes on the variant readings in the Arabic versions, and some of the variant readings themselves, in vol. 6, section 8. However, he loaned several important manuscripts, and seems to have read the proof-sheets as they were issued and sent his suggestions to Walton, a valuable service which Lightfoot at Cambridge also provided.

Walton, in his preface, bestows particular praise on Hyde, whom he calls 'a youth of the highest promise, who has made great progress,

[291] The letter is printed Greaves, *Works*, vol. i, pp. lxiii–lxvi.
[292] Twells, 215–18.

beyond his years, in the Oriental Tongues'. Hyde took over the tasks
which his teacher Wheelock had been expected to do, including
correction of the Arabic, Syrian, and Persian texts, and especially transcribing the Persian translation of the Pentateuch by Jacob Tawusi
from the Hebrew characters (in which it had been printed by Soncino
at Constantinople in 1546) into standard Persian script, a feat which
amazed Archbishop Ussher. According to Twells, Hyde was recommended to Walton by none other than Pococke, an interesting fact
in view of the distant, not to say strained relationship between the
two after Hyde migrated to Oxford. The high regard in which
Hyde's learning was held by his colleagues at Queen's College,
Oxford, which he had recently joined, is evidenced by the dedication
'ad Doctissimum Juvenem Thomam Hide Pentateuchi Persici restaura-
torem diligentissimum' by William Burton of his speech on the
remains of the ancient Persian language.[293] Hyde, who was to display a
wider knowledge of oriental languages than anyone in England in the
seventeenth century, was particularly drawn to Persian.

If we look back over the twenty years of the 'English Revolution'
we can fairly conclude that they represent the high-water mark of
Arabic studies in England during the seventeenth century. Despite the
disruptions caused by the Civil War and its aftermath, Arabic language
and literature was being taught and cultivated, not only at both universities, but also for a while at London. Facilities for printing Arabic
were established in London and Oxford, and significant contributions
to scholarship were published, including all the works of John Greaves
and Pococke's seminal books, the *Specimen* and *Porta Mosis*. Finally,
the Polyglot Bible represented a kind of manifesto of English commitment to oriental scholarship. Although much important work was done
in the field later in the century, in comparison with these two decades
the next four appear as a period of gradual and then increasing decline.

---

[293] In his *Graecae Linguae Historia* (London, 1657): Madan, *Oxford Books*, iii, no.
2321.

8

Arabic Learning after the Restoration

GIVEN the remarkable success of Arabic studies in England in the difficult period following the Civil War, it might have been expected that the Restoration would carry it to even greater heights; and indeed at first the prospects seemed very bright. Most of those who had lost their positions at the universities because of Royalist leanings or failure to conform regained them. Pococke was restored to the canonry which was his by right as Regius Professor of Hebrew,[1] and henceforward, till the end of his life, resided in his lodgings at Christ Church. He was also, by the King's command, advanced to the degree of Doctor of Divinity on 20 December 1660.[2] Samuel Clarke had already returned to Oxford. In May 1658, through the influence of Langbaine, he was appointed 'Architypographus', the office of Superior Bedel of Law, to which that post had been attached, having finally fallen vacant. Soon the University Press with which he was charged underwent remarkable changes and improvements under the influence of the man who put his own stamp on post-Restoration Oxford, John Fell.[3] Thomas Marshall was elected to a fellowship at Lincoln College in 1668, but continued to reside in Dordrecht, where he was chaplain to the English merchants, for several more years. We shall see that in Holland he was of great service to the university in obtaining types for the University Press and in other matters.

[1] An effort to do this before the Restoration was made by John Wallis in March 1660 (Twells, 231–4). Even when Pococke was granted a canon's stall and lodging it was, as before, not the one traditionally annexed to the Hebrew Chair, and he seems to have refused to occupy the lodgings until this was rectified. A letter to Boyle of 5 Oct. 1660, in which he complains of those who 'keep me out of my right', is written from Balliol College (Boyle, *Works*, vi. 323–4). For the controversy and its resolution see Twells, 236–8.

[2] But for his wife's social ambitions Pococke might not have received the degree, as appears from the letter of Thomas Lamplugh recommending the grant to Joseph Williamson (secretary to Secretary of State Nicholas), 12 Aug. 1660 (PRO, SP 29,10, fo. 132^r): 'You know Mr. Pococks deserts, & his Modesty, he doth not speak out, but I perceev his wife, beeing to live in Oxon, would not have, almost, every one to take place of her; & he himself is willing to accept of that Degree.'

[3] Fell, who had fought for the King while a Student of Christ Church, had been ejected in 1648, but continued to reside in Oxford, where he privately maintained the rites of the Church of England. In 1660 he was made canon and then Dean of Christ Church, in which position, and later as Vice-Chancellor, he ruled as an autocrat.

Furthermore, a promising new crop of Arabic scholars who had come to Oxford in the comparatively tranquil period of the Protectorate[4] was maturing. These included Edward Bernard, Robert Huntington, Thomas Smith, Narcissus Marsh, and Thomas Hyde. At the same time, however, there were disquieting signs that all was not well with this discipline, and that in particular a kind of public contempt for it had developed.[5] The promise of the younger generation was to remain largely unfulfilled.

(1) POCOCKE

In any event, in the dozen years following the Restoration much was accomplished. Pococke's first task was to publish the complete *Abū 'l-Faraj*, with translation, thus providing the Republic of Letters with its first reliable history written in Arabic. As early as 16 May 1660 Convocation had voted that the surplus of the Schools Money should be devoted to 'setting up and maintaining a learned Typographie', and that £140 of it be granted to print 'Gregorius Abul Pharagius' in Arabic and Latin.[6] The book was in the press in 1661,[7] but its size and difficulty delayed publication until 1663. In the mean time another work by Pococke, the *Carmen Tograi*, had been printed at Oxford.[8] This, although much slighter, is of considerable interest as the only textbook that he published. The *Lāmiyyat al-'Ajam* ('the poem ending in *lām* of the Persians') was written by Ḥassān b. 'Alī al-Ṭughrā'ī in the early twelfth century. A Persian in origin, he composed this Arabic poem in 59 stanzas, each ending in the same letter (*lām*), which was much admired in Arabic-speaking lands for its

---

[4] Cromwell was Chancellor of Oxford from 1651 to 1657, and did much to benefit the university and little to interfere with it.

[5] Writing to Boyle on 2 Dec. 1662 with a gift of his *Abū 'l-Faraj*, Pococke hopes that he may 'vindicate it from that contempt, which, with other men used to writings of another kind, it is likely to find'. He expressed similar sentiments to Thomas Greaves at the same time (Twells, 254). A year earlier Samuel Clarke, in the preface to Pococke's *Carmen Tograi*, had characterized the study of Arabic as 'ubíque ferè spretae, ac, proh dolor! jacenti scientiae parti'.

[6] Madan, *Oxford Books*, iii, pp. xxx, 176. The text is given by Johnson and Gibson, *Print and Privilege at Oxford*, 37–8. Carter, *History of Oxford University Press*, 43 explains that the money was not an outright grant but a loan to the printer which the Architypographus was expected to repay eventually.

[7] Clarke was already looking forward to its being printed on 3 Sept. 1659, according to his letter in Lightfoot, *Letters*, 403–4.

[8] Madan, *Oxford Books*, iii, no. 2576.

elegance and ethical content. Golius had introduced its use as an Arabic textbook into Europe by publishing an edition, consisting of the Arabic text alone (together with other elementary material), at Leiden in 1629,[9] and it had become, and remained, a standard reading-book for students of Arabic.[10] As Clarke explains in the preface, this edition was intended as a simple but interesting reading-book for students of Arabic. Pococke provides a fully vocalized Arabic text, on ten pages, with facing literal translation into Latin. The bulk of the book (233 pages) is devoted to the notes, which are directed towards the beginning student. Almost every word of the text is explained, including such terms as 'Abū'. The notes are mainly on grammatical and lexicographical points, with many references to Erpenius' grammar, and Raphelengius' and Golius' dictionaries, as well as native dictionaries and commentaries on the poem. But scholarly themes are not entirely absent. There are a good many incidental references to other Arabic authors which beginning students would hardly have read.[11] These notes certainly represent the substance of the course of lectures on the poem which Pococke had been regularly delivering.[12] The book is provided with copious indices of words and subjects. It is preceded by the lecture with which Pococke prefaced this course,[13] and which contains *inter alia* a justification for learning Arabic. He describes the reasons given by the 'Arabum magistri' as 'ut planè futilia explodenda', namely that it is the language of God and used by those admitted to Paradise.[14] Much more weighty are the claims for the clarity, elegance, and immense richness of the language. He praises the harmonious sound of Arabic, attributing the harshness which it appears to have to English ears to what they are habituated to. Concerning the wealth of Arabic he mentions that Hamza of Isfahān said that there are 12,305,412 words in it (a precision which occasioned much mirth amongst those who scorned these studies).[15] After dwelling on the love

[9] Schnurrer no. 196.

[10] See Schnurrer, pp. 185–92, for editions and translations. Vattier had issued a French translation in the year preceding Pococke's publication. For an example of the use of Golius' edition by a student of Pococke's in the 1650s see p. 200, n. 253.

[11] For example Maimonides (Pococke incidentally corrects his notes to *Porta Mosis*), ibn Khallikān, al-Mutanabbī, and Abū 'l-Fidā'.

[12] For Pococke's edition and translation of a section from al-Safadī's commentary on the poem, which Wallis had inserted in his *Mathesis Universalis*, see below, p. 248.

[13] Paraphrased by Twells, 248–52.

[14] He leaves the reader to draw his own conclusions about similar claims by Jews and Christians for Hebrew, about which he says nothing.

[15] See below, p. 309.

of poetry amongst the pre-Islamic Arabs, he celebrates the contributions of the Arabs to philosophy and the sciences, and their role in passing on the heritage of the Greeks. He cites Sir Henry Savile for the superiority of the Arabs to the Greeks in mathematics and medicine, and says that he had heard from Bainbridge that the astronomical observations that they had made long ago could hardly be bettered by any of Tycho or the other moderns.[16] Deploring the injuries done to the Arabic philosophers by the barbarous medieval translations, he expresses the hope that some day 'we may read al-Farābī, ibn Sīnā, and ibn Bājja in the language in which they wrote, and then finally we may freely express our judgement on the learning of the Arabs'. Historians, he says, should read Arabic to avoid propagating ridiculous stories, e.g. about Muḥammad's promise to return, 'lest, attributing false errors to the Muslims, we render ourselves ridiculous in trying to refute their real errors'. He strongly affirms that, as far as the humanities are concerned, the Arabs have as much to teach others as to learn from them. Coming to theology, the point usually stressed in sixteenth- and seventeenth-century arguments for learning Arabic, he expresses himself in a cool and ambiguous way. If, he says, it should be considered appropriate for Christian theologians to know and refute Muslim doctrines, they cannot hope do so without knowledge of this language.[17] He is more positive about the use of the language in illuminating the study of the Hebrew Scriptures, particularly since Maimonides and some of the other principal rabbinic authorities wrote in Arabic. At the end of the book, to fill up a blank page, an excerpt from Pococke's inaugural lecture of 10 August 1636 (otherwise lost) is printed. This, appropriately, discusses the high regard that the Arabs had for poets and poetry. Almost certainly destined for Pococke's pupils was the printed sheet, from 1673, containing the Arabic text of a poem by Abū 'l-ʿAlā al-Maʿarrī, some proverbs, etcetera, of which the only five copies known were seen in the Bodleian by Madan.[18]

The *Carmen Tograi* provides the best evidence for the content of Pococke's teaching of Arabic, but there are also some fragments of his

[16] Fo. *7ʳ, 'vix minutulum aliquid vel ex ipsius Tychonis, aliorumve seculi nostri Atlantum, lucubrationibus, illis quæ pridem in Oriente observata addi posse, doctissimi Professoris Joh. Bainbrigii, quo nemini libentius in arte sua crediderim, judicium est.'

[17] Fo. *8ᵛ, 'si impia Mohammedis dogmata vel nosse vel refellere Christianos deceat Theologos, neque illis minus necessaria erit huius linguae notitia, sine qua frustra haec conentur.'

[18] *Oxford Books*, iii, no. 2959. These could no longer be located when I asked for them at the Bodleian. Golius had published poems of al-Maʿarrī in his reissue of Erpenius' grammar of 1656 (Schnurrer no. 81).

lecture notes among the Pococke manuscripts in the Bodleian Library. Only Holt has examined these in detail, and what follows is derived from his thesis.[19] As we saw, Golius had published a collection of proverbs attributed to ʿAlī in the same book as the *Carmen Tograi*, and this too became part of the standard reading for beginners in Arabic. Pococke lectured on these *Proverbia Quaedam Alis* when he began teaching in 1636,[20] and continued to do so, probably for the rest of his career. MS Pococke 424 is a fragment of his lecture-notes on these proverbs. The notes are primarily grammatical, with references to Erpenius' *Libellus centum regentium*.[21] MS Pococke 425 also contains (besides a 'Parsing-list of Arabic words') lecture-notes on the proverbs of ʿAlī, with references to Erpenius' *Rudimenta Linguae Arabicae*, but these notes are apparently by one of Pococke's pupils. MSS Pococke 427 and 428[22] contain small parts of Pococke's lecture-notes on Golius' reissue of Erpenius' *Linguae Arabicae Tyrocinium* (1656). The reading-matter in this included the first *Maqāma* of al-Ḥarīrī, and the beginning of Pococke's lecture on this celebrated monument of Arabic *belles-lettres* is preserved.[23] It is mostly devoted to an explanation of the complicated system of nomenclature, using al-Ḥarīrī as an example, but as in his notes on the *Carmen Tograi*, the lecturer's enthusiasm and appreciation for Arabic poetry[24] and literature shine through the factual and grammatical minutiae.

Pococke's Arabic translation of Grotius' *De Veritate Religionis*

---

[19] Holt, 'Arabic Studies in Seventeenth-Century England', 61–2, with appendices 3 and 4.

[20] Twells, 38–9.

[21] This was a grammatical work of al-Jurjānī, published by Erpenius in 1617, together with his edition of the Arabic grammar of ibn Ajūrrūm: *Grammatica Arabica dicta Gjarumia, et Libellus centum regentium cum versione Latina et Commentariis* (Schnurrer no. 53, cf. Jones, 'Learning Arabic', 183).

[22] MS Poc. 427, pp. 110 and 227–32, and MS Poc. 428, pp. 1–2, according to Holt, 'Arabic Studies in Seventeenth-Century England', 62.

[23] MS Poc. 428, p. 1. Excerpted by Holt, ibid., appendix 4, pp. 108–9. On the reputation of this work Pococke justly remarks: 'Est vero unus instar omnium liber hic almakamat dictus, (in omnium oribus, omnibus manibus liber), cui primas (post Alcoranum suum) eloquentiae laudes, & summa elogia tribuunt Arabes.'

[24] I lack the expertise to pass judgement on the merits of Pococke's own Arabic poems, published in *Britannia Rediviva*, a volume celebrating the King's return, and *Epicedia Academiæ Oxoniensis in Obitum Celsissimi Principis HENRICI Ducis Glocestrensis*, both published at Oxford in 1660 (see Madan, *Oxford Books*, iii, nos. 2466–7, with some amusing remarks about those contributors who had shown equal adulation in a volume of verses addressed to Cromwell in 1654, including Ralph Button, who soon lost his place, and John Locke, who retained his). These verses, and the dedication of *Abū 'l-Faraj* to Charles II, are the only gestures of Pococke towards the court that I have found.

Christianae also appeared after the Restoration, but it had gone to press in the preceding year.[25] We saw that Pococke had completed the work long before, and that he had consulted Grotius himself about it in 1641. That it was published now was due to the Honourable Robert Boyle, who had become acquainted with Pococke while resident in Oxford during the 1650s. Boyle provided not only the money but also the enthusiasm without which it is unlikely that Pococke would ever have ventured on publication. Boyle, although an accomplished Hebraist, had only a modest knowledge of Arabic, by his own account in *Considerations touching the Style of the Holy Scriptures* (1661): 'I confess my self too unskilful in the Arabick tongue, to be a competent judge [of the eloquence of the Koran]; my other studies and distractions having made me forget most of the little knowledge I had once acquired of that flourishing language.'[26] Boyle's motives for supporting Pococke's translation are best stated in a letter which he sent to Hartlib and which the latter quoted to Worthington:

What you write conc. the Translation of the Bible into the Turkish tongue,[27] is most welcome. For to speak in the phrase of the times, it has been much upon my heart to have the propagation of the Gospel attempted, not by making an Independent a Presbyter, or Presbyter an Independent, but by converting those to Christianity that are either enemies or strangers to it. . . . Nor are we here altogether regardless of such matter, for Mr. Pocock is at my request printing a translation of Grotius's Book of the Truth of the Christian religion into Arabick, and I need not tell you, how fit he is for such a work.[28]

In other words, Boyle's primary purpose was missionary, the conversion of non-Christians to Christianity. To this end he supported a number of translation and publication projects, including the Turkish translation of the New Testament by William Seaman, and the Malay translation of the Gospels and Acts, published at Oxford in 1666 and 1677 respectively.[29] Pococke had indeed envisioned the possibility of

[25] Clarke mentions that it is being printed, and that Boyle had contributed £50 towards the costs of printing, in his letter to Lightfoot of 3 Sept. 1659 (Lightfoot, *Letters*, 403–4); Madan, *Oxford Books*, iii, no. 2498. For later partial reprints see, besides Madan, Millies, 'Over de Oostersche Vertalingen van *De Veritate Religionis Christianae*', who was the first to give a correct account of the history of Pococke's translation.

[26] Boyle, *Works*, ii. 298. Burnet's claim, repeated in the *Life* (ibid. i, p. cxliv) that but for the infirmity of his eyes Boyle would have gained a thorough knowledge of Arabic, seems ill founded.

[27] This refers to the abortive project of printing a Turkish translation of the whole Bible, which Levinus Warner was hoping to get done in the Netherlands.

[28] Worthington, *Correspondence*, i. 160–1 (7 Nov. 1659).

[29] Madan, *Oxford Books*, iii, nos. 2727 and 3164. Seaman, who had spent years in

converting Muslims with the book when he spoke to Grotius,[30] but by the time it came to be published it is doubtful whether he still thought this possible or even desirable.[31] Certainly what he stresses, as before, is the help it might bring to Arabic-speaking Christians by confirming them in their faith[32] and dissuading the several sects from dissension with each other. To this end he must have viewed Book VI, which is directed against Islam, as a deterrent to conversion to Islam for Christians rather than a likely way of converting Muslims to Christianity. Nevertheless he was anxious to avoid making the book look ridiculous to Muslims, and so took care to excise some silly fables which Grotius had attributed to them,[33] but which had no basis whatever in Arabic sources. Grotius had given Pococke permission to do this, as he explained to Boyle in his letter of 5 October 1660:

In the sixth book, I thought it necessary to put no other things for matter of history, than will be acknowledged by the *Mahometans*. And indeed *Grotius* himself was of that opinion. And therefore I have left out what is said of the pigeon flying to *Mahomet*'s ear; and that the mouse was bred of camels dung; and that half the moon came into his sleeve; and some few things are so altered, as that they might rather agree with what themselves affirm, than what others rhetorically descant on the story.[34]

To avoid arousing suspicion in Muslim countries, the copies sent to those places contained only the Arabic text, with no indication of origin, author, or translation. Even so, when Robert Huntington, as chaplain at Aleppo, distributed copies of the book which Boyle had sent to him, he sometimes took the precaution of removing Book VI altogether. He wrote to Pococke on 13 May 1675:

Constantinople in the service of Ambassador Wyche, was considered the foremost English expert in Turkish of his time.

[30] Grotius, *Correspondence,* xii. 103: 'aut etiam convertendis mahumetistis'. This may be an optimistic elaboration by Grotius himself. See above, p. 146, for a translation of the whole passage.

[31] In a letter to Vossius of 8 Apr. 1642 the only reason he gives for making the translation is for the sake of the Christians in oriental regions 'crassissimis ignorantiae tenebris miserè demersorum' (Vossius, *Epistolae,* ii, no. 336).

[32] Cf. the sentiment with which he ends his introduction to the *Carmen Tograi*: 'Eorum qui jam miserâ sub Turcae jugo tyrannide oppressi vix altius aliquid spirare audent, ignorantiae, si horum studiorum beneficio succurri aliquo modo posset, vel hoc nomine habendam esse eorum rationem suaderet pietas.'

[33] According to Pococke, *Specimen,* 191–2, 'Nobilissimus et Doctissimus' Grotius told him that he had derived these myths mainly from Scaliger. They have their origin in medieval anti-Islamic polemic.

[34] Boyle, *Works,* vi. 322–3. Cf. what Pococke says in the introduction to the Latin version of his translation, quoted by Juynboll, *Zeventiende-eeuwsche Beoefenaars van het Arabisch in Nederland,* 198 n. 2.

I have several of the Grotius's, yet by me, rather out of the apprehension I have of the malice of some Christians (who will hardly allow that a man of a different opinion should be instrumental to the propagation of the right faith) than from the unprompted accusation and downright danger by the Turks. I did cut out the last book in two or three copies.[35]

Boyle was active in the dissemination of this and his other 'missionary' publications overseas through contacts in the Levant Company and other trading companies. Pococke used the opportunity to ask Boyle to obtain for him from Aleppo copies of Jewish works in Arabic which he was interested in.[36]

Pococke's concern for the welfare of the Arabic-speaking Christians was certainly the motive for two other translations that he undertook. The first was a little booklet containing his Arabic translation of the catechism of the Church of England, apparently printed in Oxford at his own expense.[37] Huntington, in Aleppo, had requested him to send some copies of the Grotius. Pococke sent, besides these, three dozen copies of the Arabic catechism, as he informed Huntington in a letter of 23 August 1671.[38] Huntington thereupon urged him to translate the Anglican Book of Common Prayer into Arabic, offering to pay for it himself, and Pococke eventually complied, in an abbreviated form.[39] Huntington's chief aim in disseminating this work was to combat the influence of Roman Catholic missionaries amongst the Greek Christians. He appears to have been one of those who still harboured hopes of union between the Greek Orthodox and Anglican Churches. What Pococke thought of this interdenominational rivalry, which was at odds with the whole spirit of Grotius' book, is not recorded.

The *Philosophus Autodidactus*, which appeared in 1671, was the one work of Pococke which became well known outside the world of scholarship, and indeed had a long and profound influence on European thought. Strictly speaking the author of the book was Pococke's

---

[35] Twells, 298–9. The Christians whose malice he feared were not local eastern Christians, but European Catholics.

[36] Letter of 3 Jan. 1661 (Boyle, *Works*, vi. 324); cf. ibid. 324–5. The work he particularly wanted was the *Kitāb al-Bayān* of Rabbi Tanḥūm, which Huntington eventually obtained for him.

[37] He had at least envisioned this, and perhaps completed it, as early as 8 Apr. 1642, when he wrote to Vossius about his translation into Arabic of 'Catechismus brevior, & Articuli Ecclesiae nostrae' (Vossius, *Epistolae*, ii, no. 336).

[38] Twells, 288–9, who gives details of the contents of the catechism. The booklet, which is very rare, is entirely in Arabic, with no indication of translator, place, or date of printing: see Madan, *Oxford Books*, iii, no. 2885.

[39] For details see Twells, 296–7, or Madan, *Oxford Books*, iii, no. 3000. The book was published at the Sheldonian Theatre, at the university's expense, in 1674.

eldest son Edward, now 23 years old and a Student of Christ Church. In fact the whole project was conceived and directed by the father, who owned the manuscript from which the translation was made, wrote the introduction, and supervised the translation itself.[40] No doubt the time was opportune for his son, whom he saw as his successor in the Arabic Professorship, to make a name for himself, but there may have been other reasons for Pococke's not publishing the work under his own name.

The Arabic original is by the twelfth-century philosopher from Spain, ibn Ṭufayl,[41] who taught the young Averroes. It consists of a philosophical introduction followed by a story about the life of Ḥayy ibn Yaqẓān, who appears as a baby on an uninhabited island in the Indian Ocean. At first he is nurtured by a gazelle, but he gradually learns by experience and his native intelligence to fend for himself. As he matures he begins to speculate about the nature of what he observes, and about himself. By exercising the innate power of reason, he comes to understand the nature of the world (described, in the story, in Aristotelian terms), of mind, and ultimately of God. Thus he comprehends not only the natural sciences, but also morality and theology, without any assistance from outside. Ultimately he achieves, if only momentarily, a kind of mystical union with the divine. This existence is interrupted by the arrival of a man from a neighbouring island, Absāl, who teaches Ḥayy his language, and is astonished to find that his new friend has discovered by himself the truths which he was taught only by revealed religion.[42] He takes Ḥayy back home with him, but there Ḥayy finds, to his dismay, that most men are governed not by reason but by their appetites, and that the restraints of government and traditional religion are needed to maintain a semblance of civility. Accompanied by Absāl, he returns in disgust to his island and a life of contemplation.

[40] He writes (*Philosophus Autodidactus*, preface) that the book was done 'suasu atque hortatu meo', and says that anyone who dislikes the literal style of the translation should blame him, 'cum eas Interpreti leges praescripserim, ut à genuina verborum Arabicorum significatione, quam minimè fieri posset, recederet'. On Edward Pococke junior's incompetence in Arabic when unsupervised by his father see below, p. 295.

[41] On the author see Gauthier, *Ibn Thofail, sa vie, ses œuvres*. Gauthier also produced a modern edition with French translation (*Hayy ben Yaqdhân, roman philosophique d'Ibn Thofaïl*). Goodman's *Ibn Tufayl's Hayy Ibn Yaqzân* provides an adequate translation into modern English, but his commentary is of little help on the kind of questions raised below.

[42] Ibn Ṭufayl avoids referring specifically to Islam, mentioning only 'one of the sound religions, derived from one of the ancient prophets' (مِلّة من الملل الصحيحة المأخوذة عن بعض الانبياء المتقدمين, *Hayy ben Yaqdhân*, ed. Gauthier, 136), which could equally well apply to Christianity.

This summary can give but a poor notion of ibn Ṭufayl's masterly and subtle narrative, which has no single obvious moral, but which can be (and has been) read in different ways by differently prejudiced people. Whatever one's predilections, however, it is hard not to see it as threatening established religion (whether Islam or Christianity), with its exaltation of individual reason and rejection of revelation (whether through prophets or inspired books) except as a means of keeping the multitude in line. It is not surprising that the original work was condemned by Muslim theologians, and its European translations by Christian pastors. However, the Pocockes' work struck chords which resonated in current intellectual and religious movements. The book was soon translated from Edward junior's Latin into other languages, including English (twice) and Dutch (only a year after the Pocockes' edition).[43] The first English translator, George Keith, was a Quaker. What he and other Quakers of the time found attractive in the book is made clear by his 'Advertisement to the Reader': 'he speaks of a degree of knowledge attainable, that is not by *premisses premised and conclusions deduced*, is a certain truth, the *which is enjoyed in the conjunction of the mind of man with the supreme Intellect*',[44] in other words the personal communion with the Deity which the Quakers valued beyond any rites or dogma. Deists, on the other hand, liked the argument that reason alone was sufficient to attain to a knowledge of God.[45]

Pococke must have been aware that such controversial interpretations would be derived from the book. His own interest in it was of long standing,[46] and he was certainly the first European to study it deeply. Although the medieval Hebrew translation embedded in the commentary by Moses of Narbonne[47] had been examined by Pico della Mirandola, the work was little known in Europe until Pococke acquired his manuscript. He started to make an English translation of

[43] See Russell, '*The Philosophus Autodidactus*', 255 n. 16. It is disputed whether the German translation of J. G. Pritius (Frankfurt, 1726) was based on Pococke's Latin or on Ockley's English version of 1708, made directly from the Arabic. There was no French translation until modern times. On the reasons for this (despite the contemporary interest in the work in France described by Twells, 285–6) see Ekhtiar, '*Hayy ibn Yaqzan*'.

[44] [George Keith], *An Account of Oriental Philosophy* . . . (1674), quoted by Russell, '*The Philosophus Autodidactus*', 248.

[45] A book on the influence of the *Philosophus Autodidactus* in the 17th and 18th centuries is promised by Russell, ibid. 265 n. 157. In the mean time she has assembled some material on its use by the Society of Friends (ibid. 247–50).

[46] See above, p. 135 for the suggestion that he was introduced to it by Jacob Roman at Constantinople about 1639.

[47] See Steinschneider, *Die hebräischen Übersetzungen*, 365–8.

the work in 1645.[48] Whether he ever completed it is not known, although it seems likely that he did, since in 1660–1, as we shall see, there was some talk of publishing it. However, this did not happen, probably because of Pococke's cautiousness. During the Civil War and the Interregnum it would have been extremely imprudent for one in Pococke's precarious position to publish a work which could readily be interpreted as an attack on revelation and organized religion. Even after the Restoration, when Puritanism had lost its influence in England, there would be many who might take offence at such a book, particularly if published in English. So it is not surprising that when Pococke did eventually bring it to the public, he did it in his son's name, and in Latin (so that it would appear as a scholarly, not a controversial publication). Furthermore, his preface includes a disclaimer asking the reader to make allowances for the differences between now and the time in which the work was written, and to make up his own mind about the work's purpose.[49] In his own discussion of the author's intentions he claims that, after showing how far reason alone can go in attaining knowledge of God, the work demonstrates that further progress is possible only by divine revelation.[50] This interpretation is, to say the least, disingenuous, since to a contemporary English reader 'divine revelation' would mean the word of God as embodied in the Scriptures, and ibn Ṭufayl, as Pococke very well knew, meant nothing of the kind, but rather some kind of mystical personal communion of the individual with God. I can interpret this obfuscation only as an attempt by Pococke to provide a cover of orthodoxy for a treatise which he knew to be, if rightly understood, profoundly subversive of conventional morality.

To discuss how the work was interpreted by Pococke's contemporaries would take us too far from our topic, but I will mention its possible influence on two friends of Pococke. G. A. Russell has argued at length that Locke's *Essay on Human Understanding*, the first drafts of which belong to 1671, was influenced by the account of the development of the human mind from childhood to maturity in the

[48] Holt, the discoverer of the fragments of this translation (see above, p. 156), transcribed the opening of the narrative in appendix 8 of his 'Arabic Studies in Seventeenth-Century England'.

[49] 'Sed quid sibi proposuerit Author noster, Lector ipse, perlecto, si libet, opere, melius perspiciet, qui interim ut aequum de eo judicium ferat, rogandus est ut secundum istorum temporum quo vixit ille, non praesentis aetatis genium, qui in multis forsan ab eo discrepat, statuere velit.'

[50] 'ultra quod, nisi divinae revelationis ope, perveniri vix aut ne vix possit. Ad eam demum confugere cogitur Ratio.'

Philosophus Autodidactus, published in the same year.[51] We must agree that, given his friendship with both elder and younger Pocockes, Locke surely knew the book, despite the absence of explicit mention of it by him; but the thesis that it inspired his own ideas about the human mind remains, as yet, an interesting speculation.[52] Even more speculative is the connection with another friend of Pococke, Robert Boyle. Some small fragments are preserved of a work by Boyle which he described as 'a short Romantick story' and called 'The Aspiring Naturalist'.[53] These are part of the account of a man, named Authades ('self-willed'), who lives on an island 'in the Southern Ocean', narrating to some visiting Europeans the discoveries in natural philosophy of the inhabitants of the island. The similarities, at least in externals, to the story of Ḥayy ibn Yaqẓān could be explained as mere coincidence (there are also obvious similarities to Bacon's *New Atlantis*, to which Boyle himself refers). However, it is worth noting that Boyle, who in the 1650s and early 1660s was in close touch with Pococke, as we have seen with reference to the Grotius, knew the *Philosophus Autodidactus* in Pococke's English version by 1660. On 30 January 1660 Hartlib wrote to Worthington: 'The ingenious Arabick Fiction doth neither delectare not prodesse, because it is not yet extant in English. I shall urge so much the more the truly noble Mr. Boyle, he being in town at present.'[54] The implication is that Boyle is considering getting the work published (made 'extant') in English. That this is indeed a reference to Pococke's translation is proven by Hartlib's letter of 1 January 1661: 'O that I had received but an hour sooner your letter, for then I might have sent you exactly word, what you desire to be ascertain'd from Mr. Boyle concerning the printing or dispersing of Grotius, and of Pocock's Arabick Fiction.'[55] Boyle could of course have read Pococke's manuscript translation long before, but at present it seems impossible to determine whether he had read it when he composed 'The Aspiring Naturalist'.[56]

---

[51] Russell, '*The Philosophus Autodidactus*'.

[52] Russell's further conjecture (p. 245) that Locke may have been responsible for the 'resurrection' of this treatise by Pococke and for the title *Philosophus Autodidactus* seems utterly implausible to me.

[53] In MS Royal Society, Boyle Papers, vol. 9, fos. 43–4, and vol. 8, fos. 206–7. I owe my knowledge of this work to Dr Lawrence Principe.

[54] Worthington, *Correspondence*, i. 176.

[55] Ibid. 259. This and other relevant passages in the correspondence of Hartlib with Worthington and Boyle in 1660–2 are reproduced by Nahas, 'A Translation of Ḥayy B. Yaqẓān by the elder Edward Pococke', 89–90.

[56] The surviving fragments were written down in 1672 and even later, but there are

This is an appropriate place to consider Pococke's attitude towards religion in general, and towards Christianity and Islam in particular. To all appearances he was a pious clergyman of the Church of England, punctilious in the observation of its ordinances, even, as far as he safely could, during the period of the Revolution when the Book of Common Prayer was outlawed. However, Anglicanism, then as always, covered a wide range of beliefs. Pococke's admiration of Grotius' *De Veritate* clearly marks him as one of those who believed in a rational Christianity characterized by tolerance of differences in belief among Christians.[57] His personal loyalty to his patron Laud would not have extended to approval of Laud's iron-fisted attempts to enforce conformity throughout Charles I's dominions. It is not difficult to read into Pococke's account of the Islamic sects in the *Specimen* a veiled contempt for the interdenominational squabbles of Christians on doctrinal points;[58] such opinions could not be expressed freely in 1648. More difficult is any attempt to infer his personal theological beliefs from his work (including the biblical commentaries reprinted by Twells in *The Theological Works of the Learned Dr. Pocock*). It is clear that he was very interested in the content of the *Philosophus Autodidactus*, but interest in it does not imply acceptance of any particular aspect of it, nor make him an early deist or believer in mystical communion with the Deity. The most that can safely be said is that its emphasis on the power of human reason would have been congenial to anyone who, like Pococke, favoured a rational Christianity.

Even more enigmatic is Pococke's attitude towards Islam. It certainly lies far from the two extremes represented by Henry Stubbe's admiring biography of Muḥammad[59] and Humphrey Prideaux's tendentious *The True Nature of Imposture fully display'd in the Life of Mahomet*.[60] Interestingly, both men had been taught by Busby at

references to the story in Boyle's *Occasional Reflections*. Dr Principe tells me that he is inclined to date these passages to the early 1650s, which would predate Boyle's acquaintance with Pococke.

[57] For Anglicans this was best expressed in the *Religion of Protestants* of Chillingworth, whom Pococke knew personally (letter to Vossius of 2 Mar. 1630, Vossius, *Epistolae*, ii, no. 107).   [58] See above, p. 161.

[59] *An account of the rise and progress of Mahometanism with the life of Mahomet and a vindication of him and his religion from the calumnies of the Christians.* This could not be published in Stubbe's lifetime, for obvious reasons. On the work and later printed editions of it see Holt, *A Seventeenth-Century Defender of Islam*, who points out that Stubbe displays no knowledge of Arabic.

[60] On this work, and its use of the *Specimen*, see below, pp. 291–2.

Westminster School (where Prideaux at least must have learned Arabic), both had presumably attended Pococke's Arabic lectures, and both used his *Specimen* as the main source for their historical information. However, their apologetical and polemical purposes were completely alien to his own ends in that work. Pococke, in his published work, refrains from the ritual abuse of Islam and its Prophet which was normal, even in scholarly works of the time, and which we have seen exemplified in the shrill tones of Wheelock advocating his refutation of the Koran. However, his attitude towards Muḥammad himself is clearly one of dislike: he regularly uses the title 'false prophet' by which his contemporaries commonly referred to the founder of Islam.[61] Although he is careful to deny the frivolous legends about Muḥammad propagated in medieval Christian polemic,[62] he does not refrain from sarcasm about the Prophet's ignorance, and recites unimpeachable Muslim sources to support the standard Christian charge against him of libidinousness.[63] He disapproves of the ferocious aspect of early Islam in which it appears as a religion propagated by the sword, talking of Muḥammad 'laying the bloody foundations of his religion and his empire at the same time'.[64] On the other hand, he knew better than anyone, and especially in the *Specimen* he demonstrated, that Islam was not a simple entity, but had developed many different aspects in its history, to some of which he seems to have felt a profound sympathy. On pp. 269–86 of the *Specimen* he gives a long quotation and translation from al-Ghazālī outlining the basic tenets of the Islamic faith. This is presented with perfect objectivity, and is the more noteworthy since Pococke never characterizes its author (whose *Iḥyā' 'ulūm al-dīn* is one of his principal sources for Islamic beliefs) in any terms except those of admiration and respect,[65] and even points out a coincidence of one quotation from al-Ghazālī with the words of St Paul.[66]

[61] 'Pseudopropheta', e.g. *Carmen Tograi*, preface; cf. 'blasphemi impostoris', *Specimen*, 190. He quotes, ibid. 186–7, a passage from Maimonides about how to detect a false prophet, which he clearly considers applicable to Muḥammad.

[62] On p. 186 of the *Specimen* he says of these, 'haec cum *Mohammedistis* recitantur, risu exploduntur, ut nostrorum, in ipsorum rebus, inscitiae argumentum'. Cf. above, p. 217, on his excision of such matter from the Grotius (previously mentioned, *Specimen*, 191–2).

[63] *Specimen*, 175, 186–7.

[64] *Carmen Tograi*, preface, *6ʳ: 'sub Mohammede, cruenta religionis simul & Imperii fundamenta ponente'.

[65] e.g. 'magnus ille Philosophus & Theologus *Algazali*', *Carmen Tograi*, preface, *2ʳ, cf. *Specimen*, 269.

[66] *Specimen*, 205.

Pococke was confronted with a dilemma. He had a deep and genuine love for Arabic literature, and an intense interest in the history and culture which engendered it. Ideally, no doubt, he would have liked to treat these things as his scholarly contemporaries treated Greek and Roman antiquity, with respect and admiration for a civilization in which the practice of religions other than Christianity was recognized but did not diminish their admiration. Unfortunately this kind of approach to Arabic culture was not acceptable in seventeenth-century Europe, for which Islam, in the form of the Ottoman Empire, presented a threat to Christianity. Furthermore, Pococke, from his own experience of Muslim scholars and his immersion in Arabic literature, must have known well that Islam is not incidental to Arabic culture, but an integral part of it. We must not forget that in the East, especially at Aleppo, he had formed friendships with Muslims. He knew that, like his 'old scheich' Faṭhallah who did not doubt that he would meet Pococke in Paradise under the banner of his Jesus,[67] there were tolerant Muslims who believed that all the good would be saved.[68] Was Pococke's Christianity more exclusive? The question can be raised, but not answered, for to suggest otherwise would have been to invite the kind of controversy which Pococke always detested.

These ambiguities are also relevant in considering a question raised by Twells, namely why after the Restoration Pococke received no further ecclesiastical preferment or other favour from the court beyond his DD.[69] There is surely no doubt that, had Pococke shown any inclination to be a bishop, he had the reputation, the record of suffering for his Royalist sympathies, and influential friends enough to have obtained a mitre.[70] We must conclude that he did not want this kind of advancement. With his two professorships, his prebend at Christ Church, and his living at Childrey, he had sufficient income to be comfortable even with a large family. Pococke's devotion to scholarship was reason enough for such modesty. A bishopric entailed duties which would have put an end

[67] Twells, 30–1.

[68] Or at least those who were 'people of the Book', i.e. Jews and Christians, besides Muslims. In the *Specimen*, 256–7, Pococke reports without comment the views of those Muslim sects who denied that any would be condemned to eternal punishment.

[69] pp. 256–7. Twells's own answer, that there was not sufficient public esteem for Arabic studies, takes a very narrow view of the grounds for preferment.

[70] His claims would have been at least as good as those of Walton, who was appointed Bishop of Chester almost immediately after the Restoration, in Dec. 1660. It is instructive to read Wood's account (*Life and Times*, i. 364–5) of how Thomas Barlow, an Oxford contemporary of Pococke's with a record of compromise under the Interregnum, nevertheless contrived to procure a bishopric after the Restoration.

to serious scholarly work, as Pococke's pupil Narcissus Marsh was to find as he made his way up the ecclesiastical ladder. But we may speculate that Pococke also wished to avoid the public pronouncements on dogma and church politics which were expected from a bishop. To take part in the controversies on such matters as the treatment of Nonconformists and Catholics, which were to plague the careers of Anglican bishops for the rest of the century, would not have been to the taste of one who counted Muslims, Jews, Catholic missionaries, and even Presbyterians among his friends.

(II) SAMUEL CLARKE

Pococke's favourite pupil, or at least the one about whom he expressed the highest expectations, was Samuel Clarke. After his labours on the Polyglot Bible Clarke was associated with Castell in the successor to that work, the Heptaglot Lexicon, but soon after moving to Oxford as Architypographus he abandoned that. His *Scientia Metrica* was published together with Pococke's *Carmen Tograi*, which it resembles in being designed for students of Arabic. It is not the first European work on the intricate subject of the metrics of Arabic poetry. Something on the topic is found in Kirsten's *Grammatices arabicae liber I, sive Orthographia et Prosodia arabica*,[71] but the most extensive treatment hitherto was in Guadagnoli's *Breves Arabicæ linguæ institutiones*,[72] which Clarke refers to, although not by name, when he criticizes 'cuiusdam, qui Poeseos Arabicae doctrinâ explicandâ satis infeliciter sibi susceptâ'. Clarke's book is in fact more comprehensive and correct than Guadagnoli's, no doubt in part because he had access to the manuscripts and advice of Pococke, whose help he warmly acknowledges. However, it lacks the famous poem on metrics by Khazrajī (*al-Qaṣīda al-Khazrajīya*), which is in Guadagnoli's treatise. Clarke had prepared an edition with translation and notes, but was dissuaded from printing it now on the grounds that it would make the book too big. He promised to publish it later, but this, along with Clarke's other projects, came to nothing. His only other published work (apart from his contributions to the Polyglot Bible) is an edition and translation of a small tractate of the Mishnah, 'Beracoth', printed in 1667, no doubt at Fell's expense, for the use of students of Hebrew at Christ Church.[73]

---

[71] Breslau, 1608 (Schnurrer no. 45).

[72] Rome, 1642 (Schnurrer no. 72, *PO* no. 220).

[73] Madan, *Oxford Books*, iii, no. 2763. Although the editor's name does not appear in

Clarke planned several other projects. One, which Pococke enthusiastically welcomed,[74] was a general treatise on oriental chronology and geography. There is no evidence that this was ever begun, but Clarke did a great deal of work towards an edition of the whole of Abū 'l-Fidā''s *Geography*. The Bodleian MSS S. Clarke 1–4 are what remains of his enterprise.[75] The first three volumes contain Clarke's transcription and collation of the *Geography* (some 300 folios in all), while the fourth contains additions and variants. By 1669 Clarke was in two minds about publishing this, since he offered to turn over what he had done to Thévenot, who had been working on the same author. We learn this from a letter of Thomas Marshall, in Dordrecht, to Clarke:

At Leiden I spent an hour with Monsieur Thevenot, & mentioned the offer of your preparations for Abulfeda, which he took thankfully, & showed me his Copie with the Lat. Translation, intended for the Presse. Whether this Translation was his, or the deceased Monsieur Vatier's, I know not: but the Arab. was transcribed for, & said to be translated by the Latter. Since, considering what Mr Bernard hath told me concerning your ample provision for that noble Work; I wish you to bethink your self, whether your edition out of severall good Copies, with Annotations &c would not more gratify the publick, than this which supposedly will fall much short in the same particulars.[76]

Clarke bestowed his greatest efforts on a projected 'Seventh Volume of the Polyglot', which was conceived as a supplement to the Polyglot Bible. There are numerous references to this project in contemporary correspondence,[77] but the best evidence for its scope is a printed sheet headed 'Concerning an Additionall Volume to the Biblia Polyglotta', the Bodleian copy of which is annotated in Clarke's hand.[78] The texts

the pamphlet, there is no doubt that it was Clarke, since he claims it in his letters to Lightfoot (e.g. Lightfoot, *Letters*, 408, where Clarke says it is in the press, 8 Oct. 1667).

[74] Preface to *Abū 'l-Faraj*: he gives credit for supervising the publication to Clarke, 'cujus ideo libentius mentionem facio, quo ad opus, quod meditatur, Chronologicum & Geographicum, omnibus, qui Historias Orientales lecturi sint, utilissimum futurum, perficiendum ipsius fidem obstringam'.

[75] See Uri nos. 1006–1008 and 1010, p. 219, and *SC* ii/2, p. 788.

[76] MS BL 22905, fo. 90 (12/22 Feb. 1669).

[77] The earliest that I have found is Pococke's letter to Clarke of 25 Jan. 1658 (MS BL Add. 4276, fo. 57). Walton gave Clarke his blessing to the project, but warned of the difficulties of getting subscriptions, on 11 Aug. 1659 (MS BL Add. 4274, fo. 91). There is a useful notice of the work in Todd, *Life of Walton*, i. 245–7.

[78] Θ fol 663, no. 36. This is undated, but internal evidence suggests that it was printed in the early 1660s.

proposed for publication are: the 'Targum or Chaldee Paraphrase of the two Books of the Chronicles' (from a Cambridge manuscript[79]); the 'Evangelists in Syriacque', from a copy made by Pococke from the Bodleian manuscript; the 'Pentateuch in Arabick of a Christian Translation from the Greeke', of which there are two manuscripts in the Bodleian; the Psalms in Arabic, from a copy in Sion College[80] which had been collated with one in the possession of Ussher, and from one owned by 'Sam. Cromleholme',[81] Master of St Paul's; the prophecies of Isaiah, Jeremiah, Ezekiel, and the minor prophets in Arabic, from a Bodleian manuscript; the rest of the Old Testament in Ethiopic, if, as is hoped, a copy can be obtained; and other pieces not named. The volume will be published by the university, and the price proposed for subscription is 40 shillings (although no subscriptions seem to have been collected). The only remains of Clarke's work on this project concern the first item, but they are considerable. His text and Latin translation of the Chaldee paraphrase of the two books of Chronicles, dated 15 November 1662, survives as MSS S. Clarke 8 and 9,[82] and a short printed specimen of the Hebrew text, with the translation, is bound into the first volume. In a letter to Samuel Bochart, probably from late 1666, Clarke informs him that he has completed this work, but has been prevented from publishing it by lack of paper caused by the war with the Dutch.[83] On 8 October 1667 he told Lightfoot, who had been correcting his translation, that he now had the types and paper ready, and hoped to go to press soon.[84] However, writing to Lightfoot on 17 December of the same year, he tells him that he is ready to return the Cambridge manuscript, as demanded by Dobson, the University Librarian, although he had intended to keep it until the work was in press. Nothing further is heard about the publication from Clarke himself, but in the preface to the Heptaglot Lexicon, published in the year of Clarke's death, Castell says that he has used Clarke's edition of the Chaldee paraphrase for the Lexicon, and that the additional volume to the Polyglot Bible is 'ready at Oxford'.[85]

---

[79] This was one of the Erpenius manuscripts, which was lent to Clarke under bond in 1659: see Oates, 230.

[80] This is probably one of the Sion College manuscripts lost in the Great Fire.

[81] The name appears as 'Cromeholme' in the Clarke correspondence.

[82] Neubauer, *Hebrew Manuscripts*, nos. 183–4.

[83] MS BL 22905, fo. 96. The second Anglo-Dutch war did not end until July 1667.

[84] Lightfoot, *Letters*, 407–8.

[85] 'Cujus [Clarke's] etiam opera ac studiis laudatissimis in parato est apud Oxonienses septimum Bibliorum Polyglottōv Volumen, cum Versionibus antiquissimis, nec ad huc unquam editis, non Chaldaica tantum hac, sed Syriacis insuper, Æthiopicis,

Clarke's failure to publish this and his other planned works is in part due, no doubt, to his death at the age of 41 in December 1669, caused, according to George Hicks, by studying in winter in the unheated Bodleian Library.[86] But in the last years of his life he was very busy with his work as Architypographus, as the plans for a learned press and printing-house at Oxford were energetically forwarded by Fell. Clarke's role in this is illustrated by his correspondence with Thomas Marshall in Holland,[87] which indicates that he was concerned not only with the acquisition of new types, but also with acquiring books and manuscripts for projected Oxford publications, and negotiating for the rights to publish other books;[88] all this in addition to his regular duties of overseeing books printed at Oxford by licence from the university. Nevertheless, had he lived longer, he might have fulfilled the hopes of Pococke and others[89] that he would make a great contribution to oriental studies. His learned correspondence with Bochart at Caen (to whom he entrusted the education of his little son), with Buxtorf at Basel, and with Lightfoot at Cambridge shows the width of his reading in Hebrew and Arabic, and he was evidently at home in all the languages represented in the Polyglot Bible.

(III) JOHN FELL AND THE UNIVERSITY PRESS

The early history of the University Press at Oxford[90] is intimately connected with plans for publication in Arabic and other oriental languages, which are of considerable interest, although few of them came to fruition. The prominence of Arabic and Hebrew publications

Copticis, Arabicis, Persicis contextum.' In April 1669 Fell also stated that 'we have in hand a Seventh volume to be added to the Polyglott bible' (Carter, *History of Oxford University Press*, 51).

[86] Carter, ibid. 49–50, citing MS Ballard 12, fo. 125.

[87] Preserved in the MS BL Add. 22905, some of which is excerpted below in connection with the plan to publish Apollonius' *Conics*.

[88] An example of this was the attempt by Oxford to acquire the sheets of Golius' edition of al-Farghānī, left in press incomplete at his death. Marshall writes to Clarke on 8 Dec. 1667: 'Your overtures about Alfargani are noble, & would meet with acceptance if you were here: but I cannot think that the purchaser of the imperfect Impression will venture a Copie into England.' The same letter mentions a Persian translation of the Old Testament which might also be available in Holland.

[89] Lightfoot, who was a good judge, rates Clarke together with Pococke in the 'first classis of learned pens' (letter to Clarke of 13 Apr. 1662, MS BL 22905, fo. 52).

[90] This is adequately recounted by Carter, *History of Oxford University Press*, chs. 5–6, to which the reader is referred for sources and further details. Madan, *Oxford Books*, iii, pp. xxxii ff., gives additional information.

is not surprising in view of Pococke's membership in the new board of Delegates to the Press which was constituted in 1662. Carter puts the beginning of Fell's activities about the University Press in 1668, but Madan says that he was negotiating with Amsterdam about types for the press as early as 1666 (the first year of his Vice-Chancellorship), and evidence for earlier activity is also provided by letters of Thomas Marshall from Holland in 1667. From these it appears that Marshall had been commissioned to look out for material for books which the university was interested in publishing, including the *Conics* of Apollonius, which will be discussed below in connection with Edward Bernard. Fell persuaded Gilbert Sheldon, now Archbishop of Canterbury, to allow the basement of the Theatre named after him, which was being built next to the Bodleian Library at his expense, to be used for the activities of the press. A printing-press was bought in 1668, and Marshall was soon busy in Holland looking for types.[91] The earliest surviving minutes of the Delegates, from September 1668, record their decision to publish the collection of canons of the Eastern Church. Besides the Greek and Latin versions, this included the Arabic canons, taken from the famous Roe manuscript. The original plan was for the printing to be undertaken by the London bookseller Robert Scott, but when the book finally emerged in 1672 it had been printed by the new University Press at the Sheldonian Theatre. It was in fact the first book to be printed there, since the composition began in 1669. Madan calls this magnificent folio volume 'the first of the Great Books of the Oxford University Press'.[92] The editor was William Beveridge, a graduate of Cambridge (BA St John's College, 1656), who had assisted Castell for a while on the Heptaglot Lexicon, and while working in London had published there a Syriac grammar in which he claimed that the language could be learned in a month, together with a tract *De Linguarum Orientalium. praesertim Hebraicae, Chaldaicae, Syriacae, Arabicae & Samaritanae praestantia, necessitate & utilitate,*[93] precocious but unimpressive works. He was incorporated at Oxford in 1669, no doubt in connection with his work on this 'Synodicon'. He applied to Pococke for help with the Arabic, but it appears that much credit for the Arabic and other parts is due to

[91] Correspondence between Marshall and Fell 'as to the purchase in Holland of Punches, Matrices & Types for the University of Oxford' is printed as appendix III, part II in Hart/Carter. That correspondence covers the years 1670–2, but Marshall was investigating the possibilities at least as early as 1668.

[92] *Oxford Books,* iii, no. 2916, q.v. for details of its printing.

[93] London (Roycroft), 1658.

Narcissus Marsh, who says that in 1671 he was engaged by Fell to correct the translation of Balsamon and Zonaras's commentary on the canons of the Greek councils, to revise Beveridge's notes, and to supervise the whole work.[94]

Fell's plans for other learned publications were ambitious, but largely unfulfilled. These are best seen in a list that he drew up early in 1672 of books that 'we purpose to Print, if we may be encouraged'.[95] I single out those items which are of Arabic or oriental interest:

'2. The Targum on the books of Chronicles, as also the Comments of R. Tanchum & other learned Rabbins on several parts of the Old Testament neuer yet printed, both in Heb: & Arab.' In this item Pococke combined one of his own favourite authors, Rabbi Tanḥūm, with Clarke's already completed Chaldee paraphrase.

'3. The Coptick Gospels neuer yet extant, out of a copy of Venerable antiquity in the hands of Dr: Marshall, & by him fitted for the presse. 4. The Coptick Psalter from a MS. in the Same Hands, together with the Ancient Latin Psalter of the Western church.'

'10. Maimonides, More novochim, as written by himself in Arab:, Arab: lat:' As we shall see, Hyde later proposed to publish the original (Arabic) version of Maimonides' *Guide of the Perplexed*, but not until after Fell's death, which suggests that at this time Fell had someone else in mind. The most likely candidates are the elder and younger Pocockes.[96]

'11. The history of Tamerlain in Arab: & Persian, with the lat:' In 1636 Golius had published the Arabic text only of Aḥmad ibn ʿArabshāh's life of Timur[97] (known in Europe as Tamerlane). Nothing had come of his promise to publish a translation and commentary, although this was considered highly desirable. This is obviously an attempt to fill that need. This too came to nothing, but once again Hyde later promised to edit it.[98]

'15. The ancient Mathematicians Greek & latin in one and twenty Volumes; part not yet Extant, the rest collated with MS. perfected from

---

[94] 'Archbishop Marsh's Diary'. Beveridge later moved from scholarship to homiletics, for which he found a more appreciative audience, and became a bishop.

[95] Printed by Carter, *History of Oxford University Press*, 63, from MS All Souls 239, fo. 241.　　　　　　　　　　　　　　　　　　　　　[96] See below, p. 277.

[97] Schnurrer no. 166, q.v. for much interesting information on later attempts to translate the work. A French translation by Vattier was published in 1658 (ibid., p. 137).

[98] An undated prospectus for this work is printed in Hyde, *Syntagma Dissertationum*, ii. 439–43.

the Arabick versions, where the originals are lost, with their Scholia & comments: & all illustrated with Annotations.'

This last item was the brain-child of Edward Bernard, who wrote a detailed programme of publication at Fell's request, which has been preserved and was published by Thomas Smith with his life of Bernard.[99] According to Smith this was composed about 1673, but Fell's list comes from 1672, and it is clear from Fell's preface to Wallis, *Archimedes' Sandreckoner* (quoted below) that the idea goes back to 1668.[100] This 'Synopsis' of Bernard is a remarkable document. It lists the ancient mathematical works that have survived either in the original Greek or in later (usually Arabic) versions. 'Mathematics' is taken in the broadest sense to include not only geometry and arithmetic, but also astronomy, optics, mathematical geography, and even astrology. Bernard includes the location of the manuscripts from which the projected editions could be made, usually at Oxford, in the Bodleian, the colleges, or private possession, but also in Cambridge, Golius' library at Leiden, and elsewhere. Even where the original Greek survives he lists the Arabic versions, although whether the intention was to publish these or merely use them for collating the text, as Fell indicates, is not clear. The whole was to comprise fourteen volumes, but each of these would have had to be of enormous size, for Bernard included not merely Arabic translations of Greek works but also original works in Arabic that were partly derived from ancient sources. For instance vol. XIII is to contain, besides Ptolemy's *Geography*, those of al-Idrīsī and Abū 'l-Fidā', as well as other minor Arabic geographers. Since each of these is to be accompanied by a translation into Latin, the notion that all could be crammed even into a folio volume is probably impractical. The *Synopsis* covers 39 octavo pages in Smith's edition.[101] An annotated edition, identifying the

---

[99] 'Veterum Mathematicorum, Graecorum, Latinorum, et Arabum, Synopsis', at the end of Smith, *Life of Bernard*. Dating it is difficult because, according to Smith, it was expanded by Bernard many years after it was first hastily composed for Fell. The detailed analysis of the materials available for Apollonius' *Conics* must have been composed after Bernard's journey to Leiden in 1669. I have not compared Bernard's manuscript original (MS Lat. misc. f. 3, *SC* no. 8767).

[100] Bernard was canvassing for financial support in June 1671, when Oldenburg wrote to him: 'we are generally thoughtfull how to procure Patronage and Encouragement for the design of reprinting the Ancient Mathematicians.' The only possible contributor mentioned is the Bishop of Salisbury (Seth Ward), who said that he would be willing if he found that others were (MS Smith 45, p. 68).

[101] It is followed by two more pages listing Greek works which are lost but which Bernard had reason to suppose existed in Syriac or Arabic translation.

manuscripts which Bernard hoped to use, would be a valuable guide to the resources for this kind of work available at Oxford, and also to Bernard's knowledge of them, both of which are astonishingly wide. Here I give as an example some excerpts from the list of treatises which were to be published as auxiliary to the edition of Ptolemy's *Almagest*:

II Al-Suphius de Stellis fixis Arab. & Lat. cum figuris geminis, e codd. MSS D. Pocockii, D. Thevenoti, & forte ex museo D. Golii, V. praeclarissimi, cum notis.

III Liber egregius de erroribus in canone fixarum. Arab. & Lat. e codd. MSS. in bibl. Bodl. Con. Apoll. & bibl. D. Golii.

IV R. Abrahae Aben. Ezrae Astronomia. MS. Lat. Dig. & κόλουρος inter MSS. Seld. Opus excellens: & forte MS. Pembr. 67.

V Nasireddini Institutiones Astronomicae, cum commentario luculento Arabico Husain Ebn Mohammed Nisaburiensis, qui Noddam vocatur, Arab. & Lat. ex MS. Coll. Joan. Oxon. . . .

VIII Albategnius (Albatani) Lat. ex edit. Venet. 1552 & MSS. Lat. Digb. & Savil.

IX Alfragani Astronomia Arab. Lat. ex editione ac illustratione D. Golii, collatis etiam MSS. Latt. Digb. & Savil. & Laud. E. 107.

Accedant . . . Excerpta ex Institutionibus Astronomicis Arab. MSS. in Coll. D. Joan. B. & Almagesto, i.e. Astronomia Averrois. MS. Arab. D. Pocock.[102]

As a publication programme this was of course ludicrously impractical. Bernard himself possessed the combination of mathematical competence and linguistic knowledge to undertake this kind of work, but it would have taken twenty such men a lifetime of dedicated labour to carry out what he proposed, and we shall see that even he lacked the application to complete it for the one part of the work that he seriously undertook, Books V–VII of Apollonius' *Conics*. Even had there been men available to do the work, publication on this scale would have been impossible without enormous subventions which were not available to Fell's Oxford Press. The far less ambitious project of the Polyglot Bible had been made possible by subscription, but the number of those willing to subscribe to such an abstruse topic as ancient mathematical texts (let alone Arabic versions of them) would have been much too small to support the kind of expense which typesetting folio volumes in exotic languages would have entailed. Fell had recognized this by 1676, when he wrote the preface to John Wallis's edition of Archimedes' *Sandreckoner*:

[102] pp. 19–23.

Some years ago we proclaimed publicly that we had the intention of preparing here an edition of all the ancient mathematicians, and printing it at our press. Furthermore, to that end we divided the authors into classes according to the time when they lived and the subject which they treated, adding thereto such discoveries of the moderns as either advanced the science or made it less laborious. In addition, we thoroughly examined the shelves of the Bodleian, Savilian, and other libraries in this country which are rich in manuscripts; and since for some unedited treatises we lacked exemplars, we took the trouble to procure these by sending suitable men into foreign parts. Namely we saw to it that the three last books of Apollonius of Perga in Arabic, and Serenus on the section of the cylinder and cone in Greek, were transcribed at Leiden and Paris [respectively]. Furthermore, since it seemed most appropriate that Euclid should lead the array, we entrusted the care of that matter to our most learned Mr Edward Bernard, Savilian Professor of Astronomy; who was not only straining every nerve to see that the book itself should be edited as perfectly as possible, but had at his own expense provided for the elegant delineation and engraving of the diagrams for the whole work, commissioning a printed specimen of a few pages in addition.[103] But after all this, when our efforts were so far from finding some Maecenas that they could scarcely find one or two to even recommend them, we voluntarily abandoned this plan as completely hopeless.[104]

Fell goes on to say that the present edition of Archimedes' *Sandreckoner* and *Measurement of the Circle* by Wallis is intended to show how useful the study of ancient mathematics is. The little book, however, falls far short of what Bernard had envisioned. Wallis consulted no manuscripts, but simply took the text from earlier printed editions and added his translation and notes (which include some textual emendations based on his conjectures). The great plan for the edition of the ancient mathematicians produced, besides this, only one other small treatise edited by Wallis. This, the treatise of Aristarchus on the sizes and distances of the sun and moon, was previously unpublished in the original Greek, and also contained a hitherto unknown fragment of Book II of Pappus' *Synagoge*. Wallis's edition, although hardly a critical one, did have the merit of incorporating some variants that Bernard had noted from other sources in the Bodleian, including two Selden manuscripts containing the Arabic version of Aristarchus.

One may perhaps regard Halley's translations of Apollonius' *Cutting off of a Ratio* and *Conics* V–VII in the early eighteenth century

---

[103] A copy of this printed specimen of Euclid is extant: see below, p. 299.

[104] My translation from the Latin. Although the preface is unsigned, Madan (*Oxford Books*, iii, no. 3095) is certainly correct in attributing it to Fell.

515

as distant consequences of the plan to publish the ancient mathematicians, since they relied on materials which Bernard had assembled and, in the first case, on his unpublished translation. But for most of the Greek texts that were listed in Bernard's *Synopsis* the learned world had to wait until the late nineteenth and early twentieth centuries for adequate critical editions.[105] As for the Arabic versions of the Greek texts, and the original Arabic works on his list, most had to wait until the twentieth century for any edition at all, let alone a critical one,[106] and not a few remain unpublished to this day. Impractical as it was, the *Synopsis* and its compiler deserve great credit for their vision of what scholarship could and should attain in the history of scientific endeavour.

(IV) THE ARABIC APOLLONIUS

Before turning to the story of the university's efforts to obtain materials for the edition of Apollonius' *Conics* intended as part of the 'Ancient Mathematicians', I should say something about the two principals involved in this endeavour, Thomas Marshall and Edward Bernard.

Marshall, as we saw, had left Oxford after it fell to the Parliamentary forces,[107] and served for many years as chaplain to the English Merchant Adventurers, first at Rotterdam (from at least 1650), and from 1656 at Dordrecht (Dort). During the many years of his exile in the Netherlands Marshall cultivated friendships with Dutch scholars, including Franciscus Junius the younger[108] and Golius. After the

---

[105] Pappus' *Synagoge* was not fully published until the edition of Hultsch (Berlin, 1876–8). J. L. Heiberg single-handedly edited many of the other Greek mathematical and astronomical texts listed by Bernard.

[106] The principal exception is Abū 'l-Fidā''s *Geography*, which was published by Reinaud and Guyard (3 vols., Paris, 1848–83). The only other original Arabic work listed by Bernard which has been published in a critical edition is the *Tadhkira* of al-Ṭūsī, ed. Ragep (New York, 1993). Arabic versions of Greek mathematical works of which critical editions of all or part exist are: Heron, *Mechanics*, ed. Nix (Leipzig, 1900); Euclid, *Elements*, I–VI, ed. Besthorn and Heiberg (Copenhagen, 1897–1932); Menelaus, *Spherics*, ed. Krause (Göttingen, 1936); Pappus, *Commentary on Euclid X*, ed. Junge and Thomson (Cambridge, Mass., 1930); pseudo-Archimedes, *On Touching Circles*, ed. Dold-Samplonius *et al.* (Stuttgart, 1975); Diophantus, *Arithmetica*, IV–VII, ed. Sesiano (New York, 1982); Ptolemy, *Almagest* star catalogue, ed. Kunitzsch (Wiesbaden, 1986); Apollonius, *Conics*, V–VII, ed. Toomer (New York, 1990).

[107] He was formally expelled from Lincoln College by the Visitors in July 1648 (Burrows, *Register of Visitors*, 165), but was then already in Holland ('beyond sea', ibid.).

[108] The two produced the *editio princeps* of the Codex Argenteus (the Gothic translation by Ulfilas) of the Four Gospels (Dordrecht, 1665).

Restoration he renewed his ties with Oxford, taking his BD *in absentia* by the licence of Archbishop Sheldon,[109] but continued to serve as chaplain in Dordrecht, visiting England only from time to time even after he was elected Fellow of Lincoln College in 1668. However, when he became Rector of Lincoln in 1672 he returned to Oxford, where he spent the rest of his life. His surviving correspondence with Clarke, Bernard, and Fell shows how diligent he was in finding manuscripts, procuring type, and otherwise acting as an intermediary between Oxford and Dutch scholars and printers.

Edward Bernard[110] had attended Merchant Taylors' School, where he had presumably already learned Hebrew. After entering St John's College as a scholar in 1655, he applied himself to mathematics (which he studied privately with the Savilian Professor of Geometry, Wallis), and also to Arabic, making himself familiar with the Arabic manuscripts in St John's College library, which, thanks to Laud, was the best equipped of any Oxford college in that respect.[111] Graduating BA in 1659 and MA in 1662, he became a fellow of his college, and his prowess in Arabic at that time is shown by the invitation of Castell, at the suggestion of Clarke, to come and work with him on the Heptaglot Lexicon.[112] Perhaps fortunately for himself, Bernard did not accept the offer. His mathematical ability is attested by his appointment, in about 1669, as deputy to the Savilian Professor of Astronomy, Christopher Wren (who had to be absent from his post to attend to the rebuilding of London after the Great Fire of 1666). When Wren resigned in 1673 Bernard was named as his successor.

The earliest evidence that I have found for interest at Oxford in publishing the Arabic Apollonius is in a letter from Marshall to Clarke of 8 December (NS) 1667:

Whether <u>Apollonius Pergaeus</u> be in D. Golius his Library, I know not: sure I am that he procured some Arabick pieces of that Author (now not found in Greek) for the publique Library of Leiden: and have been assured that some-

[109] MS Tanner 45, no. 29.

[110] Smith's *Life of Bernard*, although better than the other biographies he wrote (as one would expect, since the lifelong friendship of the two men is attested by the voluminous correspondence between them preserved in the Smith MSS in the Bodleian), needs correcting in some particulars, and can be supplemented in many others.

[111] MS Or. 218 (Nicoll–Pusey no. 302, pp. 301–2) is Bernard's copy, made in 1659, of an astronomical work of Abū 'l-Fidā' in St John's College. He used it later for his *De Mensuris* (see p. 219 of that).

[112] Castell to Clarke, 4 and 5 Apr. 1661 (MS BL 22905, fos. 48, 50). Bernard was then only 22 years old.

thing of the said author in Arab. was found among the books of Mr John Greaves: which I presume, you have known or heard off before.[113]

The enquiry presumably originated with Bernard, who, hearing of Golius' death earlier that year,[114] knew that it might now be possible to get hold of his manuscript of the part of Apollonius lost in Greek. By 2 March 1668 Marshall had confirmed that there was indeed a copy of the desired book in the Leiden University Library:

It is very probable that the Arabique copie of Apollonius Pergeus in Leiden Library is the same in substance with that in the Medicean Library of Florence, from whence the late Latine copie[115] was translated, the title of the book in the Leiden Catalogue being, Apollonii Pergæi Conicarum sectionum lib. V. VI. et VII. hactenus desiderati, which well agreeth with the said Latine translation. But whether that Leiden Codex be better conditioned than the other, of which both Translator & Annotator so much complain, would be matter of further enquiry. To this as yet I can say nothing, being deprived of my honourable friend, the most competent judge both for Mathematique & Arabique Literature, Dr Golius: who had himself about 30 years agoe promised the Edition of those 3. books of Apollonius, but this designe with some other of that nature, have proved onely designes, for so much as I have ever heard, either from himself or otherwise.[116]

By 20/30 March the university (i.e. Fell) had evidently decided to obtain a copy of the above-mentioned Leiden codex, for Marshall reports that he had asked Allard Uchtman, Professor of Hebrew at Leiden, to negotiate for having a copy made, and Uchtman had reported that Shahin Qandi (an Armenian scribe who had acted as amanuensis for Golius) was asking a rijksdollar per leaf for copying, so that the cost would amount to £10 for the whole manuscript of about forty leaves.[117] Although the price was considered very high both in Holland and England, the bargain was concluded, but Shahin Qandi worked very slowly and refused to draw the diagrams, to Marshall's great dissatisfaction. On 9 November (NS) 1668 he wrote to Clarke: 'The Transcript of the Leiden Apollonius undertaken by the indisposed & idle Shahin Candy, advanceth most slowly: so that I am

[113] Ibid., fo. 70. The manuscript of Greaves to which he refers is Apollonius' *De sectione rationis*, which, as we saw, had passed after his death into the hands of Selden and thence to the Bodleian.

[114] Marshall announced this to Clarke in his letter of 17/27 Oct. (ibid., fo. 57).

[115] i.e. the Ecchellensis–Borelli publication of 1661.

[116] Marshall to Clarke, ibid., fo. 71.

[117] Marshall to Clarke, ibid., fo. 72. Forty leaves turned out to be a gross underestimate, for when Uchtman reported to Marshall on 5 Dec. 1668 that Qandi had completed about half the task, he had already covered 36 leaves (MS BL 4277, fo. 172).

resolved to seek another Scribe.'[118] Meanwhile, however, Marshall had been busily engaged on related matters. He started to look for other oriental translations of Apollonius' *Conics*, with so much success that in the same letter he could report 'I have now 3. Arab. Copies & one Persian of Apollonius'. The identification of at least one of these copies is certain. It was none other than Ravius' manuscript of the *Conics*, which he had shown to John Greaves in England in 1641, which Pell had translated in Amsterdam in 1644–5, and which Ravius had carried with him to England in 1647 and to Sweden in 1650. By a strange chance it now came to England for the third and last time.[119]

In 1651 Ravius, after being solicited by Claude Hardy for many years to sell him his manuscript of Apollonius, finally agreed, alleging as his reason Pell's failure to produce his translation. On 12 November of that year he sent the manuscript from Stockholm, with an accompanying letter, to Johannes Morianus (Moriaen) in Amsterdam. The agreement was supposed to be that Morianus would forward the manuscript to Hardy in Paris, and receive payment from him, 120 Joachimsthaler for the manuscript itself, plus another 80 for Ravius' translation (which he claimed was at the moment unavailable in Uppsala). Morianus would then send the money to England (presumably to pay debts that Ravius had left behind there). However, for some reason Morianus never sent the manuscript on, and when he died it must have been sold off with his other books to the bookseller Elias Ratelbandt, whose shop was near Morianus' dwelling on the Princengracht. There Marshall found it[120] some time in the first half of 1668, bought it and carried it to England in June of that year, where he showed it to Castell in London,[121] and presented it to the Bodleian Library before he returned to Holland later that summer.

---

[118] MS BL 22905, fo. 84. An extract from this most interesting letter was printed in Hart/Carter, 194.

[119] Most of the intricacies of this story were unravelled by K. M. P[ogson], 'The Wanderings of Apollonius', who did not, however, know about Pell's translation or Marshall's negotiations in Holland in 1668.

[120] As he records on the cover of the manuscript (now MS Thurston 3): 'Liber Bibliothecae Oxonii: quem ex Ratelband cujusdam Bibliopolae officinâ librariâ, propè novum Templum Amstelodami, redimendum pretio persoluto curavit Tho. Marschallus, è Collegio Lincolniensi apud Oxonienses'. Macray, *Annals*, 129 was misled by this inscription into supposing that the manuscript had formerly belonged to the Bodleian, had been purloined, and was now being restored.

[121] Castell to Clarke, MS BL 22905, fo. 79 (24 June 1668): 'Mr. Marshal of Dort ha's been twice with mee, is going to Cambridg this week, about a fortnight after intends for Oxford, he ha's sundry very choice books, amongst which Apollonius Pergaeus, so much desired.'

Marshall acquired other material for the Apollonius. Golius had arranged for all the figures for Books V–VII[122] to be drawn and engraved. Marshall bought these plates on behalf of the university for £3, and dispatched them to England. Unfortunately the ship on which they were being carried sank, and although Marshall could see the wreck from the shore, he was unable to recover anything. He was able to offer some consolation:

Yet though we have lost the substance, I hope to furnish you with some shadows conducent to your intended edition of Apollonius Pergeus: for I have got by speciall favour, a large bundle of Notes written by Jacobus Golius his own hand, upon severall Theorems of the said Mathematician, which (though destitute of his Arab. observations) will, I think, shew much of his judgment about the Translation. I am also promised as many of the said figures upon paper, as can be found in his study: & these I call the shadows, whereof Mr Bernard of St Johns may expect further account from me when I shall have passage by ship to convey them to you.[123]

Bernard saw Golius' notes in London (where Marshall had sent them) on his way to Holland in January 1669, and expressed a low opinion of them.[124] They seem to have vanished, but a few of the diagrams survive amongst Bernard's materials for his edition of Apollonius.[125]

Bernard, no doubt with the agreement of Fell, had volunteered to go to Leiden at the university's expense, and take over the copying of the manuscript himself. We first hear of this in a letter from Marshall to Clarke on 4/14 December 1668, in which he expresses his doubts about the wisdom of such a journey in winter.[126] Bernard was determined, however, and his journey is announced as a certainty by Wallis, writing to Oldenburg for Hevelius on 9 December: 'D. Bernard jam statim in Bataviam abiturus est quo Apollonij Pergaei Conicorum libros septem quos hic Arabice habemus cum eorundem codice uno et altero ibidem conferat, ut deinceps emendatius edat.'[127] Accompanied by Wallis's son, Bernard took ship from Harwich to Holland in mid-January 1669, and spent about three months in Leiden. There he thoroughly enjoyed him-

---

[122] Although Marshall does not state that these are the books which are covered, the number of the plates (93) fits this assumption, since those books would have required something over 200 figures.

[123] Marshall to Clarke, 9 Nov. (NS) 1668 (MS BL 22905, fo. 84, cf. fo. 81).

[124] Letter to Clarke, MS BL Add. 4275, fo. 30.

[125] In MS Lat. Class. e. 2: see below, p. 242.

[126] MS BL 22905, fo. 87. Bernard was granted leave by his college to travel overseas on 26 Dec.

[127] Oldenburg, *Correspondence*, v, no. 1038a, p. 233; 'quos hic Arabice habemus' can refer only to Ravius' manuscript, now in the Bodleian.

self, buying books for himself and others, cultivating the acquaintance of scholars, and investigating the libraries. Through the good offices of Marshall he was introduced to Golius' eldest son, Theodorus, and was allowed to inspect Golius' manuscripts[128] and in particular his famous copy of the Arabic Apollonius. However, he did not forget the primary object of his visit, completion of the copying of the Leiden library's exemplar of Apollonius, which he took over from Shahin Qandi. On 20 March (NS) he reported to Clarke: 'I have six dayes worke to doe on Apollonius & then I hope the transcribeing will bee finisht',[129] but he still hoped to collate it against Golius' own manuscript with the help of an amanuensis of Golius. This he seems not to have done, at least to judge by the copy of Apollonius that he made. This is now Bodleian MS Thurston 1,[130] a fairly careful copy of Books V–VII of Apollonius' *Conics* in the version of the Banū Mūsā. Book V (about half of the total) is in the hand of Shahin Qandi. Books VI and VII, on different paper, and in a different ink and much less practised hand, were copied by Bernard, as I verified by comparing his Arabic handwriting in his own manuscripts. That it is copied not directly from Golius' manuscript, but from an intermediary, is shown by the subscription on fo. 117[v], according to which the copy was completed by Darwīsh Aḥmad on Friday 15 Dhu 'l-Hijja AH 1036 (17 August 1627), exactly as in MS Leiden Or. 14(1).[131] Blanks have been left for the figures, and these have been filled in, presumably by Bernard, only up to V. 44, but rough sketches of the remaining figures have been bound in at the front. This manuscript contains no collations from other sources, although Bernard has inserted a few references to notes by Golius. It was not only the principal basis of Bernard's projected edition of Apollonius, but was also the source from which Halley made his translation of *Conics* V–VII for his 1710 edition of Apollonius, since its grandparent was sent over for his use from Ireland by Archbishop Marsh only shortly before the book went to press.

---

[128] Theodorus Golius and the other heirs were trying to sell these at the time, and both Oxford and Cambridge universities were interested in buying them: see below, p. 252.

[129] MS BL 22905, fo. 89.

[130] Uri no. 885, p. 192, where the MS itself is wrongly ascribed to AH 1036. Uri says 'Scriptura peregrinam manum redolet' (which is true only of the part copied by Bernard). Pusey (Nicoll–Pusey, p. 599) asserts 'Codex e cod. Marsh. 667 non una manu transcriptus est'. This must be the 'Arabick MS., bought by Mr. Bernard' for which the Library paid £10. 15s. in 1669 (Macray, *Annals*, 135).

[131] See Voorhoeve, *Handlist*, 180; Leiden Oriental Catalogue, iii, no. 979. Darwīsh Aḥmad made his copy in Aleppo from the manuscript which is now MS Marsh 667 before the latter was bought for Golius by David Leleu de Wilhem.

The subsequent history of Bernard's abortive edition of Apollonius' *Conics*, which covers many years, is best summarized here. This was originally intended to be part of the Oxford 'Ancient Mathematicians', but when that was seen to be a chimera, Bernard may have agreed to an arrangement with the London publisher Robert Scott for a translation of Books V–VII of the Apollonius to be printed as part of a volume containing other ancient mathematical texts. At least, this was implied by John Collins, who was trying to get Barrow to allow his version of the first four books of Apollonius' *Conics*, made long before, to be published.[132] Collins wrote to J. Gregory in March 1672:

The said Mr. Bernard is a good mathematician, and understands the Arabic tongue well; he hath found in the libraries there [Oxford] two entire copies of the first seven books of Apollonius his Conics, (and some other tracts of that author,) the one of Ben Musa, the other of Abdelmelech, and one of them hath Eutocius his notes. The three latter books, when translated and put into Dr. Barrow's method, may probably be printed with Dr. Barrow's comment on the first four, and be sold together.[133]

Similar information was transmitted by Collins to Beale and by Oldenburg to de Sluse and Huygens later in the year.[134] But Bernard had second thoughts about publishing the translation before the Arabic text was printed, as Wallis wrote to Collins on 14 November:

what concerns Apollonius I have acquainted Mr. Bernard with, who hath written, he tells me, his mind concerning it to Mr. Scot, which I think is this purpose, that he thinks it more proper to print Apollonius at large before the Epitome of him. For printing the other first would rather endanger the loss of the author himself, it having been found in experience, that Commandine having printed the translation before the original, hath so far hazarded the loss of the original, as that to this day it is not published.[135]

The plan was still alive in some form in May 1675, when Collins informed Oldenburg that Scott intended to publish a volume with, *inter alia*, 'an abridgment of Pappus, Serenus, the 3 latter Bookes of Apollonius . . .',[136] but that is the last we hear of it. The evidence for the work that Bernard actually did on the projected edition is contained in two documents bought for the Bodleian after his death. The first of these is Bernard's copy of the Ecchellensis–Borelli translation of

---

132 On this see Feingold, 'Isaac Barrow', 76–7.
133 *Correspondence of Scientific Men*, ii. 217.
134 Ibid. i. 196; Oldenburg, *Correspondence*, ix, nos. 2093 and 2094, pp. 316, 319.
135 *Correspondence of Scientific Men*, ii. 552.
136 Oldenburg, *Correspondence*, xi, no. 2644, p. 316.

Conics, V–VII, interleaved with blank pages, and heavily annotated both on the original and the interleaves.[137] The annotations contain frequent references to 'Beni Musa'. i.e. the Arabic version which Bernard had copied at Leiden, and indeed whole propositions are translated from that version. Bernard also refers to Golius' notes and occasionally to translations 'Ex schedis Golianis Apollonii Pergaei', and to the version of 'Abdo'lmelek' or 'Abdolmelik', i.e. the version in Ravius' manuscript. Occasionally, as for the definitions at the beginning of Book VI, he transcribes the actual Arabic text. All this, however, is done quite unsystematically, and there are many propositions with no annotations at all. It is clear that this could never have served as the basis for an edition. More promising is MS Lat. Class. e. 2, which is entitled 'Apollonii Pergaei Conicorum pars Altera: Sive Libri posteriores à quarto Ex Arabico vertit E. B. An. Dni MDCLXXIV', evidently begun as the fair copy for the printer in 1674. It contains only the Latin translation, mainly from the Banū Mūsā version, but with references also to 'Abdolm.' and 'Borellus'. There are annotations by Bernard himself, with references to the lemmata of Pappus and the notes of Borelli. For the first eleven propositions printed figures are pasted in, evidently those made from Golius' plates which Marshall had found among his notes. Bernard also had a copy of the specimen page which had been printed for Golius, containing his translation of the beginning of Book V,[138] for on fo. 3ᵛ he inserts the instruction 'Put here Apollonius's Ep[ist]le to Attalus out of Golius's version a 4to page'. From Prop. V. 8 onwards the translation becomes highly abbreviated, and the whole thing ends in the middle of Prop. V. 45, where Bernard had clearly run out of patience or interest.[139] It is possible that he filled other notebooks on the *Conics* which are lost, but the state of this one, which started off as the printer's copy, indicates that he never got close to finishing the projected edition and translation. We shall see that this was not the only major scholarly project that he abandoned after devoting a great deal of time and energy to it.

---

[137] MS Lat. misc. c. 65.

[138] On this elusive specimen page see Toomer, *Apollonius*, pp. lxxxvi–lxxxvii.

[139] The middle of the book is blank, but the other end is occupied by his translation of the pseudo-Archimedean *Lemmata*, preceded by a very interesting preface on their history in Greek and Arabic, with some intelligent conjectures about their real origin.

(V) THOMAS SMITH

Thomas Smith,[140] while still an undergraduate, became a friend of Bernard, and the two remained close for the rest of Bernard's life.[141] They shared a common devotion to scholarship and piety. Smith was a precocious student of oriental languages, and was nicknamed 'Rabbi Smith' and 'Tograi Smith' at Oxford for his devotion to rabbinical and Arabic literature. In order for him to take his BA in 1660 the Provost of Queen's College recommended that he be given two terms' seniority 'for his progress in learning far beyond his age and standing'.[142] Two years later he published his learned *Diatriba de Chaldaicis Paraphrastis* on the Chaldee translations of various parts of the Old Testament.[143] Smith acknowledges his indebtedness to his recently deceased namesake of Christ's College, Cambridge and to Pococke, but above all to Samuel Clarke, who had allowed him to use the translation of the Chaldee paraphrase of the Chronicles on which he was engaged. Smith was chosen Fellow of Magdalen College in 1666, and some of the lectures he delivered there while serving as Hebrew lecturer in the 1660s survive.[144] In 1668 he was chosen by Sir Daniel Harvey, who had been nominated by the King as ambassador in Constantinople, to accompany him there as his chaplain.[145] One would assume that Smith sought this post because he desired to increase his knowledge of oriental languages as Pococke had done forty years earlier. This is certainly the impression one gets from reading the letters sent from Oxford in June and July 1668 bidding him farewell. His friend Bernard talks of 'my longings after those MSSts of Orientall

---

[140] There is an excellent short account of Smith's life, with a detailed list of his writings, in Bloxam, *Register of Magdalen College*, iii. 182–204.

[141] In 1677 he wrote to Bernard: 'you and I have been friends for almost twenty yeares' (MS Smith 57, p. 15) and writing to Bernard's widow after his death in Jan. 1697 he mentions 'my almost forty years acquaintance with him' (ibid., p. 617). In 1661 the two men published poems on adjoining pages, Bernard in Arabic, Smith in Hebrew, in the Oxford volume mourning the death of Princess Mary, sister of Charles II (Madan, *Oxford Books*, iii, no. 2543).

[142] Bloxam, *Register of Magdalen College*, iii. 182 n. q.

[143] Madan, *Oxford Books*, iii, no. 2613. On the contents and sources of this work see Feingold, 'The Oxford Oriental School'.

[144] MSS Smith 113 and 114. These have been examined by Feingold, who mentions their occasional references (at second hand) to Arabic sources ('The Oxford Oriental School').

[145] Smith was recommended by Joseph Williamson (formerly Fellow of Queen's College), whom he later served as chaplain. Smith's sermon to the London Levant Merchants before his departure, in which he displays his expertise in Hebrew and Chaldee, was preached on 2 June 1668.

learning which you will have occasion to see digest & buye',[146] while Hyde, who had been Smith's colleague at Queen's College, and remained on good terms with him for the rest of their lives, more directly asked him to buy books on his behalf, and, like a good librarian, tells him that 'it would be a very good worke to procure a Catalogue of all such bookes as are extant about Constantinople in any of the Eastern languages, with the prices of each'.[147] The journal that Smith kept of his voyage out, which he published many years later,[148] displays no interest in things Arabic, although he incidentally reveals in a letter to Bernard in 1691 that when he was at Tangier in September 1668 he 'tooke particular notice of the monument in Arabick in bass a kind of bass viliaco, the letters being protuberant, just without the English Protestant Church'.[149] Evidently he did not copy the inscription into his journal,[150] since he says 'these things are out of my mind it being above two and twenty yeares since I saw the stone'. Moreover, his experiences in Constantinople and Asia Minor during the two years of his stay seem to have given him an invincible disgust for all things having to do with Muslims, and although he devoted most of his life to scholarship, he turned away completely from the path of study of his youth.

Smith's narrow and bigoted Christian piety prevented him from treating his experiences in the East as anything but a confirmation of his prejudices against the Turks. Shortly after returning to Magdalen, he published a little book, in the form of two letters addressed to Williamson, on the Turks and on the tour he made to the Seven Churches of Asia.[151] This proved so popular that he produced an English edition (*Remarks upon the Manners of the Turks*) in 1678, from which my quotations are taken. Smith's general attitude is immediately apparent in the 'Preface to the Reader':[152]

---

[146] MS Smith 47, fo. 33.

[147] MS Smith 50, p. 219.

[148] Smith, '*Journal of a Voyage from* England *to* Constantinople'.

[149] MS Smith 57, p. 181.

[150] I have not examined MS Smith 141 (*SC* no. 29820), containing his diary and note-book from 1668 to 1708.

[151] Smith, *Epistolae Duae* (Madan, *Oxford Books*, iii, no. 2948); reissued in an expanded form in 1674 (ibid., no. 3026).

[152] It is instructive to contrast the sober and objective account of Muslim beliefs and religious practices penned by Isaac Barrow during his few months in Constantinople in 1658: 'Epitome Fidei et religionis Turcicae' (Barrow, *Theological Works*, ix. 386–410). However, the long poem he wrote on the same topic ('De Religione Turcica anno 1658', ibid. 481–510) is far more pejorative.

being more and more convinced by such kind of relations, of the brutish ignorance and horrid barbarousness of the Turks, and of the dotages and follies of their worship, you may the more thankfully and seriously reflect upon that most blessed and merciful providence, which has cast your lot in *Christendom*, and in a Country especially, where the *Christian Doctrine* is profest in its primitive purity and integrity, and where civility and learning and all ingenuous Arts flourish, and are in their heigth and perfection.

His narrative begins 'The Turks are justly branded with the character of a Barbarous Nation'; this is due mainly 'to the intolerable Pride and Scorn, wherewith they treat all the World besides'. Smith claims that the Turks have contempt of learning and hatred of all other religions, and we may suspect that this conviction was reinforced when he was stoned by children in the streets of Constantinople for being a Frank, and by his experience 'in a voyage I made to *Prusia* in *Bithynia*, in which I narrowly escaped having my throat cut upon mount Olympus by several *Janizaries*'.[153] While noting the Turks' hatred of the Jews, he manages to show his contempt for both: 'their [the Jews'] wit and cunning is shew'n and exercised better about Merchandise, and Brocage, and Usury, wherein they do great service to the *Turks*, who are pitiful Accomptants.'[154] He does not fail to remark that Islam is 'a religion, which is made up of folly, and imposture, and gross absurdities', and was greatly offended by being asked 'in the Portico of *Sancta Sophia*, why will you not turn *Musulman*, and be as one of us?' However, he notes the great decorum observed in the mosques at services.[155] He also recounts the hospitality and kind treatment he met with from a Turk at Bursa, and how, as the only Frank crossing the Propontis, he was given a 'Dish of Coffee', as well as the civility with which he was received by the Cadi of Smyrna,[156] but appears quite unconscious of any discrepancy between these experiences and his general aspersions on the Turkish character. He obviously regards it as a fault in the Turks that they are 'excessively pitiful and good natured towards dumb creatures', since they will chide or beat a Christian who kicks a dog.[157]

While still at Constantinople Smith seems to have decided to abandon his oriental studies. I infer this from an incidental remark he made in a letter to Bernard of 7 February 1691, in which he reveals that he no longer possesses such a standard work as Pococke's

---

[153] Smith, *Remarks upon the Manners of the Turks*, 5, 206.
[154] Ibid. 16.   [155] Ibid. 27, 32, 55.   [156] Ibid. 37–8, 59, 209.
[157] Ibid. 103, 107.

Abū 'l-Faraj, 'having left it with a great many other Oriental books at Constantinople, for the use of such as should succeed me in that post'.[158] He certainly never published anything further on Arabic or Hebrew. The principal effect on his scholarship of his stay in Constantinople was an abiding interest in the condition of the Greek Orthodox Church under Ottoman rule. This is already apparent in his correspondence with Paul Rycaut, consul of the Levant Company at Smyrna, which began while Smith was at Constantinople. The two had met in November 1668 when Sir Daniel Harvey's party changed vessels at Smyrna on the way out,[159] and Smith encouraged Rycaut to pursue his work on the Greek and Armenian Churches,[160] although he was privately critical of it when Rycaut finally published his book in 1679.[161] In the mean time Smith himself had published in 1676 at Oxford a small book *De Graecae Ecclesiae hodierno statu*, which was reissued two years later in London in an enlarged form. A valuable part of this was the account of the death of the Patriarch Cyril Lucaris which Smith had taken from the mouth of Pococke himself. An English translation was published in London in 1680.[162] However, Smith's enthusiasm for such matters was not sufficient to persuade him to return to Turkey in 1677 to collect manuscripts of the Greek Fathers, although urged thereto by Fell and others.[163] After the Revolution of 1688 Smith became a prominent 'non-juror', refusing to take the oath of loyalty to the new monarchs. He left Oxford in 1689 for London, where he spent the rest of his life, most of it as the librarian of the Cotton Library. However, he maintained a lively correspondence with Bernard and others at Oxford, the survival of which, together with many other papers that he collected, constitutes an invaluable resource for the history of scholarship at Oxford in the last part of the seventeenth century.[164] Smith maintained an interest in the history of Arabic studies in England in his own time and the immediately preceding period, and the series of small biographies which he published towards the end of his life, although superficial,

---

[158] MS Smith 57, p. 189.

[159] Smith, '*Journal of a Voyage from* England *to* Constantinople', 614; cf. Anderson, *An English Consul in Turkey*, 148.

[160] Letter of 17 May 1669 in MS Smith 53, fo. 153, quoted by Anderson, *An English Consul in Turkey*, 216.

[161] Ibid. 221.

[162] Madan, *Oxford Books*, iii, nos. 3121 and 3279. Cf. Twells, 51. These works were reissued again in Smith's *Miscellanea* (London, 1686), in which I have examined them.

[163] Bloxam, *Register of Magdalen College*, iii. 187.

[164] Most of this material is in the Smith MSS in the Bodleian Library.

afford useful information on that topic. His accounts of the lives of his contemporaries and friends Bernard and Huntington, and of Bainbridge and Greaves amongst his predecessors, show how conscious he was of the importance of Arabic in the intellectual currents of the seventeenth century.[165]

(VI) JOHN WALLIS

One of those who had some interest, but little skill in Arabic was John Wallis. He had been appointed Savilian Professor of Mathematics by the Visitors in 1649, having earned the gratitude of Parliament by deciphering some royal letters written in code captured at the battle of Naseby. Despite this, he managed to retain his position at Oxford after the Restoration,[166] having acquired considerable influence in the university, where he had succeeded Langbaine as Keeper of the Archives.[167] He exerted himself on behalf of Pococke in the latter's difficulties during the 1650s, and the two remained good friends ever afterwards.[168] Wallis's interest in Arabic was strictly practical, as a means of access to interesting points in mathematics and astronomy. He certainly knew enough to read the numerals in Arabic and Persian astronomical tables. Writing to Oldenburg in 1664 he tells him that he had compared Hyde's translation of Ulugh Beg's star catalogue with the original Persian manuscripts 'as to numbers'.[169] However, the most famous example of the use of Arabic in Wallis's mathematical work is the translation of al-Ṭūsī's 'proof' of Euclid's parallel postulate which he inserted in his *Opera Mathematica*.[170] The earliest version of this occurs in the handwritten copy of the lecture that he delivered on 7 February 1652, in which he says that he did the translation 'not without the help' of Pococke.[171] He also inserted in his *Mathesis*

---

[165] Smith, *Life of Bernard* and *Vitae*.

[166] According to Kennett's reminiscences in MS BL Lansdowne 987, fo. 156ʳ, Wallis had prudently suppressed certain passages in the deciphered letters, for which he earned royal favour.

[167] Contrary to the Savilian statutes and in a very dubious election: see Madan, *Oxford Books*, iii, nos. 2325 and 2371 for this scandalous incident.

[168] Wallis was one of the overseers named in Pococke's will.

[169] Oldenburg, *Correspondence*, ii, no. 310, p. 163.

[170] ii. 669–73. In this he attributes the translation unreservedly to Pococke.

[171] 'non sine auxilio Edw. Pococke', MS Don. d 45, fo. 94ʳ, as quoted and summarized by Mercier, 'English Orientalists and Mathematical Astronomy', 199–201, q.v. for a discussion of the different versions and of Pococke's role.

Universalis of 1657 a long Arabic quotation from and translation of a passage in al-Safadī's commentary on al-Ṭughrā'ī's poem, concerning the famous story of the man who asked a king for a reward of the number of grains which could be placed on a chessboard, one on the first square, two on the second, four on the third, and so on. Wallis explicitly says that he owes this to Pococke.[172]

(VII) THOMAS HYDE

On 1 February 1668, in response to a query from Oldenburg about the study of Arabic in Oxford, Wallis wrote:

For those skilled in Arabick; we have here, (beside Dr Pocok) Mr Clark one of our Bedles & Mr Hyde our Library keeper, (both heretofore imployed in ye Biblia Polyglotta), Mr. Huntington, a fellow of Merton College; Mr Bernard a fellow of St Johns College, & now Procter; Mr Marsh a fellow of Exeter College; Mr Smith of Magdalene College.[173]

Noticeably absent from this list is the name of George Hooper. Hooper, currently a Student and Lecturer at Christ Church, had learned Arabic under Busby at Westminster, continued to study it under Pococke, presumably after graduating BA in 1661, and remained interested in it, in an amateurish way, all his life.[174] But in a letter to Pococke of 1682 he excused himself 'for not having made a suitable proficiency therein';[175] Wallis was undoubtedly right to omit his name. The contributions of Robert Huntington and Narcissus Marsh will be considered in the following chapter, where it will be seen that it lay primarily in forwarding the work of others, especially by the collections of manuscripts that they assembled. Unlike them, Thomas Hyde produced major works of scholarship. He has been generally and rightly considered the most learned orientalist in seventeenth-century England after Pococke. He had an extraordinarily wide interest in oriental tongues, and was concerned to master the spoken as well as the written languages by conversing with native speakers. His linguistic

---

[172] Wallis, *Mathesis Universalis*, 271–80, republished in Wallis, *Opera Mathematica*, i. 159–64. This is the passage referred to by Twells, 328.

[173] Oldenburg, *Correspondence*, iv, no. 763, p. 141.

[174] See Marshall, *George Hooper*, especially pp. 2, 5, and 176–7 (on Hooper's oriental books, now in Wells Cathedral library).

[175] Twells, 325.

interests extended as far as Malay,[176] the languages of India,[177] and even Chinese. In a letter to Thomas Bowrey of 30 March 1701, Hyde offers him for publication the Chinese translation of the Creed, the Ten Commandments, and other things.[178] In 1687 he entertained a Chinese scholar at Oxford to catalogue the Chinese books in the Bodleian, from whom he learned the language. This man, who had been brought back from Nanking to Paris by the Jesuits, also gave Hyde information about Chinese games and customs.[179] Hyde told Bowrey: 'My Chinese Michael Shin Fo-Çung (for that was his name) was bred a Schollar in all the Learning of their country, read all their Books readily, and was of great honesty and sincerity, and fit to be relyed upon in every thing . . . could speak Latine, whereby I conversed with him freely and easily.'[180] Hyde's considerable knowledge of Arabic is apparent from his scholarly publications, but the majority of these are concerned with Persian, the language in which he was most skilled.

When Thomas Lockey resigned as Bodley's Librarian in 1665, Hyde, then Under-Keeper, was elected as his successor, and retained the post into the eighteenth century. During his tenure the library acquired more oriental manuscripts than under any librarian before or since, with the major accessions of Pococke's and Huntington's manuscripts, and the smaller but still substantial collections of Thomas Greaves and Hyde himself (who sold his manuscripts to the university in 1692). Although the credit for these acquisitions belongs primarily to the enlightened authorities in the university who managed to find the substantial sums necessary to make the purchases, Hyde too deserves praise for his consistent advocacy of this kind of expansion of the library. His own record of scholarly publication, although substantial, was erratic. He seems often to have chosen to do or not do an edition on the basis of prospective profit or favour. His first major work was his edition of the star catalogue in the tables of Ulugh Beg, published

[176] He supervised, together with Marshall, the printing of the Gospels and Acts in Malay (from earlier Dutch editions) published at Oxford, at Boyle's expense, in 1677: Madan, *Oxford Books*, iii, no. 3164.

[177] He told Bowrey on 20 Nov. 1700 that he had written to a chaplain in India for some things in the 'Hanscreet' language; 'to which he answered that I must not call it Hanscreet, but Sanscreet, and accordingly he sent me papers in the ould Brachman language'. In the same letter Hyde also deals with the language of Ceylon and 'Telinga' (Telugu?) and his desire to get the 'Tartar Alphabet of Kithay' (India Office MS Eur. E. 192 4, fo. 2).

[178] India Office MS Eur. E. 192 11, fo. 1.

[179] Hyde gave him a letter of recommendation to Boyle when he left Oxford (Boyle, *Works*, vi. 574). Cf. Hyde, *De Ludis Orientalibus*, preface.

[180] India Office MS Eur. E. 192 15, fo. 1.

at his own expense at Oxford in 1665. Hyde tells us that he had some
time before translated this into Latin for Seth Ward (then Savilian
Professor of Astronomy),[181] but had abandoned it on Ward's elevation
to a bishopric, and had only recently returned to it at the urging of his
friends. Hyde notes that John Greaves had published a part of the catalogue in Bainbridge's *Canicularia*, but was prevented by death from
publishing the whole.[182] The Persian text, collated from three manuscript copies, with facing Latin translation, is followed by 72 pages of
Hyde's notes, mostly on the star names. For assistance on these he
gives effusive thanks to Pococke, from whom he had also borrowed
one of the manuscripts of Ulugh Beg and a manuscript of al-Ṣūfī's
Arabic star catalogue. Negotiations with members of the Royal Society
for Hyde to produce an edition and translation of the whole work, for
the benefit of Hevelius, came to nothing.[183] In fact Hyde produced no
other major publication for another twenty-five years,[184] and his later
work will be discussed in the next chapter. No doubt this silence is
partly to be explained by the distractions of his office, especially his
labours on the printed catalogue of the Bodleian Library, which finally
emerged in 1674. However, he was engaged on other scholarly enter-
prises during the 1670s and 1680s, not all of which bore fruit. In
particular, he says that he had intended to edit Abū 'l-Fidā''s
Geography, at the urging of Fell,[185] but that Fell's death put an end to
the project.

(VIII) ARABIC AT CAMBRIDGE

When Charles II returned home in 1660 Cambridge, like Oxford,
witnessed expulsions of those who had been intruded by Parliamentary

---

[181] Hyde, *Ulugh Beg*, Praefatio ad Lectorem. It is not clear whether Ward paid him
for this. More probably the grant of a prebendary at Yetminster which, as Bishop
of Salisbury, he made Hyde in 1666 was the reward for the translation and for Hyde's
fulsome praise of him in the present work.

[182] The exemplar in the Bodleian Library, 4° Rawl. 156, is corrected by Hyde himself
using Greaves's manuscript notes. The corrections were incorporated by Sharpe in the
reissue of *Ulugh Beg* in Hyde, *Syntagma Dissertationum*, vol. i.

[183] See e.g. Wallis's letter to Oldenburg in the latter's *Correspondence*, ii, no. 310 (6
April 1664). Probably the Society, or Hevelius, was unwilling to produce the £20 or £30
which Hyde thought he deserved for the work. See further nos. 313, 314, 316, 321, 344,
352, and 388 in the same volume.

[184] Hyde, *Peritsol* (1691), although the first part of *Historia Shahiludii* (in *De Ludis
Orientalibus*, 1694) was originally published in 1689.

[185] Hyde, *Peritsol*, preface. Presumably this happened after Clarke's death in 1669.

interference, and restitutions of some who had lost their places. However, all this had very little effect on Arabic studies there, which had been insignificant since the death of Wheelock and the consequent cessation of Arabic lectures. One of those expelled was John Worthington, Master of Jesus, who, although he never published any-thing on the topic, was interested in Arabic. When asked by Hartlib, on behalf of John Beale, for his advice on the study of the oriental languages, he replied in a letter which reveals his own attitude. After expressing great expectations for Castell's forthcoming Polyglot Lexicon, and hoping 'that the original Arabic of the Alcoran may be printed, which would better direct and enable Christians to deal with Mahometans',[186] and before giving a list of available Arabic printed books, he remarks:

As for the enquiry concerning books in such languages (without which the pains and time spent upon grammar will not receive a due recompence) I must say, that my pursuit of those languages was cooled by that very consideration, that there were no printed books, none but MSS. which are kept close, and are not for common use; nor did I much care for to trouble myself about the keys when there was no treasure of things to be come at. But I have often wished that there were a corban for the advancement of such studies, that out of some public stock some (and they would not be many) might be encouraged to study those languages, and to travel into Egypt, Persia, &c., and be enabled to purchase those intellectual treasures for the enriching of others. But we are rather for their gums and spices, for what may minister to luxury and pride, than for what is intellectual, or the preserved remains of such ancients who were the glory of their times.[187]

The principal development at Cambridge after the Restoration was the decision of Thomas Adams (who had been made a baronet in 1660 for his loyalty to the royal cause) not only to revive the Arabic Professorship but to endow it permanently. This was finally settled in 1666, after more than a year of negotiations between Sir Thomas and the university. The first professor was Edmund Castell, who had estab-lished a reputation as the best Arabist among Cambridge graduates by his work on the Polyglot Bible, and more recently on the Heptaglot Lexicon, still unpublished but already eight years in the making. He had also published, in 1660, a pamphlet entitled *Sol Angliae Oriens*, a

---

[186] Cf. Worthington's remarks in his *Miscellanies* (p. 253, quoted by Abrahams, 'Isaac Abendana's Cambridge Mishnah and Oxford Calendars', 103): 'If Christians would more knowingly and pertinently deal with Jews and Mahometans, they should be acquainted with Mishnaioth and the Alcoran.'

[187] Worthington, *Correspondence*, ii/1, 26 (9 Sept. 1661).

collection of poems in all the languages represented in the Polyglot, to celebrate the return of Charles II, in which he took the opportunity to insert a plea for support for the lexicon.[188] Castell duly delivered his inaugural lecture (on the use of Avicenna's medical work in elucidating plants mentioned in Scripture), and even published it,[189] but it is significant of the state of Arabic in Cambridge that it had to be printed in London, at Roycroft's press. Moreover Castell, while urging his audience to attend his lectures faithfully, promises to deliver them faithfully only after he has completed his great work of the lexicon. This was to take him another three years of labour and misery, during which he lived in London supervising the printing. He stayed in Cambridge, where Lightfoot provided him with rooms in St Catharine's Hall, only as long as required for the delivery of his lectures. In 1668–9 he was excused by the Heads from delivering them.[190] Even after the publication of the lexicon he spent much time in London trying to arrange for the sale of copies. It was not until 1671 that he had a permanent *pied-à-terre* in Cambridge, where he was attached to St John's College.

Castell did, however, attempt to improve the Arabic holdings of Cambridge University Library by getting the university to acquire Golius' Arabic manuscripts. After Golius' death his two sons determined to sell all his manuscripts in a single lot. Leiden seems to have been either unable or unwilling to buy them, but in England there was considerable interest in acquiring them. The earliest evidence for this that I have seen is in a letter from Marshall to Clarke of 8 December (NS) 1667, saying that he had received letters from both Clarke and Castell expressing interest, and promising to send the printed catalogue of the collection which was in preparation. The only serious competitor that he feared was Colbert in France. Marshall was still waiting for the catalogue to be sent to him from Leiden on 4/14 December 1668, but by then he had learned that the price demanded for the manuscripts was the equivalent of £400.[191] By 12/22 February 1669 Marshall had sent copies of the catalogue to both Oxford and

---

[188] 'Sic erit ut sudans respiret Lexicon, atque / Laetius hinc totum progrediatur opus.' Arberry, *The Cambridge School of Arabic*, 11–12, gives excerpts from the 'somewhat odd Arabic and Persian effusions'.

[189] Castell, *Oratio*. There is some account of this in Norris, 'Edmund Castell and his *Lexicon Heptaglotton*', 79–80.

[190] Letter to Clarke of 24 June 1668, MS BL Add. 22905, fo. 79.

[191] Ibid., fos. 70 and 87. On 10/20 Dec. Marshall repeats his anxiety that Thévenot, who was then in Leiden, might buy the manuscripts for Colbert (ibid., fo. 88).

Cambridge, and had requested Theodorus Golius to hold off selling until he had a reply from England. He continues:

I have received large account of the activity of Cambridge-men in the designe of the books for themselves; & our good friend Dr. Castell hath with incomparable industry moved both in Court, & City of London. The Result is this: His Majestie would buy the Chymicall books (as is said) almost at any rate; & some friends offer to advance some monys toward the purchase of the whole for Cambridge: but still Commissio is wanting. Our eyes now are onely upon Oxford, of whose activeness I should gladly have heard first.[192]

However, inspection of the printed catalogue dampened the enthusiasm of Oxford. Bernard, writing to Clarke from London on his way to Holland in January 1669, says: 'I mervayle at the Catalogue, which Mr Marshall sends you, for Golius had many more manuscripts & better than are there mentioned.'[193] Pococke expresses himself to the same effect and in much more detail in his letter to Bernard, now at Leiden, of 8 February 1669:

The printed copy of Golius's Manuscripts I have perused, very faulty and defectively put out. that which I conjecture from it, is that the best and noblest of his bookes are taken out, for nobler Authors then any of those he useth to cite. and if I be not deceived I have formerly seene at leaste one book belonging to him which I finde not here. and without the best of Lexicons he could not be, wheras here is neither Kamus nor Gieuhary nor any other of the best note.[194]

Clarke evidently wrote in similar terms to Marshall, for Marshall responded that since the 'missing' books were in the Leiden Library Golius had had no need to acquire them himself, and argued that although £400 might seem high, it was only an asking price, and the heirs might well accept a lesser offer.[195]

It seems clear that no offer at all was made by Oxford. Pococke's view that the price was too high[196] was justified by Marsh's acquisition

[192] Marshall to Clarke, ibid., fo. 90.

[193] MS BL Add. 4275, fo. 40.

[194] MS Smith 45, p. 133. There is a fuller transcript of the letter in Wakefield, 'Arabic Manuscripts in the Bodleian Library', 138. 'Nobler Authors then any of those he useth to cite' means 'He frequently cites more important texts than any of those (in the catalogue).'

[195] Letter of 12/22 Feb. 1669, MS BL Add. 22905, fo. 90.

[196] Whether he was also correct in thinking that some items had been held back from inclusion in the printed catalogue must await detailed comparison of that catalogue with the auction catalogue of 1696 and other information about Golius' manuscripts. I have not seen the 1668 catalogue, but according to Wakefield, 'Arabic Manuscripts in the Bodleian Library', 146 n. 197, there is a copy in All Souls College library.

of the bulk of the manuscripts, including all the choice items, for only
£220 when the collection was auctioned in 1696. Marshall's report
that the asking price had dropped to £300 seems to have made no
difference.[197] Cambridge, however, continued to show interest.
According to Thomas Smith, the university actually made an offer of a
'huge price' to Golius' heirs in 1668/9, but this was refused.[198] Oates,
who was unable to find any evidence for this offer in the Cambridge
archives, suspects that this was simply a false rumour put about by the
heirs. While it is true that Smith is often unreliable, in this case he was
in a position to get the information directly from Bernard, who was
present in Leiden for three months in 1669. Furthermore, as we have
seen, Castell was active in London soliciting friends of Cambridge in
this matter. He was still trying to get the manuscripts for Cambridge in
1673–4. According to Twells, he wrote to Pococke in 1673 that 'a
private person of his acquaintance' was willing to advance £700.[199] It
seems incredible that if this were really true the bargain would not
have been concluded. A little light is shed on the negotiations by the
correspondence of Bernard. In November 1671 he told Thomas Gale,
Regius Professor of Greek at Cambridge, that Uchtman had written to
him about the slippery behaviour of the Golii, but that he expected that
they would manage to reconcile themselves to such a large sum.[200]
This suggests that Cambridge had indeed made a definite offer. On
5 March 1673/4 Bernard asked Lightfoot: 'Pray is there any hope of
Your purchasing the Golian Books?' Lightfoot, after first replying that
there was no progress and that he had not seen Castell, later told him:
'The business about the Golian library begins to have some life in it
again: through the importunity of Dr. Castle, & the zealous forwarding
of our Vicechancelour' (John Spencer, Master of Corpus Christi
College). Bernard replied on 8 July:

Dr Marshall (who presents his love to you) is very much concerned that the
Golian affair be prosecuted & will doe his utmost to beate down the price &
effect the very much desired purchase. nay he professes to mee his readinesse
to come over to Cambridge & explaine all that that he knoweth of the busi-
nesse & what he conceives best to be done.

---

[197] Letter to Bernard of 2 Dec. 1669 (MS Smith 45, p. 109).

[198] Smith, *Life of Bernard*, 49, quoted by Oates, 431 n. 33.

[199] Twells, 291–2. The dates hereabouts in Twells's narrative are very vague.

[200] 'D. Utchmannus Professor, Ling. Hebr Leidae non ita pridem ad me scripsit &
monuit de tergiversatione Goliorum: sed, ut reor, redibunt illi in gratiam cum tantâ
pecuniarum summâ, non abhorrent enim iste homines a nummis, quamvis regios vultus
ferunt' (MS BL Add. 4277, fo. 19).

Presenting his service to Dr Castell, he congratulates him for his 'zeale & the likely successe of it for the procureing Golius his books'.[201] Despite Bernard's optimism, this is the last we hear of Castell's efforts,[202] and they certainly came to nothing.

(IX) CASTELL AND THE HEPTAGLOT LEXICON

The work for which Castell is remembered, and on which he spent a substantial part of his life, is the *Lexicon Heptaglotton*.[203] This project grew out of the Polyglot Bible, and although its origins remain obscure, it seems likely that, as the printing of the Bible drew to its close, the question of further employment of the press and types which had been acquired for printing it arose. The idea was mooted to publish a lexicon covering all the oriental languages employed in the Polyglot Bible, namely the six related (Semitic) tongues, Hebrew, Chaldee, Syriac, Samaritan, Ethiopic, and Arabic, and also Persian. Presumably those who had subscribed to the Polyglot would also be interested in subscribing to this aid to reading it.[204] Furthermore, it would continue to provide employment not only to the presses and their operators, but also to some of those who had been engaged in overseeing the publication of the Polyglot. It is not certain whose idea this was. Castell later claimed that he was dragooned into the project by certain 'great men', who are unnamed but certainly include Walton.[205] At the beginning, however, he was enthusiastic. This is

[201] Lightfoot, *Correspondence*, 454–9. My quotations are taken from the originals in MSS BL Lansdowne 1055, fo. 122, Smith 45, pp. 85 and 90, and Lansdowne 1055, fo. 123.

[202] Except for the bequest of £100 'towards the purchasing of Golius's Library' in the will of Robert Mapletoft (Oates, 428–30), which was drawn up in 1676. Oates's conjecture (pp. 432–4) that the abortive negotiations of the university with the bookseller Robert Scott in 1677 for the purchase of a nameless collection of manuscripts also concerned the Golian manuscripts seems implausible to me.

[203] On this Norris, 'Edmund Castell and his *Lexicon Heptaglotton*', provides some useful material, but is very far from comprehensive.

[204] The *Lexicon* was issued in the same format as the Polyglot, and copies in bindings contemporary with the publication are not infrequently bound uniformly with accompanying sets of the Polyglot.

[205] e.g. Castell, *Lexicon*, preface: 'literis insuper quamplurimis, à viris magni nominis, quà in Ecclesia, quà in Rep. domi, forísque ad me missis, . . . me submisi invitus admodum, animóque . . . multùm horrescente, quodque satis supérque noverunt illi omnes summi viri, qui me promissis tum auxilii, tum etiam remunerationis ad isthaec non pellexerunt tantum, sed vi quadam urgenter impulerunt.' On 22 Feb. 1664 he told Lightfoot that he had been 'called to this unhappy destructive undertaking by letters and

evident from the letter that he wrote to Lightfoot on 2 December 1657, enclosing a draft of the prospectus for the work which, he says,

> was not, at least for the present, so much contrived and undertaken by us, as by some with importunity pressed and urged upon us. . . . For above the moiety of those years I have lived, I must confesse, I have at times, been meditating and doinge somwhat in tendency to such a work: providence has now, with the assistance of so able & excellent a Coadjutor as Mr. Clarke, singularly, & indeed eminently experienced in the same studies, made some overture for the production of what wee have both for not a few years been in travell with.[206]

Early in 1658 he issued a printed prospectus and specimen entitled *Lexicon Linguarum Orientalium*, which invited subscriptions to the work, and was recommended by the signatures of Walton and Pococke, amongst others.[207] The scholars chosen to supervise the work were, besides Castell, Samuel Clarke and Alexander Huish. Huish had played a prominent role in correcting the Polyglot, but we have little information about his skills in oriental languages, for according to Walton he was mainly occupied with the Greek and Latin texts. He was an Oxford graduate who had been deprived of his benefices because of his Royalist and Laudian leanings.[208] Castell, Clarke, and Huish signed a petition to Lord Protector Cromwell, undated but certainly also from 1658, requesting the same privilege that had been granted to the publishers of the Polyglot for the importation of 5,000 reams of royal paper free of duties. After announcing that the Polyglot Bible is nearly completed, the petitioners continue:

> for as much as there is no lexicon extant for all these languages together, and for some of them not at all, without which that most excellent work cannot be so useful, as otherwise it might be, your petitioners . . . have upon the request of divers persons of worth and learning undertaken the composing and publishing of such a work, wherein the labours of former lexicographers may be

promises from the very highest persons both in church and commonwealth' (MS BL Lansdowne 1055, fo. 50; Lightfoot, *Correspondence*, 366–7).

[206] MS BL Lansdowne 1055, fo. 42, printed in Lightfoot, *Correspondence*, 387–8.

[207] This specimen is mentioned by Walton in his preface to the Polyglot: 'viri quidam docti et linguarum periti, qui in hac editione operam fidelem nobis praestiterunt, in animo habent aliud volumen edere; in quo . . . Lexicon generale absolutum *Hebraicae, Samaritanae, Chaldaicae, Syriacae, Arabicae, Æthiopicae*, et *Persicae*, secundum Schindleri Methodum in Pentaglotto suo, conficere decreverunt, in eorum usum qui subsidium ad sumptus perferendos conferre velint, Cujus Specimen luculentum nuper impressum ediderunt.'

[208] On all of this see Todd, *Life of Walton*, i. 269–76.

completed by their observations, and the same be had at a far cheaper rate, than some lexicons of one language, could heretofore be had.[209]

Castell originally proposed a subscription price of 40 shillings, but by the time that the prospectus was issued this had gone up to 50 shillings, and by 22 February 1664 to £4.[210]

The plan of the work was based on the *Lexicon pentaglotton* of Valentin Schindler, first published posthumously at Hanau in 1612, and since often reprinted and adapted.[211] The 'five tongues' represented in this were Hebrew, Chaldee, Syriac, 'Talmudo-Rabbinic', and Arabic. All five languages were treated together under the Hebrew roots, and all were printed with Hebrew types. The *Lexicon Heptaglotton* prints each language in its own script, and the 'Talmudo-Rabbinic' (which is not really separate from Chaldee and Hebrew) is abandoned in favour of Samaritan and Ethiopic, but the principle of arrangement under the Hebrew roots is retained, except for Persian, which is so different from all the others (being, according to modern classification, an Indo-European language, although it contains many words derived from Arabic) that it had to be treated separately. The Persian lexicon is accordingly printed by itself at the end of vol. I. The principal sources[212] of the Heptaglot Lexicon were already existing lexicons: for Arabic, Golius, but Bedwell's manuscript dictionary was also used, for the first (and probably last) time; for Hebrew, Schindler and Buxtorf; for Chaldee, besides these two, Sebastian Münster's dictionary; for Syriac, the dictionaries of Trostius and Buxtorf, as well as the native dictionary of Bar Bahlul (borrowed from Cambridge); for Samaritan, Morinus' *Dictionarium Trilingue* (of Samaritan, Chaldee, and Arabic), which Marshall had copied and sent to Castell from Holland; and for Ethiopic, Ludolf's dictionary. For Persian the main source was a dictionary compiled by Golius, still in manuscript, which had been sent from Leiden under bond through the agency of Marshall.[213] However, Castell and his associates also consulted

---

[209] Quoted from Baker's transcript (Cambridge MS Mm.1.47, pp. 349–50) by Norris, 'Edmund Castell and his *Lexicon Heptaglotton*', 81–2. The last part of the petition is quoted by Twells, 210.

[210] Letters of Castell to Lightfoot, MS BL Lansdowne 1055, fos. 62, 50 (Lightfoot, *Correspondence*, 368–70, 366–7).

[211] *PO* no. 106, with illustration. Todd, *Life of Walton*, i. 176–7, notes that in Sidney Sussex College, Cambridge is an interleaved copy of Schindler, in three parts, with Castell's notes.

[212] Castell gives a meticulous list of all of his sources in the preface to the lexicon. Here I notice only those which can be assumed to have been of most use.

[213] MS CUL Dd.6.4, fo. 45 is Castell's draft of a letter to Golius of 8 Aug. 1661, promis-

numerous original texts, both printed and in manuscript, as additional
sources of vocabulary. The great majority of these were biblical,
liturgical, and rabbinical texts, but they included some secular works;
for instance, among the Arabic treatises consulted was the Avicenna
printed at Rome. Notably absent from Castell's list of sources are the
Arabic historical texts edited by Erpenius, Golius, and Pococke.

Castell was soon beset by problems, the most urgent of which concerned his collaborators. In May 1658 Clarke was appointed Architypographus, and soon after removed from London to Oxford.
Although he did not immediately give up his participation in the lexicon, it was apparent that as long as the printing was done at London it
would be very difficult for him to help supervise the work. For a while
Castell contemplated moving the operation to Oxford, including himself, by the 'exchange of a benefice near Oxford for mine in Essex'.[214]
This seems to have received a chilly response from Oxford, since we
hear no more of it after 1658. In the mean time Castell was trying in
vain to find a replacement for Clarke. His approach to Thomas
Greaves was 'answerd with repuls',[215] and similar pleas to Pococke (if
the work could be removed to Oxford) and to James Lambe were of no
avail.[216] Huish was causing difficulties: Castell complains in the same
letter about 'Mr Huish's violent intemperant passions that we determin
his work to be don in the Country, against which he is imperiously
bent', and declares to Clarke that 'it would bee the greatest eas & joy
to my heart to be discharged of this most oppressive burden'. He was
also about to lose the services of Hyde (who had become Hebrew
lecturer at Queen's College, Oxford). On 2 December 1658 he sent
Clarke an ultimatum demanding that he resolve either to quit or to join

ing him a number of copies of the lexicon in return for the loan of his Persian
dictionary. The same MS, p. 404, is a letter from Caesar Calandrinus to Golius dated 9 May
1665 announcing that he is releasing Castell from his bond of £100 since he is returning
the manuscript of the dictionary to Golius. The negotiations between Golius, Castell,
and Roycroft, in which Marshall at Dordrecht acted as intermediary, are summarized by
Witkam, *Jacobus Golius en zijn Handschriften*, 60–1, from the correspondence in MS
Marsh 714. Golius' Persian–Latin dictionary is now MS Marsh 213.

[214] Castell to Clarke, 1 July 1658, MS BL Add. 22905, fo. 13. Cf. Clarke to Lightfoot,
16 June 1658 (Lightfoot, *Correspondence*, 402).

[215] Castell to Clarke, 5 Aug. 1658 (MS BL Add. 22905, fo. 15). The letter to Greaves
is preserved in MS BL Add. 4162, fos. 63ᵛ–64ʳ.

[216] MS BL Add. 22905, fo. 15. Lambe was a Canon of Westminster who died in
1664. His collections for an Arabic grammar and lexicon, in nine volumes, were given to
the Bodleian (MSS Lambe 1–9, see Uri, pp. 242, 247, and Macray, *Annals*, 135). I know
nothing more about his Arabic studies. Wood (*Athenae Oxonienses*, iii. 668) simply
mentions these Bodleian manuscripts.

in the project with himself and Huish. He was relieved when Clarke finally resigned.[217] I have not been able to determine exactly when Huish also abandoned the enterprise, but conjecture that it was after he regained his benefices at the Restoration.[218]

Castell was to spend much time, money, and complaints over the following years in recruiting and supervising helpers, most of whom proved unsatisfactory and stayed with the project only briefly. In fact the only one who stayed with him for more than a year or two was Martin Murray, who despite his name was a young German from Greifswald. Murray never published anything himself, but is praised for his skill in Arabic by Castell both in his letters and in the preface to the lexicon, where he describes Murray as 'vir non minus doctus, quam admodum ingenuus, cui per septennii fere spatium Arabicas meas concredideram collectiones'. Since Castell first mentions 'Mr Murray, skilld somwhat in al the languages' in his letter of 17 November 1658,[219] he must have stayed with the lexicon until 1665.[220] However, Moller, who met Murray in Hamburg in 1682, maintains that he spent ten years with Castell,[221] which would imply that he stayed almost until the final publication in 1669. On 27 March 1659 Castell reported to Clarke that Murray was his only assistant, but by 21 November of that year he had five working (besides himself and Huish), and on 4 April 1661 he says:

I have had not so fewe as 10. or 12. assistants, homeborn or forrainers, some of very excellent parts & polyglottique learning, especially in some one of the Languages, who have consumed mee great summes of mony, & stood me in very little stead, less than you can wel imagine, makinge this crushing, heavy ponderous burden upon mee, only their play & recreation.[222]

Clearly these assistants were not all working at the same time. Some of them can be identified. We have already noticed that Bernard was invited to join, but refused. In the preface to the lexicon Castell mentions, besides Murray, William Beveridge as helping him with the

---

[217] Mayor, *Cambridge under Queen Anne*, 492; MS BL Add. 22905, fo. 22 (23 Dec. 1658).

[218] Castell, who makes no mention of him whatever in the preface to the *Lexicon*, told Lightfoot on 22 Feb. 1664 that both his original partners had been taken away by other offers (MS BL Lansdowne 1055, f. 50; Lightfoot, *Correspondence*, 366–7).

[219] MS BL Add. 22905, fo. 20.

[220] He is mentioned as still being in London on 9 May 1665 in the letter from Caesar Calandrinus to Golius, MS CUL Dd.6.4, p. 404.

[221] Moller, *Cimbria Literata*, ii. 565.

[222] MS BL Add. 22905, fo. 48.

Syriac and J. M. Wansleben with the Ethiopic. In a draft of a letter to Beveridge of 4 February 1662, Castell complains about having to advance him money and about his shoddy work, 'in regard after you have done I am fain to examine al you do & continually find many omissions'.[223] The best information I have about the participation of Wansleben (or Wansleb) occurs in a letter from Robert Huntington to John Covel (then chaplain at Constantinople, where he had met Wansleben) of 19 October 1674: 'Wansleben is a German the sonne of a Minister in or neare Erfurt, formerly employd by Dr Castell for 2 or 3 yeares in looking after the Æthiopick part of his Lexicon.'[224] Wansleben was certainly in London in 1661, when he supervised the printing of Ludolf's Ethiopic lexicon (on which see below). The period of his stay might be fixed more precisely if we could determine the date of the brawl that he had with another of Castell's assistants, Theodorus Petraeus, which is recounted by Moller, who got the story from Job Ludolf. Some of Petraeus' Ethiopic manuscripts had been stolen, and had 'come into the hands' of Wansleben, who was engaged in copying them when Petraeus found out and forcibly removed them.[225] After returning to Germany Wansleben was sent to Egypt by Duke Ernst of Saxe-Gotha, but converted to Catholicism, became a Dominican, and collected manuscripts on behalf of the French minister Colbert.[226] Petraeus, who came from Schleswig-Holstein, was · in England in November 1659[227] and again in 1661. He was interested in Ethiopic and also in Coptic.[228] His work on Castell's lexicon may belong to either or both periods. On 9 September 1661 Worthington wrote to Hartlib that 'Petræus and some others that were engaged by him [Castell] to assist, were forced to desist, as being unable to endure such Herculean labours'.[229]

That, no doubt, was the reason alleged by Castell. However, the torrent of whining complaints running through the many letters of Castell that survive from the twelve years of his labours on the lexicon

---

[223] MS CUL Dd.6.4, fo. 211.

[224] MS BL Add. 22910, fo. 79. Huntington thoroughly despised Wansleben on account of his conversion to Catholicism.

[225] Moller, *Cimbria Literata*, i. 491, quoted by Rahlfs, 'Nissel und Petraeus', 301, who dates the incident to the summer of 1661.

[226] See above, p. 34, and Hamilton, 'The English Interest in the Arabic-Speaking Christians', 40 and 51–2, for Wansleben's book on the history of the Copts.

[227] Castell to Clarke, MS BL 22905, fo. 35.

[228] See Rahlfs, 'Nissel und Petraeus', for a good account of his life and his pioneering efforts in Ethiopic printing.

[229] Worthington, *Correspondence*, ii/1, 21.

makes it clear that Castell, unlike Walton, was a very bad manager. We may suspect that one reason why the project took so long, and why his assistants refused to stay, is that he insisted on redoing all their work himself. His unsuitability to direct a project of this kind appears most glaringly in his mismanagement of the finances. The plan was that the advance subscriptions would cover the expenses of running the press and also the pay of the supervisors,[230] and presumably the original subscription price of 50 shillings was calculated on the assumption that the work would be completed within a few years. It seems that the presses were set to work almost immediately, which meant that the typesetters and other workmen had to be paid. But the delays caused by Clarke's withdrawal and Castell's indecisions, combined with a paucity of subscribers and defalcations by some who had subscribed, soon led to an empty treasury. There were other difficulties not of Castell's making. He reported indignantly to Clarke on 17 November 1658 that 'Dr Walton yesterday made a strange motion to mee, not desiring it of mee by consent, but imperiously requiring it, that because the letters & presses, were his, after we had printed our ful number of every sheet, hee would likewise buy paper & pay workmen to print off so many sheets of our Lexicon for him, as he has Copies of his bible by him'.[231] Walton continued to press this demand for 250 free copies even after Roycroft bought the presses and types from him, but fortunately for Castell Walton died before anything of substance issued from the press.

Castell tried various solutions to his problems. He hired additional assistants in an effort to speed up the work, but, as we have seen, these were often unsatisfactory to him, and furthermore had to be paid. He tried to drum up more subscriptions with the help of powerful friends. In 1660 the newly restored King sent a letter recommending the work to the episcopacy, peerage, and others, and in 1663 Archbishop Sheldon sent a similar letter of recommendation to all the bishops.[232] However, these appeals produced only £700, most of it collected by the efforts of Seth Ward, Bishop of Salisbury, and far less than the amount Castell had already spent from his own funds. Castell also tried to manage the use of the presses better. After the withdrawal of

---

[230] MS CUL Dd.6.4, fo. 231 is a note of Huish's consent that Castell and Clarke should pay themselves £100 a year out of the 'Treasury' as long as they were working on the lexicon.

[231] MS BL Add. 22905, fo. 20.

[232] These letters are printed in the preface to the lexicon. Cf. Todd, *Life of Walton*, i. 173.

Clarke and Huish, the printer Roycroft agreed to become a partner with Castell in the enterprise. Castell realized that he had made a mistake in printing the work as it became ready for the press; for the slow progress tied up the presses, which became unavailable for other work. The first volume (lacking the preface and other introductory material, and the Persian lexicon) was finished, probably in 1661, and sent to the subscribers.[233] Worthington explained Castell's change of plan for the second volume to Hartlib on 3 February 1662:

> The second volume of the Lexicon Polyglotton is not yet in the press, nor will it be begun till they have prepared the whole. . . . They found the inconvenience of undertaking to print the first volume of the Lexicon before they had wholly prepared it for the press, which made the press sometimes to stand, and yet the workmen must be paid, else they would hardly be kept together, so that by this means the work was more chargeable.[234]

While the presses were waiting for the completion of the volume, Castell and Roycroft tried to put them to good use and profit by printing other books. Thus in 1661 they printed the Ethiopic lexicon of Job Ludolf, which Wansleben supervised. It is possible that they intended to publish something in the same year for Petraeus, since he came to London then, and Roycroft had printed for him a specimen page containing the first Psalm in Coptic, Arabic, and Latin two years earlier.[235] At this time, however, there was no Coptic type available in England, and the Coptic had to be printed with Greek types. But on the specimen sheet the intention of printing the whole Coptic Psalter, with Coptic types, is expressed.[236]

Despite these efforts, the enterprise was running at a loss, and on 30 September 1663 Castell told Clarke that Roycroft had withdrawn as a partner. In the same letter he said: 'So I am now selling the very last part of my estate, with no smal regret, so very convenient a patrimony convayed to mee from my Auncestors, as far as the bignes of it, I know not the like in Essex, all for want of Subscriptions.'[237] He had

---

[233] Thomas Smith quotes from it on p. 99 of *De Chaldaicis Paraphrastis* (1663), and Lightfoot had ordered a copy before 22 Feb. 1664 (Lightfoot, *Correspondence*, 366).

[234] Worthington, *Correspondence*, ii/1, 104.

[235] The possibly unique example of this is in Sion College library, ARC A 10.1s, *Psalmus Primus Davidis*, a single sheet 'Typis Thomae Roycroft', 1659. The date is confirmed by a mention in a letter from Castell to Clarke of 21 Nov. 1659 (MS BL Add. 22905, fo. 35).

[236] 'subsequetur integrum Psalterium Copticum seu Ægyptiacum cum Versione Arabica et Latina, typis genuinis (faveat modo fortuna virtuti!) excudendum.'

[237] MS BL Add. 22905, fo. 57.

been subsidizing the publication for some years from his own funds, gradually selling off his landed property.[238] In the end Castell claimed that he had spent no less than £12,000 of his own money on the lexicon.[239] Nor was this his only misfortune. Three hundred copies of vol. I, together with some of Castell's books, were destroyed in the Great Fire of London in 1666. In July 1667 he was imprisoned for a short time, ironically for debts incurred by his deceased brother.[240] Even after the work was finally finished in 1669 he was left with a great part of the press run on his hands. In June 1673, as he wrote to a colleague at St John's College, he still had more than 1,000 copies.[241] This despite his appeals for help to bishops, to whom he had written almost a hundred letters, resulting in five subscriptions. Most of these copies were still in his possession at the time of his death in January 1686, for in his will, dated 24 October 1685, he bequeathed 100 copies of the lexicon to Henry Compton, Bishop of London, and 100 copies each to five of his relatives.[242] A sad epilogue is recounted by Nichols in his *Literary Anecdotes*:[243]

It is supposed, that about five hundred of his Lexicons were unsold at the time of his death. These were placed by Mrs. Crisp, Dr. Castell's niece and executrix, in a room of one of her tenant's houses at Martin, in Surrey, where, for many years, they lay at the mercy of the rats, who made such havock among them, that when they came into the possession of this lady's executors, scarcely one complete volume could be formed out of the remainder, and the whole load of learned rags sold only for seven pounds.

It is not easy for one who has read Castell's letters from the years during which he worked on the lexicon, almost every one of which is filled with self-pity and complaints, to sustain the sympathy which has often been expressed for his devotion to scholarship. Furthermore, this did not go entirely unrewarded. He was made a royal chaplain in 1665, and given a prebend at Canterbury (with dispensation from attendance) in 1667. In addition he was made Professor of Arabic at Cambridge,

---

[238] As early as 21 Nov. 1659 he had told Clarke that he was borrowing money (ibid., fo. 35), and in Dec. 1660 he wrote to Worthington that he had been forced to sell property worth £20 per annum, and expected to be reduced to selling off his whole patrimony unless subscriptions improved (Worthington, *Correspondence*, i. 243–4).

[239] Letter to Clarke quoted by Mayor, *Cambridge under Queen Anne*, 493. Cf. Castell to Lightfoot, 24 Oct. 1670 (Lightfoot, *Correspondence*, 399–400).

[240] Letter to Lightfoot of 5 Aug. 1667 (ibid. 382–4).

[241] MS BL Add. 22905, fo. 97.

[242] PRO PROB 11,382 no. 2, fo. 15ᵛ. Cf. Norris, 'Professor Edmund Castell, Orientalist and Divine', 155–8.

[243] iv. 27.

although characteristically he complained to Clarke in 1667: 'My Arabique office in Cambridge is equally damagable to mee as tis beneficial, & wilbe to mee rather more chargable whilst I am upon this publique work.'[244] Nevertheless, the ravages caused by his devotion to his task, both to his estate and to his person, especially to his eyesight,[245] were real enough. One cannot help admiring the determination which brought the work to completion after so many years, even if much of the delay was due to Castell's own ineptitude. Unfortunately, it is difficult to claim that the result justifies the enormous expenditures of labour and money. Rather, the project as a whole was misconceived. The decision to follow Schindler's outdated book in grouping the six principal languages together under the Hebrew roots was a disastrous one. A 'comparative Semitic lexicon' has some use today, when we have a better understanding of the relationships of the different languages, but in the seventeenth century, when the conviction that all were descended from the 'mother' Hebrew held sway, could only lead to confusion and error. To attempt to use the *Lexicon Heptaglotton* for any one of the six related languages is an exercise in patience, if not frustration. This was evident to many of Castell's knowledgeable contemporaries even before the work was published. As early as 7 March 1659, Castell told Clarke that 'Mr Cromeholm, Mr Wood, Mr Litleton etc the best Arabitians heer I know & many others, wisht mee by al means to chang the Method described in our Specimen, & to place al the Languages by themselves',[246] but of course he refused. Thus although the lexicon allegedly took in everything that was in Golius' Arabic lexicon, and more besides, it never replaced the Golius. The work as presented by Castell was useless as a practical aid for the student reading the Polyglot Bible or any other text. It contained much of value, but this had to be extracted from it with considerable pain. That was in fact done for Syriac by one of the foremost eighteenth-century biblical scholars, J. D. Michaelis.[247] Nevertheless, the failure

[244] MS BL Add. 22905, fo. 62. Cf. his remark in the preface to the lexicon: 'munus aliud (in quo laboris multum, emolumenti vix quidquam) quod mihi demandatum est in Academia Cantabrigiensi'.

[245] In the preface to the lexicon he refers to 'Oculorum lumen, perpetuis atque indefessis vigiliis tantùm non ademptum', and that he was indeed virtually blind towards the end of his life is indicated by letters written by an amanuensis and signed very painfully by Castell in 1684 and 1685 (MS BL Add. 22905, fos. 99, 101).

[246] Ibid., fo. 27. 'heer' is London: Cromeholm was Master of St Paul's School, Littleton second master at Westminster School (see below); I have not identified 'Mr Wood'.

[247] *Edmundi CASTELLI Lexicon Syriacum ex eius lexico heptaglotto seorsim typis*

of the lexicon to attract a sufficient number of subscribers cannot be ascribed solely, or even mainly, to its scholarly deficiencies. The number of those willing to buy a sacred text such as the Polyglot Bible was far greater than the number of those who would actually try to read the exotic languages in it, and it was to those readers that the lexicon was primarily directed. Even so, had it appeared with or immediately after the Polyglot, as was originally intended, its chances would have been better. Castell's delays brought the publication into the period when interest and respect for oriental studies in England was already declining, especially among the clergy to whom his appeals for support were directed.

(X) ARABIC AT WESTMINSTER SCHOOL

One of the most remarkable features of the study of Arabic in seventeenth-century England is that it became part of the curriculum in a grammar school, namely Westminster School. This was due entirely to the enthusiasm of one man, Richard Busby, whose long reign as headmaster of Westminster began in 1638. There is a passage of Evelyn's *Diary* which has often been cited in this connection. On 13 May 1661 he records:

I heard, & saw such Exercises at the Election of *Scholars* at *Westminster Schoole* to be sent to the Universitie, both in *Lat: Gr: & Heb: Arabic* &c in Theames & extemporary Verses, as wonderfully astonish'd me, in such young striplings, with that readinesse, & witt, some of them not above 12 or 13 years of age: & pitty it is, that what they attaine here so ripely, they either not retaine, or improve more considerably, when they come to be men: though many of them do.[248]

Hebrew had long been established at Westminster School, having flourished there since Lancelot Andrewes was Dean of Westminster early in the century. Busby had evidently decided to embellish the curriculum by introducing Arabic as well. Almost all the evidence relating to Arabic at Westminster School, like Evelyn's above, comes from after the Restoration. For instance Castell wrote to Clarke on 17 · July 1667:

describi curavit atque sua adnotata adiecit Joannes David Michaelis (Pars 1–2; Göttingen, 1788).

[248] Evelyn, *Diary*, iii. 287–8. The election to places at Christ Church was conducted at Westminster. Fell, as Dean of Christ Church, was present on this occasion.

I also send you som papers from Dr Busby who presents his kind respects to you, desires the cast of your eye, & your most exact censure, alteration & emendation of the Hebr. Chaldee, Arabique etc. papers which he sends you; as also that you would with his service present them to Dr Pococke (to whom also I beseech you my most humble service) I had writ to him, & so had the Dr but not knowing his condition, wee feared least they might com unseasonably to him. Our request is, that he also would be pleased to doe the like with you, to read, censure, etc with as much severity as may be. After this expectation Dr Busby do's excuse you from that trouble he requested of you for the translating those parts you promised.[249]

The earliest specific evidence that I have seen comes from Hoole's book of 1660 (written 1659): 'it is no small ornament, and commendation to a Schoole, (as *Westminster*-Schoole at present can evidence) that Scholars are able to make Orations and Verses in Hebrew, Arabick, or other Oriental Tongues, to the amazement of most of their hearers, who are angry at their own ignorance'.[250] The interest of Hoole and Evelyn in these public demonstrations of Hebrew and Arabic learning by Westminster boys just before and after the Restoration suggests that they began at about that time, and this may reflect the excitement aroused in London by the publication of the Polyglot Bible in the 1650s.[251] When Busby himself began to be interested in Arabic,[252] and when it began to be taught at Westminster, cannot be determined. However, since those alumni of Westminster who showed an interest in Arabic at Oxford were at the school in the 1650s (for instance Henry Stubbe and George Hooper[253]) or the 1660s (Humphrey Prideaux), one might conjecture that it did not pre-date the 1650s as an element in the curriculum. In 1659 Hoole talks of the 'excellent Improvement that noble-spirited Mr. *Busbie* hath of late

[249] MS Rawl. D. 317A, fo. 17ʳ. The passage is quoted by Holt from Baker's transcript at Cambridge in *A Seventeenth-Century Defender of Islam*, 11–12. Holt assumes that the 'papers' were compositions by Westminster boys, but I think it more likely that they had been written by Busby himself.

[250] Hoole, *New Discovery Of the old Art of Teaching Schoole*, 194.

[251] Busby was one of those whose advice Castell sought concerning the proper way to proceed with the *Lexicon Heptaglotton*, as appears from his letters to Clarke of 5 Aug. and 23 Dec. 1658 (MS BL Add. 22905, fos. 15, 22).

[252] Russell, 'The Philosophus Autodidactus', 236–7 suggests that it goes back to his attending Pasor's lectures on Arabic at Oxford. However, this seems unlikely, since, as we have seen, Pasor stopped lecturing on Arabic in 1627, and Busby did not become BA until 1628.

[253] On Stubbe see above, p. 223, where we remarked that there is no evidence that he actually knew Arabic. Hooper, who was at Westminster from 1652 to 1657, certainly learned Arabic there, since the Arabic and Hebrew grammars he used then survive at Wells (Marshall, *George Hooper*, 2).

made at *Westminster* Schoole, where the Easterne Languages are now become familiar to the highest sort of Scholars'.[254] Busby's teaching of Arabic seems to have been one of the points of contention between him and Edward Bagshaw, who was second master at Westminster from 1656 to 1658, and said that Arabic was valueless.[255] Bagshaw's successor as second master, Adam Littleton, was named by Castell as one of the best Arabists in London in 1659. He had himself been taught by Busby at Westminster, and was elected a Student at Christ Church, but was ejected by the Visitors,[256] and then appointed by Busby as an usher at the school. Presumably both Busby and Littleton (who stayed only until 1661) were responsible for teaching Arabic, but there is not much evidence concerning either what they taught or to whom. It seems clear that not every Westminster boy learned Arabic. The boast in a contemporary Latin elegiac poem in praise of Westminster School that 'the boy who had entered here as an Englishman goes out as an Arab'[257] must be taken as a pardonable exaggeration. As we saw, Hoole says only that at Westminster the eastern languages were taught 'to the highest sort of Scholars'. William Taswell, who was at Westminster from 1660 to 1670, and was later appointed Busby Lecturer in Hebrew at Christ Church, makes no mention in his *Autobiography* of learning Arabic, although he gives a fairly full account of his education at Westminster and praises Busby's teaching. Nor is there anything to show that John Locke, who was a King's Scholar at Westminster and took part in the Westminster 'election' to Christ Church in 1652, ever knew Arabic at all.[258]

As far as the content of Busby's Arabic teaching is concerned, it must necessarily have been centred on grammar. Busby himself is supposed to have composed an Arabic grammar, but unlike his Greek grammar this has not survived.[259] However, Busby's strong interest in Arabic grammar is amply demonstrated by his library, still preserved as

---

[254] Hoole, *New Discovery Of the old Art of Teaching Schoole*, 220.

[255] According to Sargeaunt, *Annals of Westminster School*, 86 (no source given).

[256] On Littleton see Nichols, *Literary Anecdotes*, ii. 58–60, who says that he 'was also well skilled in the Oriental languages, and in Rabbinical learning; in prosecution of which he exhausted great part of his fortune, in purchasing books and manuscripts from all parts of Europe, Asia, and Africa. Some time before his death, he made a small essay towards facilitating the knowledge of the Hebrew, Chaldee, and Arabic tongues; which, if he had had time, he would have brought into a narrower compass.'

[257] 'Qui puer huc Anglus venerat, exit Arabs': MS Rawlinson D. 1111, fo. 56ᵛ.

[258] Russell, '*The Philosophus Autodidactus*', 236–8, assumes that he must have learned Arabic simply because he was a scholar at Westminster. Yet, as she herself notes (258 n. 57), at the election he gave orations only in Latin and Hebrew.

[259] See Sargeaunt, *Annals of Westminster School*, 116.

a separate entity at Westminster School. This contains every edition of Erpenius' or Erpenius' and Golius' Arabic grammars and reading-books published in Busby's lifetime, as well as Golius' Arabic lexicon and the dictionaries of Raphelengius and Giggei. However, there are many more Arabic items, including not merely grammars such as Ravius' *Generall Grammer*, Metoscita's *Institutiones Linguae Arabicae*,[260] and Obicini's *Grammatica arabica Agrumia appellata*,[261] but several items from the Medicean Press,[262] and a number of scholarly works. The latter include the Elichmann–Salmasius edition of the *Tabula Cebetis*, Pococke's *Specimen*, and nearly all of Pococke's other Arabic works. Busby kept up his interest in such material to the end of his long life, as is evidenced by the presence of Hyde's *De Ludis Orientalibus* of 1694, the year before Busby's death. Several of the Arabic books in the collection were once owned by John Pell,[263] who was given lodging by Busby during his financial difficulties in the 1670s and 1680s. These include a copy of Pococke's translation of Grotius containing the Arabic text only, which is the subject of a letter from Prideaux to Pell (then staying at Westminster) on 17 August 1674.[264]

The significance of the teaching of Arabic at Westminster does not lie in its effect on the development of Arabic studies. Those Westminster alumni who are known to have pursued the language after leaving were few, and the only one of them who left any mark in the field was Prideaux, whose *Life of Mahomet* reflects little credit on either Westminster or Oxford. As an element in the curriculum of the school it did not outlast Busby, and perhaps did not endure very long even under his iron rule. Rather, that Arabic was taught in at least one English grammar school[265] during the 1650s and 1660s is a reflection of the high regard in which the study of the language was held at the time among educated men both within and outside the universities. However, this estimation of its value was soon to change.

---

[260] Rome, 1624 (Schnurrer no. 59).   [261] Rome, 1631 (Schnurrer no. 63).

[262] The *Alphabetum Arabicum* of 1591–2, the Gospels in Arabic of 1591, the Euclid of 1594, and Raimondi's edition of the *Liber Tasriphi* (1610).

[263] In Westminster School library there is a handwritten catalogue of the books owned by Pell, most of which he gave to Busby. The latest publication date in this catalogue is 1683, the year before Pell died.

[264] The letter, which concerns the meaning of the marginal numerals in that edition, is also preserved in the school library.

[265] Although I know of no evidence that it was taught at any other school, it is worth recording that in the 1650s Cromeholme, Master of St Paul's School, and John Boncle, Fellow of Eton, were considered competent Arabists. On the latter see Katz, *Philo-Semitism*, 209 with n. 62. Boncle was among those whom Wheelock wished to judge his version of the Koran (Hartlib Papers 33/4/3).

9

The Decline of Arabic Studies in England

WE noted at the beginning of the previous chapter that soon after the Restoration a decline in the esteem for Arabic studies set in. Twells remarks on what he calls 'this change in the public taste' with reference to the contrast between the enthusiastic reception accorded to Pococke's *Specimen* in 1650 and the indifference with which his publication of the complete *Abū 'l-Faraj* in 1663 was greeted. Pococke dedicated the historical appendix to this work to Gilbert Sheldon (then Bishop of London, soon to be Archbishop of Canterbury), in gratitude for his help with the restitution of the privileges connected with the Hebrew Professorship. When Pococke presented him with a copy of the *Abū 'l-Faraj* Sheldon merely asked 'if there were any remarkable passages in it', obviously not intending to do more than glance at those. Sheldon was not the boor that this question might suggest, but rather a cultured man, who was to become a great patron of Oxford University. Pococke, taken aback by this reception of a book which he rightly considered a major contribution to historical knowledge, simply replied 'that I thought there were many'. Later, writing to Thomas Greaves about the incident, he asked him to point out some particular passages to Sheldon, and to do his best to publicize the book, adding: 'for I perceive it will be much slighted; the genius of the times, as for these studies, is much altered since you and I first set about them; and few will be persuaded they are worthy taking notice of.' Greaves agreed with him about the unfashionableness of Arabic studies, telling him that 'in these parts . . . they are not much followed or regarded, and receive small encouragement from those, who, I thought, would have been fautors and promoters of them'. Twells percipiently observes that this decline in public esteem for Arabic was not confined to England, citing a letter written by Bernard from Holland in 1669, relating to Pococke the sad state of affairs there too.[1] The reasons for this decline in public interest and support for Arabic studies, in

---

[1] Twells, 254–6.

England and in Europe generally, will be discussed in the final chapter. It inevitably affected those scholars working in the field, at both Oxford and Cambridge.

(I) CAMBRIDGE FROM 1680 TO 1700

The situation at Cambridge may be treated briefly, since almost nothing of interest happened there after the permanent establishment of the Professorship of Arabic. Castell remained in that post until his death in 1686, and after the publication of his Heptaglot Lexicon in 1669 no doubt delivered the required lectures, but these were soon so poorly attended that as a joke Castell once put up the following announcement of his forthcoming lecture: 'Arabicae Linguae Praelector cras ibit in desertum.'[2] He published nothing after the Heptaglot, devoting most of his energies to disposing of the copies left on his hands. As we saw, his efforts to acquire Golius' manuscripts for Cambridge met with no success. His successor as Arabic Professor, John Luke, who occupied the chair until 1702, was a man of education and intellectual curiosity, as is shown by the travel diaries which he kept while chaplain of the Levant Company at Smyrna in the 1660s and again from 1676 to 1682, which incidentally reveal his skill in the local languages.[3] However, as Arabic Professor he distinguished himself by publishing nothing except 'a poem in rather strange Ottoman Turkish' in the volume *Genethliacon* issued at Cambridge in 1688 to celebrate the birth of the future Old Pretender.[4]

This volume incidentally reveals that by that date types were available at Cambridge for printing Arabic. These first appear in John Spencer's *De Legibus Hebraeorum*.[5] That learned work, of great significance for Hebrew scholarship in England, is apart from its typography of little consequence for Arabic, since it contains only a few short quotations in that language, from well-known printed works such as Pococke's *Abū 'l-Faraj* and Bochart's *Hierozoicon*. Although it was not finally published until 1685, the first two books were printed (by John Hayes, the University Printer) in 1683 and the third in 1684.

---

[2] Twells, 214 (from Thomas Baker).

[3] The unpublished diaries are in MS BL Harley 7021, fos. 354 ff.

[4] Roper, 'Arabic Printing and Publishing in England', 20.

[5] This was first stated by Smitskamp in *Smitskamp Oriental Antiquarium Catalogue 592*, no. 296, and fully discussed, with reproductions of the Raphelengius types in Spencer's book, in his *Catalogue 594*, no. 375.

The use of Arabic type commences in the second book, where on
p. 237 the Raphelengian types, which had been lying unused in
Cambridge for more than fifty years, suddenly make their appearance.
On p. 431 they are abruptly replaced by the Selden Arabic types,
which are used consistently from then on (except for a stray
Raphelengian *kāf* on p. 552). These Selden types, which had somehow
migrated from London to Cambridge after nearly forty years of disuse,
were employed thenceforward at Cambridge for occasional printing of
short pieces of Arabic (e.g. in Ockley's *Introductio ad Linguas
Orientales* of 1706) until the university finally acquired a fount of the
Caslon Arabic in the 1730s.[6] The Raphelengius types which Bedwell
had spent so much money and effort in acquiring seem to have been
finally discarded at this time by an ungrateful university. No Arabic
text of any substance was published at Cambridge in the seventeenth
century or for many years thereafter. The university did at last find in
Simon Ockley a worthy occupant of the Arabic chair, but this belongs
to the history of the eighteenth century.

(II) THE LAST TWO DECADES OF POCOCKE'S CAREER

At Oxford, as we have seen, the dozen years or so following the
Restoration witnessed remarkable activity in oriental and particularly
Arabic studies. However, the rest of the century, although far from
barren in this respect, presents for the most part a history of unfulfilled
plans and promises. In particular Pococke, although he lived until
1691, published no Arabic texts (apart from his own Arabic translation
of parts of the Prayer Book) after the *Philosophus Autodidactus* of
1671. Twells indeed says that he contemplated publication of his
edition and translation of al-Maydānī's Proverbs in 1673, but the fact
seems to be that he had abandoned interest in it, and that it was
Bernard who was projecting an edition at this time, for which he
intended to enlarge Pococke's collections. For in a letter to Boyle of
13 May 1673, Bernard says that he is sending a specimen of the
Arabic proverbs, issued by the publisher Robert Scott, which would be
published, preferably with a Latin translation and commentary for

---

[6] For details see Roper, 'Arabic Printing and Publishing in England', 20, who, however, fails to recognize the identity of the Cambridge types with those of Selden.
Cursory examination of Ockley's Arabic poem in *Threnodia Academiae Cantabrigiensis*
(1700) suggests that a few supplementary types may have been cast, but the essential
identity with the Selden fount is beyond question.

students, if 100 subscribers could be found at Oxford, Castell already
having promised that many at Cambridge.[7] Whether through a lack of
subscribers or for some other reason, this was one of the many projects
of Bernard's which remained uncompleted in manuscript.[8] There was
another Arabic text, however, which Pococke did make a serious effort
to get published. This was an abridgement of the book on the wonders
of Egypt by 'Abd al-Laṭīf al-Baghdādī, composed in the early thirteenth
century, of which Pococke possessed the unique copy, in the author's
autograph.[9] With his unerring eye for such things, Pococke had seen
the interest of a medieval eyewitness account of the animals, plants,
monuments, and natural phenomena peculiar to that fascinating
country. He had owned the work at least since 1665, when he sent
Bochart a passage from it about the hippopotamus, to correct a passage
in his *Hierozoicon*; Bochart had quoted 'Abd al-Laṭīf in that work, but
only at second hand from al-Damīrī.[10] In the 1680s Pococke decided to
publish it, but once again, like the *Philosophus Autodidactus*, by the
hand of his son Edward, whom he was grooming to succeed him as
Arabic and Hebrew Professor. The younger Pococke completed a Latin
translation (no doubt carefully overseen by his father), and work was
begun on printing the text and translation at the University Press.
However, this was abandoned after some ninety pages of both text and
translation (about a third of the whole) had been printed. There are
conflicting accounts of the reason for this. In 1746 Thomas Hunt, who
had obtained the translation from the younger Pococke's son John
(with whom he had become acquainted while working on Twells's
reissue of Pococke's *Theological Works*), issued a proposal to publish
that translation together with the text and a commentary. In this he
says:

The *Latin translation* is the work of the reverend and learned Mr. *Edward*

[7] Boyle, *Works*, vi. 585. Twells, 290–1, evidently misunderstood letters of Castell to
Pococke on the matter. On the work, which Pococke had completed 37 years earlier, see
p. 124 above.

[8] Smith, *Life of Bernard*, 68, lists 'Proverbiorum Arabicorum, partim à D. Pocockio,
partim à se Latine versorum, Collectiones' among Bernard's aborted works. What
survives of it is now MS Bodl. Or. 573 (Nicoll–Pusey no. 348, p. 344).

[9] Now MS Poc. 230 (Uri no. 714, p. 174). See Stern, 'A Collection of Treatises by
'Abd al-Laṭīf al-Baghdādī', 56 (the whole article is valuable for its account of
al-Baghdādī's life and thought).

[10] Bochart to Clarke (MS BL Add. 22905, fo. 60): 'maximas habeo gratias viro prae-
stantissimo Domino Eduardo Pocockio pro insigni. illo loco de hippopotamo quem
propria manu ad me mittere dignatus est . . . Abdollatif historicus Bagdadensis, ex quo
locus ille excerptus est, etiam a me citatur . . . Sed post Damirem.'

Pocock, undertaken at the instance, and carried on under the direction of his father, the celebrated Dr. *Edward Pocock* . . . who brought the original manuscript out of the *East* with him. . . . Mr. Pocock had translated the book, and had begun to print his version, but his father dying, he laid aside the work, being discouraged from pursuing it any further by the disappointment he receiv'd in not succeeding him in the Hebrew-professorship.[11]

However, a very different reason had been entered by Hearne in his diary for 12 April 1706:

A Book in Arabick written by Abdollatiphi, containing a compendious History of Egypt was begun to be translated by Dr. Pocock and printed at the Theatre in Bishop Fell's time at the expense of Dr. Marshall Rector of Lincoln College, & was a pretty way advanc'd; but on a sudden the Bishop having an occasion for the Latin Letter the Book stop'd, which so vex'd the good old man Dr. Pocock that he could never be prevail'd to go on any farther. Neither would Dr. Hyde, tho' often desir'd by Dr. Aldrich when Vice-Chancellor, finish the same, unless somebody would give him a good sum of money for it; which was highly resented by the said Dr. Aldrich, who still offers to be at the Expense of finishing the Book.[12]

Although both of these accounts are second-hand, Hearne's is not only closer in time to the incident, but is almost certainly derived directly from Henry Aldrich, Fell's successor as Dean of Christ Church and in an excellent position to know the truth.[13] It also provides a clue to the year in which this happened, since Fell died in 1686 and Marshall in 1685. This is confirmed by a letter of Huntington to Pococke from late 1685 or early 1686, in which he says: 'I hear nothing of your son's Arabic History, which you once told me he had put into the press, with his Version of the same. If it be confined there, let me know what will bring it forth into the open air, and you shall have the money, as soon as you let me know the sum.'[14] So in 1685 at the latest, and probably a little earlier, a considerable part of the book was printed, and then the project was abandoned. Edward Pococke junior's disappointment did not occur until 1691, so it was not the reason for the interruption of the printing. At most it was the reason for his not taking the project

---

[11] 'Proposals For Printing Abdollatiphi', 5–6. There is a copy of this rare pamphlet among the Rawlinson MSS in the Bodleian: MS Rawl. letters 96, fos. 245–8.

[12] Hearne, *Diaries*, i. 224.

[13] The misattribution of the translation to the elder, rather than the younger Pococke is a mere technicality.

[14] Twells, 334. Twells then proceeds to give the same reason for the lack of completion as Hunt, namely the younger Pococke's disappointment at his failure to succeed his father in the Hebrew Professorship. No doubt he derived this version from John Pococke.

up again. However, there are difficulties with Hearne's account. The publication was intended, as we saw, to advance the younger Pococke's reputation. Why would his father allow his own pique against Fell to stand in the way of that? Furthermore, if he was so incensed at Fell, why did he dedicate his *Commentary on Hosea*, which was published in 1685 (hence after the alleged incident), to the bishop? We might conjecture rather that the death of Marshall, who was paying for the printing, interrupted the project. On the other hand, Pococke himself, who was not a poor man, could presumably have afforded to pay for the rest; and, as we have seen, Huntington offered to do so. The affair remains open to speculation.

There are also unanswered questions connected with Hyde's participation in later publication plans. According to Schnurrer, Hyde made a new Latin translation with a commentary, and even had some plates engraved, but his work vanished without trace.[15] This is partly confirmed by other sources, including Hyde himself. According to the accounts of the Oxford University Press, a four-page specimen of 'Dr. Hyde's History of Egypt' was typeset in 1693–4, and in the *Catalogus Librorum Impressorum* issued by the press in 1694 is the item 'Historiae Aegypti Compendium, Arab. Lat. per Tho. Hyde'.[16] The latter item was never published, and I know of no extant copy of the former. However, on 9 June 1701, in a letter to Humphrey Wanley, who had asked Hyde whether he had anything to contribute to a series of travel books which friends of his in London were thinking of publishing, he replied: 'I have by me a Latine translation of the naturall history of Egypt written by a learned physician Abdollatîph Bagdadensis. This I would willingly have printed in Arabick and Latine, with some short notes.'[17] In another letter written six days later he enlarges on this with information about the author and his book, and makes it clear that he will only undertake the publication if he can make some money from it, adding 'The translating the Book took me the best part of a year; and the correcting at the press, and adding some notes, will be the best part of another year, and therefore I am disposed rather to burn it, than to throw away any more time about it.'[18] Hyde makes no mention of the younger Pococke's translation

[15] Schnurrer, p. 150. I have not discovered whence Schnurrer derived this information.

[16] Carter, *History of Oxford University Press*, 423, who, however, has been led into inextricable confusion by identifying the work mentioned with the partially extant version of the younger Pococke.

[17] MS BL Harley 3779, fo. 366.

[18] MS BL Add. 4063, fo. 96, printed in Hyde, *Syntagma Dissertationum*, i, pp. xxx–xxxi.

and its partial printing, and in this he is being, to say the least, dis-ingenuous, for although it was never formally published, copies of the printed work were in the hands of individuals and libraries, including the Bodleian Library, of which Hyde had until recently been librarian.[19] Hyde must have seen the printed version, and certainly knew that Pococke's translation already existed, when he undertook his own trans-lation, since he could not have had access to the Arabic manuscript until it came to the Bodleian after the elder Pococke's death. He deliberately suppressed all mention of it in his correspondence with Wanley, and in his second letter went so far as to say 'The author was never known in this part of the world', which he must have known to be untrue.

The subsequent history of attempts, unsuccessful or only partially successful, to publish the work, up to Silvestre de Sacy's definitive translation (*Relation de l'Égypte par Abd al-Latif*, Paris, 1810), is well told by Schnurrer,[20] who was not aware, however, of the unpublished version of Benjamin Marshall in the early eighteenth century.[21] Hunt's proposal to publish the complete Pococke translation came to nothing, but the text, with some of Pococke's translation and the rest his own, was printed by Joseph White, Laudian Professor of Arabic, in his unsatisfactory edition of 1800.[22] Since its use by White the manuscript of Pococke's translation seems to have disappeared.[23]

Much of the elder Pococke's scholarly effort in the last fifteen years of his life was devoted to his commentaries on the minor prophets. In undertaking these he was to some extent bowing to the predilections of the times. In the preface to the *Commentary on Malachi*, addressed to his old friend Thomas Lamplugh (now Bishop of Exeter), he reveals

[19] The copy of Pococke's printed version in the library of the School of Oriental and African Studies is annotated at the top 'Editio rarissima Tho. Hyde', which is probably derived from the note in the Bodleian Library copy (transcribed by Carter, *History of Oxford University Press*, 423) which states that the book is very rare, that an edition was begun by Hyde, and that this version is by 'Pocock fil.' In the card catalogue (repro-duced as *Library Catalogue of the School of Oriental and African Studies*, Boston, 1963, 50) this has led (among other errors) to the book being misdescribed as Hyde's trans-lation.

[20] pp. 150–5.

[21] I know of this only from Tindal Hart, *William Lloyd*, 169, and have been unable to confirm that vague account. Benjamin Marshall, a competent Arabist, was Bishop Lloyd's nephew. According to Hearne, *Diaries*, i. 240 (5 May 1706), Marshall also intended to publish Pococke's edition of al-Maydānī, but abandoned it for lack of encouragement.

[22] Schnurrer no. 177.

[23] A slip pasted in MS Rawl. letters 96 states that 'The MS. of Ed. Pococke, jun., "Abdollatiphi Hist Ægypti compendium", has not been found in the Bodl. collections. G[eorge]. P[arker]. Feb. 1895.'

that Lamplugh had asked him to comment on 'some of the lesser Prophets'. I have no doubt that these commentaries grew out of an abortive plan of Fell's to publish an annotated English Bible at Oxford. The documents detailing this, from 1672, are printed by Madan.[24] Among those designated as contributors were Pococke, Marshall, and Marsh. The plan was to publish a single folio volume with a brief commentary 'rendring the mind of the Text, so as to be understood by the unlearned reader' and reinforcing 'the Orthodoxe truth'. The only thing resembling this that emerged from Fell's press was Obadiah Walker's *Paraphrase and Annotations upon the Epistles of St. Paul* of 1675.[25] It is probable enough that Pococke had undertaken the minor prophets as his contribution to the task,[26] and that when it became clear that the commentated Bible would never appear, he continued with the commentary, but in a way that suited his own taste. The remnant of the original plan is that Pococke's commentaries are in English, but in almost every other way it is so different from what Fell had in mind that Madan could declare confidently: 'The scale and style of the work make it impossible that it should be part of the Annotated Bible.'[27] Indeed, Fell's exhortations to 'be sparing in heaping vp diuerse readings' and in 'introducing original or exotick words' are completely ignored by Pococke, who has no hesitation in introducing quotations in Hebrew, Syriac, and Arabic in his discussion of the correct reading and meaning of the text. On the other hand, he does very little to 'enforce the meaning of such Texts, as establish the Orthodoxe truth', and perversely, one passage that might be said to do so, an appendix to the *Commentary on Malachi* refuting the claims of the Jews concerning the Messiah, the son of Joseph, of the tribe of Ephraim, is written not in English but in Latin. The principal concern of the commentaries is with the text and its meaning. Pococke used his profound knowledge of other oriental languages, including Arabic, and of the rabbinic commentaries (several of which were written in Arabic) to establish his conclusions. His tendency, in the main, is to defend the soundness of the generally received Hebrew text, and to justify (and occasionally improve) the English translation of it in the Authorized

---

[24] *Oxford Books*, iii. 413–15. Cf. Carter, *History of Oxford University Press*, 86–7.

[25] Madan, *Oxford Books*, iii, no. 3081.

[26] This was stated as a fact by his son Edward, who said that his father's commentaries grew out of that (Twells, 306). The doubts expressed by Twells and Madan (see below) are unjustified.

[27] *Oxford Books*, iii. 353.

Version.[28] But he often presents alternative interpretations, so that some readers complained that he tended to recite the opinions of others rather than pronounce a judgement of his own.[29]

There is a clue to Pococke's reason for choosing this form of publication in his later life in his dedication to Bishop Seth Ward in the *Commentary on Micah*, where he says: 'there is in it much stress laid on such part of Learning (the Orientall I mean,) which of late, if not all along, hath had that unhappiness, as to be scarce able to keep itself, not only from neglect, but contempt, as needless; at least of no great use or necessity.' Knowing from experience the difficulty of getting the kind of works published which he considered to be of serious interest, he acceded to the taste of the times by producing biblical commentaries instead. However, he was determined to demonstrate that even here oriental learning was useful and even necessary. The first two commentaries, on Micah and Malachi, both came out in 1677. That on Hosea (longer than the other three combined) followed in 1685, and the last, on Joel, in 1691, the year of his death. It is not clear whether he ever intended to continue with the other minor prophets.[30] The books enjoyed a modest success: the commentaries on Micah and Malachi were reprinted in 1692 (by which time the original runs of 500 copies must have been exhausted). A reprinting of all four commentaries formed the major part of the edition of Pococke's *Theological Works*, which Twells and John Pococke hoped would induce the public to buy the book (which had started out only as a biography of Edward Pococke).[31]

One other possible project of Pococke deserves mention. This was an edition of the original (Arabic) text of the great philosophical work of Maimonides, 'The Guide of the Perplexed'. The medieval Hebrew translation by Samuel ibn Tibbon, with the title מורה נבוכים, had long been known in Europe, and had been translated into Latin by the younger Buxtorf.[32] From a letter of Castell to Pococke in 1673 Twells

[28] In the *Commentary on Hosea* he cautiously says: 'to adjust that of our last deservedly approved translation with the original, I look on as my main business.' Twells, who quotes this (308 n.), interprets it to mean 'defend our authorized translation', which is a distortion of Pococke's meaning and procedure.

[29] Twells, 309, 336. Twells's discussion (328–36 and 306–9) of Pococke's procedures, especially with regard to alleged inconsistencies between the Septuagint and the Hebrew text, is valuable, if partial on the side of 'orthodoxy'.

[30] Madan, *Oxford Books*, iii. 353 calculated from the signatures in the commentaries on Micah and Malachi that Pococke in 1677 contemplated publishing about 1,500 folio pages in two volumes. That is half as much again as the four published commentaries contain, but is a slender basis on which to build any hypothesis.

[31] John Pococke to Thomas Rawlins, 20 Sept. 1734 (MS Ballard 28, fo. 25).

[32] Basel, 1629: *PO* no. 174.

inferred that the latter was then preparing 'something of . . .
Maimonides' More Nebochim, for the public'.[33] Since Judaeo-Arabic
was one of Pococke's lifelong interests, and since Twells couples this
with 'Rabbi Tanchum', another Jewish author who wrote in Arabic, we
may fairly conclude that Pococke was concerned with the Arabic text
of Maimonides' work, of which he possessed more than one manuscript, and from which he quoted extensively as early as the *Specimen*.
Furthermore, we have seen that among the books that Fell announced
that 'we purpose to print' in 1672 was 'Maimonides, More novochim,
as written by himself in Arab:'.[34] Twells thought that the project was
undertaken by Edward Pococke junior, but that is because he misdated
a letter of Locke to the elder Pococke mentioning a translation of
Maimonides by his son. Replying on 29 May 1680, Pococke says: 'He
had translated a piece of Maimonides, but there was that unhappines in
it that it was such that the Jew Abendana here had before translated
and made ready for the presse, how ever it be not yet printed. I shall
exhort him to set on some other having so good incouragement to it.'[35]
The reference to Isaac Abendana makes it certain that the piece
in question was part of Maimonides' *Mishneh Torah*, כלי בית המקדש
('Vessels of the Sanctuary'),[36] which is written in Hebrew. The
younger Pococke's Latin translation of Maimonides' Preface to the
Mishnah was published with Guise's *Zeraim* in 1690. It seems unlikely
that Pococke, knowing his son's limited powers in Arabic, would have
set him on producing an edition and translation of so long and difficult
a text as 'The Guide of the Perplexed'. In any case, there is no trace of
any edition by either Pococke. It is significant, however, that Hyde
presented a proposal to edit and translate the work. This is a four-page
leaflet, headed 'PROPONITUR *Maimonidis* More Nevochim *typis
mandandum Lingua Arabica, qua ab Authore primò scriptum est*'.
After explaining the reasons why the edition was desirable, including
the inaccuracies in Buxtorf's translation, which was in any case no
longer obtainable, Hyde presents a three-page specimen, with the
Arabic text (transcribed from the Hebrew characters of the manu-

[33] Twells, 290–1.
[34] See above, p. 231.
[35] Locke, *Correspondence*, ii. 185.
[36] Abendana mentioned that it was ready for the press in a letter to Bernard of Oct.
1673, published by Macray, 'A Letter from Isaac Abendana'. Previously Isaac Abendana
had produced a Latin translation of the Mishnah at Cambridge: see Abrahams, 'Isaac
Abendana's Cambridge Mishnah and Oxford Calendars', and Katz, 'The Abendana
Brothers and the Christian Hebraists of Seventeenth-Century England'.

script[37]), facing Latin translation, and notes at the bottom on both the Hebrew and Arabic versions. Although the pamphlet is not dated, the copy in the Bodleian is annotated on the first page by Hyde: 'Dec. 10, 1690'. He also informs us of its fate: 'This was offered to our Delegates, who refused to be at the charge of printing this work.'[38] The truth was not that the Delegates of the Press (who at this time still included the elder Pocoke) refused to print the work, but that they refused to pay Hyde for undertaking it. This is apparent from a letter of Hyde to Smith written six years later: 'I left for your view to take along with you a Specimen of Maimonides his *More Nevochim* which I offered to our Delegates to have don the whole work, but they would not allow anything for my paines, and so there is an end of that designe. for I would not labour 3 or 4 years for nothing.'[39] Perhaps Hyde never really intended to do the edition, but issued the prospectus as part of his campaign to succeed to the Arabic and Hebrew Professorships when it became apparent in 1690 that Pocoke could not live much longer, to demonstrate that he was capable of completing a scholarly edition which Pocoke had undertaken and abandoned. However, he was taken seriously by Bernard, who characteristically suggested making the edition even more unwieldy, laborious, and expensive by including the Hebrew translation as well.[40]

(III) THOMAS MARSHALL

Marshall had returned to Oxford permanently soon after he was elected Rector of Lincoln College in 1672. He had a working knowledge of Arabic, as is demonstrated by the appointment book he kept from November 1672 to April 1678,[41] in which he amused himself by writing the month names and year numbers in Arabic. His skill in Hebrew is shown by his correspondence with the Samaritans (which

[37] I do not know what manuscript Hyde was using, but under the circumstances it seems unlikely that it was one of Pocoke's. Possibly it was one of Huntington's copies (e.g. MS Huntington 162, Neubauer, *Hebrew Manuscripts*, no. 1237). In that case it would have been among the manuscripts donated to the Bodleian by Huntington between 1678 and 1683.

[38] Bodleian 4° M 13(2) Th. Cf. Carter, *History of Oxford University Press*, 415.

[39] MS Smith 50, p. 225.

[40] Smith to Bernard, 7 Feb. 1691: 'I wish with all my heart, that Dr Hyde were encouraged to publish Maimonides More in Arabick. I fully approve of your advice to print the Ebrew translation and Buxtorfs Latine with it columnatim' (MS Smith 57, p. 189).

[41] MS Marshall (Or.) 113.

will be dealt with below in connection with Huntington). However, his real interests lay in more exotic languages. We have already noticed his collaboration with Junius in the edition of the Gothic Gospels. While in Holland he had acquired an ancient manuscript of the Gospels in Coptic,[42] and intended to publish this. This was feasible, since the Oxford University Press had acquired Coptic types, partly through the agency of Marshall.[43] It was one of the items in the list of proposed publications announced by Fell in 1672,[44] and its publication is announced as imminent in the edition of Abudacnus' *Historia Jacobitarum* in 1675, but although Marshall lived another ten years after that he never completed it. In fact the only thing having to do with the Copts with which he is associated is that work of Abudacnus. This consists of a brief history of the Copts (the name 'Jacobites' being applied at that time to all Monophysite churches), with an account of their rites and their position in Ottoman Egypt. It is preceded by an anonymous preface by the Oxford editor of the work, who says something of Abudacnus (but nothing of his stay in Oxford more than sixty years earlier), and claims that Abudacnus had composed this work 'recently'. The origin of the work is mysterious, since the manuscript from which it was printed no longer exists, and it is not known how it got to Oxford. The suggestion that it had been composed by Abudacnus in Oxford in about 1612 and had been sitting there unnoticed until disinterred in 1674 seems utterly implausible. It is far more likely, as Hamilton suggests,[45] that Abudacnus had composed the work in Constantinople during the 1640s, and that it had been brought back from there by a visiting Englishman.[46] It is commonly accepted that the Oxford editor was Marshall, but although that is likely enough, given his interest in Coptic, I know of no contemporary evidence to confirm it.[47] The work, although a slight one, was an immediate success. It was translated into English, and republished more than once on the Continent in the eighteenth century.[48] Even more successful was

[42] He announced his purchase of the manuscript (which Petraeus and Thévenot had also wanted to buy) to Clarke on 29 Nov. 1668 (MS BL Add. 22905, fo. 85).

[43] More were acquired in 1686 from Nicholas Witsen through the agency of Bernard: Smith, *Life of Bernard*, 43–4.   [44] See above, p. 231.

[45] 'An Egyptian Traveller', 146.

[46] Compare the case of the notes of the Polish renegade and interpreter Albertus Bobovius (Bobowski) on various customs of the Turks, which had been brought back from Constantinople by Thomas Smith, and were later given by him to Hyde to publish together with his *Peritsol* (1691).

[47] Madan (*Oxford Books*, iii, no. 3041), who is usually knowledgeable about such matters, cites only *DNB* for Marshall's authorship of the preface.

[48] For details of all of this see Hamilton, 'An Egyptian Traveller', 147–50.

a publication by Marshall himself, which went through countless editions. However, this had nothing to do with his oriental studies, but consisted of notes on the Anglican Catechism which Marshall had composed at the suggestion of Fell.[49] Marshall's contribution to oriental studies was not in his own publications, but in acquiring manuscripts for others (as we have seen with respect to the Arabic Apollonius in 1668–9) and for himself. His manuscripts and many of his printed books were bequeathed to the Bodleian Library after his death in 1685. Although many of the 159 manuscripts were oriental, only nineteen were Arabic, and those of not much account.[50]

(IV) ROBERT HUNTINGTON

Huntington was considered by Pococke to be a promising Arabic scholar, and it was Pococke who persuaded him to apply for the post of chaplain at Aleppo in 1670.[51] No doubt he expected Huntington to pursue the same course there that he himself had followed forty years earlier, perfecting his knowledge of Arabic and other languages, and collecting manuscripts. Huntington, however, was of a vastly different temperament from his teacher, and also from his friend Thomas Smith. He enjoyed travelling to strange places, and was clearly fascinated by the countries of the East and the culture of their inhabitants. He stayed in his post eleven years, during which he managed to visit Jerusalem (several times), other parts of Palestine and Syria, Baalbek, Palmyra, Sinai, Constantinople, Egypt (twice), and Cyprus. This was not idle sightseeing. He was constantly on the look-out for manuscripts of interest to himself and his English correspondents (who included Pococke, Marshall, Bernard, Smith, and Marsh, as well as John Covel, his fellow chaplain at Constantinople). He was also interested in the exotic communities of the region. He visited the Samaritans at Sichem (modern Nablus) more than once, and initiated a correspondence

---

[49] Madan, *Oxford Books*, iii, no. 3216, with details of subsequent editions and the translation into Welsh.

[50] See Macray, *Annals*, 154 and Wakefield, 'Arabic Manuscripts in the Bodleian Library', 134.

[51] These details are given by Smith in the life of Huntington which he wrote at the request of his widow Mary Huntington (as for instance in her letter to Smith of 22 May 1702, MS Smith 50, p. 197). This was published with his *Life of Bernard* and a selection of Huntington's correspondence, and is still the most complete account of his life, although much could be added from the many letters of Huntington that survive in the Smith collection and elsewhere.

between them and England. The Mandaeans of Iraq were too remote for him to visit personally, but he obtained some of their books and information about them from Agathangelus a S. Theresia of the Carmelite mission at Basra. He was in communication with several other clerics in the region, most of them native Christians of various denominations, and derived both books and scholarly information from them. He must have become an expert linguist, at least in Arabic and Turkish, to accomplish what he did. His surviving letters[52] reveal his sharp eye, curiosity, and ironic wit, but also a diffidence concerning his own abilities and a constant self-deprecation. Even after he had returned to England, he declined requests to publish accounts of his travels, although these would surely have been of the greatest interest.[53] Writing to Smith in December 1698, he says: 'You invite me to publish some Observations on Egypt & Palestine. But I have few worthy the perusall of judicious men, which have not bin printed already: And it will be very improper I think to set forth a Discovery now, which was made above 20 years since.'[54]

Huntington manifested his interest in and concern for the Eastern Christians by disseminating Pococke's Arabic translations of Grotius, the Catechism, and the Book of Common Prayer, and Seaman's Turkish translation of the Catechism.[55] Twells seems to suggest that Huntington was one of those Englishmen who still hoped for union between the Greek Orthodox and Anglican churches,[56] but the following extract from a letter he wrote to Smith in April 1674, about a scene he had witnessed in Jerusalem, suggests a more detached attitude:

notwithstanding all the late pretence of a perfect agreement between the Greek Church and the Roman in reference to the H. Eucharist, yet is there certainly a most unchristian enmity amongst them; for to the scandall of our Religion,

[52] Those published by Smith with his *Life of Bernard* are concerned with scholarly matters and reveal little of the man. The letters to Pococke quoted or paraphrased by Twells are more characteristic; but it is the personal letters to his friends Bernard, Smith, and Covel which give the best sense of Huntington's character. These are unpublished, but one can get some idea of the style from the letter he wrote to John Locke soon after arriving in Aleppo (Locke, *Correspondence*, i. 352–3).

[53] As is apparent from his sole publication, the short account of 'the Porphyry Pillars in Egypt' which appeared in the *Philosophical Transactions* of 1684, no doubt through the efforts of Bernard.

[54] MS Smith 50, p. 195.

[55] On this see Madan, *Oxford Books*, iii, no. 2480, who dates it dubiously to 1660, and is unsure whether Seaman was the translator. It is dated to 1661 (1660 Old Style), and Seaman's authorship proved, by letters from Seaman to Clarke of February and March of that year concerning proofs of the book (MS BL Add. 22905, fos. 44, 45).

[56] e.g. 294–5.

the Fathers themselves fell together by the eares in the Church of the H.
Sepulcher, and upon no new account, but because the Latins accidentally made
use of th'others Ladder to addorn some places they judg'd convenient for the
Reception of the French Embassador. The Greekes were supplyed with
Cudgells flung down to them from their adjoyning Monastery, and being 8 or 9
to 4, may be suppos'd to have gott the Conquest, but it was with the losse of
one of their number, who dyed 5 dayes after, but not of any wounds he rec'd
in the scuffle; as both sides, recover'd of their phrensy, gave it in before the
Cady, who by vertue of the Embassadors presence & Authority gave an
Hodgiet accordingly, whereby they have escaped, for a while at least, a most
terrible and deserved Avania.[57]

Among the eminent Christian clerics with whom Huntington corresponded were the Maronite Patriarch of Mount Libanus, Estefān
al-Duwayhī[58] (whom he called 'Stephen Peter') and Johannes Lascaris,
Greek Orthodox Archbishop of Mount Sinai (whom he had met in
Cairo). Although his principal interest in maintaining this correspondence was to use their good offices in obtaining manuscripts, he had
other objectives too. For instance, in 1675 he sent Stephen Peter a
copy of Pococke's translation of Grotius and asked his opinion on
its usefulness to native Arabic speakers.[59] Writing to Fell on 24
November 1680 about his encounter with Johannes Lascaris, whom he
calls 'a Person Learned & Intelligent, beyond what I expected to find
amongst the Greeks', he says 'He was glad to find himself inform'd
by our Liturgy[60] (which I presented Him) & rectify'd concerning
th'Opinion . . . that there was no such as the Church of England, that
we had neither Bishops nor Priests, Sacraments nor Service.'[61]

Huntington became very interested in the Mandaeans, and was
responsible for some important information about them coming to
Europe.[62] He wrote enquiring about these 'Johannis-Christians' to
Angelus a S. Joseph,[63] then at the Carmelite mission in Basra, in 1677.
Hearing from him that this sect called themselves 'Sabaeans', he had
hopes of recovering from them the books of Thābit ibn Qurra and

[57] MS Smith 50, p. 187. A 'Hodgiet' is a judicial decision and an 'Avania' a fine
imposed by the Turkish authorities.
[58] On this man see Hamilton, 'The English Interest in the Arabic-Speaking
Christians', 46 with n. 51.
[59] 'Huntingtoni Epistolae' (in Smith, *Life of Bernard*), 3. Cf. letter of Stephen, 3 July
1675, ibid. 106–7.
[60] Presumably Pococke's Arabic translation of it.
[61] MS BL Add. 23206.
[62] This was published by Smith in his *Life of Huntington*, in the form of letters from
Angelus a S. Joseph and Agathangelus a S. Theresia.
[63] For his later public dispute with Hyde in the Bodleian Library see below, p. 296.

other ancient so-called Sabaeans which he knew about from Arabic bibliographical sources.[64] That was a chimera, but Huntington later received reliable information about the beliefs of the Mandaeans and their sacred books from another Carmelite missionary at Basra, Agathangelus a S. Theresia.[65] He returned to England before Agathangelus could comply with his request to get copies of these books, but he kept up the correspondence after his return, and in 1683 announced to Pococke that he had bought three of the sacred books and already received two of them, characteristically adding 'But to what purpose am I at all this expence, if none of you will make out the language?'[66]

Huntington's most famous achievement during his stay in the East was his initiation of the correspondence between the Samaritans and England. There had long been interest in Europe in the beliefs, practices, and books of the Samaritans, already almost confined to the small community at Sichem. Scaliger had sent that community a letter, but died before the reply arrived. We have seen how Ussher and others succeeded in acquiring copies of the Samaritan Pentateuch and other works, but there remained many unanswered questions about the ways in which they differed from the Jews. Pococke had asked Huntington to make enquiries on the subject, and accordingly in 1674, on his way to Jerusalem, he visited the Samaritan community at Sichem, hoping to get information and to acquire manuscripts. Twells gives the following account of what happened:

The Samaritans asked the Doctor if there were any Hebrews in his country, not meaning Jews, as he afterwards perceived, whom they hate, but Samaritans, to whom only they allow the name of Israelites and Hebrews: the doctor, supposing they asked about Jews, innocently answered in the affirmative; and at the same time, read some sentences out of their sacred books, and written in their own character. Hereupon they cried out with transports of joy, these are truly Israelites, and our dearest brethren. The Doctor took pains to undeceive them, affirming that the persons to whom his answer related were unquestionably Jews; but they hugged their mistake, and would by no means be set right. After this, the Doctor told them, that they would do well to send a book of their law, with an account of their religion, times of prayer, sacrifices, high priests, feasts, fasts, and all their books, from which it would certainly appear

---

[64] Letter of 18 July 1677, 'Huntingtoni Epistolae', 39–41.

[65] On Agathangelus see Gollancz, *Chronicle of Events relating to the Order of Carmelites in Mesopotamia*, which consists largely of the diary written by Agathangelus and continued by his successors. Agathangelus' letter of 28 Nov. 1681 to Huntington about the Mandaeans is printed in 'Huntingtoni Epistolae', 84.

[66] Twells, 326–7.

whether they were of the same faith or not. Accordingly they sent a copy of their law, and such letters as he described, which were transmitted to Dr. Marshal, Rector of Lincoln College in Oxford, and answered by him; and to this they again replied, the correspondence continuing many years.[67]

The contents of the correspondence and the history of its publication do not concern us here,[68] except to note that since some of the letters were in Arabic, they required Marshall's expertise in that language. Most, however, as Bernard remarks in his letter to Lightfoot of 5 March 1674 reporting Huntington's experience,[69] were written in Biblical Hebrew, as were Marshall's replies. There was some uneasiness at Oxford about fostering the hopes of the tiny community of Samaritans at Sichem that there was a large and prosperous population of their 'brothers' in England. Bernard told Lightfoot 'care is to be taken that we do not dissemble with them', but Marshall cannot be acquitted of deception in his replies. Although he does not claim to be a Samaritan or 'Hebrew' he does not disclaim it either, and his assurances that 'we' (i.e. the Anglican Church) had many beliefs in common with the Samaritans, but that the Messiah had already come, sorely puzzled his Samaritan readers. Although Bernard's Latin translation of the first letter of the Samaritans was eventually published by Job Ludolf,[70] most of the letters remained unpublished until 1831, when Silvestre de Sacy included those that could still be found with later correspondence initiated by the French.

Despite the excitement aroused by these events, Huntington's principal contribution to scholarship was his success in collecting oriental manuscripts. He was tireless in pursuit of items which Pococke requested him to find, and also acquired Coptic manuscripts in Egypt for Marshall. Some of Narcissus Marsh's manuscripts too came from Huntington,[71] although Marsh did not begin collecting seriously until after Huntington's return to England. However, Huntington also collected manuscripts on his own account on a grand scale. Since all of the above manuscript collections, as well as his own, eventually came to the Bodleian, there is no doubt that Huntington's efforts contributed

---

[67] Twells, 302–3.

[68] That can be found in the exemplary and definitive publication by Silvestre de Sacy, 'Correspondance des Samaritains de Naplouse'.

[69] MS BL Lansdowne 1055, fo. 122, printed in Lightfoot, *Correspondence*, 452–4.

[70] A manuscript version of Bernard's translation of some of these letters survives in the Bodleian (*SC* no. 15635).

[71] For examples see Wakefield, 'Arabic Manuscripts in the Bodleian Library', 145 n. 169.

more to the Bodleian oriental collections in general, and to the Arabic in particular, than any other individual's, at least as far as numbers are concerned. While he may have lacked Pococke's taste in selecting interesting authors, there are nevertheless several remarkable items among those manuscripts which he acquired, including autographs of Maimonides,[72] and some rare and early Arabic pieces.[73] Huntington donated some of his manuscripts to his own college, Merton, in 1673[74] and to the Bodleian in 1678, 1680, and 1683. But the great bulk, consisting of some 600 manuscripts, of which more than 200 are Hebrew and about 320 Arabic, was purchased by the university in 1692 for the enormous sum of nearly £1,100.[75]

By that time Huntington had obviously decided that he himself would never make any use of the manuscripts.[76] He had finally abandoned oriental studies, and indeed academic life, in August of that year, when he was granted the living of Great Hallingbury near Bishop's Stortford, and promptly married. Previously he had been Provost of Trinity College, Dublin, a post in which he reluctantly succeeded his friend Narcissus Marsh in 1683, and from which he had been driven for a while by the upheavals in Ireland during the Revolution of 1688. He now looked to the Church for advancement, but when, through the influence of his friend (now Archbishop) Marsh, he was offered the Irish bishopric of Kilmore in 1693 he refused, since it had become available only through the deprivation of the incumbent, Sheridan, for being a nonjuror. Huntington was finally elevated to the episcopacy in 1701, when he was consecrated Bishop of Raphoe (also an Irish see) by Archbishop Marsh in Dublin on 21 August. He died only twelve days later, and was buried in Trinity College chapel.

---

[72] MS Huntington 117 (part of Maimonides' commentary on the Mishnah; Pococke had long before acquired other parts of this autograph edition and used them for his *Porta Mosis*); also MS Huntington 80 (part of the *Mishneh Torah*): see Stern, 'Autographs of Maimonides in the Bodleian Library', 182, 191.

[73] For a brief summary of these see Wakefield, 'Arabic Manuscripts in the Bodleian Library', 135–6. For others (including the Mandaean books) see Macray, *Annals*, 161–3.

[74] Coxe, *Catalogue of College MSS*, i, Merton, 130–2; most of these are Hebrew.

[75] Philip, *The Bodleian Library in the Seventeenth and Eighteenth Centuries*, 60 and 125 n. 52. The figure of £700 given by Macray, *Annals*, 161 is erroneous.

[76] That he had intended to sell his manuscripts much earlier is indicated by a letter from Bernard to Boyle, undated but written in the early 1680s, since Huntington is said to have lately returned from the East, and is referred to as 'Mr', not 'Dr' (he became DD in 1683). Bernard hopes that the manuscripts will not be dispersed, but rather bought by 'any gentleman' that has 'a desire to advance the study of the oriental languages, which open to us the divine word' (Boyle, *Works*, vi. 585). Boyle did not take the hint, and for the time being the manuscripts remained in Huntington's possession.

(V) NARCISSUS MARSH

Marsh,[77] a contemporary and friend of Bernard, Smith, and Huntington, attended Pococke's Arabic lectures before the Restoration, and
remained on good terms with Pococke thereafter, as their correspondence quoted by Twells indicates. Marsh records that while still an
undergraduate (he entered Magdalen Hall in May 1655) 'I betook
myself seriously to the study of philosophy, mathematicks & oriental
languages'. He became a Fellow of Exeter College in 1658, and for the
next fifteen years pursued his scholarly interests at Oxford, despite
offers of ecclesiastical advancement. He published nothing in his own
name, but was entrusted by Fell with the partial revision and general
supervision of Beveridge's edition of the *Canons*.[78] He was also one of
the participants named by Fell in the abortive annotated Bible,[79] and
was responsible for the revision of Du Trieu's *Manuductio ad Logicam*
published by Fell's press in 1678.[80] However, in 1673, again through
the influence of Fell, Marsh entered on the career of an administrator
which was to occupy him for the rest of his life, and effectively put an
end to his scholarly career. After five years as Principal of St Alban's
Hall, Oxford, in which he was successful in reviving a declining institution, he was appointed Provost of Trinity College, Dublin in January
1679, where he was faced with a similar task. He found the 340 young
scholars there 'both rude and ignorant in this lewd and debauched
town'. Here too his success was rewarded with further advancement:
he was appointed Bishop of Leighlin and Fernes in 1683, and from
then on his career advanced steadily through the ranks of the Irish
ecclesiastical hierarchy, culminating in his appointment as Archbishop
of Armagh and Primate of all Ireland in 1702.

Although he undertook no further scholarly work after leaving
Oxford, Marsh maintained a keen interest in scientific and scholarly
matters, as is apparent from his correspondence with Bernard and
Pococke.[81] In the 1690s he decided to use some of the wealth which

[77] A valuable source for Marsh's life is the diary which he kept from 1690 to 1696,
preserved in the library of Trinity College, Dublin, and published by J. H. T. ('Archbishop Marsh's Diary'). Marsh preceded the actual diary with a summary of the chief
events in his life up to 1690.

[78] See above, p. 231. No doubt Fell had concerns about Beveridge's competence.

[79] See above, p. 276.

[80] Madan, *Oxford Books*, iii, no. 3173. Madan was unaware of Marsh's authorship,
which is recounted in his diary.

[81] MS Smith 45 contains several letters from Marsh to Bernard on astronomical
matters; for his letters to Pococke see especially Twells, 313–18.

his advancement had brought him to establish a 'benefaction' for his Alma Mater. He already owned a few oriental manuscripts, some of which had been given him by Huntington, others by the widow of William Guise,[82] but he began to collect in a sustained way in 1693. He had hoped to buy some of Huntington's manuscripts before he learned that Huntington had sold them to the university.[83] Instead, using Huntington as an intermediary, he commissioned William Hallifax to buy manuscripts for him at Aleppo.[84] Marsh confided in a letter to Bernard of 26 November 1695 that he hoped to assemble a good enough collection to befit a gift to Oxford: 'if I could get so many MSS of note together, as might be worth the giving, I might happily be inclin'd to bestow them where you desire; but then, I must have more and better than I am yet owner of before I can think them worth the giving.'[85] However, Hallifax was not lucky or energetic enough to find more than a few of the list that Marsh sent him, and I do not know whether his successor at Aleppo, Henry Maundrell, from whom Marsh requested the same service through Bernard and Smith, ever sent the archbishop anything.[86] Fortunately a splendid opportunity arose in 1696. Golius' heirs finally decided to put his manuscripts up to public auction at Leiden. Marsh, no doubt alerted to this by Bernard, commissioned him to bid on his behalf. He recorded in his diary for 16 September 1696: 'I returned £220 to Dr. Edw. Bernard of Oxford, who takes a journey into Holland, Friday the 18th, on purpose therewith to purchase the choicest of Jacobus Golius his oriental manuscripts that will be exposed to sale by auction at Leyden, on Oct. 6 next ensuing.'[87] Although this journey cost Bernard his life, he succeeded in securing the bulk of the manuscripts, including the most desirable items, for Marsh, and was happy to see them landed in England before

---

[82] Frances, stepdaughter of Dr Bury, Rector of Exeter, with whom Marsh stayed in 1689 when he fled Ireland during the troubles following the Revolution of 1688. Marsh's friendship with Guise himself is attested by Bernard (preface to Guise, *Zeraim*).

[83] Letter to Bernard of Feb. 1693 (MS Smith 45, p. 19).

[84] Hallifax's letter to Hyde and Bernard, 7 Dec. 1694 (MS Smith 45, p. 49). Hallifax was, like Pococke, a Fellow of Corpus Christi College who went as chaplain to Aleppo (1688–95). He is remembered chiefly for his explorations of Palmyra and his copies of Palmyrene inscriptions. Smith published these with his own and Bernard's emendations (*Inscriptiones Graecae Palmyrenorum*, Utrecht, 1698), to Hallifax's annoyance, who claimed that he could have done it better himself (letter to Smith of 17 Dec. 1698, MS Smith 50, p. 13).

[85] MS Smith 45, p. 24a.

[86] Bernard to Smith, 15 Jan. 1696 (MS Smith 47, fo. 188ʳ). In this letter Bernard tells Smith that Marsh's object is 'a benefaction like that of Archbishop Laud'.

[87] 'Archbishop Marsh's Diary', 132.

he died. In due course they were forwarded to Marsh in Dublin, who had now definitely decided, as he wrote to Smith on 4 May 1700, 'to leave all mine Oriental MSS. to the Bodleian Library when I die'.[88] Accordingly after his death in 1713 the Golian manuscripts came with the rest of Marsh's collection to Oxford.[89] Since that had been the object of his assembling them in the first place, we may properly regard Marsh's collection as the last of the great seventeenth-century accessions of Arabic manuscripts to the Bodleian. Even in his lifetime Marsh had the satisfaction of seeing one of his greatest treasures, the manuscript of Apollonius' *Conics* which Golius had brought back from Aleppo, used for Halley's definitive edition of the *Conics* published at Oxford in 1710.[90]

(VI) HUMPHREY PRIDEAUX

Among the generation of scholars who came up to Oxford after the Restoration only three men made any mark on Arabic studies, Humphrey Prideaux, Edward Pococke junior, and William Guise. Prideaux and Pococke were of the same age (both born in 1648), but matriculated at Christ Church in 1668 and 1661 respectively; both were Students there. The younger Pococke soon embarked on an ecclesiastical career,[91] becoming canon at Salisbury in 1675, but nourished hopes of returning to a professorship at Oxford after his father's death. We have already discussed his editions of ibn Ṭufayl and ʿAbd al-Laṭīf, and noted his translation of Maimonides' preface to the Mishnah. It is certain for the first, and highly probable for the other two, that his father had a very large hand in the work. Prideaux[92] remained at Christ Church for nearly

---

[88] This, with other letters between Marsh and Smith on the archbishop's designs for improving the library at Trinity College, Dublin, were published by Mant, *History of the Church of Ireland*, ii. 110–19.

[89] The remainder of Marsh's substantial library went to Trinity College, Dublin. The superficial life of Marsh by Stokes, *Some Worthies of the Irish Church*, Lectures III–VI, contains on pp. 762–74 an interesting note by the editor on Marsh's oriental printed books, which shows that he had assembled most of the Arabic books available in print in his time.

[90] He expressed his pleasure in a letter to Arthur Charlett of 3 Mar. 1708 (MS Ballard 8, fo. 14), from which it is clear that he had already sent the manuscript to Oxford for Halley's use. No doubt that occurred on 1 Nov. 1707, when a note was made on the manuscript that it belonged to the archbishop, signed by Marsh himself (MS Marsh 667, fo. 2ʳ).

[91] As early as Dec. 1672 his father was enquiring from Arthur Charlett senior about the possibility of getting a living for 'Ned' (MS Tanner 43, fo. 56ʳ).

[92] The anonymous 18th-century *Life* of Prideaux is more informative on his ecclesiastical than his academic career, but is not without use.

twenty years, and was considered a serious candidate for both the Arabic and Hebrew professorships, but eventually he too resigned himself to the life of a country parson. However, he did not renounce publication after bidding farewell to the university, but turned instead from scholarly to popular composition, producing at least one extremely successful book. While at Christ Church he was a favourite of Fell, who used him during the 1670s as a factotum to oversee the production of books at the University Press, which was being run by a syndicate of which Fell was the most active member. Many sidelights on this activity appear in Prideaux's letters to John Ellis, in which his comments on contemporary matters and individuals are enlivened by a coarse wit. Fell also pressed on the reluctant Prideaux editions of scholarly works. He was supposed to take over the edition of Malalas which John Gregory had left unfinished, but managed to avoid producing that 'horrid musty foolish booke'.[93] However, with many complaints, he did get into the press his edition of the *Marmora Oxoniensia* (1676). The Arundel marbles, after suffering considerable losses, had been presented to Oxford in 1667. Fell had decreed that these should be published together with other ancient inscriptions given to the university, notably by Selden. Unfortunately his choice for editor, Prideaux, was ill equipped for the task both in temperament and in erudition. The result was a disaster, greatly inferior to Selden's original publication of the Arundel inscriptions.[94] Prideaux was conscious of its deficiencies even at the time, writing to Ellis 'I fear I shall be put to the necessity of inserteing in many things which I shall after be ashamed of',[95] but blamed them on Fell's hurrying the work along rather than his own carelessness.

It was in oriental studies, however, that Prideaux had a claim to be a scholar. The only work that he produced in this field while he was at Christ Church was an edition and translation of two short tracts from Maimonides' *Mishneh Torah*.[96] Prideaux had recently been appointed

[93] Prideaux, *Letters*, 22 (27 Sept. 1674). Cf. *Life*, 3: he 'thought it a very fabulous and trifling book, not worth the printing; and upon his giving this judgment of it, the design was quite laid aside'.

[94] See the discussion of Madan, *Oxford Books*, iii, no. 3092, with a quotation from Hearne ('Dr Prideaux's book is wonderfully defective'). In 1710 Hearne told Dodwell that Prideaux when publishing the *Marmora* 'thought it more for the honour of himself, to write long notes, than to take accurate copies of the several inscriptions' (*Letters written by Eminent Persons*, i. 204).

[95] Prideaux, *Letters*, 28. Hearne, in 1710 and 1719, reports that he was indeed ashamed of it.

[96] *R. Moses Maimonides de Jure Pauperis et Peregrini apud Judaeos*, Oxford, 1679 (Madan, *Oxford Books*, iii, no. 3215).

as the first holder of the Hebrew Lectureship founded at Christ Church by his old teacher, Busby, and this publication might be viewed as a justification of his position, since its avowed purpose was 'to introduce young Students in the *Hebrew* language into the knowledge of the *Rabbinical* Dialect'.[97] However, Prideaux may also have wished thereby to establish a claim to be Pococke's successor in the Hebrew Professorship, since as early as 1675 he reported to Ellis that he did not expect the old man to live very long. He praises Pococke highly as a teacher: his death will 'deprive me of the best freind I have in this place, and utterly spoile me for a linguist; since the greatest encouragement I have to follow those studys is the more then ordinary helpe which I hope to receive from him'.[98] But he was probably already looking forward to succeeding him, as he certainly was in 1682, when he wrote that 'I shall have but one competitor, which is Mr Huntington, and perchance not him'.[99] However, Pococke lived another nine years, by which time Prideaux had tired of waiting and of Oxford, which he left for good in 1685, telling Ellis: 'As to Dr Pococks place, I have no expectation of it, the Earle of Rochester haveing engaged to get it for his kinsman . . . besides I am not fond of the place.'[100] Despite this pessimistic view, after Pococke's death he claimed that he had been offered the place and refused it, for two reasons: 'the first is, I nauseate that learning, and am resolved to loose noe more time upon it; and the 2d is, I nauseate Christ Church.'[101] In any event, Prideaux married and spent the rest of his life in Norfolk, most of it as Dean of Norwich. It was there that he wrote the work by which he is best known today, his *Life of Mahomet*.

Although Prideaux told Ellis 'I had much adoe to get it printed, for it laye a year in towne before any bookeseller would venture on it',[102] this was an instant and longlasting success, going through three editions in 1697–8, and reprinted many times in England and America, as well as being translated into other European languages. As the title indicates, it is a polemical work directed not only against Islam ('The

[97] Prideaux, *Life*, 8.

[98] Prideaux, *Letters*, 43 (2 Sept. 1675). No doubt he received such help for his edition of Maimonides (see the favourable analysis of it by Feingold, 'The Oxford Oriental School').

[99] Prideaux, *Letters*, 132.

[100] Ibid. 144–5. According to Maunde Thompson ad loc. the 'kinsman' was Hyde, which I doubt.

[101] Ibid. 150 (12 Oct. 1691). The second reason shows that the 'place' alluded to was the Hebrew Professorship.

[102] Ibid. 185 (May 1697).

True Nature of Imposture Fully Display'd'), but also against contemporary sects ('Offered to the Consideration of the Deists of
the present Age'). As such it is crudely effective, but as a work of
scholarship it is contemptible, despite Prideaux's parade of scholarly
apparatus. He tells the reader in the preface that this is a mere excerpt
from a larger work he had planned on 'The History of the Ruin of the
Eastern Church', and that he has 'been careful to set down all my
Authorities in the Margin'. Examination of these marginal annotations
reveals that all the oriental works quoted are taken at second hand from
European editions with translations, many of them from Pococke's
Specimen. There is no indication that Prideaux read any Arabic work in
the original, with the possible exception of the Koran.[103] The *Specimen*
could have pointed Prideaux towards many good Arabic sources on the
life of Muḥammad available in the Bodleian or in Pococke's own collection, but he obviously paid no attention to such things during his many
years in Oxford. Indeed his ignorance of Arabic is such as to permit him
to make the astonishing statement, in regard to 'the great agreement
which the Arabic hath with the English both in the power of its Letters,
and the pronunciation of its Words', that there is 'no language in the
World more akin to ours, than the Arabic is in these particulars'.[104]
Moreover, in his selection and use of sources Prideaux is utterly uncritical (despite his claims to the contrary). Everything is grist to his mill,
provided that it presents the subject of his biography in a bad light. Thus
he draws freely on medieval compilations such as the *Confutatio legis
Saraceni* of Ricoldo da Montecroce (whom, following his source,
Bibliander, he calls 'Ricardo'), and Nicholas of Cusa's *Cribratio
Alcorani*. Holt well characterizes the resulting farrago as 'an unskilful
combination of Muslim tradition and Christian legend, inspired by a
sour animosity towards its subject'. The popularity of this book, which is
a primary witness for the decline of Arabic studies in England, tells us
much about public taste in Europe in the eighteenth century. Prideaux's
one great service to the study of Arabic was his recommending Ockley
to take it up.[105]

---

[103] That he had first-hand knowledge even of the Koran is denied by Holt, 'The
Treatment of Arab History by Prideaux, Ockley and Sale', who gives an excellent
analysis of Prideaux's sources and his use of them on pp. 51–4.

[104] Prideaux, *Mahomet*, preface, p. xxii. This is reinforced by orthographical errors
such as 'Al Fragani'. Aldrich, in his severe criticism of Prideaux as a scholar, said that
though this 'unaccurate muddy headed' man's 'chief skill was in orientals, . . . even
there he was far from being perfect in either' (Hearne, *Diaries*, xi. 382).

[105] Arberry, 'Simon Ockley', 13.

(293)

(VII) WILLIAM GUISE

Guise[106] had a very different attitude towards oriental learning from his kinsman Prideaux.[107] There is unanimous admiration for his stupendous erudition in that field among his contemporaries at Oxford, not only Wood, but also Smith, Bernard, and Prideaux.[108] Coming from a wealthy and noble family, he graduated as BA at All Souls College in 1674, but resigned his fellowship to marry in 1680. He continued to live privately in Oxford, working steadily in the Bodleian Library, as his extant remains attest. His sudden death in 1683, at the age of about 30, cut off a promising scholarly career. Apart from a juvenile expression of his precocious oriental learning, a Syriac poem printed in the university's volume commemorating the death of the Duchess of York,[109] the only work of his which has been published is his translation of and commentary on *Zeraim* (a tractate of the Mishnah). This appeared posthumously, by the efforts of Edward Bernard, together with the younger Pococke's translation of Maimonides' preface to the Mishnah. The commentary illustrates Guise's extraordinarily wide learning, not only in Hebrew, but also in other oriental languages, especially Arabic. He quotes from a variety of sources, most of them available to him only in manuscript, including not only lexicons, but writers on materia medica (ibn al-Bayṭār, ibn Jazla, ibn Sīnā, al-Zahrāwī [Abulcasis], al-Damīrī), and geographers (notably Abū 'l-Fidā'). Interestingly, he also quotes Arabic poets, although I have not determined whether he knew these at first hand[110] or only from quotations in the lexicographers. His interest in Arabic is further illustrated by collections that he made from various Bodleian Arabic codices, which were given by his widow to Narcissus Marsh

[106] I follow the spelling of his name which is commonly accepted. However, it seems that he himself preferred the spelling 'Gise' (see e.g. the note in Wood, *Athenae Oxonienses*, iv. 114).

[107] I do not know what the relationship was, but it was probably through Guise's wife, Frances, née Southcote, who, like Prideaux, came from the south-west. Prideaux claims him as kin in a letter to Ellis of 8 Nov. 1681 (*Letters*, 119).

[108] The latter calls him 'the greatest miracle in the knowledge of [Arabic] that I ever heard of, he haveing made himself a perfect master of that copious and difficult language' (ibid. 43, written when Guise was only 25).

[109] Madan, *Oxford Books*, iii. 249–50. At the time Guise was a commoner at Oriel College, aged about 18.

[110] That he did is suggested by Bernard's statement in his preface to the work that Guise 'Arabum philologos, & praecipue poetas eorum, facundiae antiquae . . . magistros, assidue consuluit'.

and later came to the library (e.g. MS Marsh 88[111]). But it was above all Abū 'l-Fidā"s *Geography* which attracted him. Before his death he had prepared a text of the whole work, with notes of variants from different manuscripts, which he intended to accompany with a Latin translation and notes. This was donated by his widow to All Souls College, where it has reposed undisturbed ever since.[112] The above is far from an exhaustive account of Guise's learning: for instance MS Marsh 253 is an English–Turkish vocabulary that he compiled, and Sharpe says that Marshall gave an Armenian lexicon compiled by 'Fr. Rivola' to Guise, who considerably augmented it. Prideaux considered that he would be a worthy successor to Pococke when he matured. There is no doubt that he was the most assiduous and widely read Oxford oriental scholar of his generation, but whether the depth of his erudition would ever have equalled its width is a question which his very early death made moot.

(VIII) EDWARD POCOCKE JUNIOR

Edward Pococke junior seems to have belonged to that unfortunate class of people who are pushed by an ambitious parent into a career for which they have little aptitude and no inclination. He was only 23 when he appeared as the 'author' of a book, the *Philosophus Auto-didactus*, designed by his father to show the son's prowess in Arabic, but in fact assumed by all (correctly) to be essentially the work of the father. His other published work, the translation of Maimonides' preface to the Mishnah, also appeared in his father's lifetime (1690), and was doubtless supervised by him. However, since it was likely that he would not live much longer, it was important for the son to publish something on Hebrew to assert his claim to succeed his father. In the event, after the elder Pococke died on 10 September 1691, his son failed to be elected to either of his professorships. The Arabic chair went to Hyde (who was at least a far better scholar than the younger Pococke), but the much more lucrative position in Hebrew, with its attached prebend at Christ Church, went to Roger Altham, a nonentity as a scholar but a man with powerful friends.[113] Pococke retired to his

---

[111] Nicoll–Pusey no. 390, p. 386. Cf. MS Marsh 533 (Uri no. 46, p. 52), Guise's text of the Koran made from collating three different manuscripts.

[112] Coxe, *Catalogue of College MSS*, ii, All Souls no. 287, pp. 76–7. See Sharpe's account in Hyde, *Syntagma Dissertationum*, i, pp. xix–xx.

[113] According to Hearne, *Diaries*, i. 228, Altham obtained the post through the

country parsonage in dudgeon and gave up scholarship altogether, refusing to publish the edition of 'Abd al-Laṭīf which he had embarked upon at his father's behest.[114] Hearne was undoubtedly right in attributing his failure to succeed his father to his want of 'Friends to get him into the Professorships',[115] but his assertion that he 'understands Arabick & other oriental Tongues very well' may be doubted. The only surviving performance in Arabic by the younger Pococke which was not done under the eye of his father is the translation of a letter by the dervish Aḥmad, which he made for Humfry Smith, and which is printed by Twells.[116] In this brief document I find no less than eighteen errors of translation.

(IX) THE LATER CAREER OF HYDE

Hyde, as we saw, published nothing (apart from the Bodleian Library Catalogue) for many years after his edition of the Ulugh Beg star catalogue. He did indeed make translations from Arabic and Persian for Boyle's benefit.[117] However, round about 1690, when Pococke's death seemed imminent, Hyde bestirred himself to appear as a suitable candidate to succeed him in both professorships. In 1689 appeared the first instalment of his work on a topic which had long interested him, oriental games.[118] This consisted of three short Hebrew works (with Latin translation) on chess, the most substantial of which (although Hyde concealed the fact) was a modern composition by Isaac

influence of Dr Radcliffe with the Earl of Portland. In 1674 Prideaux had contemptuously referred to Altham, his contemporary at Westminster and Christ Church, as 'a very mean schollar' (*Letters*, 28). Cf. Wood, *Life and Times*, iii. 375 (Altham is Hebrew Professor, 'but doth not read because he is no Hebritian'). On the rumours surrounding the election to the Hebrew Professorship and the names of possible candidates, including Bernard and Prideaux, both of whom said that they refused to stand, see Feingold, 'The Oxford Oriental School'.

[114] See above, p. 273.

[115] Hearne, *Diaries*, ii. 63 (18 Oct. 1707).

[116] pp. 31–3. See above, p. 122, for my partial translation.

[117] e.g. those sent with his letter to Boyle of 14 Feb. 1667 (Boyle, *Works*, vi. 557). In 1663 he had volunteered to translate geographical coordinates out of Abū 'l-Fidā''s *Geography* for Boyle after Pococke had refused to do so. Wallis commented sagaciously: 'I suppose he will expect some gratuity for his pains' (ibid. 456–7), and indeed Hyde enjoyed Boyle's patronage thereafter.

[118] In his letter to Smith of 8 June 1668 (MS Smith 50, p. 219) he asks him to send from Constantinople 'any booke that treateth of Playes and Games, or Chesse and Tables'. He announced his intention of publishing a book on the topic in a letter to Thévenot in 1673, printed in Hyde, *Syntagma Dissertationum*, ii. 464.

Abendana, currently teaching Hebrew at Oxford. This is revealed in an indignant letter by Bernard to Smith, undated but obviously written shortly after Pococke's death:

You see how our acquaintance [Hyde] gloryes upon the coffin of a great man [Pococke]: as if the master of Oriental & Arabe learning could not interpret an African epistle. He should of all the candidates avoyd the Topic of disprayse, being so very liable both his own manners and his consorts, & also his mistakes in turning of Perisol, & his barbarisms both, with translation & in his Scacchiludium:[119] besides his imposing upon the world as a peice of auctority a Tract of Chesse made for his recreation in a florid style by my master Abendana; which he shew'd me in MSt & not onely so but also acquainted me that he was his ayder in the turning of Perisol in the difficult places.[120]

The last sentence refers to Hyde's *Peritsol* (1691), an edition and translation of a slight sixteenth-century cosmography in Hebrew.[121] The book contains copious learned notes, in which the various exotic languages used are set in the appropriate types. These include, beside Arabic and Hebrew, Samaritan, Syriac, Turkish, Persian, Ethiopic, and Tamil. On pp. 102–4 is a long dissertation on plant names (another lifelong interest of Hyde's[122]) with quotations from numerous unpublished Arabic writers. The book is enlivened by the addition of notes in Latin by Albertus Bobovius on various Turkish customs, written down at Smith's instance and brought back by him from Constantinople; and by Hyde's 'castigation' of Angelus a S. Joseph's *Pharmacopeia Persica*. Hyde was involved in a feud with this man (a Carmelite whose original name was de la Brosse), because he had criticized the edition of the Persian version of the Gospels in the English Polyglot, with which Hyde had been involved. Hyde describes how he discomfited the friar in an oral dispute, both speaking Latin and Persian, in the Bodleian Library in January 1688.

---

[119] On 31 Dec. 1694 Bernard wrote a long letter to Job Ludolf criticizing passages (mainly about chess) in Hyde's *De Ludis Orientalibus* (printed in Hyde, *Syntagma Dissertationum*, ii. 475–8).

[120] MS Smith 47, fo. 92r.

[121] On Abraham Farissol see Steinschneider, *Hebräischen Übersetzungen*, 81. The work is notable for its mention of the recent discoveries in America. See *PO* no. 372 (the copy which Hyde gave to Smith).

[122] According to Sharpe (Hyde, *Syntagma Dissertationum*, i, p. xxv), Hyde had contributed notes from Arabic sources to Bobart's edition of Morison's *Plantarum Historiae Universalis Oxoniensis pars tertia* (1699, see Carter, *History of Oxford University Press*, 433), but he was uncertain whether these were actually incorporated. There is no mention of Hyde in that work, but his intention is confirmed by Bernard in a letter to Smith of 1692: 'Dr Hyde . . . also makes notes out of the Eastern books upon Dr Morison De Plantis' (MS Smith 47, fo. 118r).

As we saw, Hyde obtained the Arabic Professorship in 1691, but was passed over for the Hebrew in favour of Altham. When Altham was forced to resign in 1697 for refusing to swear loyalty to King William, Hyde succeeded to this chair too, and held both until his death in 1702. However, after the publication of *De Ludis Orientalibus* in 1694 (with its considerable Arabic and Hebrew content) he produced nothing of consequence in either language.[123] His remaining energies were devoted to his great work on the religion of the ancient Persians, published by subscription at Oxford in 1700.[124] This embodied immense learning, but because Hyde did not have access to the Pahlavi (much less Old Persian) literature, it was rendered largely obsolete when these became available later in the eighteenth century.[125] Hyde got very few subscribers, a failure which John Cleland[126] attributed to the decline of public taste: 'Need I mention the celebrated Dr. Hyde's boiling his tea-kettle, with almost the whole impression left on his hands, of that profoundly learned treatise of his: "De Religione Veterum Persarum", admired by all literary Europe, and neglected at home: so low was the taste for literature in this country, already sunk!' The picture that this paints of Hyde is unfortunately of a piece with the mixture of amusement and contempt in which his contemporaries in late seventeenth-century Oxford held him. This is true even of those, like Bernard and Smith, who recognized and encouraged his learning (criticizing his Latin or Hebrew the while). Hyde's first wife was a subject of Oxford scandal, Anthony Wood bluntly calling her 'a quondam whore, now a madwoman, a convert [to Rome] ever since last October [1686] (i.e. uxor Thomas Hyde)'.[127] Years before, Prideaux had recounted with gusto the story of how Hyde was beaten by his wife on suspicion of making love to their maid.[128] Even Hearne, who admired Hyde's learning unreservedly, tells a disparaging story about him being so 'slow of speech, and his delivery very low' that after he had been preaching inaudibly at Christ Church for a long time the Vice-Chancellor ordered him to come down from the pulpit.[129]

---

[123] His inaugural lecture as Arabic Professor (printed in *Syntagma Dissertationum*, ii. 449–59) is completely without interest, except for the passage mentioned above, p. 20.

[124] *Historia religionis veterum Persarum*, etc. (Carter, *History of Oxford University Press*, 435; see also 390–1).

[125] Hyde spent much money on having types cut for the Old Persian characters, and did try to get the Zend-Avesta from the Parsee community in Bombay (letter to Boyle of 29 Nov. 1677; Boyle, *Works*, vi. 567). On the contempt expressed by its first European editor, Anquetil Duperron, for Hyde's work see Marshall, 'Oriental Studies', 558.

[126] Reported by Nichols, *Literary Anecdotes*, ii. 457.

[127] Wood, *Life and Times*, iii. 213.

[128] Prideaux, *Letters*, 46–7.

[129] Hearne, *Diaries*, xi. 368–9.

Just as Bernard and others cast doubt on Hyde's command of Hebrew, his knowledge of Arabic too was belittled by Prideaux. Writing to Ellis in 1682, he expresses indignation that, for the job of translating Arabic diplomatic correspondence, Pococke had been passed over in favour of 'so egregious a donce in [Arabic] as Hyde', who 'hath the least skil in this language of any that pretend to it in the University'.[130] Whatever his failings in this regard, Hyde evidently had the confidence of the government, since a number of his translations of such documents survive in the Public Record Office.[131] Moreover, in 1699 he was approached by the Secretary of State to 'instruct and bring up some young man in the knowledge of the Oriental Languages . . . that there may be a succession of such as may serve the public in the same manner as you have done'. A government grant of £100 a year was allotted for this, of which £40 went to each of two students, and £20 to the professor who was to teach them Arabic.[132] Nothing is known about Hyde's instruction, but since one of the two students chosen was John Wallis,[133] Hyde's disastrously bad successor as Arabic Professor, the result reflects no credit on him. Nevertheless, Wallis seems to have been a favourite of Hyde's, for when he resigned as Bodley's Librarian, after a tenure of thirty-five years, he tried to get Wallis appointed as his successor,[134] claiming that with his knowledge of eastern languages he was more suitable than the other candidate, John Hudson. Fortunately Hudson was chosen, for with all his faults (duly noted by his assistant Hearne) he was not as supremely idle as Wallis. In his letter of resignation to the pro-Vice-Chancellor William Wake,[135] Hyde remarks that 'Lectures (though we must attend upon them) will do little good, hearers being scarce and practicers more scarce', a telling comment on the state of Arabic and Hebrew studies at Oxford at the beginning of the new century.

---

[130] Prideaux, *Letters*, 132–3.

[131] See Hopkins, *Letters from Barbary*, 93. Cf. the letters in Hyde, *Syntagma Dissertationum*, i, pp. xxii–xxiv.

[132] Sutherland, 'The Origin and Early History of the Lord Almoner's Professorship', 167–9. Hyde was characteristically disgruntled at the smallness of his reward.

[133] No relation to the Savilian Professor. The other student was Benjamin Marshall, allegedly a good Arabist, although he never published anything to prove it.

[134] Letter of 9 Mar. 1701 to Archbishop Tenison, published by Todd, *Life of Walton*, i. 265–6.

[135] Printed by Macray, *Annals*, 170–1.

(X) EDWARD BERNARD

For all his shortcomings, Hyde produced a very respectable body of scholarly work, in which his knowledge of Arabic was prominent. His exact contemporary Bernard, who prided himself as a critic of Hyde and was often privately scornful of him, in the end produced much less. We have already seen the miserable failure of his proposed edition of Apollonius. This was but one example of a pattern which was to repeat itself throughout his life. He would embark enthusiastically on a new project, only to become enmired, lose interest, and leave only a trail of undigested notes. Other examples are his editions of Euclid and Josephus. The first may be dealt with briefly, since it apparently did not involve the Arabic versions. It too was an outcome of the abortive plan for the collected works of the ancient mathematicians, as is clear from the preface to Wallis, *Archimedes' Sandreckoner*. Fell says there that Bernard had figures engraved and a specimen of a few pages printed. Two such specimens, in different formats, are preserved in MS Bodley 886, which consists of Bernard's collections on Euclid VII and other books. Another specimen and many plates of figures are in MS Bodley 887.[136] These specimens are undated, but were probably all in existence by 1676, the date of Fell's preface. There the edition is already despaired of, but Bernard tried to revive it in 1684[137] and again in 1694, when he mentioned it several times in his letters to Smith. The last comment I have seen, on 4 December, is: 'Euclide must be the charge of a bookseller or our Tenants for the imprimery, or else must go abroad: I hope the second. I am glad Sr Chr. W[ren] & yourselfe do like the specimen.'[138]

The sad story of Bernard's edition of Josephus is told by Carter.[139] The decision to publish the Greek text of Josephus' *Jewish Antiquities* and *Jewish War* was made (by Fell) in 1669, and Bernard was entrusted with the task. He set to work, compiling copious notes, but the work went very slowly. In 1678 specimens were printed, and the work itself began to be set in type. But examination of the proof-sheets

[136] See Madan, *Oxford Books*, iii, no. 3141, with references to other collections of Bernard on Euclid which I have not seen.

[137] An encouraging letter was written by Boyle to Bernard in 1684 (MS Smith 45, pp. 141–3).

[138] MS Smith 47, fos. 147^r–154^r. No doubt this is why Carter, *History of Oxford University Press*, 423, dates the specimen in MS Bodley 887 to 1694 (certainly wrongly).

[139] Ibid. 88–90, following Havercamp in his 1726 edition of Josephus (which I have not consulted).

by the Delegates and others induced horror. Apart from alleged errors, 'the length of the commentaries, in which whole dissertations were inserted without any apparent necessity' led to a decision to abandon publication and to coldness between Bernard and Fell. Clement Barksdale's doggerel couplet of 1684 must have sounded ironical to contemporaries:

> Savilian Bernard, a good Learned Man,
> Will give us his Josephus, when he can.[140]

At some point, however, printing was resumed, and a fragment of the edition of the *Jewish War* came out in 1687, with brief notes. No doubt as a result of Fell's death in 1686, nothing more appeared during Bernard's lifetime, although in 1694 a new specimen was issued by three Oxford booksellers, announcing that the edition was being undertaken at the Sheldonian. The result of this is presumably the crippled 1700 edition,[141] which consists of a reissue of the 1687 fragment of the *Jewish War* plus Books I–IV and part of V (out of twenty) of the *Jewish Antiquities*. The voluminous notes printed with the latter section give some idea of the commentary which Bernard had projected, since they frequently take up much more room than the text and translation. Oriental learning is prominent, with quotations set in Hebrew, Arabic, Syriac, and even Samaritan type. The Arabic references are mainly from geographical authors, and show Bernard's acquaintance with the resources of the Bodleian, since he quotes, besides Abū 'l-Fidā' and al-Idrīsī, lesser-known authors such as al-Qalqashandī and ibn Ḥawqal. Historians cited include not only printed texts, such as Eutychius' *Annals*, but also works that Bernard found in manuscript, including al-Maqrīzī's *History of Cairo* and the Arabic 'Samaritan Chronicle'. Bernard was familiar with the Huntington manuscripts that had recently come to the Bodleian, since he refers often to the 'falsi Josephi exemplar Huntingtonianum', and has an Arabic quotation from 'Tanchumus Lexicographus'. The work as published reveals both Bernard's wide but undirected learning and his lack of any sense of proportion, since the scale of the commentary, if extended to the whole work, would have filled many years and many folio volumes.

Bernard's restless temperament prevented him from finishing any of

---

[140] As quoted by Hearne, *Diaries*, vi. 235.

[141] For details see Bibliography (Bernard, *Josephus*) and Carter, *History of Oxford University Press*, 435.

the major projects which his wide-ranging curiosity and interests led him to undertake. As early as 1677 Smith, disturbed by Bernard's sudden notion to give up his Savilian Professorship and go with Princess Mary to Holland as her chaplain, warned him: 'The world expects justly some great matter from you in point of study & learning and therefore let mee desire you to fix upon some what speedily and let that be your onely busines.'[142] The advice had no effect on Bernard, whose discontent with Oxford (often expressed in his letters) had already led him, in 1676, to a stay in Paris as tutor to the bastard sons of Charles II by the Duchess of Cleveland. The result was predictable: on 24 February 1677 Prideaux reported that Bernard 'hath been soe affronted and abused there by that insolent woman that he hath been forced to quit that employment and return'.[143] However, while in Paris Bernard formed friendships with the leading French scholars and augmented his already impressive library. In 1683 he again tried to obtain a post away from Oxford. During a long stay at Leiden, where he had gone for the sale of Nicolaus Heinsius' library (from which he acquired some choice items for himself), he was encouraged by his friends at the university there to hope for the post of Professor of Arabic, which had been vacant since the death of Golius. According to Smith,[144] Bernard wanted the post because the climate of scholarship and the opportunities for publication there were far better than in England. However, this came to nothing, although Smith was still advising Bernard against accepting a 'Professorship in Leyden' on 14 July 1692.[145] By that time Bernard had resigned the Savilian Professorship, having obtained the rectorship of Brightwell in 1692. However, he continued to spend much time in Oxford, where since 1692 he had been engaged on the one major scholarly enterprise which he brought to fruition, the *Catalogi Librorum Manuscriptorum Angliæ et Hiberniæ in unum collecti*.[146] This list of all manuscripts in public collections (and in many private ones) in England and Ireland was compiled under his supervision, and for the Bodleian and Oxford

---

[142] MS Smith 57, p. 15 (1 Nov.). In the event the chaplaincy was not conferred on Bernard, but first on William Lloyd and then on George Hooper, both of whom were unfortunate in the post (see Marshall, *George Hooper*, 20–8).

[143] Prideaux, *Letters*, 58.

[144] *Life of Bernard*, 44. This is the only evidence that I have seen for the attempt, but the close relationship between Smith and Bernard is sufficient guarantee of its truth.

[145] MS Smith 57, p. 281.

[146] Published at Oxford, nominally in 1697, but the preface, which explains Bernard's role in the enterprise, is dated 1698. The bulk of the work was already set up in type before Bernard's death.

college libraries he did much of the work himself. It was a remarkable achievement for its time, and is still not without use.

Bernard's other scholarly publications are on a small scale, and mostly of an occasional nature. Thus in 1689 he issued *Orbis eruditi literatura*, a single large engraved sheet exhibiting the development of writing. This took the form of twenty-nine tables arranged chronologically from 'Adam' (i.e. the oldest Hebrew alphabet) through the various western oriental alphabets, Greek, Latin, and modern scripts (including Runic, Coptic, Russian, and Armenian). Although rendered largely obsolete by later archaeological discoveries, it could hardly have been done better at that time, and exhibits to good effect Bernard's wide knowledge of manuscripts, inscriptions, and coins in many different languages. On a somewhat larger scale was the treatise on the measures and weights of antiquity appended by Bernard to Pococke's *Commentary on Hosea* of 1685, as a typically Bernardian enormous annotation on one passage of that prophet. It was reissued separately in an expanded form in 1688.[147] Arabic measures are prominent in the book, gathered from a variety of sources both printed and manuscript. Bernard also retells the story of the measurement of one degree of the earth's surface under al-Ma'mūn (p. 251), from a number of authorities, including al-Bīrūnī (presumably Greaves's copy of the *Canon Masudicus*, which Bernard had acquired). In general, however, the work is an uncritical compilation of terms and facts from whatever sources lay to hand. The same could be said of two short articles which Bernard published in the *Philosophical Transactions* on the coordinates of 'the chiefest fixt stars according to the best Observers' and 'the Observations of the Ancients concerning the Obliquity of the Zodiack'.[148] These include numerous data from Arabic and Persian sources, but with no attempt at evaluation.[149] In such matters Bernard seems to have been acting as a mere purveyor of information to practising astronomers who hoped to use such historical data to improve modern astronomical parameters, but were unable to read the relevant authors themselves. The second of the above-mentioned articles is addressed to John Flamsteed, the Astronomer Royal, and in

[147] Bernard, *De Mensuris*.

[148] Vol. 14 (1684), 567–76 and 721–5. These are analysed by Mercier, 'English Orientalists and Mathematical Astronomy', 178–89, with some account of the oriental manuscripts which Bernard consulted for them.

[149] The conclusion drawn at the end of the second article, that the obliquity had always been the same, is completely contrary to the evidence adduced: Bernard was merely adopting Flamsteed's erroneous belief.

fact Flamsteed had been in communication with Bernard about such matters since 1678.[150] Flamsteed used historical information supplied by Bernard in his Gresham Lectures of 1681–4, especially in Lecture 11 on the obliquity of the ecliptic.[151] But it was above all in the preface to vol. III of his posthumously published *Historia Coelestis Britannica* (1725) that Flamsteed divulged historical information that he had derived, directly or indirectly, from Bernard.[152]

Flamsteed was only one of the many scholars throughout Europe with whom Bernard kept up a learned correspondence on an astonishing variety of topics.[153] His opinions were held in high regard by such notable classical scholars as Richard Bentley, who addressed him as 'Eruditissime et Amicissime',[154] and Jacobus Gronovius, who published a letter from Bernard containing emendations to the fragment of Stephanus of Byzantium which Gronovius had discovered,[155] to mention two out of a long list. Throughout his life he continued to pile up notes on numerous topics, many of which survive among his manuscripts and printed books which the university bought after his death, but none of which (among those that I have seen) are in a form remotely suitable for publication. However, Bernard may be considered as ultimately responsible for two publications of considerable importance in Arabic studies which eventually emerged through the efforts of Edmund Halley. One of the manuscripts which Bernard left at his death was his partial transcription and Latin translation of the Arabic version of Apollonius' lost treatise *Cutting off of a Ratio*.[156]

---

[150] For details of the correspondence between Flamsteed and Bernard see Forbes, *The Gresham Lectures of John Flamsteed*, 75 n. 149. Cf. Mercier, 'English Orientalists and Mathematical Astronomy', 190, who also discusses Bernard's correspondence on such matters with John Collins and Thomas Street.

[151] The 'Manuscript Paper in which these obliquitys of the Zodiac were transmitted to me' (Forbes, 213) is simply the letter which Bernard later published in the *Philosophical Transactions* and not (as Forbes imagines, p. 396) the 'Arabick manuscript lately brought out of the East which describes the Instruments used by both the ancient Greekes and Arabians' (p. 392). The latter was Huntington's copy of a work by Abū 'Alī al-Marrākushī (now MS Huntington 201), which Flamsteed could have known of only from Bernard. Cf. Chapman, *The Preface to Flamsteed's Historia Coelestis Britannica*, 44, from which it appears that Bernard contemplated a partial publication of that treatise.

[152] A modern annotated version of this has been published by Chapman, *The Preface to John Flamsteed's Historia Coelestis Britannica* (unfortunately based an a very defective English translation). See especially pp. 44, 49 ff.

[153] Thomas Smith acquired Bernard's correspondence from his widow after his friend's death, so that a great many letters to Bernard, as well as Bernard's own letters to Smith, are preserved among the Smith MSS in the Bodleian.

[154] Bentley, *Correspondence*, i. 13.

[155] *Fragmentum Stephani Byzantini Grammatici de Dodone* (Leiden, 1681).

[156] Among the Selden MSS, although it had originally been acquired by John

Halley, who at the time knew no Arabic at all, came upon this in the Bodleian Library, and used it as a key to the language and eventually to the decipherment of the whole of the original work, as he explains in the translation which he published in 1706.[157] His success in this encouraged him to undertake the translation from the Arabic of Books V–VII of Apollonius' *Conics* as part of his edition of the whole treatise. Here again he owed much to Bernard, for although he seems not to have made any use of Bernard's own collections on the *Conics*, the principal manuscript that he used was the one which Bernard had brought back from Leiden in 1669 and had himself in large part copied.[158] Before the actual publication of Halley's edition in 1710, Narcissus Marsh sent him the ancestor of this manuscript, the famous codex that had belonged to Golius, to consult. This too would not have been possible without the efforts of Bernard, for it was he who had urged Marsh to buy the Golian manuscripts and had acted as his agent.

That was Bernard's last contribution to learning during his lifetime, and was indeed the proximate cause of his death. When he heard in June 1696 that the manuscripts of Golius would finally be disposed of by auction at Leiden on 16 October (NS), he wrote to Smith informing him of his intention of attending it if someone whom he refers to as 'un amy' and 'a person of honour' will employ him. This was a reference to Marsh, who had already used Bernard as an intermediary in buying oriental manuscripts. Marsh, as we saw, transmitted £220 to Bernard for the purpose on 16 September, and Bernard set off, accompanied by his wife, on the 18th. His health, as he himself recognized, was not good, and his friends were dubious about the wisdom of such a journey in winter,[159] but Bernard could not bear to miss such an opportunity. He reached Rotterdam safely by 28 September and by 3 October was at Leiden,[160] where he duly attended the auction and carried off in triumph the most and the best of Golius' manuscripts. On the return journey in November, however, he was severely troubled by a cough and dysentery, as he told Smith after arriving back at Brightwell on 20 November. He was confined to bed, in great anxiety

Greaves: see above, p. 177. Bernard's excerpts are in MS Bodl. Or. 250 (Nicoll–Pusey no. 372, p. 364).

[157] Halley, Apollonius' *Cutting off of a Ratio*, preface (where he says that Bernard had completed less than a tenth of the work); partially translated by Molland, 'The Limited Lure of Arabic Mathematics', 221.   [158] See above, pp. 239–40.

[159] John Wallis, writing to Smith on 8 Sept., says 'I should not encourage' the voyage (*Letters written by Eminent Persons*, i. 77).

[160] MS Smith 47, fo. 207; MS BL Add. 4275, fo. 43.

whether the manuscripts, which had been sent by a different ship, would arrive safely, and importuning Smith in London to oversee their clearing customs. His last letter to Smith of 2 January 1697, written by his wife because he was too weak, reflects his agitation. He probably never saw Smith's reply assuring him that all would be well,[161] for he died on 12 January, in his fifty-ninth year, a martyr to the scholarship to which he had devoted much of his life.

[161] The correspondence between Smith and Bernard on this matter is contained in MSS Smith 47, fos. 204 ff. (letters of Bernard) and Smith 97, pp. 613 ff. (letters of Smith).

IO

Epilogue

THE death of Edward Bernard is an appropriate event with which to end our account of Arabic studies in the seventeenth century, since he was the last of the pupils of Pococke from whom there was still an expectation that he might produce something worthy of his great teacher. In the event, as we have seen, none of those pupils did fulfil such hopes, and it was clear that there would not be another generation of Arabists to follow them at Oxford.

The decline which was already apparent well before the end of the seventeenth century continued precipitately in the eighteenth,[1] at least at the universities. Hyde's successor as Arabic Professor, John Wallis, did nothing whatever in the way of either teaching or studying during his thirty-five years in the chair. The next occupant, Thomas Hunt, possessed both scholarly ability and interests, but the only projects of his that came to fruition involved reprinting the works of his predecessors Pococke and Hyde.[2] Even Joseph White, who came under the influence of Silvestre de Sacy, was mainly concerned with publishing or republishing works which Pococke had been engaged on,[3] rather than opening new avenues. Ironically it was a Cambridge man, Simon Ockley, who made the best use of the Arabic resources of the Bodleian Library during the eighteenth century.[4] Ockley, who became Professor of Arabic at Cambridge in 1711, had already distinguished himself by producing a new English translation of ibn Ṭufayl's 'Ḥayy ibn Yaqẓān', made from the Arabic (unlike previous versions, which had

[1] It is not my purpose to give even a sketch of the study of Arabic in the eighteenth century. The account of it at Oxford by Marshall, 'Oriental Studies', is inadequate, although it does give some useful illustrations of the neglect of instruction in the subject there. I have not seen the unpublished Ph.D. dissertation by S. D. Khairallah, 'Arabic Studies in England in the Late Seventeenth and Early Eighteenth Centuries' (London, 1972).

[2] He collaborated with Twells on the publication of Pococke's *Theological Works*. See above, p. 272, for his unsuccessful attempt to get the work of ʿAbd al-Laṭīf published. In 1760 Hyde's *Historia religionis veterum Persarum* was reprinted by his efforts.

[3] Edition of ʿAbd al-Laṭīf, 1800; re-edition of Pococke's *Specimen*, 1806.

[4] A sympathetic account of Ockley's life and work is given by Arberry, 'Simon Ockley'. On Ockley's *History of the Saracens* see also Holt, 'The Treatment of Arab History by Prideaux, Ockley and Sale', 54–7 (for the Arabic historians consulted by Ockley in the Bodleian), and *L'Europe et le monde arabe*, 114–17.

been made from the younger Pococke's Latin). He had also published the first volume of his *History of the Saracens*, based in part on manuscripts which he had studied at Oxford. The work, supplemented by a second volume in 1718, covers the first two centuries of the Caliphate from the death of Muḥammad, and, being based on first-hand knowledge of original sources, is the one major contribution to Arabic studies to emerge from England in the eighteenth century. It had a powerful effect on the young Gibbon, who later made good use of it in his *Decline and Fall*. Otherwise, however, Cambridge was even more of a desert than Oxford.[5] Even though some attempt was made to mitigate the effects of the refusal of the professors to lecture, by the creation of an additional professorship in Arabic at each university under the name 'Lord Almoner's Professorship', these were often absorbed into the emoluments of the Laudian or Adams Professor. The only holder of this post who actually published an Arabic text was John Gagnier, a Frenchman who for religious reasons found refuge in England. During the twenty-five years or so that he held the professorship he not only gave lectures (on Hebrew as well as Arabic), but worked diligently on the Arabic manuscripts in the Bodleian Library (as his collections there attest) and produced an edition and translation of a small part of Abū 'l-Fidā''s *History*. Although industrious, he was a poor scholar, to judge by Reiske's harsh verdict on that work.[6]

The universities were in fact largely irrelevant to the study of Arabic (as to many other aspects of culture and scholarship in England) during this period. Much of what was significant in the field was produced outside of Oxford and Cambridge. In this respect the activity of two native Christian Arabs, known as Salomon Negri and Carolus Dadichi,[7] was of importance. Both came from Syria, and were in London in the earlier eighteenth century, where Negri made Arabic versions of the Scriptures for the Society for Promoting Christian Knowledge, and Dadichi was for a time the King's Interpreter. George Sale knew both men, and Dadichi is said to have given him instruction in Arabic. Sale seems to have attended neither university, but was

---

[5] Arberry, *The Cambridge School of Arabic*, 16–22, gives a bright survey of this dismal period. The one real scholar in his list, David Wilkins, should not have been included, for Wilkins, although indeed holder of the Lord Almoner's Professorship, was appointed to teach Anglo-Saxon, not Arabic (see Sutherland, 'History of the Lord Almoner's Professorship', 170–2).

[6] See Schnurrer, 118–19.

[7] There is a brief account of them in Fück, *Die arabischen Studien in Europa*, 95–7 (more on their activity in Germany than in England). I have not seen Negri's autobiography, mentioned by Schnurrer, 218.

trained in the law. In 1734 he published his English translation of the
Koran, the first reliable version in a modern language. It was preceded
by a long 'Preliminary Discourse' on the early history and doctrines of
Islam, which is distinguished by its calm objectivity. Sale probably
owed much to Marracci's Latin translation of the Koran. He certainly
drew heavily on Marracci's 'Prodromus' for the factual content of his
'Discourse' and explanatory notes,[8] although he preferred to cite
Pococke's *Specimen* wherever possible, and acknowledged it as his
principal authority. Sale directly criticizes Prideaux's *Life of Mahomet*
only occasionally, but the whole work is an antithesis to Prideaux's,
being an outstanding example of early 'enlightenment'. In its treatment
of Islam it had a forerunner in the *De Religione Mohammedica* of
Adriaan Reeland, Professor of Oriental Languages at Utrecht.[9] That the
spirit of Prideaux still flourished in England is shown by the absurd
accusations of being a covert Muslim that were levelled at Sale for
failing to denigrate the Prophet of Islam. Nevertheless, his translation
was popular enough to go through several reprintings, and was another
important source for Gibbon's *Decline and Fall*.

Other examples of translation from the Arabic outside the universities could be cited. For instance the antiquary Richard Mead
commissioned the translation of several biographies from ibn Abī
Uṣaybiʿa's *History of the Physicians* for John Freind's *History of
Physick*.[10] But it must be emphasized that the demand was only for
translations. Even though the elegant Arabic types of William Caslon
(modelled on the smaller Granjon Medicean types) were available
from 1725 on, these found little use in England outside the publications of the Society for Promoting Christian Knowledge for which they
were originally designed, under the supervision of Negri. Despite
the 'enlightened' view of Islam held by some cultured men, and
the interest in Islamic lands to which the publication of numerous
splendid books of travel, in England as in the rest of Europe, bears
witness,[11] the actual study of the languages was a matter of neglect, if
not positive contempt. This is illustrated by an anecdote told by

---

[8] In the preface he remarks that the notes Marracci 'has added are indeed of great
use; but his refutations, which swell the work to a large volume, are of little or none at
all' (Sale, *Koran*, p. xiv).

[9] Utrecht, 1705, second edition 1717 (Schnurrer nos. 388 and 389). See Brugman
and Schröder, *Arabic Studies in the Netherlands*, 23–5. Sale cites the work not infrequently.

[10] 2 vols., London, 1725–6; see Klein-Franke, *Die klassische Antike in der Tradition
des Islam*, 98.

[11] Some of the finest examples of these are depicted in *L'Europe et le monde arabe*.

Crossley about William Warburton, who epitomizes all that was worst in the literary culture of eighteenth-century England: 'Bishop Warburton, who had not the highest reverence for Oriental learning, often in joke mentioned to young students the number of words in Arabic, which Pococke has given (12,350,052), as a wonderful inducement to the study of the language.'[12] Towards the end of the century attitudes began to change, partly under the influence of William Jones, especially his *Poems, consisting chiefly of translations from the Asiatick Languages*;[13] but that belongs to the history of the Romantic movement.

(I) CAUSES OF THE DECLINE OF ARABIC STUDIES

The remarkable contrast between the flourishing state of Arabic studies in England in the 1640s and 1650s, and their gradual and then rapid decline after the Restoration to a nadir in the mid eighteenth century, invites some enquiry into the cause of that decline. The matter was discussed by Holt,[14] whose explanations may be summarized as follows. The principal arguments for studying Arabic adduced by those who advocated it in the seventeenth century were its use in establishing the texts of the Scriptures, its necessity for spreading Christianity (more specifically Protestant Christianity) in Muslim lands, and its application in revealing the wisdom locked up in Arabic scientific and especially medical texts. With the passage of time all three of these claims were seen to be exaggerated or invalid. After the publication of the London Polyglot, Arabic seemed to have little more to contribute to the biblical texts. Besides, after the Restoration the interests of Anglican theologians moved away from minute textual arguments to greater concern with ethics and the use of reason. The almost complete lack of success of Protestant missions in Muslim lands was bound to lead to disillusionment with the linguistic efforts involved. As for the

[12] Worthington, *Correspondence*, ii/1, 103–4. Warburton knew the passage only from Twells, from whom he copied the incorrect number.
[13] First edition 1772. At the time Jones was a Fellow of University College, Oxford. One would like to think that he had been influenced by his father's friend Thomas Hunt, Laudian Professor of Arabic until 1774. But the truth seems to be that Jones gained his expertise in oriental languages from native speakers outside Oxford. Jones's views and reputation counted for so little in his own university that when, in 1780, he was a candidate for the Lord Almoner's Professorship he was passed over in favour of the nonentity Henry Ford.
[14] Holt, 'Arabic Studies in Seventeenth-Century England', 93–100, stated more briefly in 'An Oxford Arabist', 19–22.

hopes of gaining new knowledge from Arabic scientific texts, their content was rapidly made obsolete by the rise of organized experimental science (typified by the founding of the Royal Society) in the second half of the seventeenth century.

Most of Holt's arguments are persuasive. Only his second point seems weak. Whatever the lack of success of the missionary efforts by Englishmen (and also other Europeans, both Protestant and Catholic) in Muslim countries, this had very little effect on their continuation. Holt himself points to the energetic support of missionary endeavours by Boyle (seconded in Oxford by Pococke, Hyde, and Marshall, and in Aleppo by Huntington), after the Restoration; and we have seen that in the eighteenth century the activity of the Society for Promoting Christian Knowledge was responsible for printing Arabic texts and supporting Arabists. One must agree, however, that the Arabic and other oriental versions are of limited use in establishing the text of the Bible,[15] and that the interests of most theologians moved away from such matters in the later seventeenth and eighteenth centuries. Furthermore, it is certainly true that the enormous scientific progress made throughout the seventeenth century overtook the discoveries of antiquity and the Middle Ages. An apt illustration of this is provided by the fate of the later books of Apollonius' *Conics*, which survived only in Arabic. Had these been published and translated in Europe (as Raimondi had intended) when a manuscript containing them was first brought there in the 1580s, they would have provided much that was new to contemporary mathematicians. But progress in mathematics was so rapid in the first half of the seventeenth century that by the time the Ecchellensis–Borelli version was published in 1661 (to say nothing of Halley's translation of 1710), there was little that mathematicians could learn from the book. The same could be said of geographical knowledge, for which the sixteenth-century Arabists held out such high hopes after Postel brought back his manuscript of Abū 'l-Fidā'. European exploration and navigational and cartographical advances made the maps and geographical treatises that survived in Arabic largely obsolete, and even when these covered areas not yet penetrated by European travellers, the demonstrable errors in the co-ordinates they assigned to known places made their other information suspect.[16] The astronomers of the later seventeenth century were

[15] See above, p. 85, for a similar opinion expressed by Ussher, who was one of the principal supporters of the Polyglot Bible.

[16] See above, p. 173, for John Greaves's remarks about the unreliability of Abū 'l-Fidā'.

indeed interested in obtaining Arabic observations, particularly of
eclipses, in order to establish long-term mean motions, but this interest
was very limited in scope, and the contemporary attitude towards the
bulk of astronomy in Arabic astronomical treatises is probably well
expressed by William Wotton when he says:

There have been so many Thousands of *Arabick* and *Persick MSS.* brought
over into Europe, that our learned Men can make as good, nay, perhaps, a
better Judgment of the Extent of their Learning, than can be made, at this
distance, of the *Greek.* There are vast Quantities of their Astronomical
Observations in the *Bodleian* Library, and yet Mr. *Greaves* and Dr. *Edward
Bernard,* two very able Judges, have given the World no Account of any
Thing out of them, which those *Arabian* Astronomers did not, or might not
have learnt from *Ptolemee*'s *Almagest,* if we set aside their Observations
which their *Grecian* Masters taught them to make.[17]

In other words, because the Arab astronomers had not achieved the
results of Hevelius and Newton, their writings were of no interest.

If, then, one takes the reasons for studying Arabic advanced by
Erpenius in his Orations and by his many imitators, including Pasor,
Thomas Greaves, Castell, Hyde, and even Thomas Hunt, as the true
motives of those who did study it, we have a ready explanation for its
decline. We should certainly not discount such motives, but we must
also distinguish between what is uttered for the benefit of listening
patrons and students, and what really interests the speaker. There
were certainly some Arabists (Wheelock is an obvious example) who
fervently believed that they were promoting Christianity by their
studies. But to say that Erpenius was impelled by other motives is not
to accuse him of hypocrisy. He was convinced that he was serving
Christianity by his publication of biblical texts in Arabic. Nevertheless,
it was probably true of him, as it certainly was of Golius and Pococke,
that the primary motivation was intellectual rather than utilitarian.
Both these men, who had spent years in Muslim countries, were deeply
interested in the history and culture of Arabic-speaking lands, and
clearly thought it worth studying for its own sake. Pococke is the one
who comes closest to actually enunciating such an unfashionable
idea,[18] but Golius' choice of authors for his students to read, and his
delight in rhyming prose in his Arabic letters, exhibits both his taste
and his knowledge of the range of Arabic literature.

However, even if the best European Arabists of the seventeenth

---

[17] Wotton, *Reflections upon Ancient and Modern Learning,* 142–3.
[18] See the quotation from the *Specimen* above, p. 161.

century had a much wider vision of the value of Arabic than is implied
by the contemporary apologias for its study, they were few in number,
and unsuccessful, both in the Netherlands and in England, in establishing a tradition to perpetuate that vision. Our review in the preceding
two chapters of the aims and achievements of Pococke's pupils reveals
that with the possible exception of Clarke and Guise, both of whom
died prematurely, none of them shared his wide interests in and
sympathy with Arabic culture. Much the same might be said of Golius,
whose pupils, if they achieved anything, did so, like Petraeus, within
the narrow field of biblical studies. Such scholars as Golius and
Pococke, and, in a more limited way, Erpenius, Selden, and John
Greaves, who seem to anticipate the nineteenth century in their
intellectual curiosity about the whole civilization to which the Arabic
language gave access, were ahead of their time. Moreover, they lived
in an age that valued learning and enquiry for its own sake, but which
began to give way to a very different temper in the lifetimes of some
of them. We have seen how Pococke and his correspondents lamented
the change in public respect for the study of Arabic after the
Restoration. While this was true enough, it was only part of a much
wider phenomenon. Anthony Wood's remarks on the universal
degeneration of learning at Oxford after the Restoration, although
hardly impartial, are full of interest.[19] These changes were not confined
to Oxford or even England. Twells gives illustrations from Pococke's
correspondence of the decline of Arabic studies in the Netherlands at
the same time.[20] It would be interesting, but too far outside the bounds
of my topic, to review the development throughout Europe of learned
periodicals and societies at the same time as certain kinds of scholarship, especially those based on the study of original texts, were decay-
ing both in practice and in reputation. The eighteenth century, or at
least its first two-thirds, witnessed an acceleration of these trends. This
has been well described with respect to Hebrew studies by Manuel,[21]
who emphasizes the contrast between the eighteenth-century second-
hand 'encyclopaedic' approach and the real familiarity with Hebraic
sources displayed by such seventeenth-century scholars as Selden, the
Buxtorfs, Pococke, and Lightfoot.

---

[19] Wood, *Life and Times*, i. 360–1, cf. 423.
[20] See above, p. 52.
[21] *The Broken Staff*: see especially 228 ff., on the works of Augustin Calmet, published from 1719 onwards.

(II) DECLINE OF ARABIC STUDIES IN EUROPE

In Arabic studies too during the eighteenth century, the unhappy state of affairs which we have glimpsed in England was not confined to that country. One might have supposed that the decline in England was caused solely by the general decay of the universities, in enrolment, scholarship, and public esteem, brilliantly illustrated by Gibbon's account in his autobiography of his own experience at Oxford. However, while this peculiarly English phenomenon undoubtedly aggravated the situation there, the study of Arabic elsewhere in Europe too was far from flourishing. Even in those areas where Arabic texts were published and studied, notably the Netherlands and Germany, Arabic was viewed primarily as a handmaiden of biblical exegesis, to elucidate difficulties in the Hebrew text or Israelite customs. This concept was forcefully and successfully advocated by Albert Schultens, who as Professor of Oriental Languages at Leiden from 1729 on established it once again as the foremost centre of Arabic studies in Europe. While the editions of Arabic texts which he and his successors produced were by no means contemptible, the approach to Arabic of which he was the foremost proponent was stifling. The fate of the one Arabist of the mid-century who refused to follow this path, and strove instead to understand Arabic literature for its own sake, in all its diversity, J. J. Reiske, might serve as a warning to all heretics. He saw scholars vastly inferior to him in knowledge and critical judgement, such as Schultens at Leiden and J. D. Michaelis at Göttingen, preferred to honours and influence, while he was forced to accept their contemptuous patronage to enable him to scrape together a living while preparing his editions of Arabic authors (most of which were published in such small numbers that they sank without trace). In the end he was glad to find a haven as a schoolmaster, and to turn his philological gifts to the more acceptable channel of classical literature.[22] Reiske had enormous respect for the achievement of the English in Arabic studies in the previous century, and although he realized that the situation had changed,[23] he fondly imagined that

[22] There is a good account of Reiske by Fück, *Die arabischen Studien in Europa*, 108–24, but to fully appreciate the tragedy of his life one must read his *Autobiography* and *Letters*.

[23] Letter to Wesseling, 12 June 1748 (Reiske, *Letters*, 270–1): 'non tamen novi [Angli] aeque Arabicis nostra hac aetate faventes, atque ante saeculum, quum in vivis essent Archepiscopus Laudius, Seldenus, Pocokius, praeclari homines'.

if he could somehow get to England his projected edition of Abū
'l-Fidā' would be welcomed and printed. He was probably fortunate in
never having the chance to put this to the test.

This gloomy account of the eighteenth-century decline should not
make us forget the real and permanent achievements of the seventeenth
century in Arabic studies. A firm foundation was established for knowledge of the language in grammar and lexicography. In this respect the
work of the Dutch scholars, Erpenius and Golius, was fundamental.
Equally important was the setting up of Arabic presses, and the publication of Arabic books. Here again, the Netherlands took the lead from
Italy, but English Arabists also played a major part. Thirdly, some
progress was made in disseminating knowledge (and even understanding) of a civilization about which ignorance and prejudice were still
the general rule in Europe. Here the work of Pococke, notably in his
Specimen, was outstanding, and of lasting value and influence.
Fourthly, great collections of manuscripts were formed, which were to
be the foundation of the progress of nineteenth-century Arabic scholarship. In this respect Oxford became one of the most important
repositories, not merely in the numbers, but also in the choice of
manuscripts assembled there. The final achievement was the establishment of a system for teaching the Arabic language at the universities.
In England the structures established by Laud and Sir Thomas Adams,
and fostered by Pococke and Wheelock, survived the lean years of the
eighteenth century to flourish again in later and better times.

Bibliography

ABRAHAMS, I., 'Isaac Abendana's Cambridge Mishnah and Oxford Calendars', *Transactions of the Jewish Historical Society of England* (1915–17), 98–121.

Abudacnus, *Historia Jacobitarum*: Historia Jacobitarum, Seu Coptorum, In Ægypto, Lybia, Nubia, *Æthiopia* tota, & parte *Cypri* Insulae habitantium. Opera *Josephi Abudacni, seu Barbati*, nati Memphis Ægypti Metropolii (Oxford, 1675).

ADLER, MICHAEL, *Jews of Medieval England* (London, 1939).

AL-HĀSHIMĪ, 'ALĪ IBN SULAYMĀN, *The Book of the Reasons behind Astronomical Tables (Kitāb fī 'ilal al-zījāt)* . . . A facsimile reproduction of the unique Arabic text contained in the Bodleian ms. Arch. Seld. A. 11 with a translation by Fuad I. Haddad and E. S. Kennedy and a commentary by David Pingree and E. S. Kennedy (New York, 1981).

AL-SHARĪF AL-IDRĪSĪ, *Kitāb Nuzhat al-Mushtāq*, Reprint of the Edition Rome 1592, ed. Fuat Sezgin (Publications of the Institute for the History of Arabic-Islamic Science, Islamic Geography, 1; Frankfurt am Main, 1992).

ALTANER, BERTHOLD, 'Die Durchführung des Vienner Konzilsbeschlusses über die Errichtung von Lehrstühlen für orientalischen Sprachen', *Zeitschrift für Kirchengeschichte*, 52 (1933), 226–36.

—— 'Raymundus Lullus und der Sprachenkanon (can. 11) des Konzils von Vienne', *Historisches Jahrbuch*, 53 (1933), 190–219.

D'ALVERNY, M. T., 'Deux traductions latines du Coran au Moyen Age', *Archives d'histoire doctrinale et littéraire du Moyen Age*, 16 (1948), 69–131.

—— 'Avicenne et les médecins de Venise', in *Medioevo e Rinascimento: Studi in onore di Bruno Nardi*, i (Florence, 1955), 177–98.

—— 'La Connaissance de l'Islam en Occident du IXᵉ au milieu du XIIᵉ siècle', in *L'Occidente e l'Islam nell'alto medioevo* (Settimane di studio del Centro Italiano di studi sull'alto medioevo 12; Spoleto, 1965), ii. 577–602.

ANDERSON, SONIA P., *An English Consul in Turkey: Paul Rycaut at Smyrna, 1667–1678* (Oxford, 1989).

ANNERSTEDT, CLAES, *Upsala Universitets Historia*, 2 parts with appendices (Uppsala, 1877–1909).

ARBERRY, ARTHUR J., *The Cambridge School of Arabic: An Inaugural Lecture delivered on 30 October 1947* (Cambridge, 1948).

—— 'The Pioneer Simon Ockley', in his *Oriental Essays* (London, 1960), 11–47.

'Archbishop Marsh's Diary': 'Diary copied from a MS. in Archbishop Marsh's Library, Dublin' [edited by J. H. T.], *The British Magazine, and Monthly Register of Religious and Ecclesiastical Information, Parochial History*, etc., 28 (1845), 17–36 and 115–32.

Bainbridge, *Canicularia*: Cl. V. IOHANNIS BAINBRIGII Astronomiae, *In celeberrimâ Academiâ Oxoniensi Professoris Saviliani* CANICVLARIA. Unà cum demonstratione Ortus *Sirii* heliaci, Pro parallelo inferioris Ægypti. *Auctore* IOHANNE GRAVIO, *Quibus accesserunt Insigniorum aliquot Stellarum Longitudines, & Latitudines* Ex Astronomicis Observationibus *Vlug Beigi, Tamerlani Magni* nepotis (Oxford, 1648).

BARANOWSKI, BOHDAN, 'F. Mesgnien-Meninski et l'enseignement des langues orientales en Pologne vers la moitié du XVIIe siècle', *Rocznik Orjental- istyczny*, 14 (1938), 63–71.

BARKSDALE, CLEMENT, *Memorials of Worthy Persons . . . The Fourth Decad* (Oxford, 1663).

Barrow, *Theological Works*: The Theological Works of Isaac Barrow, D.D. In nine volumes. Ed. Alexander Napier (Cambridge, 1859).

BATAILLON, MARCEL, 'L'Arabe à Salamanque au temps de la Renaissance', *Hespéris*, 21 (1935), 1–17.

Bedwell, *Via Regia*: Via Regia ad Geometriam. The VVay to Geometry. Being necessary and usefull, FOR Astronomers . . . Written in Latine by Peter Ramus, and now Translated and much enlarged by the Learned Mr. William Bedwell (London, 1636).

BENFEY, THEODOR, *Geschichte der Sprachwissenschaft und orientalischen Philologie in Deutschland seit dem Anfange des 19. Jahrhunderts mit einem Rückblick auf die früheren Zeiten* (Geschichte der Wissenschaften in Deutschland, Neuere Zeit, 8; Munich, 1869).

Bentley, *Correspondence*: The Correspondence of Richard Bentley, D.D. Master of Trinity College, Cambridge [ed. C. Wordsworth] (2 vols., London, 1842–3).

BERNARD, AUGUSTE, *Antoine Vitré et les caractères orientaux de la Bible poly- glotte de Paris* (Paris, 1857).

Bernard, *De Mensuris*: EDVARDI BERNARDI DE MENSURIS ET PON- DERIBUS ANTIQUIS LIBRI TRES. *Editio altera, purior & duplo locuple- tior* (Oxford, 1688).

Bernard, *Josephus*: FLAVII JOSEPHI Antiquitatum Judaicarum LIBRI QUATUOR PRIORES, *Et Pars magna Quinti*, Gr. Lat. Cum Exemplaribus MSS. collati, & illustrati Notis amplissimis D. *EDVARDI BERNARDI* S.T.P. ITEM HISTORIARUM DE BELLO JUDAICO LIBER PRIMUS, *Et Pars secundi*. Gr. Lat. Ad Codices MSS. itidem recogniti & emendati (Oxford, 1700).

BERNARD, NICHOLAS, *The Life & Death of the Most Reverend and Learned Father of our Church Dr. James Usher . . .* (London, 1656).

BLOXAM, JOHN ROUSE, *A Register of the Presidents, Fellows, Demies, Instruc- tors in Grammar and in Music, Chaplains, Clerks, Choristers, and other members of Saint Mary Magdalen College in the University of Oxford, from the foundation of the College to the present time, 2: The Instructors in*

Grammar (Oxford, 1863).

BOCHART, SAMUEL, *Hierozoicon Sive bipartitum opus de animalibus Sacrae Scripturae* (2 parts; London [Roycroft], 1663).

Bodley, *Letters to James*: Letters of Sir Thomas Bodley to Thomas James First Keeper of the Bodleian Library. Edited with an Introduction by G. W. Wheeler, M.A. (Oxford, 1926).

Bodley, *Letters to Oxford*: Letters of Sir Thomas Bodley to the University of Oxford, 1598–1611. Edited by G. W. Wheeler (Oxford, 1927).

BOURNE, HENRY RICHARD FOX, *The Life of John Locke* (2 vols., London, 1876).

BOUWSMA, WILLIAM J., *Concordia Mundi: The Career and Thought of Guillaume Postel (1510–1581)* (Harvard Historical Monographs, 33; Cambridge, Mass., 1957).

Boyle, *Works*: The Works of the Honourable Robert Boyle in six volumes. To which is prefixed The Life of the Author. 2nd edition (London, 1772).

BRAHE, TYCHO, *Historia Coelestis . . . cum Commentariis Lucii Barretti et Paralipomenis ex Rec. et Mss. Guil. Schikardi* (Augsburg, 1666).

BRODRICK, GEORGE C., *Memorials of Merton College* (Oxford Historical Society, 4; Oxford, 1885).

BRUGMAN, J., and SCHRÖDER, F., *Arabic Studies in the Netherlands* (Publications of the Netherlands Institute of Archaeology and Arabic Studies in Cairo, 3; Leiden, 1979).

BUC, SIR GEORGE, *The Third Vniversitie of England, or A treatise of the Foundations of all the Colledges, ancient Schooles of Priuiledge, and of Houses of Learning, and liberall Arts, within and about the most famous City of London . . . by G. B. Knight* [printed at the end of] Iohn Stow, *Annales, or a Chronicle of England* (London, 1631) [and also earlier editions].

BURNETT, CHARLES (ed.), *Adelard of Bath: An English Scientist and Arabist of the early Twelfth Century* (Warburg Institute Surveys and Texts, 14; London, 1987).

BURROWS, MONTAGU (ed.), *The Register of Visitors of the University of Oxford from A.D. 1647 to A.D. 1658, with some account of the state of the University during the Commonwealth* (Camden Society, 1881).

CABANELAS RODRÍGUEZ, DARIO, *El Morisco Granadino Alonso del Castillo* (Granada, 1965).

CALAMY, EDMUND, *An Account of the Ministers, Lecturers, Masters and Fellows of Colleges and Schoolmasters, who were Ejected or Silenced after the Restoration in 1660* [Vol. 2 of *An Abridgment of Mr. Baxter's History of his Life and Times*], 2nd edn. (London, 1713).

CARTER, HARRY, *A History of the Oxford University Press, Vol. I to the year 1780* (Oxford, 1975).

Casaubon, *Letters*: Isaaci Casauboni Epistolae, insertis ad easdem Responsionibus quotquot hactenus reperiri potuerunt [3rd edition] curante Theodoro

Janson. ab Almeloveen (Rotterdam, 1709).

CASIRI, MICHAEL, *Bibliotheca arabico-hispana Escurialensis, sive Librorum omnium mss. quos arabice ab auctoribus magnam partem arabo-hispanis compositos bibliotheca coenobi Escurialensis complectitur, recensio et explanatio* (2 vols., Madrid, 1760, 1770).

Castell, *Lexicon*: LEXICON HEPTAGLOTTON, HEBRAICUM, CHAL-DAICUM, SYRIACUM, SAMARITANUM, ÆTHIOPICUM, ARABICUM, Conjunctim; Et PERSICUM, Separatim . . . *Authore* EDMUNDO CASTELLO, *S.T.D. Regiae M. à Sacris, linguae Arabicae apud Cantabrigienses Professore, Atque Ecclesiae* CHRISTI *Cantuarensis praebendario* (2 vols., London, 1669).

Castell, *Oratio*: ORATIO IN Scholis Theologicis HABITA AB *EDMUNDO CASTELLO* S.T.D. ET LINGUÆ ARABICÆ IN Academia Cantabrigiensi PROFESSORE, CUM Praelectiones suas in secundum Canonis Avicennae Librum auspicaretur, quibus via praestruitur ex Scriptoribus Orientalibus ad clarius ac dilucidius enarrandum Botonologicam S.S. Scripturae partem, Opus a nemine adhuc tentatum (London, 1667).

DE CASTRIES, HENRY (ed.), *Les Sources inédites de l'histoire du Maroc. Première Série — Dynastie Saadienne. Archives et Bibliothèques de France*, 3 (Paris, 1911); *Archives et Bibliothèques d'Angleterre*, 2 (Paris and London, 1925); *Archives et Bibliothèques des Pays-Bas*, 3 (Paris and The Hague, 1912).

Catalogi Librorum Manuscriptorum Angliæ et Hiberniæ in unum collecti (2 vols., Oxford, 1697).

CHAPMAN, ALLAN (ed.), *The Preface to John Flamsteed's Historia Coelestis Britannica or British Catalogue of the Heavens (1725)* (Maritime Monographs and Reports, 52; Greenwich, 1982).

CHARRIÈRE, ERNEST (ed.), *Négociations de la France dans le Levant* (Collection de documents inédits sur l'histoire de France, 1; Paris, 1848).

CHAUVIN, VICTOR, and ROERSCH, ALPHONSE, *Étude sur la vie et les travaux de Nicolas Clénard* (Mémoires couronnés par la Classe des lettres de l'Académie Royale de Belgique, Tome 60 in-8°; Brussels, 1900).

CHEW, SAMUEL C., *The Crescent and the Rose, Islam and England during the Renaissance* (New York, 1957).

Clarke, *Scientia Metrica*: علم العروض والقوافي SCIENTIA METRICA & RHYTH-MICA Seu TRACTATVS DE Prosodia Arabica, EX Authoribus probatissimis eruta, Operâ SAMUELIS CLERICI, inclytae Academiae *Oxoniensis* Architypographi (Oxford, 1661).

CLÉNARD, NICOLAS, *Correspondance,* ed. Alphonse Roersch (Académie Royale de Belgique, Classe des Lettres, Collection des Anciens Auteurs Belges, NS 2), 1 (Brussels, 1940).

CODAZZI, ANGELA, 'Leone Africano', in *Enciclopedia Italiana*, xx (1932), 899.

COLL, JOSÉ MA., 'Escuelas de lenguas orientales en los siglos XIII y XIV

(Periodo Raymundiano)', *Analecta Sacra Tarraconensia*, 17 (1944), 115–38.

COLOMESIUS, PAULUS, *Gallia Orientalis sive Gallorum qui linguam Hebraeam vel alias Orientales excoluerunt vitae, Variis hinc inde praesidiis adornatae* (The Hague, 1665).

——*Italia et Hispania Orientalis sive Italorum et Hispanorum qui linguam Hebraeam vel alias orientales excoluerunt Vitae* ex ΑΥΤΟΓΡΑΦΩι Auctoris nunc primum editae et notis instructa a Jo. Christophoro Wolfio (Hamburg, 1730).

CORNELISSEN, J. D. M., 'Thomas Erpenius en de "Propaganda"', *Mededeelingen van het Nederlandsch Historisch Instituut te Rome*, 7 (1927), 121–46.

Correspondence of Scientific Men of the Seventeenth Century, including letters of Barrow, Flamsteed, Wallis, and Newton, printed from the originals in the collection of the right honourable the Earl of Macclesfield [ed. Stephen Jordan Rigaud] (2 vols., Oxford, 1841).

Coxe, *Catalogue of College MSS*: Catalogus Codicum MSS. qui in Collegiis Aulisque Oxoniensibus hodie asservantur confecit Henricus O. Coxe (2 vols., Oxford, 1852).

COX-JOHNSON, ANN, 'Lambeth Palace Library, 1610–1664', *Transactions of the Cambridge Bibliographical Society*, 2 (1954–8), 105–26.

Crosfield, *Diary: The Diary of Thomas Crosfield*, selected and edited by Frederick S. Boas (London, 1935).

DANIEL, NORMAN, *Islam and the West: The Making of an Image* (Edinburgh, 1958; 2nd rev. edn. Oxford, 1992).

DANNENFELDT, KARL H., 'The Renaissance Humanists and the Knowledge of Arabic', *Studies in the Renaissance*, 2 (1955), 96–117.

DAVIES, HUGH WM., *Bernhard von Breydenbach and his journey to the Holy Land 1483–4: A Bibliography* (London, 1911).

DELISLE, LÉOPOLD, *Le Cabinet des Manuscrits de la Bibliothèque Nationale [Impériale]* (4 vols., Paris, 1868–81).

Dickenson, *Delphi Phoenicizantes*: DELPHI PHOENICIZANTES, *sive, Tractatus, in quo Graecos, quicquid apud Delphos celebre erat . . . è Josuae historia, scriptisque sacris effinxisse . . . ostenditur . . . Authore* EDMUNDO DICKINSONO (Oxford, 1655).

DNB: The Dictionary of National Biography, founded in 1882 by George Smith, edited by Sir Leslie Stephen and Sir Sidney Lee. From the Earliest Times to 1900 (22 vols., Oxford, 1921–2).

Doctrina Christiana en lengua Arauiga y Castellana; compvesta, e impressa por mandado del Illustrissimo y Reuerendissimo Señor don Martin de Ayala Arcopispo de Valencia, para instrucción de los nueuamente conuertidos deste Reyno (Valencia, 1566) (Photographic reproduction of original edition, ed. Roque Chabás, Valencia, 1911).

DOZY, R. P. A. (ed.), *Catalogus Codicum Orientalium Bibliothecae Academiae*

Lugduno Batavae, i (Leiden, 1851).

DSB: Dictionary of Scientific Biography, ed. C. C. Gillispie (16 vols., New York, 1970–80).

DUVERDIER, GÉRALD, 'Savary de Brèves et Ibrahim Müteferrika, Deux drogmans culturels à l'origine de l'imprimerie turque', *Bulletin du Bibliophile* (1987), 322–59.

—— 'Les Impressions orientales en Europe et le Liban', in *Le Livre et le Liban*, 157–279.

Ecchellensis–Borelli: Apollonii Pergaei Conicorum Lib. V.VI.VII. Paraphraste Abalphato Asphahanensi Nunc primùm editi Additus in calce Archimedis Assumptorum Liber, Serenissimi Magni Ducis Etruriae Abrahamus Ecchellensis Maronita In Alma Vrbe Linguar. Orient. Professor Latinos reddidit. Io. Alfonsus Borellus In Pisana Academia Matheseos Professor curam in Geometricis versioni contulit, & notas vberiores in vniuersum opus adiecit (Florence, 1661).

Ecchellensis, *Eutychius Vindicatus*: EVTYCHIVS PATRIARCHA ALEXANDRINVS VINDICATVS, Et suis restitutus Orientalibus; Siue Responsio *AD IOANNIS SELDENI ORIGINES in duas tributa Partes*, Quarum Prima est *De Alexandrinae Ecclesiae Originibus* Altera *De Origine nominis PAPÆ*; Quibus accedit Censura in Historiam Orientalem IOHANNIS HENRICI HOTTINGERI Tigurini à pag. 283 ad 495. *Omnia ex Orientalium excerpta monumentis AUCTORE ABRAHAMO ECCHELLENSI* Maronita è Libano (2 vols., Rome, 1661, 1660).

EKHTIAR, SHELLEY, '*Hayy ibn Yaqzan*, the eighteenth-century reception of an oriental self-taught philosopher', *Studies on Voltaire and the Eighteenth Century*, 302 (1992), 217–45.

ELLIS, SIR HENRY (ed.), *Original Letters of Eminent Literary Men of the Sixteenth, Seventeenth, and Eighteenth Centuries* (Camden Society, 1843).

Enciclopedia Italiana di Scienze, Lettere ed Arti (36 vols., Milan and Rome, 1929–39).

Evelyn, *Diary: The Diary of John Evelyn*, ed. E. S. de Beer (6 vols., Oxford, 1955).

FEINGOLD, MORDECHAI, 'Isaac Barrow, Divine, Scholar, Mathematician', in *Before Newton, The Life and Times of Isaac Barrow*, ed. M. Feingold (Cambridge, 1990), 1–104.

—— 'Patrons and Professors, the Origins and Motives for the Endowment of University Chairs—in Particular the Laudian Professorship of Arabic', in Russell, *The 'Arabick' Interest of the Natural Philosophers*, 109–27.

—— 'The Oxford Oriental School', in *The History of the University of Oxford*, iv: *The Seventeenth Century* [forthcoming].

FORBES, ERIC G. (ed.), *The Gresham Lectures of John Flamsteed* (London, 1975).

FOSTER, JOSEPH, *Alumni Oxonienses, The Members of the University of Oxford*,

1500–1714 (4 vols., Oxford and London, 1891–2).

FOSTER, SAMUEL, *Miscellanea, sive Lucubrationes Mathematicae* (London, 1659).

FÜCK, JOHANN, *Die arabischen Studien in Europa bis in den Anfang des 20. Jahrhunderts* (Leipzig, 1955).

GABRIELI, FRANCESCO, and SCERRATO, UMBERTO (eds.), *Gli Arabi in Italia. Cultura, contatti e tradizioni* (Milan, 1979).

GARCIA BALLESTER, LUIS, 'The Circulation and Use of Medical Manuscripts in Arabic in 16th Century Spain', *Journal for the History of Arabic Science*, 2 (1979), 183–99.

GAUTHIER, LÉON, *Ibn Thofail, sa vie, ses œuvres*, Publications de l'École des Lettres d'Alger, Bulletin de Correspondance Africaine, 42 (Paris, 1909).

——(ed. and tr.), *Hayy ben Yaqdhân, roman philosophique d'Ibn Thofaïl*, 2nd edn. (Beirut, 1936).

GIOVANNOZZI, GIOVANNI, 'La versione Borelliana di Apollonio', *Memorie della Pontificia Accademia Romana dei Nuovi Lincei*, serie 2, vol. 2 (1916), 1–32.

GOLDSTEIN, BERNARD R., *The Arabic Version of Ptolemy's Planetary Hypotheses*, Transactions of the American Philosophical Society NS, 57.4 (Philadelphia, 1967).

Golius, *Auction Catalogue*: *Catalogus Insignium in omni facultate, linguisque, Arabica, Persica, Turcica, Chinensi, etc. librorum M.SS, quos . . . Jacobus Golius . . . ex variis Regionibus . . . collegit. Quorum auctio habebitur . . . Ad diem XVI. Octobris St. Novo . . .* (Leiden, 1696).

Golius, *Catalogus*: Catalogus rarorum Librorum, quos ex Oriente nuper advexit, et in publica Bibliotheca inclytae Leydensis Academiae deposuit Clariss. et de bonis artibus meritiss. vir Jacobus Golius, in illa eadem Academia et Linguarum orientalium et matheseos Professor insignis (Paris [Vitray], 1630).

Golius, *Lexicon*: JACOBI GOLII LEXICON ARABICO-LATINUM, CONTEXTUM EX PROBATIORIBUS ORIENTIS LEXICOGRAPHIS. ACCEDIT INDEX LATINUS COPIOSISSIMUS, QVI LEXICI LATINO-ARABICI VICEM EXPLERE POSSIT (Leiden, 1653).

GOLLANCZ, SIR HERMANN (ed. and tr.), *Chronicle of Events between the years 1623 and 1733 relating to the Settlement of the Order of Carmelites in Mesopotamia (Bassora) . . .* (London, 1927).

GÓMEZ DE CASTRO, ALVAR, *De Rebus Gestis a Francisco Ximenio, Cisnerio, Archiepiscopo Toletano, libri octo* (Complutum [Alcalá de Henares], 1569); [Spanish translation by José Oroz Reta:] *De las Hazanas de Francisco Jiménez de Cisneros* (Madrid, 1984).

GOODMAN, LENN EVAN, *Ibn Tufayl's Hayy Ibn Yaqzân: A Philosophical Tale*, translated with introduction and notes, 3rd edn. (Los Angeles, 1991).

GRAFTON, ANTHONY, *Joseph Scaliger: A Study in the History of Classical*

Scholarship (2 vols., Oxford, 1983, 1993).

Greaves, *Astronomica quaedam*: Astronomica quaedam ex traditione Shah Cholgii Persae una cum Hypothesibus Planetarum, Studio et opera Johannis Gravii nunc primum publicata (London, 1650).

Greaves, *Chorasmiae Descriptio*: Chorasmiae et Mawaralnahrae, hoc est, Regionum extra fluvium Oxum Descriptio, Ex Tabulis *Abulfedae Ismaelis*, Principis Hamah (London, 1650).

Greaves, *Elementa*: Elementa Linguae Persicae, authore Johanne Gravio, Item Anonymus Persa de Siglis Arabum & Persarum Astronomicis (London, 1649).

Greaves, *Pyramidographia*: Pyramidographia, OR A DESCRIPTION OF THE PYRAMIDS IN ÆGYPT By IOHN GREAVES, Professor of Astronomy in the University of OXFORD (London, 1646).

Greaves, *Roman Foot*: A DISCOVRSE OF THE ROMANE FOOT AND *DENARIVS*, From whence, as from two principles, THE MEASVRES AND WEIGHTS, used by the Ancients, may be deduced. *By* IOHN GREAVES, *Professor of Astronomy in the Vniversity of Oxford* (London, 1647).

Greaves, *Tabulae Geographicae*: Binae Tabulae Geographicae una Nassir Eddini Persae, altera Vlug Beigi Tatari. Operâ, & Studio Johannis Gravii nunc primùm Publicatae, et Commentariis ex Abulfedae Aliisque Arabum Geographis illustratae (London, 1648).

Greaves, *Works*: Miscellaneous Works of Mr. John Greaves, Professor of Astronomy in the University of Oxford . . . Published by Thomas Birch (2 vols., London, 1737).

GREAVES, THOMAS, *De Linguae Arabicae Vtilitate & Praestantia. Oratio Oxonii habita 19. Jul. 1637* (Oxford, 1639).

Gregory, *Notes and Observations*: NOTES AND OBSERVATIONS UPON SOME PASSAGES OF SCRIPTVRE. *By* I. G. *late Master of Arts of* Christ=Church OXON. *The second edition* (London, 1650) [first edition Oxford, 1646].

Gregory, *Posthuma*: GREGORII *Posthuma, OR*, Certain Learned Tracts, VVRITTEN By JOHN GREGORIE, M.A. and Chaplain of *Christ-Church* in *OXFORD*. . . . Published by his Dearest Friend *J.G[urgany]*. B.D. of *Merton* College (London, 1650) [first issued 1649].

GRIFFITHS, JOHN (ed.), *Statutes of the University of Oxford Codified in the Year 1636 under the Authority of Archbishop Laud* (Oxford, 1888).

GRONOVIUS, JOH. FREDERICUS, *Laudatio Funebris, recitata in exsequiis cl. Viri Jacobi Golii Arabicae Linguae & Mathematicorum professoris ante diem IV. Nonas Octobr. MDCLXVII* (Leiden, 1668).

Grotius, *Correspondence*, xii: *Briefwisseling van Hugo Grotius*, Twaalfde deel 1641 uitgegeven door Drs. Paula P. Witkam (Assen and Maastricht, 1986).

DE GUBERNATIS, ANGELO, *Matériaux pour servir à l'histoire des études orientales en Italie* (Paris, Florence, Rome, Turin, 1876).

DE GUIGNES, J., *Essai historique sur l'origine des caractères orientaux de l'Imprimerie Royale, sur les ouvrages qui ont été imprimés à Paris, en Arabe, en Syriaque, en Arménien, &c., et sur les caractères grecs de François Ier appelés communement Grecs du Roi*, Notices et Extraits des Manuscrits de la Bibliothèque du Roi, 1, ix–cii (Paris, 1787).

Guise, *Zeraim*: Misnae Pars, Ordinis Primi Zeraim Tituli Septem. Latinè vertit & Commentario illustravit *GVLIELMVS GVISIVS, Accedit* Mosis Maimonidis *Praefatio* in Misnam Edv. Pocockio *Interprete* (Oxford, 1690).

GUNTHER, R. T., 'The First Observatory Instruments of the Savilian Professors at Oxford', *The Observatory*, 60 (1937), 190–7.

Halley, Apollonius' *Conics*: *Apollonii Pergaei* Conicorum Libri Octo et Sereni Antissensis de Sectione Cylindri & Coni Libri Duo. Opera & studio Edmundi Halleii (2 vols., Oxford, 1710).

Halley, Apollonius' *Cutting off of a Ratio*: Apollonii Pergaei de sectione Rationis Libri Duo Ex Arabico MSto. Latine Versi. Opera & studio Edmundi Halley (Oxford, 1706).

Halliwell, *Collection of Letters*: *A Collection of Letters illustrative of the Progress of Science in England from the Reign of Queen Elizabeth to that of Charles the Second*, edited by James Orchard Halliwell (London [Historical Society of Science], 1841).

HAMILTON, ALASTAIR, 'The Victims of Progress, the Raphelengius Arabic type and Bedwell's Arabic Lexicon', *De Gulden Passer, Bulletin van de 'Vereeniging der Antwerpsche Bibliophielen'*, 61–3 (1983–5), 97–108.

——'"Nam Tirones Sumus". Franciscus Raphelengius' *Lexicon Arabico-Latinum* (Leiden 1613)', *De Gulden Passer, Bulletin van de 'Vereeniging der Antwerpsche Bibliophielen'*, 66–7 (1988–9), 557–89.

——*William Bedwell the Arabist 1563–1632*, Publications of the Sir Thomas Browne Institute, NS 5 (Leiden, 1985).

——'Eastern Churches and Western Scholarship', in *Rome Reborn: The Vatican Library and Renaissance Culture*, ed. Anthony Grafton (Washington and New Haven, 1993), 225–49.

——'The English Interest in the Arabic-Speaking Christians', in Russell, *The 'Arabick' Interest of the Natural Philosophers*, 30–53.

——'An Egyptian Traveller in the Republic of Letters: Josephus Barbatus or Abudacnus the Copt', *Journal of the Warburg and Courtauld Institutes*, 57 (1994), 123–50.

HAMMOND, PAUL, 'Thomas Smith, a Beleaguered Humanist of the Interregnum', *Bulletin of the Institute for Historical Research*, 56 (1983), 180–94.

Harmar, *Vindiciae Academiae Oxoniensis*: Vindiciae ACADEMIÆ OXONIENSIS, SIVE ORATIO APOLOGETICA, Quâ Exercitiorum Academicorum in Trimestre VACATIO A crimine vindicatur; nec non Academiae fama, &, ἐν παρόδῳ, Ἐπισκοπὴ asseritur; habita *OXONIÆ*

Postridie Iduum Octobris in pleno Termino, A *JOANNE HARMARO* Lingue Gr. apud *Oxonienses* Praelectore Regio, & M. L. (Oxford, 1662).

Hart/Carter: Hart, Horace, *Notes on a Century of Typography at the University Press Oxford, 1693–1794*. A photographic reprint of the edition of 1900 with an Introduction and additional notes by Harry Carter (Oxford, 1970).

HARTWIG, O., 'Die Uebersetzungsliteratur Unteritaliens in der normannisch-staufischen Epoche', *Centralblatt für Bibliothekswesen*, 3 (1886), 161–90, 223–5, and 505–6.

HARVEY, JOHN, 'Coronary Flowers and their "Arabick" Background', in Russell, *The 'Arabick' Interest of the Natural Philosophers*, 297–303.

HASKINS, C. H., *Studies in the History of Medieval Science*, 2nd edn. (Cambridge, Mass., 1927).

HAYWOOD, JOHN A., *Arabic Lexicography: Its History, and its Place in the General History of Lexicography* (Leiden, 1960).

Hearne, *Diaries: Remarks and Collections of Thomas Hearne*, ed. C. E. Doble, D. W. Rannie, H. E. Salter, *et al.*, Oxford Historical Society, vols. 1, 7, 13, 34, 42, 43, 48, 50, 65, 67, 72 (11 vols., Oxford, 1884–1921).

Hefele–Leclercq: Hefele, Charles-Joseph, *Histoire des conciles d'après les documents originaux*, nouvelle traduction française faite sur la deuxième édition allemande corrigée et augmentée de notes critiques et bibliographiques par Dom H. Leclercq, 6 pt. 2 (Paris, 1915).

HENKEL, WILLI, *Die Druckerei der Propaganda Fide: Eine Dokumentation* (Munich, Paderborn, and Vienna, 1977).

D'HERBELOT, BARTHÉLEMY, *Bibliothèque orientale, ou Dictionnaire universel, contenant généralement Tout ce qui regarde la connoissance des Peuples de l'Orient. Leurs Histoires et Traditions véritables ou fabuleuses. Leurs Religions, Sectes et Politique. Leurs Gouvernements, Loix, Coutumes, Moeurs, Guerres, & les Révolutions de leurs Empires. Leurs Sciences, et leurs Arts... Les Vies et Actions remarquables de tous leurs Saints, Docteurs, Philosophes, Historiens, Poètes, Capitaines, & de tous ceux qui se sont rendus illustres parmi eux, par leur Vertu, ou par leur Savoir. Des jugemens critiques, et des extraits de tous leurs Ouvrages* ... (Maastricht, 1776) [reprint of original edition, Paris, 1697].

d'Herbelot (Reiske): Orientalische Bibliothek oder Universalwörterbuch, welches alles enthält, was zur Kenntniss des Orients nothwendig ist. Verfasst von Bartholom. D'Herbelot (4 vols., Halle, 1785–90) [essentially the same in content as the French version published The Hague, 1777–9, for which see *L'Europe et le monde arabe*, 36].

HERVEY, MARY S. F., *The Life Correspondence & Collections of Thomas Howard Earl of Arundel* (Cambridge, 1921).

HILL, CHRISTOPHER, *The World Turned Upside Down: Radical Ideas During the English Revolution* (London, 1972).

Holsten, *Epistolae*: Lucae Holstenii Epistolae ad diversos, quas ex editis et ineditis codicibus collegit atque illustravit Jo. Franc. Boissonade (Paris, 1817).

HOLT, P. M., 'Arabic Studies in Seventeenth-Century England with special Reference to the Life and Work of Edward Pococke', B.Phil. thesis (Oxford, 1952).

——*A Seventeenth-Century Defender of Islam: Henry Stubbe (1632–76) and his Book*, Friends of Dr. Williams's Library, 26th Lecture (London, 1972).

——'An Oxford Arabist, Edward Pococke (1604–91)', in Holt, *Studies in the History of the Near East* (London, 1973), 3–26.

——'The Study of Arabic Historians in Seventeenth-Century England, the Background and the Work of Edward Pococke', *Bulletin of the School of Oriental and African Studies,* 19 (1957), 444–55, reprinted in Holt, *Studies in the History of the Near East* (London, 1973), 27–49.

——'The Treatment of Arab History by Prideaux, Ockley and Sale', in *Historians of the Middle East,* ed. Bernard Lewis and P. M. Holt (London, 1962), 290–302, reprinted in Holt, *Studies in the History of the Near East* (London, 1973), 50–63.

HOOLE, CHARLES, *A New Discovery Of the old Art of Teaching Schoole* (London, 1660) [reprinted as no. 133 of English Linguistics 1500–1800 (Menston, 1969)].

HOPKINS, J. F. P., *Letters from Barbary 1576–1774: Arabic Documents in The Public Record Office*, Oriental Documents, 6 (London and New York, 1982).

HOTTINGER, J. H., *Promtuarium; sive Bibliotheca Orientalis exhibens Catalogum, sive Centurias aliquot, tam authorum, quam librorum Hebraicorum, Syriacorum, Arabicorum, Aegyptiacorum, Aethiopicorum &c. Addita Mantissa Bibliothecarum aliquot Europaearum . . .* (Heidelberg, 1658).

——*Bibliothecarius Quadripartitus. I. Pars quae Prolegomenis absolvitur, agit de officio Bibliothecarij, Bibliothecis, &c. II. De Theologia Biblica. III. De Theologia Patristica: cum Appendice Leonis Africani hactenus* ἀνεκδότῳ, *de Scriptoribus Arabicis. IV. De Theologia Topica; Symbolica, & Systematica; tam universali, quàm Particulari* (Zurich, 1664).

HOUTSMA, M. TH., *Uit de Oostersche Correspondentie van Th. Erpenius, Jac. Golius en Lev. Warner: Eene bijdrage tot de geschiedenis van de beoefening der oostersche letteren in Nederland*, uitgegeven door de Koninklijke Akademie van Wetenschappen te Amsterdam (Amsterdam, 1887).

HOWARTH, DAVID, *Lord Arundel and his Circle* (New Haven and London, 1985).

[HUDSON, JOHN (ed.)], GEOGRAPHIÆ VETERIS SCRIPTORES GRÆCI MINORES. *Accedunt Geographica Arabica &c.,* vol. 3 (Oxford, 1712).

Hunt, *Laudian Manuscripts: Bodleian Library, Quarto Catalogues II. Laudian Manuscripts*, by H. O. Coxe. Reprinted . . . with an historical introduction by R. W. Hunt (Oxford, 1973).

[HUNT, THOMAS], Proposals For Printing by Subscription, Abdollatiphi

326 Bibliography

Historiae Aegypti Compendium quod, Sexaginta abhinc annis, Ab EDVARDO POCOCKIO, clarissimi EDVARDI filio, A.M. Aedis Christi Alumno, Ex Linguâ Arabica in Latinam versum, Nunc Primum Utrâque edidit, Notisque illustravit THOMAS HUNT, S.T.P. *Lingue Arabicae* Professor, & R.S.S. è Collegio Hertfordiensi ([?Oxford], 1746).

——*De usu dialectorum orientalium, ac praecipue Arabicae in Hebraico Codice Interpretando, Oratio Habita Oxonii, in Schola Linguarum, VII Kalend Martii MDCCXLVIII* (Oxford, 1748).

R[OBERT] H[UNTINGTON], 'A *Letter from* Dublin *to the* Publisher *of these Tracts, concerning the* Porphyry Pillars *in* Egypt', *Philosophical Transactions*, vol. 14, no. 161 (20 July 1684), 624–9. Reprinted by John Ray, *Collection of Curious Travels and Voyages*, ii (1693), 149–55.

Hyde, *De Ludis Orientalibus*: De Ludis Orientalibus libri duo, quorum prior est duabus partibus, viz. 1. Historia Shahiludii Latine, deinde 2. Historia Shahiludii Heb. Lat. per tres Judaeos. [Mandragorias *etc.* horis succisivis olim congessit Thomas Hyde.] Liber posterior continet historiam reliquorum ludorum orientis [Historia Nerdiludii, hoc est dicere, Trunculorum cum quibusdam aliis Arabum, Persarum, Indorum, Chinensium, & aliarum Gentium ludis *etc.*] (Oxford, 1694) [The second part was first printed separately in 1689, *De Historia Shahiludii Tria Scripta Hebraica*].

Hyde, *Peritsol*: אגרת אורחות עולם ID EST, ITINERA MUNDI, SIC DICTA NEMPE COSMOGRAPHIA, AUTORE ABRAHAMO PERITSOL Latinâ VERSIONE donavit & NOTAS passim adjecit THOMAS HYDE S.T.D. è Coll. Regine *Oxon.* Protobibliothecarius Bodlejanus. Calce exponitur Turcarum LITURGIA, PEREGRINATIO MECCANA, ÆGROTORUM VISITATIO, CIRCUMCISIO, &c. Accedit CASTIGATIO In *Angelum à Sto Joseph*, al. dictum *de la Broße*, Carmelitam discalceatum, sui Ordinis in Ispahân Persidis olim Praefectum (Oxford, 1691).

Hyde, *Syntagma Dissertationum*: SYNTAGMA DISSERTATIONUM QUAS OLIM AUCTOR DOCTISSIMUS THOMAS HYDE S.T.P. SEPARATIM EDIDIT ACCESSERUNT NONNULLA EJUSDEM OPUSCULA HACTENUS INEDITA; NECNON DE EJUS VITA SCRIPTISQUE ΠΡΟΛΕΓΟΜΕΝΑ. CUM APPENDICE DE LINGUA SINENSI ALIISQUE LINGUIS ORIENTALIBUS UNA CUM QUAMPLURIMIS TABULIS ÆNEIS, QUIBUS EARUM CHARACTERES EXHIBENTUR. OMNIA DILIGENTER RECOGNITA A GREGORIO SHARPE LL. D. REG. MAJ. A SACRIS TEMPLI MAGISTRO. SS.R ET A.S. (2 vols., Oxford, 1767).

Hyde, *Ulugh Beg*: جداول مواضع ثوابت در طول وعرض که برصد یافته است الغ بیك بن شاهرخ بن تیمور SIVE TABVLÆ LONG. AC LAT. STELLARUM FIXARVM EX OBSERVATIONE ULUGH BEIGHI TAMERLANIS Magni Nepotis, Regionum ultra citráque GJIHUN (i. Oxum) Principis potentissimi. Ex tribus invicèm collatis MSS Persicis jam primùm Luce ac Latio donavit, & Commentariis illustravit, THOMAS HYDE A.M. è Coll. Reginae Oxon. In

Calce Libri accesserunt MOHAMMEDIS TIZINI TABULÆ Declinationum & Rectarum Ascensionum. Additur demum ELENCHUS Nominum Stellarum (Oxford, 1665).

INNES SMITH, R. W., *English-Speaking Students of Medicine at the University of Leyden* (Edinburgh and London, 1932).

Isaacson, *Lancelot Andrewes*: An exact Narration OF THE LIFE and DEATH OF THE Reverend and learned Prelate, and painfull DIVINE, LANCELOT ANDREWES, Late Bishop of WINCHESTER. [By the Rev. H. Isaacson] (London, 1650).

Jacob, *Philologiae* ἀνακαλυπτήριον: PHILOLOGIAE ᾽ΑΝΑΚΑΛΥΠΤΗΡΙΟΝ *Oratione celebratum Inaugurali,* Quam *publicè habuit ad Oxonio-Mertonenses* HENRICUS IACOBIUS; Publicavit à Quindecennio H.B. è Coll. Omn. Animar. Cum Appendice *luculentâ* (Oxford, 1652).

James, *Catalogus*: Catalogus Librorum Bibliothecae Publicae quam Vir Ornatissimus Thomas Bodleius Eques Auratus in Academia Oxoniensi nuper instituit . . . Autore Thoma James (Oxford, 1605) [facsimile reprint:] *The First Printed Catalogue of the Bodleian Library 1605: A Facsimile* (Oxford, 1986).

JOHNSON, JOHN, and GIBSON, STRICKLAND, *Print and Privilege at Oxford to the year 1700* (Oxford, 1946).

JONES, JOHN ROBERT, 'The Arabic and Persian Studies of Giovan Battista Raimondi (c. 1536–1614)', M.Phil. dissertation (Warburg Institute, June 1981).

——'Learning Arabic in Renaissance Europe (1505–1624)', Ph.D. thesis (School of Oriental and African Studies, London University, July 1988), forthcoming in the series 'Brill's Studies in Intellectual History'.

——'Thomas Erpenius (1584–1624) on the Value of the Arabic Language', *Manuscripts of the Middle East*, 1 (1986), 15–25.

——'The Medici Oriental Press (Rome 1584–1614) and the Impact of its Arabic Publications on Northern Europe', in Russell, *The 'Arabick' Interest of the Natural Philosophers*, 88–108.

JUSTEL CALABOZO, BRAULIO, *La Real Biblioteca de El Escorial y sus manuscritos arabes* (Madrid, 1978).

JUYNBOLL, WILHELMINA MARIA CORNELIA, *Zeventiende-eeuwsche Beoefenaars van het Arabisch in Nederland* (Utrecht, [1931]).

KATZ, DAVID S., 'The Abendana Brothers and the Christian Hebraists of Seventeenth-Century England', *Journal of Ecclesiastical History*, 40 (1989), 28–52.

——*Philo-Semitism and the Readmission of the Jews to England 1603–1655*, Oxford Historical Monographs (Oxford, 1982).

KAYSERLING, M., 'Richelieu, Buxtorf père et fils, Jacob Roman. Documents pour servir à l'histoire du commerce de la librairie juive au XVIe siècle', *Revue des Études Juives*, 8 (1884), 74–95.

328   *Bibliography*

KEMKE, JOHANNES, *Patricius Junius (Patrick Young): Mitteilungen aus seinem Briefwechsel*, Sammlung Bibliothekswissenschaftlicher Arbeiten, 12 (Leipzig, 1898).

KEPLER, JOHANNES, *Gesammelte Werke*, vols. 13–17: *Briefe*, ed. Max Caspar (Munich, 1945–59).

KLEIN-FRANKE, FELIX, *Die klassische Antike in der Tradition des Islam*, Erträge der Forschung, 136 (Darmstadt, 1980).

Knös, *Analecta Epistolarum*: ANALECTA EPISTOLARUM, IN PRIMIS *HISTORIAM ET RES LITTERARIAS* SVECIÆ ILLUSTRANTIUM. . . . COLLEGIT, RECENSUIT ET EDIDIT OLAVUS ANDREAE KNOES (9 parts; Uppsala, 1786–96).

Koran (Bibliander): MACHVMETIS SARACENORUM PRINCIPIS, EIVSQVE SUCCESSORVM VITAE, AC DOCTRINA, IPSEQUE ALCORAN . . . opera & studio Theodori Bibliandri (Basel, 1543).

KRITZECK, JAMES, *Peter the Venerable and Islam*, Princeton Oriental Studies, 23 (Princeton, 1964).

KUNITZSCH, PAUL, *Der Almagest: Die Syntaxis Mathematica des Claudius Ptolemäus in arabisch-lateinischer Überlieferung* (Wiesbaden, 1974).

Laud, *Works*: *The Works of the Most Reverend Father in God, William Laud, D.D.* (7 vols., London, 1847–60).

LEFRANC, ABEL, *Histoire du Collège de France* (Paris, 1893) [reprint, Geneva, 1970].

Leiden Oriental Catalogue: *Catalogus Codicum Orientalium Bibliothecae Academicae Lugduno Batavae* ediderunt P. de Jong et M. J. de Goeje, iii (Leiden, 1865).

Le Livre et le Liban: Camille Aboussouan (ed.), *Exposition Le livre et le Liban jusqu'à 1900* (Paris, 1982).

Leo Africanus, tr. Épaulard: Jean-Léon l'Africain, *Description de l'Afrique*, nouvelle édition traduite de l'italien par A. Épaulard et annotée par A. Épaulard, Th. Monod, H. Lhote et R. Mauny (2 vols., Paris, 1956).

Letters written by Eminent Persons in the Seventeenth and Eighteenth Centuries . . . now first published from the originals in the Bodleian Library and Ashmolean Museum, with biographical and literary illustrations. [By Rev. John Walker, M.A., Fellow of New College] (2 vols., Vol. II in 2 parts; London, 1813).

L'Europe et le monde arabe. Cinq siècles de livres de lettrés et voyageurs européens choisis dans les bibliothèques de l'Arcadian Group, ed. Alastair Hamilton (Paris, 1993).

LEVI DELLA VIDA, G., *Ricerche sulla formazione del più antico fondo dei manoscritti orientali della Biblioteca Vaticana*, Studi e Testi, 92 (Città del Vaticano, 1939).

——*Documenti intorno alle relazioni delle chiese orientali con la S. Sede durante il pontificato di Gregorio XIII*, Studi e Testi, 143 (Città del Vaticano,

1948).

Levinus Warner and his Legacy: Three Centuries Legatum Warnerianum in the Leiden University Library (Leiden, 1970).

Lightfoot, *Letters*: The Whole Works of the Rev. John Lightfoot, D.D. Master of Catharine Hall, Cambridge. Edited by John Rogers Pitman. Volume XIII, containing the Journal of the Proceedings of the Assembly of Divines, from January 1, 1643 to December 31, 1644, and letters to and from Dr. Lightfoot (London, 1824).

LLOYD, DAVID, *Memoires of the Lives, Actions, Sufferings and Deaths of those . . . Personages That suffered . . . In our late Intestine Wars, . . . with the Life and Martyrdom of King Charles I* (London, 1667).

LLOYD JONES, G., *The Discovery of Hebrew in Tudor England: A Third Language* (Manchester, 1983).

——(ed. & tr.), *Robert Wakefield on the Three Languages [1524]*, Medieval and Renaissance Texts and Studies, 68 (Binghamton, 1989).

Locke, *Correspondence*: *The Correspondence of John Locke*, ed. E. S. de Beer (8 vols., Oxford, 1976–89).

LONG, P., *A Summary Catalogue of the Lovelace Collection of the Papers of John Locke in the Bodleian Library*, Oxford Bibliographical Society Publications, NS 8, 1956 (Oxford, 1959).

LOSSEN, MAX (ed.), *Briefe von Andreas Masius und seinen Freunden 1538 bis 1573*, Publikationen der Gesellschaft für Rheinische Geschichtskunde, 2 (Leipzig, 1886).

LUCCHETTA, FRANCESCA, *Il Medico e filosofo bellunese Andrea Alpago (†1522) traduttore di Avicenna: Profilo biografico* (Padua, 1964).

McKITTERICK, DAVID, *Cambridge University Library: A History*, ii: *The Eighteenth and Nineteenth Centuries* (Cambridge, 1986).

MacLAUGHLIN, TREVOR, 'Une lettre de Melchisédech Thévenot', *Revue d'Histoire des Sciences*, 27 (1974), 123–6.

MACRAY, WILLIAM DUNN, *Annals of the Bodleian Library with a notice of the earlier library of the University*, 2nd edn. (Oxford, 1890).

——'A letter from Isaac Abendana', in *Festschrift zum achtzigsten Geburtstage Moritz Steinschneider's* (Leipzig, 1896), 89–90.

——*A Register of the Members of St. Mary Magdalen College, Oxford. From the Foundation of the College*, New Series, 4: *Fellows, 1648–1712* (London, 1904).

MADAN, FALCONER, *Oxford Books: A bibliography of printed works relating to the University and City of Oxford or printed or published there*, vol. 1, *The Early Oxford Press, 1468–1640* (Oxford, 1895); vol. 2, *Oxford Literature 1450–1640, and 1641–1650* (Oxford, 1912); vol. 3, *Oxford Literature 1651–1680* (Oxford, 1931).

MALLET, CHARLES EDWARD, *A History of the University of Oxford*, ii: *The Sixteenth and Seventeenth Centuries* (London, 1924).

MANT, RICHARD, *History of the Church of Ireland* (2 vols., London, 1840).

MANUEL, FRANK E., *The Broken Staff: Judaism through Christian Eyes* (Cambridge, Mass., and London, 1992).

MARSHALL, P. J., 'Oriental Studies', in *The History of the University of Oxford*, v: *The Eighteenth Century* (Oxford, 1985), 551–63.

MARSHALL, WILLIAM M., *George Hooper 1640–1727 Bishop of Bath and Wells* (Sherborne, 1976).

MATTHEWS, A. G., *Walker Revised ('Sufferings of the Clergy during the Grand Rebellion 1642–60')* (Oxford, 1948).

MAYOR, J. E. B., *Cambridge under Queen Anne illustrated by Memoir of Ambrose Bonwicke and Diaries of Francis Burman and Zacharias Conrad von Uffenbach* (Cambridge, 1911).

MERCIER, RAYMOND, 'English Orientalists and Mathematical Astronomy', in Russell, *The 'Arabick' Interest of the Natural Philosophers*, 158–214.

Mersenne, *Correspondance*: Correspondance du P. Marin Mersenne, religieux minime, publiée par Mme. Paul Tannery, éditée et annotée par Cornelis de Waard [*et al.*] (17 vols., Paris, 1932–88).

Mersenne, *Synopsis*: VNIVERSÆ GEOMETRIÆ, MIXTÆQVE MATHE-MATICÆ SYNOPSIS ET BINI REFRACTIONVM DEMONSTRATA-RVM TRACTATVS. *Studio & Operâ* F.M. MERSENNI M. (Paris, 1644).

METLITZKI, DOROTHEE, *The Matter of Araby in Medieval England* (New Haven, 1977).

[Michaud], *Biographie universelle ancienne et moderne*, nouvelle édition (45 vols., Paris, n.d.).

MILLIES, H. C., 'Over de Oostersche Vertalingen van het beroemde Geschrift van *Hugo Grotius, De Veritate Religionis Christianae*'. *Verslagen en Mede-deelingen der Koninklijke Akademie van Wetenschappen*, Afdeeling Letter-kunde, 7 (1863), 109–34.

MOLLAND, GEORGE, 'The Limited Lure of Arabic Mathematics', in Russell, *The 'Arabick' Interest of the Natural Philosophers*, 215–23.

Moller, *Cimbria Literata*: Johannis Molleri Flensburgensis *CIMBRIA LITERATA, sive Scriptorum ducatus utriusque Slesvicensis et Holsatici, quibus et alii vicini quidam accensentur, historia literaria tripartita* (3 vols., Copenhagen, 1744). Tomus Primus. *Scriptores universos Indigenas, hisqve immistos complures, qvorum Patria explorari necdum potuit, compre-hendens.* Tomus Secundus. *Adoptivos sive Exteros, in Ducatu utroque Slesvicensi & Holsatico vel officiis functos publicis, uel diutius commoratos, complectens.*

MONNERET DE VILLARD, UGO, *Lo Studio dell'Islam in Europa nel XII e nel XIII secolo*, Studi e Testi, 110 (Città del Vaticano, 1944).

——*Il Libro della Peregrinazione nelle Parti d'Oriente di Frate Ricoldo da Montecroce*, Institutum Historicum FF. Praedicatorum, Dissertationes Historicae, 13 (Rome, 1948).

MORES, EDWARD ROWE, *A Dissertation upon English Typographical Founders and Founderies (1778) with A Catalogue and Specimen of the Typefoundry of John James (1782)*, edited with an Introduction and Notes by Harry Carter and Christopher Ricks (Oxford [The Oxford Bibliographical Society], 1961).

MORISON, STANLEY, *John Fell, the University Press and the 'Fell' Types* (Oxford, 1967).

MÜLLER, MAX, *Johann Albrecht v. Widmanstetter 1506–1557: Sein Leben und Wirken* (Bamberg, 1907).

MYNORS, R. A. B., *Catalogue of the Manuscripts of Balliol College* (Oxford, 1963).

NAHAS, MICHAEL, 'A Translation of Ḥayy B. Yaqẓān by the elder Edward Pococke (1604–1691)', *Journal of Arabic Literature*, 16 (1985), 88–90.

NALLINO, C. A., 'Il valore metrico del grado di meridiano secondo i geografi arabi', in *Raccolta di Scritti editi e inediti*, 5 (Rome, 1944), 408–57.

—— 'Le fonti arabe manoscritte dell'opera di Ludovico Marracci sul Corano', in *Raccolta di Scritti editi e inediti*, 2 (Rome, 1940), 90–134.

—— 'Filosofia «orientale» od «illuminativa» d'Avicenna?', in *Raccolta di Scritti editi e inediti*, 6 (Rome, 1948), 218–56.

NEUBAUER, AD., *Catalogue of the Hebrew Manuscripts in the Bodleian Library and in the College Libraries of Oxford*, Catalogi Codd. Mss. Bibliothecae Bodleianae, 12 (Oxford, 1886).

NICHOLS, JOHN, *Literary Anecdotes of the Eighteenth Century* (9 vols., London, 1812–16).

Nicoll: *Bibliothecae Bodleianae Codicum Manuscriptorum Orientalium Catalogi, Partis Secundae Volumen Primum Arabicos complectens* confecit Alexander Nicoll (Oxford, 1821).

Nicoll–Pusey: *Bibliothecae Bodleianae Codicum Manuscriptorum Orientalium Catalogi, Partis Secundae Volumen Secundum Arabicos complectens* confecit Alexander Nicoll, J. C. D. edidit et catalogum Urianum aliquatenus emendavit E. B. Pusey, S. T. B. (Oxford, 1835).

NIJENHUIS, WILLEM, *Matthew Slade 1569–1628: Letters to the English Ambassador*, Publications of the Sir Thomas Browne Institute, New Series, 6 (Leiden, 1986).

NORRIS, H. T., 'Professor Edmund Castell (1606–85), Orientalist and Divine, and England's Oldest Arabic Inscription', *Journal of Semitic Studies*, 29 (1984), 155–67.

—— 'Edmund Castell (1606–86) and his *Lexicon Heptaglotton* (1669)', in Russell, *The 'Arabick' Interest of the Natural Philosophers*, 70–87.

NUOVO, ANGELA, 'Il Corano arabo ritrovato', *La Bibliofilia*, 89 (1987), 237–71; reprinted in Angela Nuovo, *Alessandro Paganino (1509–1538)*, Medioevo e Umanesimo, 77 (Padua, 1990), 107–31, chapter 'Il Corano'.

Oates: *Cambridge University Library: A History*, i: *From the Beginnings to the Copyright Act of Queen Anne*, [by] J. C. T. Oates (Cambridge, 1986).

OATES, J. C. T., *The Manuscripts of Thomas Erpenius*, Bibliographical Society of Australia and New Zealand, Occasional Publications, 1 (Melbourne, 1974).

OEHME, RUTHARDT, 'Der Geograph und Kartograph', in Seck, *Wilhelm Schickard*, 310–75.

Oldenburg, *Correspondence*: *The Correspondence of Henry Oldenburg*, Edited and Translated by A. Rupert Hall and Marie Boas Hall (13 vols., Madison and London, 1965–86).

[OMONT, HENRI], *Missions archéologiques françaises en Orient aux XVII et XVIII siècles*, Documents publiés par Henri Omont (2 vols., Paris, 1902).

Pasor, *Inaugural Lecture*: ORATIO *PRO* LINGVÆ ARABICÆ *PROFESSIONE, PVBLICE* ad Academicos habita in Schola Theologica *Universitatis Oxoniensis* XXV Octob. 1626. à MATTHIA PASORE (Oxford, 1627).

Pasor, *Vita*: Parentalia in piam memoriam Reverendi & Clarissimi D. Matthiae Pasoris . . . Oratio Funebris ab Abdia Widmario, in Choro Templi Academici 6. Febr. Ann. 1658; Vita Matthiae Pasoris, ab hoc ipsomet vivo pleniùs consignata . . . (Groningen, 1658).

PEARSON, JOHN B., *A Biographical Sketch of the Chaplains to the Levant Company, maintained at Constantinople, Aleppo and Smyrna. 1611–1706* (Cambridge and London, 1883).

PEILE, JOHN, *Biographical Register of Christ's College 1505–1905 and of the earlier foundation God's House 1448–1505* (2 vols., Cambridge, 1910, 1913).

Peiresc, *Dupuy Correspondence*: Lettres de Peiresc aux Frères Dupuy, publiées par Philippe Tamizey de Larroque (Collection de Documents Inédites sur l'Histoire de France, Deuxième Série, Paris, I, 1888; II, 1890; III, 1892).

PHILIP, IAN, *The Bodleian Library in the Seventeenth and Eighteenth Centuries* (Oxford, 1983).

Philologia Arabica. Arabische studiën en drukken in de Nederlanden in de 16de en 17de eeuw, onder redactie van Dr. Francine de Nave, Catalogus. Tentoonstelling Museum Plantin-Moretus 25 oktober – 21 december (Antwerp, 1986).

PINKE, WILLIAM, *The Triall of a Christian's Sincere Love unto Christ*, 5th edn. (Oxford, 1659) [1st edn. 1630].

Pococke, *'Abd al-Laṭīf*: مختصر اخبار مصر لعبد اللطيف البغدادى *ABDOLLATIPHI* HISTORIÆ ÆGYPTI *COMPENDIUM* [tr. Edward Pococke junior (Oxford, ?1685)].

Pococke, *Abū 'l-Faraj*: تاريخ مختصر الدول HISTORIA COMPENDIOSA DYNASTIARVM, AUTHORE Gregorio Abul-Pharajio *Malatiensi Medico* Historiam complectens universalem, à mundo condito, usque ad Tempora Authoris, res Orientalium accuratissimè describens *Arabice edita, & Latine versa*, ab EDVARDO POCOCKIO Linguae Hebraicae in Academia Oxoniensi Professore Regio, nec non in eadem L. Arabicae Praelectore (Oxford, 1663).

Pococke, *Carmen Tograi*: لامية العجم Lamiato'l Ajam CARMEN TOGRAI, Poetae ARABIS Doctissimi; Unà Cum *versione Latina, & notis* Operâ EDVARDI POCOCKII, *LL HEBR. & ARAB. Profess.* Accessit TRACTATUS DE PROSODIA ARABICA (Oxford, 1661).

Pococke, *Commentary on Hosea*: A Commentary on the Prophecy of Hosea, by Edward Pocock, D.D. (Oxford, 1685).

Pococke, *Commentary on Joel*: A Commentary on the Prophecy of Joel, by Edward Pocock, D.D. (Oxford, 1691).

Pococke, *Commentary on Malachi*: A Commentary on the Prophecy of Malachi, by Edward Pocock, D.D. (Oxford, 1677).

Pococke, *Commentary on Micah*: A Commentary on the Prophecy of Micah, by Edward Pocock D.D. (Oxford, 1677).

Pococke, *Eutychius*: نظم الجوهر *Contextio Gemmarum* SIVE, EUTYCHII Patriarchae Alexandrini ANNALES. Illustriss. IOHANNE SELDENO, τοῦ μακαρίτου, *Chorago*. Interprete EDWARDO POCOCKIO Linguarum *Hebraicae & Arabicae* in Academia OXONIENSI Professore Publico (2 vols., Oxford, 1656, 1654).

Pococke, *Grotius*: كتاب فى صحة الشريعة المسيحية نقل من اللاطيني الي العربي Hugo Grotius de Veritate Religionis Christianae. Editio Nova cum Annotationibus, Cui accessit versio Arabica (Oxford, 1660).

Pococke, *Philosophus Autodidactus*: PHILOSOPHUS AUTODIDACTUS SIVE EPISTOLA ABI JAAFAR, EBN TOPHAIL *DE HAI EBN YOKDHAN*. In quâ Ostenditur quomodo ex Inferiorum contemplatione ad Superiorum notitiam Ratio humana ascendere possit. *Ex Arabicâ in Linguam Latinam versa* Ab EDVARDO POCOCKIO A.M. (Oxford, 1671).

Pococke, *Porta Mosis*: באב מושי Porta Mosis, sive, Dissertationes aliquot à R. Mose Maimonide, suis in varias Mishnaioth, sive textus Talmudici partes, Commentariis praemissae . . . Nunc primùm Arabicè prout ab ipso Autore conscriptae sunt, & Latinè editae . . . operâ & studio Edvardi Pocockii (Oxford, 1655).

Pococke, *Specimen*: Specimen Historiae Arabum; auctore Edvardo Pocockio. . . . Edidit Josephus White (Oxford, 1806) (original edition, لمع من اخبار العرب Specimen Historiae Arabum, sive Gregorii AbulFarajii Malatiensis, de *Origine & Moribus* Arabum *succincta Narratio, in linguam Latinam conversa, Notisque è probatissimis apud ipsos Authoribus, fusiùs illustrata.* Operâ & Studio Edvardi Pocockii . . . Oxford, 1650).

Pococke, *Syriac Epistles*: Epistolae Quatuor, Petri secunda, Johannis secunda & tertia & Iudae, fratris Jacobi, una Ex Celeberrima Bibliothecae Bodleianae Oxoniensis MS. exemplari nunc primum depromptae et Charactere Hebraeo, versione Latina, notisque quibusdam insignitae, Operâ & studio EDVVARDI POCOCKE, Angli-Oxoniensis (Leiden [Elzevirs], 1630).

K. M. P[OGSON], 'The Wanderings of Apollonius', *The Bodleian Quarterly Record,* 3 (1921), 152–3.

334   *Bibliography*

POPE, WALTER, *The Life of the Right Reverend Father in God, Seth, Lord Bishop of Salisbury* . . . (London, 1697) [repr. Oxford, 1961].

POSTEL, CLAUDE, *Les Écrits de Guillaume Postel publiés en France et leurs Éditeurs 1538–1579* (Geneva, 1992).

PRESCOTT, WILLIAM H., *History of the Reign of Philip the Second, King of Spain* (Boston, 1859).

Prideaux, *Letters*: *Letters of Humphrey Prideaux to John Ellis 1674–1722*, ed. Edward Maunde Thompson (Camden Society, 1875).

Prideaux, *Life*: The Life Of the Reverend *Humphrey Prideaux*, D.D. Dean of *Norwich*. With several tracts and letters of his upon various subjects (London, 1748).

Prideaux, *Mahomet*: The True *Nature of Imposture* Fully Display'd in the Life of Mahomet. With A Discourse annexed, for the Vindication of Christianity from this Charge; Offered to the Consideration of the Deists of the present Age. By Humphrey Prideaux, D.D. The Second Edition Corrected (London, 1697).

PRYNNE, WILLIAM, *Canterburies Doom, or the first part of a complete History of the Commitment, Trial,* . . . *of William Laud* (London, 1646).

RADEMAKER, C. S. M., *Life and Work of Gerardus Joannes Vossius (1577–1649)* (Assen, 1981).

RAHLFS, ALFRED, 'Nissel und Petraeus, ihre äthiopischen Textausgaben und Typen', *Nachrichten der Königlichen Gesellschaft der Wissenschaften zu Göttingen, Phil.-hist. Kl.* (1917), 268–348.

Ramusio: Gian Battista Ramusio, *Navigationi et Viaggi* (photographic reprint of edn. of Venice, 1563–1606), Mundus Novus, First Series, 2–4 (3 vols., Amsterdam, 1967–70).

Ravius, *Alcoran*: Prima XIII Partium Alcorani Arabico Latini Versionis geminae, alterius parallelae loco interlinearibus, textualis alterius; ubi Arabicae voces 6400, ob defectum typorum Arabicorum, Latinis litteris sunt expressae . . . Praemittitur gemina Dissertatiuncula, 1. de vastissimo campo S. orientalis lingvae, 2. de ratione versionis suae. Accedit Catalogus CCLXI. MSStorum Arabicorum Bibliothecae S. Laurentii in Escuriali Regis Hispaniae, a Licent. Castillio A. 1583 confectus . . . opera et studio Christiani Ravii Berlinatis (Amsterdam, 1646).

Ravius, *Apollonius*: Apollonii Pergaei Conicarum Sectionum Libri V. VI. & VII in Graecia deperditi jam vero ex Arabico Manuscripto ante quadringentos annos elaborato operâ subitaneâ Latinitate donati à CHRISTIANO RAVIO Berlinate Oriental. LL. Prof. Reg. Upsal. (Kiel, 1669).

Ravius, *De scribendo Lexico*: CHRISTIANI RAVII BERLINATIS *DE SCRIBENDO LEXICO* Arabico-Latino DISSERTATIO. AD Nobilissimum & Amplissimum SENATVM TRAIECTINVM Orientalium Rerum & Linguarum PATRONUM (Utrecht, 1643).

Ravius, *Discourse*: A Discourse of the Orientall Tongues viz. Ebrew,

Samaritan. Calde, Syriac, Arabic, and *Ethiopic. Together with a Generall Grammar for the Said Tongues.* By Christian Ravis (London, 1649).

Ravius, *Generall Grammer*: A Generall Grammer For the ready attaining of the Ebrew, Samaritan, Calde, Syriac, Arabic, and the Ethiopic Languages. With a Pertinent Discourse of the Orientall Tongues. Also a Sesquidecury, or a number of Fifteene Adoptive Epistles sent together out of divers parts of the World concerning care of the Orientall Tongues to be promoted. By Christian Ravis of Berlin (London, 1650).

Ravius, *Orthographia*: CHRISTIANI RAVII BERLINATIS ORTHO-GRAPHIÆ ET ANALOGIÆ (vulgò Etymologiae) EBRAICÆ Delineatio juxta vocis partes abstractas. I CONSONAS II. VOCALES III. ACCENTVS (Amsterdam, 1646).

Ravius, *Panegyrica Prima*: CHRISTIANI RAVII BERLINATIS PANE-GYRICA PRIMA ORIENTALIBVS LINGVIS *DICTA* Illustrissimo & Frequentissimo Auditorio *RHENO-TRAIECTINO* Propridie Nonarum Octobris ANNI MDCXLIII (Utrecht, 1643).

Ravius, *Panegyrica Secunda*: CHRISTIANI RAVII BERLINATIS PANE-GYRICA SECVNDA, ORIENTALIBUS LINGVIS DICTA, In Splendidissimo & Florentissimo Auditorio Rheno-Trajectino, *Postridie Nonarum Octobris Anni* MDCXLIII (Utrecht, 1644).

Ravius, *Sesqui-Decuria*: Christiani Ravii Berlinatis Sesqui-Decuria Epistolarum adoptivarum. Ex Varijs orbis partibus commissarum Circa Orientalium Studiorum promovendorum Curam (London, 1648).

RAVIUS, CHRISTIANUS, *Specimen Lexici Arabico-Persici-Latini* (Leiden, 1645).

Reading, *Sion-College*: The History of the Ancient and Present State of Sion-College Near CRIPPLEGATE, London; and of The London-Clergy's Library there. By W. Reading, M.A. Library-Keeper (London, 1724).

REED, TALBOT BAINES, *A History of the Old English Letter Foundries*, new edition revised and enlarged by A. F. Johnson (London, 1952).

Reiske, *Autobiography*: D. Johann Jacob Reiskens von ihm selbst ausgesetzte Lebensbeschreibung (Leipzig, 1783).

Reiske, *Letters*: Johann Jacob Reiske's Briefe herausgegeben von Richard Foerster, Königl. Sächs. Ges. d. Wiss., phil.-hist. Cl. Abh. 16 and 34.4 (Leipzig, 1897, 1917).

REX, RICHARD, 'The Earliest Use of Hebrew in Books Printed in England, Dating some Works of Richard Pace and Robert Wakefield', *Transactions of the Cambridge Bibliographical Society*, 9 (1990), 517–25.

DE RICCI, SEYMOUR, *English Collectors of Books and Manuscripts (1530–1930) and their Marks of Ownership* (Cambridge, 1930).

ROBERTS, JULIAN, and WATSON, ANDREW G., *John Dee's Library Catalogue* (London, 1990).

ROPER, G. J., 'Arabic Printing and Publishing in England before 1820', *British Society for Middle Eastern Studies Bulletin*, 12 (1985), 12–32.

ROSENTHAL, FRANZ, 'An Ancient Commentary on the Hippocratic Oath', *Bulletin of the History of Medicine*, 30 (1956), 52–87.

——'Al-Mubashshir ibn Fâtik. Prolegomena to an abortive edition', *Oriens*, 13–14 (1961), 132–58.

——*The Classical Heritage in Islam* (Berkeley and Los Angeles, 1975).

ROSSI, ETTORE, *Elenco dei manoscritti persiani della Biblioteca Vaticana*, Studi e Testi, 136 (Città del Vaticano, 1948).

ROSTENBERG, LEONORA, 'Republican Credo, William Dugard, Pedagogue & Political Apostate', in her *Literary, Political, Scientific, Religious & Legal Publishing, Printing & Bookselling in England, 1551–1700, Twelve Studies* (2 vols., New York, 1965), i. 131–59.

ROTH, CECIL, 'Jews in Oxford after 1290', *Oxoniensia*, 15 (1950), 63–80.

——'Edward Pococke and the First Hebrew Printing in Oxford', *Bodleian Library Record*, 2 (1948), 215–19.

RUSSELL, G. A., 'The Impact of *The Philosophus Autodidactus*, Pocockes, John Locke, and the Society of Friends', in Russell, *The 'Arabick' Interest of the Natural Philosophers*, 224–65.

——(ed.), *The 'Arabick' Interest of the Natural Philosophers in Seventeenth-Century England*, Brill's Studies in Intellectual History, 47 (Leiden, 1994).

SABRA, A. I., 'Simplicius's Proof of Euclid's Parallels Postulate', *Journal of the Warburg and Courtauld Institutes*, 32 (1969), 1–24.

Sachau–Ethé: *Catalogue of the Persian, Turkish, Hindûstânî, and Pushtû Manuscripts in the Bodleian Library*, begun by Ed. Sachau, continued, completed, and edited by Hermann Ethé. Part I: *The Persian Manuscripts*, Catalogi Codd. Mss. Bibliothecae Bodleianae, 13 (Oxford, 1889).

Sale, *Koran*: The Koran, commonly called the Alcoran of Mohammed, translated into English . . . with . . . a Preliminary Discourse, by George Sale, Gent. A new Edition (2 vols., London, 1825) [original edition London, 1734].

Salmasius, *Epistolae*: Claudii Salmasii, Viri Maximi, Epistolarum Liber Primus Accurante Antonio Clementio (Leiden, 1656).

SALMASIUS, CL., *De Annis Climactericis et Antiqua Astrologia Diatribae* (Leiden, 1648).

SALMON, VIVIAN, 'Arabists and Linguists in Seventeenth-Century England', in Russell, *The 'Arabick' Interest of the Natural Philosophers*, 54–69.

SALTINI, GUGLIELMO ENRICO, 'Della Stamperia Orientale Medicea e di Giovan Battista Raimondi', *Giornale Storico degli Archivi Toscani*, 4 (1860), 257–308.

SARGEAUNT, JOHN, *Annals of Westminster School* (London, 1898).

SAYILI, AYDIN, *The Observatory in Islam and its Place in the General History of the Observatory*, Publications of the Turkish Historical Society, Series VII, No. 38 (Ankara, 1960).

SC: *A Summary Catalogue of Western Manuscripts in the Bodleian Library at*

Oxford which have not hitherto been catalogued in the Quarto series, by Falconer Madan, H. H. E. Craster, N. Denholm-Young, R. W. Hunt, and P. D. Record (7 vols., Oxford, 1895–1953).

SCHIAPARELLI, C. (ed.), *Vocabulista in Arabico pubblicato per la prima volta sopre un codice della Biblioteca Riccardiana di Firenze* (Florence, 1871).

Schnurrer: Bibliotheca Arabica. Auctam nunc atque integram edidit D. Christianus Fridericus de Schnurrer (Halle, 1811) [reprinted Amsterdam, 1968, together with Victor Chauvin, 'Table Alphabétique de la Bibliotheca Arabica de Chr. Fr. de Schnurrer', Réimpression du Tome I de la Bibliographie des Ouvrages Arabes (Liège, 1892)].

Sclater, *Crown of Righteousnes*: THE CROWNE OF RIGHTEOUSNES; OR. The glorious Reward of FIDELITY In the Discharge of our DUTY. As it was laid forth in a Sermon, preached in S. *Botolphs Aldersgate, London*, Sept. 25. 1653. At the solemn Funerall of Mr. *Abrah. Wheelock*, B.D. The first Publick Professor, and Reader of *Arabick*, and of the *Saxon*, in the University of CAMBRIDGE. Whereunto is added, An ENCOMIUM of HIM. By WILLIAM SCLATER Doctor in Divinity . . . (London, 1654).

SECK, FRIEDRICH (ed.), *Wilhelm Schickard 1592–1635: Astronom Geograph Orientalist Erfinder der Rechenmaschine*, Contubernium, Beiträge zur Geschichte der Eberhard-Karls-Universität Tübingen, 25 (Tübingen, 1978).

SECRET, F., 'Guillaume Postel et les études arabes à la Renaissance', *Arabica*, 9 (1962), 21–36.

Selden, *De Dis Syris*: IOANNIS SELDENI I. C. DE DIS SYRIS SYNTAG-MATA II. EDITIO ALTERA; emendatior & tertia parte auctior (Leiden, 1629).

Selden, *De Synedriis Liber Tertius*: *Ioannis Seldeni* De Synedriis & *Praefecturis Iuridicis* Veterum Ebraeorum *Liber Tertius & Vltimus* (London, 1655).

Selden, *Eutychius*: Eutychii *Aegyptii,* Patriarchae Orthodoxorum *Alexandrini* . . . Ecclesiae suae Origines. Ex ejusdem Arabico nunc primùm typis edidit ac Versione & Commentario auxit *Ioannes Seldenus* (London, 1642).

Selden, *Mare Clausum*: *Ioannis Seldeni* MARE CLAUSUM SEU *De* Dominio Maris *Libri Duo* (London, 1635).

Selden, *Opera*: Joannis Seldeni Jurisconsulti Opera Omnia, Tam Edita quam Inedita. In tribus voluminibus Collegit ac Recensuit, Vitam Auctoris, Praefationes, & Indices adjecit, David Wilkins (3 vols. in 6 parts; London, 1726).

SILVESTRE DE SACY, [Baron Antoine Isaac], 'Correspondance des Samaritains de Naplouse, pendant les années 1808 et suiv.', *Notices et Extraits des Manuscrits de la Bibliothèque du Roi et autres bibliothèques,* 12 (1831), 1–235.

SIRAISI, NANCY, *Avicenna in Renaissance Italy: The Canon and Medical Teaching in Italian Universities after 1500* (Princeton, 1987).

Smith, *Life of Bernard*: Admodum Reverendi & Doctissimi Viri, D. Roberti Huntingtoni, Episcopi Rapotensis, Epistolae, et Veterum Mathematicorum, Graecorum, Latinorum, & Arabum, Synopsis, Collectore Viro Clarissimo & Doctissimo, D. Edwardo Bernardo, Astronomiae in Academia Oxoniensi Professore Saviliano. Praemittuntur D. Huntingtoni & D. Bernardi Vitae. Scriptore Thoma Smitho, S. Theologiae Doctore (London, 1704).

Smith, *Remarks upon the Manners of the Turks*: Remarks Upon the Manners, Religion And Government of the Turks. Together with A Survey of the Seven Churches of Asia, As they now lye in their Ruines, and A Brief Description of Constantinople. By Tho. Smith; B.D. and Fellow of St. Mary Magdalen College, Oxon. (London, 1678).

Smith, *Sermon*: A SERMON Preached before the RIGHT WORSHIPFUL Company OF MERCHANTS Trading into the LEVANT, AT St. *OLAVES HART-STREET* LONDON, Tuesday *JUNE*, 2. M.DC.LXVIIII, BY THO. SMITH, MA *Fellow of MAGDALEN COLLEGE in Oxford, and* CHAPLAIN *to the* RIGHT HONOURABLE Sr. *DANIEL HARVEY, His* MAJESTIES EMBASSADOUR TO CONSTANTINOPLE (London, 1668).

Smith, *Vitae*: Vitae Quorundam Eruditissimorum et Illustrium Virorum . . . Scriptore Thoma Smitho (London, 1707). (The biographies are separately paginated.)

SMITH, THOMAS, *Epistolae Duae, Quarum altera de Moribus ac Institutis Turcarum agit: Altera Septem Asiae Ecclesiarum notitiam continet* (Oxford, 1672).

——'A Journal of a Voyage from England to Constantinople, made in the Year 1668. by T. Smith *D.D.* & *F.R.S.*', *Philosophical Transactions*, 19 (1695–7) [published 1698], 597–619.

——*An Account of the Greek Church . . . to which is added . . . An Account of the State of the Greek Church, under Cyrillus Lucaris Patriarch of Constantinople, with a Relation of his Suffering and Death* (London, 1680).

——*Miscellanea* [including] *Brevis & succincta narratio de vita, studiis, gestis, & Martyrio D. Cyrilli Lucarii, Patriarchae Constantinopolitani* (London, 1686).

SMITSKAMP, RIJK, *Philologia Orientalis: A description of books illustrating the study and printing of Oriental languages in 16th- and 17th-century Europe* (Leiden, 1992) [Titelauflage, with additions, of an E. J. Brill catalogue originally published in three parts, 1976, 1983, and 1991].

Spencer, *De Legibus Hebraeorum*: De legibus Hebraeorum ritualibus et earum rationibus, libri tres. . . . Authore Joanne Spencero, S.T.D. Ecclesiae Eliensis Decano & Colleg. Corp. Christ. apud Cantabrig. Praefecto (Cambridge, 1685 [in fact 1683–5]).

Stationers' Registers: A Transcript of the Registers of the Worshipful Company of Stationers 1640–1708 A.D., i: 1640–1655, ed. Eyre and Rivington (London, 1913).

STEINSCHNEIDER, MORITZ, *Die arabischen Übersetzungen aus dem Griechischen* (Graz, 1960) [reprint of four periodical articles from 1889–96].

——*Die hebräischen Übersetzungen des Mittelalters und die Juden als Dolmetscher* (Berlin, 1893; repr. Graz, 1956).

STERN, S. M., 'Autographs of Maimonides in the Bodleian Library', *Bodleian Library Record*, 5 (1955), 180–202, reprinted in S. M. Stern, *Medieval Arabic and Hebrew Thought*, ed. F. W. Zimmermann (London, 1983), no. xix.

——'A Collection of Treatises by 'Abd al-Laṭīf al-Baghdādī', *Islamic Studies*, I (1962), 53–70, reprinted in S. M. Stern, *Medieval Arabic and Hebrew Thought*, ed. F. W. Zimmermann (London, 1983), no. xviii.

STOKES, GEORGE THOMAS, *Some Worthies of the Irish Church*, ed. H. J. Lawlor (London, 1900).

STROTHMANN, WERNER, *Die Anfänge der syrischen Studien in Europa*, Göttinger Orientforschungen, I. Reihe, Syriaca, 1 (Wiesbaden, 1971).

SUTHERLAND, L. S., 'The Origin and Early History of the Lord Almoner's Professorship in Arabic at Oxford', *Bodleian Library Record*, 10 (1978–82), 166–77.

Taswell, *Autobiography*: Autobiography and Anecdotes by William Taswell, D.D. . . . A.D. 1651–1682, edited by George Percy Elliot, The Camden Miscellany, vol. 2 [6th item] (Camden Society, 1852).

Thomason Tracts: *Catalogue of the Pamphlets, Books, Newspapers etc collected by George Thomason, 1640–1661* (2 vols., London, 1908).

TINDAL HART, A., *William Lloyd 1627–1717: Bishop, Politician, Author and Prophet* (London, 1952).

TINTO, ALBERTO, *La Tipografia Medicea Orientale*, Studi e Ricerche di Storia del Libro e delle Biblioteche, 1 (Lucca, 1987).

Todd, *Life of Walton*: Memoirs of the Life and Writings of Right Rev. Brian Walton, D. D. Lord Bishop of Chester, Editor of the London Polyglot Bible, with notices of his coadjutors in that illustrious work; of the cultivation of oriental learning, in this country, preceding and during their time . . . To which is added, Dr. Walton's own vindication of the London Polyglot. By the Rev. Henry John Todd (2 vols., London, 1821).

Toomer, *Apollonius*: *Apollonius Conics Books V to VII: The Arabic Translation of the Lost Greek Original in the Version of the Banū Mūsā*, edited with translation and commentary by G. J. Toomer (2 vols., New York, 1990).

TOOMER, G. J., 'The Solar Theory of az-Zarqāl, A History of Errors', *Centaurus*, 14 (1969), 306–36.

——'Lost Greek Mathematical Works in Arabic Translation', *The Mathematical Intelligencer*, 6 (1984), 32–8.

TREVOR-ROPER, HUGH, *Archbishop Laud 1573–1645* (London, 1940).

——*Catholics, Anglicans and Puritans: Seventeenth Century Essays* (London and Chicago, 1987, 1988).

TURNBULL, G. H., *Hartlib, Dury and Comenius: Gleanings from Hartlib's Papers* (London, 1947).

Twells, *Life of Pococke*: in The Theological Works of the Learned Dr. POCOCK, Sometime Professor of the HEBREW and ARABICK Tongues, in the University of Oxford, and Canon of Christ-Church, CONTAINING His PORTA MOSIS, And ENGLISH COMMENTARIES on HOSEA, JOEL, MICAH, and MALACHI, To which is prefixed, An Account of his LIFE and WRITINGS, never before printed; In Two Volumes, i, By Leonard Twells (London, 1740).

[The Life is reprinted in] THE Lives OF DR. EDWARD POCOCK, THE CELEBRATED ORIENTALIST, BY DR. TWELLS; OF DR. ZACHARY PEARCE, BISHOP OF ROCHESTER, AND OF DR. THOMAS NEWTON, BISHOP OF BRISTOL, BY THEMSELVES; AND OF THE REV. PHILIP SKELTON, BY MR. BURDY, i (London, 1816), 1–356.

ULLMANN, MANFRED, 'Arabische, türkische und persische Studien', in Seck, *Wilhelm Schickard*, 109–28.

UNTERKIRCHER, FRANZ, 'Sebastian Tengnagel (1608–1636)', in *Geschichte der Österreichischen Nationalbibliothek*, ed. Josef Stummvoll, i, Museion, NF Reihe II, 3 (Vienna, 1968), 129–145.

Uri: Bibliothecae Bodleianae Codicum Manuscriptorum Orientalium, videlicet Hebraicorum, Chaldaicorum, Syriacorum, Arabicorum, Persicorum, Turcicorum, Copticorumque Catalogus jussu curatorum Preli Academici a Joanne Uri Confectus. Pars Prima (Oxford, 1787).

Ussher, *Letters*: A Collection of Three Hundred Letters Written between the most Reverend Father in God James Usher, Late Lord Arch-bishop of Armagh, and Primate of all Ireland, and others . . . Collected and published from Original Copies . . . by Richard Parr, D.D. his Lordship's Chaplain many Years (London, 1686) [published with, but separately paginated from] The Life Of the Most Reverend Father in God, James Usher . . . by Richard Parr (London, 1686).

Ussher, *Works*: The Whole Works of the Most Rev. James Ussher, D.D, Lord Archbishop of Armagh, and Primate of all Ireland. Now for the first time collected, with a life of the Author, and an Account of his Writings, by Charles Richard Elrington, D.D. (17 vols., Dublin, 1829–64).

VACCARI, ALBERTO, 'I Caratteri Arabi della «Typographia Savariana»', *Rivista degli Studi Orientali*, 10 (1923–5), 37–47.

VAN DER WALL, ERNESTINE G. E., '"Without Partialitie Towards All Men", John Durie on the Dutch Hebraist Adam Boreel', in *Jewish-Christian Relations in the Seventeenth Century: Studies and Documents*, ed. J. van den Berg and Ernestine G. E. van der Wall, International Archives of the History of Ideas, 119 (Dordrecht, 1988), 145–9.

VAN KONINGSVELD, P. SJ., *The Latin-Arabic Glossary of the Leiden University Library*, Asfār, 1 (Leiden, 1977).

VAN MAANEN, JOHANNES ARNOLDUS, *Facets of Seventeenth Century Mathematics in the Netherlands*, Proefschrift ter Verkrijging van de Graad van Doctor in de Wiskunde an Natuurwetenschappen aan de Rijksuniversiteit te Utrecht (Utrecht, 1987).

VAUGHAN, ROBERT, *The Protectorate of Oliver Cromwell and the State of Europe during the early part of the reign of Louis XIV illustrated in a series of letters between John Pell . . . Sir Samuel Morland, Sir William Lockhart, Mr. Secretary Thurloe, and other distinguished men . . .* (2 vols., London, 1839).

Velschius, *Dodecas Epistolarum*: Gerardi Joan. Vossii et Clarorum Virorum ad eum Epistolae, collectore Paulo Colomesio, . . . Nunc accuratius recussae, . . . Quibus accessit Dodecas Epistolarum Clarissimi Viri Georgii Hieronymi Velschii (Augsburg, 1691).

VENN, JOHN, and VENN, J. A., *Alumni Cantabrigienses*, Part I (4 vols., Cambridge, 1922–7).

VERVLIET, H. D. L., 'Robert Granjon à Rome (1578–1589). Notes préliminaires à une histoire de la typographie romaine à la fin du XVIe siècle', *Bulletin de l'Institut Historique Belge de Rome*, 38 (1967), 177–231.

——(ed.), *The Type Specimen of the Vatican Press 1628: A Facsimile* (Amsterdam, 1967).

——*Sixteenth Century Printing Types of the Low Countries* (Amsterdam, [1968]).

Viccars, *Decapla*: DECAPLA IN PSALMOS: SIVE COMMENTARIUS EX DECEM LINGUIS MSS. ET IMPRESSIS, Heb. Arab. Syr. Chald. Rabbin. Græc. Rom. Ital. Hispan. Gallic. CUM Specimine linguæ Cophticæ, Pers. & Ang. MSS. Ex Antiquis Patribus S. *August*. S. *Chrysost*, S. *Theod*. &c. Rab. Historicis & Poetis In Duodecim SECTIONES digestus. . . . A JOANNE VICCARS Anglo (London, 1639).

VOGEL, E. G., 'Ueber Wilh. Postel's Reisen in den Orient', *Serapeum, Zeitschrift für Bibliothekwissenschaft, Handschriftenkunde und ältere Litteratur*, 14 (1853), 49–58.

VOORHOEVE, P., *Handlist of Arabic manuscripts in the library of the University of Leiden and other collections in the Netherlands* (Leiden, 1957).

Vossius, *Epistolae*: Gerardi Joan. *Vossii et Clarorum Virorum ad eum Epistolae, collectore Paulo Colomesio* (London, 1690).

Vossius, *Funeral Oration*: GERARDI JOANNIS VOSSII ORATIO IN OBITUM *Clarissimi ac praestantissimi viri*, THOMÆ ERPENII, Orientalium linguarum in Academia Leidensi Professoris. Habita statim ab exsequiis in auditorio Theologico, XV Novemb. Anno MDCXXIV, in *Gerardi Joannis Vossii Opuscula varii Argumenti* (Amsterdam, 1698), 84–91 (Vossius, *Opera*, iv), originally published Leiden, 1625.

WAKEFIELD, COLIN, 'Arabic Manuscripts in the Bodleian Library, the Seventeenth-Century Collections', in Russell, *The 'Arabick' Interest of the*

Natural Philosophers, 128–46.

Wakefield, *De laudibus trium linguarum*: ROBERTI VVAKFELDI SAcrarum literarum professoris eximij oratio de laudibus & vtilitate trium linguarum Arabicę Chaldaicæ & Hebraicę atque idiomatibus hebraicis quæ in vtroque testamento inueniuntur. Londini apud VVinandum de Vorde (n.d. [*c*.1528]).

Wallis, *Archimedes' Sandreckoner*: ΑΡΧΙΜΗΔΟΥΣ ΤΟΥ ΣΥΡΑΚΟΣΙΟΥ Ψαμμίτης, καὶ Κύκλου Μέτρησις, ΕΥΤΟΚΙΟΥ ΑΣΚΑΛΩΝΙΤΟΥ εἰς αὐτὴν ὑπόμνημα ARCHIMEDIS SYRACUSANI Arenarius, Et Dimensio Circuli. EUTOCII ASCALONITÆ, in hanc Commentarius. Cum Versione & Notis *Joh. Wallis*, SS. Th. D. Geometriae Professoris Saviliani (Oxford, 1676).

Wallis, *Aristarchus*: ΑΡΙΣΤΑΡΧΟΥ ΣΑΜΙΟΥ Περὶ μεγεθῶν καὶ ἀποστημάτων Ἡλίου καὶ Σελήνης ΒΙΒΛΙΟΝ. ΠΑΠΠΟΥ ΑΛΕΞΑΝΔΡΕΩΣ Τοῦ τῆς Συναγωγῆς ΒΙΒΛΙΟΥ Β´ Ἀπόσπασμα. ARISTARCHI SAMII De Magnitudinibus & Distantiis Soli & Lunae, LIBER *Nunc primum Graece editus cum* Federici Commandini *versione Latina, notisque illius & Editoris.* PAPPI ALEXANDRINI SECUNDI LIBRI MATHEMATICÆ COLLECTIONIS, *Fragmentum* Hactenus Desideratum. *E Codice MS. edidit, Latinum fecit, Notisque illustravit JOHANNES WALLIS*, S.T.D. Geometriae Professor Savilianus; & *Regalis Societatis Londini, Sodalis* (Oxford, 1688).

Wallis, *Mathesis Universalis*: in Johannis Wallisii, . . . Geometriae Professoris *Saviliani* in Celeberrimâ Academia Oxoniensi; *Operum* Mathematicorum *Pars Prima* (Oxford, 1657).

WALLIS, JOHN, *Opera Mathematica* (3 vols., Oxford, 1695, 1693, 1699).

WALTON, BRIAN, Introductio ad lectionem linguarum Orientalium Hebraicae, Chaldaicae, Samaritanae, Syriacae, Arabicae, Persicae, Aethiopicae, Armenae, Coptae. Consilium de earum Studio foeliciter instituendo, & de libris quos in hunc finem sibi comparare debent studiosi. In usum tyronum qui linguas istas addiscere desiderant, præcipuè eorum qui sumptus ad Biblia Polyglotta (jam sub prelo) imprimenda contulerunt. Praemittitur praefatio, in qua de hisce linguis, & de Textuum & versionum, quæ in dictis Bibliis habentur, Antiquitate, Authoritate & Usu, breviter disseritur, quidque in hac Editione præ reliquis expectandum sit. Editio secunda priori emendatior (London, 1655).

WARD, G. R. M. (tr.), *Oxford University Statutes*. Vol. I *containing the Caroline Code or Laudian Statutes* (London, 1845).

WARD, JOHN, *The Lives of the Professors of Gresham College, To which is prefixed The Life of the Founder, Sir Thomas Gresham* (London, 1740).

WEBSTER, CHARLES, *The Great Instauration: Science, Medicine and Reform 1626–1660* (London and New York, 1975).

WEISS, ROBERT, 'England and the Decree of the Council of Vienne on the teaching of Greek, Arabic, Hebrew, and Syriac', *Bibliothèque d'Humanisme et Renaissance*, 14 (1952), 1–9.

W[HEELER], G. W., 'Bibliotheca Rabbinica (1629)', *Bodleian Quarterly Record*, 3 (1921), 144–6.

WIEGERS, G. A., *A Learned Muslim Acquaintance of Erpenius and Golius: Ahmad b. Kâsim al-Andalusî and Arabic Studies in the Netherlands* (Leiden, [1990]).

WIJNMAN, H. F., 'De Hebraicus Jan Theunisz. Barbarossius alias Johannes Antonides als lector in het Arabisch aan de Leidse universiteit (1612–1613)', *Studia Rosenthaliana*, 2 (1968), 1–29, 149–77.

WIJNNE, J. A., *Resolutiën, genomen bij de Vroedschap van Utrecht, betreffende de Illustre School en de Akademie in hare stad, van de jaren 1632–1693*, Werken van het Historisch Genootschap, gevestigt te Utrecht, Nieuwe Serie, 52 (Utrecht, 1888).

WITKAM, J. J., *Jacobus Golius (1596–1667) en zijn Handschriften*, Oosters Genootschap in Nederland, 10 (Leiden, 1980).

WOOD, ALFRED C., *A History of the Levant Company* (Oxford, 1935; reprinted London, 1964).

Wood, *Athenae Oxonienses*: Athenae Oxonienses. An exact history of all the writers and bishops who have had their education in the University of Oxford. To which are added the Fasti, or Annals of the said University. By Anthony a Wood, M. A. of Merton College. A new edition, with additions and a continuation by Philip Bliss (4 vols., London, 1813–20).

Wood, *History and Antiquities*: The History and Antiquities of the University of Oxford in two books, by Anthony à Wood . . . now first published in English . . . by John Gutch, Vol. 2 (2 parts; Oxford, 1796).

Wood, *Life and Times*: The Life and Times of Anthony Wood, antiquary, of Oxford, 1632–1695, described by Himself, collected by Andrew Clark, Oxford Historical Society, vols. 19, 21, 26, 30, 40 (5 vols., Oxford, 1891–1900).

WORTHAM, JOHN DAVID, *British Egyptology 1549–1906* (Newton Abbot, 1971).

Worthington, *Correspondence*: Diary and Correspondence of Dr. John Worthington edited by James Crossley, Vols. 1 & 2 Part 1 (Printed for the Chetham Society, 1847, 1855).

WOTTON, WILLIAM, *Reflections upon Ancient and Modern Learning* (London, 1694).

Index

coffee 166; on Ussher's MSS. 205 n.;
grievances against Walton 206, 255,
261; learned Arabic at Cambridge 86,
182; borrowed Bedwell's dictionary
63, 257; his opinion of that work 63;
Sol Angliae Oriens 251; inaugural
lecture 99 n., 252, 311
Castell, Edmund, correspondence: to
Clarke 63 n., 156 n., 166 n., 208 n.,
236 n., 238 n., 252 n., 258 nn., 259 n.,
260 n., 261, 262 nn., 263 nn., 264,
266; to Golius 257 n.; to Thomas
Greaves 258 n.; to Lightfoot 206 n.,
255 n., 256, 257 n., 263 n.; to Pococke
254, 272 n., 277
Castell, Edmund, *Heptaglot Lexicon* 63,
182, 206, 236, 251, 252; origins of
255; specimen for 205 n., 256;
prospectus for 256; plan of criticized
264; price 257, 261; solicitation of
subscriptions 261; scholars associated
with 207, 256, 259–60; sources of
257–8; MSS. borrowed for 63, 208,
257; Clarke's Chaldee Paraphrase used
for 228; format 255 n.; delays in 261,
265; first volume issued 262; finally
published 263; copies left on Castell's
hands 263, 270; destruction of copies
263; deficiencies of 264; reasons for
its failure 265
Catholic Church: attempts to establish
communion with Eastern Churches 15,
22; missionaries sent to Ottoman
Empire 15
Caussin de Perceval, publishes extracts
from ibn Yūnus 175 n.
Cavendish, Charles (royalist commander),
toured Asia Minor with Ravius 145
Cavendish, Sir Charles: letter to Mersenne
185 n.; correspondence with Pell 145
n., 183, 184, 185
Cayet de la Palme, Arabic excerpts
published by 29
'Cebetis Tabula', Arabic version
published 51
Celestinus de Sancta Liduina, *see* Golius,
Petrus
censorship of Islamic books: in England
200; in Italy 24
Cerigo, Giorgio 140 n.; helped Greaves
and Pococke at Constantinople 135,
137 n.; observed eclipse at Galata 139
'Chaldee': meanings of 10 n.;

paraphrases of Old Testament 41; *see
also* Clarke
Charles I, King 145, 198, 223; in Madrid
72 n.; given Codex Alexandrinus 141
n.; Laud's influence with 92, 105;
letters to Levant Company in name of
108, 109, 124; made Oxford
headquarters in Civil War 147, 149;
seized college plate 149; removed
Brent as Warden of Merton 155;
named Pococke Hebrew Professor
157; executed 158; allegedly forbade
importation of Koran 201; library of
205 n.
Charles II, King 243; Restoration 250,
252; Polyglot Bible dedicated to 205;
named Pococke DD 211; Oxford
volume of verses addressed to 215 n.;
book dedicated to by Pococke 215 n.;
recommended Heptaglot 261; interest
in buying Golius' MSS. 253; sons of,
tutored by Bernard 301
Charlett, Arthur, senior, letter from
Pococke 289 n.
Charlett, Arthur, junior: and Pococke's
correspondence 4; letter from Marsh
289 n.
Charterhouse, Thomas Greaves at 132–3
Chasteigner, account of Arabists in Paris
by 33 n.
Chievely, Pococke's father vicar of 116
Childrey: Fettiplace family at 120;
Pococke rector of 120, 148, 159, 225;
soldiers quartered at 157
Chillingworth, William: corresponded
with Laud 107 n.; known to Pococke
223 n.; *Religion of Protestants* 223 n.
Christians, Eastern: importance as
Arabists in Europe 25; colleges for
established at Rome 15; contacts with
western Europe 15; Huntington's
contacts with 282–3; Pococke's
concern for 217–8; *see also* Catholic
Church
Christina, Queen of Sweden: appointed
Kirsten as her physician 36; Grotius
ambassador of 145; tutored by
Johannes Matthiae 189; offered Ravius
post in Sweden 197; gave Ravius
money 186
Christmann, Jacob 86, 100: career as
Arabist 37–8; translation of al-
Farghānī 37

Marmora Oxoniensia 290; edition of part of *Mishneh Torah* 290; *Life of Mahomet* 223, 268, 291–2, 308
Prideaux, John, learned Arabic from Pasor 98
printing: Muslim suspicion of 20, 23 n.; *see also* Arabic, printing of; type, Arabic
Propaganda Fide, Sacra Congregatio de: oriental publishing by 24, 47; refutation of Koran published by 25; employed Stefano Paolino 31 n.; tried to recruit Erpenius 47
proverbs, Arabic: collected by Scaliger and published by Erpenius 43, 46; *see also* 'Alī; al-Maydānī
Prynne, William, accuser of Laud 148 n.
Psalms: polyglot 20, 40, 67, 76 n., 85, 94, 100; Arabic (Savary de Brèves) 30, 67, 76 n., 100; exemplar for that 30 n.; Ussher's MS. of Arabic 82; specimen in Coptic and Arabic 262; *see also* Viccars
Ptolemy: observed at Alexandria 138; *Geography* 232
Ptolemy: *Almagest*: translated from Arabic into Latin 11; edition promised by Bainbridge 72; John Greaves's Arabic MS. of 137 n.; proposed edition 233
Ptolemy: *Planetary Hypotheses*: Arabic version brought back by Golius 49, 74; *editio princeps* of Greek 75
Pythagoras, Arabic version 51

Qāmūs: used by Europeans 49, 62, 178; lent by Selden to Golius 62 n., 69 n.
Qandi, Shahin: copied MSS. for Golius 50, 237; copied Arabic Apollonius for Oxford 237, 240
Queen's College, Oxford: Arabic MS. at 103; book at borrowed by Gregory 103 n.

Radcliffe, Dr John, interceded with Earl of Portland for Altham 295 n.
Radtmann, Bartholomaeus, Arabic grammar of 38
Raimondi, Giovanni Battista: director of Medicean press, 22; his publishing plans 22 n., 23, 24, 25, 310; problems with censorship 24 n.; attempts to acquire MSS. 23 n.; death 24; taught

J.-B. Duval 32; employed Stefano Paolino 30 n.; grammatical studies of 22 n., 28; cites decree of Council of Vienne 10 n.; *see also* Medicean oriental press
Ramusio, *Navigationi et viaggi* 21, 28, 172 n.
Raphelengius, Franciscus: son-in-law of Plantinus 41; studied Arabic with Postel 27; moved to Leiden 42; Professor of Hebrew there 42; his Arabic lexicon 42, 46, 60, 69, 213; owned Latin-Arabic glossary 11 n.; used Pedro de Alcalá's vocabulary 18 n.; used Scaliger's thesaurus 43; borrowed Arabic books from Franciscus Junius the elder 37 n.; Arabic types of 42; Arabic books published with these 45, 46, 60; mentioned by Pasor 100; *see also* type, Arabic
Raphelengius, Franciscus: sons of: publish father's Arabic lexicon 46; publish Theunisz.' Arabic book 60; publish Bedwell's Arabic book 59–60; abandoned printing of Arabic 46; sold Arabic type to Bedwell 60
Ratelbandt, Elias (Amsterdam bookseller) 238
Ravius, Christianus: career 37, 83 n., 189–97; first visit to England 84; travel to orient subsidized by Ussher 83–4, 142, 189; met scholars and dignitaries in Paris 142–3; arrival at Constantinople described 143; in Constantinople 84, 144; visit to Smyrna 143; travels in the East 118, 143–5; visited Ephesus 144; voyage from Smyrna to London 121 n.; in Cyprus 145; return to England (1641) 145, 150; visited Oxford and Cambridge 151–2; went to Leiden 152; lectured at Utrecht 183, 186, 189; tried to get post at Amsterdam 189; return to England (1647) 189; anglicizes name to 'Ravis' 190; Professor of Oriental Languages in London 90, 187 n., 190–5; connection with Sion College 191–2; petition of 197; appointed Fellow of Magdalen 196; moved to Sweden 197; career in Sweden 83 n., 186, 189, 197; married niece of Johannes Matthiae 189;